SOUTH AFRICAN

WINE BUYER'S GUIDE

DAVE HUGHES

1994 EDITION

STRUIK

Struik Publishers (Pty) Ltd
(a member of the Struik Group (Pty) Ltd)
Cornelis Struik House
80 McKenzie Street
Cape Town
8001

Reg. No.: 54/00965/07

First published 1986
Second edition 1987
Third edition 1988
Fourth edition 1989
Fifth edition 1990
Sixth edition 1991
Seventh edition 1992
Eighth edition 1993

Editor Hilda Hermann
Editorial assistants Wenda Pace, Susannah Coucher
Designer Neville Poulter
DTP Suzanne Fortescue, Struik DTP
Reproduction Hirt & Carter (Pty) Ltd, Cape Town
Printing and binding CTP Book Printers, Parow

ISBN 1 86825 402 X

Contents

PREFACE

It is a source of constant amazement to me that there is such a demand for information on wine. Each year brings not only a new vintage, but a host of new books on wine and the up-dates of guides such as this eighth edition of *The South African Wine Buyer's Guide*.

The idea of this book is simple – to help you get as much enjoyment out of South African wine as possible. For this reason you will only find wines available on the South African market reviewed in it. It contains none of the myriad export labels that have been developed in recent times – only those you can buy locally. Many of those export labels are wines we know simply by different labels. Some are wines blended for the overseas customer to give them their 'own' wine with names such as 'Klippen Kop' and 'Cape Levant'. Personally, I think it is a pity that these other labels are necessary as I prefer the proud promotion of our well known names. This, in fact, does happen and it is good to see just how well our great names continue to do in overseas competition.

The encouraging trends of relaxation of the KWV's tight controls at the producers end of the industry will eventually work through to the consumer end. At this stage, no one can predict what these effects will be. Hopefully they will slow the ever-climbing cost of wine. It is also pleasing to see the greater range of overseas wines beginning to appear on the shelves of the better wine merchants. The world's healthiest wine markets are those where local production has to compete with imports. Because of our exchange rates, surcharges etc., this has not been the case in South Africa for very long.

Hopefully the growing success of increased exports of Cape wines will benefit the industry. Competing in the big, wide world should have an effect on our wines as the wine makers tune their wines to cope with international tastes. I only hope we do not lose our own identity, and our wine makers must ensure that they are not dictated to by the overseas buyers to our detriment.

I do hope that this year's *South African Wine Buyer's Guide* is as useful to you as past comments seem to have proved.

My sincere thanks go to Hilda Hermann for once again editing the work with such good humour, and to the sisters Jaci and Laura van Niekerk for all their assistance.

Cheers!

Dave Hughes
Stellenbosch

HOW TO USE THIS BOOK

For easy reference, the book is divided into the wine assessments, a listing of wine according to star rating and a wine index. The index is a list of the wines presented alphabetically according to the producer. Each wine appears with its star rating and price symbol, and the page on which you will find the assessment. The wine assessments provide more detailed descriptions and are divided into six broad categories: Red, White, Blanc de Noir/Rosé, Nouveau, Sparkling, Perlé, and Fortified. Within these sections you will find further divisions into cultivars, types and styles of wine. The wines in each section are then presented alphabetically together with their star rating and an indication of price.

I have given my indication of quality on a scale of 0 to 5 stars. One must remember that wine is a living entity, and changes with the vintage are perfectly natural. Also, if a wine is not correctly cared for it might not be at its best when you try it, and if you are not at your best, a wine might seem different from when you tried it last.

no stars	an unremarkable or poorly made wine
★	a sound wine without any special attributes
★★	a well-made wine of average quality
★★★	a good wine
★★★★	an excellent wine
★★★★★	a masterpiece, a tribute to the wine makers' art.

In instances where I have felt the wine to be worthy of slightly more than, say, three stars but not quite the standard of a four-star wine, I have included a fourth star in brackets. Similarly a rating of ★★★★(★) indicates more than four stars but not quite five.

To give a firm retail price for the wines in the book would be foolhardy, but as an indication I have included with each assessment a symbol to indicate roughly the price range within which that wine falls. The symbols are based on bottle-store prices at the coast and I stress that the following is an indication only and in no way should be seen as fixed:

A = Less than R4,99 a bottle	D = R15,00 – R19,99 a bottle
B = R5,00 – R9,99 a bottle	E = R20,00 – R29,99 a bottle
C = R10,00 – R14,99 a bottle	F = more than R30,00 a bottle

In some instances I have included a vintage guide, to indicate the readiness of particular vintages for consumption.

CULTIVARS

The big, fleshy grapes one eats at the table do not usually produce good wine and in most cases the small, juicy, wine-making grapes have far more flavour than the table varieties. The most commonly used cultivars for wine, and in South Africa the only ones permitted by law, are those of the species *Vitis vinifera*. It is from the juice of ripe grapes that wine is made and a wine maker can only make good wine from good grapes. The following represent the better-known grape varieties used.

White Cultivars

Chenin Blanc (Steen)

Pride of place goes to this remarkably versatile white grape. It is the most widely planted of all our wine cultivars, making up more than 31,9% of the area under vine. Good quality Steen makes fine, fruity, dry wines as well as wines of any degree of sweetness, right through to the fullest botrytis wines. It makes our best sherries and is used in most of our finer sparkling wines. It is also used for sweet fortified wines and in brandy production. Grown in all the producing areas, it is an early mid-season ripening grape. Vines produce medium-sized, compact bunches with small, oval, thinnish-skinned berries.

White French (Palomino)

Known locally as White French or Fransdruif, this is the same cultivar used in Spain for sherry production and is known there as Palomino. Locally, it is rapidly declining in popularity owing to its vulnerability to the disease anthracnose. White French vineyards produce 9,7% of the area under vine. Vines produce large, loose bunches with medium-sized, round berries with tough skins. It is an early mid-season ripener.

Clairette Blanche

A late-maturing grape giving a low acid wine which is much appreciated in the making of sparkling wines. The vines produce medium-sized, loose bunches of medium-sized, long, oval, tough-skinned grapes which ripen right at the end of the vintage. Clairette Blanche represents 3,8% of national plantings.

Cape Riesling (South African Riesling)

This grape made Riesling synonymous with top quality, dry, white wines in South Africa. The cultivar, however, represents only 3,6% of the national crop and is grown mainly in the Coastal Region. Vines produce medium-sized, compact bunches with round or slightly oval, thin-skinned berries.

Weisser Riesling (Rhine Riesling)

This variety is a relative newcomer to South Africa and produces a more fragrant wine than our traditional Cape Riesling which, incidentally, is a totally unrelated variety. It is grown mainly in the Coastal Region with scattered plantings in the Breede River Valley Region. Short, cylindrical, compact bunches are produced with medium-sized berries with medium-thick skins. It represents less than 1% of the national plantings.

Colombar (Colombard)

Originally grown for brandy production, this cultivar has in recent years been used to produce very attractive, fruity wines especially in the Breede River Valley Region. It is also grown in the Coastal Region and in total now represents 6,2% of the national plantings. It ripens late mid-season and has medium-sized, conical bunches with short, oval berries.

Sémillon (Green Grape)

One of the grapes which was very popular in the early days of South African wine making and is the variety used in France for dry Graves and sweet Sauternes wines. Locally its use is dwindling and it now represents only 1,5% of national plantings. It ripens early mid-season. Medium-sized, compact bunches comprise soft-skinned, short, oval berries.

Gewürztraminer

This important variety of Alsace in Europe does not always develop the true 'gewürz' (spicey) flavour in our growing conditions. Grown mostly in the Coastal Region, including Tulbagh, it does in some localities, however, produce wines of good spice, as proven in recent international competitions. It makes up only a fraction (0,3%) of the total national plantings. The fairly short and mostly compact bunches have slightly pinkish berries, round to short oval and with tough skins. Gewürztraminer is an early season ripener.

Bukettraube

Introduced to South Africa only in the 1970s, this vigorous grower now comprises some 0,4% of all plantings, giving wines with slight Muscat aroma. Medium to large, fairly compact bunches are produced with medium-large, firm, thin- but tough-skinned berries. The variety is an early season ripener.

Kerner

Though introduced at the same time as Bukettraube, plantings of this variety represent only 0,1% of the national crop. It gives a distinctive if somewhat stern wine. It is an early ripener, bearing medium-large, compact bunches of medium-large, round, thick-skinned berries.

Sauvignon Blanc

A remarkable variety which, when used with Sémillon and Muscadel in Bordeaux in France, produces some of the most exceptional wines, including the driest Graves and sweetest Sauternes. It is also famous on the upper Loire for the striking wines of Sancerre. Although once popular in South Africa, it fell from favour but has now made a reappearance and recent efforts have shown some most encouraging wines. The variety has been planted in large quantities in recent years and now makes up almost 3,6% of the national plantings and produces medium-large, compact bunches with medium-large, round, thick-skinned grapes.

Chardonnay

The grape of the famous white wines of Burgundy, Chablis and Champagne in France, and now responsible for some of the finest wines in California. At this stage it is grown only in minimal quantities locally (1,04% of the total national crop), mainly in the Coastal Region and on a few farms in the Breede River Valley Region. The small, compact bunches have small, round, tough-skinned berries.

Chenel

This cross of Chenin Blanc and Trebbiano produced by Professor Chris Orffer of the University of Stellenbosch already represents over 0,7% of the national crop. The medium-sized, cylindrical bunches have short, oval, medium-sized, thin- but tough-skinned grapes. It is grown mostly in the high production inland areas, with much lesser amounts in the Coastal Region.

Muscat d'Alexandrie (Hanepoot)

One of the world's oldest cultivated grape varieties and definitely South Africa's favourite grape flavour. It is planted in a higher percentage in local vineyards than anywhere else in the world and currently produces 5,7% of the national plantings. Grown in all areas, its large, loose bunches have large, obovoid, thin- but tough-skinned berries. The grapes ripen in late mid-season and the wines have unmistakable Muscat character.

Raisin Blanc/Servan Blanc

These two names refer to the same grape which has been grown in the Cape over a long period. It is grown mainly in the Klein Karoo Region and later in the Worcester and Robertson districts. It is not a good quality wine grape and is better suited to brandy distillation. It represents 1,7% of the total crop.

Fernão Pires

This Portuguese cultivar was introduced to South Africa in the 1970s. It appears to be suited to the Cape (where 0,2% of the national crop is grown). It is an early ripener.

Red Cultivars

Cabernet Sauvignon

'King' Cabernet produces a great deal of the best Bordeaux wines and has been transplanted to the vineyards of the New World probably more successfully than any other noble variety. In Bordeaux its greatest successes are in blends in varying proportions with Cabernet Franc, Malbec, Merlot and Verdot. Cabernet Sauvignon makes very distinctive wines of remarkable range in style and individuality. It contributes 2,6% to national plantings and produces small, fairly loose, conical bunches of small, round, thick-skinned, dark berries.

Cinsaut

Formerly known as Hermitage, and although reducing in popularity, it is still by far the most widely planted red grape in South Africa, making up 7% of national plantings. Today it is not one of the fashionable varieties, nevertheless most of South Africa's red wine is made from it. It is grown in all areas but mainly in the Coastal Region. Cinsaut vines produce large conical bunches with large, oval berries which ripen early mid-season.

Pinotage

South Africa's first commercially successful crossing, this variety was produced by Professor A.I. Perold in 1925 from Pinot Noir and Hermitage, as Cinsaut was then known. It makes wines with a very distinct 'Pinotage ester' nose when young, but which age into good, soft reds. Pinotage vineyards, mainly in the Coastal Region, produce about 2% of the national crop. It has medium-sized, compact bunches with small, oval, tough, thick-skinned, dark berries.

Pinot Noir

This is the great red cultivar of Burgundy and Champagne, but it has not transplanted well in the New World. Locally, it is grown only in small amounts in the Coastal Region where it makes up about 0,3% of national plantings. The small, fairly compact bunches have small, round, thick and tough-skinned, dark violet berries which ripen early mid-season.

Shiraz

One of the major grapes of the Rhône Valley. It makes well-flavoured wines with a peculiar nose described as 'smokey'. It makes up 0,9% of national plantings almost all of which are in the Coastal Region but with some notable exceptions in the Breede River Valley Region. Shiraz vines bear medium-sized, fairly loose bunches with small, oval berries which ripen in mid-season.

Merlot

There is not much Merlot yet in the Cape, but encouraging quantities are being planted. Its ability to age more quickly makes it a great asset in softening the harder wines made from Cabernet Sauvignon, hence its importance in Bordeaux-style blends. It produces soft, full, attractive wines. It makes up 0,5% of the national crop.

Cabernet Franc

Belonging to the same family as Cabernet Sauvignon, its wine is occasionally not easily identified from its relation; they are generally softer, however, and so make ideal blending partners. Cabernet Franc makes up only a small fraction of the national crop.

Gamay Noir

Second in importance only to Pinot Noir in Burgundy, this is the great grape of Beaujolais. Producing excellent, full-flavoured wine ready for early drinking in the Nouveau style, it can also produce very acceptable wines for ageing. It makes up a small fraction of the national crop.

THE SOUTH AFRICAN WINE OF ORIGIN SYSTEM

Legislation came into force on 1 September 1973, providing for one of the most advanced and comprehensive wine control systems in the world. It draws from the best features of wine legislation in France and Germany and is geared for our specific requirements. It was also recognized by the authorities of the European Economic Community (EEC) until 1993. It encompassed the following elements which form the 'Wine of Origin Seal' appearing on the capsule of many bottles of wine.

Estate
To qualify for the description 'Estate' a wine must be made from grapes grown and produced on a proclaimed Estate. It need not, however, be bottled on the Estate.

Origin (Blue band)
The legislation has divided the wine-producing areas into clearly defined Regions, which are further divided into Districts, which in some cases are made up of smaller Wards. The last-mentioned are still being determined and each year more are added to the list.

Cultivar (Green band)
If the type of grape used to make the wine is stated on the label the wine must contain a minimum of 75% of that cultivar.

Vintage (Red band)
This refers to the year in which the grapes are harvested and at least 75% must be derived from the vintage stated.

During the course of 1990 Superior certification fell away. This certificate was given to wines of exceptional quality. The Wine of Origin law will, however, continue to guarantee vintage, cultivar, origin and Estate, but not superior quality.

In 1993 the colour banded seal was replaced with a much smaller black and white, rectangular seal. It carries an identity number which confirms the strict controls that apply right from the pressing of the grapes to the final certification by the Wine and Spirit Board.

Only about 10% of the total wine crop is certified. A wine maker is under no obligation to certify his wine. But if he wants to claim origin, vintage and cultivar, then the wine must be certified.

The South African Winelands in terms of Regions, Districts and Wards:

REGION	DISTRICT	WARD

REGION	DISTRICT	WARD
		NUY
		GOUDINI
	WORCESTER	SLANGHOEK
		SCHERPENHEUVEL
		AAN-DE-DOORNS
		MCGREGOR
		KLAASVOOGDS
		VINKRIVIER
BREEDE RIVER VALLEY		EILANDIA
	ROBERTSON	BOESMANSRIVIER
		AGTERKLIPHOOGTE
		LE CHASSEUR
		HOOPSRIVIER
		BONNIEVALE
	SWELLENDAM	BUFFELJAGS
BOBERG	TULBAGH	WELLINGTON
	PAARL	FRANSCHHOEK
	SWARTLAND	RIEBEEKBERG
		GROENEKLOOF
COASTAL		DURBANVILLE
		CONSTANTIA
	STELLENBOSCH	SIMONSBERG-STELLENBOSCH
		JONKERSHOEK
KLEIN KAROO		MONTAGU
		TRADOUW
		SPRUITDRIFT
OLIFANTSRIVIER		KOEKENAAP
		LUTZVILLE-VALLEI
		VREDENDAL
	PICKETBERG	CEDERBERG
		BENEDE-ORANJE
	OVERBERG	WALKER BAY
		ELGIN
		ANDALUSIA
	DOUGLAS	RUITERBOSCH

1. The Ward of Bonnievale now lies entirely in the Robertson District.
2. The Ward of Klaasvoogds has been determined in the Robertson District.
3. The Boberg Region is only recognized for fortified wines.
4. Tulbagh, excluding Wolsely, is included in the Coastal Region.
   Wolseley is included in the Breede River Valley.
5. Buffeljags is a Ward in the Swellendam District.
6. Wellington is a Ward in the Paarl District.
7. Durbanville and Constantia are Wards in the Coastal Region.
8. Elgin and Ruiterbosch are new Wards on their own.
9. Tradouw is a new Ward in the Klein Karoo region.

WINE PRODUCERS

Aan-de-Doorns Co-op PO Box 235, Worcester 6849. Tel: (0231) 72301. Wine maker: Alwyn Mostert. Open weekdays 07h30–12h00, 13h00–17h30; Saturdays 09h00–11h00.

Agterkliphoogte Co-op PO Box 267, Robertson 6705. Tel: (02351) 61103. Wine maker: Helmard Hanekom. Open weekdays 08h00–12h00, 13h30–17h00. Saturdays – visitors by appointment only.

Allesverloren Estate PO Box 23, Riebeek-West 6800. Tel: (02246) 320. Wine maker: Fanie Malan. Visitors by appointment only.

Alphen *see* Kleine Zalze

Alto Estate PO Box 184, Stellenbosch 7599. Tel: (02231) 93884. Wine maker: Hempies du Toit. Visitors by appointment only.

Altydgedacht Estate PO Box 213, Durbanville 7550. Tel: (021) 961295. Wine maker: Oliver Parker. Vineyards: John Parker. Open weekdays 09h00–17h30; Saturdays 09h00–13h00.

Ashton Co-op PO Box 40, Ashton 6715. Tel: (0234) 51135. Fax: (0234) 51284. Manager: Willem Joubert. Wine maker: Kas Huisamen. Open weekdays 08h00–12h30, 13h30–17h30; Saturdays 09h00–12h30.

Aufwaerts Co-op PO Box 51, Rawsonville 6845. Tel: (0231) 91750. Wine maker: Hennie de Villiers. Visitors by appointment only.

Avontuur Estate PO Box 1128, Somerset West 7129. Tel: (024) 553450. Fax: (024) 554600. Wine maker: Jean-Luc Sweerts. General Manager: Manie Kloppers. Open weekdays 08h30–17h00 and Saturdays 09h00–13h00.

Backsberg Estate PO Box 1, Klapmuts 7625. Tel: (02211) 5141. Fax: (02211) 5144. Sydney Back. Wine maker: Hardy Laubser. Vineyards: Michael Back. Open weekdays and public holidays 08h30–17h30; Saturdays 08h30–13h00.

Badsberg Co-op Grootvlakte, PO Box 72, Rawsonville 6845. Tel: (0231) 91120. Wine maker: Gerrit van Zyl. Open weekdays 08h00–17h00.

Barrydale Co-op PO Box 59, Barrydale 6750. Tel: (028572) 1012. Fax: (028572) 5721541. Wine maker: Bob de Villiers. Open weekdays 08h30–17h00.

Belcher Wine Farm PO Box 541, Suider Paarl 7624. Tel: (02211) 631458. Fax: (02211) 632076. Proprietor: Ronnie Belcher. Wine maker: Ernst Gous. Open weekdays 09h00–12h00, 13h00–17h00; Saturdays 09h00–13h00.

Bellingham PO Box 13, Groot Drakenstein, 7680. Tel: (02211) 41011. Fax: (02211) 41712. Wine maker: Charles Hopkins. November to April: four tastings per day at 09h30, 10h30, 14h30, 15h30; Saturdays at 10h30. Closed to the public during the rest of the season and on public holidays.

Bergkelder PO Box 184, Stellenbosch 7599. Tel: (02231) 72440. Fax: (02231) 99533. Cellar master: Dr Pierre Marais. Regular cellar tours offered weekdays and Saturdays at 10h00, 10h30 and 15h00, or by special arrangement.

Bergsig Estate PO Box 15, Breërivier 6858. Tel: (02324) 603/721. Fax: (02324) 658. Proprietor: B W (Prop) Lategan. Wine maker: De Wet Lategan. Open weekdays 08h45–16h45; Saturdays 09h00–12h00. Cellar tours by appointment.

Bertrams Wines/Gilbey Distillers & Vintners PO Box 137, Stellenbosch 7599. Tel: (02231) 906111. Fax: (02231) 906003. Operations Manager: Martin van der Merwe. Wine maker: Leo Burger. Not open to members of the public.

Beyerskloof PO Box 107, Koelenhof 7605. Tel and Fax: (02231) 92135. Wine maker: Beyers Truter. Open weekdays 09h00–13h00.

Blaauwklippen PO Box 54, Stellenbosch 7599. Tel: (02231) 900133/4. Fax: (02231) 901250. Wine maker: Jacques Kruger. Open weekdays 09h00–17h00; Saturdays 09h00–13h00.

Bloemendal Estate PO Box 466, Durbanville 7550. Tel: (021) 962682. Wine maker: Jackie Coetzee. Open Wednesdays 13h00–17h00; Saturdays 09h00–12h00.

Bodega Farm Joostenbergvlakte 7570. Tel: (021) 9882929. Owners/Wine makers: Eddie and Julianne Barlow. Visitors by appointment only.

Bolandse Co-op Daljosaphat cellar: PO Box 2, Huguenot 7645. Tel: (02211) 626190/626191. Fax: (02211) 625379. Wine maker: Anthony de Jager. General Manager: Altus le Roux. Open weekdays 08h00–17h00; Saturdays 08h00–13h00. Noorder Paarl cellar: PO Box 7007, Noorder Paarl, 7623. Tel: (02211) 21747/21748/21766. Fax: (02211) 23866. Wine maker: Jacques du Toit. General Manager: Altus le Roux. Open weekdays 08h00–17h00; Saturdays 08h30–13h00.

Bon Courage Estate PO Box 589, Robertson 6705. Tel: (02351) 4178. Fax: (02351) 3581. Wine maker: André Bruwer. Open weekdays 09h00–17h00; Saturdays 09h00–12h30. Cellar tours conducted by appointment only.

Bonfoi Estate PO Box 9, Vlottenburg 7580. Wine maker: Johannes van der Westhuizen. Not open to the public.

Bonnievale Co-op PO Box 206, Bonnievale 6730. Tel and Fax: (02346) 2795. Wine maker: Piet Linde (to end 1993), Gerrit van Zyl (from 1994). Open weekdays 08h30–12h30, 13h30–17h00.

Boplaas Estate PO Box 156, Calitzdorp 6660. Tel: (04437) 33326/33397. Fax: (04437) 33750. Proprietor and wine maker: Carel Nel. Open weekdays 08h00–13h00, 14h00–17h00; Saturdays 09h00–13h00. Cellar tours by appointment and lunches served during December school holidays. Ruiterbosch is the name for Boplaas Estate's Mossel Bay vineyards. (Note: these wines can only be tasted at Boplaas.)

Boschendal Estate PO Groot Drakenstein 7680. Tel: (02211) 41031. Fax: (02211) 41413. Cellar master: Hilko Hegewisch. Viticulturist: Gerrie Wagener. Taphuis open weekdays 08h30–16h30; Saturdays 08h30–12h30. Daily lunches 12h30. Picnics available 1 November–30 April, 12h30. Also audiovisual presentations and vineyard tours, manor house and waenhuiswinkel.

Botha Co-op PO Botha 6857. Tel: (02324) 740. Wine maker: Andre Stofberg. Open weekdays 07h30–12h30, 13h30–17h30; Saturdays 09h30–12h00.

Bottelary Co-op PO Box 16, Koelenhof 7605. Tel: (02231) 92204. Fax: (02231) 92205. Wine maker: Frikkie Botes. Manager: H de Preez. Open weekdays 08h30–12h30, 13h30–17h00; Saturdays 08h30–13h00.

Bouchard Finlayson PO Box 303, Hermanus 7200. Tel: (0283) 23515. Fax: (0283) 22317. Wine maker: Peter Finlayson. Open weekdays 09h00–13h00, 14h00–17h00.

Bovlei Co-op PO Box 82, Wellington 7655. Tel: (02211) 31567/641283. Fax: (02211) 31386. Wine maker: Martinus Broodryk. Open weekdays 08h30–12h30, 13h30–17h30; Saturdays 08h30–12h30.

Brandvlei Co-op PO Box 595, Worcester 6849. Tel and Fax: (0231) 94215. General Manager: Theuns le Roux. Wine maker: Willie Burger. Open weekdays 07h30–12h30, 13h30–17h30.

Buitenverwachting PO Box 281, Constantia 7848. Tel: (021) 7945190/1. Fax: (021) 7941351. Proprietor: Christina Mueller. Wine maker: Hermann Kirschbaum. Open for sales weekdays 09h00-17h00; Saturdays 09h00-13h00. Cellar tours weekdays 11h00 and 15h00; Saturdays (booking essential) 11h00.

Calitzdorp Co-op PO Box 193, Calitzdorp 6660. Tel: (04437) 33328. Wine maker: Alwyn Burger. Open weekdays 08h00–13h00, 14h00–17h00; Saturdays 08h00–12h00.

Cederberg Kelders Dwarsrivier, PO Cederberg 8136. Tel: (02682) 1531. Wine maker: Flippie Nieuwoudt. Sales from premises during office hours: weekdays 08h30–12h30, 13h30–17h30; Saturdays 08h30–12h30, 14h00–17h30.

Chamonix PO Box 28, Franschhoek 7690. Tel: (02212) 2494/2498. Wine made at Franschhoek Vineyards Co-op. Visitors by appointment only. Wine sales and tasting: Franschhoek Vineyards, Le Quartier Français, Die Binnehof.

Citrusdal Co-op PO Box 41, Citrusdal 7340. Tel: (02662) 94 x 121. Fax: (02662) 94. Wine maker: Michael de Beer. Manager: HJ Cruywagen. Open weekdays 08h00–12h30, 14h00–17h00; Saturdays 09h00–12h30. Cellar tours by appointment. Wines distributed under Goue Vallei label.

Clairvaux Co-op PO Box 179, Robertson 6705. Tel: (02351) 3842. Fax: (02351) 5052. Wine maker: Kobus van der Merwe. Open weekdays 08h30–12h30, 13h30–17h30; Saturdays 08h30–12h00.

Clos Cabrière Estate PO Box 245, Franschhoek 7690. Tel: (02212) 2630. Fax: (02212) 3390. Wine grower and Managing Director: Achim von Arnim. Visitors by appointment only.

Clos Malverne PO Box 187, Stellenbosch 7599. Tel: (02231) 92022. Fax: (02231) 92518. Proprietor: Seymour Pritchard. Wine maker up to and including 1991 vintages: Jeremy Walker. Wine maker from May 1991: Guy Webber. Open weekdays 08h30–17h30, Saturdays 09h00–13h00 and certain public holidays. 'Valley lunch' offered during December and January, and cellar tours by appointment.

De Doorns Co-op PO Box 129, De Doorns 6875. Tel: (02322) 2100. Fax: (02322) 2100. Wine maker: Pieter Hamman. Open weekdays 08h30–12h30, 13h30–17h00; Saturdays 08h30–12h00.

De Helderberg Co-op PO Box 71, Firgrove 7110. Tel: (024) 422370. Fax: (024) 422373. Wine maker: Inus Muller. Open to the public for sales and lunches weekdays 09h00–17h30; Saturdays 09h00–15h00.

Delaire Wines PO Box 3058, Stellenbosch 7602. Tel: (02231) 91756/91213. Fax: (02231) 91270. Proprietors: Storm and Ruth Quinan. Wine maker: Christopher Keet. Open to the public weekdays, Saturdays and most public holidays 10h00–17h00. Lunches served all year round, from Tuesdays to Saturdays, 12h00–14h00.

Delheim Wines PO Box 10, Koelenhof 7605. Tel: (02231) 92033. Fax: (02231) 92036. Vintner: Spatz Sperling. Wine maker: Philip Costandius. Wine tasting and sales: weekdays 08h30–17h00; Saturdays 08h30–15h00. Tours weekdays 10h30 and 14h30, 1 October – 30 April only. Tour of production cellar Saturdays all year round at 10h30. Vintner's platter served from October to April, and soup lunch from May to September, Mondays to Saturdays 11h00–14h00.

De Leuwen Jagt PO Box 505, Suider Paarl 7624. Tel:(02211) 633495/6. Fax: (02211) 633797. Consultant wine maker: Gideon Theron. Open weekdays 08h30–17h00; Saturdays 09h00–13h00. Light lunches served, Mondays to Fridays.

De Wet Co-op PO Box 16, De Wet 6853. Tel: (0231) 92710/92760. Fax: (0231) 92723. Wine makers: Kobus de Wet and Zakkie Bester. Manager: Zakkie Bester. Open weekdays 08h00–17h00; Saturdays 09h00–12h00.

De Wetshof Estate PO Box 31, Robertson 6705. Tel: (0234) 51853/7. Fax: (0234) 51915. Proprietor and wine maker: Danie de Wet. Open weekdays 08h30–17h00; Saturdays 09h30–13h00. Cellar tours by appointment only.

De Zoete Inval Estate PO Box 591, Suider Paarl 7624. Tel: (02211) 632375. Fax: (02211) 632817. Wine makers: Adrian and Gerard Frater. Open weekdays and Saturdays 09h00–17h00.

Die Krans Estate PO Box 28, Calitzdorp 6660. Tel: (04437) 33314. Fax: (04437) 33562. Wine makers: Boet and Stroebel Nel. Open weekdays 08h00–17h00; Saturdays 09h00–12h30. Wine tasting, cellar and vineyard tours when requested. Lunches served December and April holidays; book for rest of year.

Diemersdal Estate PO Box 27, Durbanville 7550. Tel: (021) 963361. Fax: (021) 961810. Proprietor and wine maker: Tienie Louw. Open Wednesdays 13h30–18h00; Saturdays 09h00–16h00. Cellar tours and group functions by appointment.

Die Poort PO Box 45, Albertinia 6795. Tel: (02952) 2030. Wine maker and Proprietor: Jannie Jonker. Open to members of the public weekdays 08h00–18h00; Saturdays 08h00–13h00. Restaurant booking essential.

Dieu Donné Vineyards PO Box 94, Franschhoek 7690. Tel: (02212) 2493. Fax: (02212) 2102. Wine maker: François Malherbe. Proprietor: Robert Maingard. Open weekdays 09h00–17h00; Saturdays (only December and January) 09h00–12h30.

Domein Doornkraal PO Box 104, De Rust 6650. Tel: (04439) 6715/ 2556. Fax: (04429) 2548. Wine maker and Proprietor: Swepie le Roux. Open weekdays 09h00–17h00; Saturdays 08h00–13h00. During school holidays open weekdays 08h00–18h00.

Douglas Co-op PO Box 47, Douglas 8730. Tel: (053) 2981910. Fax: (053) 2982445. Wine maker and Manager: W H (Pou) le Roux. Open weekdays 08h00–17h00.

Douglas Green Bellingham PO Box 246, Wellington 7655. Tel: (02211) 31001. Not open to members of the public. PO Box 4617, Randburg 2125. Tel: (011) 8868290. Fax: (011) 7894503. Production: Johan Bruce. Marketing: Henry Kempen. Not open to members of the public.

Drakenstein Co-op Now known as Simondium Winery Co-op.

Drostdy Co-op PO Box 9, Tulbagh 6820. Tel: (0236) 301086. Cellar master: Frans du Toit. Open weekdays 08h00–12h00, 13h30–17h00; Saturday tours at 11h00 and 15h00.

Du Toitskloof Co-op PO Box 55, Rawsonville 6845. Tel: (0231) 91601/91936. Fax: (0231) 91581. Wine maker: Philip Jordaan. Open weekdays 08h30–17h30; Saturdays 08h30–12h00.

Eersterivier Kelder PO Box 2, Vlottenburg 7604. Tel: (02231) 93870/1. Fax: (02231) 93102. Wine maker: Manie Roussouw. Open weekdays 08h30–17h00; Saturdays 09h00–13h00.

Eikendal Vineyards PO Box 2261, Dennesig 7601. Tel: (024) 551422. Fax: (024) 551027. Wine maker: Josef Krammer. Open weekdays 09h00–17h00; Saturdays 09h00–12h30.

Fairview Estate PO Box 583, Suider Paarl 7624. Tel: (02211) 632450. Fax: (02211) 632591. Wine makers: Charles and Cyril Back. Open weekdays 08h30–18h00 (in winter, 17h30); Saturdays 08h30–17h00 (in winter, 13h00).

Franschhoek Vineyards Co-op PO Box 52, Franschhoek 7690. Tel: (02212) 2086. Fax: (02212) 3440. Wine makers: Deon Truter and Driaan van der Merwe. Manager: Deon Truter. Open to members of the public, weekdays and non-religious public holidays 08h30–13h00, 14h00–17h30 (May to August open 09h00–13h00, 14h00–16h30); Saturdays 09h00–13h00 (May to August open 09h30–13h00).

Gilbeys Distillers & Vintners PO Box 137, Stellenbosch 7600. Tel: (02231) 906111. Fax: (02231) 906000. Operations Manager: Martin van der Merwe. Visitors by appointment only.

Glen Carlou PO Box 23, Klapmuts 7625. Tel: (02211) 5528. Fax: (02211) 5314. Wine maker: Walter Finlayson. Open weekdays 09h00–12h00, 14h00–16h30; Saturdays 09h00–12h30.

Goede Hoop Estate PO Box 25, Kuils River 7580. Tel: (021) 9036286. Wine maker: PJ Bestbier. Open to the public by appointment only.

Goedvertrouw Bot River, Tel: (02824) 49769. Proprietor and wine maker: AH Pillmann. Open weekdays and Saturdays 08h00–18h00. Light lunches and teas by appointment (held in wine tasting room).

Goudini Co-op PO Box 132, Rawsonville 6845. Tel: (0231) 91090. Wine maker and Manager: Hennie Hugo. Open weekdays 08h00–12h00, 13h00–17h00. Cellar tours by appointment.

Goudveld Wynkelder PO Box 1091, Welkom 9460. Tel: (057) 28650. Wine maker: Merkil Alers. Open weekdays and Saturdays 08h30–18h00.

Grangehurst PO Box 206, Stellenbosch 7599. Tel: (024) 553625. Fax: (024) 552143. Wine maker: Jeremy Walker. Visitors by appointment only.

Groot Constantia Estate Private Bag Constantia 7848. Tel: (021) 794 5128. Fax: (021) 794 1999. Wine maker: Martin Moore. Manager: Danie Appel. Open to visitors Monday to Sunday 10h00–17h00.

Groot Eiland Co-op PO Box 93, Rawsonville 6845. Tel: (0231) 91140. Fax: (0231) 91801. Manager and wine maker: Willem Loots. Open weekdays 08h00–12h30, 13h30–17h30. Cellar tours by appointment.

Hamilton Russell Vineyards Hemel-en-Aarde Valley, PO Box 158, Hermanus 7200. Tel: (0283) 23441/23595. Tasting Room Tel: (0283) 21791. Fax: (0283) 21797. Chairman: Timothy Hamilton-Russell. Managing Director: Anthony Hamilton Russell. Wine maker: Storm Kreusch-Dau. Open weekdays 09h00–17h00; Saturdays 09h00–13h00.

Hartenberg Estate PO Box 69, Koelenhof 7605. Tel: (02231) 92541. Fax: (02231) 92153. Proprietor: Kenneth Mackenzie. Resident Director: JS Krige. Wine maker: Carl Schultz. Open weekdays 08h30–17h00; Saturdays and most non-religious holidays 09h00–15h00. Cellar tours weekdays 10h00 and 15h00,; Saturdays 10h00. Lunches served Mondays to Saturdays 12h00–14h00.

Haute Provence PO Box 211, Franschhoek 7690. Tel: (02212) 3195. Fax: (02212) 3118. Proprietor: Peter Younghusband. Open weekdays 10h00–12h00, 14h00–16h00; Saturdays 10h00–12h00.

Hazendal Estate PO Box 19, Kuils River 7580. Tel: (021) 903 5035. Wine maker: Michael Bosman. Open weekdays 09h00–17h00; Saturdays 09h00–13h00.

H C Collison made by The Bergkelder.

Huguenot Wines PO Box 275, Wellington 7655. Tel: (02211) 641277. Fax: (02211) 32075. Wine maker: P Matthee. Not open to the public.

Jacobsdal Estate Kuils River 7580. Wine maker: Cornelius Dumus. Not open to the public.

John Platter Wines Clos du Ciel, PO Box 3162, Stellenbosch 7602. Tel: (024) 553497. Fax: (024) 554 775. Wine maker: John Platter. Not open to members of the public.

Jonkheer Farmers' Winery PO Box 13, Bonnievale 6730. Tel: (02346) 2137. Fax: (02346) 3146. Wine makers: Nicholaas Jonker and Erhard Roothman. Not open to the public. Also make Bakenskop Wines.

Kaapzicht Estate PO Box 5, Sanlamhof 7532. Tel: (021) 9033870. Fax: (021) 9036272. Wine maker: Danie Steytler. Wine tastings and cellar tours by appointment only. Wine sales: weekdays 09h00–12h30, 13h30–18h00; Saturdays 08h00–12h00

Kango Co-op PO Box 46, Oudtshoorn 6620. Tel: (0443) 226065. Fax: (0443) 291038. Wine maker: C Langenhoven. Manager: Pieter Conradie. Open weekdays 08h30–13h00, 14h00–16h45. Close 16h00 on Fridays. Also make Rijkshof wines.

Kanonkop Estate PO Box 19, Muldersvlei 7606. Tel: (02231) 94656. Fax: (02231) 94719. Proprietors: Paul, Johann and Jannie Krige. Wine maker: Beyers Truter. Open weekdays 08h30–17h00; Saturdays 09h00–12h30. Cellar tours and lunches for visitors by appointment only.

Klawer Co-op PO Box 8, Klawer 8145. Tel: (02724) 61530. Fax: (02724) 61561. Wine maker: Manfred van Heerden. Manager: Hennie Snyders. Open weekdays 08h00–17h00; Saturdays 09h00–12h00.

Klein Constantia Estate PO Box 375, Constantia 7848. Tel: (021) 7945188. Fax: (021) 7942464. Proprietors: Duggie and Lowell Jooste. Wine maker: Ross Gower. Open weekdays 09h00–17h00; Saturdays 09h00–13h00.

Kleine Zalze Estate c/o Gilbeys, PO Box 137, Stellenbosch 7600. Tel: (02231) 906152. Fax: (02231) 900630. Wine maker: Marius Lategan. Tours by appointment only.

Kloofzicht PO Box 101, Tulbagh 6820. Tel: (0236) 300658. Wine maker: Roger Fehlmann. Open weekdays 10h00–16h00, weekends and public holidays, however, it is advisable to telephone beforehand. Estate tours and guest farm facilities available.

Koelenhof Co-op PO Box 1, Koelenhof 7605. Tel: (02231) 92020/1. Fax: (02231) 92796. Wine maker: Pieter Carstens. Manager: Helmie de Vries. Open weekdays 08h30–13h00, 14h00–17h00; Saturdays 08h30–12h30.

Koopmanskloof Estate PO Box 92, Koelenhof, 7605. Tel: (02231) 92225. Fax: (02231) 92355. Proprietor: Stevie Smit. Wine maker: Stefan Smit. Open weekdays and Saturdays 09h00–17h00.

KWV PO Box 528, Suider Paarl 7624. Tel: (02211) 73911. Fax: (02211) 73000. Chief of production: Charl Theron. Wine maker: SH de Wet and Johan Schreuder. Cellar tours Monday, Wednesday, Friday 09h30 and 14h15, Afrikaans. Monday, Wednesday and Friday 11h00 and 15h45, English. Tuesday and Thursday 09h30 and 14h15, English. Tuesday and Thursday 11h00 and 15h45, Afrikaans.

La Belle Provence PO Box 60, Franschhoek 7690. Tel: (02212) 2135. Proprietor: Chris Enslin. Not open to the public.

Laborie Estate (owned by KWV) PO Box 632, Suider-Paarl 7624. Tel: (02211) 73095/4. Fax: (02211) 73000. Wine maker: Jorrie Jordaan. Open weekdays 09h00–17h00; Saturdays 09h00–13h00.

La Bourgogne PO Box 78, Franschhoek 7690. Tel: (02212) 2115. Fax: (02212) 2689. Proprietors: Michael and Sonny Gillis. Open by appointment only. Wine tastings at Franschhoek Vinyards Co-op.

La Bri PO Box 180, Franschhoek 7690. Tel: (02212) 2593. Fax: (02212) 3197. Proprietors: Michael and Cheryl Trull. Manager: Xagene de Villiers. Open weekdays 11h00–12h30; 14h00–16h00.

La Couronne PO Box 84, Franschhoek 7690. Tel: (02212) 3000/3508. Fax: (02212) 2252. Proprietor: Mike Stander and Dr Glennie van Hoogstraten. Wine maker: John Goschen. Tasting and sales at the Co-op and at the Franschhoek Wine Tasting Centre. Wine tastings at La Couronne: weekdays 10h00–17h00; Saturdays 10h00–13h00.

Ladismith Co-op PO Box 56, Ladismith 6885. Tel: (028) 5511042. Fax: (028) 5511930. Wine maker: AS Simonis. Open weekdays 08h00–13h00, 14h00–17h00. Cellar tours by appointment. Also make Towerkop wines.

La Motte Estate PO Box 45, La Motte 7691. Tel: (02212) 3119. Fax: (02212) 3446. Proprietors: Paul and Hannelie Neethling. Wine maker: Jacques Borman. Open for wine tasting and sales: weekdays 09h00–16h30; Saturdays 09h00–12h00. Closed on public holidays.

Landskroon Estate PO Box 519, Suider Paarl 7624. Tel: (02211) 631039/631059. Fax: (02211) 632810. Wine maker: Paul de Villiers Jnr. Open weekdays 08h30–17h30; Saturdays 08h30–12h30.

Landzicht Co-op PO Box 94, Jacobsdal 8710. Tel: (053212) 132/99. Fax: (053212) 113. Wine maker: Ian Sieg. Open weekdays 08h30–13h00, 14h00–17h00; Saturdays 08h30–12h00.

Langverwacht Co-op PO Box 87, Bonnievale 6730. Tel: (02346) 2815. Fax: (02346) 3059. Wine maker: Johan Gerber. Open weekdays 08h00–12h30, 13h30–17h00.

La Provence PO Box 393, Franschhoek 7690. Tel: (02212) 2542. Fax: (02212) 2616. Wine maker: François Malherbe. Manager: N Maree. Wine tastings and sales weekdays 09h30–17h00; Saturdays 09h30–12h30.

Lebensraum Estate PO Box 36, Rawsonville 6845. Tel: (0231) 91460/91260. Wine maker: Kobus Deetlefs. Open weekdays 14h00–18h00, or by appointment.

Le Bonheur Estate PO Box 56, Klapmuts 7625. Tel: (02211) 5432. Wine maker: Michael Woodhead. Not open to the public.

Le Grand Chasseur Estate PO Box 439, Robertson 6705. Tel: (02351) 4635. Wine makers: Wouter and Albertus de Wet. Not open to the public.

Lemberg Estate PO Box 108, Tulbagh 6820. Tel: (0236) 300659. Fax: (0236) 301540. Proprietor and wine maker: Janey Muller. Visitors by appointment only.

Lievland PO Box 66, Klapmuts 7625. Tel: (02211) 5226. Fax: (02211) 5213. Proprietor: Paul Benadé. Wine maker: Abraham Beukes. Open weekdays 09h00–17h00; Saturdays 09h00–13h00.

Loopspruit Winery PO Box 855, Bronkhorstspruit 1020. Tel: (01212) 24303. Wine maker: B Myburgh. Open weekdays 08h00–16h00; Saturdays by appointment only.

L'Ormarins Estate Private Bag Suider Paarl 7624. Tel: (02211) 41026. Owner: Anthonij Rupert. Wine maker: Nico Vermeulen. Open weekdays 08h30–17h00; Saturdays 08h30–12h30 for visitors and sales.

Louisvale PO Box 542 Stellenbosch 7599. Tel: (02231) 92422. Fax: (02231) 92633. Proprietors: Hans Froehling and Leon Stemmet. Wine maker: Marinus Bredell. Open weekdays 10h00–17h00; Saturdays 10h00–13h00. Lunches served: May to October, bookings essential; November to April, á la Carte menu available and bookings unnecessary.

Louwshoek-Voorsorg Co-op PO Box 174, Rawsonville, 6845. Tel/Fax: (0231) 91110. Wine maker and manager: Jaco Potgieter. Open weekdays 08h00–12h30, 13h30–17h00.

Lutzville Co-op PO Box 50, Lutzville 8165. Tel: (02725) 71516. Fax: (02725) 71435. Wine maker: Johan Theron, assisted by JA Rush. Open weekdays 08h00–12h30, 14h00–17h00; Saturdays 08h30–12h00. Cellar tours and lunches by prior arrangement.

Madeba (Graham Beck Winery) PO Box 88, Robertson 6705. Tel: (02351) 2650. Fax: (02351) 5164. Cellar master: Pieter Ferreira. Open weekdays 08h00–17h00; Saturdays 08h00–14h00.

Mamreweg Wine Cellar Co-op PO Box 114, Darling 7345. Tel: (02241) 2276/7. Fax: (02241) 2647. Wine makers: François Weich and P Rossouw. Manager: François Weich. Open Monday to Thursday 08h00–17h00; closes at 16h00 on Friday. Saturday 09h00–12h00. Available from Groenkloof Drankhandelaars.

McGregor Co-op Private Bag X619, Robertson 6705. Tel: (02353) 741. Fax: (02353) 829. Wine maker: Carel van der Merwe. Open weekdays 08h00–12h00, 13h00–17h00.

Meerendal Estate PO Box 2, Durbanville 7550. Tel: (021) 961915. Fax: (021) 969083. Wine maker: W Starke. Not open to the public.

Meerlust Estate PO Box 15, Faure 7131. Tel: (024) 43587. Fax: (024) 43513. Wine maker: Giorgio Dalla Cia. Owner: Hannes Myburgh. Visitors by appointment only.

Meinert PO Box 7221, Stellenbosch 7599. Tel: (02231) 92120. Wine maker: Martin Meinert. Visitors by appointment only.

Merwespont Co-op PO Box 68, Bonnievale 6730. Tel: (02346) 2800. Fax: (02346) 2734. Wine maker: Dirk Cornelissen. Open weekdays 08h00–12h30, 13h30–17h00.

Merwida Co-op PO Box 4, Rawsonville 6845. Tel: (0231) 91301. Fax: (0231) 91953. Wine maker: Jacobus Wolhuter. Open weekdays 07h30–12h00; 13h30–17h30.

Middelvlei Estate PO Box 66, Stellenbosch 7599. Tel: (02231) 3308. Wine maker: Jan Momberg. Not open to the public.

Monis of Paarl PO Box 266, Paarl 7620. Tel: (02211) 21811.

Mons Ruber Estate Private Bag X629, Oudtshoorn 6620. Tel: (04439) 6550. Wine maker: CJ Meyer. Open weekdays 08h30–17h00; Saturdays 08h30–13h00.

Montagu Co-op PO Box 29, Montagu 6720. Tel: (0234) 41125. Wine maker: Sonnie Malan. Open weekdays 08h30–12h30, 13h30–17h00.

Mont Blois Estate PO Box 181, Robertson 6705. Tel: (02351) 3872. Proprietor: Ernst Bruwer. Wine maker: Raymond Kirby. Visitors by appointment only.

Montpellier Estate PO Box 24, Tulbagh 6820. Tel: (0236) 300723. Proprietors: Jan and Hendrik Theron. Wine maker: Jan Theron. Open weekdays 09h00–12h30, 13h30–16h30; Saturdays 09h00–12h00.

Mooiuitsig Wynkelders PO Box 15, Bonnievale 6730. Tel: (02346) 2143. Fax: (02364) 2675. Wine makers: Chris Versveld, Francois Claassen and Wrench Roux. Executive Director: NL (Boet) Jonker. Open weekdays 08h00–17h30. Also make Bonwin, Monte Vista, Overberg, Overberger, Ouderust and Rusthof wines.

Môreson PO Box 114, Franschhoek 7690. Tel: (02212) 3055. Fax: (02212) 2348. Proprietors: Charles and Pauline Friedman. Wines made by and sold at Franschhoek Vineyards Co-op. Not open to members of the public.

Morgenhof PO Box 365, Stellenbosch 7599. Tel: (02231) 95510. Fax: (02231) 95266. Wine maker and General Manager: Jean Daneel. Open weekdays 09h00–16h30; Saturdays 09h00–12h30 (May to September), 09h00–15h00 (October to April). Summer lunches (picnics) and winter lunches served 12h00–14h00.

Moutonne-Excelsior PO Box 54, Franschhoek 7690. Tel: (02212) 2071. Fax: (02212) 2177. Wine consultants: Jan (Boland) Coetzee and Prof. Niel Matthee. Farm Manager: Johann Oldewager. Wines can be tasted at Die Binnehof by appointment only.

Muratie Wine Farm PO Box 133, Koelenhof 7605. Tel: (02231) 92330/6. Fax: (02231) 92790. Proprietor: Ronnie Melck. Wine maker: Johan Joubert. Manager: Hennie van der Westhuizen. Open weekdays 09h30–17h00; closes 16h00 on Friday. Saturdays 09h00–13h00.

Mulderbosch PO Box 548, Stellenbosch, 7599. Tel: (02231) 92488. Fax: (02231) 92351. Proprietor: Larry Jacobs. Wine maker: Mike Dobrovic. Not open to the public.

Nederburg Wines Private Bag X3006, Paarl 7620. Tel: (02211) 623104. Fax: (02211) 624887. Wine maker: Newald Marais. For daily tours, phone to book. Open weekdays 08h30–17h00; Saturdays (November to March only) 09h00–13h00.

Neethlingshof Estate PO Box 104, Stellenbosch 7599. Tel: (02231) 98988. Fax: (02231) 98941. Wine maker and Vintner: Hein Hesebeck. Open weekdays 09h00–17h00; Saturdays 10h00–16h00. Cellar tours by appointment. Reservations essential for group tastings and tours.

Neil Ellis Wines PO Box 917, Stellenbosch 7599. Tel: (02231) 92960. Fax: (02231) 92644. Wine maker: Neil Ellis. Visitors by appointment.

Nordale Co-op PO Box 105, Bonnievale 6730. Tel: (02346) 2050. Fax: (02346) 2192. Wine maker: Emile Schoch. Open weekdays 08h00–12h30, 13h30–17h00.

Nuy Wynkelder PO Box 5225, Worcester 6850. Tel: (0231) 70272. (0231) 74994. Wine maker and Manager: Wilhelm Linde. Open weekdays 08h30–16h30; Saturdays 08h30–12h30. Cellar tours conducted by appointment only.

Onverwacht Estate PO Box 438, Wellington 7655. Tel: (02211) 34315. Fax: (02211) 32237. Proprietor: Trevor Harris. Wine maker: Ian Naudé. Manager: Fanie Louw. Open for sales, tastings and cellar tours weekdays 10h00–16h00.

Opstal Estate PO Box 27, Rawsonville 6845. Tel: (0231) 91066. Wine maker: Stanley Louw. Open weekdays 09h00–11h00, 15h00–17h00; Saturdays by appointment.

Oranjerivier Wynkelders PO Box 544, Upington 8800. Tel: (054) 25651. General Manager: Noel Mouton. Open weekdays 08h00–12h45, 14h00–17h00; Saturdays 08h30–12h00.

Oude Nektar Estate PO Box 389, Stellenbosch 7599. Tel: (02231) 70690/7049. Fax: (02231) 70647. Proprietor: Hans-Peter Schröder. Open weekdays 09h30–17h00; Saturdays 11h00–16h00; non-religious public holidays 09h30–17h00. (Closed to the public on Saturdays from May to October.) Picnic lunches by appointment during December and January.

Overgaauw Estate PO Box 3, Vlottenburg 7604. Tel: (02231) 93815. Fax: (02231) 93436. Proprietor and wine maker: Chris Joubert. Assistant wine maker: Braam van Velden. Open weekdays 09h00–12h30, 14h00–17h00; Saturdays 10h00–12h30. Cellar tours conducted Wednesdays 14h30.

Overhex Co-op PO Box 139, Worcester 6849. Tel: (0231) 71057. Fax: (0231) 71057. Wine makers: Hennie Verster and Alkie van der Merwe. Manager: Hennie Verster. Open weekdays 08h30–17h00; Saturdays 09h00–12h00. Cellar tours by appointment.

Paddagang Vignerons Tulbagh. Tel: (0236) 300242. Fax: (0236) 300433. Manager: Jan Bester. Wine house open seven days a week 09h00–17h00 for breakfast, tea, lunch, wine sales and wine tasting.

Perdeberg Co-op PO Box 214, Paarl 7620. Tel: (02211) 638112. Fax: (02211) 638245. Wine maker: Joseph Huskisson. Open weekdays 08h00–12h30, 14h00–17h00.

Porterville Co-op PO Box 52, Porterville 6810. Tel: (02623) 2170. Fax: (02623) 2171. Wine maker: Klaas de Jongh. Open weekdays 08h30–13h00, 14h00–17h00; Saturdays 08h30–12h00.

Rhebokskloof PO Box 7141, Noorder Paarl 7620. Tel (02211) 638386. Fax: (02211) 638504. Wine maker: John Reagh. Open seven days a week 09h00–16h30 for wine tasting and sales. Also open on public holidays.

Riebeek Wine Farmers' Co-op PO Box 13, Riebeek-Kasteel 6801. Tel: (02244) 213/632. Fax: (02244) 281. Wine maker and Manager: Sias du Toit. Open weekdays 08h00–12h30, 13h30–17h30; Saturdays 08h30–12h00.

Rietrivier Co-op PO Box 144, Montagu 6720. Tel: (0234) 41705. Wine maker: Piet Frick. Open weekdays 08h00–13h00, 14h00–17h00.

Rietvallei Estate PO Box 386, Robertson 6705. Tel: (02351) 3596. Wine maker and proprietor: Johnny Burger. Open to the public by appointment only.

Robertson Co-op PO Box 37, Robertson 6705. Tel: (02351) 3059. Wine maker: Estesan Bruwer. Manager: Bowen Botha. Open Mondays to Thursdays 08h00–12h30, 13h30–17h00; Fridays 08h00–12h30, 13h30–16h30.

Romansrivier Co-op PO Box 108, Wolseley 6830. Tel: (0236) 311070/80. Fax: (0236) 311102. Manager and wine maker: Olla Olivier, assisted by Johan Louw. Open weekdays 08h30–12h00, 13h30–17h00; Saturdays 08h30–10h30.

Roodezandt Co-op PO Box 164, Robertson 6705. Tel: (02351) 2912/3020. Fax: (02351) 5074. Wine maker: Christie Steytler. Cellar Master/Manager: Abe Rossouw. Open weekdays 08h00–13h00, 14h00–17h30; Saturdays 08h30–12h30. Cellar tours by appointment.

Rooiberg Co-op PO Box 358, Robertson 6705. Tel: (02351) 3124. Fax: (02351) 3295. Wine maker: Tommy Loftus. Cellar master: Dassie Smith. Open weekdays 08h00–17h30; Saturdays 08h00–13h00.

Rozendal Farm PO Box 160, Stellenbosch 7599. Tel: (02231) 76855. Fax: (021) 8876854. Wine maker: Kurt Ammann. Open to the public by appointment only.

Ruiterbosch Mountain Vineyards *see* Boplaas Estate.

Rustenberg PO Box 33, Stellenbosch 7599. Tel: (02231) 73153. Fax: (02231) 78466. Proprietor: Simon Barlow. Wine maker: Etienne le Riche. Open weekdays and non-religious public holidays 09h00–12h30, 14h00–16h30; Saturdays 09h00–12h30.

Rustenburg Farm Claridge Wines. PO Box 407, Wellington 7655. Tel: (02211) 641241. Fax: (02211) 643620. Wine maker: Roger Jorgensen.

Rust-en-Vrede Estate PO Box 473, Stellenbosch 7599. Tel: (02231) 93881/93757. Fax: (02231) 93000. Proprietor: Jannie Engelbrecht. Wine maker: Kevin Arnold. Open weekdays 08h30–12h30, 13h30–16h30; Saturdays 09h00–12h00. Cellar tours by appointment only.

Saxenburg (Saxenheim) PO Box 171, Kuilsrivier 7580. Tel: (021) 9036113. Fax: (021) 9033129. Wine maker: Nico van der Merwe. Open weekdays 09h00–17h00; Saturdays 09h00–16h00.

Simondium Winery Co-op (formerly known as Drakenstein Co-op) Box 19, Simondium 7670. Tel: (02211) 41659. Wine maker and manager: WD Wagenaar. Open weekdays 08h30–17h00; Saturdays 08h30–12h30.

Simonsig Estate PO Box 6, Koelenhof 7605. Tel: (02231) 92044. Fax: (02231) 92545. Proprietors: Malan brothers. Wine maker: Johan Malan. Wine sales weekdays and non-religious public holidays 08h30–17h00; Saturdays 08h30–12h30. Cellar tours weekdays 10h00 and 15h00; Saturdays 10h00. Light meals served during December and January. 'Simonsig Snuffelwinkel' open at above times.

Simonsvlei Co-op PO Box 584, Suider Paarl 7624. Tel: (02211) 633040. Fax: (02211) 631240. General Manager: Kobus Louw. Production Manager and cellar master: Philip Louw. Wine maker: Bennie Wannenberg. Open weekdays 08h00–17h00; Saturdays 08h30–13h00. Lunches during December holidays and cellar tours weekdays by appointment.

Slanghoek Co-op PO Box 75, Rawsonville 6845. Tel: (0231) 91130. Wine maker: Kobus Rossouw. Open to the public, weekdays 07h30–12h30, 13h30–17h30. Closes at 16h30 on Fridays. Saturdays 10h00–12h00.

Soetwynboere Co-op PO Box 332, Montagu 6720. Tel: (0234) 41340. Wine maker: Mr Laubser. Open weekdays 08h00–12h30, 13h30–17h00; Saturdays 08h00–12h00.

Spier Estate PO Box 28, Vlottenburg 7604. Tel: (02231) 93725. Fax: (02231) 93514. Owner: Chris Joubert. Wine maker: Jan Smit. Open weekdays 08h30–13h00, 14h00–17h00; Saturdays 08h30–13h00.

Spruitdrift Co-op PO Box 129, Vredendal 8160. Tel: (0271) 33086/7. Fax: (0271) 32937. Wine maker: Johan Roussouw. Open weekdays 08h00–17h30; Saturdays 08h00–12h00. Cellar tours and wine tasting during office hours. Wine tasting and lectures offered to large groups and snoekbraai for groups of 10–40 can be arranged by appointment.

Stellenbosch Farmer's Winery (SFW) PO Box 46, Stellenbosch 7599. Tel: (02231) 73400. Production director: Duimpie Bayly. No cellar sales.

Stellenzicht Vineyards PO Box 104, Stellenbosch 7600. Tel: (02231) 901103. Fax: (02231) 78171. Wine maker: Hein Heesebek. Vintner: François Theron. Visitors by appointment.

Stettyn Co-op Private Bag 3011, Worcester 6850. Tel: (0231) 94220. Wine maker: Tienie Crous. Not open to the public.

Swartland Co-op PO Box 95, Malmesbury 7300. Tel: (0224) 21434/21134. Fax: (0224) 21750. Wine makers: Johan de Villiers and Christo Koch. Marketing manager: Albie van Vuuren. Open weekdays 08h00–17h00; Saturdays 09h00–12h00.

Talana Hill Chardonnay Wine Estate, Blaauwklip Rd, Stellenbosch. Enquiries: Doug Smollen. Tel: (011) 6407634. Proprietors: Doug Smollen and others. Wine maker: Jan Coetzee.

Thelema Mountain Vineyards PO Box 2234, Dennesig 7601. Tel: (02231) 91924. Fax: (02231) 91800. Wine maker: Gyles Webb. Open weekdays 09h00–17h00; Saturdays 09h00–13h00.

Theuniskraal Estate Tulbagh 6820. Tel: (0236) 300689/300690. Wine maker: Kobus Jordaan. Visitors by appointment.

Trawal Wynkelders PO Box 2, Klawer 8145. Tel: (02724) 61616. Fax: (02724) 61616. Wine maker: Frank Meaker. Manager: Kobus Basson. Open weekdays 08h00–13h30, 14h00–17h00, Saturdays 09h00–12h00. Not open on public holidays.

Tulbagh Co-op PO Box 85 Tulbagh 6820. Tel: (0236) 301001. Wine makers: Stephan Smit and Len Knoetze. Open weekdays 08h00–12h30; 13h30–17h15; Saturdays 08h30–12h00.

Twee Jongegezellen PO Box 16, Tulbagh 6820. Tel: (0236) 300680. Fax: (0236) 300686. Wine maker: Nicky Krone. Open for wine tasting weekdays 09h00–12h30, 14h00–17h00; Tours 11h00, 15h00; Saturdays 09h00–12h00. Large groups preferably by appointment.

Uiterwyk Estate PO Box 15, Vlottenburg 7604. Tel: (02231) 93711. Fax: (02231) 93776. Wine maker: Chris and Daniël de Waal. Open weekdays and Saturdays 09h00–16h30; 1 May–31 August Saturday 10h00–16h30.

Uitkyk Estate PO Box 3, Elsenburg 7607. Tel: (02231) 94710. Manager: Mr Cotze. Not open to the public.

Vaalharts Co-op PO Box 4, Hartswater 8570. Tel: (05332) 425111. Wine maker: Roelof Maree. Open weekdays 08h30–13h00 14h00–17h00.

Van Loveren PO Box 19, Klaasvoogds 6707. Tel: (0234) 51505. Fax: (0234) 51336. Wine maker: Wynand Retief. Viticulturist: Nico Retief. Open weekdays 08h30–13h00, 14h00–17h00; Saturdays 09h30–13h00.

Vergelegen PO Box 17, Somerset West 7129. Tel: (024) 517060. Fax: (024) 515608. Owned by Anglo American Farms Ltd. Wine maker: Martin Meinert. Vineyards: Felix Faure. Open to members of the public.

Vergenoegd Estate PO Box 1, Faure 7131. Tel: (024) 43248/43417. Proprietors: Jac and Brand Faure. Wine maker: John Faure. Open Wednesdays 14h00–17h00, or by appointment.

Villiera Estate PO Box 66, Koelenhof 7605. Tel: (02231) 92002/3/4. Fax: (02231) 92314. Wine maker: Jeff Grier. Viticulturist: Simon Grier. Open weekdays 08h30–17h00; Saturdays 08h30–13h00. Cellar tours by appointment only.

Villiersdorp Co-op PO Box 14, Villiersdorp 7170. Tel: (0225) 31120. Wine maker: JP Steenekamp. Kelkiewyn wine tasting and sales centre open weekdays 08h00–13h00, 14h00–17h00; Saturdays 08h00–13h00.

Vlottenburg Co-op PO Box 40, Vlottenburg 7604. Tel: (02231) 93828/9. Fax: (02231) 93357. Wine maker: Kowie du Toit. Open weekdays 08h30–17h00; Saturdays 09h00–12h30.

Vredendal Co-op PO Box 75, Vredendal 8160. Tel: (0271) 31080. Fax: (0271) 33476. Wine maker: Giel Swiegers. Open weekdays 08h00–12h30, 14h00–17h30; Saturdays 08h00–12h00.

Vredenheim Estate Wines (Made on the farm Vredenburg.) PO Box 369, Stellenbosch 7599. Tel: (02231) 93637/93878. Proprietor: CJ Bezuidenhout. Wine maker: Elzabé Bezuidenhout. Open weekdays 08h00–17h00; Saturdays (except May) 09h00–12h00.

Vriesenhof PO Box 155, Stellenbosch 7599. Tel: (02231) 900284/900214. Fax: (02231) 901503. Wine maker: Jan 'Boland' Coetzee.

Waboomsrivier Co-op PO Box 24, Breërivier 6858. Tel: (02324) 730. Fax: (02324) 731. Wine makers: Chris van der Merwe and Wim Viljoen. Open weekdays 08h30–17h00; Saturdays 08h00–10h00.

Wamakersvallei Co-op PO Box 509, Wellington 7657. Tel: (02211) 31582. Fax: (02211) 33194. Wine makers: Chris Roux and Pieter Rossouw. Open to visitors, weekdays 08h00–12h30, 14h00–17h00; Saturdays 08h30–12h30.

Warwick Estate PO Box 2, Muldersvlei 7606. Tel: (02231) 94410. Fax: (02231) 94025. Proprietor and wine maker: Norma Ratcliffe. Visitors by appointment only.

Welgemeend Estate PO Box 69, Klapmuts 7625. Tel: (02211) 5210. Fax: (02211) 5239. Wine maker: Louise Hofmeyr. Open Saturdays 09h00–12h30.

Wellington Wynboere Co-op PO Box 520, Wellington 7657. Tel: (02211) 31163. Fax: (02211) 32423. Wine maker: Gert Boerssen. Open weekdays 08h00–12h30, 14h00–17h00; Saturdays 08h30–12h00.

Welmoed Co-op PO Box 465, Stellenbosch 7599. Tel: (02231) 93800/1. Fax: (02231) 93434. Wine maker: Nicky Versveld. Open weekdays 08h30–17h30; Saturdays 08h30–17h00.

Weltevrede Estate PO Box 6, Bonnievale 6730. Tel: (02346) 2141/46. Fax: (02346) 2460. Proprietor and wine maker: Lourens Jonker, assisted by Kevin Grant. Open weekdays 08h30–17h00; Saturdays 10h00–16h30.

Windmeul Co-op PO Box 2031, Windmeul 7630. Tel: (02211) 638043/638100. Fax: (02211) 638614. Wine makers: Bernhard Luttich and Hein Koegelenberg. Manager: Bernhard Luttich. Wine sales open weekdays 08h00–12h30, 13h30–17h00; no tasting.

Zandvliet Estate PO Box 36, Ashton 6715. Tel: (0234) 51146/51823. Fax: (0234) 51327. Wine maker: Paul de Wet Jnr. Open weekdays 08h30–17h00; Saturdays 09h30–13h00. Cellar tours by appointment.

Zandwijk PO Box 2674, Paarl 7620. Tel: (02211) 632368. Fax: (02211) 631884. Proprietors: Cape Gate (Chairman: Mendal Kaplan). Wine maker: Leon Mostert. Open weekdays during business hours.

Zevenwacht PO Box 387, Kuils River 7580. Tel: (021) 9035123. Fax: (021) 9033373. Wine maker: Eric Saayman. Open weekdays 08h30–12h30, 13h03, 17h00; Saturdays 09h00–12h30.

Sugar Level Laws

In 1980 regulations were introduced which strictly define any claims made on a label as to the wine's degree of dryness or sweetness.

Extra Dry
Residual sugar not more than 2,5 grams per litre.

Dry
Residual sugar not more than 4 grams per litre.

Semi-dry
Residual sugar more than 4 but not more than 12 grams per litre (if more than 9, the total acid content shall not be more than 2 grams per litre lower than the sugar content).

Semi-sweet
Residual sugar more than 4 but not more than 30 grams per litre (if the sugar is less than 12 grams per litre then the total acid content must be lower than for semi-dry per litre).

Late Harvest
Residual sugar more than 20 but less than 30 grams per litre.

Special Late Harvest
Residual sugar more than 20 but less than 50 grams per litre.

Noble Late Harvest
Residual sugar more than 50 grams per litre.

Further requirements for Late Harvest wines are stated in the Government Gazette of 19 December 1980:

Late Harvest
a. Shall be obtained by the complete or partial fermentation of must;
b. Shall not be fortified;
c. Shall have an alcoholic strength of at least 10% alcohol by volume;
d. Shall have a residual sugar content, expressed as invert sugar, of more than 20 grams per litre but less than 30 grams per litre, irrespective of whether such residual sugar content has been obtained through the addition of sweet must or concentrated must to the wine concerned.

Special Late Harvest
a Shall be produced from must of which the sugar content prior to fermentation is at least 20 Balling; provided that:
• grapes of a sugar content of less than 21 Balling may not be pressed to obtain such must;
• such must may not be concentrated (dehydrated);
• no sweetening agent of any kind whatsoever may be added to such must;
b. Shall be obtained from partial alcoholic fermentation of such must;
c. Shall not be fortified;
d. Shall have an alcoholic strength of at least 10% alcohol by volume;

e. Shall have a residual sugar content of more than 20 grams per litre but not more than 50 grams per litre, provided that such residual sugar content will be derived solely from the grapes from which such wine has been produced, and that no sweetening agent of any kind whatsoever may be added to such wine;

f. Shall have a sugar-free extract of not less than 19 grams per litre;

g. Shall possess the character which is distinctive of wine which was produced from grapes which were harvested at a full-ripe stage.

Noble Late Harvest

a. Shall be produced from grapes of which the sugar content at the time of pressing thereof is at least 28 Balling;

b. Shall be obtained from the partial alcoholic fermentation of the must of such grapes, provided that:

- such must may not be concentrated (dehydrated);
- no sweetening agent of any kind may be added to such must;

c. Shall not be fortified;

d. Shall have a residual sugar content, expressed as invert sugar, of more than 50 grams per litre, provided that such residual sugar content shall be derived solely from the grapes from which such wine has been produced and that no sweetening agent of any kind whatsoever may be added to such wine;

e. Shall have a sugar-free extract of not less than 30 grams per litre;

f. Shall have the character which is distinctive of wine which was produced from grapes that were harvested late.

Sweet Natural

Must be more than 30 grams per litre, but need not be botrytis infected.

Sparkling Wines

Extra dry: 15 grams per litre or less;

Dry: 15–35 grams per litre;

Semi-sweet: 35–50 grams per litre;

Sweet: more than 50 grams per litre.

CAPE VINTAGE GUIDE

The following table is an attempt to indicate the range of quality between the vintages as experienced in the Cape generally. For details on different wines, consult the wine assessments.

Vintage	White Wines	Red Wines	Vintage	White Wines	Red Wines
1974	4	8-9	1984	4	8-9
1975	3	4	1985	6	4
1976	4	7-8	1986	5-6	9
1977	5	4	1987	6	8-9
1978	6	7-8	1988	4-7	6-7
1979	5	4-5	1989	4-6	6-8
1980	4	6-7	1990	5-8	8-9
1981	7	4-5	1991	6-9	8-10
1982	6	6-7	1992	5-9	7-9
1983	3	4	1993	6-9	7-9

Key to the vintage ratings:

1-2	=	Poor
3-4	=	Fair
5-6	=	Good
7-8	=	Excellent
9-10	=	Magnificent

1974 This year is considered by many as the outstanding vintage of the decade for reds. In general the whites suffered, although some Steens proved exceptional. The overall crop was down in quantity owing to poor setting conditions. Generally, the 1974 Cabernets are still showing well, although many have now reached their best.

1975 A fairly dry vintage with an exceptionally hot February which resulted in whites of very low acid; late rains tended to spoil the late-ripening reds, especially Cabernet, although there are some outstanding exceptions. This was the largest crop since 1971.

1976 A long, cold winter with late rains and snow. The vintage took place in almost ideal conditions and all cultivars produced good quantity and quality. Some reds have proved to be outstanding.

1977 A cool winter which was followed by a wet spring and poor berry set. The harvest was troubled with rain and was plagued by extensive downy mildew damage which resulted. The Cape Riesling crop was small but produced some excellent wines. High acids benefited all whites and gave reds a very French character, although they generally lacked colour. All red varietals showed well, although most have peaked by now.

1978 Another cool wet winter followed by rains which kept sugars low. Considered overall to be a vintage of good quality and quantity.

1979 The driest and also warmest winter since 1926. Warm and wet conditions resulted in a high incidence of botrytis which in some areas developed into noble rot. March was dry and cool so late-ripening reds showed rather well. Some have developed well, but most are not great.

1980 Overall a good vintage. Hot dry weather gave sound grapes with good sugars, but low acids. Cabernets are beginning to show very well.

1981 The year of the great flood at Laingsburg. This deluge did untold damage to vineyards in the Robertson, Montagu and Bonnievale areas. The cool weatherresulted in relatively higher fruit acids. There was large variation of quality within wine types with some exceptionally good white wines. Red grapes lacked sugar and colour; wines were generally lighter.

1982 The biggest crop to date. Almost perfect climatic conditions enabled superb wines to be made. Some reds are showing excellent character.

1983 The crop was up some 5% on the record harvest of 1982 and it was a sound vintage, although the acid and sugar levels were generally lower. Some exceptional wines were made. Wines are well-balanced and developing better than expected.

1984 The 1984 vintage was disease-free but slightly down on 1983. It was preceded by one of the wettest winters in ten years. Late bud burst meant that the harvest began some 10 days later than in 1983. A long, dry period from October to February resulted in some white varieties ripening under stress. This gave high sugars but low acid which led to rather neutral wines. The reds were magnificent. The late red cultivars produced excellent colour and a variety of red wine styles which are ageing well.

1985 A greater range of style and variety of wine was produced. The total crop was almost 10% down on 1984. Whites were generally better than reds. Cool conditions and frequent rains during the ripening period produced grapes with good acid/sugar ratio. Red wines have good flavour but are lighter than those of 1984.

1986 The hottest, driest summer for a couple of decades.Overall crop was down in quantity. Wine makers were delighted with the quality of the grapes and some excellent wines have resulted as fruit acid was good.

1987 The overall yield was down 10% on the 1986 vintage, due mainly to rot attacking the grapes, but the long, cool growing season ensured optimum ripeness in healthy grapes. The outstanding characteristic of the vintage was the balanced combination of high fixed acidity, low pH and good sugar, resulting in fruity whites and reds with good cellaring potential.

1988 The long, cool ripening season ended abruptly mid-vintage with four weeks of excessive heat. This brought much of the crop to ripeness simultaneously.The cooler areas seem to have potentially good wines from the better cultivars, such as Cabernet Sauvignon, Cape Riesling, Steen and Pinotage. Some magnificent sweet dessert wines were made.

1989 A good winter chilling occurred and the vines experienced normal and natural bud burst. It was a dry year with no late rains, although a cool spring lasted through to the end of December. This gave rise to slightly later ripening conditions. Improved quality and a greater concentration of flavour resulted. This was the first 'real' Chardonnay vintage.

1990 This was not an easy vintage as much of the top quality crop ripened at the same time, instead of being well spaced. This was the first vintage with sufficient earlier-ripening clones to have a marked effect on the picking programme. The relatively cool ripening period ended abruptly. Sugars suddenly developed and a lot of Steen and Pinotage ripened rapidly. Rain followed that caused rot in the Steen. Fortunately the Cape Doctor (south-easterly wind) blew strongly after the rain and dried the vineyards well. The pride and joy of this year's vintage was Cabernet Sauvignon. All of the cellars had excellent colours, good sugar/acid ratios and fine flavours. This, backed with the best-ever Merlot, made the first vintage of the 1990s potentially very exciting. All the reds are developing well. Sauvignon Blancs and Chardonnays are generally good.

1991 The 1991 vintage has been hailed as one of the best ever. Certainly it was one of the most favourable weather-wise. There was a lower than usual rainfall from September to December in 1990, followed by a very mild, almost cool spring and a cool, early summer. Cool evenings and good dew eased the summer strain on the vines and ensured constant moisture supply. All this resulted in some of the finest quality fruit from which some excellent wines have been made. Some of the earlier and mid-season varieties had almost perfect sugar/acid/pH balance. The late hot spell helped to increase the sugar content in some of the latest ripening varieties. Some excellent whites have appeared and early reds have good noses and lots of fruit.

1992 From all accounts this is another very good vintage and early releases of whites have shown some fine wines. Early reds are good and fruity, while those in wood are, in general, excellent.

1993 Overall, a smaller crop than the record 9,9 million hectolitre harvest of 1992. Flowering took place in cool conditions and ripening period was generally cool, but wind did considerable damage. All areas were affected by very hot weather in January. The main quality areas have produced better than average quality whites, but with a lot of Sauvignon Blanc not showing much varietal nose, and some decidedly disappointing. Chardonnays from Paarl, Stellenbosch and other areas, are generally flavourable and show good character. Early reds, such as Pinotage and Merlot, show good potential, with some late Cabernet Sauvignons a little disappointing. There are some good Cinsauts and Shirazes. Worcester and Robertson produced good, well-balanced wines, although generally lacking prominent cultivar nose. This should be a reasonable year for lower-priced Colombars and Steens.

AGEING WINES

South Africans are often chided about drinking their wines too young and then concluding that they do not like red wines because they 'bite' too much. This is a gross misapprehension, resulting from drinking the right wine at the wrong time. Although vintage is not reputed to play a very important role in South African wines, knowing the vintage year is relevant to the ageing or maturing of wines in the bottle. Traditionally, South African red wines are full-bodied, needing 10 or, if you can wait that long, 20 years of maturation. Today, however, there is an increasing number of light-bodied and some distinctly fruity red wines available on the market. These are either ready for immediate drinking or need far less maturation. Buy across the spectrum and choose a light red wine to drink through the year and at least two bottles a month of select red wines to put away. In this way you will soon build up your cellar and be in that enviable position of being able to match a memorable occasion with an equally memorable wine.

Red wines

It is generally held that the older a red wine, the better.

Cabernets require about 10 years or longer to reach their peak.

Pinotages may vary from three to nine years. For a typically young Pinotage taste with a flowery flavour keep the wine for three years, but if you prefer a more full-bodied bottle with mature character, store it for five or six years or more. Research carried out in 1984 showed most people prefer Pinotage of eight years and older.

Shiraz wines are generally soft and drinkable after three years but with a further three years can mature to a very rewarding full-bodied roundness and softness.

Tinta Barocca does not require long bottle maturation, so store it for three years and then drink it.

Cinsaut reaches its peak at three years but can also be left to mature for up to 10 years. Most Cinsauts are produced for early drinking.

The ageing times related here are, however, no more than rules of thumb – the actual time will depend on how the wine was made and how it is stored. Judging the optimum time for an individual wine comes only with experience.

Nouveau wines

The concept of Nouveau wine may be fashionable but it is not new, for as long as man has made wine, much of it has been drunk before fermentation is complete. The concept of bottling young wine and marketing it as a product for early consumption is, however, relatively new.

In 1982 Stellenbosch Farmers' Winery launched the idea in South Africa with their Nouveau Range. Walter Finlayson was quick to follow with the Blaauwklippen Nouveau and Spatz Sperling with an early Pinotage Rosé. It took the wine master, Günter Brözel, however, to produce a Gamay, the traditional grape used for this style of wine in Beaujolais. The Nederburg Gamay appeared at the Nederburg Auction on 20 April 1985, 55 days after pressing. In 1986, it was released just 30 days after harvesting. KWV and Simonsig are now both producing white variations and others who are joining the Nouveau trend are Fairview, Villiera, Woolworths, and Buitenverwachting with its colourful L'Arrivée.

Production is traditionally by carbonic maceration. The wine is normally chaptalized and early fermentation occurs at fairly warm temperatures (25–30°C) to extract good colour. This fresh red wine should be enjoyed young and chilled as an ideal picnic drink or with a hot breakfast in winter.

White wines

White wines, unlike the reds, do not need long bottle maturation; in fact, most of them should be drunk immediately. One can, however, drink a white wine any time within one or two years from vintage, when the flavour is delicate, fruity and characteristically young and fresh. Some wines, especially those that are semi-sweet, benefit from storing for some two to three years from vintage.

Nederburg Edelkeur, the honey-sweet, golden-hued wine, considered the pride of the wine maker's art in South Africa, should be stored for ten years after vintage, according to Patrick Grubb, the respected British wine auctioneer. In all, very few local dry white wines will benefit with age, notable exceptions being some dry Rieslings which need two or three years to reach full development. Some of the 'new wave' wood-aged whites will benefit with a few years of bottle age.

Sparkling wines

Most bubblies are released at the time the wine maker believes they are ready for drinking. The important part of ageing bubblies is the time spent on the lees. Once degorged, not much more dramatic development will take place other than ageing. Some Méthode Cap Classique wines are at their best when degorged but will still develop in the bottle. The English tend to enjoy very old and almost flat champagne. Most people prefer their bubblies relatively fresh. A couple of years after degorging is usually as much as one should let bubblies age. Most tank-produced bubblies don't really benefit from more than a year or two in the bottle unless the wine used was exceptional, as is the case with some of the top-class German Sekts.

GLOSSARY

Acidity All grapes contain fruit acids and these stay in the liquid when the grapes are crushed, ending up in the final wine. High fruit acid produces sharp wines, a little less produces fresh, fruity wines and very little results in soft wines.

Aftertaste *See* Farewell

Ampelography The scientific study of the description and classification of the vine and the grape.

Appearance The first step in wine appreciation which is the assessment of colour and clarity.

Aroma A term used to describe the fragrance of a wine owing to the fruit.

Astringency The quality in a wine which makes the mouth pucker. The degree of astringency depends on the amount of tannin absorbed by the wine from the skins, pips and stalks of grapes.

Balling The concentration of sugar in the grapes, expressed in degrees.

Blanc de Noir White wine made from red grapes. The skins are removed at the time of pressing and thus impart only the slightest blush.

Blending The art of 'mixing' wines of different grape varieties, vintages, areas and qualities to achieve a particular end.

Body The consistency or substance of a wine. It refers to the quantity of solid matter or extract in solution in the wine.

Botrytis cinerea (Noble rot) This is a fungoid infection that attacks ripe grapes under certain climatic conditions. In its development the fungi evaporates moisture from the grapes, causing them to shrivel and concentrate the relative sugar content. Wine makers use this process of 'noble rot' to make rich, sweet wines such as Nederburg Edelkeur and various other Noble Late Harvest wines. If the weather conditions are other than 'optimum', the fungus can rapidly turn to vulgar rot, thereby ruining the harvest.

Bottle age Mellow development observed in the bouquet of a wine and its smoothness across the palate.

Bottle sickness A loss of flavour and bouquet caused by excessive contact of the wine with air at the time of bottling.

Bouquet Fragrance derived from fermentation, maturation and ageing.

Bordeaux Famous wine-producing region on the western coast of France where the main red grapes are Cabernet Sauvignon, Cabernet Franc, Merlot, Malbec, etc. and the wines are blends of those varieties. The white wines of the area are mainly Sauvignon Blanc, Sémillon and Muscadel and the wines are blends of these. Hence the term 'Bordeaux Blend' for wines using combinations of the varieties.

Brut French term for dry. Generally applied to sparkling wines and champagne with a sugar content of 1,5% or less.

Carbonic maceration Vinification without crushing grapes. Whole bunches are placed into pressure tanks and intercellular fermentation under oxygen-free conditions occurs. This process is used in Beaujolais Nouveau production.

Cask A wooden wine barrel, varying in capacity; it is usually made of oak and bound with steel hoops.

Chaptalization The addition of sugar to grape musts, either before or during fermentation, to increase the alcohol content of wine.

Charmat In short: tank-produced. Méthode Charmat is a patent method of producing sparkling wine where the bubbles are produced when the wine undergoes secondary fermentation in a tank. The wine is then bottled under pressure. It is a lot less expensive than doing it in individual bottles. The name Charmat is applied to most tank-produced bubblies.

Chateau Though meaning 'castle', it is today the name given to properties such as wine estates and vineyards in the Bordeaux region famous for their wine: Chateau Mouton-Rothschild, Chateau Loudenne, etc.

Clarity A wine must be attractive to the eye, clean and bright, not cloudy or dull.

Clean No foreign smell or taste.

Closed A descriptive term used when the potential of a young wine remains 'locked in' and does not show.

Cooper An artisan who makes and/or repairs wooden casks.

Corked 1. A wine adversely affected by an infected cork. 2. Any wine sealed with a cork.

Crisp Good acid; a clean and refreshing wine.

Crust Sediment precipitated on the inside of a bottle of wine, especially Port, after long bottle maturation.

Cultivar A term used for a grape variety used in viticulture.

Cuvée Literally, the contents of a cask, generally applied to a specially prepared blend of wine.

Decanting Process of pouring wine from the original container into a decanter, care being taken to ensure that sediment is not disturbed in the process in the case of old wines. In the case of young wines decanting serves to aerate it, thus enhancing bouquet and aroma.

Dessert wine A generic term frequently used to describe very sweet fortified wines.

Dry wine Legally a dry wine cannot exceed four grams of residual sugar per litre. However, a wine completely without sugar can taste very smooth and almost sweet if low in acid, whereas a wine with relatively high sugar appears drier if the acid content is high.

Elegant Harmonious and refined, with good style.

Extract The soluble solids that are non-volatile, and non-sugars.

Farewell A term used to describe the flavour and the length of time that the flavour remains in the mouth after swallowing the wine.

Feel The term used to describe the sensation that the wine gives in the mouth before swallowing.

Fortification The addition of brandy or grape spirit to wine. The process is used in making Ports, Sherries and Dessert wines.

Fresh A young, lively wine.

Fruity A wine of good acidity which gives off the aroma of fruits, not only grape; for example, Steen wines often have a guava aroma.

Full-bodied A wine high in all its individual components.

Gewürz Spicey flavour of bouquet.

Hard High tannin gives wines a hardness which will soften with age.

Heavy This need not be derogatory and is usually used to describe a wine high in alcohol and flavours, which often needs time to mellow.

Honest No great attribute, but a good, clean, well-made wine.

Late Harvest, Special Late Harvest, Noble Late Harvest South African terms to describe a sweetish, medium- to full-bodied white wine having sugar levels from 20 g/l upwards.

Lees The deposit at the bottom of the fermenting vessel. Mainly made up from the dead yeast cells. Prolonged contact of wine with lees can influence the character of the wine.

Light Low in alcohol and body, but this can be an attribute.

Maderized A term used to describe a particular aged condition of wine; a baked taste usually owing to storing conditions being too hot.

Malolactic fermentation The conversion of malic acid to lactic acid in wine, resulting in a wine which tastes less acidic.

Maturation Process whereby wines are left in wood or bottles to age, improve and mellow. The period of maturation depends on the type and character of the wine.

Mellow Softened with age.

Méthode Champenoise The method of making sparkling wine employed in Champagne in the north-east of France in which the all-important second fermentation takes place in the bottle in which the wine is ultimately sold. The method is being used more and more in the Cape.

Mousse The froth or foam produced when Perlé or Sparkling wines are poured.

Must Freshly-pressed, unfermented grape juice, with or without skins and pips.

Natural wine Unfortified table wine to which nothing extraneous has been added.

New clone This is a term used not quite correctly. New clone should imply recently developed new clones of particular cultivars. However, it is generally used to describe virus-free vines.

Noble Well bred, classy.

Nose A term for the bouquet and aroma of the wine. A wine with a good nose produces pleasant sensations when smelled.

N.V. Non-vintage; meaning no claim to the year of production.

Oak This is the preferred wood used for the casks and barrels in which wine is matured. All the finest red wines, most of the fortified wines and some white wines owe part of their quality to the flavour imparted by oak.

Oaky An odour of oak apparent in wines aged too long in casks. It is desirable in fine red table wines but is unpleasant when excessive and especially so in white table wines.

Oenology The science of wine and wine making. The cellar as opposed to the vineyard (vineyard = viticulture).

Open A fully developed wine, showing all its characteristics.

Organoleptic Scientific term for the evaluation of wines using the senses of sight, smell and taste.

Oxidized A fault in wine owing to excessive exposure to air, and which can be detected by both the nose and palate.

Perfumed The aroma usually derived from the grape, e.g. Muscadel.

Perlé, Perlant Not quite a still wine, but not a sparkling wine either. Some bubbles of carbon dioxide have, however, been introduced, giving it a slight effervescence.

Perlé wine Slightly effervescent wine, as opposed to sparkling wine which effervesces vigorously.

Pétillant A word the French originated and is now more widely used to describe wines which, like Pérle wines, contain a little gas, being lightly sparkling.

pH This is the measure of strength of acidity and not the amount of acid. The measurement scale is such that above the value seven is alkaline and below is acid, and the lower the figure the stronger the acid. The warmer the growing climate, the higher the pH of the wine made and the cooler the climate, the lower the pH. This explains why many of the finest wines come from the cooler growing areas. Lower pH also helps to prevent bacterial spoilage, allows more effective sulphur dioxide use and gives wine a better colour.

Pipe A cask made of oak and tapered sharply towards the ends, it is used to mature Port. It comes in varying sizes, the most common holding 522 litres; the standard Madeira pipe is considerably smaller.

Port Name for the classic fortified wines produced in the Douro Valley of Portugal and shipped from Oporto. Port-style wines, both red and white, are produced in most wine-producing regions.

Premier Grand Crû A term used in South Africa as a name for a class of blended dry wines. This type of wine should be as dry as vinification techniques allow.

Red wine Made by fermenting red grapes in the presence of their skins so that the pigments in the skin can colour the wine. Red wines usually contain more tannin than whites and are often aged for a year or two in wooden barrels before being bottled.

Residual sugar (RS)
All grapes contain sugar and it is the conversion of this sugar by yeast into alcohol and carbon dioxide that gives wine. If not all the sugar is converted and some remains behind in the wine, this portion is termed residual sugar.

Rosé Rosé wines are made by fermenting red grapes in contact with their skins for only a matter of hours until the wine maker judges he has obtained that degree of pink colour which gives Rosé wine its name. The juice is then separated from the skins so that no further coloration takes place and the fermentation continues as for white wine. Rosés can be semi-sweet or dry.

Rough Lacking in finesse.

Round Well-balanced and mature.

Semi-sweet A term used in South Africa to describe wines that have an excess of four grams per litre of residual sugar but not more than 30 grams. In practice wines so described normally have about 20 g/l and are usually white.

Sharp A wine with high acid, which will mellow with age.

Smooth Soft texture.

Solera A system of maturing and blending Sherry to produce a consistent product year after year. The process evolved in Spain and is employed for the best sherries in South Africa. The casks are arranged in three tiers, with each supplying the one below, wine for bottling being drawn from the bottom cask.

Sound Well-made wine but without great attributes.

Sour Applied to wine spoiled by acetic acid bacteria and which is therefore vinegary. Not to be confused with Dry, Tart or Astringent.

Sparkling wine An effervescent wine owing to the presence of carbon dioxide gas.

Spicey Rich and aromatic.

Spumante Italian style of sparkling wine usually with Muscat in character and, in South Africa, usually sweet.

Stein A name used in South Africa for an extremely popular class of blended semi-sweet wines. They are characterized by a good, fruity flavour and sugar levels of 1–2% by volume. Not to be confused with 'Steen' (Chenin Blanc), which is the most widely grown grape.

Sulphur dioxide (SO_2) The use of sulphur to sterilize wine is almost as old as wine itself. In the modern wine cellar small but effective amounts of sulphur dioxide are used as the standard sterilizing agent for casks and barrels. It is also extensively used in the vineyards to control vine disease. Compared with some European countries the sulphur level in South African wines is very low. For natural table wines the permitted maximum is 200 parts per million. This can be exceeded only in Noble Late Harvests.

Sur lie Means 'on the lees' and is usually applied when bottled directly from the casks which have not been racked. Such wines usually possess greater freshness and can have a slight 'prickle' or pétillance. More loosely applied in South Africa to wines that have spent some time on their lees prior to bottling and are not necessarily bottled direct from the cask.

Tannin A group of organic compounds occurring in the bark, wood, roots, skins, pips and stems of many plants and fruits, including the grape. It is most pronounced in red wines which pick up tannin from the skins and pips during maturation in oak barrels.

Tart Natural and agreeable fruity-acid taste in wine.

Tawny 1. Applied to wines which have turned from red to a brownish colour with maturation. 2. A type of port.

Thin Lacking alcohol, watery and feeble.

Total acidity (TA) This is the collective amount of fruit and volatile acids in a wine and is usually expressed as grams per litre.

Tough Full-bodied but needing age to soften.

Traditional Blend A phrase that I think I was possibly the first to use. I applied it to South African red blends that contained Cabernet and another cultivar or numerous other cultivars including Shiraz, Pinotage, Cinsaut and various Port varieties.

Varietal *See* Cultivar

Vermouth A fortified herbal wine, dry or sweet, flavoured with aromatic herbs. Most wine-producing countries produce vermouth-type wines.

Vin gris A pale pink wine made, as with Blanc de Noir wines, from red grapes. Not to be confused with the cultivar Pinot Gris.

Vin ordinaire An inexpensive wine often sold by the glass or carafe. Taken to mean everyday or house wine.

Vinho Verde A type of natural wine made in Portugal near to Oporto. Usually finished with a slight pétillance.

Vinosity The depth or degree to which a particular wine shows vinous qualities.

Vintage 1. Used to signify the grape-gathering season: the yield is known as the harvest. 2. The year in which a wine was made. 3. A 'vintage year' is a year in which excellent wines were made.

Virus free This is a term applied to grapes that have been cleared of virus infection and therefore perform better than those infected.

Volatile acid Fruit acids should not be confused with volatile acid which is the acid of vinegar, better known as acetic acid. It is not found in the grape and develops after the alcoholic fermentation. In minute quantities it can be quite attractive, especially in red wines, but larger amounts are unpleasant and make the wine too vinegary.

Weight A term applied to the feel of the wine in the mouth.

BEST BUYS OF THE YEAR

Some buys are good value for money, and those that really appeal to me, have been marked with a ★. The other wines on the list are those that appeal to me, no matter the cost.

Alphen Le Fevre 1993
Backsberg Merlot 1990 ★
Bertrams Shiraz 1986
Beyerskloof Cabernet
  Sauvignon 1991
Blaauwklippen
  – Pinot Noir 1989
  – Zinfandel 1989
Boplass Vintage Reserve
  Port 1989
Boschendal Jean Garde
  Gewürztraminer 1990
Buitenverwachting
  – Christina
  – Gamay L'Arivee 1993
  – Merlot 1989
Claridge Chardonnay 1992
Craighall
  – Chardonnay
  – Sauvignon Blanc
Delaire Chardonnay 1992
Delheim
  – Cabernet Sauvignon ★
  – Grand Reserve
Du Toitskloof
  – Cinsaut ★
  – Special Late Harvest
Eersterivier Sauvignon
  Blanc 1992
Eikendal
  – Chardonnay 1992
  – Merlot 1991 ★
Fairview
  – Gamay Noir
  – Reserve Shiraz
Fleur du Cap
  Gewürztraminer 1991
Glen Carlou
  Chardonnay 1992
Glen Carlou Les Trois ★
Graham Beck Cap
  Classique NV ★
Grangehurst
Hamilton Russell
  – Chardonnay 1992
  – Pinot Noir 1991
Hippo Creek Sauvignon
  Blanc/Chardonnay 1992

John Platter Chardonnay
Kanonkop
  – Paul Sauer 1989
  – Pinotage 1989/1990
Klein Constantia
  – Blanc de Blanc 1991
  – Chardonnay 1990
  – Marlbrook 1988
L'Ormarins
  Chardonnay 1991
La Motte
  – Millenium 1989 ★
  – Shiraz 1988
Le Bonheur Cabernet 1984
Lievland
  – Lievlander ★
  – Shiraz 1990
Louisvale
  Chardonnay 1992
Meerlust
  – Merlot 1989
  – Rubicon 1989
Mulderbosch Sauvignon
  Blanc 1992
Nederburg
  – Chardonnay
  – Eminence
  – Sauvignon Blanc ★
Neethlingshof
  Cabernet 1989
Neethlingshof
  – Noble Late Harvest
    Sauvignon Blanc
  – Noble Late Harvest
    Weisser Riesling
Neil Ellis
  – Cabernet
  – Sauvignon Blanc
Nuy Muscadels
Overgaauw
  – DC Classic Merlot
  – Tria Corda 1988
Roodezandt
  White Muscadel ★
Rust en Vrede
  – Blend
  – Cabernet Sauvignon
  – Shiraz

Rustenburg
  – Cabernet
  – Gold
Simonsig
  – Adelberg ★
  – Adelblanc ★
  – Pinotage
  – Tiara
Stellenryck
  – Cabernet Sauvignon
  – Gewürztraminer
Stellenzicht
  – Grand Vin Blanc ★
  – Grand Vin Noir
Swartland Steen ★
Talana Hill Royale 1989
Tassenberg ★
Thelema
  – Cabernet
  – Chardonnay
  – Sauvignon Blanc
TJ Krone Borealis
Villiera
  – Crû Monro ★
  – Merlot
  – Sauvignon Blanc ★
  – Tradition de Charles
    de Ferve NV ★
Vriesenhof
  – Cabernet
  – Kallista
Warwick
  – Cabernet Franc
  – Merlot
  – Trilogy
Welgemeend
Weltevrede
  – Chardonnay ★
  – Prive du Bois 1991 ★
Woolworths
  – Cabernet Sauvignon-
    Merlot 1990★
  – Grand Rouge 1991 ★
  – Sauvignon Blanc 1991
  – Shiraz 1989 ★
Zonnebloem
  – Pinotage
  – Shiraz

BORDEAUX BLENDS

Alto Rouge ★★★(★) D

I have, to date, included this entry under Cape Traditional Blends. However, the modern character is very much along the style of Bordeaux Blends (as mentioned in the 1993 edition) and even though it still contains a proportion of Shiraz, I have decided to move it here. Always one of the aristocrats of South African traditional blends, it is now almost lost among the range of high quality, small oak aged blends of Cabernet Sauvignon, Cabernet Franc and Merlot. Until 1985 it was usually a blend of Cabernet Sauvignon, Shiraz and Tinta Barocca, although the proportions varied with the vintage. In 1985 the blend changed to include Cabernet Franc and Merlot, and had a much-reduced Shiraz content. I am sad to see this wine lose its traditional character and follow the latest red wine fashion as it really was one of our earliest surviving blends. The wines of the 1970s all developed well over 12–15 years with the 1987 (to my mind) being the best and still very good in 1993. The wines of the 1980s have varied in character and style with a major change in blend for 1985. The 1984 is developing well and the 1985 is drinking very well now. The 1986 still needs time to develop its full potential while the 1987 drinks well now and is considered to be one of the best wines from Alto's cellar. It will be well worth ageing through to the end of the century. The 1989 is a beautiful wine with everything; rich and full with big 13,5% alcohol, and will develop over the years.

75 ★★★★ drink up. 76 ★★★★★ ready. 77 ★★★ past its best, drink up. 78 ★★★★★ ready, will still improve. 79 ★★★ ready. 80 ★★★★ ready, will still improve. 81 ★★★★ ready. 82 ★★★★(★) ready, will still improve. 83 ★★★ ready. 84 ★★★★ ready, will still improve. 85 ★★★★ ready, will still develop. 86 ★★★★(★) not ready, age further. 87 ★★★★(★) ready, will age further. 88 ★★★★ not ready, age further. 89 ★★★★ not ready, age further. 90 ★★★★ not ready, age further.

Arthur Freedberg Beau Rouge (Rebel) ★★★(★) B/C

This is a big, full-flavoured wine from Cabernet Sauvignon and Merlot. Although non-vintaged, it showed lots of youth and full tannins late in 1992, which will allow good ageing over five to six years.

Avontuur Avon Rouge ★★★★ B

A good-value, non-vintaged red blend with early releases being predominantly Cabernet Sauvignon with 30% Merlot and about 15% Cabernet Franc. More recent releases are almost two thirds Cabernet Sauvignon with Merlot and Cabernet Franc making up the balance. It shows good varietal character and, despite a youthful release, is not tannic but soft on the palate with just a hint of oak. It was awarded Gold at the 1992 Veritas Awards.

Avontuur Baccarat ★★★★ D

The first release from the 1989 vintage has developed very well in the bottle. The 1990 is much along the same lines with 70% Merlot and 30% Cabernet Sauvignon, but with much deeper flavours. They drink well now, but both will benefit with four to six years ageing. The 1991 continues with this winning style. Baccarat is pronounced without the 't', thus Baccara, and is the name of a deep red, almost black, rose that has been the inspiration for Avontuur's labelling of their inky, black-red wine.

Backsberg Klein Babylonstoren ★★★★(★) D

This, the flagship of Backsberg reds and in keeping with the cellar style, is easy to drink within three years of vintage, yet has the ability to develop with benefit over six to eight years. The first release from the 1984 vintage was predominantly Cabernet Sauvignon with as much as 40% Merlot, and well-wooded in new oak. It developed well and now needs to be enjoyed. The 1985 is a little more reserved, elegant and stylish and about at its best now. The 1986 is 50% of each of the two varieties and is a delicious, full-flavoured wine. Soft yet fruity, it makes delightful drinking now but will still develop over another two to three years. The 1987 is 40% each of Cabernet Sauvignon and Merlot, and 20% Cabernet Franc with far more intense character. The 1988 went back to being a 50/50 blend of Merlot and Cabernet Sauvignon. The 1989 and 1990 are 70% Cabernet Sauvignon and 30% Merlot. Since 1988 more and more new clone Cabernet Sauvignon has been used, with the 1990 Cabernet Sauvignon content all from new clone. This has resulted in great berry character and made it a more forward, fruity, and most appealing early-drinking wine. All have good wood, lovely flavours and are easy to drink when released.

84 ★★★★ ready, drink up. 85 ★★★★ ready, will still keep. 86 ★★★★★ ready, will develop. 87 ★★★★(★) ready, will develop. 88 ★★★(★) ready, will develop. 89 ★★★★ allow to develop. 90 ★★★★(★) allow to develop.

Barrydale Co-op Tradeaux Reserve ★★★★ C

A surprisingly good first attempt from the 1991 vintage bodes well for this area not noted for red wine. Less than 30 cases were blended from 60% Cabernet Sauvignon and 20% each Cabernet Franc and Merlot. The 1992 will give more commercial quantity while the 1993 should give a couple of hundred cases.

Bertrams Robert Fuller ★★★★(★) E

This blend, with its first release from the 1984 vintage, is a major departure from the traditional style of Bertrams' reds. Made under the guidance of Martin van der Merwe and now continued by Leo Burger, the 1984 is 70% Cabernet Sauvignon and 30% Merlot. It was aged first in large wood and then spent about half a year in small new Nevers oak casks. It has the Bertrams fullness and is drinking very well in 1992. In the 1985 vintage, Merlot has been reduced to 20%, but it has more wood, giving slightly lighter but better flavoured wine. The 1986 is an excellent wine with some 70% Cabernet Sauvignon and 30% Merlot. Launched in May 1991, this is a much bigger, fuller wine, and the best so far under this label. It was awarded Double Gold in 1992. Good wood and tannin will ensure good and long ageing. This is another wine to see in the new century. The 1987 is 85% Cabernet Sauvignon and 15% Merlot and has been a slow starter. It is not as open as previous excellent wines, but is now beginning to develop well.

84 ★★★★(★) *ready, enjoy now.* 85 ★★★★ *ready, will develop further.* 86 ★★★★★ *ready, will develop further.* 87 ★★(★) *allow to develop.* 88 ★★★★(★) *allow to develop.*

Blaauwklippen Cabriolet ★★★(★) D

The first release from 1983, is a delightful lightish red wine, comprising almost three-quarters Merlot, the balance Cabernet Sauvignon, and aged for two years in small wood. Walter Finlayson opted to sell the wine without any mention of the fact that it was rated Superior. It has aged with interest and drinks particularly well now, but has probably reached the limit of its development. It will still hold its maturity. The 1988 release, which was sold at the Cape Independent Winemakers' Guild annual auction, is 80% Cabernet Sauvignon and 20% Merlot and is much better wine than previous vintages. This wine received a Gold at the 1992 Veritas Awards.

Boplaas Grand Vin Rouge ★★★★ D

A very limited quantity (120 cases) of the 1987 was made available mid-1990. The 90% Cabernet and 10% Merlot give a very attractive fruity nose and good, concentrated, elegant flavours backed by fine oak. It is developing beautifully in the bottle and the 13,6% alcohol and good tannins will no doubt allow many years before it reaches its full potential. There was no 1988; the next release was from the 1989 vintage. In this one the Cabernet Sauvignon was reduced to 50% and the balance made up of Cabernet Franc and Merlot. It is not as dramatic as the 1987, but give it time to develop. There was no 1990. The next release will be the 1991 which is 70% Cabernet Sauvignon and 30% Merlot.

Boschendal Grand Vin ★★★(★) E

The first release from the 1985 vintage has proved to be somewhat disappointing. The 1986 release is considerably better and easily four-star material. It apparently has less Merlot than the 1985 and is an elegant, restrained wine with good wood backing. The 1985 vintage is not developing with any excitement; it has browned considerably and should be drunk up. The 1986 is developing better than 1985. The 1990, however, is a great improvement – comprising 90% Merlot with 10% Cabernet Sauvignon and lots of oak. Future vintages could prove this Estate, which has a reputation for fine white wines, and may make it into the major league reds.

Bovlei Co-op Grand Rouge ★★(★) A

Early offerings of this non-vintaged wine were easy-drinking blends of Shiraz and Pinotage. The latest offerings are a blend of unwooded Cabernet and Merlot which gives a full-flavoured, early drinking wine. Good value for money.

Buitenverwachting Buiten Keur ★★★(★) D

The blend from the 1986 vintage was the cellar's entry into the Bordeaux style of wines made in the Cape. Released late in 1990 it spent 14 months in new Nevers oak before bottling. A little more than half the blend is Cabernet with a balance of 40% Merlot and a fraction Cabernet Franc. Deep in colour and character, with the Cabernet showing strongly through good oak, it is developing well. The next offering is from the 1987 vintage and is almost 70% Cabernet Sauvignon, a little more than 15% Merlot and 15% Cabernet Franc. Also out of Nevers barrels, it has a little more body and firmer tannin. The 1988 is about half Merlot, one-third Cabernet Sauvignon and the balance Cabernet Franc. It is slightly subdued but will develop.

Buitenverwachting Grand Vin ★★★★ E

The first release from the 1988 vintage is a particularly full-flavoured, berry-type wine made from 70% Cabernet Sauvignon, 20% Merlot, and 10% Cabernet Franc, with nice toastiness from new oak. It carries a classy new label. The 1989 is a deep, dark wine, packed with character and fully deserving its Double Gold at the 1992 Veritas Awards.

Calitzdorp Co-op Vin Rouge ★★(★) B

From the 1991 vintage comes a blend of 60% Cabernet Sauvignon and 40% Merlot, resulting in a wine with attractive fruity nose, good flavour and sound oak backing. It makes for enjoyable drinking and is a good attempt from a region not known for its quality reds.

Cape Vintners Members Only Grand Reserve ★★★★ D

The 1988 is predominantly Cabernet with Merlot and Cabernet Franc, aged for a year in second–fill Allier and Nevers barrels. Good character with lots of tannin. The 1989 is a fine wine with good berry character, from 80% Cabernet Sauvignon and 20% Merlot, backed by nice oak. It should develop well.

Claridge Red Wellington ★★★★ D

From this new Wellington-based cellar comes an excellent entry into the world of wine. It is a blended red with a power-packed 14% alcohol, containing 60% Cabernet Sauvignon, 20% Merlot and 10% Cabernet Franc. It is sold in attractive and very sensible 500 ml bottles. It should develop with great benefit.

Clos Malverne Auret ★★★★ E

Clos Malverne only produce red wine and Auret is their flagship. Only 500 cases containing six bottles each were produced from selected barrels of the 1988 vintage. This wine, which was released late in 1990, is a very distinct, rich, intense wine that should develop well into the late 1990s. It is all Cabernet that had been selected from 20 new 225 litre Nevers barrels where it spent 10 months. The second release was from the 1989 vintage: 1 100 cases made up of 82% Cabernet Sauvignon and 18% Merlot that has aged in new and second–fill Nevers for 14 months. The 1990 has more Merlot (24%), and should develop well over five to seven years.

Clos Malverne Auret Reserve ★★★★(★) F

A limited quantity, about 120 cases of numbered bottles, of 1990 Auret Reserve was produced. A blend of 75% Cabernet and the balance Merlot, it had 16 months in new Nevers and Allier barrels. It was the South African Champion Wood-matured Dry Red at the 1990 Young Wine Show and is a real mouthful of powerful flavour that will need many years to reach its potential.

Delaire Barrique ★★★★ E

The first release, from 1988 vintage, is a well-wooded blend of equal proportions of Cabernet and the 1988 Gold Medal South African Champion Merlot. A deep, rich, full-flavoured wine with lots of fruit and good wood, it is developing well and should be at its best in eight to twelve years. The 1989 is predominantly Merlot (85%), with Cabernet Sauvignon giving a luscious, full-flavoured wine, soft in the mouth yet with lots of good oak backing. As well as it drinks now, its tannin and almost 13% alcohol will allow further development. This cellar produces deep rich reds and the 1990, which is 35% Merlot and 65% Cabernet Sauvignon, is again top quality with cassis, cherries and vanilla that will all develop with time. The 1991 continues the same good character.

De Leuwen Jagt Rood ★★★(★) E

From the 1990 vintage comes a blend of 70% Cabernet Sauvignon and 30% Merlot with lots of fruit, eucalyptus, and herb characters.

Delheim Grand Reserve ★★★★★ F

This is now firmly established as one of the Cape's great reds. Originally released from the 1981 vintage, and along with the 1982 and 1983, it was entirely Cabernet Sauvignon. Excellent small new-wood-ageing gave these wines beautiful character. From 1984 these wines have contained varying proportions of Cabernet Franc, with the 1986 comprising 65% Cabernet Sauvignon, 11% Cabernet Franc and 24% Merlot (the lowest Cabernet content yet). This will rank as one of South Africa's real greats. Previously, the blend was more or less 65–75% Cabernet Sauvignon and Merlot and usually no Cabernet Franc, whereas the 1988 and 1989 vintages are both 75% Cabernet Sauvignon and 25% Merlot, and the 1990 is 100% Cabernet Sauvignon. As always, they are all matured in new Nevers oak for a year or more. Beautiful berry flavours, vanillas, with good tannin. The wines are surprisingly easy to drink when released, but are well worth keeping for five to six years, and are even more rewarding if you can resist the temptation a while longer. The early vintages of 1982 and 1983 are probably at their best now, while subsequent vintages should continue to mature. This wine has been acclaimed by critics, both locally and internationally, and has achieved excellent prices at the Independent Winemakers' Guild and Nederburg Auctions. It has also been selected as a SAA Wine of the Month and was awarded a gold medal at the International Wine and Spirit Competition in 1988. It remains one of the leaders in this style of Cape wine. Small quantities are bottled in magnums.

81 ★★★★★ ready. 82 ★★★★★ ready. 83 ★★★★★ ready. 84 ★★★★★ ready, will still improve. 85 ★★★★★ ready, will still improve. 86 ★★★★★ ready, will still improve. 87 ★★★★★ ready, age further. 88 ★★★★★ allow time to develop. 89 ★★★★★ allow to develop. 90 ★★★★★ allow to develop.

Diemersdal Private Collection ★★★ D

The first release from the 1988 vintage was fairly heavy, while the 1989 was much lighter in style. Both were labelled Droë Rooi. The 1990 is labelled Private Collection. All are made from equal quantities of Cabernet Sauvignon and Cabernet Franc with 20% Merlot. The 1990 is the best to date and shows good potential.

88 ★★★ well rounded, ready to drink. 89 ★★★ needs more time. 90 ★★★★ good potential; allow to develop further.

Eikendal Classique ★★★★ E

First released from the 1987 vintage, this is a well-wooded blend of 60% Cabernet Sauvignon and 40% Merlot, and has shown good development. The 1988 has less Merlot (30%), but is a more elegant wine. The 1989 has the same make-up and is an even better wine, with good berry character, nice tannin and good oak. The 1990 contains 70% Cabernet Sauvignon and 30% Merlot, and is a most attractive, fruity wine. All vintages need four to five years to develop.

Fairview Charles Gerard Reserve ★★★★ C

From the 1987 vintage comes a deep red blend of 60% Merlot and 40% Cabernet Sauvignon with big, bold, deep flavours. It should develop with interest over the next four to six years. The next release, from the 1990, is a big, full-flavoured wine with 60% Cabernet Franc, 30% Merlot and 10% Cabernet Sauvignon. It has deep colour and intense flavours, and will probably develop earlier than the 1987. The 1991 is 60% Cabernet Sauvignon and 40% Merlot; a lovely, rich wine that will develop well.

Fairview Merlot Reserve ★★★★★ E

Although called Merlot Reserve, this wine, with the first release from the 1989 vintage, contains almost one-quarter Cabernet Franc. Aged in six different woods, a barrel of each has been bottled for interest. The balance was blended and bottled for sale. Deep rich, full berry-like character; soft in the mouth now, but will develop well over five to six years. Following the well-received 1989 is an excellent 1990 of much the same composition, but it is a much fruitier, fresher wine with good oak. It will need five to six years to mellow out.

Glen Carlou Grande Classique ★★★★★ F

The first release from the 1989 vintage is a gorgeous wine that is only now beginning to show its full potential. The 1990 is a great wine with lots of everything – a good blend of almost 70% Cabernet Sauvignon, 23% Merlot, 3% Cabernet Franc and 5% Petit Verdot, all giving great complexity and depth of fruit flavours, and backed by good new oak. It will age beautifully. I'm looking forward to the 1991.

Glen Carlou Les Trois ★★★★(★) E

The first release from the 1989 vintage is a very New World red, blended from Cabernet Sauvignon (72%, almost half of which is new clone) with Merlot and Cabernet Franc. Ageing in new Nevers barrels for 14 months gave it a deep, rich flavour. It drank very well on release, has aged beautifully and will continue to do so for another four to five years. The 1990 is a slightly lighter, but still lovely wine, made up of 50% Cabernet Sauvignon, 30% Petit Verdot and 20% Merlot. The 1991 follows the same good drinking style, yet has the ability to develop well over some six years.

Groot Constantia Gouverneurs Reserve ★★★★ F

The first release, launched late in 1990 from the 1986 vintage, is a medium-bodied, wood-aged wine blended from Cabernet Sauvignon and Cabernet Franc. It is, to my mind, the best red yet to be produced by this cellar. Aged in 500 litre Nevers barrels it has subdued but definite oak backing and good fruity, berry flavours. It is already very drinkable, but age it for six to eight years for full reward. The 1987, a Cabernet Sauvignon and Merlot blend, is more elegant than the 1986, but has all the ability to develop. The 1988 continues in good style. The 1989 has some 80% Cabernet Sauvignon with the balance Cabernet Franc. Lovely wine.

86 ★★★ ready. 87 ★★★★ ready, will still improve. 88 ★★★★ allow to develop. 89 ★★★★ allow to develop.

Hamilton Russell Vineyards Premier Reserve ★★★★ E

Tim Hamilton Russell is always ready to challenge the authorities over their sometimes silly regulations, and the name of this wine is a result of one of those actions. It is a fine wine that is often overlooked because of the cellar's very fine Pinot Noir and Chardonnay. The 1988 is probably the best release to date, with layers of deep flavours that will develop magnificently with five to seven years and should last well into the new century. It drinks amazingly well now, but time will be worth the wait. The 1989 is a Cabernet-Merlot blend, a little austere in 1993, but with potential to develop with benefit.

84 ★★★(★) ready, will still improve. 85 no release. 86 ★★(★) ready, will still improve. 87 no release. 88 ★★★★ ready, will develop further. 89 ★★★(★) not ready, allow to develop.

Kanonkop Auction Reserve ★★★★★ F

This is made up specially each year for the Independent Winemakers' Guild Auction and is more or less a blend of the best barrels of Paul

Sauer and Kanonkop Cabernet Sauvignon. The result is always excellent. The 1987 vintage was sold at the 1990 Auction. The 1988 and 1991 are both developing extremely well in the bottle. They are big, powerful wines with full strong nose that have lots to give. The 1989, sold at the 1992 Auction, is a beautiful wine that will age with benefit late into the 1990s. It is decidedly New World in style and will require many years to show its full potential.

Kanonkop Paul Sauer ★★★★★ F

This wine was planned by Jan 'Boland' Coetzee over many years. He planted a vineyard comprising 55% Cabernet Sauvignon, 25% Cabernet Franc, 10% Malbec and Souzão, and 10% Merlot, all of which are harvested and crushed together. The 1981 was the first release and the wine is now accepted as one of the Cape's greats. Beyers Truter, who has proved himself to be a great wine maker, intends to keep Paul Sauer a great wine, and will alter the blend as the vintage determines to ensure only the very best goes into the wine. Over six to ten years, the wines develop dramatically. The 1984 is a splendid, five-star product. The wine maker sold 50 cases of this vintage, of which half of the bottles in each case were closed with a patent screw top, and the other half with traditional corks, the intention being to obtain the opinion of collectors concerning the development of wine closed by different methods. The 1985 was the champion red at the Stellenbosch Wine Show and has a Cabernet content as high as 75%, with the balance being Cabernet Franc and Merlot. Blends nowadays are usually 70–75% Cabernet Sauvignon with some 15% Cabernet Franc, 10% Merlot, and sometimes fractions of Malbec and Souzão. The ageing programme can be anything from 13 months to nearly two years in Nevers small casks using 50% new barrels and the balance second fill. The 1986 release is superb and the 1987 is very promising and may be more drinkable earlier than the 1986. The 1988 vintage promises to be another great, though the 1989 could very well turn out to be the best.

82 ★★★★★ ready. 83 ★★★★ ready. 84 ★★★★★ ready, will improve. 85 ★★★★★ ready, will still improve. 86 ★★★★★ ready, will still improve. 87 ★★★★★ not ready, age further. 88 ★★★★★ not ready, age further. 89 ★★★★★ allow to develop.

Klein Constantia Marlbrook ★★★★★ E

From the 1988 vintage comes a great red blend of 60% Cabernet Sauvignon and 40% Merlot. It was judged the South African Young Wine Champion in 1988 and gained a Double Gold at the 1992 Veritas Awards. It was only released in 1992 after spending two years in small French oak barrels and the remaining two years in the bottle. It carries the name of the vineyard at Klein Constantia named by Hendrik Cloete towards the end of the 18th Century in honour of the Duke of Marlborough, who was known as Marlbrook.

Kloofzicht Alter Ego ★★★★ E

The Tulbagh Estate with its five-hectare vineyard has produced its first wine from the 1989 vintage – mainly Merlot with some Cabernet Sauvignon. It has a deep rich colour, full nose, great concentrated fruit, and deep layers of flavour backed by good French oak. As good as it tastes now, another four to six years will allow it to reach full potential. This is an amazing red wine for a valley known for its whites. It is followed by a very similar 1990.

KWV Cathedral Cellars ★★★(★) (no price available)

This unlikely name is KWV's range of improved quality wines for export. It is predominantly Cabernet (60%), with equal amounts of Merlot and Cabernet Franc. The first two vintages are the 1987 and 1988, with the latter being the better. Both aged less than six months in new Nevers barrels. The grapes originate as far afield as Faure and Durbanville. The 1989, which is still to be released, is an improvement, while the 1990 might be the best to date.

La Motte Millenium ★★★(★) D

The first release from the 1988 vintage is 60% new clone Cabernet Sauvignon and 40% Merlot, aged almost 18 months in Nevers oak. The 1989 is 50% Cabernet Sauvignon, 45% Merlot and 5% Cabernet Franc, aged in the same way. Both are lovely wines that drink very well on release, but will reward well into the mid 1990s.

Landskroon Premiere Reserve ★★★ C/D

This wine has developed out of the Estate's Bouquet Rouge which, in 1987, was equal portions Cabernet Sauvignon, Cabernet Franc and Merlot, and was aged for eight months in small wood. This resulted in a medium-bodied wine with light texture that developed well over a short period. The 1988, released under a new label, is somewhat subdued in character. It is a blend of half Cabernet Sauvignon and almost equal quantities of Cabernet Franc and Merlot. Good tannins should allow reasonable development. The 1989 is about 40/40 Cabernet Sauvignon and Cabernet Franc, with nearly 20% Merlot. A good, sound wine without complexity.
87 ★★★ ready, will still develop. 88 ★★★ not ready, age further. 89 ★★★(★) not ready, age further.

Le Bonheur Blend ★★★★ D

The first release from the 1989 vintage is 75% Cabernet Sauvignon and 25% Merlot, and well oaked in new Nevers. It is big, full and showy in its youth, but will be well worth keeping until the mid 1990s.

Lievland Blend ★★★(★) E

This is the first release from the 1989 vintage. It is a blend of 65% Cabernet Sauvignon and 35% Merlot, and was aged in small oak. The 1990 shows greater promise with 59% Cabernet Sauvignon, 33% Merlot and 9% good old Cinsaut that has spent more than a year in small oak. Very drinkable wine.

L'Ormarins Optima Reserve ★★★★(★) F

The 1987 and 1988 are beautiful Bordeaux blends of Cabernet Sauvignon and Cabernet Franc with Merlot. Good fruit, nice spice, fine oak and lots of all. It will age beautifully. The upcoming 1989 is a big, bold, full wine.

Lutzville Co-op Fleermuisklip Robyn ★★(★) C

A beautiful, deep, ruby-coloured wine that takes its name from a well-known local rock feature in the area. It is made from predominantly Ruby Cabernet with small portions of Cabernet Franc and Cabernet Sauvignon. The 1992 is 35% Cabernet Sauvignon with the balance Ruby Cabernet, but no Cabernet Franc.

Meerlust Red ★★★★ D

A second label from this famous red wine estate. It is very similar to the Rubicon style and from the 1985 vintage, which was not considered up to quality to carry the Rubicon label. It is developing very well. The second release, from 1990, is a very attractive wine and excellent value for money. It needs time to develop.

Meerlust Rubicon ★★★★★ E/F

A consistently excellent blend of Cabernet Sauvignon, Cabernet Franc and Merlot. The first vintage was 1980: a lovely, soft, full-flavoured wine of great complexity which developed well in the bottle and now needs to be enjoyed. The 1981 and 1982 seem to be even better than the original, and will help to confirm that this is one of the best of South Africa's new-style reds. The 1983 does not contain Cabernet Franc and is showing well. The 1984 is drinking well but will be even better with time. It contains the Cabernet that was Champion Red at the Stellenbosch Young Wine Show and South African Champion Red at the Goodwood Show. Despite how good I thought cellar samples of the 1985 Rubicon were, the Estate's stringent quality parameters kept them from releasing it as they believed it just wasn't good enough. Instead they followed well-proven Bordeaux practice and released the wine under a second label (Meerlust Red) at a lower price. The 1986 more than makes up for the missing vintage with its magnificence. It has more Cabernet Sauvignon than usual (70%), and more Merlot (20%), but less Cabernet Franc (10%). The 1987 is really super wine. The 1988 is a lovely, luscious wine.

80 ★★★★ ready. 81 ★★★★★ ready. 82 ★★★★★ ready, will still improve. 83 ★★★★(★) ready. 84 ★★★★★ ready, will still improve. 85 no release. 86 ★★★★ not ready, age further. 87 ★★★★(★) not ready, age further. 88 ★★★★★ not ready, age further.

Meinert Blend ★★★★(★) D

This, the first wine to be released from the delightful Devon Valley winery where Cindy Meinert, wife of Vergelegen wine maker Martin, is in charge, comes from the 1991 vintage. Grapes from nearly 20 year old shy bearing vines have been used, combining 55% Italian clone Merlot and 45% old clone Cabernet Sauvignon. It is a lovely wine with great individual character and certainly one to watch.

Nederburg Private Bin R109 ★★★★ E

A garnet-coloured wine with good depth of flavour from the 1985 vintage; a blend of almost 50/50 Cabernet Sauvignon and Merlot which spent time in large oak. Some 420 cases were sold for the first time at the 1989 Nederburg Auction. This is a lovely wine that will be at its best in the mid 1990s. The next release, from the 1986 vintage, sold at the 1991 and 1992 Nederburg Auctions. It is deep, full, soft wine that drinks very well right now but will still develop in the bottle over another four to six years. *85 ★★★★ ready to drink, will still improve. 86 ★★★★ ready to drink, will still improve.*

Neil Ellis Cabernet ★★★★(★) E

1991 saw 17% Merlot being introduced to this well-oaked wine which contained 15% in 1990. Both releases are beautiful, bold wines with lots of berry character that will benefit with six to eight years of ageing and should develop great complexity.

Neil Ellis Reserve Selection ★★★★ D

The 1987 is the first release of this super wine. It is a delicious, full-flavoured New World wine in Bordeaux-blend style. It is 62% Cabernet Sauvignon, 30% Merlot and 8% Cabernet Franc, and is showing well early in 1993. It has good attractive nose with lots of oak showing, together with good fruit. Keep with patience as it should continue to develop with great benefit.

Overgaauw DC Classic ★★★★ D

A deep, rich wine bottled for the Cape Independent Winemakers' Guild Auction. It usually comprises mainly Merlot and 20% Cabernet Franc with lots of wood-ageing. (DC are the initials of winemaker Braam van Velden's dad, Dawid Conradie.) Thirty to fifty cases are sold each year. The 1990 has deep colour with great berry flavours and excellent oak. It will age with great benefit. Collector's stuff!

Overgaauw Tria Corda ★★★★★ E

One of the Cape's first Bordeaux blends with the 1981 vintage. It was made up of Cabernet Sauvignon, with Merlot providing the balance. The Estate previously made good individual wines from these cultivars and now, in blending and good oak ageing, seems to have consistently brought out the best in both. This is one of the Cape's most popular Bordeaux blends. The 1981 did exceptionally well at the 1982 South African Championship Young Wine Show. The Merlot content has been increased over the years, reaching 34% in 1983. With the 1984 vintage, however, Cabernet Franc was added, resulting in a composition of 62% Cabernet Sauvignon, 22% Cabernet Franc and 16% Merlot. Since 1985 the blend has been more or less 60–65% Cabernet Sauvignon, 20% Cabernet Franc, and 15% Merlot, giving finer wines than before. With the 1988 the

Merlot content has been increased to 25% and the Cabernet Franc scaled down to 10%. All the vintages have developed well.

81 ★★★★ ready. 82 ★★★★★ ready. 83 ★★★★★ ready. 84 ★★★★★ ready, will improve. 85 ★★★★(★) ready, will still improve. 86 ★★★★★ ready, will still improve. 87 ★★★★ not ready, age further. 88 ★★★★★ not ready, age further.

Paddagang Vignerons Paddamanel ★★(★) D
A full-bodied, dry red with Cabernet and Merlot.

Pick 'n Pay Meritage ★★★(★) D
From 1988 vintage comes a fine blend of Cabernet Sauvignon, Cabernet Franc and Merlot made by Fairview. This is well-balanced wine with good tannin that will allow good bottle development.

Rozendal ★★★★★ C
From 1986 onwards this wine no longer contains Cinsaut, although that year was a blend of 50/50 Cabernet Sauvignon and Merlot. It is a great wine, and achieved a gold at the International Wine and Spirit Competition. It continues to develop well in the bottle. The 1987 is mainly Merlot with 15% Cabernet Sauvignon and 5% Cabernet Franc. It has beautiful berry flavours, is medium-bodied, yet has good tannin. There was no 1988. The 1989 remains mainly Merlot, with the balance Cabernet Sauvignon, and although concentrated now, will develop well.

Rustenberg Gold ★★★★★ E/F
The first release, from the 1985 vintage, was 55% Merlot, 25% Cabernet Franc and 20% Cabernet Sauvignon. It is a lovely, medium-bodied wine, full of fine flavours. The 1986 is a much bigger wine, comprising 60% Cabernet and the balance, equal amounts of Merlot and Cabernet Franc. It was rated highly by visiting authorities for the New World Wine Auction and those of the Nederburg Auction. The 1987 is the same blend as the 1986 and another big wine. The 1987 received a Double Gold at the 1992 Veritas Awards, while the 1988 was selected for SAA as a first class Wine of the Month, among other accolades. The 1988 is also magnificent wine, as is the 1989, at 60% Cabernet Sauvignon, 30% Merlot and 10% Cabernet Franc.

85 ★★★★★ ready, will still develop. 86 ★★★★★ ready, will still develop. 87 ★★★★★ not ready, age further. 88 ★★★★★ not ready, age further. 89 ★★★★★ not ready, age further.

Rust-en-Vrede ★★★★★ E
Simply carrying the name of the Estate, this label will be given to the Estate's finest wine of each vintage. The product could vary dramatically. The first release, from 1986 vintage, is 75% Cabernet and 25% Merlot, with lots of good new oak. It is packed with penetrating aromas and berry flavours. There was no 1987 vintage, but this was more than made up for with a magnificent 1988, which is 75% Cabernet Sauvignon, 10% Merlot and 15% Shiraz. The 1989 is magnificent and packed with berry flavours

from 70% Cabernet Sauvignon and 15% each Merlot and Shiraz. It was awarded Double Gold at the 1992 Veritas Awards. Aged in special thin Bordeaux barriques that have given a decided Bordeaux character, these are beautiful wines in every way. They drink very well when released but should be allowed to develop to reach their full potential.

86 ★★★★★ ready, develop further. 87 no release. 88 ★★★★★ ready, develop further. 89 ★★★★★ not ready, age further.

Saxenburg Private Collection Novum ★★★(★) E

Brash but attractive young wine from 1990 with good berry character and hard tannins from 50% Cabernet Sauvignon, 25% Cabernet Franc and 25% Merlot. It will need time to soften.

Simonsig Tiara ★★★★★ F

The first release from the 1990 vintage is 80% new clone Cabernet Sauvignon and 20% Merlot, aged for 16 months in predominantly new small oak. It was selected as the Wine of the Month Club's best wine for 1992 and as the Stellenbosch Young Wine Champion in 1990. A great wine that will develop beautiful complexity over six to eight years.

Simonsvlei Co-op Classique Reserve ★★★ B

25% Cabernet Sauvignon, 25% Merlot and 50% Ruby Cabernet have resulted in a pleasant enough wine, if not exactly classic. Good, fruity nose and nice oak backing makes pleasant drinking.

Talana Hill Royale ★★★★ E

The first release from the 1988 vintage numbered only 530 cases. It is made from 50% Cabernet Sauvignon, 37% Merlot and 13% Cabernet Franc, and was aged for 16 months in small French oak. It is a good firm wine with New World wine character, fine flavours and good oak backing. It would be a pity to drink it at this early age when it shows so much potential for development, so give it another five to eight years for a real treat. The 1989 is bigger and better, but will need longer to develop. The 1990 will be the next release.

Vergenoegd Reserve ★★★★ E

The first release from the 1988 vintage heralded a great departure from the Estate's traditional style. It is now a classic Bordeaux blend of mainly Cabernet Sauvignon with Merlot and Cabernet Franc that is aged for a year in small Nevers. The 1989 is a well-structured wine with good berry fruit and deserved its 1992 Veritas Double Gold. The 1990 is a more intense wine that should develop great complexity.

Villiera Crû Monro ★★★★★ D

Traditionally, Monro is the middle name of the men of the Grier family who own Villiera and has been given to the red and white flagship wines of the Estate. The first release of the red is from the 1984 vintage and is a blend of 60% Cabernet Sauvignon and 40% Merlot, which is aged in small French wood and then aged for a further ten months in the bottle before being released. It is a very good blend which, nine years later, has developed beautifully. A further selection of this wine is made from the best barrels and bottled for the Independent Winemakers' Guild Auction under the label 'Private Reserve'. An excellent wine, it needs time to show its potential. The second release from the 1985 vintage is particularly good considering the generally light vintage. The 1986, a blend of 60% Cabernet Sauvignon and 40% Merlot, is developing beautifully. The 1988 puts this wine firmly in the ranks of South Africa's best Bordeaux-type blends and achieved a Veritas Double Gold in 1992. There was no release in 1989, but in 1990 a blend of 50/50 Cabernet Sauvignon and Merlot was released that maintains the top quality. It was also awarded Double Gold in 1992. Time should allow these wines to reach their full potential.

84 ★★★★ ready. 85 ★★★(★) ready. 86 ★★★★(★) ready, will improve. 87 ★★★★ ready, will improve. 88 ★★★★★ allow to develop. 89 no release. 90 ★★★★★ allow to develop.

Vriesenhof Kallista ★★★★(★) E

Destined to be Jan 'Boland' Coetzee's best blend and most prestigious wine, Kallista is blended in varying proportions to take the best that each vintage has to offer. The first release was from the 1984 vintage and is predominantly Cabernet Sauvignon (88%) with the balance, Merlot. Ageing in small Nevers oak yields a fine wine that will be accessible earlier than the Vriesenhof Cabernet Sauvignon. The 1985 release has 25% Merlot, making it a much softer wine, while the 1986 has greater character intensity. The 1987 content is 30% Merlot, 10% Cabernet Franc, and 60% Cabernet Sauvignon. It has lovely berry flavours and is almost sweet. The 1987 has developed beautifully and is truly a five-star wine although it still needs more time. The 1988 continues the same style but is not showing its best yet. These wines all need plenty of time to develop. It is sold at the Independent Winemakers' Guild Auction and for export. The 1989 is made up of over one-third Merlot blended with Cabernet Sauvignon and 60% Cabernet Franc, and is considered to be one of the Cape's best from this vintage. The 1990 is a stricter wine that will need time. Wait for the 1991 – Jan considers it the best vintage ever.

84 ★★★★(★) ready. 85 ★★★★ ready. 86 ★★★★(★) ready, will still improve. 87 ★★★★★(★) ready, will still improve. 88 ★★★★ allow to age. 89 ★★★★★ allow to develop. 90 ★★★★ allow to develop.

Warwick Trilogy ★★★★★ F

The first release, from the 1986 vintage, is a blend of 70% Cabernet Sauvignon, 23% Merlot and 7% Cabernet Franc. This is a beautiful wine, matured for 18 months in small oak, half new and half second fill. Norma Ratcliffe tries to use natural methods wherever possible with her wine making, does no filtration and refines only with egg white. A special Trilogy Reserve – with more Merlot – was prepared for the New World Wine Auction, resulting in a wine that was ready to drink much earlier than non-NWWA wine. The 1987 is equally good and packed with developing flavours. The 1988 is a fuller-flavoured yet softer wine than the previous two vintages. It contains 75% Cabernet Sauvignon, 15% Merlot and 10% Cabernet Franc. It drinks well now, but should be allowed time, six to eight years more, to develop full potential. The 1989 is the same blend as the 1986 but a much richer wine, soft on the palate, and more accessible earlier. The 1990 continues the Estate's quality and slightly lighter style.

86 ★★★★(★) ready, will still improve. 87 ★★★★ ready, will still improve. 88 ★★★★★ not ready, allow time. 89 ★★★★★ not ready, will develop ahead of the 88. 90 ★★★★(★) not ready, age further.

Welgemeend ★★★★★ E

A multiple blend dominated by Cabernet Sauvignon, with Cabernet Franc, Merlot, Petit Verdot and Malbec playing lesser roles. From the 1986 vintage onwards Malbec was dropped from the blend. Early vintages show well, with fine wood treatment adding to the overall dimension of the wine. It needs time in the bottle to mellow, but the wait will be worthwhile. Each vintage has shown improvement: the 1982 is five-star material, as is the 1983, which is by far the softest of the wines to date. The 1984 is a rich, full, powerful wine while the 1985 is somewhat reserved. The 1986 is a magnificent wine. The 1987 is half Cabernet Sauvignon, some 24% Cabernet Franc, and Merlot making up the rest, with a fraction of Petit Verdot. The result is a deep, full-flavoured wine with great character, backed by good wood, and is well worth ageing. The 1988 is much the same blend, although the 1987 does not have quite the same depth. The 1989 is as stylish as ever and drinks remarkably well already – but have resolve and allow it to age and develop. The same goes for the 1990. The 1991 has only 38% Cabernet Sauvignon, the same amount of Merlot, 21% Cabernet Franc and 3% Petit Verdot. Delicious wine that will develop very well.

82 ★★★★★ ready. 83 ★★★★★ ready. 84 ★★★★★ ready, will still improve. 85 ★★★★★ not ready, age further. 86 ★★★★★ not ready, age further. 87 ★★★★★ not ready, age further. 88 ★★★★(★) not ready, age further. 89 ★★★★★ not ready, age further. 90 ★★★★★ not ready, age further. 91 ★★★★★ allow to age.

Welgemeend Douelle ★★★★ C

This is an intriguing blend of Cabernet Sauvignon and Malbec which develops well in the bottle. The 1987 is the best yet – deep and rich, but easy drinking. The 1988 and 1989 have a good range of flavours but are not quite up to the 1987. All are good value. Regret, no 1990 or 1991.

85 ★★★ ready. 86 ★★★★ ready. 87 ★★★★ ready, will still improve. 88 ★★★(★) ready, will still improve. 89 ★★★(★) drinkable, will improve.

Woolworths Cabernet Sauvignon-Merlot ★★★★(★) D

An excellent blend of 70% Cabernet Sauvignon and 30% Merlot from the 1990 vintage. Lovely deep colour and great depth of flavour. It will benefit from another four to six years in the bottle. Made by Neil Ellis.

Woolworths Grand Rouge ★★★★ C

This is made in the La Motte cellars from 1991 vintage and is a blend of about 60% Cabernet Sauvignon and balance Merlot and Cabernet Franc. Good fruity nose, fine flavours and long finish.

Woolworths Le Cinquieme 895R ★★★★ D

Part of the Woolworths' Vintage Collection. 89 denotes the vintage, the 5, the fifth in the range, and R is for red. It comes from the La Motte cellars and is a blend of Merlot and Cabernet Sauvignon. It has good character, nice tannin and long finish. This is wine that drinks very well now and has great development potential.

Woolworths Le Premier 881R ★★★★ D

Part of the Woolworths' Vintage Collection. The number 88 indicates the vintage, the 1 indicates the first release, and the R is for red. It is made up of about half Cabernet Franc and the balance Cabernet Sauvignon and Merlot from the cellars of Warwick. It has fruity nose, deep flavour and good oak backing. It is good to drink now, but has the potential to age over six to eight years.

Woolworths Rubato ★★★(★) B

The 1987 is a blend of 60% Merlot and 40% Cabernet Sauvignon, with good nose, full flavour and good oak. This is followed by a very good four-star 1988. This wine is excellent value for money and decidedly good drinking at an early age. It should develop well over four to five years. Has been discontinued.

Zevenwacht ★★★★(★) E

From 1987, the vintage has decided New World character. It is full, rich wine from new clone Cabernet Sauvignon, Cabernet Franc and Merlot. It should age with interest.

Zonnebloem Lauréat ★★★★ D/E

The first release of Zonnebloem's flagship red from 1988 comes as a limited edition. It is Cabernet Sauvignon-based, softened with Merlot and touched off with Cabernet Franc – all grapes from the Stellenbosch area. All components have been aged for nine months in Nevers oak casks at 30°C. It is easy to drink now, but will develop with interest.

CAPE TRADITIONAL BLENDS

Aan-de-Doorns Co-op Dry Red ★★ B
This used to be a blend of Pinotage and Cabernet Sauvignon that developed well after three years in the bottle. Nowadays it is 50% each Cinsaut and Pinotage. This is a deep coloured, fruity, unwooded red.

Altydgedacht Dry Red ★★★ B
A most attractive wine from Merlot and Gamay, which made an excellent drinking wine. Very good value, but no recent production.

Ashton Co-op Droë Rooi ★★(★) B
An everyday, non-vintaged red wine with distinct Pinotage character for the 60% content. The 30% Cabernet Sauvignon is not all that evident, while the 10% Tinta Barocca adds to the fresh tannic finish.

Backsberg Dry Red ★★★ B
Consistently one of the Cape's best value for money wines, if not the Cape's best wine bargain. The blend varies to cater for the vintage but always gives a lighter than medium wine with good flavours. Although ready for drinking at the time of release, it is worth keeping for a year or more. It develops well in the bottle, giving nice softness and a pleasant fruity nose. The blend always contains Cabernet Sauvignon, but has also included Shiraz, Pinotage, Pinot Noir, and even Merlot. The 1991 is as delightful as always but has more Merlot and Pinotage which gives deeper character. It remains a very remarkable wine.

Bellingham Classic Thirteen ★★★ C
A light, blended dry red wine made from 13 different varieties, including Steen, but usually none of them commanding more than 20%. Six of the varieties are Port types. The first release, in 1985, was not vintage-dated and this procedure has been followed with subsequent releases. However, each release is easily recognized by the Roman numeral in the gable window on the label. The first had I, the second II, the third III, and so on. They all age well over three to five years. Besides being a blend of many cultivars, the age of the wines used can vary by as much as five years, although number IV is mainly from the 1987 vintage.

Bergendal Bergenrood ★★★ C
The original release was a full-flavoured dry red. The next release, from the 1988, is mainly Cabernet Sauvignon with some Pinotage. It is much lighter, but pleasant and easy drinking with good character.

Blaauwklippen Red Landau ★★★ C
An interesting wine, the components of which have changed over the years. Originally, the blend comprised Zinfandel, Pinotage, Cinsaut and a little Cabernet Sauvignon. Since then, the blend has varied with great interest and has always been good value for money. The 1988 is super, with over 60% Cabernet, 30% Merlot and the balance Zinfandel. It is

lovely for early drinking but will age with benefit. The 1989 follows the same lines. What would have been 1990 is in fact labelled non-vintage, as it contains more Merlot from other vintages than the system allows. It is a lovely wine with 64% Merlot (not all 1990), 31% Cabernet Sauvignon from 1990 and 5% Zinfandel. The next release will be from 1991.

80 ★★★ ready. 81 no release. 82 ★★★ ready. 83 ★★★ ready. 84 ★★★(★) ready. 85 no release. 86 ★★★★ ready, will still improve. 87 ★★★(★) ready, will still improve. 88 ★★★★ ready, will still improve. 89 ★★★★ ready, will still improve. 90 ★★★★ very drinkable, will still develop.

Bolandse Co-op Bon Vino Red ★★★ A

The cellar has three wines in 500 ml screw-top bottles, of which this red is a blend of mainly Cinsaut with Cabernet Sauvignon, Shiraz, and Merlot. It is a well-flavoured, easy-drinking wine.

Boplaas Dry Red ★★★ B

This is a blend of a number of varieties which usually contains some Cabernet Sauvignon and Shiraz and others, all aged in small wood, giving an attractive deep red wine with a good nose and full, fruity flavour. The latest releases are better balanced, and contain some Merlot.

Boschendal Lanoy ★★★(★) D

The first release was the 1979 blend of Cabernet Sauvignon and Shiraz. The 1980 was much the same, but subsequent vintages have contained more Merlot. The 1988, 1989 and 1990 are fuller, showing more Cabernet character. The wines of the early-to-mid 1980s seemed to reach their best in four to five years, while those produced since 1988 will age longer. The 1991 has good berry concentration and is a good drinking wine.

79 ★★★ past its best. 80 ★★★ drink up. 81 ★★★ past its best. 82 ★★★(★) drink. 83 ★★★(★) ready. 84 ★★★★(★) ready. 85 ★★★ ready. 86 ★★★(★) ready. 87 ★★★(★) ready. 88 ★★★(★) ready, will still improve. 89 ★★★(★) ready, will still improve. 90 ★★★(★) ready, will still improve. 91 ★★★(★) ready, will still improve.

Bottelary Co-op Adelrood ★★★ A

Earlier releases were easy-drinking, inexpensive blends in which Pinotage gave pleasant, refreshing fruitiness. Later bottlings have been a great improvement and are basically blends of various vintages of unwooded Cabernet Sauvignon and some Pinotage. Adelrood is now heading the Bordeaux route with nearly 50% Cabernet Sauvignon, 37% Merlot and the balance Pinotage.

Cantori Vino Rosso (Gilbeys) ★★★ B

This is Gilbeys' Italian-style red. I'm not so sure this qualifies for the Traditional section, but it does contain some Cabernet Sauvignon and Cinsaut plus a good amount of mature Shiraz. On account of these three, it must qualify. The odd grape is Grenache. The combination gives a very drinkable, flavourful non-vintaged wine, and is packed in an attractive Italian-style, cork-closed bottle.

Cape Selection Grand Vin Rouge (Pick 'n Pay) ★★ A/B

A very typical traditional blend of Shiraz, Pinotage and Cabernet Sauvignon resulting in a softish, easy-drinking dry red.

Carnival Dry Red (Spar) ★★ A

An easy-drinking blend of Tinta Barocca and Cinsaut with a touch of Cabernet Sauvignon.

Chateau Libertas (SFW) ★★★(★) B/C

The grandfather of South African blended reds, Chateau Libertas celebrated its 60th anniversary at the end of 1992. In 1985 it gained the Monde Selection gold award with palm leaves, the logical culmination of honours won consistently over a 50-year period, though it struggled through a comparatively indifferent patch while part of the Taskelder range. With the 1978 vintage, it regained all its former glory and reappeared under its own label. Recent blends are comparable to the legendary wines of the 1930s and 1940s. The 1982 was very good, but the 1983 has been much lighter – in character with the vintage. The 1984 was the best of the decade when released and, at the age of four, it was excellent value for money. It received Superior certification in 1988. Although modern techniques allow it to be drunk when young, it ages superbly. The 1985 is a much lighter wine which has improved dramatically since its release. The 1986 is a very good wine and has developed well. The 1987 is a very good wine but, with a small amount of Merlot and Cabernet Franc being included in the blend, this is another old favourite in danger of losing its identity. This should not be allowed to happen. The 1988 is a lovely wine and will develop with great benefit. It has a meaningful amount of Merlot which changes the character of this very traditional wine. The 1989 has been acclaimed as the best of the decade of the 1980s. Chateau Libertas often came on the market without Superior rating, but later labellings usually gained this controversial certification. A limited number of magnums are issued some two years after the 750 ml bottlings. The first release was from the 1978 vintage.

78 ★★★★ ready. 79 ★★★ ready. 80 ★★★ ready. 81 ★★★★ ready. 82 ★★★★ ready. 83 ★★★ ready. 84 ★★★★ ready, will still improve. 85 ★★★ ready, will still improve. 86 ★★★★ ready, will still improve. 87 ★★★ ready, will still improve. 88 ★★★★ ready, will still improve. 89 ★★★ ready, will still improve.

Delaire Cuvée Rouge ★★★ B

This was originally a dry blend of Cabernet Sauvignon and a touch of Pinotage, with wood-ageing showing strongly soon after it was released. Fairly light and definitely pleasant when young, it developed into a satisfying wine over 12–18 months. The second release was better, a combination of almost 50% Cabernet Sauvignon, 40% Pinotage and the balance Merlot, produced from the 1988 vintage. The 1989 has decided Pinotage character which is not surprising – it is 85% Pinotage with only 15%

Cabernet Sauvignon. The 1990 is a well-made wine with good oak backing and consists of 65% Pinotage, 25% Merlot and 20% Cabernet Sauvignon. The latest release is the non-vintaged 1992, made from 70% Merlot and 30% Pinotage. Technically it doesn't fit into this category, but stays here on its history.

Delheim Roodenwijn Dry Red ★★★ B

Over the years this non-vintaged blend has undergone many changes, but it has always been a worthwhile buy and very rewarding if kept for a year or two in the bottle. Latest blends are well-made, good-flavoured, easy-drinking wines, with unlikely blends of a third each Cabernet Sauvignon and Pinot Noir, and about 20% Pinotage and others.

De Helderberg Co-op Vin Rouge ★★★ B

This wine replaced the Co-op's Dry Red and Special Red. It has varied over the years with blends including Pinotage, Cabernet Sauvignon, Cinsaut, Merlot and Pinot Noir, giving a pleasant-flavoured, medium-bodied wine that drinks well. It will develop with a year or two in the bottle.

De Zoete Inval Grand Rouge ★★ A

A full-flavoured, fruity, dry red wine with unusual flavours, this is a blend of Cabernet Sauvignon and Cinsaut. The 1986 is still available.

Douglas Green St Augustine ★★★(★) C

A fine blend of Shiraz, Pinotage, Tinta Barocca and, more recently, increasing quantities of Cabernet Sauvignon. No varietal dominates. It is wood-aged for almost two years in large old vats so the wood is not too apparent, although it has obviously done its work in bringing the wine together. It develops well over the years. The 1988 is a good, full-flavoured wine in the traditional style, that should develop well over the next seven to nine years.

77 ★★(★) ready, drink up. 78 ★★★ ready, drink up. 79 ★★★ ready, drink up. 80 ★★★★ ready. 81 ★★★(★) ready. 82 ★★★★ ready. 83 ★★★(★) ready. 84 ★★★★ ready. 85 ★★★ ready. 86 ★★★(★) ready, will still improve. 87 ★★★(★) ready. 88 ★★★(★) not ready, age further.

Drostdy-Hof Claret Select (Kaapwyn) ★★ B

A smooth, off-dry, wood-aged blend of many cultivars, including Cabernet Sauvignon, Pinotage, Shiraz and Tinta Barocca, resulting in a pleasant, easy-drinking red.

Drostdy-Hof Vin Noir ★★★ B

A Cabernet/Pinotage blend from the 1987 vintage that is medium-bodied with good berry character and freshly finished. Good value for money.

Edward Snell Special Reserve Dry Red ★★★ B

Originally an unusual blend of Cabernet Sauvignon, Pinotage and Pinot Noir – now a traditional Cape blend of Shiraz, Pinotage and Cabernet Sauvignon, making it medium-bodied and soft in the mouth with good finish. It will develop well over a year or two. It is not vintaged, so mark the label.

Goue Vallei Chianti (Citrusdal Co-op) ★★ **B**

A wine that has reappeared on the market after a break of a few years. It was originally Grenache but is now a wood-aged blend containing 60% Grenache, 30% Cinsaut and the balance Cabernet Sauvignon. The next blend also contained some Tinta Barocca, while the latest has dropped the wood and the Cabernet Sauvignon. This is a big, powerful wine that is surprisingly smooth and fruity.

Groot Constantia Heerenrood ★★★(★) **E**

Heerenrood was introduced to the range of famous Constantia reds with the 1975 vintage. This first making, blended from at least four cultivars, was a well-balanced wine of fine maturing promise. It was not considered a success, however, and from 1976 onwards it has been made from more-or-less equal quantities of Cabernet Sauvignon and Shiraz, the quantities varying with the vintage. Despite the apparent potential, the earlier vintages never really lived up to expectation. The Estate invested in new wood which, along with the higher proportion of Shiraz, resulted in the 1984 being distinctly better. The 1985 developed rapidly, but the 1986 had the deepest character when released and is developing well. The 1987 is a richer, fuller wine with good wood backing, and should improve with great benefit well into the late 1990s. The 1988 and 1989 are 50/50 well-wooded Cabernet Sauvignon and Shiraz, giving good, full, easy-drinking wine.

80 ★★★ ready. 81 ★★★ ready. 82 ★★★(★) ready. 83 ★★★ ready. 84 ★★★★ ready. 85 ★★★ ready. 86 ★★★ ready, will still improve. 87 ★★★ ready, will still improve. 88 ★★★(★) ready, will still improve. 89 ★★★(★) ready, will still improve.

Groot Constantia Rood ★★★ **B**

After I had described this non-vintage wine in the first Wine Buyer's Guide as a good braai wine, the wine maker, Pieter du Toit, responded by sending me six bottles and a bag of braai wood. His driver deposited them outside my office and, at the end of the day, when I left for home, the wood had been 'taken' but the wine left behind! It was a rugged blend of Cabernet Sauvignon, Shiraz and Pinotage, the good Constantia Shiraz showing through quite distinctly. A few years in the bottle is well worth the wait. It is not usually vintage-dated (except for the 1984 vintage). The addition of Merlot and Cabernet Franc, and 18 months in new Yugoslavian wood have resulted in a totally different wine. The bottling from the 1986 vintage is also atypical, as it is a Bordeaux-style blend aged in Nevers oak – a very different red. There was no 1987, but a very acceptable 1988 was developed from equal quantities of Cabernet Franc and Shiraz, with Cabernet Sauvignon and Merlot making up the balance. It is already very good drinking, but it should develop with benefit over four years. The 1990 is very drinkable, and comes from a good blend of Cabernet Franc, Shiraz and Merlot.

Hartenberg Bin 9 ★★★ C

A non-vintaged dry red blend sold only at the Estate, and always a full-flavoured, bold wine with the original containing well-aged Cabernet Sauvignon, Shiraz and Tinta Barocca. Although not vintaged, there was a particularly interesting release from the 1987 vintage which is 40% each Cabernet Sauvignon and the unusual cultivar, Pontac. The balance is Shiraz, all backed with a bit of good oak. The 1989 followed the same make-up but is a better wine. The 1990 vintage is a Shiraz-Tinta Barocca blend. It is good value for money and well worth maturing for a couple of years.

Hartenberg Paragon ★★★(★) E

This wine succeeds the Estate's Premium Red Blend which was mainly an export wine with small amounts released locally. The 1986 is predominantly Cabernet (60%), with Shiraz (30%) and the balance of 10% Pontac from the Estate's more than 40-year-old Pontac vines. This is a most unusual blend that had two years in oak to bring it all together. The previous release was 1984. The 1987 is a more refined wine with good tannic finish. Good, strong flavours are evident. The blend will change while the old Pontac vineyard is being replanted.

Inglewood Dry Red (Neil Ellis) ★★★ C

A full-flavoured blend based on Cabernet with some Pinotage. It is a good wine for drinking now, but will develop with benefit in the bottle.

Kaapzicht Kaaproodt ★★★ B

This wine with 60% Pinotage and 40% unwooded Cabernet Sauvignon from the 1992 vintage is full of clean flavour and should develop well.

Kanonkop Kadette Rooiwyn ★★ B

Described by the wine maker as 'informal' wine which should be served chilled, this is a well-flavoured, good-value-for-money blend that varied from vintage to vintage, but is now firmly Pinotage based.

Kleindal Cuvée Rouge ★★ B

A good, well-flavoured wine that makes for enjoyable early drinking yet has the potential to improve after a year or more in the bottle. This blend varies with the vintage, although the wine is non-vintaged, but is predominantly Pinotage with Cabernet Sauvignon and Shiraz.

Kleindal Roodewyn (Vinimark) ★★★(★) C

From the 1989 vintage comes a good character Cabernet Sauvignon-based blend with Pinotage.

Koelenhof Co-op Koelenberg ★★★ B

This is a fruity, dry blend containing Cabernet Sauvignon, Pinotage and lesser quantities of Shiraz and Cinsaut. It is most suitable for casual occasions and is good value for money.

KWV Roodeberg ★★★ (no price available)

A wine with a remarkable reputation as it is available only to wine farmers and for export. Recent vintages show considerable change away from the old-fashioned 'Dikvoet' style. This applies especially to the 1984. The blend contains at least four varieties – Cabernet Sauvignon, Shiraz, Pinotage, Tinta Barocca – but seldom does any one exceed 25%. Regrettably, the 1985 does not have the quality of the 1984. More recent vintages are better, with the 1987, 1988 and 1989 being softer, more drinkable wines.

Laborie (KWV) ★★★ D

The first vintage of this wine was the 1979. It was deep in colour, with considerable Cabernet Sauvignon character and, although blended with Pinotage, Shiraz and Tinta Barocca, the individual cultivars were not discernible. Originally somewhat severe, it has softened with age, yet it still has to reach its best. The 1980 is a much softer wine and the 1981 showed a disturbing browning within six years of age. The 1983 has developed a rich but curious character – attractive to some people but not to others. The 1988 was somewhat ordinary with lots of wood.

Laborie Taillefert (KWV) ★★★ E

A wine from the same cellar as Laborie and of much the same blend – Cabernet Sauvignon, Shiraz, Pinotage and Cabernet Franc – but with a very different result. Medium-bodied, it lacks fruit but has good wood and is reasonably smooth on the palate. The 1984 has been a bit disappointing as it has aged, but the 1983 shows fresher wood and has developed well. It featured at the 1990 Nederburg Auction. The 1985 is a better wine showing good oaking; a fuller wine with cleaner Cabernet character. The 1987 has good fruit with the 1988 the best to date.

Landskroon Bouquet Rouge ★★★(★) B

Originally a medium-bodied blend of Shiraz and the Estate's exceptional Cinsaut, this wine has a good, fruity bouquet. The first vintage, the 1978, has developed beautifully in the bottle and now needs to be enjoyed. The 1979 was given Superior certification and has developed much like the 1978, as has the 1980, and also need drinking. The 1981 has more Shiraz, less Cinsaut and a touch of Cabernet Sauvignon, changing the character considerably. It has developed very well and is probably at its best now. The 1982 and 1983 releases are blends of 60% Shiraz and 40% Cinsaut, and have softened amazingly well in the bottle yet still seem to have lots of life. The 1987 is equal proportions of Cabernet Sauvignon, Cabernet Franc and Merlot, aged for eight months in small wood, giving yet another very interesting wine under this label. The 1988 is half Cabernet Sauvignon and the balance equal quantities of Cabernet Franc and Merlot. It has enough tannin to develop well. It is, however, no longer available, having given way to the Estate's Premier Reserve.

78 ★★★★ ready, drink up. 79 ★★★(★) ready, drink up. 80 ★★★(★) ready, drink up. 81 ★★★(★) ready. 82 ★★★(★) ready. 83 ★★★(★) ready. 84 no release. 85 no release. 86 no release. 87 ★★★★ ready. 88 ★★★ ready.

Landzicht Dry Red (Jacobsdal Co-op) ★★ A

Basically a Pinotage with bright colour, fruity nose, and fairly sharp on the palate.

Lievland Lievlander ★★★ C

Originally a delightfully bright, easy-drinking wine made from Cinsaut with some Cabernet Sauvignon. The blend varies with the vintage but is a vin ordinaire with 'class' and contains some Merlot and Cabernet Franc plus good oaking. It is excellent value for money.

Nederburg Baronne ★★★(★) C

The first four vintages of Baronne – 1973, 1974, 1975 and 1976 – varied considerably but were all excellent wines and have matured magnificently. A very definite style of wine has now emerged, not far removed from the Nederburg Selected Cabernets of old, which were reputed to be blends containing predominantly Cabernet Sauvignon and lesser quantities of Shiraz, Pinotage and Cinsaut. Whatever the composition, the result is a fine, full-flavoured, deep-red wine which is acceptable when young but has every potential for fine ageing. This wine has very good berry-like aroma and flavour, and will bring true delight if aged for five years or more. The 1976 vintage was very good, as was the 1979. The 1980 and 1981 have proved their early potential and are excellent now. The 1984 is a fuller wine and is tremendous in 1991. The 1985 is more austere and needs drinking. The 1986 is bigger, fuller and better than previous vintages and will develop well. The 1987 drinks very well at this early age and may peak earlier than previous vintages. The 1988 is fine, full wine to be followed by an elegant 1989.

73 ★★★★★ drink up. 74 ★★★★★ ready. 75 ★★★ drink up. 76 ★★★★ ready. 77 ★★★ drink up. 78 ★★★★ ready. 79 ★★★(★) ready. 80 ★★★★ ready. 81 ★★★ ready. 82 ★★★★ ready. 83 ★★★ ready. 84 ★★★★ ready. 85 ★★★(★) ready. 86 ★★★★ ready. 87 ★★★(★) ready, will still develop. 88 ★★★★ ready, will still develop. 89 ★★★(★) not ready, develop further.

Nederburg Edelrood ★★★★ D/E

Edelrood is a top-quality dry red in which no particular variety shows, but as a harmonious whole it is hard to beat. Originally launched as an uncomplicated, pleasant dry table wine of light body and acid with moderate tannin, recent vintages have taken on a more definite and demanding style: it is now a wine to be reckoned with and one that needs time to show its best. The 1979, 1980, 1981, 1982, 1983, 1984, 1985 and 1986 vintages carry Superior certification and have been major award winners in many overseas competitions. Edelrood ages extremely well and is destined to be the best of Nederburg's regular range. The 1988 is very good.

78 ★★★★★ drink. 79 ★★★★★ drink. 80 ★★★★★ ready. 81 ★★★★ ready. 82 ★★★★ ready. 83 ★★★★ ready. 84 ★★★★ ready. 85 ★★★★ ready. 86 ★★★★ ready, will still improve. 87 ★★★★ ready, will still improve. 88 ★★★★ ready, will still improve.

Nederburg Private Bin R115 ★★★★(★) E

Originally a light, elegant blend of almost equal quantities of Shiraz and Cabernet Sauvignon and, although a traditional Cape blend, it was done in a style new to the Cape. The first release, from the 1980 vintage, was launched at the 1986 Nederburg Auction and the 1981 and the 1982 were sold at the 1987 and 1988 Auctions respectively. The Cabernet Sauvignon, not the Shiraz, has been wood-aged, giving a light, red wine, full of flavour and beautiful bouquet. The 1982 is a bigger wine and requires more time to soften than the earlier vintages. The dark-purple 1983 needs time to develop and will probably reach its best in the mid-1990s. The 1984, sold at the 1991 Auction, is very fruity and although very drinkable now, still has the ability to develop. The 1985 at the 1992 Auction is fine wine; good to drink now, but will still develop for a few years. The 1986 sold at the 1993 Auction is firmer and finer.

80 ★★★★ ready. 81 ★★★★ ready. 82 ★★★★★ ready. 83 ★★★★ ready. 84 ★★★★(★) ready, will still improve. 85 ★★★(★) ready, will still improve. 86 ★★★★★ ready, will still improve.

Nederburg Private Bin R103 ★★★★★ F

One of the classic South African red wines and a worthy successor to the much-vaunted Nederburg Selected Cabernets of pre-Wine of Origin days. Exceptionally smooth, it is bold and dry with good Cabernet Sauvignon character touched off with Shiraz and Cinsaut – the traditional South African blend. This is a rich, glowing wine which needs plenty of ageing (10 or more years) to bring it to its best. The 1976 vintage is magnificent yet still has considerable life to come. It is sold only at the Nederburg Auction. The vintages released to date have been 1975, 1976, 1978, 1979, 1980, 1981 and 1982. The last three vintages are magnificent wines and will probably develop longer than any of the previous vintages. The 1982 is particularly good and demanded higher average prices at the 1991 Auction than previous vintages. The 1983, sold at the 1992 Auction, is excellent to drink now and over the next two to three years. The 1984 is the best release to date.

75 ★★★★★ drink. 76 ★★★★★ drink. 77 no release. 78 ★★★★★ ready. 79 ★★★★★ ready. 80 ★★★★★ ready. 81 ★★★★★ ready. 82 ★★★★★ ready. 83 ★★★★★ ready. 84 ★★★★★ ready, will still develop.

Neethlingshof Rouge ★★★(★) D

The 1983 was an interesting blend of equal proportions of Tinta Barocca and Cabernet Sauvignon aged in new small oak. It aged with benefit. The 1984 is disappointing (just three stars) and has not shown the class of the 1983 vintage. The 1986 is a major improvement with lots of flavour. The 1987 was a great improvement with the 1988 being the best to date and deserving its four stars. With the good quality developments at this cellar, this should be a wine to watch in the future.

Nuy Co-op Rouge de Nuy ★★★ B

The first release from 1989 was 100% Pinotage. The 1990 is a total departure for this popular cellar and the first time it has bottled a wood-aged wine. 20% Cabernet Sauvignon aged for three months in small French oak blended with 80% Pinotage gives a very attractive and drinkable wine that is excellent value. The 1991 follows in similar fashion.

Oude Nektar Grand Vin ★★★(★) C

The 1989 is good value for money with good character and potential. It is made from Cabernet Sauvignon and Shiraz. The 1990 is in the same stern, clean-flavoured style.

Paddagang Vignerons Paddarotti ★★ C

More fun from Paddagang. A good, full-bodied red in which Pinotage features along with some Cabernet.

Pick 'n Pay Dry Red ★★★ B

A good-flavoured, good-drinking wine from 1990 made by Lievland. It is a blend of Cinsaut, Cabernet Sauvignon and Shiraz, with good oak backing. Soft and good to drink now and over the next few years.

Roodendal Reserve (SFW) ★★★★ C

From 1982 vintage comes a blend of Cabernet Sauvignon, Merlot and Shiraz aged in seven different oaks. A very different wine.

Roodezandt Co-op Roode Huiswyn ★★(★) B

Over the years this has changed from being 100% Cabernet Sauvignon in 1983 and 1984 to a blend of Cabernet Sauvignon, Tinta Barocca and Cinsaut. They are always full, earthy wines that develop well. The 1990 has Ruby Cabernet as well as Cabernet Sauvignon and a small amount of Tinta Barocca and Cinsaut. It is a little more full in the mouth and should develop well in the bottle.

Rooiberg Co-op Roodewyn ★★★ B

An early-drinking smooth blend, originally of Cabernet Sauvignon, Pinotage and Tinta Barocca, which has a good touch of wood. More recent wines are heading for Bordeaux blends. The 1990 contains both Cabernets, Merlot, Pinotage and good oak. When the Pinotage goes it will move category. Meanwhile it's a lovely wine.

Rozendal ★★★★ E/F

The 1983 vintage is a blend of Cinsaut and Cabernet Sauvignon which has improved with time beyond all recognition. The 1984 contains more Cabernet Sauvignon and is showing better character at an earlier stage than the 1983, though it will need longer to develop its full potential. These two vintages have unusual character and show great promise. In subsequent vintages Merlot replaced Cinsaut. There was no release of a 1985. The 1986 is the first with Merlot.

Rustenberg Dry Red ★★★★(★) D

Previously known as Rustenberg. A classic among South African wines, Rustenberg is always interesting and, given time in the bottle, rewards the taster with elegantly fine flavours. Traditionally, it comprises two-thirds Cabernet Sauvignon and one-third Cinsaut, blended at the crusher so that the combined cultivars ferment together. Softer and fruitier than many local reds, its excellence has brought it to many Nederburg

Auctions. (A case of 1974 sold at the 1990 Auction for R7 100!) The 'odd' year vintages of the 1970s seem better than the 'even' years, but all are good. In the 1980s, quality continued to improve with each year, the 1980 to 1983 vintages seeming more elegant than their predecessors. The 1982 vintage is more full-bodied than the others and will need longer than the usual five to seven years to peak. The 1983 is a fine wine and the 1984 is full of character with everything that rewards many years of patient ageing. The 1985 has full Cabernet Sauvignon character, with lots of fruit and good wood-backing, and is probably the last of the really 'old' style. With the ageing of the Cinsaut vineyards, lesser quantities of Cinsaut are being used and a typical blend would be 60% Cabernet Sauvignon, 20% Cinsaut and then 10% each of Cabernet Franc and Merlot. The 1987 is a slightly sterner wine while the 1988 is lovely, soft and flavourful. Replanted Cinsaut vineyards are now bearing, and from the 1989 vintage the wine reverts to the original combination.

78 ★★★★★ ready. 79 ★★★★ ready. 80 ★★★★★ ready. 81 ★★★★ ready. 82 ★★★★★ ready. 83 ★★★★ ready, will still improve. 84 ★★★★★ ready, will still improve. 85 ★★★★ ready, will still improve. 86 ★★★★★ ready, will still improve. 87 ★★★★ not ready, develop further. 88 ★★★★ drinking well, will still improve. 89 ★★★★ drinking well, will still improve.

Rusthof Dry Red (Mooiuitsig Wynkelders) ★ A

A medium-bodied dry red from Cabernet Sauvignon and Pinotage.

Saxenburg Connoisseurs Blend ★★★ C

A wood-aged blend of Cabernet Sauvignon, Cinsaut and Tinta Barocca from the 1990 vintage. It needs some time to smooth out. The 1991 is more robust, from Cabernet Franc, Merlot, Tinta Barocca and Cinsaut and is already soft and easy to drink.

Simonsig Adelberg ★★★(★) B

This good blend is usually made from Cabernet Sauvignon and Shiraz, and ages with reward. The 1983 vintage shows good potential, while the purple-coloured 1984 is less woody. The 1985 is the most complex release, yet it is light and elegant. The 1986 was a little disappointing but the 1987 is a much fuller, fine-flavoured wine. The 1988 is a fruitier, finer wine with good oak backing, as is the 1989. The 1990s are fine, more Pinotage-based wines and definitely four-star quality. They develop well over three to five years, drink well and are exceptional value for money.

Simonsvlei Co-op Simonsrood ★★(★) A

This wine was formerly labelled Claret, and was a good example of a medium-bodied Cinsaut. It then became a Cinsaut-Pinotage blend with a short term in wood giving better depth; and subsequently Cinsaut and Shiraz with some 10% Cabernet Sauvignon. Then a proportion of Zinfandel was introduced. The 1992 is mainly Pinotage with some Merlot and Cinsaut. A short period in large wood gives good drinking wine. It is available in either corked-closed bottles or less expensive screw-top bottles.

Springlands Classique Rouge (Drop Inn) ★★★ **B**

A blend of Cabernet Sauvignon, Shiraz and some Merlot, giving a robust, full-flavoured dry red that is good value for money. It will develop well.

Swartland Co-op Dry Red ★★★ **B**

A good dry blend originally of Cinsaut, Tinta Barocca and Pinotage, with a touch of Cabernet Sauvignon. Nowadays it is 60% Pinotage with Tinta Barocca and Cabernet Sauvignon. A big, full wine.

Tassenberg Reserve (SFW) ★★★ **C**

A very good value blend of Cabernet Sauvignon, Merlot and Cinsaut, with lots of flavour which should develop well over three to four years.

Vaughan Johnson's House Red ★★★★ **C**

A typical, well-made traditional blend of reducing amounts of Cinsaut, Shiraz and Cabernet Sauvignon and some Pinotage. It has full flavour, good nose, is easy drinking and good value for money.

Vredenheim 200 ★★ **B**

From 1989 vintage, comes this complex blend of Cabernet Sauvignon, Carignan, Shiraz and Tinta Barocca; a light, aromatic wine.

Vredenheim Dry Red ★★(★) **B**

An unwooded blend of Cabernet Sauvignon and Pinotage. Nice light wine for easy drinking.

Warwick Femme Bleu ★★★★ **E**

A non-vintaged wine produced before Warwick certified their wines. It has developed very well and is now very much a collector's item.

Welmoed Co-op Rouge Sec ★★★ **B**

Originally an unusual blend of 75% Shiraz and 25% Pinotage, giving a pleasant dry red. It then became a blend of Shiraz and Pinotage, and later a blend of some 50% Cabernet Sauvignon and 25% each Shiraz and Pinotage, aged for more than a year in large oak. Now it contains 50/50 Shiraz and Pinotage, giving a good, easy-drinking wine with the ability to develop in the bottle. This is good value for money.

Woolworths Selected Cape Red ★★★ **A**

This is a most agreeable dry red blend based on Cinsaut and Shiraz with small amounts of Cabernet Sauvignon and Merlot. It has good nose and flavour. A bargain at the price, and as easy-drinking as it is at the time of purchase, it is well worth ageing (you will have to keep your own records as it is not vintage-dated). From Eikendal.

Zevenwacht ★★★(★) **C**

The 1983 is a little light, while the 1984 is a luscious, four-star wine with good fruit supported by good wood. The earlier vintage was matured in big wood, while the latter spent a year in small oak and large oak successively. It is a very good example of the traditional South African blend of Cabernet Sauvignon and Shiraz. The 1985 needs time to develop, while the 1986 and the 1988 are well-made wines with Cabernet Sauvignon showing nicely. There was no 1987.

DRY RED BLENDS

Aan-de-Doorns Vin Rouge ★★ A

A flavourful dry red blended from Pinotage and Tinta Barocca. Although it makes easy drinking on release, it improves in the bottle and is best after four to five years.

Altydgedacht Tintoretto ★★★★ C

The 1981 was a most unusual deep-flavoured wine, the good fruit and meaty flavours of which are due to its equal quantities of Barbera and Shiraz grapes. This is a wine that, as attractive as it is when young, has definitely benefited with time in the bottle and after ten years drank very well. This wine was originally launched under the name Barbiraz, but the Wine and Spirit Board rejected the name as it too closely resembled the cultivars from which it was made. (I thought it a fine name.) The next release from the 1986 vintage is a blend of 75% Shiraz and 25% Barbera. Don't be fooled by the wine's lightish colour or pass it off as an insignificant wine – it isn't. Its alcohol exceeds 13,5% and in 1993 is super in every respect. The 1987 is a quieter wine, while the 1988 is probably the 'biggest' so far, having 70% Shiraz and 30% Barbera with lots of good wood. The next release is from the 1989 vintage.

81 ★★★★ ready. 86 ★★★★ ready, will still develop. 87 ★★★(★) ready, will still develop. 88 ★★★★ ready, will still improve. 89 ★★★(★) needs time to develop.

Ashton Co-op Dry Red ★★★(★) B

This is a good value wine available in convenient screw-top bottles. The latest release is a blend of Pinotage and Tinta Barocca and some Cabernet Sauvignon. It is a fresh, fruity wine that drinks easily when young, and is non vintaged.

Autumn Harvest Country Claret (SFW) ★★ A

This is a smooth, easy-drinking red blend in which no particular varietal is obvious. It is only available as a so-called box wine and is not intended for ageing.

Beaufort Claret (Solly Kramer) ★★ A

Remarkable value for a dry red, this wine has plenty of good nose and deep, soft flavours.

Beaufort Dry Red (Solly Kramer) ★★(★) A

A fruity dry red blend of Cinsaut and Tinta Barocca.

Botha Co-op Droë Rooiwyn ★★ A

An attractive, easy-drinking wine made from equal proportions of unwooded Cinsaut and Pinotage, with the latter showing strongly. Neither 1988, the first vintage, nor 1989 are certified. No longer produced.

Calitzdorp Co-op Dry Red ★★ B

A very pleasant wine from unwooded Cabernet Sauvignon.

Cape Vintry Dry Red (Picardi) ★★★(★) B

From 1989 vintage comes a well wooded dry red from Cabernet and Pinotage, made by Neethlingshof. Very good value for money. It is drinkable now, but will still develop over a few years.

Casal da Serra Vinho Tinto Seco (Delheim) ★★★ B

A respectable dry red with good nose and soft, generous flavour from a collection of varietals including Cabernet Sauvignon, Ruby Cabernet, Pinotage and Pinot Noir. It drinks easily on its own and makes an ideal accompaniment to a meal.

Cederberg Kelders Cedar Rouge ★★★ B

A Pinotage aged in new oak; easy-drinking, non-vintaged red.

Cellar Cask Premier Claret ★★(★) B

A dry red of the Cellar Cask brand, but presented in a 750 ml bottle and closed with a cork. Despite the advertisement claiming that the wine is 'corked', I found it to be a very pleasant, dry red blend that is good value for money.

Cellar Reserve Dry Red (Hyperama) ★★ A

A good blend of half Cinsaut and equal quantities of Tinta Barocca and Pinotage. A soft, easy-drinking red.

Checkers Smooth Red ★★ B

A Pinotage-based blend with Cinsaut.

Cheers (Picardi) ★★★ B

A very drinkable dry red at a good price.

De Wet Co-op Dry Red ★★★ A

A blend of equal proportions Cabernet Franc and Cinsaut. A nice combination that smooths out after a year or so in the bottle.

Domein Doornkraal Kannaland ★★ B

A blend of Pinotage and Merlot with a full, soft, almost sweet taste.

Douglas Co-op Dry Red ★★(★) B

Made from Ruby Cabernet and Pinotage from 1992 vintage. Full, fruity and easy-drinking.

Douglas Green St Raphael ★★ B

A popular non-vintaged wine. Recent blends have shown an improvement. It is Pinotage-based with some Cinsaut, giving a light-bodied, pleasant wine.

Du Toitskloof Co-op Vino Uno Rosso Secco ★★★ A

This cellar's effort to keep the cost of drinking down. Inexpensive 500 ml screw-top bottles of good-drinking Cinsaut-based wine.

Eersterivier-Valleise Kelder Le Foyer Dry Red ★★ A

In an effort to keep the price down, the range of Le Foyer wines are packed in 500 ml screw-top bottles and are available only at the cellar. The dry red is a Pinotage-based braai wine.

Eersterivier-Valleise Kelder Vin Rouge ★★ A

Pleasant-flavoured quaffer of mainly Pinotage and 25% Cinsaut.

Eikendal Vineyards Rouge ★★★ B

Originally under the Duc de Berry label, but from 1991 onwards under Eikendal. Early releases of this dry blend are predominantly wood-aged Shiraz and have developed well. From the 1986 vintage onwards, the blend contains 70% Cinsaut, 20% Shiraz and small quantities of Cabernet Sauvignon and Merlot, resulting in easy drinking sooner than usual.

Fairview Paarl Red ★★(★) B

Originally a non-vintaged blend containing aged Pinotage and Shiraz; then a light Pinot Noir which progressed to a Cabernet Sauvignon-based full wine; then back to a light Pinot Noir. It is now a blend of unwooded Cabernets.

Goede Hoop Vintage Rouge ★★★(★) D

Originally an interesting blend of Shiraz, Tinta Barocca and Cinsaut. The 1974, 1975 and 1976 vintages were all very good and developed well in the bottle. There were no releases in 1977 and 1979, but a very different wine was released with the 1978 vintage. Said to be a blend of equal parts of Cabernet Sauvignon, Shiraz and Pinotage, it carried Superior certification, and needed considerably longer to achieve the smoothness of the earlier blends. The 1980 is excellent and differs again in its make-up with Shiraz, Tinta Barocca and Carignan being used. The 1981 is a full, firm wine, but has not developed well. The 1982 is a lovely wine – a true blend in which no cultivar dominates – and is touched off with new oak. The 1983 is similar but shows more wood. The 1988 is Shiraz and Pinotage with a fraction of Cabernet Sauvignon. The 1989 is much the same and should develop well.

74 ★★★★ drink up. 75 ★★★ drink up. 76 ★★★★ ready. 77 no release. 78 ★★★★ ready. 79 no release. 80 ★★★★ ready. 81 ★★ ready. 82 ★★★★ ready. 83 ★★★(★) ready. 86 ★★★(★) ready. 87 ★★★★ ready. 88 ★★★★ ready. 89 ★★★(★) needs time to develop.

Goue Vallei Classique Rouge (Citrusdal Co-op) ★★★ B

An unwooded multiple blend of Cinsaut, Grenache, Pinotage and Tinta Barocca, giving fairly smooth wine.

Goudveld Soewenier ★ B

A medium-bodied dry red made from Pinotage on the Orange Free State's only wine estate.

Hemel-en-Aarde Valley Vin Rouge ★★★★ C

A delightful, easy-drinking, medium-bodied wine, with a good range of flavours in the mouth. The lightness in colour comes from the 75% Pinot Noir that has been aged in oak for a short period. The balance is well-flavoured Shiraz. The wine is non-vintaged but usually released about a year after vintage. It will develop with two to three years in the bottle. It will no longer be produced as the cellar is concentrating on its classics.

Huguenot Wine Farmers Smooth Red ★★ B

An almost sweet, easy-drinking wine from Cinsaut.

Huguenot Wine Farmers Zellerhof Smooth Red ★★(★) B
A Cinsaut-Pinotage blend for early drinking.

Jonkerskloof (OK) ★★(★) A
A multiple blend of Tinta Barocca, Cinsaut, Pinotage and some Cabernet Sauvignon for early, easy drinking.

KWV Bonne Esperance Red ★★ (no price available)
A light, easy-drinking, unremarkable dry red available to KWV members, and for export, in one-litre, screw-top bottles.

Louwshoek-Voorsorg Co-op Dry Red ★ A
A light dry red made from Cinsaut.

Mamreweg Co-op Claret ★★ B
It was previously known as a dry red – a wood-aged, dry red blend which varied with the vintage, but usually contained Cinsaut, Pinotage and Tinta Barocca. More recently it is a 50/50 blend of Cinsaut and Pinotage. This is always a good-value, quaffing wine. It is not vintage-dated.

Mons Ruber Conari ★★ A
An unusual, early-drinking dry red in which Cabernet dominates. It has an almost marzipan aftertaste.

Monterey Rouge (Western Province Cellars) ★★ A
Current releases are an improvement on earlier wines. Good value.

Morgenhof Dry Red ★★★ C
Easy, everyday drinking wine from the 1990 vintage, from Pinotage.

Onverwacht Rouge de Noir ★★ B
A fruity-nosed, simple wine with a definite Cinsaut base and some Tinta Barocca from the 1989 vintage.

Oranjerivier Wynkelders Droë Rooi ★ A
Originally a light-bodied Pinotage but now made from Grenache.

Overgaauw Overtinto ★★★★ B
A very good blend of Port varieties, including Tinta Barocca, Comifesto, Francisca, Malvasia Rey and Souzão. This is one of the more unusual South African red wines tasting, not surprisingly, like a dry Port. It is full-bodied and ages well. It is no longer being produced and it is a pity to see such an interesting wine disappear. Most of the vintages are still developing but the earlier ones will soon need to be consumed – I'm sure with great satisfaction.

Overmeer Selected Red (SFW) ★★ B
Good, easy-drinking wine in which Cinsaut dominates.

Party Pack Dry Red (Drop Inn) ★★(★) A
This wine is obviously Pinotage-based from the clean, distinctive nose. It is young, bright and easy on the palate. Good value.

Paddagang Vignerons Paddajolais ★★★ B
When chilled, this bright-red blend, originally of Cabernet Sauvignon, Shiraz and Merlot – later of Pinotage and Tinta Barocca – drinks incredibly well as a young wine.

Paradyskloof Rouge (Vriesenhof) ★★★(★) C

This non-vintaged blend of Merlot with Cabernet Sauvignon and Shiraz has replaced the Roodewyn and Claret labels. It has good character with fine oak backing and is good value for money. It drinks easy on release yet has the potential to develop over three to five years.

Pascali Rosso (Bergkelder) ★★★ B

For its price, this was a particularly enjoyable dry red wine which went well with Mediterranean food. It was a blend of Merlot, Pinotage and Shiraz with some oak age. It had good nose and full, deep flavour which showed a rare complexity for a wine of this price. Regretfully now culled.

Porterville Co-op Dry Red ★★ A

Mainly Pinotage with some Cinsaut.

Ravenswood Dry Red (Pick 'n Pay) ★★ A

Sold only in the five-litre box, this wine is shy on the nose but pleasant enough on the palate. A simple blend of Cinsaut and Pinotage.

Rebel Dry Red ★ A

The best of the Rebel range: a dry red braai wine.

Rhebokskloof Dry Red ★★★ C

A good, clean-flavoured, easy-drinking dry red. This is a blend with Cinsaut, Pinotage and a touch of Cabernet Sauvignon crossing vintages that makes nice, early drinking. The non-vintaged bottles need to be marked with the purchase date to give you an indication of the age. Two to three years will give gratifying development.

Rijckshof Claret (Kango Co-op) ★★(★) A

The first release was an exceptional wine although it did not meet the normal quality criteria. It was blended from 70% Cabernet with an unusually high alcohol content of 16,5% and 30% (less alcoholic) Tinta Barocca. Aged in 500 litre Nevers puncheons for 18 months and developing well over the year, this is a full-bodied, bold wine with vague porty tones. The fresh, fruity, unwooded 1989 release is a very different wine, comprising predominantly Tinta Barocca with 10% Cinsaut and 10% 'other reds'. The 1991 offers small quantity and light quality and the 1992 is an almost pink Pinot Noir.

Romansrivier Co-op Vino Rood ★★ A

This replaces the former Rood which was a surprisingly full blend of Cabernet Sauvignon and Pinotage. The replacement is a light-blend Cinsaut and Pinotage which is ready for early drinking but develops over a year in the bottle. It is good value for money.

Rooiberg Co-op Selected Red ★★(★) B

This wine varies in composition year by year. Recent years have been Pinot Noir, Shiraz and Merlot with the latest, Pinot Noir, Shiraz and Cinsaut.

Rozendal Val de Lyn ★★★(★) E

Mostly Merlot with some Cinsaut from the 1989 vintage; a very nice drinking wine at this early stage.

Simondium Co-op Claret ★★ A

A dry red from Cinsaut.

Stellenbosch Wine Route Vin Rouge (Delheim) ★★★ B

A label available on 1,5 litre returnable plastic flasks. Pinotage-based, it is good, easy drinking wine.

Tassenberg (SFW) ★★★ B

Our most popular red – quaffed by some, but drunk with respect by those who know and understand wine.

Taverna Rouge (Bergkelder) ★★ B

A somewhat light, dry red.

Tulbagh Co-op Claret ★★ A

An unwooded blend of Cinsaut, Pinotage and Tinta Barocca giving a medium-bodied dry red.

Vaalharts Co-op Overvaal Dry Red ★★ B

A light, easy-drinking dry red from Pinotage.

Valley Dry Red (Gilbeys) ★★ A

A good, no-nonsense dry red of predominantly Cinsaut.

Valley Smooth Red (Gilbeys) ★★ A

A light-bodied, easy-drinking, off-dry red from Pinotage and Cinsaut.

Villa Rossini Rosso (DGB) ★★(★) B

This was Union Wines' venture into Italian-style wines; made from Cinsaut and Shiraz, giving a full-flavoured, relatively light red that makes easy drinking and is sold in screw-top, one-litre bottles.

Vino Roma Rosso (SFW) ★★★ B

SFW's red entry into the current Italian fashion. Surprisingly good, it is made from unwooded Shiraz (two-thirds) with the balance, Pinotage. It is easy, early-drinking wine, but develops well over a year.

Vinovat Dry Red (Marcows) (★) A

A very ordinary dry red.

Vin Rouge (Picardi) ★★★★ C

A very drinkable dry red from Walker Bay. The blend includes Cabernet Sauvignon, Pinot Noir and others.

Vintner's Choice Grand Vin Rouge (Drop Inn) ★★ A

A good, honest, medium-bodied red wine with a pleasing taste. Made from Cinsaut, Tinta Barocca and Pinotage, it has every potential to develop with a few years in the bottle.

Vredenheim Léger ★★ A

A light-bodied, ordinary dry red.

Welgemeend Amadé ★★★(★) B

This wine was first produced in 1979 from equal quantities of Grenache, Pinotage and Shiraz, crushed and fermented together. In 1983 the blend changed considerably, becoming 50% Grenache, 44% Shiraz and 6% Pinotage, which produced a much better, fruitier wine. The 1983 has developed in the bottle and is drinking well in 1990. The 1985 was the

Alphen Wine of the Month for non-Cabernet blends during 1988. Matured in good wood, the 1986 has as little as 12% Pinotage with Grenache and Shiraz making up almost equal parts of the balance. The 1987 is very good with a blend of some 50% Grenache, 40% Shiraz, and the balance Pinotage. It drinks very well in 1993. The 1988 is a lighter wine but has very pleasant flavours. The 1989, 1990 and 1991 are back to being mainly Shiraz and Grenache and as little as 10% Pinotage. A lovely, fruity wine with a very pleasing palate, even at an early stage. With a few years, this smooth, medium-bodied wine, full of lovely flavour, develops with great benefit.

85 ★★★ ready. 86 ★★★ ready. 87 ★★★★ ready, will improve. 88 ★★★(★) ready, will develop. 89 ★★★★ ready, will develop. 90 ★★★(★) ready, will develop. 91 ★★★★ ready, will develop.

Woolworths Blue Label Rouge ★★(★) C

Fairview's nouveau-style wine from Gamay without added sulphur dioxide. This is for cool, early drinking if you still have some – it has been discontinued.

Woolworths Petit Vin Dry Red ★★★ A

A good-drinking dry red in 250 ml Tetrapak from Villiera.

Yellow Label Red (Checkers) ★★ A

An easy-drinking red with Pinotage character and Cinsaut sweetness.

Zevenwacht Zevenrood ★★ B

A non-vintaged bold, full-flavoured, wood-aged wine which has good character and was based on Shiraz with small amounts of Pinotage and Pinot Noir. From 1991 onwards it will be Pinot Noir and Merlot.

CABERNET FRANC

Landskroon Cabernet Franc ★★★(★) D

The first of these wines on the market was the 1979 vintage. In general, it is a medium-bodied, well-flavoured wine which ages with distinction. The 1989 is the best yet. It has good, full nose, and lots of fine flavours with some wood backing. It will develop well over four or more years. The 1990 is not quite as full and will probably peak slightly earlier.

79 ★★★★ past its best. 80 ★★★ ready. 81 ★★★ past its best, still enjoyable. 82 ★★★★ ready. 83 ★★★ ready. 88 ★★★ ready, will still develop. 89 ★★★★ ready, will still develop. 90 ★★★★ ready.

Warwick Cabernet Franc ★★★★ D

Initially bottled only for export to the UK. The 1988 made an appearance here in limited quantities. A special selection of 1989 was at the 1992 Cape Independent Winemakers' Guild Auction. A clean, lively wine with lots of attractive fruit. The 1990 is superb and should develop beautifully by 1995. It is really worth seeking out and, to my mind, a five-star wine.

CABERNET SAUVIGNON

Aan-de-Doorns Co-op Cabernet Sauvignon ★★ B
This is a dry red which has shown continual success in local competitions. In general, it ages over three to four years to become a smooth wine with distinct Cabernet Sauvignon character. The 1987 is a softish, dry wine suitable for relatively early drinking and not for ageing like those of the early 1980s. The 1988 and 1990 are unwooded wines and ready for early drinking.

Allesverloren Cabernet Sauvignon ★★★★ D/E
Until the 1982 vintage, this was usually full-bodied Cabernet made in the traditional style. Thereafter there was a difference in style with the prominence of new oak. The 1982 has a deep, full flavour, developed beautifully, but now needs to be enjoyed. Of the earlier vintages, the 1978 was good and the 1979 one of the better wines of a poor vintage. The 1980 needs drinking. The 1981 is a superb, full, rich wine from a vintage which has been discounted by many, but is now ready for drinking. The 1982 is as good as the 1984 and developing just as well. The 1983 is lighter, like so many others of that vintage, and now needs to be enjoyed. The 1984 has made good use of new oak, which adds an extra dimension to the wine – probably one of the best of the decade. The 1985 was a gold medal winner at the Cape Young Wine Show. Its appearance in the bottle, however, has shown it to be a little reserved compared with the 1982 and 1984. The 1986 is a fine, big, complex wine with good oak. The 1987 is a big, full wine that will need plenty of time to develop. The same applies to the 1988 which is a massive wine, full of character, lots of tannin and 13,5% alcohol. It will need lots of time to tame. The next release is from the 1989 and is also very good, but needs time to develop.
74 ★★★★★ ready. 75 no release. 76 ★★★★★ ready. 77 ★★★ past its best. 78 ★★★★ ready. 79 ★★★ ready. 80 ★★★★ ready. 81 ★★★★ ready. 82 ★★★★★ ready. 83 ★★★★ ready. 84 ★★★★(★) ready. 85 ★★★★ ready. 86 ★★★★(★) not ready, age further. 87 ★★★★ not ready, age further. 88 ★★★★ not ready, age further. 89 ★★★(★) not ready, age further.

Alphen Cabernet Sauvignon ★★★★ C
Alphen upgraded their wines in 1980 and have revised their style and operation, again making the wines at Kleine Zalze, a South African champion cellar, drawing grapes from a wide area around Stellenbosch, Helderberg and Somerset West. The 1980 is rich, smooth and not entirely dry, and has improved in the bottle. The 1982 is a four-star wine and should not be underrated. The 1983 is drinking well and the 1984 was ready for consumption on release. The 1985 is a lighter wine and should be drunk now. The 1986 is good and needs time to show. The 1987 is the first from the new style, with the 1988 being a very good drinking wine at

an early age. This will be followed by a very pleasant 1989. Most of the early- to mid-1980s need to be enjoyed now.

80 ★★★★ ready. 81 no release. 82 ★★★★ ready. 83 ★★★ ready. 84 ★★★(★) ready. 85 ★★★ ready. 86 ★★★(★) ready. 87 ★★★★ ready, will still develop. 88 ★★★★ ready, will still improve with time. 89 ★★★(★) not ready, age further.

Alto Cabernet Sauvignon ★★★★ F

A big, specially matured, full-bodied, deep-coloured Cabernet. The 1970 had a lot of tannin and took years to round out and to realize its potential. This wine was not bottled between 1972 and 1975, but supplies were resumed in 1976 with a fine, less powerful wine. The 1977 vintage is a light wine of which very little appeared on the South African market. The 1978 was also a lighter-styled wine than usual for Alto. The 1979 was definitely a more medium-bodied wine which, although appealing, was not as fruity as other vintages, yet developed beautifully over ten years. The 1980 was only released in 1986 and shows Alto's true style. The 1982 is a big, alcoholic wine that has developed beautifully over ten years and is super now. It was selected by SAA as a Wine of the Month during 1990 and has done well on auction. The 1984 is a big, powerful, full-flavoured wine that will be at its best in the early 1990s. There was no 1985, but the 1986 followed in outstanding style and is developing very well.

76 ★★★★★ ready. 77 ★★★ ready. 78 ★★★★ ready. 79 ★★★ ready. 80 ★★★★ ready. 82 ★★★ ready, will still improve. 84 ★★★★ ready, will still improve. 85 no release. 86 ★★★★ allow time to develop.

Altydgedacht Cabernet Sauvignon ★★★(★) E

Altydgedacht is an interesting Estate where, many years ago, Mrs Jean Parker made outstanding Cabernets until she decided to send her grapes to Nederburg. Today her sons are in business, John looking after the vineyards and Oliver making the wine. Oliver's first release of Cabernet is from the 1982 vintage: a light, stylish wine which has developed beautifully. The 1985 was the next release and is surprisingly full for the vintage – a most attractive wine which is developing well. The 1986 is a big wine that is only smoothing out now. The 1987 is a big strong wine with plenty of potential, as is the 1988, which will be at its best at the end of the century. It will be followed by a 1989.

82 ★★★ ready. 83 no release. 84 no release. 85 ★★★★ ready. 86 ★★★★ ready, will still develop. 87 ★★★★ not ready, age further. 88 ★★★★ not ready, age further.

Ashton Co-op Cabernet Sauvignon ★★ B

The heavily-wooded 1984 was followed by a 1987 wine which is pleasant, light and fruity. It is developing well but is not designed to last long, and is at its best now. The 1988 has good wood backing and is a nice, fruity wine. The 1989 is an improvement, with good wood, and the 1990 is the best to date.

Avontuur Cabernet Reserve ★★★(★) D

The 1987 is a firm, full wine, but the 1989 seems curiously light and lacks the character of the 1987.

Avontuur Cabernet Sauvignon ★★★(★) D

The 1987 is a well-made dry wine with good cultivar character backed by fine wood. This old and established farm has returned to making its own wine in a well-equipped winery. The 1988 is a lovely rich, full-flavoured wine that will develop well; the 1989, an acceptable medium-bodied wine.

Backsberg Cabernet Sauvignon ★★★★(★) D

This was the first wine to be awarded Superior status under the Wine of Origin legislation and is a regular prizewinner. Most vintages were awarded Superior status when this certification still existed, are undoubtedly excellent, and all have considerable varietal character. Backsberg is one of the few cellars that can offer older vintages of their Cabernets and usually have three or four available. They are surprisingly consistent wines. All are ageing well, and it is hard to choose between the years. The 1981 was lighter than previous vintages, the 1982 much fuller, with a good oakiness not previously noticeable. The 1983 and 1984 are the last of the Estate's earlier-style wines. The 1985 shows a very different, fuller wine which should age with great benefit over eight to ten years. The 1986 was the best Cabernet Sauvignon to date from this Estate, but the 1987 is even better, with great Cabernet character backed by good wood. It will definitely age with benefit. The 1988 is a little shy and will drink earlier than the 1987. The 1989 is showing new clone Cabernet character and is a delicious wine that will develop with great benefit, as will the very tasty 1990. New clone and style of wine-making makes this wine very drinkable at an early age, though it still has the ability to develop further.

72 ★★★★ drink. 73 ★★★ past its best. 74 ★★★★ drink. 75 ★★★★★ past its best. 76 ★★★★★ drink. 77 ★★★ past its best. 78 ★★★★ ready. 79 ★★★ drink. 80 ★★★★ ready. 81 ★★★ ready. 82 ★★(★) ready. 83 ★★★ ready. 84 ★★★ ready. 85 ★★★★ ready. 86 ★★★★(★) ready, will still improve. 87 ★★★★(★) ready, will improve. 88 ★★★(★) ready, will still improve. 89 ★★★★ ready, will still improve. 90 ★★★★ ready, will still improve.

Bellingham Cabernet Sauvignon ★★★★(★) E

The first release of this wine was the 1980 vintage and heralded a dramatic change in the quality of Bellingham products. The 1980 has very good Cabernet nose and just a hint of fresh oak, giving subtle complexity which has developed well with time. It has probably reached its best, but has the ability to hold. The 1981 is just as good. The 1982 is a good, full wine which is developing well. The 1983 is a little lighter and needs to be drunk. The 1984 and 1985 are similar in that they are much more forward wines. The 1986 is the best so far. It is a fine, deep wine and will probably peak in the mid-1990s.

80 ★★★★ ready. 81 ★★★ ready. 82 ★★★★ ready. 83 ★★★(★) ready. 84 ★★★★ ready. 85 ★★★(★) ready. 86 ★★★(★)ready, will still improve.

Bergkelder Cabernet Sauvignon (Cellarmaster's Choice) ★★★★★ F

A special release from the 1987 vintage. The best casks available were selected and blended by Dr Laszlo to produce remarkable wine. It was aged in new French oak and shows great style and character, and will develop well over time.

Bergsig Cabernet Sauvignon ★★★ D

The early wines were very soft, yet full-flavoured and nicely wooded. The wines of the 1980s had better fruit. All develop well and drink easily at four to five years. The 1988, 1989 and 1990 have more oak and a soft finish, and are ready for drinking when released – although they will develop over two to three years. The 1991 and 1992 are finer in character but still in the same easy-drinking style.

Bertrams Cabernet Sauvignon ★★★★ F

In the middle-to-late 1970s, this was one of the finest Cabernets of the Stellenbosch district and was judged champion red wine at the South African Championship Wine Show at Goodwood in 1975, 1978 and 1979. It had its own distinct, full-bodied character with deep aroma and moderately high tannin; a powerful wine with an excellent ageing potential of ten years plus. The 1982 and 1983 were still of the old Bertrams style and are showing well now. The 1984 is very different, with a slightly subdued nose, but every potential to develop over many years. The 1985 is of a more modern style and is a finer, more elegant wine. The 1986 shows a developing style that is very pleasing and the 1987 continues to show improving style. The cellar is to be congratulated on releasing their wines when they are a full five years old and have developed good bottle age. These wines now make regular appearances at the Nederburg Auction.

79 ★★★ ready. 80 ★★★★ ready. 81 ★★★★ ready. 82 ★★★★ ready. 83 ★★★★(★) ready. 84 ★★★★ ready, will still improve. 85 ★★★★ ready, will still improve. 86 ★★★★ ready, will still improve. 87 ready, with lots of development potential.

Beyerskloof Cabernet Sauvignon ★★★★★ F

The first production from this small cellar on the lower slopes of the Koelenhof hills comes from the 1989 vintage. The wine has full Cabernet character and lots of berry, backed by wood. It is well-packed in traditional Bordeaux-tapered bottles with a most attractive label. The pack received a 1991 Loerie award and the wine was selected as the Alphen Wine of the Month for the best 1989 Cabernet Sauvignon. The 1990 is another beauty, with the 1991 being an absolute stunner. Expensive, but worth the search – they will all age majestically.

Blaauwklippen Cabernet Sauvignon ★★★★(★) E

A light style of Cabernet with a decidedly Bordeaux character. The well-rounded 1980 vintage won the then wine maker, Walter Finlayson, the

Diners Club Award in 1982 for the second year running. It is definitely a five-star wine, which is still developing extremely well in the bottle. The 1981 was a lighter wine, in keeping with the vintage, but has developed well in the bottle. The 1982 is a fine wine, but the 1983 is slightly out of character. The 1984 is magnificent, however, and the 1986 and 1987 are even better. The 1985 has not lived up to my original expectations. As good as it is, it is not developing as well as the 1984, 1986 and the potentially stunning 1987. Winemaking now rests in the hands of Jacques Kruger who was the assistant for many years. He has a particular touch for red wine as witnessed in the 1987 and 1988 wines. The 1989 is very good. These wines need six to eight years to develop to their full potential. Also available in 375 ml (half) bottles.

78 ★★★★ drink. 79 ★★★★ drink. 80 ★★★★★ ready. 81 ★★★ ready. 82 ★★★★★ 83 ★★★ ready. 84 ★★★★★ ready, will still develop. 85 ★★★★ ready, will improve. 86 ★★★★★ ready. 87 ★★★★ ready, will still develop. 88 ★★★★★ not ready, age further. 89 ★★★★★ not ready, age further.

Blaauwklippen Reserve Cabernet Sauvignon ★★★★★ D

This wine is produced for the Cape Independent Winemakers' Guild Auction. Small quantities are selected and bottled with the Guild's Auction label. They are always deep, magnificent wines packed with Cabernet character, shown off with excellent oak. The 1985 was chosen by SAA as a Wine of the Month. The 1986 is a big, powerful wine with lots of berry flavours, as is the 1987. The great complexity of the wine ensures superb development in the bottle over many years to come.

82 ★★★★★ ready. 83 ★★★★★ ready. 84 ★★★★★ ready, will still improve. 85 ★★★★★ ready, will still improve. 86 ★★★★★ not ready, age further. 87 ★★★★★ not ready, age further.

Bloemendal Cabernet Sauvignon ★★★★ E

The first release was from the 1987 vintage which was launched in 1990. It is an elegant, fruity wine, full of berry character, good tannin and nice oak background. The 1988 is a delicious, elegant wine with layers of fruit and berry flavours backed by good wood. Next up, the 1989, is a little lighter and more elegant wine, but with the same good fruit and wood.

Bodega Cabernet Sauvignon ★★★(★) D

The first release from the 1990 vintage is a very creditable production, with good fruit and friendly tannins. The next release will be from the 1991.

Bolandse Co-op Cabernet Sauvignon ★★★(★) B

Many of the earlier vintages were indifferent but, during the late 1970s and 1980s, they have shown great promise – the 1977 having aged with elegance over the years. The 1982 vintage has performed surprisingly well and is regularly rated higher in tastings than many of the more fancied wines. The 1983 is as full-bodied as the others and, in 1989, was selected for sale at the Nederburg Auction. The 1984 shows more wood and will develop greater complexity than earlier vintages. The 1985 has benefited from maturing for a year in wood. The 1986 is showing very well and has good development potential. Some of the 1985, 1986 and 1987 vintages have been bottled in magnums. A portion of the 1987 has been aged in American oak with a decidedly woody effect. The 1988, 1989 and 1990 vintages are in keeping with the cellars quality and are excellent value for money.

82 ★★★ ready. 83 ★★★ ready. 84 ★★★★ ready, will still improve. 85 ★★★★ ready. 86 ★★★★(★) ready, will still improve. 87 ★★★★ not ready, age further. 88 ★★★★ not ready, age further. 89 ★★★(★) not ready, age further. 90 ★★★★ age further.

Boplaas Cabernet ★★★(★) D

A surprisingly good Cabernet from this inland area. The 1985 has good cultivar character touched with good new wood, and has developed well over the years. The 1986 is a fruity, lean wine, with the 1987 showing more character. The 1988 and 1989 show improved style and will develop better than earlier vintages. These satisfying wines are probably at their best in five to seven years. The 1990 is fuller bodied but continues the improvement in style.

Botha Co-op Cabernet Sauvignon ★★★ B

This is a consistently good wine which is usually released within one year of production. Most develop well over six to eight years. There was no release of the 1984 vintage, and the full-wooded 1985 was released before it was a year old; the 1986 at about six months. The 1986 tastes almost sweet, is amazingly soft, and was a wine for early consumption. The 1987 was released before the year was out and needed more ageing before drinking. The 1988 is medium-bodied, has good flavours, and is fairly forward. I missed the 1989 but the 1990 has got lots of wood with good fruit. Good value wine.

85 ★★★ ready. 86 ★★★ ready. 87 ★★(★) ready. 88 ★★★ ready, will still improve. 90 ★★★ ready, will still improve.

Bottelary Co-op Cabernet Sauvignon ★★★ B

Early vintages like the 1976 were full-bodied and fairly robust Cabernets that aged with great benefit over six to eight years. Recent vintages are much lighter and more medium-bodied. Those of the 1980s are on the light side, but have developed quite well over a year or so. The 1989, however, is a wooded wine with deeper style, but still for early drinking.

82 ★★★ drink. 83 ★★★ drink. 84 ★★ drink. 85 ★★ drink. 86 ★★★(★) ready. 87 ★★★ ready. 88 ★★★ ready, will still improve. 89 ★★★ ready, will still improve.

Bovlei Co-op Cabernet Sauvignon ★★★ B

A regular medal winner, this full-bodied wine needs time to show its best. The 1987 is a light, elegant, fruity wine which was easy drinking when young and followed by a big, heavier 1988. The 1989 is very different, with lots of wood and good fruit, and has done well in competition.

Calitzdorp Co-op Cabernet ★★ B

The 1989 is a fairly ordinary, light-bodied wine and was followed by a similar style wine in 1991. The 1992 is wooded and, with this vintage, the name Buffelskroon has been dropped in favour of Calitzdorp Co-op.

Cape Vintners Members Only Cabernet Sauvignon ★★★ D

From the 1988 and 1989 vintages comes a berry-flavoured wine with good, deep tones.

Cederberg Kelders Cabernet Sauvignon ★★★ B

This unusual cellar has improved its Cabernet vintage by vintage. The 1978 was a dramatic Grand Champion Red at the Olifants River Young Wine Show and winner of a gold medal at the Goodwood show. The wines of the early 1980s were for early consumption. The 1986 vintage heralded a total change of style and quality, and deserves three stars. A portion of the wine is aged for a year in large old vats, with the balance aged in new American and French oak, producing a lovely flavoured wine. The 1987 is a much bigger, fuller-flavoured wine that should develop with great interest. I have not tasted the 1988, but the 1989 is a very acceptable wine, and cellar samples of the 1992 show a fruity, flowery soft wine that drinks easy.

Chamonix Cabernet Sauvignon ★★★ C

The 1986 vintage was specially made to celebrate the Huguenot tercentenary and is a nice, light-style wine which has good cultivar character balanced with new wood. The 1987 is a fuller, better-flavoured wine. There was no 1988 or 1989, but new ownership produced a very acceptable 1990. Keep a look out for better things to come.

Clairvaux Co-op Cabernet Sauvignon ★★ A

The initial offerings were medium-bodied and rather ordinary. The 1984 was a clean wine with good character, albeit on the light side. The next release carries no vintage date as it is a blend of the 1985 and 1986. It is a fuller wine that is ready for drinking now. The 1988 is medium-bodied, easy-drinking wine that is now showing its age. The 1989 appears to be much the same.

Clos Malverne Cabernet Sauvignon ★★★★ E

The first release from this Devon Valley cellar came from the 1988 vintage and numbered 450 cases. Small quantities were produced from the 1986 and 1987 vintages, and show great character. The 1989 has good complexity and is a rich, full-flavoured wine which will develop well. The 1990 follows the same dense style, with deep colour and lots of berry flavours. It should also develop well. The 1991 is more elegant and will develop well.

De Helderberg Co-op Cabernet Sauvignon ★★★ B

Wines from this Co-op have changed for the better over the past few years and the Cabernet probably best illustrates this change in style. From the mid-1980s, the Cabernets are full in style. The 1986 was full of tannin and is only now softening out. The 1987 is also big and deep with lots of flavours, and makes an unusual change to this kind of wine as it is without any wood influence. The 1988 has developed well. There is very little 1989 and no 1990. The 1991 is particularly good and the 1992 continues the same unwooded style. Excellent value for money.

85 ★★(★) ready. 86 ★★ ready. 87 ★★★ ready. 88 ★★★ ready, will improve. 89 ★★★ ready. 90 no release. 91 ★★★(★) not ready, age further. 92 ★★★(★) not ready, age further.

De Leuwen Jagt Cabernet ★★★ D

The 1989 is a medium-bodied, well-wooded wine, and the 1990 is a more elegant, deeper flavoured wine. Cellar samples look good for the future.

Delheim Cabernet Sauvignon ★★★★ D

One of the Cape's top-quality wine bargains. Although this used to be a fairly light-bodied wine, it had most attractive qualities which made pleasant drinking at four to five years. The 1982 vintage showed considerable change in quality and was full of good cultivar character. This vintage has been particularly well wood-treated: the cultivar still dominates, but the wood has added complexity and softened the wine. The 1983 reflects the vintage with a lighter but well-flavoured wine. The 1984 is a deep, beautiful wine packed with character and has tremendous potential to develop very well in the bottle. The 1985 was launched in May 1987 and made easy drinking sooner than the 1984. The 1986 contains 25% Merlot that gives it greater depth of character. It is very drinkable now and has every potential to develop in the bottle over five to eight years. It was the Alphen Wine of the Month in August 1988. The 1987 is a good successor with 18% Cabernet Franc and 4% Merlot, backed with very good wood. The 1988 is a very good, complex wine and the 1989 has a most attractive nose and flavour. The 1990 is looking very good, with lots of concentrated character. It is going to develop very well.

82 ★★★★ ready. 83 ★★★★ ready. 84 ★★★★ ready. 85 ★★★★ ready, will still improve. 86 ★★★★(★) ready, will still improve. 87 ★★★★(★) ready, will still improve. 88 ★★★★(★) not ready, age further. 89 ★★★★(★) not ready, age further. 90 ★★★★(★) not ready, age further.

De Zoete Inval Cabernet Sauvignon ★★ C

A wine with a very distinctive character. It has its devotees, although I didn't like it when I drank it young; it probably needs time to develop. The 1980 carries the now extinct Superior certification and is showing good development in the bottle. Three vintages are available, the youngest being the 1981. The cellar believes in selling well-aged, old-style wines.

Die Krans Cabernet ★★★ B

The first release is a good, well-wooded, full-flavoured wine from the 1991 vintage.

Diemersdal Cabernet Sauvignon ★★★ D

The first release from the 1988 vintage is a robust wine with good fruit and fair tannin that should allow it to age well. The 1989 is full of berry and vanilla flavours, and has good wood backing. The 1990 has the same full, woody character.

Dieu Donne Cabernet ★★★(★) **C**

One of the cellar's best wines. The first release from the 1991 vintage is a medium-bodied wine with a good fruity nose and oaky background. It will develop with time. The next release is from the 1992.

Douglas Green Cabernet Sauvignon (DGB) ★★★(★) **D**

Many South African Cabernets have improved a great deal over recent vintages and this wine is no exception. Originally a Cabernet and Cinsaut blend of fairly full body and high tannin, the 1979 saw a change in style from an early-drinking wine to one requiring some bottle-ageing, and was by far the best seen under this label up to that time. The 1980, 1981 and 1982 carry Superior certification. The 1981 is past its best and the 1980 and 1982 need to be consumed. There was very little of the 1983 vintage. The 1984 is a very light wine, rather like a Rosé, and has little cultivar character. The 1985 is very pleasant, with attractive fruit and pleasant palate, and is a good example of the traditional-style Cape Cabernet. It was selected for the 1989 SAA Wine List. The 1986 has more character and is more attractive. The 1987 was somewhat reserved. The 1988 release is a better wine, having spent 18 months in large vats. It should develop well in the bottle over six to eight years. The 1989 was released in a new pack, and will be followed by a 1990.

78 ★★★ drink. 79 ★★★★ drink. 80 ★★★ ready. 81 ★★★ past its best. 82 ★★★★ ready. 83 ★★★ ready. 84 ★★★ ready. 85 ★★★★ ready. 86 ★★★★ ready, will still improve. 87 ★★★ ready. 88 ★★★★ ready, will still improve. 89 ★★★(★) ready, will still improve.

Du Toitskloof Co-op Cabernet ★★★ **C**

This attractively labelled 1988 vintage is a rich, full wine with good wood backing. It is the best wine from this cellar, and should develop with interest. The 1989 is slightly lighter, medium-bodied and fruity, with fine wood. The 1990 is a more elegant wine and will develop better than previous vintages.

Eersterivier-Valleise Kelder Cabernet Sauvignon ★★★ **B/C**

The early vintages of 1977 and 1979 were light, easy-drinking wines that did not develop well. There were no further releases until 1982, when a fuller-bodied, deeper-style wine came onto the market. This was followed by a similar wine in 1983. Both developed well in the bottle and were at their best in 1989. The 1984 was surprisingly light and should have been drunk by now. The 1985 was also fairly ordinary but the 1987 was a much more attractive, wood-aged, medium-bodied wine that drank well when young. The 1988 is also a medium-bodied, but better flavoured wine from new, early ripening clones. No 1989 was bottled. The 1990 continues the improvement shown in the 1988. This is good wine for drinking four to five years from the vintage.

Eikendal Cabernet Reserve du Patron ★★★(★) E

This is a more extensively wood-aged wine than the cellar's regular Cabernet and sales are reserved to just two bottles per person. The first release from the 1984 vintage has developed beautifully. The next release, from the 1987, is a super, four-star wine. Powerful flavours and good tannin should allow it to age with benefit.

Eikendal Cabernet Sauvignon ★★★ D

This cellar made a fine début with the blending of a small amount of Shiraz, giving its Cabernets greater complexity and the potential to develop well. The 1984 contains some softening Cinsaut, having spent ten months in small wood. It is a good, rich, deep-coloured wine, drinking very well in 1992. The 1985 was lighter, but the 1986 is an excellent deep, full-flavoured wine with good fruit and wood. The 1987 is developing well, while the 1988 is already drinking well. The 1989 has 30% Merlot which makes it very drinkable. The 1990 is a little reserved at this early stage, but should develop well.

Fairview Cabernet Sauvignon ★★★★ B

This is a regular award-winner. Early vintages were powerful, robust wines needing seven to ten years to smooth out, but in the late 1970s and early 1980s the style changed. These wines are now medium-bodied, far more elegant, and drink well much earlier than previous vintages. The 1983 is fairly full for the vintage and shows fine Cabernet character without wood influence. There is a small amount of the extremely fine, wood-aged 1983, which was only available from the Estate. The 1984 shows some of the old style of robustness tempered with a bit of wood. The 1985 is a lighter wine, while the 1986 and 1987 are considerably richer and finer. 1988 was skipped, but the 1989 is firm wine with good cultivar character. The 1990 is unwooded but very drinkable.

Fairview Reserve Cabernet ★★★★ D

From both the 1986 and 1987 vintages come very good, deep, full-flavoured, small-wood-aged wines. As good as they taste now, they will benefit from six to eight years of development.

Fleur Du Cap Cabernet Sauvignon (Bergkelder) ★★★★(★) D

These are always good, medium-bodied, elegant Cabernets with good varietal nose. They are well-balanced, with clean, full Cabernet character which makes pleasant drinking when relatively young, yet they always have the potential to age well. The 1976 vintage was excellent at six years. The 1978 is probably the best of the 1970s' vintages, with the 1979 not far behind. Those of the early 1980s are outstanding: full of fruit and delightful cultivar character. The 1982 and 1984 are excellent – they drink very well now and are beautiful examples of fine wine-making. They used to carry Superior certification when this still existed. It appears that the 1983 was not launched. The Superior 1985 is good, but not as full as the 1984. The 1986, 1987 and 1988 are all very good, with lovely depth of flavour and excellent oak backing. Although they drink well on release, they have enough tannin to age with distinction.

82 ★★★★(★) ready. 83 no release. 84 ★★★★(★) ready, will still improve. 85 ★★★(★) ready, will still improve. 86 ★★★★ ready, will still improve. 87 ★★★★ ready, will still improve. 88 ★★★★ not ready, allow to age.

Fleur Du Cap Oak Collection (Bergkelder) ★★★★ D

This is a collection of six 750 ml bottles of Cabernet Sauvignon. Five of these are aged in different kinds of oak; three French (Nevers, Allier and Limousin), and the other two in Spanish and American oak. The sixth Cabernet is a fine blend with a deep purple/red colour, packed with varietal fruit and a good underlay of oak. All are from the 1986 vintage.

Glen Carlou Cabernet Sauvignon ★★★★(★) E

The first release from the 1990 vintage is a super wine from new clone Cabernet Sauvignon, richly packed with all the best Cabernet can give, and with the potential to develop into one of the Cape's best. The 1991 continues in the high quality, deeply intense style.

Goede Hoop Cabernet Sauvignon ★★★ E

The 1987 vintage is beginning to show well after a quiet start. There was no 1988 release and the next will be from the 1989.

Goedvertrou Cabernet Sauvignon ★★★★ E

The first release is from the 1991 vintage and is showing good berry character and nice wood. A cellar to watch.

Goue Vallei Cabernet Sauvignon (Citrusdal Co-op) ★★★ D

The 1984 was a pleasant, light-bodied wine with a slight woody character. The 1986 is a better wine and will need a year to smooth out. The 1988 has lots of wood and high tannin, and needs time to smooth out. The 1989 is an improvement on previous releases and the 1990 better still; a big, alcoholic wine with good wood backing. Good value for money.

Groot Constantia Cabernet Sauvignon ★★★★ D

The Cabernets of Groot Constantia have an enviable reputation of elegance and refinement. They were consistently good during the 1970s. The vintages of the early 1980s are pleasant enough but do not seem to be improving as dramatically as Cabernets shown by other Cape cellars. The later 1980s are very different, with better fruit and fine oak character. The 1985 was good for a generally poor year. The 1986 is an improvement in all respects, while the 1987 and 1988 are very good wines. The 1989 is gorgeous.

78 ★★★★ ready. 79 ★★★ past its best. 80 ★★★★ ready. 81 ★★★ ready. 82 ★★★★ ready. 83 ★★★ ready. 84 ★★★★ ready. 85 ★★★★ ready. 86 ★★★★(★) ready, will still improve. 87 ★★★(★) not ready, age further. 88 ★★★★ not ready, age further. 89 ★★★★ not ready, age further.

Hartenberg Cabernet Sauvignon ★★★(★) F+

The 1979 was the first vintage of this wine since the classification of the farm as an Estate. It is a good, soft Cabernet which developed well over ten years and has the potential for further ageing. The 1980 is a more substantial wine with better complexity and will probably live even longer than the 1979. The 1981 is much lighter. The 1982 and 1983 are in keeping with the cellar's full-flavoured style, but they drink well earlier than the 1979 and 1980. The 1983 is medium-bodied and more forward than earlier vintages. The 1984 is a big, full wine that will develop well with time. The 1985 release is not the usual full Hartenberg style, but a fine wine all the same, and makes for good drinking. The 1986 release is much better in all respects – a full-bodied wine that drinks well now but has lots of development potential. The 1987 is somewhat lighter and more refined wine.

79 ★★★ ready. 80 ★★★★ ready. 81 ★★★ ready. 82 ★★★★ ready.
83 ★★★★ ready, will still improve. 84 ★★★★(★) ready, will still improve.
85 ★★★ ready, will still improve. 86 ★★★★ ready, will still improve.
87 ★★★(★) not ready, age further.

HC Collison Cabernet Sauvignon (Bergkelder) ★★★(★) D

The first release was a 1981 Cabernet which has fine features and carries Superior certification. The next release, from the 1982 vintage, is far better wine and excellent value for money: the kind of wine one should buy to age in the cellar. Considering the vintage, the 1983 is very good and has developed well. The 1984 is an excellent example of good Cabernet Sauvignon. The 1985 is a surprisingly good wine for the vintage and was certified Superior. All of these wines have developed well. The 1985 was the last to be released.

81 ★★★ ready. 82 ★★★★ ready. 83 ★★★ ready. 84 ★★★★ ready, will still improve. 85 ★★★(★) ready, will still improve.

Huguenot Cabernet Sauvignon ★★★ B

Soft, old-style, but not unattractive wine.

Kanonkop Cabernet Sauvignon ★★★★★ F

A deep, rich, elegant wine of powerful character. The Cabernets vary with the vintage but are always very good and feature regularly at the Nederburg Auction. The 1973 wine, the first to be bottled at Kanonkop under its own label, was a full-bodied and rather robust Cabernet carrying plenty of wood. It took a gold medal at the 1975 Stellenbosch Young Wine Show. The early 1970s all developed well into the early 1990s. The wines of the later 1970s are all good, and needed a full ten years to reach their best. The 1979 vintage is probably the best of the 1970s, but the 1980 set the new decade off to a grand start. The 1980s are all good and will show their best 12–15 years from vintage. The 1987 is everything a Cabernet should be, with lovely fruit flavours and excellent wood, without the intensity of the 1986. The 1988 is developing more quickly – it could be great in eight to ten years and not the regular 15 years! The 1989 is great. The 1990s have all been intense, deep wines and their release is eagerly awaited.

73 ★★★★★ *drink. 74* ★★★ *drink. 75* ★★★★ *drink. 76* ★★★★ *ready.*
77 ★★★ *drink. 78* ★★★★★ *ready. 79* ★★★★ *ready. 80* ★★★★ *ready, will still*
improve. 81 ★★★★★ *ready. 82* ★★★★★ *ready, will still improve. 83* ★★★★
ready. 84 ★★★★★ *ready, will still improve. 85* ★★★★ *ready, will still*
improve. 86 ★★★★★ *ready, will improve. 87* ★★★★(★) *not ready, age further.*
88 ★★★★★ *not ready, age further. 89* ★★★★★ *not ready, age further.*

Klein Constantia Cabernet Sauvignon ★★★★★ E

Ros Gower has produced magnificent wines at the revamped Constantia
Estate and the Cabernets have accumulated all kinds of awards including South African Championship for cultivar and overall champion, as
well as much acclaim from overseas critics. The first release from the
1986 vintage is a stunner and, as good as it tastes now, will develop over
many years to come. The 1987, released mid-1991, is a big, beautiful
wine with a very high alcohol content of 13,7%, layers of flavour and
good firm tannins that will carry the wine well into the next century. The
1988 is slightly toned down but is a delicious wine that, with time, will
develop with benefit.

86 ★★★★★ *good now, but will age with distinction. 87* ★★★★★ *good now,*
but will age with distinction. 88. ★★★★★ *not ready, allow to age.*

Kleindal Cabernet Sauvignon ★★★ D

Early releases were good, non-vintage wines, without complexity, that
have developed well in the bottle. Latest releases have better body and
are bolder in style.

Kleindal Director's Reserve ★★★(★) C

A very good Cabernet from the 1987 vintage. It has nice fruit, good wood
backing, and has developed very well in the bottle. There was no 1988
release, but the 1989 is a big, bold wine. The 1990 release is more fruity
and elegant wine.

Koelenhof Co-op Cabernet Sauvignon ★★(★) C

A dry, oaky wine (the 1985 being somewhat too oaky) with insufficient
cultivar character. The 1986 is better balanced and deserves three stars.
It drank well in 1990, when it was probably at its best. The 1987 is better still. The 1988 is on the light side although it is a good improvement
on previous releases. The 1989 has good fruit and tannin backing, and
just the right amount of oak.

KWV Cabernet ★★★ (no price available)

Clean, sound wines without much vintage variation which are supplied
to members and for export. These wines are not of the same quality as
the Cape's commercial Cabernets, but have old-style appeal and make
pleasant drinking.

La Cotte Cabernet Sauvignon (Franschhoek Vineyards) ★★ B

This wine is produced in limited quantities with the 1988 rather better
than usual, and the 1989 showing good fruit. The 1990 is a bigger, more
attractive wine.

La Motte Cabernet Sauvignon ★★★★ E

Although labelled Cabernet Sauvignon, the wines from 1986 onwards contain 15% or more Merlot. The first was from the 1985 vintage and was released in 1990. Lightish in colour, this Cabernet has deep, concentrated, intense cultivar character, lots of nose and good backing of new wood. The 1986 is a more rounded wine but both are good and will develop well. Cellar samples show vintages to come will be stunners.

85 ★★★(★) ready. 86 ★★★★ ready. 87 ★★★(★) ready. 88 ★★★★ ready, will still develop. 89 ★★★★ needs time to develop.

Landskroon Cabernet Sauvignon ★★★★ D

This Cabernet has good varietal character with a rather unusual minty nose and good wood. A fair amount of bottle age is needed before it settles down. The 1978 has Superior certification. The 1979, 1980 and 1981 are more medium-bodied and made good drinking by the end of the 1980s. The 1982 is a big, bold wine which is now reaching its full potential. The 1983 is lighter and past its best. There were no releases from the 1985 and 1986 vintages. The 1987 shows a change in style, with new wood very evident. The 1988 is the best ever but will need time to develop. The 1989 follows the trend and 1990 is altogether better with depth of character and layers of flavour.

78 ★★★★ ready. 79 ★★★★ ready. 80 ★★★★ ready. 81 ★★★ ready. 82 ★★★★ ready. 83 ★★★ past its best, still enjoyable. 84 ★★★★ ready, will still improve. 85 no release. 86 no release. 87 ★★★(★) ready, will still improve. 88 ★★★★ not ready, age further. 89 ★★★★ not ready, needs time. 90 ★★★★ not ready, age further.

La Provence Rougeance ★★★ C

An attractive young Cabernet with distinct oak backing.

Le Bonheur Cabernet Sauvignon ★★★(★) F

It seems that whenever Michael Woodhead sets out to make a wine, he does so with distinction. The 100% Cabernet Sauvignon from the 1982 vintage was a beautiful, full-flavoured wine which has developed very well in the bottle and has become one of the Cape's great Cabernets. After ten years the wine is beautiful and has loads of life to go. Keep an eye on the corks, however, as they are rather inferior, which is a pity. The 1983 is a lighter wine, in keeping with the vintage, but still has fine character and is probably at its best now. The 1984 and 1986 are the best so far, with the 1984 fetching the Warren Winiarski Trophy at the IWSC in 1991 for the best Cabernet. They are deep and full-flavoured wines with lots of fruit and fine wood giving great complexity. The 1987 continues the trend and is full of fruit with good oak and fine tannin. It will develop with distinction.

82 ★★★★ ready, will still develop. 83 ★★★★ ready. 84 ★★★★★ ready, will still improve. 86 ★★★★★ not ready, age further. 87 ★★★★★ not ready, age further.

Lievland Cabernet Sauvignon ★★★★ E

The 1984 vintage is the first release and is drinking particularly well in 1992. The 1985 is a lightish wine but, from 1986 onwards, this Cabernet, along with all of the reds from this cellar, has developed into a very good wine. The 1986 is a really super wine with a deep satisfying richness. The 1987 is a little leaner but elegant all the same. The 1988 is bigger and better and really brings Lievland into the top quality category. This wine was awarded the Alphen Wine of the Month selection plus a gold medal at the Stellenbosch Bottled Wine Show. The 1989 follows the same quality and is enriched with over 20% Merlot, as is the 1990.

84 ★★★ ready. 85 ★★(★) ready. 86 ★★★(★) ready, will still improve. 87 ★★★(★) ready, will still improve. 88 ★★★★ not ready, age further. 89 ★★★★ not ready, age further. 90 ★★★★ not ready, age further.

L'Ormarins Cabernet Sauvignon ★★★★ E

(These wines are sold under the name 'Maison du Roi' in honour of the first owner.) The release of the 1983 L'Ormarins Cabernet was made only in 1988. It is a deep, rich wine with a lot of good wood, and will benefit with age. The 1984 is a fuller wine, deep, rich and full of tannin, and should develop well with time. The 1986 is a magnificent, full-flavoured, beautiful wine, and the 1987 is equally grand. It will be followed by the 1988 which is of the same quality.

83 ★★★★ ready, will still improve. 84 ★★★★(★) ready, will still improve. 85 ★★★★ not ready, age further. 86 ★★★★★ not ready, age further. 87 ★★★★★ not ready, age further.

McGregor Co-op Cabernet Sauvignon ★★★ B

The 1975 was the first McGregor Cabernet to be offered to the public, and only a few hundred bottles were produced. The 1977 vintage was a better product and showed promise of improvement in the bottle. Some ten years preceded the next release, which is a light-bodied, dry, fruity red for early drinking. The 1990 has a fair amount of wood backing the clean Cabernet character.

Meerlust Cabernet Sauvignon ★★★★★ E

The Meerlust Cabernet has a superb reputation, and justifiably so. A fine wine, it is usually light-bodied and stylish. All releases have been certified Superior. The 1977, 1979 and 1985 vintages were not marketed, but the 1978 leaves no doubt over its outstanding quality and should be enjoyed now. All the 1980s are excellent, with 1980 and 1984 perhaps the best so far. The 1986 is a beautiful, big wine that will need many years to show its full potential. The 1989 is the last release for a while to come due to replanting. Existing Cabernet Sauvignon is being reserved for Auction. A feature of the Meerlust Cabernets is their complex nose and excellent flavour, set off by the judicious use of new wood. It is not surprising, then, that they have been consistent winners at young wine shows, and judged more than once as South African champion.

75 ★★★★ drink. 76 ★★★★★ drink. 77 no release. 78 ★★★★ ready. 79 no release. 80 ★★★★★ ready. 81 ★★★★ ready. 82 ★★★★★ ready. 83 ★★★★ ready. 84 ★★★★★ ready, will improve. 85 no release. 86 ★★★★★ not ready, age further.

Middelvlei Cabernet Sauvignon ★★★★(★) E

The 1981 vintage was the first release of a Cabernet from this Estate, and it won gold medals at the Stellenbosch and the South African Championship shows. It has admirable cultivar character which has obviously had good ageing in new small wood before bottling, producing a complex wine which is drinking very well right now. The 1982 is a bigger, fuller wine with good depth of character and will age longer than the 1981. The 1983 has a very different nose, but the 1984 is a big, powerful wine that will develop over many years. There was no release from the 1985 vintage, but the 1986 more than makes up for it with a lovely full-flavoured wine that will age with distinction, as will the well-made 1987, which is very fine wine.

81 ★★★★ ready. 82 ★★★★ ready. 83 ★★★★ ready. 84 ★★★★ ready, will still improve. 85 no release. 86 ★★★★(★) not ready, age further. 87 ★★★★(★) needs time to develop.

Mons Ruber Cabernet Sauvignon ★★ C

The 1986 was the first attempt I'd seen from this pocket-size Klein Karoo Estate. It has a strange but not unattractive nose and pleasant flavour, and developed well up to 1990. The 1990 was the next release – an unwooded, clean, light wine with good fruit. The 1992 follows with another unwooded wine for early drinking.

Morgenhof Cabernet Sauvignon ★★★(★) D

Morgenhof, at the foothills of the Simonsberg, has been revitalized and its 1984 Cabernet was the first release. They couldn't have picked a better vintage with which to begin. A deep-coloured, well-balanced wine with fine character backed with good wood, it has enough tannin to develop well with time and was sold at the 1991 Nederburg Auction. There was no release of the 1985 vintage, but the 1986 is available – a lighter wine which tastes good now and probably won't age as long as the 1984 vintage. The 1988 shows better and bigger, with good fruit and oak, and should develop well. The 1989 is a bit disappointing after the 1988, but the 1990 is showing better and might develop with benefit.

84 ★★★★ ready, will still improve. 85 no release. 86 ★★★ ready. 87 no release. 88 ★★★(★) not ready, develop further. 89 ★★(★) not ready, develop further. 90 ★★★ not ready, allow to age.

Mouton Excelsior Le Moutonné Cabernet Sauvignon ★★★ C

This Franschhoek cellar has bottled a very good, full-flavoured 1984 Cabernet from grapes harvested in the Stellenbosch district. This dry, deep-flavoured wine is about at its best now. The next release was an older 1982 wine which now needs to be enjoyed. The 1987 is a good wine with every ability to develop well in the bottle. I look forward to future releases of this wine.

82 ★★★ ready. 84 ★★★ ready. 87 ★★★(★) ready, will improve with time.

Muratie Cabernet Sauvignon ★★★ D

First samples of the 1990 and 1991 look far better than anything from this cellar before. Devotees of the old-style wines insist it needs long bottle-ageing, an opinion which is supported by recent tastings of the 1971 and 1976. Hopefully they will appreciate the new style. The first release from the 1992 vintage is a good start. I look forward to future releases.

Nederburg Auction Cabernet Sauvignon ★★★★★ E

The 1974 vintage is much the same as the 1972, and is regarded as one of the world's great Cabernets – its many honours include best Cabernet on show at the Club Oenologique International Wine and Spirit Competition, winning against worthy entrants from France, Italy, Spain, California and Australia. These special Cabernets from the cellar are released only after ten or more years and sold exclusively at the annual Nederburg Auction. This very elegant wine with fine features was ready for drinking when released at the Auction and has the ability to develop further. The 1982 should be released in 1994.

74 ★★★★★ ready. 75 ★★★★★ past its best, still enjoyable. 76 ★★★★★ ready. 77 ★★★★(★) ready. 78 ★★★★★ ready, will still improve. 79 ★★★★★ ready, will still improve. 80 ★★★★★ ready, will still improve. 81 ★★★★★ ready, will still improve.

Nederburg Paarl Cabernet ★★★★(★) D/E

The Cabernets of Nederburg are internationally renowned for their own distinct style of deep, red richness in which cultivar character is prominent. Delicious and full, they require good bottle-ageing before they reach their full potential (they peak between 10 and 15 years). Attractive as they are when young, they should not really be opened before they are at least five years old and beginning to show some of their promise. Patience and self-denial will be amply rewarded. Nederburg elevated Cabernet to the status of the most sought-after cultivar in South Africa. For many years, though, it could not be certified Superior because it contained less than the stipulated 75% of the cultivar required by law. Some magnificent vintages were produced during this time, however, the most outstanding being 1972, 1974, 1975 and 1976. Those of the 1980s were consistently good and always very accessible, yet all ageing well over a period of between 12 and 15 years.

72 ★★★★ drink. 73 ★★★★ drink. 74 ★★★ ready. 75 ★★★★ ready. 76 ★★★★★ ready. 77 ★★★★ ready. 79 ★★★(★) ready. 80 ★★★★ ready. 81 ★★★ past its best, still enjoyable. 82 ★★★★ ready. 83 ★★★ past its best, still enjoyable. 84 ★★★★ ready. 85 ★★★★ ready, will still improve. 86 ★★★★(★) ready, will still improve. 87 ★★★★ drinkable, but will improve. 88 ★★★★ not ready, age further. 89 ★★★★ not ready, age further.

Neethlingshof Cabernet Sauvignon ★★★(★) E

The 1975 vintage was beautiful: deep and rich with complex flavour. The 1976, lighter in style, has also developed very well and should be drunk now. The wines of the early 1980s tend to be much lighter and finer than their predecessors and this, together with the use of new oak, allows much earlier drinking. The 1982 has good character, while the 1983 has developed into an excellent wine – 13 cases being selected for sale at the 1989 Nederburg Auction. After a disappointing start the 1984 is developing well. Now that Günter Brözel is in charge, things have changed. He couldn't have made the wine, as he wasn't there yet, but the 1986 is a giant step forward: a beautiful wine with a fine oak backing. It will need time to reach its full potential. The 1987 and 1988 are beautiful well-made wines packed with character, lots of fruit and good oak, and will develop well. The 1989 will develop into a magnificent wine.

86 ★★★★ not ready, age further. 87 ★★★★(★) not ready, age further. 88 ★★★★★ not ready, age further. 89 not ready, age further.

Neil Ellis Cabernet Sauvignon ★★★★ C

The 1984 Cabernet was a creditable start to a new venture. Made from grapes selected from a vineyard in the Stellenbosch area, it is a fine wine with good cultivar character and good use of wood from an excellent vintage. It is drinking very well in 1993 and worth its four stars. The 1985 is very good, considering the vintage, and it might even age longer than the 1984. The 1986 is by far the best vintage and, as it develops, is heading for five-star status: big, deep-coloured wine filled with fruit flavour and backed by good wood. It will require lots of bottle development. After a long break the 1990 appeared under a very smart, 'up-market' label; softened with 15% Merlot and a delicate touch of oak. This is a super wine that will be followed by a 1991 that is firmer but equally attractive.

84 ★★★★ ready, will still improve. 85 ★★★(★) ready, will still improve. 86 ★★★★(★) ready, will still improve. 90 ★★★★★ not ready, age further. 91 ★★★★(★) not ready, age further.

Oude Libertas Cabernet Sauvignon (SFW) ★★★★ B

Although this range has been discontinued there are a number of good vintages still available. This underestimated wine never really became popular, but aged with great benefit. The 1976 and 1978 vintages were outstanding, and while the 1979 was not highly regarded when released, it has now aged into a delightful wine. The 1980 (the last) is probably the best and deserves four stars. It has matured into a beautiful wine. The middle 1970s wines need to be drunk. The 1979 and 1980 are excellent in 1993.

Oude Nektar Cabernet Sauvignon ★★★(★) D

The 1988 and 1989 releases are complex wines with good oak and firm tannin. The latter is developing well. The 1990 is much improved and future vintages will be well worth watching.

Oude Rust Cabernet Sauvignon (Mooiuitsig Wynkelders) ★★ **B**

A very light dry red with clean Cabernet character.

Overgaauw Cabernet Sauvignon ★★★★(★) **E**

One of South Africa's consistently good Cabernets with no less than seven vintages of the 1970s receiving Superior certification. The wine has an unmistakable cellar characteristic on the nose, and good wood treatment which complements the Cabernet without overwhelming it. An excellent wine made from some of South Africa's best Cabernet grapes, it is known to mature with rare distinction over ten years or more. The wines of the early 1980s have taken on a fine style. The 1982 has developed very well to date, while the 1983 is surprisingly slow in developing. The lightish-coloured 1984 makes up for in character what it lacks in colour and is drinking well now. It appears regularly at the Nederburg Auction. The 1985 is light and firm with fine character. The 1986 is very Bordeaux-ish, and an elegant fine wine that will develop with distinction. The 1987 is much the same and will develop equally well. The 1988 makes surprisingly easy drinking at this early age, and is full of fine flavours and good oak.

75 ★★★ ready. 76 ★★★★ ready. 77 ★★★ past its best. 78 ★★★★ ready. 79 ★★★ ready. 80 ★★★★ ready. 81 ★★★★ ready. 82 ★★★★ ready, will still improve. 83 ★★★★★ ready, will still improve. 84 ★★★★ ready. 85 ★★★★(★) not ready, age further. 86 ★★★★(★) not ready, age further. 87 ★★★★(★) not ready, age further. 88 ★★★★ enticing to drink now, but allow to develop further.

Pick 'n Pay Cabernet Sauvignon ★★★(★) **C**

Part of the 'added-value' range and made by Simonsig. The 1987 is deep in colour and has very good Cabernet character backed with clean oak. This is a good dry Cabernet that drinks well now, and has the potential to develop well over six to eight years. The 1988 is more full bodied with good complexity. It will develop well with five to seven years.

John Platter's Reserve Cabernet Sauvignon ★★★(★)

This lovely, light Cabernet Sauvignon from the 1986 vintage is full of cultivar flavour and was well-matured in oak. Half the blend was aged in new Nevers oak and half in new Limousin barrels for 17 months. It received very little cellar handling and was treated in much the same manner as practised in Bordeaux. In early 1993 it had developed beautifully. A treat to drink.

Rhebokskloof Cabernet Sauvignon ★★★★ **D**

A first release from the 1989 vintage was taken almost entirely by the Alphen Wine Club. A very good début that bodes well for the future. It has good cultivar character, backed by French oak, and will develop well in the bottle over the next four to six years. The 1990 is full of character; good fruit, fine flavours, good oak and firm tannin. It will develop well. The 1991 is still to come.

Riebeek Wine Farmers' Co-op Cabernet Sauvignon ★★ B

The 1989 Pieter Cruythoff is vastly different to the full-bodied, fiery, dry reds of the early 1980s. More recent vintages have been toned down by some wood maturation. There was a gap between vintages from 1985 to 1988. The 1989 is light-bodied, has nice fruit flavours and is very drinkable in 1993.

Robertson Co-op Cabernet Sauvignon ★★★ C

The first vintage was the 1983, which takes the place of Robroi. It showed well, with good cultivar character and reasonable wood. The 1986 and 1987 vintages were light-bodied, while the 1988 vintage is a somewhat fuller wine. The 1989 sports a handsome new label and is a bold, strong wine, and an improvement on other vintages. The 1990 has its own definite character, which is rather nice, and also shows in the 1991. A pleasant touch of oak makes for easy, early drinking.

Romansrivier Co-op Cabernet Sauvignon ★★★ B

This is a light Cabernet that has improved with each vintage and, since 1987, has been given a little wood age. They drink quite well when two or three years old. The 1989 is at its best now and should last through 1994.

Roodendal Cabernet (SFW) ★★★ C

The first appearance of Roodendal was the 1979 vintage, one that proved a remarkable bargain for such good quality wine. Unfortunately, the next vintage, the 1981, appeared not to be in the same class when it was released, but it developed surprisingly well. The 1983 vintage which carries Superior certification was very shy to show, but has developed. The 1985 is an improvement on the 1981 and 1983. The 1987 is a lighter-style Cabernet, and the 1989 a much-improved, oak-matured Cabernet. Good value.

Roodezandt Co-op Cabernet Sauvignon ★★★ B

The earliest release was a very good 1978 vintage which has aged well. The 1979 was a little coarse and has not developed well. The 1980 was good, but the floods of 1981 prevented a release from that year. The 1982 and 1983 vintages were good value for money. The 1984 is full of cultivar character and has developed well; it is probably at its best now. I have not seen a 1985 but the 1986 is a good, firm, medium-bodied wine that will develop well. There is a gap of a number of years as vineyards were replanted. The 1990 is now available and has been blended with some Ruby Cabernet, resulting in an attractive, fresh wine for early drinking.

78 ★★★★ ready. 79 ★★★ past its best, still enjoyable. 80 ★★★ ready. 81 no release. 82 ★★★ ready. 83 ★★★ ready. 84 ★★★(★) ready. 85 no release. 86 ★★★ ready. 87, 88, 89 no release. 90 ★★★(★) ready.

Rooiberg Co-op Cabernet Sauvignon ★★★ D

A Wine of Origin Robertson, with good balance of cultivar and wood, this usually light red wine ages well in the bottle. It regularly wins honours at the young wine shows (including a gold medal at Goodwood in 1982). The

1983 was a good wine, but is probably past its best. The 1984 is fuller in body and will have longer life, peaking in the early 1990s. The 1985 is much lighter in all respects and should be enjoyed now while the 1984 develops. The 1986, 1987 and 1988 are all good wines that can be enjoyed young. The 1990 is not in keeping with previous vintages.

83 ★★★ ready. 84 ★★★(★) ready, will still improve. 85 ★★★ ready. 86 ★★★ ready. 87 ★★★ ready. 88 ★★★ ready, will still improve. 89 ★★★ ready. 90 ★★★ not ready, age further.

Rozendal Colour Label Magnums ★★★★ D

In 1983, Kurt Amman produced a 100% Cabernet Sauvignon and aged it in Nevers oak for 18 months, resulting in a full, richly-flavoured wine that is developing very well in the magnums in which it was bottled. There is a range of 15 different colourful labels, 12 of these by the Stellenbosch artist, Larry Scully, from his series 'Views of Stellenbosch', one by Kurt's wife, Lyn, and two by his daughter, Natalie (one depicting the winemaking process, the other a bridal couple). Another Colour Label issue will be a 1989 Magnum series with the same blend as Rozendal: 80% Merlot and 20% Cabernet.

Rustenberg Cabernet Sauvignon ★★★★(★) E

The full-bodied Rustenberg Cabernet has not been available for as long as the dry red. Nevertheless, it has established its place as one of the Cape's best wines of this cultivar. It is difficult to place one vintage above another, but certainly the later years have greater varietal character and are more complex than the earlier ones. Of the 1975 vintage, the Estate released a special issue of 625 numbered bottles which were distributed during the Stellenbosch tercentenary celebrations. The 1982 is a magnificent wine. It is developing beautifully in the bottle and continuing to do so into the 1990s. In keeping with the vintage, the 1983 is lighter and a little disappointing. The 1984 more than compensates for the 1983: it is a beautiful wine and is developing well. The 1985 should be consumed while the 1984 develops. The 1986 is a magnificent wine – big, bold and full of cultivar character, while the 1987 is elegant with good flavour. The 1988 is a refined, elegant wine as is the 1989.

71 ★★★★ past its best, still enjoyable. 72 ★★★★★ ready. 73 ★★★★ ready. 74 ★★★★ ready. 75 ★★★★ ready. 76 ★★★★ ready, will still improve. 78 ★★★★★ ready. 79 ★★★★ ready. 80 ★★★★★ ready. 81 ★★★ ready. 82 ★★★★★ ready, will still improve. 83 ★★★★ ready. 84 ★★★★★ ready, will still improve. 85 ★★★★ ready. 86 ★★★★★ ready, will still improve. 87 ★★★★ not ready, age further. 88 ★★★★ not ready, age further. 89 ★★★★★ not ready, age further.

Rustenberg Cabernet Sauvignon Reserve ★★★★ E/F

This is big and powerful wine out of the 1984, 1986 and 1987 vintages, and is kept for special occasions; to be followed by the 1989. It is deep, rich, attention-grabbing wine for sipping and savouring.

Rust-en-Vrede Cabernet Sauvignon ★★★★ E

The Estate's maiden vintage Cabernet (1979) was good, but succeeding ones were disappointing and the critics were quick to claim beginner's luck. The 1982 is, however, an exceptionally good wine. It drank well on release, and has continued to develop to date. The 1983 was judged South Africa's champion young red wine but developed more quickly than the 1984 and is probably past its best. The 1980s all showed well, with 1985 perhaps the weakest of a very fine line-up. All develop very well in the bottle. The 1988 is the first vintage handled by Kevin Arnold and shows a more refined style that should drink well fairly early compared to previous vintages.

79 ★★★★(★) ready. 80 ★★★★ ready. 81 ★★★ ready. 82 ★★★★(★) ready, will still improve. 83 ★★★ ready. 84 ★★★★(★) ready, will still improve. 85 ★★★★ ready, will still improve. 86 ★★★★(★) not ready, age further. 87 ★★★★(★) not ready, age further. 88 ★★★★ drinkable now, but allow to develop further.

Saxenburg Cabernet Sauvignon Reserve ★★★ D

From the 1990 vintage comes a good, clean, deep-flavoured Cabernet with fine oak backing, labelled Private Collection. The 1991 Reserve is a deep-coloured, well-wooded wine that could develop with distinction.

Simonsig Cabernet Sauvignon ★★★★ D/E

South Africa produces some superb Cabernets and Simonsig is known for being consistently among the best. From SA Young Wine Championship in 1977 to the 1984 which won a gold medal at the International Wine and Spirit Competition in London and, I am proud to say, was the first winner of my trophy for the best South African red on show. Seeming to improve with each vintage, the 1986 and 1987 are great wines, while the 1988 is generally more elegant and refined. The 1989 has lots of good berry fruit flavours backed with a delicate touch of oak.

77 ★★★★(★) past its best. 78 ★★★ ready. 79 ★★★★ ready. 80 ★★★ ready. 81 ★★ past its best. 82 ★★★ ready. 83 ★★★ ready. 84 ★★★★(★) ready, will still improve. 85 ★★★★ ready, will still improve. 86 ★★★★★ ready, will still improve 87 ★★★★(★) not ready, will still develop. 88 ★★★★ not ready, age further. 89 ★★★★ not ready, age further.

Simonsvlei Co-op Cabernet Sauvignon ★★★ C

A medium- to full-bodied Cabernet with good cultivar character. Usually very full in the mouth, with enough tannin to age well, it has appeared at a number of Nederburg Auctions and has regularly won gold medals at local shows. It has been somewhat erratic over the vintages, with 1982 the best of the 1980s. Latest vintages are a little disappointing, but sales show otherwise. The 1990 shows an improvement.

81 ★★★ past its best. 82 ★★★(★) drink. 83 ★★★ drink. 84 ★★(★) drink. 85 ★★★(★) ready. 86 ★★ ready. 88 ★★★(★) ready. 89 ★★★ ready. 90 ★★★ready, will still improve.

Slanghoek Co-op Cabernet Sauvignon ★★★ B

The first release from the 1991 vintage is for early, easy drinking at a very good price.

Spier Cabernet Sauvignon ★★★ C

This is a sound wine showing definite Cabernet character – usually on the light side, with the 1985 even lighter than usual. The 1984 is the best to date, and the 1986 is much the same. The 1987 is lighter in style. There has been no subsequent release.

84 ★★★(★) ready. 85 ★★★ ready. 86 ★★★ ready. 87 ★★★ ready, will still improve.

Springlands Cabernet (Drop Inn) ★★★ A

A non-vintage, easy-drinking, soft wine with Cabernet character and some wood.

Stellenryck Collection Cabernet Sauvignon ★★★★★ E

The wines under this label are magnificent, full and deep, and reward with many years of careful ageing. There were no releases from the 1983, 1985 and 1988. The 1980 and 1982 are drinking beautifully now and will do well into the mid-nineties. The 1984, 1986 and 1987 are all developing well and will easily see in the new century in grand style. The 1989 should be the next release.

80 ★★★★★ ready, will still hold. 81 ★★★★ ready. 82 ★★★★★ ready, will still hold. 83 no release. 84 ★★★★★ ready, will still develop. 85 no release. 86 ★★★★★ drinkable, but has lots more development. 87 ★★★★★ not ready, age further. 88 ★★★★★ no release. 89 ★★★★★ not ready, age further.

Stellenryck Historic Wine Museum Cabernet Sauvignon 1975 (Bergkelder) ★★★★(★) E

This wine, which is 100% Cabernet Sauvignon, was bottled especially for the Stellenbosch tercentenary in 1979. All those fortunate enough to have some in their private cellars and have resisted drinking it should thoroughly enjoy their wine now.

Stellenzicht Cabernet Sauvignon ★★★★ E

The first release from this spectacular new cellar is from the 1987 vintage. It is well-made wine, with lots of character, that will need time to show its full potential. The 1988 is a little lighter, while the 1989 is a full-bodied wine that will develop well.

Swartland Co-op Cabernet Sauvignon ★★ C

Over the years this has gone from somewhat coarse and bold to good, harmonious wine. It is usually medium-bodied and develops well over two to three years, so it's good for fairly early drinking.

85 ★★ ready. 86 ★★★(★) ready. 87 ★★(★) ready. 89 ★★★ ready. 90 ★★★ ready, will develop further. 91 ★★★ ready, will still improve.

Thelema Cabernet Sauvignon ★★★★★ E

The release from the 1988 vintage is a good first effort with lots of exciting character. The 1989 is a bench-mark wine; a beautiful wine packed with layers of fruit flavours, entirely from new clone Cabernet, and backed with fine new French oak. It tastes good now, but patience will be well rewarded as it will develop magnificently. The 1990 takes this cellar well on its way to being consistently one of the Cape's best. The cellar samples of the 1991 confirm the quality and could be the best yet.

Uiterwyk Cabernet Sauvignon ★★★(★) E

This is a very consistent wine which regularly received Superior certification. Deep purple when young, it ages elegantly, reaching a depth of complexity not to be found in many other Cabernets. With its fine balance between cultivar and wood, the 1974 was the most outstanding of the 1970s' vintages. The 1982 is outstanding: blended with a little Merlot, and spending almost two years in wood, it has developed well into the 1990s. There were no releases from the 1989 and 1990. The 1987 and the 1988 are rich, full wines – also with a touch of Merlot. The 1991 is a great improvement and should develop well.

76 ★★★★ past its best. 77 ★★★ past its best. 78 ★★★★ ready. 79 ★★★★ ready. 80 ★★★★(★) ready. 81 ★★★ ready. 82 ★★★★ ready. 83 ★★★(★) ready. 84 ★★★★ ready. 86 ★★★ ready, will still improve. 87 ready, will still improve. 88 ready, will still improve. 89, 90 no release. 91 ★★★★ not ready, age further.

Uitkyk Carlonet ★★★★(★) F

Today's Uitkyk Carlonets taste seductively ready at an early age, but deceptively so, for they need time to fulfil their true potential. Through the late 1970s and mid-1980s, this wine developed dramatically in style and quality. There were no releases of the poorer vintages of 1979, 1981 and 1985. The 1986 is a soft, pleasant wine with good cultivar flavours and nice oak. The 1987 is a more intense wine and, although drinkable, has the structure to age with benefit through to the late 1990s. The 1988 will need time.

74 ★★★★★ past its best, still enjoyable. 75 ★★★★ ready. 76 ★★★★★ ready. 77 no release. 78 ★★★★ ready. 79 no release. 80 ★★★ ready. 81 no release. 82 ★★★★★ ready. 83 ★★★★ ready. 84 ★★★★★ ready, will still improve. 85 no release. 86 ★★★★ ready, will still improve. 87 ★★★★ not ready, age further. 88 ★★★★ not ready, age further.

Vergenoegd Cabernet Sauvignon ★★★★(★) D

The wines of the 1970s and 1980s were of a style very distinctive to the Estate, and no doubt influenced by its close proximity to the sea. This is medium-bodied wine with great depth of character giving a very long-lasting finish and an interesting complexity. Wood-aged in old vats, it was consistently certified Superior. It developed well over five to ten years and sold regularly at the Nederburg Auction and, in earlier days, was a consistent grand champion at the SA Championship Wine Show. The vintages of the early 1980s are richer, fuller and have beautiful depth of character which will reward good bottle ageing. The wines of the late

1980s show a difference in style and reflect the use of new French oak. The 1987 begins to show some new life, and the 1988 shows a change in style. The 1989 is a firm, tannic wine with good character.

72 ★★★★ drink. 73 ★★★★ past its best. 74 ★★★★★ drink. 75 ★★★ past its best. 76 ★★★★★ ready. 77 ★★★ ready. 78 ★★★★ ready. 79 ★★★ ready. 80 ★★★★★ ready. 81 ★★★★ ready. 82 ★★★★★ ready. 83 ★★★★ ready. 84 ★★★★ ready, will still improve. 85 ★★★(★) ready. 86 ★★★(★) ready, will still improve. 87 ★★★(★) not ready, age further. 88 ★★★★ not ready, age further. 89 ★★★(★) not ready, age further.

Villiera Cabernet Sauvignon ★★★(★) D

This wine was launched with the 1983 vintage. Medium-bodied, undoubtedly Cabernet, but rather too heavily wooded, the overall style nevertheless augured well for the future. The 1984 and 1986 are fuller and, to my taste, better wines in every respect, fully deserving four stars. They have good wood character coming from both French and American oak. From 1988 on, the wines are leaders in their field. The 1988 is a superb wine, full of intense character and a depth of flavour not found in any previous vintage. The 1989 is a little quieter to start, but is developing beautifully, as is the 1990. The 1991 has good fruit and fine oak and should develop with distinction.

83 ★★★(★) ready. 84 ★★★★ ready, will still improve. 85 no release. 86 ★★★★ ready, will still improve. 87 ★★★★ ready, will still improve. 88 ★★★★★ not ready, age further. 89 ★★★★ not ready, age further. 90 ★★★★ not ready, age further. 91 ★★★★ not ready, age further.

Vlottenburg Co-op Cabernet Sauvignon ★★★ B

Good value for money, this dry, honest and uncomplicated wine was originally unwooded. Nowadays it receives good wood, adding an extra dimension to the wine as evidenced in the 1986 and 1987. These last two vintages should develop with interest. The 1988 is not quite up to the same standard, but this is a factor of the year. The 1989 is an improvement with good fruit and early drinkability.

Vredenheim Cabernet Sauvignon ★★★ D

The first release, from the 1987 vintage, is a little light in all respects. There is no 1988. The next release, from 1989, is more attractive.

Vriesenhof Cabernet ★★★★★ E

The name was changed from simply Vriesenhof to Vriesenhof Cabernet with the 1984 vintage. The 1984 is a beautiful wine, with lots of Cabernet character backed with good young wood. As attractive as the wine is now, your patience will be rewarded if you can wait until 1994 before sampling. The 1985 is lighter but has good cultivar character. The 1986 is a big, beautiful wine and five-star material. The 1987 is much the same but still needs lots of time to smooth out. The 1988 appeared somewhat subdued and soft on release, but is already developing and won't disappoint. The 1989 is 50/50 new clone and old clone, giving floral-berry character wine with lots of elegance. It is probably the best so far. The 1990 has less fruit, and cellar samples of the 1991 show the best is yet to come.

84 ★★★★(★) *ready, will still improve.* 85 ★★★ *ready, will still improve.* 86 ★★★★★ *ready, will still develop.* 87 ★★★★★ *not ready, age further.* 88 ★★★★★ *not ready, age further.* 89 ★★★★★ *not ready, age further.* 90 ★★★(★) *not ready, age further.*

Warwick Cabernet Sauvignon ★★★★(★) E

Warwick Estate has produced good quality grapes for many years, but Norma Ratcliffe crushed them for the first time in 1984. The resulting wine was only for tasting at the farm. Norma's experience in Bordeaux has taught her to handle the wine as little as possible and not to use artificial agents or cold stabilization. The first release was some 1 500 cases from the 1985 vintage. It has good, clean cultivar character with fine oak backing after 16 months in small, new Nevers oak, and it will develop over the next five to eight years. The 1986 is a much more complex and impressive wine that will need many years to show its full potential. The 1987 vintage contains a portion of Warwick's gold medal-winning Merlot and the result is beautiful. The 1988 and 1989 have the potential to be tremendous. The 1990 is very good, but without the vintage advantage of the 1989.

85 ★★★★(★) *ready, will still improve.* 86 ★★★★★ *not ready, age further.* 87 ★★★★(★) *ready, will still develop.* 88 ★★★★★ *not ready, age further.* 89 ★★★★★ *not ready, age further.* 90 ★★★★★ *not ready, age further.*

Welgemeend Cabernet Sauvignon ★★★★ C

The 1986 was the last vintage as all the Estate's Cabernet was required for its blends. However, some 1990 has been bottled for release.

Wellington Wynboere Co-op Cabernet ★ B

The first Cabernet released from this Co-op was the 1984 vintage – a wood-aged wine that has improved in the bottle. The 1983 is much lighter and should be enjoyed now. The 1984 is a very good dry wine that will definitely age with benefit. The 1985, 1986, 1987 and 1988 are good, medium-bodied wines that drink well early and are excellent value.

Welmoed Co-op Légende Cabernet Sauvignon ★★★ B

These are well-made wines with good cultivar flavour and nice wood backing – and have a good record of Young Wine Show success. The 1988 shows lovely style and flavour and should develop well in the bottle. The 1989 is a good, four-star wine and very good value. The 1990 is a good, honest Cabernet Sauvignon with a light touch of oak.

Windmeul Co-op Cabernet ★★★ B

An unwooded release from the 1991 vintage for easy, early drinking.

Woolworths Cabernet Sauvignon ★★★★ C

The first release from the 1986 vintage has developed very well, as has the follow-up 1987. The 1988 has good fruit and is also developing well.

The 1990 was released ahead of the 1989 and both are in keeping with the quality of the 1990 – the best so far. All from Vriesenhof.

86 ★★★(★) good drinking now. 87 ★★★ ready, will still develop. 88 ★★★ ready, will still develop. 89 ★★★(★) drinkable, will still improve. 90 ★★★★ not ready, age further.

Woolworths Reserve Cabernet Magnum ★★★★(★) E

This comes from 1990 vintage and is made by Neil Ellis. It is a wine with lots of fruit and good, soft tannins that makes it very acceptable at an early age, yet it has all the composition to develop very well over five to six years.

Zandvliet Cabernet Sauvignon ★★★(★) E

The 1984 vintage is a surprisingly good wine and drinks very well. The 1985 is a good follow-up. The 1987 will be the next one available.

Zandwijk Cabernet Sauvignon ★★★ E

This wine is made according to Jewish religious requirements. The 1988 was released in 1991 and is a big, bold wine, full of tannin, which needs time to soften. The 1989 is easier drinking.

Zevenwacht Cabernet Sauvignon ★★★★ E

The 1983 is a firm, elegant wine, matured in small French and large Yugoslavian oak. The 1984 is much bigger, full of fruit and good wood, and has developed very well into the 1990s. The 1985 is surprisingly good for a weak vintage. The 1986 follows the same lines as the 1984 but is made with more complexity with the addition of some 15% Merlot. The 1987 is by far the best, made from new clone Cabernet blended with Merlot and Cabernet Franc. The 1988 is a fine wine and is showing good bottle development.

84 ★★★★ ready, will still improve. 85 ★★★(★) ready, will still improve. 86 ★★★★ ready, will still improve. 87 ★★★★(★) ready, will still improve. 88 ★★★★(★) developing well, age further.

Zonnebloem Cabernet Sauvignon (SFW) ★★★★(★) D

Traditionally a full-flavoured, stout wine which ages with great benefit, it has been a consistent feature of the South African market since the early 1920s and, considering the enormous volume produced over the decades, it has sustained a remarkably high standard. More recent vintages have seen a move to a more modern style, and better use of new small oak is playing a noticeable role. Up until the Coastal region was proclaimed, a wine like Zonnebloem Cabernet could not claim Superior certification. With the formation of the Coastal region, the wine received its first Superior and did so for the subsequent eleven vintages to 1986. By the time the 1987 was released in early 1991, the Superior certification system had been dropped. Zonnebloem Magnums are released some three to four years after the 750 ml bottles. To date, the Magnum releases are from the 1978, 1979, 1980, 1981, 1982, 1983 and 1984 vintages with the 1985 due in 1993. The more recent vintages are quite outstanding with the exception, perhaps, of the 1981 which, although Superior, showed less well when launched. Nevertheless, it is developing well in the bottle. The 1986 is a pleasing development in style, showing much better fruit and good wood. The 1987 has signs of the more modern style. The 1988 and 1989 could develop as well as the 1986.

76 ★★★★ drink. 77 ★★★ past its best. 78 ★★★★ ready. 79 ★★★★ past its best. 80 ★★★★ ready. 81 ★★★(★) ready. 82 ★★★★ ready. 83 ★★★(★) ready. 84 ★★★★(★) ready, will still improve. 85 ★★★★(★) ready, will still improve. 86 ★★★★(★) ready, will still improve. 87 ★★★★(★) not ready, age further. 88 ★★★★(★) not ready, age further. 89 ★★★★(★) not ready, age further.

RUBY CABERNET

Douglas Co-op Ruby Cabernet ★★ B
The first release from the 1992 vintage has a remarkable deep, dark colour and good fruit.

Louwshoek-Voorsorg Ruby Cabernet ★★★ C
The first release from the 1992 vintage is a full-flavoured, fruity, unwooded red for early consumption.

McGregor Co-op Ruby Cabernet ★★★ B
This is an interesting introduction from 1990 vintage. It has good berry flavour, no wood, and is fresh and clean. It makes easy drinking at an early age.

Vredendal Co-op Ruby Cabernet ★★★ C
The first release from the 1991 vintage is slightly wooded and looks like it could be a reasonable red for this area.

Waboomsrivier Co-op ★★ B
The 1987 was released very young and has developed pleasantly over the years. The 1988 has more body, is lively, fruity and ready for drinking. The 1990 and 1991 were ready for drinking on release.

CINSAUT

Du Toitskloof Co-op Cinsaut ★★★ A

This is a good, deep, full, well-made wine which develops splendidly after a year or two in the bottle, and is a good example of what can be done with Cinsaut. Throughout the 1980s this Co-op produced very acceptable wines from Cinsaut. The 1990 and 1991 are delightful, medium-bodied, ruby-coloured, fruity-fresh flavoured wines that drink very well now, and have enough tannin to allow development over a few years. The 1991 has a massive 13,8% alcohol and will develop with interest. Good value.

Kaapzicht Cinsaut ★★★ B

This is a not-to-be-repeated wine from the 1990 vintage. Designed to be drunk young, it is still drinking very well in 1993 and shows no negative signs of ageing. It is light-coloured, fruity wine made for easy, uncomplicated drinking.

Landskroon Cinsaut ★★★(★) B

This is a fairly fruity wine with medium body and the finesse which lacks in many lesser Cinsauts. It provides enjoyable drinking, proving that this cultivar, when correctly handled, can produce good dry reds. The 1974 aged very well and peaked at six years. The 1976 was even better, and the early 1980s' vintages maintained the attractive quality of the previous vintages, as do the more recent ones of 1986 and 1987. The 1988, 1989 and 1990 are lighter in character and have the slightest touch of oak.

Mamreweg Co-op Cinsaut ★★★ B

This is undoubtedly the cellar's best wine. The 1977 vintage developed nicely in the bottle and made easy drinking after two years. The cellar then produced South Africa's champion Cinsaut for three years in succession (1978, 1979 and 1980). All have looked good in the bottle, and the 1979 is developing particularly well. The vintages of the early 1980s have become fuller bodied, with 1986 and 1987 being particularly good for early, easy drinking. The 1989 was soft and fruity and needed to be drunk young. Releases from the 1990s' vintages are a little fresher and not to be taken lightly – the 1991 having a high 13% alcohol content and the 1992 a staggering 14,7%!

Perdeberg Co-op Cinsaut ★★(★) A

At first this Cinsaut was not produced on a regular basis, but this trend has changed over the past few vintages. It is good, honest, medium-bodied, dry red wine suitable for early quaffing.

Roodezandt Co-op Cinsaut ★★ B

Roodezandt is producing Cinsaut while their Cabernet is being replanted. The label says 'light', but the releases to date have had a respectable alcohol content of between 12,5 and 14,0%! The 1990 and 1991 have a little Ruby Cabernet added, making good-flavoured wines.

Swartland Co-op Cinsaut ★★ A

The heavy, full-flavoured 1973 vintage was sold at the 1979 Nederburg Auction and was definitely a four-star wine. Its age has given it a soft bouquet, and its heaviness, virtually unique to a Cinsaut, has rounded it out into a fine wine which goes down admirably – an astonishing achievement after all these years. Although on the full side, more recent wines do not seem to have the same depth. They drink well when young. The 1988 is a deep, full-flavoured wine, but the 1989 is not quite up to the old standard, although it is pleasant enough. The wines of the 1990s continue with popular style and demand. It is good for youthful drinking.

Vergenoegd Cinsaut ★★★(★) B

This is a really good Cinsaut that is easy to drink at two years and develops really well in the bottle. The 1978 vintage was the first Cinsaut to be certified Superior. The vintages of the early 1980s are all good, which proves just how much can be done with this much-maligned cultivar. Mother Nature did not provide good Cinsaut in 1983, 1984 and 1985, and none was bottled at Vergenoegd. The 1986 was released in 1988 and is delightful, light-bodied, well-flavoured wine that drinks very easily. The 1989 makes very good drinking and has good wood. The 1990 is very attractive wine.

Waboomsrivier Co-op Cinsaut ★★ B

A typical, light dry red. It usually makes very pleasant, early drinking.

Wamakersvallei Co-op Cinsaut ★★ A

A good, light Cinsaut.

GAMAY

Vlottenburg Co-op Gamay Noir ★★ A
First produced from the 1985 vintage, this release was not particularly good, having none of the fruit associated with the cultivar. The 1986 and 1987 vintages were an improvement and the 1988 very good. The 1989 has a nice oak background. The 1990 is pleasant and soft, with a dry finish. This light, dryish wine needs to be drunk young and chilled. The 1991 is particularly soft and pleasant for easy drinking.

GRENACHE

A number of cellars use Grenache in various blends. Citrusdal seems to be the only cellar to have labelled a wine 'Grenache' but does not appear to have done so since 1982. The Droë Rooi from Oranjerivier Wynkelders is made from Grenache, and the Citrusdal Chianti is 60% Grenache. Lutzville make a Blanc de Noir from this variety as well.

MALBEC

Backsberg Malbec ★★★(★) C
First release from 1990. This is a bright-coloured, medium-bodied wine with lots of berry flavours. It is the first certified label to carry this name. It has been jokingly referred to as 'Malback'. The label shows the profiles of Sydney Back and son, Michael and is a very different label from the rest of the range. There was no 1991.

MERLOT

Avontuur Merlot ★★★(★) **D**
This wine has very good Merlot character backed with good wood. The 1989 is a medium-bodied wine with good oak and is developing nicely. The 1990 has better fruit and is very attractive in its youth.

Backsberg Merlot ★★★(★) **C**
The first release from the 1989 vintage has a most enticing nose and is full of soft, yielding flavours and mouth-filling qualities. The 1990 is along the same lines – lovely when young, but probably best within three to four years of vintage. It will be followed by the 1991. Excellent value for money.

Boplaas Merlot ★★★(★) **C**
This has been a good wine throughout the 1980s. The 1986 is very good and probably at its best in 1992. The 1987 vintage is attractive and the 1988, although a well-made wine, seems to lack the life of the earlier vintages. The 1989 is well-made, elegant wine that should develop as well as the 1986.

Boschendal Jean de Long Merlot Auction Reserve ★★★★ **E**
This is a super wine from the 1991 vintage with only 30 cases being sold on the 1992 Cape Independent Winemakers' Guild Auction. It is fine, elegant wine, full of berry nose, soft fruit in the mouth and good oak background.

Bouchard Finlayson Merlot ★★★★ **E**
This cellar has produced an attractive wood-aged Merlot from grapes grown in Elgin. The entire quantity has been bottled for Woolworths.

Buitenverwachting Auction Reserve ★★★★ **E**
The 1989 vintage provided 100 six-bottle cases for the 1991 Cape Independent Winemakers' Guild Auction. It is big wine with lots of flavour and good oak. The 1991 was the Diners Club Wine of the Year winner.

Cape Vintners Members Only Merlot ★★★★ **D**
This is a very well-made wine with deep, soft flavours and full, fruity nose, aged in Nevers oak giving good, but not obtrusive, oak backing. It comes from the 1990 vintage. Its youthful zest needs two to four more years for it to reach its best. This is good value for money, good wine from Overgaauw.

Cederberg Kelders Merlot ★★★ **C**
The first release from 1991 had good fruit and a touch of wood. The 1992 is deep in colour but a lighter, fruitier wine.

De Leuwen Jagt Merlot ★★★ **D**
The first release was from the 1990 vintage. It has good nose and pleasant fruity flavour, with a fairly tannic finish, and should soften out over another year or two.

Delheim Merlot ★★★★ C

A small quantity of the 1986 was bottled under the Delheim Collectors label. It is a splendid wine, full of fine flavours, and is ageing with great benefit. The Collectors Label wines are not for sale, but are given away to friends of Delheim. The Merlot is also used to soften the Pinotage. An amount of the 1990 was bottled for sale.

Domein Doornkraal Merlot ★★★ B

The first release from the 1990 vintage is a medium-bodied, somewhat soft-charactered wine that makes good, early drinking. It is good value for money. No 1991 has been released.

Eikendal Merlot ★★★★ D

The first release from 1991 is a super wine with lots of fruit and flavour, and good oak backing.

Fairview Merlot Reserve ★★★★ D

The first release from 1989 is excellent, well-balanced wine with fine fruit and good wood. It is developing well. The 1990 is fuller and fruitier.

Fleur Du Cap Merlot (Bergkelder) ★★★★ D

From the 1990 vintage comes this very drinkable fruity wine, which is very soft in the mouth. This wine signifies a break in the Fleur du Cap tradition of not releasing their reds until they are five years old; they believe this wine is good at two years and will probably peak by five. It is followed by a lovely 1991.

Glen Carlou Merlot ★★★★ E/F

The first vintage, the 1988, is deep in colour and has good nose and lots of fruit backed by good wood. The 1989 is a most attractive, big, full wine which should develop well with age. The 1990 has a whole per cent more alcohol at 13,4%, and a lot more potential. It is lovely, full-flavoured wine. The 1991 promises to be an even better wine, full of berry-cherry character and, although it is not bottled on its own, has made up to 25% of the 1992 release. It will develop with benefit.

Le Mouton Merlot ★★★(★) D

The first release from 1990 is soft, easy wine. The 1991 is considerably better with 20% Cabernet Franc. Nice fruit, good oak.

Lievland Merlot ★★★ D

This wine is from the 1990 vintage. It has little fruit but good flavour with oak backing. 10% Cabernet Sauvignon gives an added dimension.

Meerlust Merlot ★★★★ E/F

The 1984, backed with good wood and touched with a small fraction of Cabernet, was a most attractive wine to drink when released and super in 1993. There was no release from 1985. The 1986 is bigger and better, while the 1987 is a five-star stunner. It will be followed by the 1988.

Overgaauw Merlot ★★★★ C

The Cape's first Merlot came from the 1982 vintage. A deep wine, full of flavour and interest, it has developed beautifully in the bottle. The 1983 is lighter and will probably not reach the height of the 1982, although the 1984 and 1986 are very good. The 1987 is a beautiful wine. It drinks very well now and is probably best enjoyed by the mid-1990s. The 1988 is a magnificent wine, full of fruity flavours and backed with good wood. It is likely to become five-star material. The 1989 is given more complexity with some 15% Cabernet Sauvignon. This is wine well worth buying.

Rustenberg Merlot ★★★★ E

The first release from 1990 is good, fruity wine that drinks remarkably well at this early age. The 1991 is better with fine fruit and good wood.

Thelema Merlot ★★★(★) D

Not yet released, but cellar samples from 1991 and 1992 auger well for the future.

Uiterwyk Merlot ★★★ E

The 1984 was a big wine with deep colour and rich flavour. It has no evident wood flavour in its make-up although it matured for a year in big old vats. It's still very good. The 1987 vintage is darker in colour but light in flavour. The 1988 is somewhat reserved and, with the evident tannin, probably needs a few years to develop. The next release from the 1991 vintage is a fine, full wine, but with a bit too much wood.

Villiera Merlot ★★★(★) D

The 1989 and 1990 are both excellent wines and it's no wonder this cellar's Merlot was judged South Africa's best. It is deep, dark wine, packed with fruit and spice, and will develop with benefit.

Vlottenberg Co-op Merlot ★★★ B

The first release from the 1989 vintage, which was a little shy on release, is now beginning to show more fruity flavours against a good oak backing. The 1990 is an improvement, with the 1991 a big, full wine with high alcohol of 13,5%.

Warwick Merlot ★★★★ E

As one would expect from Warwick, this is a fine Merlot with deep, wonderful flavours and most attractive nose. The 1989 is the first commercial release and has developed well. The 1990 is also a most attractive wine. As good as it is now, control yourself and allow another four or five years' development, when it should be great.

Warwick Special Reserve ★★★★

A beautiful, deep-coloured wine with plenty of fruit and flavour, and lots of tannin that will enable it to develop over many years. Only 20 cases were made for the New World Wine Auction in 1990. The 1990 vintage appeared at the 1992 Cape Independent Winemakers' Guild Auction. These are fine wines that are worth seeking out.

Woolworths Elgin Merlot ★★★★ E

This wine is made by Bouchard Finlayson with grapes from Oak Valley estates in Elgin from the 1991 vintage. It has good fruit and is fairly woody. It is available in limited quantities.

Woolworths Le Deuxieme 902R ★★★★ E

Part of the Woolworths Vintage Collection. The number 90 indicates the vintage, 2 the second in the range, and the R stands for red. This is excellent straight Merlot from Rustenberg and needing two to four years to develop.

Woolworths Merlot ★★★★ D

This wine is from the 1991 vintage and made by Rustenberg. It is lightly wooded, fruity, soft, and easy drinking, even at this early age.

Zevenwacht Merlot ★★★ C

This wine comes from the 1989 vintage. It has good fruit and has developed delightful softness.

Zonnebloem Merlot ★★★★ D

Zonnebloem released two vintages simultaneously – a 1988 and a 1989. Both are fine wines with good flavours and complexity from excellent use of small oak. Both drink very easily now, but will be well worth developing into the mid-nineties.

PINOTAGE

Aan-de-Doorns Co-op Pinotage ★★ B
A fruity, dry wine with typical Pinotage nose, most suitable for early drinking despite its hefty alcohol.

Altydgedacht Pinotage ★★★ C
The 1983 was a soft, well-flavoured wine with good cultivar character and nice wood. The 1986 is a very different Pinotage, having aged for 10 months in new Spanish oak. It is developing well in the bottle. The 1987 is also very oaky but from American oak. The 1988 and 1989 vintages had some American oak giving good, full, masculine wine. There was no 1990, but the 1991 is looking very good.

Avontuur Pinotage ★★★ C
This is an easy-drinking Pinotage. The 1987 vintage has good cultivar nose without the distinctive Pinotage ester which appeals to many. The flavour is good, with a nice soft feel in the mouth. The 1988 is a soft, early-drinking wine. The 1992 has some wood which refines the wine without reducing its attraction.

Backsberg Pinotage ★★★ C
This is always a delightful wine that can be consumed young, when the fruity Pinotage bouquet can be fully appreciated. It can also be aged with benefit. It develops a wide, full flavour which, together with its deep colour, gives the impression of a seemingly much heavier wine. The 1984 and 1985 vintages offer a change in style, yielding deeper, bigger wines. Recent vintages were more like the old style, but the 1988 is a much bigger wine. The 1989 is a full-flavoured delicious wine and probably the best ever. The 1990 follows in similar style. The 1991 is a gorgeous, fresh wine for early enjoyment.
88 ★★★ ready. 89 ★★★(★) ready. 90 ★★★(★) ready, will still develop. 91 ★★★★ ready, will still develop.

Beaufort Pinotage (Solly Kramer) ★★★ A
This is a good example of a Pinotage with good cultivar nose and fine flavour. The latest is a full-bodied, easy-drinking wine.

Bellingham Pinotage ★★★ B
This wine has shown improvement with each year and now has typical Pinotage fruitiness. It is delightful when young and slightly chilled. From the 1986 vintage the wine is vintage-dated. From 1988 the wines are big, bold, forceful, unwooded and, like the 1990, very drinkable.

Bergheuwel Pinotage (Drop Inn) ★★★ B
This is a light but bright wine for early drinking – preferably chilled.

Bergsig Pinotage ★★★ B
A pleasant, light wine, without the typical Pinotage nose. The 1982 was wood-aged, and by 1988 it had developed into a fine wine deserving an

extra star. The 1985 and the 1987 are good but lighter in style. The 1988 and 1989 are less fruity but drink easily. The 1990 is bigger and fuller-flavoured, yet still easy, early drinking and a Veritas Double Gold in 1992. Good value wine.

Bertrams Pinotage ★★★ D

Throughout the 1980s these were very reliable, easy-drinking, fruity wines with good cultivar character. It improved as the decade progressed and by 1987 was excellent wine. The 1988 is lighter and more elegant. There was no 1989. The 1990 is out of keeping with previous vintages.

81 ★★★ past its best, still enjoyable. 82 ★★★ ready. 83 ★★★ ready. 84 ★★★★ ready. 85 ★★★ ready. 86 ★★★★ ready, will improve. 87 ★★★★ ready, will still improve. 88 ★★★★ ready, will still improve. 89 no release. 90 ★★★ for early drinking.

Bolandse Co-op Pinotage ★★★(★) A

This is a cellar noted for its good reds, and the Pinotage is no exception. The 1976, 1977 and the 1978 developed well over about 10 years. The Pinotages of the early 1980s are all full-bodied and need to be consumed within four to six years when they are at their best. The 1986 is particularly good. The 1988 is lighter-bodied for early drinking. The 1989 is a little fuller but suitable for early drinking. The 1990 is a big, full, unwooded wine with nearly 14% alcohol. The 1991 follows the style.

Bonnievale Co-op Pinotage ★★ A

A typical medium-bodied Pinotage. The 1990s are brightly coloured wines, Nouveau in style, and for early drinking.

Botha Co-op Pinotage ★★★ A

A consistently good Pinotage with a long record of show successes. Its good balance and full flavour allow it to age well over five to seven years. The wines of the early 1980s seem to be slightly fuller-bodied, with the 1983 and 1984 already showing well – the latter having the potential to develop well into the early 1990s. From the 1985 vintage onwards some of the vintages had ageing in wood. The 1987 is the best release to date, with the 1988 good, but not outstanding. There was no release from 1989 or 1990, and the 1991 is unwooded and full of fruit flavour.

Bovlei Co-op Pinotage ★★★ A

This is a frequent prize-winner at shows. The 1986 is a very full wine, while the 1987 and 1988 are lighter in body but have good flavours. The 1989 is fuller and better. The 1991 is full, fresh and unwooded.

Calitzdorp Co-op Pinotage ★ A

Previously labelled 'Buffelskroon', this is very much a vin ordinaire without much cultivar character. This wine is not bottled with each vintage. The 1991 is unwooded.

Cape Vintners Members Only Pinotage ★★★(★) C

This is one of the new-style Pinotage wines. It has attractive, fruity nose, with the eight months of small oak ageing showing on the nose and softening the Pinotage character. It comes from the 1989 vintage and is very drinkable wine now, but will develop with benefit from another four to six years in the bottle.

Cederberg Kelders Pinotage ★★★ B

Never a typical Pinotage, the Cederberg Kelders Pinotage always seems to have more cellar character than cultivar character with lots of wood. This is nevertheless an attractive wine. The 1987 has developed with interest. I missed the 1988, but the 1989 is similar to the 1987. The 1990 has unusual nose but good flavour, and has enough tannin to age well. The 1991 is a good, fruity wine with nutty character, and the 1992 is more refined and well-wooded.

Clairvaux Co-op Pinotage ★★ A

A tough, dry wine from the 1988 vintage. Not one for ageing, and it has not been seen since. It has not improved after five years of ageing.

Clos Malverne Pinotage ★★★(★) D

This cellar is making a speciality out of Pinotage. The initial release from the 1989 vintage is a full-flavoured, well-wooded wine with lots of fruit. It is developing well in the bottle. The 1990 is a classy wine, and the 1991 continues in bold, generous style. They will all age with benefit over eight to ten years.

Culemborg Pinotage ★★★ B

An inexpensive, pleasant cultivar wine which is excellent value for money and has very good Pinotage character. It is vintage-dated. The 1986 has developed well in the bottle over four years. All subsequent vintages are along the same lines, with the 1991 having definite young Pinotage nose.

De Doorns Co-op Pinotage ★★ A

This is one of the heavy-bodied, powerful Pinotages.

De Helderberg Co-op Pinotage ★★(★) A

This is a moderate wine which has changed quite considerably from vintage to vintage. More recent ones, with their typical cultivar character, have been very light but markedly better. Released within the year of the vintage, the 1991 is a fuller wine, and the 1992 has good fruit. It is also available in sensible 500 ml bottles.

Delheim Pinotage ★★★(★) C

Up to 1986 this has been a medium-bodied, dry red with good cultivar character. Aged about a year in large Limousin vats before bottling, this gives the wine more class than most Pinotages. The 1983 vintage is particularly fruity and pleasant, while the 1985 is a fine, elegant wine. For 1986, Philip Costandius blended some 20% Merlot with the Pinotage, producing a serious wine of most unusual dimension. It has aged with interest. The 1987 has 25% Merlot and is a big, beautiful wine with soft plummy flavour that makes it most attractive – as is the 1988. The 1989 and 1990 are made in an attractive style but without blending. All develop well in the bottle.

Die Krans Pinotage ★★(★) B
This is one of the better natural wines from this cellar which benefits from some wood-ageing.

Diemersdal Pinotage ★★★ C
This is a wine that is big in character, soft in style, with lots of fruit, and a clean finish. It has enough tannin to age in the medium term. The first release came from the 1989 vintage. The 1990 follows in similar style and the 13% alcohol should allow good development.

Douglas Co-op Pinotage ★ A
From the 1990 vintage comes the first release under this label (previously sold as Dry Red). It is recognizable as Pinotage, medium-bodied, yet a little awkward in the mouth. The 1991 is fuller and better, with a touch of Tinta Barocca.

Douglas Green Pinotage ★★★(★) C
This is a fairly full-bodied Pinotage of good quality and probably slightly underrated by the wine-drinking public. Although earlier vintages were blended with Cinsaut, it is unmistakably Pinotage when young. Its slightly overbearing quality tones down with a year or two in the bottle and becomes very acceptable. It carries a vintage date. The 1978 has developed very well. The 1979 is even better but is reaching the stage where it needs to be consumed. The vintages of the 1980s are far smoother than earlier ones at the time of bottling, which adds to the wine's acceptability. The 1986 is a full, rounded wine that drinks well in 1993. The 1987 is a more dominant wine, while the 1988 is a well-made wine that might need time to develop. These wines usually carried Superior certification which is fairly unusual for Pinotage. The 1989 is in new packaging.
79 ★★★ past its best, drink. 80 ★★★★ ready. 81 ★★★★ ready. 82 ★★★★ ready. 83 ★★★ ready. 84 ★★★★ ready. 86 ★★★(★) ready. 87 ★★★ ready. 88 ready. 89 ★★★ ready, will still develop.

Du Toitskloof Co-op Pinotage ★★★ B
The first release from 1990 is a little subdued, showing as much wood as cultivar. The 1991 shows more fruit but still a lot of oak. This is early-drinking wine which might develop in the bottle.

Eersterivier-Valleise Kelder Pinotage ★★★ B
This is consistently reliable, fruity wine of a fuller-bodied style, with a good record of show successes. At the time of release, earlier vintages were ready for early drinking. The late 1980s and early 1990s are distinctly Pinotage and best when young and fresh. They are medium-bodied, fresh and fruity. Good value for money.

Fairview Pinotage ★★★ C
This is usually a full, powerful, dark-coloured wine which is distinctly different from most other Pinotages. The 1979 is the best of the 1970s' vintages and is perhaps rather less powerful. The 1980 is very good, the 1982 even better, and the 1984 has good, full body and lovely fruit.

Although the 1985 is light, it is a fine wine. The 1986 has more character. The 1987 is a good, sound wine, while the 1988 is one of the best to date. The 1989, 1990 and 1991 continue the style.

79 ★★★★ drink. 80 ★★★ drink. 82 ★★★★ ready. 84 ★★★ ready. 85 ★★★ ready. 86 ★★★ ready. 87 ★★★ ready. 88 ★★★ ready, will still improve. 89 ★★★ ready, will improve. 90 ★★★ ready, will improve.

Fairview Pinotage Reserve ★★★★ C

The 1989 is excellent value for money and one of the Cape's great Pinotage wines. It is wood aged, has good fruit, fine tannins, and is developing beautifully in the bottle.

Fleur Du Cap Pinotage (Bergkelder) ★★★★ C

When the Fleur du Cap wines were introduced, this was one of the poorest of the range. It has since developed into a really fine Pinotage – well-balanced, medium-bodied, with good fruit and fine cultivar character, it ages very well. The 1978 vintage was outstanding and rated a good four stars. The 1979, which also showed great promise, developed well up to 1993 and now needs to be enjoyed. The 1980 vintage is as good and has developed well. The 1984, released in 1989, spent 16 months in small French oak. It is a lovely wine and carries Superior. The 1985 is a firmer, harder wine. The 1987 is big, fruity and tannic. The 1988 is a lovely wine although it does not show too much cultivar character; it will develop well. The 1989 and 1990 follow in good style. These wines need some four to five years to show their pace, but develop well up to 10 years. Some will last much longer.

80 ★★★★ ready. 82 ★★★★ ready. 83 ★★★ ready. 84 ★★★★(★) ready. 85 ★★★ ready. 86 no release 87 ★★★(★) ready, will still improve. 88 ★★★★ ready, will still develop. 89 ★★★★ ready, will still develop. 90 ★★★★ ready, will still develop.

Goudini Co-op Pinotage ★★ A

A typical, unwooded, high alcohol, young Pinotage.

Goue Vallei Pinotage (Citrusdal Co-op) ★★★ B

A wine with a good fruity nose, suggesting lightness, yet remaining full of flavour and not short of body. It is receiving a little wood-ageing to add further dimension and is improving with each vintage. It is best consumed within three to four years.

Groot Constantia Pinotage ★★★ C

This is a rather robust-flavoured Pinotage, which develops into a soft, full-bodied red. The 1978 was outstanding wine and still beautiful after 12 years. The 1981, 1982 and 1983 have developed well over ten years. The 1984 is very attractive and is ageing with benefit, while the 1985 is a little lighter. The 1986 is a full-flavoured, fruity wine with lots of cultivar character and is well worth ageing. The later 1980s, especially the 1987 and 1989, are all good, powerful wines with loads of potential. This wine should age with great benefit.

Jacobsdal Pinotage ★★★(★) **D**

This Estate has consistently produced a good, full-flavoured wine with unmistakable varietal character. From the 1970s, the 1974, 1976 and 1978 are still showing well in 1993. Of the 1980s, the 1984 and 1986 have developed well and all have received some wood ageing. The high alcohol (14%) 1989 is a little out of character. The 1990 has good berry character and should age with benefit.

82 ★★★★ *ready. 83* ★★★ *ready. 84* ★★★★ *ready. 86* ★★★★ *ready. 89* ★★★(★) *ready, will still improve. 90* ★★★★ *not ready, age further.*

Kaapzicht Pinotage ★★★ **C**

This friendly cellar produced a wooded and an unwooded Pinotage from the 1991 vintage. The latter made good, easy drinking, but will not be repeated. The newer aged 1990 is a more serious wine and is already showing improvement in the bottle.

Kanonkop CIWG Pinotage ★★★★★ **E**

The 1990 is magnificent wine, full of deep rich flavours. The 1991 release is a massive, magnificent effort! Both will need a long time in the bottle to develop.

Kanonkop Pinotage ★★★★ **E**

This has long been one of South Africa's bench-mark wines: big and bold with a lot of complex cultivar character mingling well with good wood. The 1976 was one of the best Pinotages of that year. The 1978 was also extremely good, but the 1979 lacked some of the complexity of previous and subsequent vintages. The 1980 set a standard against which Pinotage wines generally could be judged. The 1981 is a little more discreet, but the 1982 and 1983 are back to full character. Both the 1984 and 1985 spent 10 months in large French oak vats. The 1984 is very similar to the 1982, and is showing well in 1992. The 1985 is a lighter wine and will peak earlier than the 1984. It was judged winner of the Diners Club Award in 1987. The 1986 is a full-flavoured, high-alcohol wine which is magnificent now, but still has lots of life to go to reach its potential. It should be magnificent. The 1987 is also a high alcohol wine (13,8%) and has been aged for 12 months, partly in big vats and partly in small casks. It is great right now but will still develop over another three to four years. The 1988, 1989, and 1990 releases continue in character and prove, without doubt, that this cellar continually makes one of the greatest Pinotage wines in the country. The 1991 is amazingly good in the mouth at this early stage, but give it time for a real treat. They are also excellent value for money.

80 ★★★★(★) *ready. 81* ★★★ *ready. 82* ★★★★ *ready. 83* ★★★★ *ready. 84* ★★★★ *ready, will still improve. 85* ★★★★ *ready. 86* ★★★★(★) *ready, will still improve. 87* ★★★★ *ready, will still improve. 88* ★★★★ *ready, will still improve. 89* ★★★★ *ready, will still improve. 90* ★★★(★) *not ready, allow to develop. 91* ★★★★ *not ready, allow to develop.*

Klawer Co-op Pinotage ★ B

The 1985 was the first vintage of this wine to come my way. Medium-bodied and fruity, this dry red is ready for early consumption. The 1988 has Pinotage esters covered by oak. The 1991 shows promise.

Kleindal Pinotage ★★★ B

Like all the wines under this label, this is a good example of the cultivar and reasonable value.

Koelenhof Co-op Pinotage ★★ B

This used to be a full-flavoured wine with real young Pinotage punch. The 1986 vintage received some wood ageing, which softened the fruit, to make for pleasant, early drinking. The 1988 was a somewhat weak effort, but the unwooded 1989 is much like the old style and full of Pinotage ester. The 1990 is in the same style and makes early, easy drinking.

KWV Pinotage ★★ (no price available)

For members and for export only. It usually has a somewhat subdued style. Although certified Superior, the 1984 is decidedly quiet and now very tired. The 1986 is in full traditional style. The late 1980s all follow a traditional style, with good flavour and ageing potential, although the 1989 shows a move towards finer style.

Landskroon Pinotage ★★★ C

Over the years this cellar has produced a deep Pinotage, without the initial full fruit associated with this cultivar. The vintages since 1977 have been very good and the 1979 is the best of the 1970s. The 1983 and 1984 are especially appealing. The 1982 is developing nicely, while the 1983 and 1988 are in keeping with the cellar's regular quality. The 1987 was selected as the 1988 Alphen Pinotage Wine of the Month. The 1988 and 1989 show good class, with the 1990 following the same style. These wines are known to age very well into good dry reds with very little hint of their cultivar.

Lanzerac Pinotage ★★★ C (refers to new release and not auction wines)

Lanzerac was the name given to the world's first commercially bottled Pinotage which was launched in 1961 from the 1959 vintage. Its owners decided to remove it from the market and, although not commercially available, old stocks are traditionally used as the first and last lots at the Nederburg Auction, where they reach incredible prices. I have come across numerous bottles in private cellars and have recently enjoyed the 1978 and 1979 vintages, both of which were very impressive. I have also had the pleasure of serving these wines on numerous occasions to overseas wine connoisseurs, who are always impressed. Fortunately the label has now returned in the familiar dewdrop bottle. The first of the new releases is from the 1989 vintage and is fairly subdued wine, but unmistakably Pinotage. The next release is from the 1990 vintage and an improvement, with attractive fruit and a fair amount of oak.

89 ★★★ might develop. 90 ★★★(★) not ready, allow to develop.

Mamreweg Co-op Pinotage ★★(★) B
Originally this was a very light Pinotage. Recent releases have been fuller
and have some wood character which tones down the very typical Pinotage nose. The 1992 is very much along the lines of the earlier style. This
wine is best enjoyed in its youth.

Meerendal Pinotage ★★★★ D
This is one of the big Pinotage wines. It is wood-matured with a good balance between wood and cultivar. It ages well in the bottle, showing great
improvement over a few years. The 1978 vintage gained a gold medal at
the 1982 International Wine and Spirit Competition, and the wines have
subsequently won other international awards. The 1983 is one of the best
ever, which is a remarkable feat considering the poor vintage. The 1984
and 1985 are big, attractive wines. The 1987 is one of the best of the
1980s – more refined than usual, with good, deep flavours and lovely
clean aftertaste. The 1988 is fine wine; the 1989 lighter and more elegant,
but it will age with benefit. The wine is only released after five years.

Meinert Winery Devon Crest Pinotage ★★★★
The first release from this modern, attractive new winery at the head of
Devon Valley is a new oak barrel-aged, full-flavoured, complex wine. A
great debut. It should develop with great benefit over six to eight years.

Middelvlei Pinotage ★★★(★) D
This is always an interesting and reliably good red wine and, although it
is medium-bodied, it has rich character. As with most good Pinotages it
tends to lose cultivar as it ages, but becomes most satisfying with time.
The 1976 vintage was still exceptionally good in 1993. More recent vintages have been lighter, the 1978 being the best of the 1970s and about
at its best now. The vintages of the early 1980s sustain the quality with
the 1980 lacking the usual Pinotage ester. The 1981 is a big wine which
has needed time to tone down. The 1982 is a big, almost old-style wine,
certified Superior, while the 1983 is a lovely four-star wine which has
benefited from good oak. There was no 1984, and the 1985 is not as
attractive as previous releases. The 1986 is a fine, rich wine with full
flavours and enough alcohol (13,7%) and tannin to develop well. The
1987 and 1988 are so far the best of the 1980s, although the 1989 to
come could top them.

*72 ★★★★ drink. 73 ★★★ past its best, drink. 74 ★★★ ready. 75 ★★★ past
its best. 76 ★★★★ ready. 77 ★★★ ready. 78 ★★★★ ready. 79 no release.
80 ★★★★ ready. 81 ★★★ ready. 82 ★★★ ready. 83 ★★★★ ready. 84 no
release. 85 ★★★ ready. 86 ★★★★ ready. 87 ★★★★ drinks well now, but
will benefit from more age. 89 ★★★★ not ready, age further.*

Nederburg Pinotage ★★★ D
Nederburg Pinotage is usually only available on the export market,
except for one local release in the early 1970s. There are occasional
releases of Nederburg Pinotage at the annual Auction.

Nederburg Auction Pinotage ★★★★ E

This is a specially selected wine sold only at the Nederburg Auction. The 1978 vintage has rich character and lingering smoothness, and became more voluptuous as it aged. The 1976 still has the grace of a fine wine. The 1981 is a beautiful wine, showing that this cultivar can hold its own among the classic varieties and proving that Pinotage, when well made, is a wine to be taken seriously. The 1981 vintage was sold at the 1992 Nederburg Auction, and the 1985 at the 1993.

Neethlingshof Pinotage ★★★ D

This is one of the most interesting wines to emerge from the Neethlingshof cellar. The early vintages had overwhelming Pinotage ester and were bottled without any wood ageing. Initially, the new owners removed Pinotage from their list, but it returned with the 1984 vintage released in 1988. This was somewhat over-wooded and lacked any real Pinotage character. The 1986 is considerably better and the 1988 is fine wine that is developing well. The 1989 is a whole step up in quality – wood-aged yet full of fruit, and described by Günter Brözel as 'Super Elegant'.

86 ★★★ ready. 87 ★★(★) ready. 88 ★★★ ready, will still improve. 89 ★★★★ not ready, age further.

Oranjerivier Wynkelder Pinotage ★ A

This is a light wine with some cultivar character and wood backing.

Oude Libertas Pinotage (SFW) ★★★★ F

This was the successor to Lanzerac Pinotage, the world's first marketed Pinotage. It had a robust style, yet tended to remain soft in the mouth, with strong, fruity varietal character which was very marked when young. It matured in the bottle, however, undergoing remarkable character change to produce a rich-flavoured, mellow wine with surprising depth which still does justice to the finest tables. It is a great pity that the 1981 vintage was the last of these historic wines: the regular Oude Libertas range has ceased to exist. The 1973 release is still remarkably good. The 1978 in magnums, released to commemorate 25 years of Pinotage as a commercial wine, is magnificent. Twenty cases were sold at the 1991 and 1992 Nederburg Auctions.

Oude Nektar Pinotage ★★(★) C

The first vintage sampled was the 1983; a fairly subdued wine of medium body but deep colour. There was no 1984, but the 1985 was a light, smooth wood-aged wine. Next was a 1986: a beautiful, full, cultivar wine that fully deserves four stars. The 1987 was not as good when released but is developing well. The 1989 is bold, full wine and will also benefit from more time in the bottle. Cellar samples look good for the future.

Overgaauw Pinotage ★★★(★) A

This was always a good wine, well-wooded and medium-bodied with good fruit. Unfortunately it is no longer being produced, although a few bottles may still be found. They are worth searching for.

Paradyskloof Pinotage (Vriesenhof) ★★★ **B**

This is a good example of pure Pinotage cultivar character which drinks well when young but is worth keeping to allow it to develop.

Perdeberg Paarl Pinotage ★★★ **A**

Usually a consistently good wine that develops quite a complex nose after a short while. It is, however, more enjoyable when on the younger side. The 1988 is a good, medium-bodied, drinking wine. The 1989 has a less typical Pinotage nose, yet is still attractive wine that drinks easily. The 1991 has the old-fashioned Pinotage ester.

Pick 'n Pay Pinotage ★★★(★) **C**

The 1990 is a typical, full, rich Pinotage with good fruit and wood in the modern style of Kanonkop. The same can be said of the 1991. Both are good to drink now, but have plenty of ageing potential.

Porterville Co-op Pinotage ★★ **A**

This is a light, typical Pinotage which drinks very easily when young.

Rhebokskloof Pinotage ★★★★ **D**

The 1991 is a very different Pinotage, aged in American oak and showing unusual character. It is deep purple, almost opaque, has deep flavour, is soft on palate and yet fairly tannic. It should develop with great interest.

Riebeek Wine Farmers' Co-op Pinotage ★★ **A**

This used to be a simple, medium-bodied Pinotage. Six months in wood, however, has made the 1984 more complex and it has developed well. The next release was from the 1988 vintage, followed by the 1991.

Romansrivier Co-op Pinotage ★★(★) **A**

This is a good cultivar wine. Recent vintages are delicate but well-bodied.

Rooiberg Co-op Pinotage ★★★ **C**

This wine has improved over the years. The 1980s were all interesting and needed four to six years to show their best. The late 1980s and early 1990s seem to be for earlier drinking and show a lot of wood.

Rouge de Nuy ★★★ **A**

The Nuy Co-operative is situated in the foothills of the Langeberg range between Worcester and Robertson. The area is better known for its white wines, but the micro-climates here produce some very interesting reds, of which this Pinotage is one. It is medium-bodied, dry and with good, fruity Pinotage nose. Though slightly sharp when young, it settles down very quickly into a pleasant drinking wine. The 1983 vintage was a medal winner at the South African Championship Wine Show. The 1985, which has an unmistakable, but not overpowering, Pinotage nose, made very good early drinking, as did the 1987. The 1988 is fuller, bigger wine that has developed well over two years. The 1989 carried the name change to Rouge de Nuy. From 1990, the entry falls under Cape Traditional Blends.

Saxenburg Private Collection ★★★(★) **C**

Released from the 1989 vintage, this is a most appealing wine. 70% was aged in French oak and 30% in American oak for 10 months. Nothing has been released from the 1990 vintage. The 1991 spent a year in wood which masks the Pinotage ester but gives an attractive wine.

Simondium Co-op Pinotage ★★ B

An early-bottled, dry, fruity wine that is without doubt a Pinotage, though it is somewhat harsh.

Simonsig Pinotage ★★★(★) C

This is a wine with a long, successful history, with some vintages ageing with incredible benefit. It frequently features as a Young Wine Champion but is always good and worth ageing. It is consistently one of the Cape's best. The 1989 and 1990 continue the quality and the 1991 is a particularly good, four-star wine.

Simonsig Pinotage Reserve ★★★★(★) E

This is a spectacular wine from 1989. It is well oak-aged and has lots of fruit, with good tannin. It will age with considerable benefit. This is one of the best and I look forward to the next one.

Simonsvlei Co-op Pinotage ★★★★ B

This wine has a long and successful history and a popular following. It is a regular award winner at regional and national shows. The 1975 and 1976 vintages were offered at the 1977 and 1978 Nederburg Auctions respectively. The 1979 still shows very well. Since 1988, it has been made lighter in style. Recent vintages are fine, firm wines with good fruit and reasonable ageing potential.

Slanghoek Co-op Pinotage ★★★ A

Slanghoek Co-operative produced a wooded and an unwooded Pinotage, but have now opted for the latter version. It has good fruit and is best enjoyed when young.

Spier Pinotage ★★★ C

Spier has a reputation for unusual Pinotage. The 1974 was an outstanding wine and the 1976 developed in a similar fashion. The wines of the 1980s are fuller and more forceful than those of the mid-1970s, but not as stylish. The 1983 is probably the best of the decade. The 1984 is a good successor but is not quite up to the same standard. The 1986 is big and powerful, but the 1987 is a lesser wine. The 1988 is a much better wine and appears to be the last release. The Estate has available various older vintages of their Pinotage.

Spruitdrift Co-op Pinotage ★★(★) A

This is a wine that is improving vintage by vintage and gaining gold medals at the South African Championship Wine Show. It has good, typical cultivar character. The 1983 was an excellent example of the Pinotage cultivar with deep colour, good ..ose and full flavour, giving a wine which has aged well over the years. Since 1986, the wine is aged for nine months in puncheons. This tames the Pinotage ester and makes it a very easy-drinking wine. The wines of the early 1990s are all very acceptable drinking wines.

Swartland Pinotage ★★★(★) A

This wine, with its full and rich Pinotage nose, was the first to evoke interest in this Co-op. The 1975 vintage needed taming at the time of release, but smoothed out and developed well over 10 years. The 1973, sold at the 1978 Nederburg Auction, had deep colour and soft flavour. Later vintages have been far less robust but have very good Pinotage character and are regular class winners at regional and national shows. Since 1986, the wines have been considerably lighter than usual and will not have the long life of the wines of the 1970s. The 1989 was a slight lapse in character, but the wines of the early 1990s are back to the regular style.

Tulbagh Co-op Pinotage ★★★ B

The first release comes from the 1991 vintage. It is light and bright wine for early drinking.

Uiterwyk Pinotage ★★★(★) D

A Pinotage of usually medium body, Uiterwyk has cultivar character toned down with wood. The 1978 vintage has aged very well, and vintages of the early 1980s all show good potential. The 1983, however, needs drinking now. The 1984 and 1985 are both better wines than the 1983 and are developing with benefit. The 1987 is developing well and the 1988 is a wine in fine traditional style. The 1986 is the best release to date; a three-star wine. No 1989 was released, but suddenly the 1990 and 1991 are four-star wines – full of fruit and good wood – with the 1991 being particularly attractive.

Villiersdorp Co-op Pinotage ★★ B

This is a wine with big, soft body and typical cultivar nose. Recent vintages have received some wood, making them easy, early-drinking wines.

Vlottenburg Co-op Pinotage ★★★ B

This is a good-flavoured Pinotage with interesting fruitiness and good use of wood.

Vredendal Co-op Pinotage ★★(★) B

A wine which is high in alcohol and fairly course.

Waboomsrivier Co-op Pinotage ★★ A

This Co-op wins an impressive number of regional show medals each year. This Pinotage is wood-aged for a year giving easy, early-drinking wine which is good value for money.

Wamakersvallei Co-op Pinotage ★★ A

This is a typical, light-style young Pinotage wine. It is a regular class winner at local shows.

Wellington Co-op Pinotage ★★(★) B

The 1991 vintage has been wood-aged and gives very drinkable wine.

Welmoed Rendition Pinotage ★★(★) C

This is usually a medium-bodied wine of good cultivar character and best for early, easy drinking.

Windmeul Co-op Pinotage ★★★ B

Very little is available from the 1992 vintage. It is a big, full, fruity wine.

Woolworths Pinotage ★★★ A

A Wine of Origin Paarl, this is unmistakably a young Pinotage – dry and full of cultivar character. It is not vintage-dated but is definitely for youthful drinking.

Woolworths Pinotage Magnums ★★★ F+

By Kanonkop and from the 1990 vintage, this is a super wine that will age with considerable benefit in the big bottle.

Woolworths Pinotage Reserve ★★★(★) C

This is a complex, unwooded, good varietal wine from the 1989 vintage, out of the Simonsig cellars. It will develop with benefit.

Zevenwacht Pinotage ★★ B

Early vintages have been overwooded to my taste. The 1987, however, is a very pleasant, lighter-bodied dry red. The 1988 is simple wine, while the 1989 is better and developing well.

Zonnebloem Pinotage (SFW) ★★★★ C

It was to be expected when Zonnebloem introduced a Pinotage to its range that it would be an outstanding addition, matching the traditional excellence of its Cabernet. This it has done with a full-bodied wine of impressive colour and depth, and of distinguished character. The wine should be given every opportunity to age and realize its full potential. Outstanding vintages of the 1970s were 1974, 1976 and 1979, while the 1975 had developed surprisingly well by the late 1980s, despite its poor reception when released. The 1979 might have been the best of the 1970s. The 1982 also promises to develop with great benefit, as will the 1983 which is a four-star wine. Although the 1983 is very good, of the 1980s the 1984, 1985, 1986, 1987, 1988 and 1989 are big, bold, beautiful wines.

74 ★★★★★ drink. 75 ★★★ drink. 76 ★★★★★ drink. 79 ★★★★★ drink. 82 ★★★★ ready. 83 ★★★★ ready. 84 ★★★★★ ready. 85 ★★★★(★) ready. 86 ★★★★ ready, will still improve. 87 ★★★★ ready, will still improve. 88 ★★★★ not ready, age further. 89 ★★★★ not ready, age further.

PINOT NOIR

Arthur Freedberg Collection Pinot Noir (Rebel) ★★★ C
Nice 'fruit-juicy', light, early drinking wine.

Backsberg Pinot Noir ★★★ C
The 1985 was the first release of this wine. The 1990 is light bodied with distinct cultivar character, fruity and very drinkable. The 1991 will be from new clone and should show greater character.

Blaauwklippen Pinot Noir ★★★★ D
This rather fickle variety has baffled most winemakers beyond the borders of Burgundy. Walter Finlayson persevered with the cultivar at Blaauwklippen and has been particularly successful with it. He has established himself as the pioneer and is now the expert in the Cape with this cultivar. The first vintage, the 1979, was well received. Beginner's luck, some might say, but the vintage variation since then has been remarkable. Practise makes perfect, however, and the 1984 was really very good and deserved its five stars. The 1985 is still one of the best Pinot Noirs produced in the Cape and was selected as a SAA Wine of the Month. The 1986 is developing well in the bottle, as is the 1987. With Walter's departure, Jacques Kruger has continued the good work. The 1988 is a fine, medium-bodied, fruity wine, followed by a particularly good 1989.
79 ★★★★ ready. 80 ★★★★ ready. 81 ★★★ past its best, still enjoyable. 82 ★★★★★ ready. 83 ★★★★★ ready. 84 ★★★★★ ready. 85 ★★★★★ ready. 86 ★★★★ ready, will still improve. 87 ★★★★ ready, will still improve. 88 ready, will develop. 89 ★★★★(★) not ready, allow to develop.

Boplaas Pinot Noir ★★★ C
From the 1989 vintage comes a good, fresh, fruity-styled wine that drinks very well. The 1990 is delicately wooded and easy drinking.

Bouchard Finlayson Pinot Noir ★★★★ E
From the 1991 vintage, with grapes from Elgin, this wine has good cultivar character with fine oak backing. It should develop well over a year or two. I expect the 1992 to be even better.

Buitenverwachting Pinot Noir ★★★ D
The first release came from the 1986 vintage. It is a full, strong Pinot Noir with a decidedly French farmyard character which developed well. There was no release from 1987 but the 1988 is a very good wine – flavourful, light, soft and elegant – as is the 1989.

Delheim Pinot Noir ★★★ C
Early attempts were fun, but in 1980 this Pinot Noir suddenly became a serious wine, its very subtle oak blending well with cultivar character. The 1981 was more complex, but has not developed as well as the 1980 and should, I believe, be drunk now. The 1982 and 1983 vintages are

good wines, but the 1984 had the best combination of wood and cultivar flavours for that time. It drinks very well now. The 1985 is a deep-coloured but much lighter-bodied wine with fine cultivar character. The 1986 is a super wine, fully deserving four stars. The 1987 may not be as good as the 1986, but it's better than any of the previous vintages, and was an Alphen Wine of the Month Club choice. The 1988 has the makings of a very good wine. It will develop well, as should the 1989. The 1990 is even better.

85 ★★★ ready. 86 ★★★★(★) ready. 87 ★★★(★) ready. 88 ★★★★ ready, will still develop. 89 ★★★(★) ready, will still develop. 90 ★★★★ allow to age.

Eikendal Vineyards Pinot Noir ★★★ D

The first release from the 1988 vintage is a medium-bodied, complex wine with good fruit and wood – an interesting first attempt that is developing well in the bottle. The 1989 is a bigger, fuller wine but has not developed much cultivar character to date. No 1990 vintage was released, but the 1991 is good and fruity.

Fairview Pinot Noir ★★★ B

It first appeared in 1982 and won a gold medal at the SA Championship Wine Show. The 1983 vintage did not show as well, but the 1984 is developing with benefit. The 1985 and 1986 are both developing well. The 1987 has good fruit flavour, backed with good wood, and the 1988 looks very promising.

82 ★★★ ready. 83 ★★★ ready. 84 ★★★ ready. 85 ★★★(★) ready, will still improve. 86 ★★★ ready, will still develop. 87 ★★★ ready, will still develop. 88 ★★★ not ready, age further.

Fairview Pinot Noir Reserve ★★★(★) B

From the 1987 vintage comes a big wine with lots of flavour and distinct wood. It is developing well and is probably at its best now.

Glen Carlou Pinot Noir ★★★★ E

Made by Walter Finlayson, one of the Cape's pioneers of quality Pinot Noir. The 1990 is very good in every respect and should develop well in five to seven years. The 1991 is slightly lighter but has good character. This is a wine to watch for future releases.

Hamilton Russell Vineyards Pinot Noir ★★★★★ F

This wine used to be labelled 'Grand Vin Noir' and did not carry Wine of Origin certification, so dating the vintage is a little difficult if unfamiliar with the labels. For a guide to the vintages, look for the large, light-red print on the neck label. For example, the P3 is the 1983 Pinot Noir, P4 the 1984 Pinot Noir. Each release seems to be better than the last, the pleasing results of a combination of cultivar, good wood and excellent cellar technique. The 1982, 1983 and 1984 are all very good, as is the 1985, which is showing very well now. It is vintage-dated, but still carries the name Grand Vin Noir. From 1985 the vintage is printed on the label. The 1986 is labelled Pinot Noir. I once wrote, 'To my mind this is the best

Pinot Noir yet produced in the Cape and compares well with any any-where', and this was proved later in 1989 when it was judged by Diners Club to be the best in South Africa. The 1987 also looks great. It seems the Finlayson brothers discovered the secret of making Pinot Noir in South Africa. Winemaking is now in the capable hands of Gail Kreusch-Dau. Both the 1988 and 1989 maintain the high standard, but the 1991 looks like it could be the best of them all!

82 ★★★★★ ready. 83 ★★★★★ ready. 84 ★★★★★ ready. 85 ★★★★★ ready, will still improve. 86 ★★★★★ ready, will still improve. 87 ★★★★★ ready, will still improve. 88 ★★★★★ ready, will still improve. 89 ★★★★★ ready, will still develop. 90 ★★★★★ not ready, allow to develop. 91 ★★★★★+ not ready, allow to develop.

Hamilton Russell Vineyards Pinot Noir Reserve ★★★★★ F

This is a wine specially selected from the 1989 vintage. Beautiful.

Landskroon Pinot Noir ★★(★) C

While others have struggled, Landskroon seemed to have mastered this cultivar quite quickly with their early releases. Each vintage since 1978 has been good. The 1980 appeared at the 1985 Nederburg Auction. The 1981 and 1982 vintages were both encouraging, but do not keep up with some of the other Cape Pinot Noirs of more recent vintages. The 1984, however, is decidedly disappointing and was the last release until the 1989. Good fruit flavours are evident that will require time to develop in the bottle. It is followed by the 1990 release which is somewhat harsh in character.

Meerlust Pinot Noir ★★★(★) E

The first release, in 1980, showed signs of class. The 1981 was even bet-ter; the 1982 fuller and more complex, yet delightfully light in body and very drinkable four years later. The cellar master, Giorgio Dalla Cia, pre-dicted a life of 10 years or more for this wine and he wasn't wrong. The 1984 is one of the better wines from this cultivar produced in the Cape. The 1985 is better still, with good flavours, medium body and 13% alco-hol. The 1986 is developing well. The 1987 is one of the best in the Cape, with concentrated character, full of live fruit. Delicious wine. The 1988 is lovely wine but will have to go some way to match the 1987. It is consis-tently one of the Cape's best.

81 ★★★★ ready, will still improve. 82 ★★★(★) ready. 83 ★★★(★) ready. 84 ★★★★ ready. 85 ★★★★(★) ready. 86 ★★★★(★) ready. 87 ★★★★★ ready, will still improve. 89 ★★★★ ready, will still improve.

Muratie Pinot Noir ★★★ D

This is one of the oldest wines with a Pinot Noir label and is very different to the modern style. The 1976, 1977, 1978 and 1979 vintages were sold at the Nederburg Auction. Vintages have varied and, although they do not compare favourably with modern efforts, they have a loyal following. Now under Melck ownership, the wine has adopted a dramatic change in

style. The 1991 is light, soft, full of flavour and should develop with benefit. The 1992 continues the improvement.

*90 ★★★ ready, will still improve. 91 ★★★ ready, will still improve. 92 ★★★
not ready, age further.*

Nederburg Pinot Noir ★★★★ D

The first release of this limited edition was from the 1982 vintage. A fine
wine with clear cultivar character and reserved use of new oak, it is high
quality and certainly good value for money. The 1983 is an even better
wine and has confounded quite a number of British connoisseurs as to
its origin. The 1984 is a firm, full wine that developed well. The 1986 is a
good wine that, on release, had a strange bitterness in the finish. With
time this has gone and the wine has developed with benefit. The 1987 is
a good example of clean winemaking with the cultivar. The 1988 is a big,
full wine but lacking the good varietal character of earlier vintages.

*82 ★★★★ ready. 83 ★★★★(★) ready. 84 ★★★(★) ready. 86 ★★★(★) ready.
87 ★★★★(★) ready, will still develop. 88 ★★★ might improve with time.*

Rooiberg Co-op Pinot Noir ★★(★) B

The 1987 vintage is a creditable Pinot Noir which has good colour, fruity
bouquet, soft palate and a little wood. It developed in the bottle. The
1988 is young and robust, with some interesting flavours, while the 1989
is an improvement and deserves three stars. The 1990 is a light, easy-
drinking, fruity wine along Nouveau lines.

Ruiterbosch Mountain Vineyards Pinot Noir ★★★ C

The 1990 Pinot Noir has good cultivar and definite farmyard character.
The 1991 is fresher and brighter, and could develop with benefit.

Rustenberg Pinot Noir ★★★★ E

A relative newcomer, this Pinot Noir has a distinctive rich aroma and
medium body, combining well to give an attractive wine. First released in
1978, it has since improved and can be considered to have come of age
with the 1982 vintage, an assessment confirmed by the 1983, while the
1984 and the 1986 were better still. The 1984 has been very successful
at many tastings and has been most acceptable to many visiting British
connoisseurs. These are very rich, full-flavoured wines which will certainly age with benefit over five to eight years, although they drink well on
release. The 1985 is a little disappointing when compared with the 1984
and 1986, but still very good. The 1987 has some Burgundy farmyard
character and will develop. The 1988 is a powerful, full-flavoured, very
fruity wine, which is soft in the mouth and very drinkable ahead of the
1987. The 1989 and 1990 both show very well.

*78 ★★★ past its best, still enjoyable. 80 ★★★ ready. 82 ★★★(★) ready.
83 ★★★(★) ready. 84 ★★★★ ready, will still improve. 85 ★★★(★) ready.
86 ★★★★ ready. 87 ★★★★ ready, will still improve. 88 ★★★★ ready, will
still improve. 89 ★★★★ ready, will still develop. 90 ★★★★ not ready, will
develop with benefit.*

Simonsig Pinot Noir ★★★(★) C

This cellar's Pinot Noir has a character all of its own. It might not appeal to all, but it is well worth trying. The 1982 has shown well in recent tastings. The 1983 and 1984 are better wines and are developing well. Although light in character, the 1984 has superb flavour, drinks very well, and is probably at its best now. There were no bottlings of 1985 and 1986. The 1987 is good, but had a strange bitter aftertaste when released. This has now disappeared. The 1988 has a delicious berry flavour and is probably the most elegant release. It is, however, the last vintage, as the grapes are now used for Kaapse Vonkel.

82 ★★★★ ready, will still improve. 83 ★★★ ready, will still improve. 84 ★★★★ ready, will still improve. 85 no release. 86 no release. 87 ★★★(★) ready, will still improve. 88 ★★★(★) ready, will still improve.

Woolworths Pinot Noir ★★★★ C

This is a very good example of the cultivar, which showed well at two different tastings. Showing good Burgundian characteristics and produced by Rustenberg Estate, it is excellent value for money and one of the best Woolworths' wines. This applies particularly to the 1987 and 1988. The 1991 is good and smooth, but does not have the high notes of the 1988.

SHIRAZ

Allesverloren Shiraz ★★★★ D/E

The first release from the 1982 vintage is a super wine, more in the style of an Australian than a South African Shiraz. It is a big wine in every way (nose, flavour, body and alcohol – exceeding 13%) so treat it with due respect. Beautiful wine in 1993. There were no releases of the 1983, 1984, and 1985, but the 1986 is a big fruity wine with lots of tannin that will allow long ageing. The 1987 is another full wine with more berry nose, deep layers of flavour, and good oak backing. The 1988 is excellent big wine with lots of alcohol and flavour; to be followed by the 1989 which is also 13%+ alcohol. It has good new oak and lots of fruit.

82 ★★★★ ready. 83 no release. 84 no release. 85 no release. 86 ★★★(★) ready, will still develop. 87 ★★★★ ready, will still develop. 88 ★★★★ ready, will still develop. 89 ★★★★ allow to age.

Altydgedacht Shiraz ★★★ C

The first release from the 1987 vintage has the smokey-type Shiraz character. It is light in style, and beginning to loosen out and develop more flavour. There was no 1988, but the 1989 is full of old style smokey, leathery nuances plus lots of good fruit and spice.

Backsberg Shiraz ★★★★ D

An extremely well-made wine with deep, distinctive Shiraz character, this has been a firm favourite over the years. The 1974, 1975 and 1976 vintages were magnificent in 1986, while those of the later 1970s developed well. All the vintages of the 1980s show great promise. The 1983 is a five-star product and the 1984 a big, full wine in all respects. The 1985 and 1986 are superb wines which are developing well. Ageing for 10 years seems to be the optimum for these wines. The 1987 and 1988 are just as full of flavour, but softer, and appear to be developing more quickly. The 1989 is another lovely, full wine that will develop over a longer period of time than the 1988. The 1990 has more tannin and will take longer to develop, and the 1991 could well be the best ever, though not yet released at the time of writing. These are lovely wines and excellent value.

74 ★★★★ drink. 75 ★★★★ drink. 76 ★★★★ drink. 83 ★★★★★ ready, will still improve. 84 ★★★★(★) ready. 85 ★★★★ ready. 86 ★★★★ ready, will still improve. 87 ★★★★ ready, will still develop. 88 ★★★★ ready, will still develop. 89 ★★★★ ready, will still develop. 90 ★★★★ ready, will still develop.

Bellingham Shiraz ★★★★ D

A far cry from the original no-star, non-vintage Bellingham product, today's wines are rich, deep and complex with plenty of Shiraz character. The four-star 1980, which led Bellingham's first appearance at the 1986 Nederburg Auction, drank beautifully 12 years later and still has plenty of life ahead. The 1981 is developing slowly, but the 1983 is not in keeping with Bellingham's usual high quality – probably due to the vintage. The 1984 is a very good wine, full of cultivar character and backed with good wood. The 1985 has the smokey character so often referred to in a Shiraz, yet seldom experienced. The 1986 continues the quality and style; it was ready for drinking on release but will still develop with time. The 1987 heralds a dramatic change with 25% Cabernet in the blend giving greater complexity. This is fine wine and regularly carried Superior.

80 ★★★★(★) ready. 81 ★★★★ ready. 82 ★★★★ ready. 83 ★★★ ready. 84 ★★★★(★) ready, will still improve. 85 ★★★★(★) ready, will still improve. 86 ★★★★ ready, will improve. 87 ★★★★ ready, will develop.

Bertrams Shiraz ★★★★ E

This is a very impressive dry red, with unusually good body for a South African Shiraz. It has been well-aged in good wood and is a most complex wine, appreciably fuller than most other Shiraz labels. The 1979 vintage is outstanding and probably at its best now. Each vintage of the 1980s seems to be better than its predecessor. The 1980 is excellent and will develop with great benefit. The 1982 is an exception, not living up to the reputation of its predecessors, but the 1983 is very good wine. The 1984 is a big beautiful wine that is one of the best of the 1980s. The 1985 is a little slow in developing. The 1986 release is truly a great wine and certainly one of the Cape's best-ever Shiraz wines. It is developing magnificently. This Shiraz carried Superior certification and regularly appears at the annual Nederburg Auction. It will be followed by the 1987 release which is another great wine.

75 ★★★★ past its best, still enjoyable. 76 ★★★★ ready. 78 ★★★★ ready. 79 ★★★★★ ready. 80 ★★★★★ ready. 81 ★★★ ready. 82 ★★★★ ready. 83 ★★★★ ready. 84 ★★★★★ ready, will still improve. 85 ★★★(★) ready, will still develop. 86 ★★★★ ready, will still develop. 87 ★★★★(★) not ready, allow to develop.

Blaauwklippen Shiraz ★★★(★) E

This is a rich, well-coloured Shiraz with a good touch of wood. The 1981 vintage was full-bodied and the 1982 even fuller, proving to be one of the best and developing into a four-star wine. The 1984 is a full-bodied wine with very typical cultivar character. The 1982 and 1984 vintages have developed well to date and must be about at their best now. The 1987 is one of the best and fully deserving four stars. The 1988 is a rich, full wine with farmyard nose and good flavour. The 1989 needs time to develop. The later vintages are ready for drinking on release but will benefit from time in the bottle.

80 ★★★ ready. 81 ★★★ ready. 82 ★★★★ ready. 83 ★★★ ready. 84 ★★★★ ready. 85 ★★★(★) ready. 86 ★★★ ready, will still improve. 87 ★★★★ ready, will still improve. 88 ★★★(★) ready, will still improve. 89 ★★★★ needs time to develop.

Bon Courage Shiraz ★★(★) B

This is a plain wine with big alcohol from the 1989 vintage, that could develop with time. The 1992, is medium-bodied and slightly oaked.

Bottelary Shiraz ★★★(★) B

This wine has developed into a very attractive, well-balanced product with definite Shiraz character. It ages well over four to five years. Bottelary Shiraz is one of the Cape's better Shiraz wines – proved by the 1987. It has good character that develops well in the bottle and is excellent value for money. The 1988 is a little paler in character and the 1989 is still no match for the 1987.

Bovlei Co-op Shiraz ★★(★) B

The first release from the 1987 vintage was a medium-bodied wine with good cultivar character unaffected by wood maturation. I did not see one from 1988, but the 1989 and 1990 both have good Shiraz character.

Cape Vintners Members Only Shiraz ★★★ D

This is an unusual Shiraz from the Van Loveren cellar which is oak-matured giving attractive softness and flavour. It is from 1987 vintage and although easy to drink now, will age well for another two to four years.

De Helderberg Co-op Shiraz ★★★ B

This is usually a fairly robust wine which softens in the bottle. It has good Shiraz character as demonstrated by the 1985, which had a smokey nose and drank well in 1988. The release from the 1990 vintage is medium bodied and very drinkable, as is the 1991. Three to five years seems to see this wine reach its best.

Delheim Shiraz ★★★★ C

This is a light South African Shiraz which rounds off beautifully after a year or more in the bottle. The 1974 and 1976 vintages were excellent and continued to develop well a decade later. The 1979 and 1980 vintages are full of interest and delivering their potential, while the 1983 is powerful in every respect and at its best now. The 1984 has equally good character but does not have 1983's astonishing alcohol content of almost 14%. It is showing very well now but will still develop. The 1985 was a tamer and more elegant wine, that is probably at its best now. Both 1986 and 1987 have excellent cultivar nose, nice flavour and a soft feel in the mouth. Overall, the 1987 is a better wine and is ageing well. The 1988 is a clearer character wine, soft in the mouth, and has developed well into 1993. The 1989 contains some Merlot, making it very easy drinking, and with its 14% alcohol will no doubt develop well. The 1990 looks equally good and will develop over another three to four years.

74 ★★★★ past its best, still enjoyable. 76 ★★★★★ ready. 80 ★★★★ ready. 82 ★★★ ready. 83 ★★★★ ready. 84 ★★★★ ready. 85 ★★★ ready. 86 ★★★(★) ready, will still improve. 87 ★★★★ ready, still improve. 88 ★★★(★) ready, will still develop. 89 ★★★(★) ready, will still develop. 90 ★★★(★) ready, will still develop.

Diemersdal Shiraz ★★★ B

This wine is available in 500 ml screw-top bottles and from the 1989 vintage. It is well wooded wine with good potential.

Die Krans Shiraz ★★★ C

The first release from the 1989 vintage has a range of pleasant aromas and full flavour, and is a very good first attempt. The 1990 is full of youthful zest and backed by good oak. It has potential to develop. As the vines age, the resulting wines will probably be even better.

Douglas Green Shiraz ★★★ C

The 1981 vintage was the first release of this wine and carried Superior certification. It had full flavour, was soft on the palate, but lacked in finish. Those in the 750 ml bottles are now past their best. The 1981 magnums carry Superior certification and are very drinkable now. After a long break a very good 1984 was released, also with Superior certification, followed by a good, old-style 1986. The 1987 has more defined nose and is considered a finer wine. The 1988 is in the new bottle and label, and has fair cultivar character. The 1989 is a bit dull, but has the potential to develop.

Fairview Reserve Shiraz ★★★★ B/C

The first release from the 1987 vintage is a super, full-flavoured and fruity wine that is developing with considerable interest. There was no 1988. The 1989 is a decidedly easy wine to drink, yet is packed with deep, rich flavours. It certainly is under-priced. The 1990 is particularly fine wine.

87 ★★★★ ready, will still improve. 88 no release. 89 ★★★★ ready, will still develop. 90 ★★★★ ready, will still develop.

Fairview Shiraz ★★★(★) D

The early wines were full of flavour and heavy in character, and used to be consistent carriers of Superior certification. This cellar now produces regular class winners at the Paarl Wine Show. Latest bottlings lack the big fullness of earlier wines. The 1982 is an excellent wine and has developed beautifully over 10 years. The 1983 is less attractive but has developed in the bottle. The 1984, 1985 and 1986 are good wines but lack the richness of earlier vintages. The 1987 is soft, full-flavoured, and one of the best of recent releases. The 1988 is medium-bodied wine and the 1990 is a super wine with very good berry character and good wood.

74 ★★★★ drink. 75 ★★★ drink. 76 ★★★★ drink. 77 ★★★ drink. 78 ★★★★ ready. 79 ★★★ past its best. 80 ★★★★ ready. 81 ★★★ ready. 82 ★★★★ ready. 83 ★★★ ready. 84 ★★★★ ready. 85 ★★★ ready. 86 ★★★ ready. 87 ★★★ ready, will still improve. 88 ready, will still develop. 90 ready, will still develop.

Fleur Du Cap Shiraz (Bergkelder) ★★★(★) D

A good, rich red wine with a noticeable Shiraz aroma and taste. In the older Fleur Du Cap wines these characteristics tended to dissipate with time, leaving a fairly robust wine with a spicy aftertaste. More recent vintages, particularly the 1978, are better balanced and have clearer cultivar character. They all improve with a few years in the bottle. The 1980 vintage is excellent and carries Superior certification. The 1981 was a lighter wine and needs to be consumed now. The 1985 was not released. By far the best is the 1986 which is a big, full-flavoured, mouth-filling wine that drinks very well now. The 1987 and 1988 are both clean in style and backed with good wood. The 1989 continues the style.

80 ★★★★ ready. 81 ★★★ past its best, still enjoyable. 85 no release. 86 ★★★★ ready. 87 ★★★★ ready, will still develop. 88 ★★★(★) ready, will still develop. 89 ★★★(★) ready, will still develop.

Groot Constantia Shiraz ★★★★ C

In the 1970s and early 1980s the Shiraz was usually Groot Constantia's best wine and consistently one of South Africa's better Shirazes – evidence that many of the country's finest reds come from the cooler growing areas. From the later 1980s the Shiraz is still very good, but the Estate is producing other excellent reds. The wines usually age well. The 1974 is truly excellent, showing the use of new wood, and should develop with great benefit in the bottle. The 1983 is a big, full, rather coarse wine, but is softening in the bottle. The 1986 is a deep, full wine which is developing very well in the bottle and was the best of the 1980s until the 1987, which is a very good wine with lots of depth and good mouth-filling qualities. The 1988 continues the style; the 1989 is as good as the 1987.

73 ★★★★ ready. 74 ★★★★ ready. 82 ★★★★ ready. 83 ★★★(★) ready. 84 ★★★★(★) ready. 85 ★★★★ ready, will still develop. 86 ★★★★(★) ready, will still improve. 87 ★★★★(★) ready, will still develop. 88 ★★★★ not ready, age further. 89 ★★★★(★) not ready, age further.

Hartenberg Shiraz ★★★★ E

The first release was a very good wine from the 1979 vintage. It was full of cultivar character and is still developing. The 1980 is even better. The 1981 reflects the characteristics normally associated with Shiraz and is a fine wine which drank well when released. It has developed beautifully and is super now. The 1982 maintains this cellar's ability to produce very good quality Shiraz. The 1983 and 1984 maintain the cellar's good reputation. The 1985 does not have quite the class of previous vintages, but is very good nonetheless. It is aged in large wood for a year and only released after six years in the bottle, making very acceptable drinking then, and with enough to go for a few more years. The 1986 has massive 14% alcohol but lots of fine character. The 1987 takes a different direction, having been given some small wood, and will need time to develop.

79 ★★★★ ready. 80 ★★★★ ready. 81 ★★★★ ready. 82 ★★★★ ready. 83 ★★★★ ready. 84 ★★★★ ready, will still improve. 85 ★★★(★) ready, will still develop. 86 ★★★★ not ready, allow to develop. 87 ★★★(★) not ready, allow to develop.

Klawer Co-op Shiraz ★★ A

This is the best red wine from this cellar and one which develops surprisingly well over four years or so. It is a regular class winner at local shows, with the 1982 receiving gold at the SA Wine Show. The 1984 developed splendidly and was at its best after six years. The 1985 is also showing pleasing development. The next release is from the 1991 vintage and is a much fuller wine.

Klein Constantia Shiraz ★★★★ D

The first release of a Shiraz from this Estate was from the 1986 vintage. It is a big, complex wine that will age with benefit. The 1987 is a beautiful, deep-flavoured wine with great elegance. Cellar samples of the 1988 show a lighter and more elegant style, and very much Cape-modern. Sensational now, these wines will be tremendous in the mid-1990s.

KWV Shiraz ★★★ (no price available)

One of the KWV's best natural wines, this Shiraz usually carried Superior certification and is made in the traditional style. It is at its best after about five to six years.

La Motte Shiraz ★★★★ D

The 1985 vintage provided the first release from this cellar. A lovely wine full of individual character, it has lots of aroma and full, distinctive flavour. The 1986 is a beautiful, deep, intense wine of the modern-style Cape Shirazes, and will age with great benefit. The 1987 continues the good quality and clean style, with the 1988 being one of the Cape's best. A super, complex wine full of character and flavour.

85 ★★★★ excellent to drink now. 86 ★★★★ ready, lots of development to go. 87 ★★★★ ready, will still develop. 88 ★★★★★ not ready, age further.

Landskroon Shiraz ★★★★ C

This is an award-winning wine with more character than most Cape Shiraz wines and, although easy to drink when young, it will develop and soften considerably in the bottle. The 1978 vintage was outstanding and all those since have been very good. However, I believe everything up to and including 1981 has passed its best. The 1982 is drinking very well in 1992. The 1983 is more advanced. The next vintage bottled was the 1987, which is super wine and developing well. The 1988 is full of flavour and, as drinkable as it is now, will probably peak in the mid-1990s. The 1989 is a little subdued and will probably develop with a few more years. It is remarkable value for money. The 1990 is fine wine with good berry flavours and one of the best produced.

78 ★★★ drink. 79 ★★★ drink. 81 ★★★ drink. 82 ★★★★ ready. 83 ★★★(★) ready. 87 ★★★★ ready. 88 ★★★★ ready, will still develop. 89 ★★★(★) ready, will still develop. 90 ★★★★ not ready, will still develop.

Lievland Shiraz ★★★★ D

The Estate's first attempt was the 1983 vintage, and the result was a very good, light-bodied wine with fine Shiraz character that developed well over eight to ten years. The 1985 is a good, wood-aged, easy-drinking wine which has developed very well. The 1986 is bigger and fuller, while the 1987 is full of flavour. It is a more elegant wine of medium body and more or less the style set for this cellar. The 1988 is softer and almost sweetish, but is equally full of flavour. It was chosen by the Alphen Wine of the Month Club as the most recommended wine in the Shiraz category. The 1989 continues in the exciting style developed over the years. The 1990 is full of fruit and spice and contains a touch of Merlot to give even greater complexity.

85 ★★★ ready. 86 ★★★(★) ready. 87 ★★★(★) ready, will still improve. 88 ★★★★ ready, will still improve. 89 ★★★★ ready, will still improve. 90 ★★★★(★) not ready, allow to develop.

L'Ormarins Shiraz ★★★★ F

The 1983, the first release, is a medium-bodied, lighter-type, yet full-flavoured Shiraz. It was launched late in 1988 in very small quantities and is retailing at a very high price. The 1984 is bold yet elegant and full of flavour; it is developing very well. The 1986 is an elegant, well-oaked wine with good depth of flavour and a soft feel in the mouth. The 1987 is softer than usual but good. The 1988 is a big wine for long keeping.

83 ★★★★ ready. 84 ★★★★ ready, will develop. 86 ★★★★ ready, will develop. 87 ★★★★ ready, will develop. 88 ★★★★ ready, will still develop.

Meerendal Shiraz ★★★(★) D

This medium-bodied dry wine develops remarkable smoothness with ageing. It has performed consistently well over the years, its own cellar character blending well with that of the varietal character. The Meerendal Shiraz (and the Pinotage) won gold medals at the 1982 International Wine and Spirit Competition in the UK. The 1980 vintage was out of character, but the 1981 is as good as ever. Later releases were certified Superior. The 1982 was a little dull at first but developed well with time. There is a large gap in the vintages, with the next release being the 1987: a big, full-flavoured wine that has a very different character. It has a strange, uncharacteristic nose but a nice flavour. It is rich, full wine that will need time to develop.

81 ★★★★ ready. 82 ★★★ ready. 83, 84, 85, 86 no release. 87 ★★(★) not ready, age further. 88 no release. 89 ★★★ not ready, age further.

Middelvlei Shiraz ★★★ C

The first release from the 1988 vintage is a very good, well-made wine, full of cultivar character. The 1989 is a deep, full wine with good fruit and wood. It will need time to develop.

88 ★★★ ready, will still develop. 89 ★★★(★) not ready, age further.

Muratie Shiraz ★★★ B

Released from the 1990 vintage comes a youthful, full, fruity wine which should develop over a few years. The 1991 is developing well, while the 1992 has had a quiet start. It is good and rich and will develop well.

Nederburg Shiraz ★★★★(★) C

The Nederburg Shiraz wines are expansive, with deep flavours which develop exceedingly well over eight or more years. To date, only the 1974, 1975, 1976, 1977, 1978, 1982 and 1984 vintages have been released, and then, only at annual Nederburg Auctions.

74 ★★★★(★) ready. 75 ★★★★ past its best, still enjoyable. 76 ★★★★(★) ready. 77 ★★★★ ready. 78 ★★★★(★) ready. 79, 80, 81 no release. 82 ★★★★(★) ready. 83 no release. 84 ★★★★(★) ready.

Oude Nektar Shiraz ★★★ C

The 1983 was a full-bodied wine with good Shiraz character. The 1984 has good wood backing the cultivar character and has developed well. The fullish 1985 has good wood and attractive flavour, while the 1986 is lighter and the cultivar smokiness is nearly lost in the woodiness. The 1987 is a nice wine and is drinking well now.

Pick 'n Pay Shiraz ★★★★ C

The 1987 comes from Simonsig, and a combination of a good red wine vintage and a year in oak has given it intense flavour concentration. It is developing beautifully and is well worth seeking out as one of the best Shirazes available.

Riebeek Co-op Shiraz ★★(★) A

This is a full-flavoured Shiraz. The 1982, 1986 and 1988 vintages have been released, and the last two are developing with benefit. The 1989 vintage is fully wooded, but the fruit should develop given a bit of time in the bottle.

Rooiberg Co-op Shiraz ★★★ C

The first release was from the 1985 vintage which is a well-wooded wine, with a small amount of Souzão giving added complexity and a greater depth of colour. It bottle-aged with interest. The 1986 was better and also developed well. The 1987 is a big wine, but lacks the attractiveness of the two earlier vintages. It will probably develop with time. The 1988 and 1989 are robust wines with interesting flavours. The 1990 is the best release to date and will age with benefit.

85 ★★★ drink. 86 ★★★(★) ready. 87 ★★(★) ready, will still develop. 88 ★★★ ready, will still develop. 89 ★★★ not ready, age further. 90 ★★★(★) not ready, age further.

Rust-en-Vrede Shiraz ★★★★ E/F

The 1979 vintage was an outstanding wine with full flavour and has developed well in the bottle. The 1982 is a great wine which, as it ages, deserves a full five stars. Ironically, the Wine and Spirit Board initially would not award it a Superior rating. The 1983 is a lighter wine and it developed beautifully over five years. The 1984 is good but not as flavourful. The 1985 is a beautiful wine, full of fine flavour and is ageing with great benefit. The 1986 is a lovely, big, tasty wine and the 1987 and 1988 are big, bold and full-flavoured.

79 ★★★★ ready. 80 ★★★★ ready. 81 ★★★★ ready. 82 ★★★★★ ready, will still improve. 83 ★★★★ ready. 84 ★★★★ ready. 85 ★★★★(★) ready, will still improve. 86 ★★★★ ready, will still improve. 87 ★★★(★) not ready, age further. 88 ★★★★ not ready, age further.

Saxenberg Private Collection Shiraz ★★★ C

From the 1990 vintage comes a rich, fruity, pleasing wine. The 1991 is more rounded and better balanced.

Simonsig Shiraz ★★★★ D

The vintages of the late 1970s were all full-bodied, deep, red wines with fine aroma, and aged very well. The early wines of the 1980s are better and lighter, with greater finesse – the 1982 being fuller in all respects and deserving four stars. It has developed well and is probably at its best now. The 1984 is very good and backed by good wood. It was selected by SAA as one of its Wines of the Month. The 1985 is a little out of character, but the 1986 is similar to the 1984. Drink the 1985 before the 1984 and 1986. The 1984, 1986 and the 1987 make this wine one of the best of the modern Cape Shirazes. The 1987 is a deep, intense wine with good soft oak in the background. The 1988 and 1989 show fine quality with lots of character, and are easy, early-drinking wines. The 1989 is developing beautifully.

80 ★★★ ready. 81 ★★★ ready. 82 ★★★★ ready. 83 ★★★ ready. 84 ★★★★ ready, will still improve. 85 ★★★ ready. 86 ★★★★ ready, will still improve. 87 ★★★★ ready, will still improve. 88 ★★★★ ready, will still develop. 89 ★★★★ ready, will still develop.

Simonsvlei Co-op Shiraz ★★★(★) C

These are good value, good quality wines. The vintages of the 1980s are worth keeping for five to eight years. The 1987, 1988 and 1989 are very satisfying wines.

Spier Shiraz ★★★ D

Although the cellar does not produce a Shiraz with every vintage, the maiden vintage of 1976 was a good one. The 1981 vintage has developed well, while the medium-bodied 1984 has good cultivar nose and flavour backed by good wood. It drinks well now. The 1986 is a fuller wine that needs a few more years in the bottle. The 1987 is a lighter-styled, fruity wine. No 1988 was released, but the 1989 is fuller-bodied wine.

Springlands Shiraz (Drop Inn) ★★★ B

A pleasant, well-made dry wine with smokey Shiraz character. It will benefit from a few years in the bottle.

Stellenzicht Shiraz ★★★(★) D

The first release, from 1989, has lots of wood behind the fruit and should develop with benefit.

Swartland Co-op Shiraz ★★ C

This is not produced every vintage but, when available, it is a full-bodied dry wine with the kind of nose described as smokey. The 1989 is developing well in the bottle. The 1991 is a big, full wine with some wood, and a good improvement.

Uitkyk Shiraz ★★★(★) D

The wines of Uitkyk are marketed by Bergkelder and their decision to discontinue this label in 1973 was a sad one. The 1973 Uitkyk Shiraz, in 375 ml bottles, was memorable: smooth, luscious, full-flavoured and, after eight or nine years, a superb wine. Consider yourself fortunate if you managed to track down a bottle or two. Fortunately, Uitkyk Shiraz was reintroduced with a fine wine from the 1981 vintage that has developed well. The next release is from the 1985 vintage, has distinct cultivar character, and is ready for drinking. The 1986 is a four-star wine in the newer Cape style, with berry rather than smokey flavours, and good wood backing. This is fine wine and is developing well.

Van Loveren Dry Red ★★★ B

The wine labelled Dry Red was 100% Shiraz with smokey character and a bit of wood. It was a robust wine that developed well over a few years. It is no longer produced.

Vergenoegd Shiraz ★★★★ C

First released on the open market in 1978, this attractive, deep red wine had the character to develop well with time, peaking in about 1985/7. Subsequent vintages have been very good. The 1982 has developed beautifully. The 1983 is lighter, in keeping with the vintage, and very different to the usual Vergenoegd Shiraz. It is a superb wine all the same but now needs drinking. The 1984 is developing a unique nose as it ages. The 1985 has the kind of cultivar character that tends towards leathery rather than smokey, which is also a characteristic of the 1986. The 1987 is a Shiraz in the old style: full leathery character and a soft, pleasing drink, but with enough tannin to develop. The 1988 shows good fruit and is soft in the mouth, and the 1989 has good old-fashioned character.

85 ★★★(★) ready, will still improve. 86 ★★★(★) ready, will still improve. 87 ★★★(★) ready, will still develop. 88 ★★★(★) needs time. 89 ★★★(★) not ready, age further.

Welmoed Légende Shiraz ★★★ C

This is the best of the cellar's reds: big and bold, with every potential to age well over the years, which it needs in order to soften. The 1984 and 1985 have not been wood-aged and show good bottle development. The 1987 is well aged in large old wood, and on release makes enjoyable drinking. The 1989 is the best release to date and good value for money.

Woolworths Shiraz ★★★ B

This wine is produced by Fairview. The 1983 and 1984 are good examples of the cultivar and are both developing well in the bottle. The 1986 is a big, alcoholic wine that should age well. The 1987 and 1989 are super wines with deep full flavours and lots of alcohol. They will develop well with time and are well worth laying down.

*86 ★★★ ready, will still develop. 87 ★★★★ ready, will still develop.
89 ★★★★ not ready, allow to develop further.*

Zandvliet Shiraz ★★★(★) D

The 1975 was apparently released only for export, but occasionally a few bottles found their way to local tastings and were considered very good. The 1976 vintage was released with a fanfare of publicity. It had excellent cultivar character, was light and fruity, soft to taste and so palatable that I wondered how well it would keep. In fact, it aged very well and after six years was beautifully soft and mellow. Floods prevented the release of a 1981 vintage, but the 1982 was acclaimed as the best ever and carried Superior certification. I believe the 1985 was better. The 1983 and 1984 are very light and probably past their best now. The 1986 is better and the 1987 better still – a lighter, more elegant wine. The 1989 continued with the same style. The next release will be from the 1990 vintage.

75 ★★★ past its best, still enjoyable. 76 ★★★★ past its best, still enjoyable. 77 ★★★ past its best. 78 ★★★★ past its best. 79 ★★★ past its best, still enjoyable. 80 ★★★ ready. 81 no release. 82 ★★★ ready. 83 ★★★★, drink up. 84 ★★★ drink up. 85 ★★★(★) ready. 86 ★★★★ ready, will still improve. 87 ★★★★ ready, will still develop. 88 no release. 89 ★★★★ ready, will still develop.

Zevenwacht Shiraz ★★★ C

The Shiraz from this cellar is usually a big, bold, Porty-type wine that develops well. The 1988 is a departure in style: a super, well-flavoured wine with all the traditional descriptions of leathery, peppery and smokey, and worthy of four stars.

Zonnebloem Shiraz (SFW) ★★★★ D

The 1974 vintage was an elegant, soft Shiraz with a very interesting character – one which developed beautifully in the bottle and is still showing magnificently in 1993. The full-bodied 1975 is soft, smooth, and voluptuous. It has developed with age into a really lovely wine. The 1976 vintage is also an excellent wine which is evolving a complexity seldom found in South African products. The 1978 and 1980 both need to be drunk now. The 1979 is excellent and lighter bodied than usual, but now at its peak. The 1981 is also very good now and, although the 1982 was a slow starter, it is developing great character in 1993. Little did I know last year when writing this that this wine would win my trophy – over all the fancied Cabernets and Bordeaux blends – at the International Wine and Spirit Competition in Britain for the best South African Red entered. This is proof of just how good this wine is. The 1983 is a textbook example of how a Shiraz should be made. Light and full of character, this is a beautiful wine which is also about at its best now. The 1984 is a bigger, bolder wine. The 1978, 1979 and 1980 vintages, which are available in magnums, were all drinking well in 1992. The 1985 is typical of the vintage and is a great wine. The 1986 is another lovely wine, while the 1987 is a little disappointing, but it should develop well. The 1988 is back on track, as is the 1989.

74 ★★★★★ *ready.* 75 ★★★★ *past its best, still enjoyable.* 76 ★★★★★ *ready.* 78 ★★★★ *ready.* 79 ★★★ *ready.* 80 ★★★★ *ready.* 81 ★★★★★ *ready.* 82 ★★★★★ *ready.* 83 ★★★★★ *ready.* 84 ★★★★ *ready, will still improve.* 85 ★★★★(★) *ready, will age further.* 86 ★★★★ *ready, will still improve.* 87 ★★★ *ready, will still improve.* 88 ★★★★ *not ready, will improve.* 89 ★★★★ *not ready, age further.*

TINTA BAROCCA

Allesverloren Tinta Barocca ★★★(★) C

Like most of the wines from this Estate, the Tinta Barocca is usually full-bodied and powerful, and requires time to mellow. The 1972 vintage was exceptional and in 1988 was amazing to drink. This just goes to show that these wines can age well over 10 to 15 years. The 1978 was not certified Superior, but 10 years later it developed into a super wine. The 1980 is big and bold, like the 1978, but the 1981 is much lighter. The 1982 is very different, aged in new wood and giving an unusually fine wine under the label. The 1983 is somewhat subdued and not up to the cellar's usual standard. There is a gap in vintages with the next one from 1986. It is big and full like the 1980, 1987 and 1988. The 1989 is an easier drinking wine at its release with fine fruit and good wood.

80 ★★★★ ready. 81 ★★★(★) ready. 82 ★★★★ ready. 83 ★★★ ready. 84 no release. 85 no release. 86 ★★★★ ready, will still improve. 87 ★★★(★) ready, age further. 88 ★★★(★) not ready, age further. 89 ★★★(★) ready, will still develop.

Die Krans Tinta Barocca ★★(★) C

This was the cellar's best offering but it was discontinued for a while after the 1979 vintage, which has developed with interest. The next release was the 1986 and is a bit disappointing. The 1987 is a pleasant wine and 1988 shows good wood. The 1989 and the 1990 are both much better wines and will develop well. Both have spent five months in oak.

Goue Vallei Tinta Barocca (Citrusdal Co-op) ★★ A

This is a full-bodied wine with the 1984 having a colossal 15% alcohol! The 1986 has good wood to back the full fruit. The 1987 had flowery, fruity, attractive character with nice wood, and has developed well into 1993. There was no release from the 1988. The 1989 is developing well and 1990 is tamed by some new oak ageing.

Mamreweg Co-op Tinta Barocca ★★ A

The first release, the 1986, showed good character, but the 1987 was very light and ready for early consumption. The 1988 and 1989 releases were pleasant, easy-drinking wines, and the 1991 and 1992 continue in the same style.

Onverwacht Tinta Barocca ★★★ B

As other producers drop the use of this cultivar for dry red wine, this cellar is making their best effort with it. The first release from 1989 was tough and tannic, but it is developing well and still available at the cellar. The 1990 had good berry flavours and new French oak backing that added an extra dimension. The 1991 is the best yet, with good layers of fruit flavours – plum, cherry and vanilla. It will drink well earlier than some of the previous vintages.

Oude Libertas Tinta Barocca (SFW) ★★★(★) B

This was the first South African label to carry the name Tinta Barocca. Though discontinued, it was popular and odd bottles are still to be found in many cellars. It was a blend and therefore better balanced than most other Tinta Baroccas. A fairly hefty wine, well-wooded, rich and mellow, it aged with benefit for eight or more years. It is a great pity that it is no longer made.

Riebeeck Co-op Tinta Barocca ★★(★) B

Despite earlier comments, the 1988 is developing well in 1993, and the 1987, which was a lesser wine, drinks well now.

Roodezandt Co-op Tinta Barocca ★★ B

This is a medium-bodied wine that has varied considerably and should be consumed in its youth. There is a gap from the 1986 vintage until the release of the unwooded 1990 which has 5% Cabernet. It is a fairly full-bodied yet somewhat plain wine. The next release, from 1991, is 100% Tinta Barocca.

Rust-en-Vrede Tinta Barocca ★★★(★) C

This is a wine of great appeal and with an excellent record in its short show history. It has good cultivar character which blossoms at an early age to make easy, rewarding drinking. It has improved with each vintage. The 1982 is delightful now and shows a finesse not found in other Tinta Baroccas. The 1983 is lighter and was a gold medal winner at the Stellenbosch show. As the 1984 has been well wood-aged, much of the cultivar character has been lost; nevertheless it is an attractive wine. The 1985 is a thinnish wine but rated Superior. The 1986 is a lot like the 1982, deep, rich and full, and could be confused with Cabernet. (It had 25% Merlot blended into it.) The 1988 is a big, earthy wine, also with over 20% Merlot, making a most attractive, good-flavoured winter wine. This was the first Tinta Barocca selected by SAA. The 1989 continues the good drinking style. The 1986, drunk in early 1992, was in peak condition. The 1990 is an early-drinking wine at a very fair price and really good value for money.

Swartland Co-op Tinta Barocca ★★ C

The 1986 and the 1988 vintages were big, full wines, but the 1987 was very light and a bit disappointing. The 1989 and those of the early 1990s are back to the regular style.

Vergenoegd Tinta Barocca ★★★ B

This is an excellent example of this variety and an easy, early-drinking wine. The 1983 has strong nose and flavour, while the 1984 has delightful character. The 1985 is lighter wine, while the 1986 is more in the traditional style of this Estate. The 1987 has strong varietal character and should age well. The 1988 is in line with the Estate's good, consistent style, as is the 1989. With regret, this wine is no longer being produced. The grapes are now being used solely for the production of Port.

ZINFANDEL

Bertrams Zinfandel ★★★(★) E

An interesting speciality from Bertrams. Usually medium-bodied and well-wooded with reasonable acid, it drinks well within three to four years. The 1984 was by far the best in the old style. The 1985 is a bit weak in character, but the 1986 is a lovely wine, full of berry fruit, and has developed well. The 1987 is a complete departure, having had some time in new French oak, as has the 1988, which is a delightful wine with fuller fruit.

Blaauwklippen Zinfandel ★★★(★) E

This Estate is famous for its Zinfandel. The 1980 vintage won the first Diners Club Award in 1981 and is a regular choice of the Wine of the Month Club and for SAA. There was no 1981, but the 1982 and 1984 have been very good. They are high-acid, medium-bodied, fruity wines that have aged well. These wines were made by Walter Finlayson, who is considered to be the father of Zinfandel in the Cape. The 1983 is lighter, in keeping with the vintage, yet has very good berry character. The 1985 and 1987 both have good fruit backed by good wood. The 1988 is a lovely, berry-flavoured wine with spicy side-tones and worthy of four stars. The 1989 is magnificent, masculine wine with an alcohol content exceeding 14% – and all the fruit and flavour to go with it. This is well-balanced, well-wooded wine that will develop with great benefit. The 1990 is as good as ever with full fruit and elegant spice.

Hartenberg Zinfandel ★★★ C

A light-bodied, full, fruity wine. The first vintage was the 1981, from vines originally planted by Walter Finlayson. The 1982 is full and fruity and has developed well. The 1983 was not up to standard but the 1984 is a good, easy-drinking wine. The 1985 and the 1988 vintages are delightful, lively wines, while the 1989 is slightly wooded, adding extra dimension to the wine.

Welmoed Co-op Zinfandel ★★ C

The first release, from the 1986 vintage, was lacking in cultivar character, but the 1988 and 1989 are much better wines with good cultivar character and a soft taste for early drinking. The 1990 is a further improvement and may mellow with a few years in the bottle.

Sweet Red Wines

Calitzdorp Co-op Semi-sweet Red ★★ A
Not as sweet as the label suggests, this Pinotage-Tinta Barocca blend is a surprise to the palate all the same. It is light-bodied yet rather filling to drink. It is no longer produced.

De Helderberg Co-op De Zoete Roodt ★★★ B
This is a semi-sweet red from unusual cultivars including Carignan. It is light, easy-drinking, low-alcohol wine.

BLENDED/NON-VARIETAL DRY WHITE WINES

Altydgedacht Tygerberg Wood-aged White ★★★ B
If you want a dry white with character, this is it. The first release was a blend of 1985 Steen with 40% 1982 Steen which had been in large oak vats, previously used for ageing red wines for more than two years. This produced a full-flavoured dry wine of considerable body and good character which, by 1993, has developed most unusual flavours. The next release was a blend of 40% of this wine with the balance Steen from the 1986 vintage. This wine did not have quite the same wood of the first release, but it was still a most attractive wine. This sort of solera process produces wines which are full of character and a welcome variation to the rather stereotyped dry whites. Both wines developed well in the bottle. The third release is predominantly 1986 Steen, which has been aged for more than a year, blended with unwooded Sauvignon Blanc and Bukettraube from the 1987 vintage. The result is a very different wine which, in 1992, had deep flavour and now probably needs to be drunk. The next release is about 50% Chenin Blanc, 30% Sauvignon Blanc (that shows well) and the balance Bukettraube. This is a good, full-flavoured wine. Wines under this label are always worthwhile buys and make for very good drinking.

Avontuur Blanc de Blanc ★★ A
This is a fresh dry white, predominantly Chenin Blanc, that develops with interest in the bottle.

Avontuur Grand Vin Blanc ★★★(★) B
The first two vintages, 1987 and 1988, differed dramatically. Both are good bone-dry wines blended from Sauvignon Blanc, Chenin Blanc and Sémillon, showing lots of pleasing character. The 1987 developed very well in the bottle and was by far the more dominant wine. The 1989 wine was a pleasing product; lighter and more neutral for early consumption. The 1990 was a blend of 50/50 Sauvignon Blanc, which had four months wooding, and Sémillon. This is a coarser wine than previous vintages which has developed well over three years and now drinks with interest. It is no longer being produced.

Badsberg Co-op Tafelwyn ★★(★) A
This wine, previously off-dry but finished dry from the 1990 vintage, is made from 20% Chenin Blanc and 80% Servan Blanc. It is light, pleasant, and easy drinking.

Beaufort Blanc de Blanc (Solly Kramer) ★★ A
A refreshing, crisp dry white which is very good value for money. In the past it was blended from Cape Riesling, Sauvignon Blanc and Sémillon, but is now mainly Chenin Blanc.

Bergendal Bergen Blanc ★★★ B

A Sauvignon Blanc-based blend with Chenin Blanc and Rhine Riesling, this is a well-made, dry, fruity wine with fresh flavours. Easy drinking.

Bergsig Blanc de Blanc ★★★ B

This is a Steen-based blend with nice fruity nose and clean flavour. Introduced from 1992.

Blue Ridge Blanc (Villiera) ★★★

A big, unwooded, full-flavoured Steen and Sauvignon Blanc blend for serious drinking.

Bolandse Co-op Bon Vino ★★★ A

This very inexpensive, very quaffable, fruity dry white from Steen is sold in 500 ml screw-top, returnable bottles.

Boschendal Blanc de Blanc ★★★(★) C

This is an established, reliable label from the cellar. Previously, it was mainly Chenin Blanc and Rhine Riesling with 15% Sauvignon Blanc, but is now decidedly Sauvignon Blanc with Chardonnay, Rhine Riesling and Colombar. Good flavour and very drinkable.

Botha Co-op Vin Blanc ★★ A

A light, dry white blend of Clairette Blanche and Riesling.

Bouchard Finlayson Blanc de Mer ★★★ C

The 1991 was a blend of mainly Rhine Riesling with Pinot Gris and Gewürztraminer that underwent malolactic fermentation, giving it a softness that makes it appear not as dry as it actually is. It is lightly flavoured, with slight muscat tones and fruity finish, and drank well. The 1992 is mainly Kerner with Schonberger and Gewürztraminer, with the latter showing clearly on the nose. Very easy drinking.

Buitenverwachting Buiten Blanc ★★★(★) B/C

This is a most refreshing dry wine with attractive nose and full flavour, and drinks very easily. The blend has varied over the vintages but seems to have settled on mainly Sauvignon Blanc with lesser quantities of Rhine Riesling and Pinot Gris. It is not wooded and develops beautifully in the bottle.

Cape Selection Blanc de Blanc (Pick 'n Pay)★★(★) B

An easy drinking, fruity dry wine.

Cape Vintners Members Only Blanc de Blanc ★★★(★) B

A delicious, light, fruity dry white blended from Sauvignon Blanc, Colombar and a touch of Muscat de Frontignan which gives enticing nose. It has a dry, clean finish and makes reliable, easy drinking.

Cape Vintry Blanc de Blanc (Picardi) ★★★ B

A very drinkable, good value for money wine made by Van Loveren.

Cape Vintry Bouquet Blanc (Picardi) ★★★ B

Another good and very drinkable wine with flowery nose. Good value for money. Made by Van Loveren from Gewürztraminer and Rhine Riesling. Finished off-dry.

Casal da Serra Vinho Branca Seco (Delheim) ★★★ B

A good, crisp, dry white with appealing nose and fruity character. It drinks easily as an appetizer but also goes well with seafood.

Chant de Nuit (Nuy Co-op) ★★★★ B

This is a very good blend of Colombar and Steen, with a touch of something that produces a finely flavoured, bone-dry white wine with a most appealing pineapple nose, coming from a grape called Ferdinand de Lesseps. This variety is not accepted by the authorities and their fine wine is uncertified, hence the change of name from Nuy (a place) to Nuit, a fantasy name. Some would have you believe that Chant de Nuy sounded too much like Chardonnay for the likes of the Wine and Spirit Board. One taste and you know it is not Chardonnay. Despite its dryness, it is soft across the palate, with a good clean finish. Recent vintages are four-star quality with good, all-round character. They are best enjoyed when young and fruity. Good value for money.

Claridge Blanc du Blois ★★★(★) C

A Chenin Blanc, part of which was barrel fermented showing just what a versatile varietal this is. It is good to see newcomers doing such good things with this varietal.

Culemborg Blanc de Blanc (DGB) ★★(★) B

A pleasant, dry, fruity blend based on Steen, with quantitites of Cape Riesling and Colombar.

De Leuwen Blanc (De Leuwen Jagt) ★★★ B

A good value, dry white made mainly from Steen. The 1992 and 1993 are well-balanced wines with good, fresh finish.

Delheim Heerenwijn ★★★ B

This is an easy-drinking, well-made wine of varying blends that is always attractive, fresh and lively. It should be enjoyed when young and is excellent value for money. If stars were issued for always being satisfying, this wine would certainly be a four-star product!

De Wet Co-op Danie de Wet Blanc de Blanc ★★★ B

This is a good value, non-wooded, easy-drinking, fresh blend of Sauvignon Blanc, Chardonnay and Cape Riesling.

De Zoete Inval Blanc de Blanc ★ B

An odd, non-vintaged dry white wine that is showing lots of bottle age and needs to be drunk immediately.

De Zoete Inval Capri ★★ B

A bottle-aged dry white wine with a strange but not unpleasant herby-type character.

Die Krans Grand Vin Blanc ★★★ A

The 1991 was an intriguing blend of 20% Colombar, 30% Fernão Pires, 40% Hárslevelü and 10% Muscat d'Alexandrie. It has a fascinating fruit salad nose and made pleasant, easy drinking as a fresh young wine. The 1992 is a balanced blend of Fernão Pires and Hárslevelü.

Dieu Donne Blanc de Blanc ★★★ B

The first release from 1992 is a Rhine Riesling and Chenin Blanc blend. It is an attractive, easy-drinking wine that is not bone-dry, yet not really off-dry.

Domein Doornkraal Serenade Droog ★★(★) A

This is a multiple blend in which Sauvignon Blanc shows, plus lots of Muscat and other fruity flavours, and is best enjoyed young.

Douglas Green Blanc de Blanc (DGB) ★★ B

A pleasant, clean, fresh, non-vintaged wine, from Steen. Pretty pack.

Douglas Green St Vincent (DGB) ★★ B

A non-vintaged, dry, white vin ordinaire of the 'Saint' series which also forms part of the new range.

Du Toitskloof Co-op Blanc de Blanc ★★★ B

The blend has varied over the vintages. The 1991 was all Steen with the 1992 being 50/50 Steen and Colombar. It has good nose, lots of fruit, nice flavours and a clean finish.

Du Toitskloof Co-op Vino Uno Secco ★★(★) A

This is a dry white wine from Steen in 500 ml screw-top bottles. It makes for easy-drinking.

Edward Snell Blanc de Blanc ★★★ B

This is a non-vintaged, dry white wine. The blend may vary, but the quality is constant.

Eersterivier-Valleise Co-op Le Foyer Dry White ★★(★) A

A good-tasting blend of Steen and Sauvignon Blanc, which is available in 500 ml screw-top bottles.

Eersterivier-Valleise Kelder Vin Blanc ★★★ B

The blend varies but is always reliable and fruity with no variety dominating. It has a crisp dry finish and is best enjoyed young.

Eikendal Blanc de Blanc ★★★ B

This Blanc de Blanc has developed vintage by vintage into a most attractive, fresh, fruity wine that is best enjoyed in its youth. It comprises mainly Steen, with about 25% Sauvignon Blanc.

Fairview Charles Gerard ★★★ B

The nineties are big, unwooded Sauvignon Blanc-Chenin Blanc blends with a touch of Pinot Gris, and make good, easy drinking wine.

Fairview Charles Gerard Reserve ★★★★(★) C

The 1991 is excellent oak-fermented wine. It is a blend of Sauvignon Blanc and Sémillon; big, full-flavoured wine with lots of character and good oak. The 1992 is even more complex, with distinct Chardonnay character – not that it contains any. This is a fine wine with lots of good wood and is excellent value for money.

Golden Alibama (SFW) ★★ A

This is an inexpensive dry wine, coloured 'brandy brown' with caramel. It has a surprisingly good flavour when chilled and served as an aperitif.

Goue Vallei Blanc de Blanc (Citrusdal Co-op) ★★★ B

This cellar has improved its quality and image over the past few years with labels depicting the flowers of Namaqualand. Latest vintages are unwooded 50/50 blends of Chenin Blanc and Sauvignon Blanc. It has a lovely fresh fruity nose, crisp acidity on the palate, but is finished off dry.

Goudini Co-op Gouvino ★★ A

A dry fruity blend in 500 ml returnable bottles.

Groot Constantia Blanc de Blanc ★★★ C

Originally this was an interesting dry white blend of varying varieties. It is now a three-way blend of Steen, Chardonnay and Pinot Gris, and finished off dry; an attractive, easy drinking wine.

Grünberger Blanc de Blanc (Bergkelder) ★★★(★) B

A lovely, dry, refreshing white wine with a broad flavour spectrum. Several varieties, including Sauvignon Blanc and Steen, are so harmoniously blended that no one predominates, but together they produce a wine of individual character. It comes in tall, slender, Rhine bottles rather than the old flask-shaped bottles.

Hamilton Russell Vineyards Grand Vin Blanc ★★★(★) D

The blend of this interesting wine has changed almost from vintage to vintage, as has the name. The latest is mainly Chardonnay, with 30% Sauvignon Blanc and an interesting touch of 10% Gewürztraminer. It is a most attractive, very satisfying drinking wine that has developed in the bottle. It is no longer being produced.

Hartenberg Bin 3 ★★★ C

An attractive dry white wine with a good, zesty character, available only at the farm. Although the blend varies, it is usually Steen based and can contain Sauvignon Blanc, Sémillon, Morio Muscat and Auxerrois.

Hartenberg Chatillon ★★(★) C

Hartenberg launched its new image as an Estate in 1985 with a range of seven wines. One of these, Chatillon, was a blend of Riesling, Steen and Sémillon, of which the last-named is the main component. The blend has varied with the vintage but is always full of interest and lots of flavour. The latest has Sauvignon Blanc, Auxerrois and some Chardonnay.

Haute Provence Blanc Royale ★★(★) B

This is a blend of 60% Sémillon and the balance Sauvignon Blanc. The 1989 and 1991 releases are wood-aged but the 1990 is not. The wine has good flavour, but is not the easiest drinking.

Haute Provence Grand Vin ★★(★) B

This is a product of the Franschhoek Vineyards Co-op scheme. The name often changes with the vintage but is pleasant, if unexciting, dry wine.

Helderberg Co-op Vin Blanc ★★ B

This is a medium-bodied wine with the blend varying with the vintage. It is Steen based but can contain Colombar, Sauvignon Blanc and Cape Riesling, giving a very popular pleasant dry white wine.

Hemel-en-Aarde Vin Blanc ★★★(★) B/C

This wine was interesting and of varying blends but usually contained Sauvignon Blanc, Chenin Blanc, Kerner and Rhine Riesling. It is matured on the lees, giving pleasing complexity. It is no longer produced, but some have aged with interest.

Hippo Creek Sauvignon Blanc/Chardonnay (Picardi) ★★★(★) C

The first release from the 1992 vintage is a fine blend of the two cultivars produced by Neethlingshof. It has good nose and flavours and is easy to drink. Excellent value for money.

Inglewood Blanc de Blanc (Neil Ellis Wines) ★★★(★) B

This is a good value, attractive drinking wine with nice flavours from Steen, Sauvignon Blanc and Sémillon. It is now 50/50 Sauvignon Blanc and Cape Riesling with a brisk finish.

Jonkheer Edelweiss Dry White ★★ A

This is a dry wine which, year after year, offers pleasant, easy drinking.

Kaapblanc ★★★ B

A big, full-bodied, dry white wine, with fresh fruity nose and full flavour.

Kango Co-op Premier White ★(★) A

A variable blend, usually of Sauvignon Blanc, various Rieslings and a touch of Muscat.

Klein Constantia Blanc de Blanc ★★★★ C

The first is a big, beautiful wine at 13% alcohol, produced because the Estate believed its Sauvignon Blanc from the 1987 vintage was not up to their style and standard. It was blended with Chenin Blanc to produce South Africa's best combination of these two varieties. As good as it tasted when released, it has developed into one of South Africa's greatest dry whites. I have regularly served it to many overseas fundis and they have all rated it as one of South Africa's best wines. The next release from the 1991 is a similar blend, with the lightest touch of botrytis. It is wonderful, and ready to drink now, but another two to three years keeping will well reward the development. Super wine.

Koelenhof Co-op Koelenhoffer ★★★ A

A surprisingly good, light, dry blend that has varied with the vintage and now contains Sauvignon Blanc among others. It makes easy drinking when young and fresh.

KWV Bonne Esperance Dry White ★★ (no price available)

This is a technically well-made dry wine, without character, presented in one litre bottles.

KWV Cape Floret ★★ (no price available)

An awkward, oak-aged Steen.

La Bri Blanc de La Bri ★★★ B

A product of the Franschhoek Vineyards Co-op scheme, this is a very fashionable wine blended from Sauvignon Blanc and Sémillon. The latter is given a little wood age, which adds extra dimension to the blend.

Although this wine is usually best enjoyed when young, a tasting of every vintage produced indicates that this wine definitely ages with interest. The 1991 is the best to date.

La Cotte Blanc de Blanc (Franschhoek Co-op) ★★ A

This is a pleasant new release from Sauvignon Blanc, Sémillon and Colombar, making dry and easy drinking.

La Couronne Richesse ★★★ B

The first release is a 50/50 blend of Sauvignon Blanc and wooded Sémillon, resulting in a full-flavoured, high-acid wine. Although a little aggressive when young, it has smoothed out over time. Later releases contain more Sauvignon Blanc and are better wines.

Ladismith Co-op Swartberg Aristaat ★★(★) A

An unusual, dry Steen which is very good value for money.

La Gratitude (SFW) ★★★(★) B

One of South Africa's famous old-timers, it was brought up to date with the 1985 vintage with a subtle touch of new small French oak. It has improved with each vintage and the 1991 is lovely. It has good wood showing, without masking the attractive fruitiness. The 1992 has 25% Chardonnay with wood-fermented Sauvignon Blanc and Cape Riesling. It is a good, complex, easy-drinking wine. La Gratitude has been around for too long to be fashionable, but is still far better than many 'new' wines. Very good value for money.

La Provence Cuvée Blanche ★★ B

The 1990 is 60% Sémillon, 34% Sauvignon Blanc and 6% Chardonnay. The last vintage was well-wooded in French and American oak, and is a big wine with lots of alcohol.

Landskroon Premier Blanc ★★★★ C

A big, oak-fermented Pinot Blanc with 13% alcohol and lots of citrus and vanilla tones. The slightly lighter 1991 is developing well and the 1992 will age with great benefit. Very good value for money.

Langverwacht Co-op Blanc de Blanc ★★(★) A

A good value Sauvignon Blanc/Colombar blend.

Loopspruit Grand Vin Blanc ★★(★) B

A dry white based on Steen with Muscat nose coming from Hanepoot.

Mamreweg Co-op Blanc de Blanc ★★ B

A fruity, fresh, dry white from Steen and Clairette Blanche, and a touch of Muscat. It is best enjoyed when very young.

McGregor Co-op Blanc de Blanc ★★(★) A

The 1990, 1991 and 1992 vintages are 40% each of Riesling and Colombar and 20% Sauvignon Blanc. Fresh and fruity, these wines are best enjoyed when young.

Mon Don Blanc de Blanc ★★ A

This is a nice, easy-drinking, good-value wine from Sauvignon Blanc, Colombar and Steen.

Mon Don Mystère ★★(★) B
The 1988 developed good bottle age over two years. The 1991 is light, dry and pleasant, and good value for money.

Monfort Blanc de Blanc (Solly Kramer) ★ A
A very ordinary, dry white.

Montpellier Blanc de Blanc ★★★ B
Originally a dry, light blend from Sémillon and Sauvignon Blanc, and now Colombar and Cape Riesling, making a pleasant, easy-drinking wine.

Mooiuitsig Wynkelders Dry White ★ A
An ordinary, dry white wine.

Morgenhof Blanc de Blanc ★★(★) C
No longer vintaged. A pleasant, easy-drinking Steen/Weisser Riesling.

Muratie Dry White ★★(★) B
Blended from Steen, Sémillon, Riesling and Palomino, this is a pleasant, easy-drinking dry white wine.

Naked White (Picardi) ★★(★) A
A good attempt to keep the price of wine drinking down. Not labelled (hence 'Naked') but very easy, acceptable drinking wine.

Nederburg Prelude ★★★★ C
The first release from the 1988 vintage appeared early in 1990, the launch coinciding with the 16th Nederburg Auction. It is a very good blend of Sauvignon Blanc and Chardonnay, that has been just sufficiently wood-aged to tone the components, but not to be obviously woody. Subsequent vintages have been progressively better.

Nederburg Private Bin D207 ★★★★ B
Produced for the first time in 1983, and then perfected in 1984. The 1985, 1986, 1987 and 1988 have followed with fruity nose and dry, refreshing flavour coming from predominantly Fernão Pires. It is excellent while young and fresh, yet has the ability to age well. The last vintage, the 1988, was released at the 1989 Nederburg Auction. It needs to be drunk.

Nederburg Private Bin D212 ★★★(★) C
A seldom-produced, absolutely dry wine packed with flavour. It ages exceptionally well. Nederburg Bin wines are prefixed 'S' for the Sweet Wines, 'D' for Dry Whites and 'R' for the Reds. The Bin Series is only released at the annual Nederburg Auction.

Nederburg Private Bin D218 ★★★ D
The first release of this wine was from the 1987 vintage at the 1989 Nederburg Auction. It was blended from 80% Sauvignon Blanc and 20% Pinot Blanc, and then aged for six months in small oak, giving a full, complex nose packed with fruit flavours and backed with good acidity. It is now mainly Chardonnay and Sauvignon Blanc, and aged in a combination of small and large oak. Releases of vintages 1988, 1989 and 1990, vary in quantity from 360 to 950 cases. High alcohol and good acid allow these wines to develop with distinction over four to five years.

Neethlingshof Lord Neethling Blanc ★★★ C
A light, dry, slightly wooded Chardonnay/Sauvignon Blanc blend.

Onverwacht Blanc de Blanc ★★ B
A dry Steen and Colombar blend.

Oom Tas (SFW) ★★(★) A
South Africa's original Blanc de Noir – although in those days the Blanc de Noir colour was not fashionable, so it was tinted with caramel. Its strong-looking hue belies the lightness of Oom Tas. This is a blend of Blanc de Noir, Cinsaut and dry Hanepoot which gives the attractive fruity nose. It is a well-balanced, well-made wine that makes a very good aperitif when chilled. It is South Africa's second biggest selling natural wine.

Oude Bos Droë Wit (Drop Inn) ★★★ B
This is a particularly good dry white made from Steen.

Oude Nektar Belladonna Blanc de Blanc ★★★ A
This is a pleasant dry white from Olasz Riesling. The label features the Belladonna lily which I find an odd choice as the name is connected with deadly poison!

Paddadundee (Paddagang Vignerons) ★★(★) C
This blend of Sauvignon Blanc, Chenin Blanc and Rhine Riesling gives a full-flavoured dry white wine.

Paddasang (Paddagang Vignerons) ★★(★) B
This is a dry white wine produced by the Paddagang Vignerons from grapes grown on their small vineyards and vinified at the local Co-op. The main varieties included in the blend are Sauvignon Blanc, Chenin Blanc and Colombar.

Paradyskloof White (Vriesenhof) ★★★ B
This is excellent value for a wooded dry white from mainly Pinot Blanc, Sauvignon Blanc and some Chardonnay. It is a good, complex wine with fine, long finish and oakiness.

Pick 'n Pay Grand Vin Blanc ★★★(★) B
A very well made, oak-matured white of predominantly Sauvignon Blanc. It has complex, fruity character that develops well over a year or two.

Rhebokskloof Grand Vin Blanc ★★★ C
A pleasant blend in which no single variety dominates; it is fermented and matured in French oak. It is a blend of several varieties including Sauvignon Blanc. It is crisp, clean, pleasantly fruity, and delightful when young, but ages well over two to three years. It drinks easily and well, especially in the ambience of the Estate's restaurant.

Rietrivier Co-op Blanc de Blanc ★★ A
An unusual blend of Colombar, Steen and Sauvignon Blanc, which is fruity and has lots of flavour.

Romansrivier Co-op Blanc de Blanc ★★★ B
This is a dry wine that varies with vintage, has good Sauvignon Blanc character and more recently dry Colombar, with a brisk, clean finish.

Roodezandt Co-op Blanc de Blanc ★★★ A

This is a dry blend that varies vintage by vintage, but is usually a good, full-flavoured, easy-drinking wine. It has been discontinued.

Rooiberg Co-op Selected Dry White ★★★ A

A very pleasant, clean, dry white wine, usually blended from Steen, Colombar and Sauvignon Blanc or Clairette Blanche. It is available with a screw-top.

Rovino Dry White (Romansrivier Co-op) ★★ A

This is an inexpensive dry white wine blended from Colombar, Clairette Blanche and Ferdinand de Lesseps. It has attractive nose and good flavour, and comes in 500 ml screw-top bottles.

Saxenburg Blanc de Blanc ★★★ B

A fresh, clean, dry wine containing Sauvignon Blanc and Chenin Blanc, and touched out with Gewürztraminer. It is best enjoyed young.

Simondium Co-op Vin Blanc ★(★) A

A rather plain and neutral dry white wine.

Simonsig Vin Fumé ★★★★ C

Originally a wood-aged blend based on Steen, with some Sauvignon Blanc and Kerner added, it is nowadays predominantly Sauvignon Blanc with some well-oaked Chardonnay. The 1981 vintage was called Blanc Fumé, and was the subject of some debate between Frans Malan and the authorities, who ruled that the name could only be used for wines made entirely from Sauvignon Blanc. Hence the change to Vin Fumé. Nowadays the cultivar 'Sauvignon Blanc' appears on the label. The quality continues through all the recent vintages. This wine drinks exceptionally well when very young, but has the ability to age with appeal over three to four years. It is good value for money.

Simonsvlei Co-op Blanc de Blanc ★★ B

This is an interesting blend with good, fruity nose and pleasant taste. Steen comes through but is tempered by other varieties, including Riesling, resulting in a well-balanced blend that varies with the vintage. It was previously labelled Selected Dry White.

Stellenbosch Wine Route Vin Blanc ★★★ B

A dry white blend, based on Cape Riesling, produced by Delheim in 1,5 litre returnable plastic flasks.

Stellenzicht Grand Vin Blanc ★★★★ D

This wine has developed over the vintages into a really super wine with almost enough Sauvignon Blanc to qualify for cultivar certification. The next biggest portion is Auxerrois, with touches of Chardonnay and Pinot Gris. It is very French in style, with lots of fine oak; delicious full flavour, and great when young, but with ageing potential.

Stellenzicht Heerenblanc ★★★★ B

A very well-made wine from Sauvignon Blanc and some Rhine Riesling. It is fine for drinking on release, but has the potential to develop.

Swartland Co-op Blanc de Blanc ★★★ B

A dry white wine where the blend varies with the vintage and can include Steen, Riesling, Sauvignon Blanc, Sémillon or Hárslevelü. The latest release includes Sauvignon Blanc, Sémillon and Cape Riesling and is delightful, fresh, drinking wine.

Twee Jongegezellen 39 ★★★ C

A wine with a pleasing, attractive, fruity bouquet and refreshing palate – a blend of the Estate's best cultivars in which the Muscat shows on the nose and Rieslings give good body. It now includes Chardonnay which seems to have added a degree of softness. Almost dry, it makes easy drinking. The 1991 is particularly good.

Valley Dry White (Gilbeys) ★★ A

A pleasant, light, dry white wine.

Van Loveren Blanc de Blanc ★★★ B

The blend differs with the vintage. Nowadays Sauvignon Blanc makes up the biggest percentage of the blend (40 to 50%) with the balance made up of Colombar with Hárslevelü and Muscat de Frontignan. It is very dry, good, fruity, full-flavoured wine, to be enjoyed when young, and good value for money.

Vaughan Johnson's Good Everyday Dry White ★★★ B

This is a multiple blend giving easy-drinking, fresh-flavoured wine, and is now available in stores other than Vaughan Johnson's. Good value for money wine.

Vaughan Johnson's Really Good White ★★(★)

A simple Sauvignon Blanc-based, easy-drinking wine.

Vaughan Johnson's Dry Fly Fishing Old Cape Wine ★★(★)

This is another easy drinker, with a fun name, and is based on Sémillon.

Villa Rossini Bianco (DGB) ★★ A

This is one of a spate of Italian-style wines which entered the market during 1989. It is not quite dry, flavoursome wine, sold in returnable one-litre, screw-top bottles.

Vino Roma Bianco (SFW) ★★ A

This is a dry white, Steen-based blend for easy drinking. It was previously called Roma White, but geared up and replaced to cater for the current Italian fashion.

Vredendal Co-op Classic Dry White ★★ A

This wine replaces the cellar's Premier Grand Crû and is a dry blend of Chenin Blanc, Colombar and Sauvignon Blanc.

Welmoed Co-op Blanc de Blanc ★★★ B

A powerful (13% alcohol) Sauvignon Blanc/Steen blend. It has good aroma and flavour, and has a brisk finish.

Welmoed Palatino Blanc ★★★ B

A dry white blend of Riesling and Sauvignon Blanc with good flavour and a brisk finish.

Weltevrede Blanc de White ★★★ B

The blend varies, with the latest recent releases having been of Steen and Colombar, but the latest is the most attractive. It is a combination of 25% each Sauvignon Blanc and Gewürztraminer, with 35% Rhine Riesling and 15% Colombar. It has a beautiful tropical fruit nose, is finished dry and packed with flavour.

Weltevrede Privé de Bois ★★★★ C

The first release was the 1979 Privé, with a touch of wood giving it added dimension. Since then it has developed into a well-made, dry, wooded white, usually from Colombar and Steen. It is now in a different league with 70% Sauvignon Blanc and 30% Chardonnay, and was awarded Double Gold Veritas. It is beautiful now, but will benefit with a few years in the bottle. Excellent value.

Woolworths Blanc de Blanc ★★★ B

From Villiera comes a very good Sauvignon Blanc/Chenin Blanc blend with lots of flavour and fruit. Good drinking wine.

Woolworths Le Troisieme 913W ★★★★

From Neil Ellis. The number 91 indicates the vintage; 3, the third in the range, and the W stands for white. Both are fine examples of Sauvignon Blanc and Chardonnay blends, with nearly 70% of the former. It has big alcohol, is cask-fermented, and gives fruity nose and lots of toasty flavours. It is good to drink now, but will develop well over a year or two.

Woolworths Petit Vin Dry White ★★ B

A dry white wine in 250 ml Tetrapak.

Zandwijk Klein Draken ★(★) A

A Steen-based, dry white blend.

Zevenwacht Blanc de Blanc ★★★ C

This is a blend of Riesling, Sauvignon Blanc and Steen, giving a fresh, dry, fruity wine that drinks well when young but has the potential to develop in the bottle. Good value.

Zevenwacht Vin Blanc ★★ B

This is a well-made, dry blend of Steen and Riesling at a budget price.

Zonnebloem Blanc de Blanc (SFW) ★★★(★) C

A very good, Steen-based blend with a pitch of nose and flavour seldom found in such a dry Cape wine. It contains as much as 25% Sauvignon Blanc, is vintage-dated and best enjoyed when young.

Zonnebloem Grand Soleil (SFW) ★★★★ C

Soleil, pronounced 'sollay', means sun, and this definitely is a warm-hearted wine, produced originally from Sauvignon Blanc, Chenin Blanc and Chardonnay. The first release was from the 1988 vintage and has a tinge of gold colour and attractive grassy nose, with a touch of new oak. It is now a blend of almost equal portions of Sauvignon Blanc and Chardonnay. It drinks easily and will develop with benefit with two to three years in the bottle.

BLENDED/NON-VARIETAL
OFF-DRY/SEMI-SWEET WHITE WINES

Arthur Freedberg Beau Blanc (Rebel) ★★(★) B
A Steen/Sauvignon Blanc-based, semi-sweet light wine.

Autumn Harvest Ausberger(SFW) ★★(★) A
A light, off-dry, consistent wine with fruity nose and good, clean palate.

Autumn Harvest Stein (SFW) ★★(★) A
A good, semi-sweet white wine with consistently pleasing character.

Avontuur Insensata ★★(★) B
A semi-sweet wine from mainly Steen with 10% Weisser Riesling.

Badsberg Co-op Badlese ★★ A
A very light, slightly fruity, semi-sweet, Steen-based white wine.

Beaufort Stein ★★ A
A pleasant, easy-drinking, semi-sweet white wine.

Belcher Bouquet Blanc ★★★ B
A fruity, semi-sweet Colombar/Steen blend of equal proportions.

Belcher Stein ★★★
This is not as sweet as the Bouquet Blanc, and has complex flavour.

Bellingham Blancenberger ★★★ B
This used to be a Sauvignon Blanc-based blend with Steen, which then became predominantly Sauvignon Blanc and 35% Sémillon. It makes easy, pleasant drinking, and is off dry.

Bellingham Johannisberger ★★★(★) B
This is a particularly pleasant wine with attractive Muscat nose followed by a full-flavoured, semi-sweet taste. It is a lovely wine and a long-time market leader in its category.

Blaauwklippen White Landau ★★★(★) B
This is an off-dry, delicate and consistently good blend of varieties, which has improved with time and the introduction of more interesting cultivars. It is lovely when young and fresh but also ages with interest, developing an elusive complexity. Good value for money.

Bloemendal Bloemen Blanc ★★★(★) B
The first release from this Estate, from the 1987 vintage, was an off-dry wine with good Steen character. Since then it has become a much more attractive wine: an off-dry blend of Cape and Rhine Rieslings. It is presented with a most attractive label showing a brightly-coloured waterblommetjie. Recent vintages continue to be similar blends and are just as attractive.

Bolandse Co-op Bon Vino Semi-sweet ★★ A
This is Bolandse Co-op's attempt to keep the cost of wine down. It is semi-sweet Steen, with a touch of Hanepoot, in 500 ml screw-top, returnable bottles.

Bolandse Co-op Stein ★★ A

This is a full-flavoured, semi-sweet Steen that is best when young and fresh, but has the potential to age and develop very well.

Bon Courage Bouquet Blanc ★★★(★) B

A dryish blend (although nearly 11 g/l sugar) of Colombar and Gewürztraminer which shows well on the nose. It is best enjoyed when young.

Bonfoi Ouverture ★★★ B

A semi-sweet white, wine based on Steen, with good acidic finish. It replaces the Chenin Blanc.

Bonistein (Mooiuitsig Wynkelders) ★ A

This is a fruity Steen which makes pleasant drinking.

Bonnievale Co-op Blanc de Blanc ★★(★) A

This is an off-dry white, blended from Sauvignon Blanc and Colombar, making pleasant drinking when young.

Boplaas Vin Blanc ★★ B

A nice, easy-drinking wine made from Chenin Blanc and Colombar with a touch of Muscat.

Boschendal Grand Vin Blanc ★★★(★) D

This wine was launched in the same year as the farm's 300th anniversary, in October 1985, with splendidly festive French flair. It was basically Sauvignon Blanc fermented and aged in French oak; a delicate wine with enticing nose and pleasant palate, which drank well at an early age. Nowadays it has settled at about 75 to 80% Sauvignon Blanc and the balance Rhine Riesling blend, giving a much more complex wine which improves with age. It has really become one of the Cape's consistently better white wines and proving itself by its popularity. With Boschendal's pedigree it is a pity the presentation is so similar to that of the really noble Baron d'L, the classic French wine from the Loire.

Boschendal Le Bouquet ★★★(★) C

Although technically semi-sweet, the high fruit-acid counteracts the sweetness, giving a refreshing, attractively flavoured wine with delightful nose. It shows good Gewürztraminer layered with fine Muscat. Recent vintages are very attractive wines.

Bovlei Co-op Stein ★★ A

Made from Steen and finished semi-sweet, this is a gold medal winner at regional shows.

Brandvlei Co-op Stein ★★ A

This is a Steen-based blend which offers a full-bodied, semi-sweet white wine with a powerful bouquet.

Breughel Stein (Aroma Group) ★★ A

A semi-sweet, Steen-based white wine.

Cantori Bianco (Gilbeys) ★★★ B

A very pleasant, easy-drinking wine from Cape Riesling, Sauvignon Blanc and Sémillon, which is finished off-dry.

Cape Vintners Members Only Bouquet Blanc ★★★ B

A very drinkable semi-sweet wine with a subtle touch of Muscat from the 1992 vintage.

Carnival Stein (Spar) ★★ A

A semi-sweet white blend based on Steen and Colombar.

Cederberg Kelders Dwarsrivier Weissberger ★★★ A

A much-improved, semi-sweet, white wine with good, fruity nose and pleasant flavour, for easy drinking. It comes in 500 ml screw-top bottles.

Cellar Cask Premier Semi-sweet ★★ A

An easy-drinking, semi-sweet wine, available in cork-closed bottles.

Cellar Cask Select Johannisberger ★★★ B

A Steen-based, semi-sweet wine, with fruity nose and brisk finish.

Cellar Reserve Stein (Hyperama) ★(★) A

A Steen-based, semi-sweet wine.

Chamonix Bouquet Blanc ★★★ B

This label has replaced the Vin Blanc. An off-dry wine with a most attractive guava nose, it develops well with a year or two in the bottle.

Culemborg Blanc de Blanc (DGB) ★★(★) B

A good, vintaged, value-for-money wine with pleasant flavour from Riesling/Steen with a touch of Colombar blend. It is finished off-dry.

Culemborg Stein (DGB) ★★ A

This is a good example of a clean, fruity, semi-sweet wine made from Steen. It is vintage-dated and very good value for money.

De Doorns Co-op Stein ★★ A

A strong-flavoured, semi-sweet white from Steen and Colombar.

Delheim Goldspatz Stein ★★★ B

This tasty, happy, semi-sweet white, which has good vinous character from multiple varieties is a smooth, fine flavoured wine. In a range of very ordinary Steins, this is in a class of its own. Latest vintages have clean botrytis touch. Good acid balances the sweetness. It is of a consistent and surprisingly high standard.

De Zoete Inval Demi Sec ★★ D

Like all the wines from this cellar, it is very individual. It has a somewhat aged character but is nevertheless intriguing. It is definitely different in a range of very similar semi-sweets. It is now a Chardonnay/Steen blend.

Die Krans Bouquet Blanc ★★(★) A

A blend of some two-thirds Colombar and the balance Hanepoot, crushed and fermented together to give a fresh, fruity, pleasant, off-dry wine.

Die Poort Fröhlich Stein ★★ A

A non-vintage, semi-sweet Steen, touched off with some Muscat.

Domein Doornkraal Kuierwyn ★★(★) A

This is a multiple blend that has varied dramatically over the vintages. It usually has Colombar, Clairette Blanche and Hanepoot. It is semi-sweet wine and comes in screw-top bottles.

Domein Doornkraal Serenade ★★ A

This is a slightly dry and semi-sweet multiple blend of varying sweetness.

Douglas Co-op Stein ★ B

A semi-sweet blend of Steen and Colombar.

Douglas Green St Anna Schloss (DBG) ★★ B

A non-vintaged, semi-sweet, fruity white in the range's attractive packaging; the label showing a decidedly Rhine river scene.

Douglas Green Stein (DGB) ★★★ D

A consistent, clean-flavoured semi-sweet wine that was selected for SAA in 1989. It is now in the range's attractive packaging.

Douglas Green St Morand (DGB) ★★★ B

The blend of some six white cultivars, all capable of producing good fruity noses, creates this wine's most attractive aroma. Although classed as off-dry, it tastes sweeter due to lack of good fruit acid. This non-vintaged wine should be consumed while fresh and young. It also appears in the range's attractive packaging.

Drostdy-Hof Stein Select (Bergkelder) ★★ B

A good, semi-sweet Steen with clean finish.

Edward Snell Johannisberger ★★★ B

A delightful fresh nose comes from the blend of Rhine Riesling, Gewürztraminer and Steen, which is finished semi-sweet. It is best when young.

Eersterivier-Valleise Kelder Le Foyer Semi-sweet ★★(★) A

This is a slightly muscaty, semi-sweet white in 500 ml screw-top bottles.

Eikendal Vineyards Duc de Berry Stein ★★ B

This is an easy-drinking, semi-sweet white wine.

Fairview Bouquet Fair ★★★★ C

Charles Back produced a delightful, off-dry, fruity wine from the 1990 vintage using Steen and Gewürztraminer. A winner. This is followed by a bright, muscaty-flavoured 1991. The 1992 is equally attractive but now a blend of Gewürztraminer and Bukettraube, making good-value, nice drinking wine.

Fleur Du Cap Emerald Stein (Bergkelder) ★★★ B

Many rather indifferent wines are offered under the name of Stein, but this one has class and quality: a semi-sweet, almost Late Harvest wine, full of flavour. It is vintage-dated and always very reliable.

Golden Mustang (SFW)★ A

A semi-sweet, golden wine sold in screw-top bottles.

Goue Vallei Blanc de Blanc ★★

This is an off-dry wine of equal quantities Sauvignon Blanc and Steen, making very pleasant drinking.

Graça (SFW) ★★★(★) B

This is a wine which has developed both in character and quality since its first release, and is now a market leader in its category. Slight pétillance sets off the good flavours of the Sémillon and Sauvignon Blanc blend. This is a well-made wine which allows easy drinking. Rapidly recognized as a good drinking wine, it is now one of South Africa's firm favourites.

Groot Constantia Bouquet Blanc ★★★ A
A good-value, Muscat-based, off-dry wine.

Groot Constantia Stein ★★★ A
Recent vintages are lively, semi-sweet wines, and are very pleasant when young and well-chilled. Good value for money.

Groot Eiland Co-op Honigtraube ★★ A
This is mainly Bukettraube with a touch of Ferdinand de Lesseps. It has an extra attractive nose and sweet finish.

Grünberger Stein (Bergkelder) ★★★ C
This is the original of the range and still its principal wine. It is blended from a Steen base, in a constant and definite semi-sweet style to suit the vintage, and is one of South Africa's most popular wines.

Hartenberg Bin 6 ★★★ C
This is a semi-sweet white wine, available only at the farm. A slight hint of Muscat and botrytis makes this a very pleasant, easy-drinking wine. Good value for money.

Haute Provence Larmes des Anges ★★(★) B
A semi-sweet blend of Steen and Muscat d'Alexandrie giving a very light-flavoured but pleasantly scented wine. The name means 'Angels Tears' and comes from the legend in which the angels wept tears of joy on tasting the fruits of a fine vintage!

Helderberg Co-op Vin Sucre ★★ A
A pleasant, light, semi-sweet wine; mainly Steen with Cape Riesling. It is also available in 500 ml bottles.

Honey Blossom (SFW) ★★ B
A well made, semi-sweet white wine.

Huguenot Stein ★★ A
A pleasant, semi-sweet wine with fresh finish.

Jonkerskloof Selected Stein (OK/Hyperama) ★★ A
A semi-sweet, fruity wine in five litre bottles.

Kango Co-op Herfsgoud ★★ B
A semi-sweet white wine showing fair fruit from the Colombar and Muscadel blend.

Kango Co-op Bouquet Petit ★★ B
This is a new release based on Morio Muscat, with Steen and Colombar. It is not too sweet.

Kango Co-op Xandré ★★ B
This is an off-dry wine made originally from Muscat d'Alexandrie, hence the name, but now a blend of Colombar and Muscadel. It is sold in inexpensive, screw-top bottles.

Kellerprinz Selected Stein (SFW) ★★ A
A semi-sweet, fresh and fruity Stein with good, clean flavour.

Klawer Co-op Blanc de Blanc ★★ A

An off-dry blend of half each Colombar and Sauvignon Blanc, and some Muscat Ottonel. It is light-bodied and refreshing when chilled.

Koelenhof Co-op Koelenheimer ★★(★) A

(Previously known as Koelenhof Co-op Stein.) Recent releases have been very good. Koelenheimer used to be Steen-based and touched off with Hanepoot, but is now Sauvignon Blanc, Riesling and Colombar with a touch of Hanepoot.

KWV Bonne Esperance Stein ★★ (no price available)

A semi-sweet white in one litre bottles.

Laborie Taillefert White (KWV) ★★★(★) C

This is one of a range of wines launched in 1988 by the KWV, as a tribute to the French Huguenot, Jean Taillefert, the original owner of Laborie. It is an off-dry blend based on Rhine Riesling with lots of bottle age.

La Bri La Briette ★★★ B

Introduced to celebrate La Bri's 10th anniversary. A blend of 'Rhine Riesling for fruitiness, Sémillon for smoothness and Sauvignon Blanc for richness' – or so the advert and back label say. This is a very pleasant, easy-drinking wine.

Ladismith Co-op Towerkop Stein ★ A

A pleasant, semi-sweet blend from Steen and Colombar.

Landskroon Bouquet Blanc ★★★ C

A Steen-based wine, with Morio Muscat giving a most attractive nose. It is finished off-dry and is delightful as a young wine.

Landzicht Stein ★ A

A semi-sweet blend of Chenel, Hanepoot and Colombar.

Le Pavillon Blanc (Boschendal) ★★★ (★) B

This is a good value, just off-dry, but so well balanced wine that it appears almost dry. It is a good blend of Chenin Blanc, Riesling and Chardonnay, and has an attractive fruity bouquet, good flavour and crisp, clean finish.

Les Chênes C'est La Vie ★★ B

This wine was previously labelled 'La Fleur' but one of the major merchants challenged the use of the name so Sarel van Vuuren used the French version of his exclamation, 'Well, that's life', as the new name for the wine. This off-dry white is a blend of predominantly Sémillon and the balance Sauvignon Blanc.

Lieberstein (SFW) ★★ A

This is the semi-sweet white wine which led the natural wine revolution of the mid-1960s, and still has a considerable following. When young and fresh, it is delightfully flavoured and pleasing.

Lievland Cheandrie ★★★ B

This lovely wine, with good scented nose, is not as sweet as most Steins. It has relatively low alcohol, but makes pleasant, easy drinking.

Mamreweg Co-op Stein ★★ **B**

An inexpensive, semi-sweet Stein.

Matin Soleil Vin Bouquet (Môreson) ★★ **B**

A pleasant Chenin Blanc, with nice fruity nose, making easy drinking.

Merwespont Co-op Blanc de Blanc ★★★ **A**

Off-dry Steen/Colombar blend with fruity nose, and fresh finish.

Monfort Stein (Solly Kramer) ★ **A**

A semi-sweet white with easy-drinking qualities.

Monterey Stein (Western Province Cellars) ★ **A**

A vintage-dated, sound, semi-sweet blend.

Montpellier Huiswyn ★★ **A**

A fruity, pleasant, good drinking wine with varying blends including Colombar, Sauvignon Blanc, Sémillon, Steen and Pinot Blanc.

Montpellier Suzanne Gardé ★★(★) **B**

An off-dry wine with intriguing flavour and a slight hint of Sauvignon Blanc. From 1990 onwards it is vintage dated.

Nederburg Elegance ★★★(★) **C**

The first release, from the 1987 vintage, was wine with a delightful fruity nose and off-dry taste, full of gentle Muscat flavours. It has improved over the vintages and now has good Rhine Riesling content which gives greater complexity. The slight fresh finish gives the impression of being drier than it really is. Easy-drinking wine.

Nederburg Fonternel ★★★ **B**

Its production has now ceased, but, as Fonternel ages with interest it is worth keeping the later vintages to enjoy the bottle-developed flavours. It was a pioneer of the off-dry, fruity type wine and many similar wines are now being produced by other cellars.

Nederburg Pinot Blanc ★★★ **C**

The first release from 1989 is a soft, off-dry, pleasant wine, without much cultivar character. Those of the nineties are better and drier.

Nederburg Private Bin S311 ★★★ **D**

This is wine made for sale at the Nederburg Auction, in a lovely Late Harvest style, that has aged well. With lots of tropical fruit and spices, this is a lovely drink and usually good value for money.

Nederburg Private Bin S312 ★★★★ **C**

In keeping with the 'S' series, this wine is sweet but not cloying. It has a most beautiful tropical-fruit nose and a flavour of great complexity. With a few years of bottle-ageing it evolves magnificently. It is sold only at the Nederburg Auction.

Nederburg Private Bin S333 ★★★★ **C**

Apparently the sweetest of the three 'S' Bins (they are all, in fact, of much the same sweetness), this wine has a special appeal which is due to the gentle touch of Muscat. It ages with great distinction. It is sold only at the Nederburg Auction and is an absolute delight.

Nederburg Private Bin S354 ★★★★(★) D

The first release, of the 1982 vintage, was sold at the 1985 Nederburg Auction. Since then there have been vintages 1982 through to 1990. It is a lovely, fruity blend of Weisser Riesling and Gewürztraminer, offering a wealth of sweet flavour balanced by good acid.

Nederburg Stein ★★★(★) B

This is a remarkably consistent wine which has been a favourite for many years. Its good, clean flavour and sprightly zest account for its attractiveness. Occasionally, releases have been certified Superior and the 1991 obtained Double Gold Veritas. It has enjoyed increased popularity during the last year.

Neethlingshof Neethlingshoffer ★★★(★) C

The first release from the 1988 vintage was an off-dry blend of some five cultivars, none of which shows on its own. It is now based on Rhine Riesling with some Cape Riesling and Sauvignon Blanc.

Onverwacht Bouquet Blanc ★★★ B

An attractive Steen/Colombar blend introduced from the 1991 vintage, and followed in 1992, with good fruity nose and clean finish.

Oranjerivier Wynkelders Stein ★ A

This is a well-made, well-balanced, semi-sweet Steen, which drinks well when young. Served chilled, it makes a good aperitif.

Overmeer Stein ★★ A

A well-balanced, easy-drinking, semi-sweet white wine.

Pick 'n Pay Bouquet Blanc ★★★

A lowish-alcohol, easy-drinking off-dry wine with Muscat flavours.

Pick 'n Pay Johannisberger ★★(★)

A very pleasant semi-sweet wine from Sauvignon Blanc, Steen and Weisser Riesling.

Platanna (Paddagang Vignerons) ★★ C

Produced from the small, unique vineyards surrounding the Paddagang Wine House, this is one of the range from the Paddagang Vignerons. The wines are as much fun as their labels. Platanna is a light, fruity, semi-sweet wine made from Steen.

Platteklip Off-dry White (Rebel) ★★ A

A Rebel housebrand with a pleasant Muscat character making for very easy drinking.

Platteklip Semi-sweet White (Rebel) ★★ A

A fairly ordinary, semi-sweet Steen in the Rebel housebrand range.

Porterville Co-op Blanc de Blanc ★ A

An off-dry Steen.

Ravenswood Selected Stein (Pick 'n Pay) ★(★) A

A Steen-based, semi-sweet white wine.

Rebel Stein ★ A

A fresh, semi-sweet, white wine.

Rhebokskloof Bouquet Blanc ★★★ C

An unwooded blend of Chenin Blanc and Colombar, resulting in a soft, easy-drinking, undemanding wine. It is best drunk within two years to enjoy its youthful fresh fruitiness.

Romansrivier Co-op Vin Blanc Special Reserve ★★★ A

A most unusual semi-sweet Cape wine, best enjoyed when young and slightly chilled. It develops an unusual attraction after a couple of years.

Rooiberg Co-op Selected Stein ★★★ B

A consistently good, fruity, semi-sweet Steen with clean finish. This is good value for money wine which is also available in screw-top bottles. Nice, easy-drinking wine.

Romansriver Co-op Rovino Semi-sweet White ★★ A

This is a blend of Colombar and Chenel, which is finished semi-sweet.

Royal King (SFW) B

A semi-sweet white wine which is coloured brown with caramel to meet market requirements.

Rusthof Stein (Mooiuitsig Wynkelders) ★★ A

A pleasant, semi-sweet wine blended from Steen, Colombar and Muscat, giving a much fruitier nose than most Steins.

Simonsig Mustique ★★★ B

An attractive, off-dry blend of various Muscat cultivars with a hint of botrytis. It does consistently well in wine club selections and has been an SAA selection. Good drinking.

Simonsig Sonstein ★★★ B

A slightly sweet, Stein-style wine which has some interesting vintage variations, and is always good, well made and well balanced. It appears under various private labels and deserves its popularity. Enjoy this wine well-chilled and in its youth.

Simonsvlei Co-op Stein ★★ B

This is usually a well-balanced, semi-sweet wine. Recent vintages are medium-bodied and pleasant.

Spruitdrift Stein ★★ A

A semi-sweet Steen.

Swartland Co-op Stein ★★ A

A semi-sweet white wine with good fruit.

Tasheimer Goldtröpfchen (SFW) ★★★ B

One of the first post-Second World War wines to appear in a semi-sweet style, it quickly became one of South Africa's most popular semi-sweet whites, and remains so today (although it did disappear for a while into Stellenbosch Farmers' Winery's Taskelder range). Once again marketed as an individual brand, the wine is fruity, well-balanced and surprisingly full-flavoured. Its smooth texture makes it a pleasure to drink and, when young, it has a delicate freshness and a good, clean, crisp finish. The 1987 was the first vintage-dated Tasheimer.

Twee Jongegezellen Schanderl ★★★★ C

This is an outstanding example of the art of blending. The inviting, flowery bouquet promises a sweetish wine, but instead it is crisp to taste, just off-dry, and makes excellent drinking within three years of the vintage. Made mainly from a unique red clone of Muscat de Frontignan and blended with Gewürztraminer and Weisser Riesling, it is especially delightful when young and fresh.

Twee Rivieren Selected Stein (Western Province Cellars) ★★ A

A semi-sweet wine with fresh nose and clean finish.

Uiterwyk Kromhout ★★★(★) C

Recent vintages have been very characterful, well-flavoured, semi-sweet wines with brisk finish. Despite the name, it is not wooded.

Vaalharts Co-op Overvaal Stein ★★ A

Semi-sweet and soft, this is the best wine from this cellar.

Villa Rossini Bianco (DGB) ★★ B

This is part of Douglas Green Bellingham's venture into Italian-style wines. Although finished off-dry it appears to be drier, and is best when young. It is sold in screw-top, one-litre bottles.

Valley Kaapse Keur (Gilbeys) ★★ A

A popular, off-dry, easy-drinking wine.

Valley Stein (Gilbeys) ★★ B

A good, clean, honest, semi-sweet white wine, based on Steen, which drinks very easily.

Villiera Sonnet ★★★ B

A delightful, off-dry wine based mainly on Steen with catching, fruity nose from small amounts of spicy cultivars.

Vin de Florence (Vergelegen) ★★★ C

The first release from 1992 vintage is a multiple blend of Gewürztraminer, Rhine Riesling, Sauvignon Blanc and Chenin Blanc. It has attractive nose, lots of flavour, and is soft across the palate. Pleasantly off-dry wine.

Vintner's Choice Premier Vin Blanc (Drop Inn) ★★ A

An off-dry white in the Vintner's Choice range, described as 'House Wines', it is based on Colombar.

Vintner's Choice Stein (Drop Inn) ★★ A

A semi-sweet wine from Steen with a nice flavour and little nose.

Virginia (SFW) ★★ A

South Africa's largest-selling wine, this is a Steen-based, semi-sweet blend which, when young, is considerably better than many of the more expensive products on the market.

Vredenheim Debuut Wit Tafelwyn ★★ B

An off-dry blend of Rhine Riesling, Steen and Sauvignon Blanc, with fruity nose and clean finish.

Wamakers Vallei Co-op Stein ★ A

A well-flavoured, off-dry Steen.

Wellington Wynboere Co-op Stein ★★ A

A good-value, Steen-based, semi-sweet white wine.

Witzenberg Stein Select (Bergkelder) ★ A

A very pleasant, fruity, semi-sweet wine with good grapey nose.

Woolworths Bouquet Blanc ★★★ B

Produced by Zevenwacht, this is an elegant, off-dry, white wine based on Gewürztraminer with a decided Muscat nose.

Woolworths Selected Cape White ★★(★) A

From Rooiberg comes a fruity, off-dry, white wine which drinks very well when chilled.

Woolworths Stein ★★(★) A

From Douglas Green Bellingham. This wine has an attractive nose and a pleasant, semi-sweet flavour, with enough acidity to give nice freshness when young. It is available in five litre boxes.

Yellow Label Stein (Checkers) ★★ A

A semi-sweet white wine with pleasant nose and good, fresh acidity.

Zellerhof Stein ★★ A

A pleasant, semi-sweet white wine.

Zevenwacht Bouquet Blanc ★★★ B

A lovely off-dry blend with lots of attractive tropical flavours. It usually has very good Muscat nose. It is good, off-dry, pleasant, well-made wine, that develops well in the bottle.

Zevenwacht Stein ★★(★) B

A good, light, fruity wine with Steen character. Very good drinking and good value for money.

Light Wines

Bernini Sparkling Grape Beverage (Castle Wine) ★★★ B
A delightfully 'grapey', fizzy, sweet wine with a low alcohol content (5%).

Bergsig Le Bouquet Light ★★(★) A
A lovely light wine with a slight bubble, with good Muscat nose, made from Hanepoot. It is semi-sweet and alcohol is usually only about 7%.

Cellar Cask Premier Light (Bergkelder) ★★(★) A
A pleasant, fruity, dryish white wine with low alcohol.

De Wet Co-op Pétillant Fronté ★★★ A
A pretty, light wine with delicate Muscat aromas from Muscat de Frontignan. It has good pétillance and a low alcohol content of 9%.

Drostdy-Hof Extra Light (Cape Wine) ★★★ B
An attractive, easy-drinking dry white wine with about 9,5% alcohol. The other Drostdy Hof Lights have been culled. Good value for money.

Fleur Du Cap Natural Light (Castle Wine) ★★★ B
This is probably the most consistent of the Light wines. It has good nose, nice flavour and still has an alcohol content of only 9%.

Twee Jongegezellen Light ★★★ B
A naturally produced product. TJ Light has nice fruitiness from Gewürztraminer, Muscat and other varieties, as well as good flavour, combining to promote easy drinking. The alcohol content is usually about 8%. This is consistently one of the best Light wines.

Vredendal Co-op Meisie ★★(★) A ★
A light, pleasant-tasting wine with crisp finish.

Woolworths Bianca Light ★★★ B
From Delheim. This wine is based on Muscat d'Alexandrie with Clairette Blanche and Riesling, giving very acceptable, easy-drinking wine. The alcohol content is under 10% and finished off-dry.

Woolworths Musque Light ★★★ B
From Simonsig, this wine has less than 10% alcohol and is just off-dry. It has lovely fresh Muscat scents and fresh flavour; a delightful light wine.

Woolworths Rosso Light ★★ B
From Villiera. Rosso Light has an alcohol content of less than 10%, and is made from Cinsaut, Carignan and Cabernet.

BUKETTRAUBE

Altydgedacht Bukettraube ★★★ B

This is attractive, just off-dry wine with good cultivar character. It makes easy drinking, has fresh finish, and is consistently one of the better examples of this cultivar, as evidenced by the 1992 release.

Ashton Co-op Bukettraube ★★(★) A

This is a good, semi-sweet wine with fine nose and flavour that finishes far drier than one would expect. There is a slight variation in quality, vintage by vintage.

Bolandse Co-op Bukettraube ★★★ A

This is an easy-drinking young wine, with good cultivar nose, and is finished off-dry. All releases are best when young.

Bottelary Co-op Bukettraube ★★★ B

A very pleasant, semi-sweet young wine with attractive nose and good cultivar character. Good, easy-drinking wine.

Bovlei Co-op Bukettraube ★★★ A

Since 1986, when this wine was first introduced, it has been of the same style. It is a semi-sweet white wine with fruity nose and flavour.

Cederberg Kelders Bukettraube ★★(★) B

This is a consistently attractive, semi-sweet, soft, fruity wine with good cultivar character when launched. It is best enjoyed while young.

Du Toitskloof Co-op Bukettraube ★★★(★) B

This Co-op has a reputation for producing Bukettraube which is usually semi-sweet, full of flavour, and with good, fresh finish. The 1992 is spicier than usual and very attractive.

Fairview Bukettraube ★★★ B

Lots of tropical fruit flavours, mingling with distinct Muscat, makes this semi-sweet wine nice, easy drinking.

Goue Vallei Bukettraube (Citrusdal Co-op) ★★★ B

This is one of the most improved Bukettraubes. Nowadays it is a good cultivar wine that is semi-sweet, tasty, Muscaty and easy drinking.

Huguenot Bukettraube ★★★ B

This pleasant, easy-drinking, semi-sweet wine, with soft Muscat flavour, is one of this cellar's better natural wines.

Koelenhof Co-op Bukettraube ★★(★) B

This is a pleasing, semi-sweet wine, with a nose that has more Muscat than Bukettraube.

Lievland Bukettraube ★★★ B

The 1989 is a lovely, fruity wine that has aged with benefit. It is still available, although it is no longer produced.

Lutzville Co-op Bukettraube ★★ A

This off-dry wine makes pleasant, easy drinking. The 1992 is better.

Neethlingshof Bukettraube ★★★ C

This is a fine, highly scented, semi-sweet wine, that drinks very easily, and is one of the more elegant wines from this varietal.

Nuy Co-op Bukettraube ★★★ A

This is a gold medal winner at regional and national shows and one of the better examples of this cultivar. It is just off-dry, lovely when young and fresh, yet has the ability to age over two to three years. Very pleasant drinking and good value for money.

Robertson Co-op Bukettraube ★★★(★) A

This is consistently one of the better examples of this cultivar. There may be slight variations in the vintage, but it is usually off-dry and full of fruit salad scents and flavours. It is best enjoyed when fresh and young. It is the best natural wine from this cellar and good value for money.

Rooiberg Co-op Vinkrivier Bukettraube ★★ A

This wine has varied since its first release in 1983. Recent vintages are off-dry and have attractive Muscat nose and sound flavour. For the best enjoyment, drink when young.

Simonsvlei Co-op Bukettraube ★★ B

A regular medal winner at regional shows, this wine is finished semi-sweet for bottling. Recent vintages are finished semi-sweet and have good, satisfying scents and flavours. This is wine which makes soft and easy drinking.

Spier Bukettraube ★★ B

This is a wine with a sweet, honeyed nose, and full almondy flavour. It is a very different style. There has been no recent production.

Swartland Co-op Bukettraube ★★ B

This is a semi-sweet wine, with good fruit and a Muscat nose, which makes for easy drinking.

Vredendal Co-op Bukettraube ★★(★) A

This is a semi-sweet wine with Muscat nose and a soft taste.

CHARDONNAY

Aan-de-Doorns Chardonnay ★★ B
First release from 1991 is an unwooded dry white. This is followed by an equally light '92. This is easy-drinking wine with little varietal character.

Aan de Wagenweg Chardonnay (Bergkelder) ★★★★ E
Only two releases – one from 1988 and the other from 1989 – both in small quantities. Made from grapes grown in the Durbanville district, these turned out to be very mean and lean, and lacked development. It is no longer produced.

Alphen Chardonnay ★★★ C
A good, clean, undemanding Chardonnay, with nice citrus tones and subtle oak backing, from the 1992 vintage.

Altydgedacht Chardonnay ★★★★ D
A 1991 Chardonnay follows the previously non-certified wine called Charade which has developed well in the bottle. The 1991 has enticing nose and layers of complex flavours with good oak backing. The 1992, like the 1991, is big, full, deep and buttery, with vanilla flavours. It drinks well now and has the potential to develop.

Ashton Co-op Chardonnay ★★ B
The first release from 1991 vintage has slight citrus nose and lots of wood. In early 1993 it drinks well and flavours have married better. The 1992 is a better effort and, as the vines develop, the future looks good.

Avontuur Le Chardon ★★★★ E
The 1990 and 1991 are a change in style, without the buttery fullness of the 1989. A harder, more acidic wine is now being made that will need time to soften and develop. The 1992 is fuller flavoured and a more easy-drinking wine than earlier releases.

Backsberg Chardonnay ★★★★(★)D
This cellar produces one of the Cape's best. The 1985 won the Diners Club award in 1986 for the best wooded white wine. The 1986 was a gold medal winner at the International Wine and Spirit Competition in London in 1988. The 1989 vintage seems to have settled into a fine, fruity style. The 1990 is a lovely, elegant wine with lots of citrus tones on subtle oak. The 1991 shows more vanilla. The 1992 continues the fine form.
81 ★★★ drink. 84 ★★★(★) drink. 85 ★★★★★ drink. 86 ★★★★★ ready. 87 ★★★★ ready. 88 ★★★★ ready. 89 ★★★★(★) ready, will still develop. 90 ★★★★ ready, will still develop. 91 ★★★★ ready, will still develop. 92 ★★★★ ready, will develop.

Bellingham Chardonnay ★★★ D
The 1991 was a light and fruity wine, with clean acidic finish, which needs some time to develop. The 1992 has lots of wood, some fruit and hard finish.

Bellingham Reserve Chardonnay ★★★★ **E**

An altogether different product, grown and produced at Bellingham. This is a barrel-fermented, big wine with lots of citrus and toasty flavours. The first release from the 1991 vintage is developing well. The 1992 is a more stylish wine, with good fruit and nice oak. It should develop well over a year or two.

Blaauwklippen Chardonnay ★★★ **E**

The 1981 vintage was the first release. The style has varied over the years but has always been good quality; the 1983 was perhaps better balanced, and the 1984 had admirable cultivar character backed with considerable wood. It showed very well in 1988, having developed greater complexity than any of the earlier vintages. No 1985 was bottled. The 1986 has developed into a lovely wine, but the 1988 could be the best of the 1980s. There was no 1989, but the 1990 is fine wine with buttery flavour, good oak and tones of lime, and is developing well. The 1991 is another big wine that will need time to settle. This wine is also available in 375 ml bottles. The 1992 continues the improved style.

83 ★★★ *ready. 84* ★★★*(★) ready. 85 no release. 86* ★★★★ *ready.*
87 ★★★★ *ready. 88* ★★★*(★) ready, will still improve. 89 no release.*
90 ★★★★*(★) ready, will improve. 91* ★★★*(★) not ready, allow to develop.*

Bloemendal Estate Chardonnay ★★★ **E**

The Bloemendal Chardonnay was yet another first from the 1989 vintage. It has good cultivar character, nice woody/vanilla backing, and has developed well. The 1990 has good citrus flavour backed by good toast from American oak. It will age well with 13,6% alcohol. The 1991 has good character and is developing well. There was no 1992 release.

Bon Courage Chardonnay ★★★★ **C**

The first attempt, from the 1988 vintage, was a good dry white, but it still has to show good varietal character. The 1989 is a great improvement – a soft, full-flavoured wine, with nice butter/toasty, woody background. The 1990 is a great improvement, with lovely vanilla, fruity flavour. The 1991 is barrel-fermented and has greater complexity than any of the earlier releases. The 1992 confirms this wine as one of the best in its price range. This is very good wine and very drinkable now.

Boland Co-op Chardonnay ★★(★) **C**

The first release from 1992 is well oaked but lacking fruit.

Boplaas Chardonnay ★★★ **B**

This is one of the least expensive Chardonnays, but it has pleasing character, good oak backing and is easy to drink. The 1992 is an improvement – big, full and nicely oaked.

Boschendal Chardonnay ★★★★ **E**

Released in July 1989, the first wine was from the 1986 vintage. It was disappointing and has not developed well. Subsequent vintages, however, have been a great improvement. The 1987 began to show improvement and has developed well in the bottle; the 1988 is a lovely soft, full-flavoured wine that is delicious now. The 1989 started well but hasn't developed. The 1990 continues with the high quality and elegant style, and the 1991 is a super wine – its quality confirmed by its selection for the 1993 Nederburg Auction.

87 ★★★ ready. 88 ★★★(★) ready. 89 ★★★ ready, will still develop. 90 ★★★★ not ready, allow to develop. 91 ★★★★ not ready, allow to develop. 92 ★★★★ not ready, allow to develop.

Bottelary Co-op Chardonnay ★★ B

This wine has little recognizable character but is pleasant to drink. The 1989 vintage was bottled as Blanc de Blanc, and the 1990 certified as Chardonnay. There was no release from 1991. The 1992 is better, but very woody.

Bouchard Finlayson Chardonnay ★★★★ E

A good first, from 1991 vintage, from grapes grown at Elgin. It has good fruity nose, nice toasty wood, fine clean finish, and should develop well. The 1992 is a big wine in all respects.

Bovlei Co-op Chardonnay ★★ C

A rather ordinary unwooded wine with little varietal character.

Buitenverwachting Chardonnay ★★★★ E

With a couple of vintages bottled, the cellar has now settled into a well-flavoured, good quality wine, full of cultivar flavour. It has lots of fruit, with some lemon backed by nice toasty wood, that will develop well over three to five years. The 1991 is a beautiful wine with good citrus and oak, and will develop well. The 1992 shows just as well.

Cape Vintners Members Only Chardonnay ★★★(★)D

Made by Vlottenburg. This is very good, well-oaked wine with citrus nose and vanilla flavours, from 1991 vintage. It makes good drinking now and should remain so over the next year or two.

Cathedral Cellars Chardonnay ★★★(★) (no price available)

Produced only for export. The 1990 is well-made wine with good early showing, yet appears not to be developing in the bottle. Given the best fruit from Durbanville, finest cellar conditions and best wood, one looks forward to exciting wine in the future.

Claridge Chardonnay ★★★

Barrel-fermented, long lees contact and malolactic fermentation make this first effort from the 1991 vintage very creditable. It is big, rich wine, with buttery and citrus tones backed by good oak. It was released mid-1992.

Danie de Wet Chardonnay ★★★★ D

Aromas bursting out of the tasting glass means high volatility from lots of alcohol – not a problem. This is big wine with layers of deep flavours of all kinds of citrus and vanilla, with fine oak backing, that will develop well. The 1989 was the first release, followed by an equally good 1990.

Danie de Wet Chardonnay Bateleur ★★★★ E

This is the most expensive of the four Danie de Wet Chardonnays, and of the 1990 vintage it is the smoothest, if not the most flavourful. It will need time to develop to its full potential.

Danie de Wet Chardonnay Bon Vallon ★★★★ C

An unwooded, well-priced wine with lots of good citrus and clean cultivar character. The first release from 1990 was followed by a similar 1991. It will develop well over a few years.

Danie de Wet Chardonnay Clos de Roche ★★★★ C

This wine was first wood-fermented and then spent only a short time in wood afterwards. It is made from grapes grown inside the rock-walled Bon Vallon 'Clos' dedicated to the late Hungarian viticulturalist, Desiderius Pongrácz, who gave Danie considerable aid during the early days. This is a very fruity wine, with deep citrus flavours backed by vanilla. The first release came from the 1990 vintage. The 1991 is a much fruitier and more elegant wine that is developing somewhat slower than the 1990.

Delaire Chardonnay ★★★★ E

The first release from 1987 showed that this cellar was going to be good for Chardonnay. The 1988 had good cultivar character with lemon taste and fine wood. The 1989 is a fresher style, with fuller, toffee-type taste, hints of citrus and good wood. It was easy to drink when released and has developed in the bottle with benefit. The 1990 is a lovely, full, luscious wine. With 13,5% alcohol, it is developing with benefit. The 1991 set the most style: lovely fresh nose with good citrus flavours, where lime shows the most. The 1992 is complex, concentrated and delicious. These wines will develop well over three to five years.

De Leuwen Jagt ★★★ B/C

The cellar sells two wines from the 1991 vintage – one slightly wooded (C) and the other totally unwooded (B). Both have good character but are a little light on fruit. The 1992 is a good improvement.

Delheim Chardonnay ★★★★ D

The first release from the 1988 vintage had high fruit that developed well in the bottle. The 1989 vintage is a great improvement, with full voluptuous character, good citrus flavours and buttery woody backing. It is one of the leading Chardonnays of 1989. The 1990 is far fruitier and more graceful, and is developing with benefit. The 1991 is a big wine with nice fruit and is also developing well. The 1992 is probably the best. It has beautiful fruit and is very drinkable now.

De Wetshof Chardonnay ★★★(★) D

The first release came from the 1981 vintage, although it contained a legally acceptable quantity from the 1980 harvest. It was launched with fanfare and received acclaim as a full, dry wine with very good wood tones. It certainly was excellent, but a year later seemed to have lost its majesty. The 1982 vintage is a much better wine, with a complexity of flavour derived from cultivar, cellar style and good wood. The 1983 began to show better use of wood, and the 1984 was an excellent wine with good fruit and fine wood. There has been very little of the 1985 available as it was judged the overall winner for the best wine at the Vinexpo Wine and Wine Machinery Exhibition at Bordeaux in 1987. I have missed the 1986, and the 1987 is a little lacking in flavours. Those that are there are very good. The 1988, 1989 and 1991 are considerably better wines and are far more complex.

81 ★★★ drink. 82 ★★★ drink. 83 ★★★(★) drink. 84 ★★★(★) drink. 85 ★★★(★) ready. 87 ★★★(★) ready. 88 ★★★★ ready. 89 ★★★★ ready, will still develop. 90 ★★★★ ready, will develop. 91 ★★★★ ready, will develop.

De Wetshof Estate Finesse ★★★★ D
This is an unwooded Chardonnay from the Cape's earliest producer of the cultivar. This light, fresh, fruity and somewhat simple wine from the 1990 vintage was followed by a similar 1991.

Diemersdal Chardonnay ★★★ C
The first release from 1990 vintage is fruity, fine wine with a touch of light oak backing. The 1991 is more citrusy and somewhat lighter in character than the 1990.

Dieu Donne Chardonnay ★★★ B
This is big, dry wine with lots of buttery/lemon flavour and woody background. It will need time to settle. The first release was from 1991. The 1992 is full in all respects and continues this cellar's improvement with the variety.

Dieu Donne Chardonnay (unwooded) ★★★ C
The first release from 1992 is fresh and fruity, with attractive citrus nose. This is repeated in 1993.

Drostdy-Hof Chardonnay (Bergkelder) ★★★(★) B
This is a very acceptable product in an everyday range of wines, with good cultivar character. It is good value for money and makes very pleasant drinking. The 1992 is fresh, clean and fruity.

Du Toitskloof Co-op Chardonnay ★★★ C
The first release from the 1991 vintage is forceful, butterscotch wine, with lots of wood, that will need time to marry and smooth. The 1992 has more varietal character and a decided citrus flavour.

Eersterivier-Valleise Kelder Chardonnay ★★★ C
The first release from 1989 had tropical fruit with reasonable oak backing. This was wine for early drinking. The 1990, 1991 and 1992 show annual improvement and a move towards more elegant wines.

Eersterivier Valleise Kelder Chardonnay Bin 7 ★★★ C
First released from the 1990 vintage. This wine is now showing good bottle development, decided citrus character and good oak. It is used by the cellar for tastings only.

Eikendal Chardonnay ★★★★ D

The 1991 is a fine wine, full of satisfying fruity flavours and nice butter-scotch character. The 1992 is even better, more elegant and fruitier. Both will develop over three to five years.

Fairview Chardonnay ★★★★ D

The first release from the 1990 vintage has lots of fruity flavour with but-terscotch overtones. The 1991 is a great improvement – full of flavour, and an elegant wine in fine style. The 1992 is a big wine in every respect, with lots of fruit and little wood. This is very good wine.

Fleermuisklip Chardonnay (Lutzville Co-op) ★★ C

Koekenaap is an unlikely name of origin but that is where the grapes for this wine come from, with an incredible yield of 32 tons per hectare in 1992! The wine has recognizable citrus-type Chardonnay character with reasonable wood backing. It is improving with the vintages.

Fleur Du Cap Chardonnay (Bergkelder) ★★★★ C

The first Chardonnay to be listed on a regular wine list was the Fleur du Cap 1988, made from grapes from eight- to ten-year-old vines grown in the Durbanville area. With almost 13% alcohol content, this wine has distinct cultivar character but is not really developing in the bottle. The 1989 is softer and better flavoured, with nice citrusy layers. The 1990 is altogether better wine with very good flavour and a most attractive nose. Wood is subdued but good and it has nice fresh finish. It should develop well. The 1991 release is an even better wine, an is followed by an equally good 1992.

Glen Carlou Chardonnay ★★★★(★) E

A beautiful wine full of nose and flavour, made from the 1988 vintage, was a first for this new 'cellar'. The 1989 is fuller, bigger wine in all respects and will certainly develop with great benefit in the bottle. The 1990 is big, full-flavoured wine with citrus, fruit and vanilla flavours, and good oak. This is a delicious wine that is developing with great benefit. The 1991 is great, and one of the Cape's best: lots of citrus and buttery flavours with good wood which will develop well. The 1992 confirms this cellar's ability to produce some of the Cape's best Chardonnays. It is rich, full yet elegant, and beautiful wine. The Reserve Chardonnays from this cellar are superb.

Goedvertrouw Chardonnay ★★★(★) F

The 1991 is an improvement on the very creditable first release from 1990. Good toast, nice citrus, hints of lemon. The 1992 shows continued improvement. Very small production, hence the high price.

Graham Beck Lone Hill Chardonnay ★★★★ C

The first release from 1991 vintage is beautiful wine with enticing nose and delicious full flavour; lots of citrus backed by good oak. The 1992 is fuller flavoured with good citrus and nice oak. Relatively large quantity for such good quality.

Groot Constantia Chardonnay ★★★★ E

The first vintage was the 1988 and heralded a promising start, with good cultivar character marrying well with new wood. It will need time to develop. The 1989 is big, better flavoured wine, with nuances of lemon backed with good wood. The 1990 brings this cellar into the top line of Cape Chardonnays. Good clean flavours and wood make this a fine wine that is developing with benefit. The 1991 shows further improvement. It is well made, with good depth of flavour and greater complexity, and ages well. The 1992 is a gorgeous wine.

Hamilton Russell Vineyards Chardonnay ★★★★(★) E

This wine used to be called Premier Vin Blanc but, since 1985, has been certified as Chardonnay. The first vintage was the 1983, which developed beautifully. The 1984 is a softer wine and, despite my original doubts, has developed beautifully. The 1985 vintage was the best to date when launched. It has the style of a well-wooded Chardonnay and was released as such. In 1993 it is showing extremely well. The 1986 is a little lighter, yet in 1993 has developed into a superb wine. The 1987 is showing very well. It has very good cultivar character, backed by good wood. It is developing with great benefit and, like the 1985, become a five-star wine. The 1988 is definitely a five-star wine and was the best release at that time. It has developed beautifully in the bottle. The 1989 was so attractive on release that some thought it would not develop, yet it looks like it will develop with benefit well into the late 1990s. The high alcohol of 13% and total acidity of 6,5% will ensure safe ageing. The 1990 is less woody. The 1991, made by Storm Kreusch-Dau, could well be the best ever. While the 1992 is still very young, it has great style and the flavour and character are already showing beautifully. Since 1989, half bottles have been available.

83 ★★★ drink. 84 ★★★ drink. 85 ★★★★ ready. 86 ★★★★ ready. 87 ★★★★(★) ready, will still improve. 88 ★★★★★ ready, will still improve. 89 ★★★★★ ready, will still improve. 90 ★★★★(★) (new style) ready, will still improve. 91 ★★★★(★) ready, will still improve. 92 ★★★★★ allow to develop further.

Hamilton Russell Vineyards Chardonnay Reserve ★★★★★ F

The first Hamilton Russell Vineyards Chardonnay label came from the 1989 vintage. Only selected bunches were used to produce this wine, as is the case for the Reserve. Wine making is in the traditional style of the Côte-d'Or and aged in small French oak for nine months. It is then held for at least another nine months in the bottle before being released. The bottle is easily recognized by its darker background and white shield on the neck label. The 1989 is a delicious wine with everything one could ever expect from this grape. The 1990 and 1992 are stunning wines. Both make tremendous drinking now, but will develop over eight to twelve years.

Hartenberg Chardonnay ★★★ D

From the 1991 vintage comes a big, barrel-fermented wine that needs time to settle down and work out its 14% alcohol. The 1992 is a fine, full-flavoured wine.

Haute Provence Chardonnay ★★(★) C

The 1990 and 1991 are acceptable dry white wines without much cultivar character. The 1992 is an improvement with fresh, clean style.

Hippo Creek Chardonnay (Picardi) ★★★ C

This is firm, fresh and fruity wine that is fermented and matured in oak. Made by Danie de Wet in Robertson. The first release is from 1992, and is followed by 1993.

John Platter Chardonnay ★★★★ D

The first release, from the 1987 vintage, seems to improve each time I taste it. It is developing a lemon character, and a slight hint of good wood is showing.

John Platter Clos du Ciel Chardonnay ★★★★

I hardly saw the 1990, but the 1991 is a delightful wine with citrus qualities and gentle oak. The bigger, more forceful 1992 will develop with benefit. There is very little available, but it is well worth the search to find. Erica sorts out the pronunciation of Clos du Ciel by saying it just like the Stellenbosch number plate 'CL'.

Klein Constantia Chardonnay ★★★★★ F

I first tasted it with Australian Chardonnay master, Len Evans, and he fully agreed that the first Chardonnay wine from the 1988 vintage was one of the best in the Cape. It has developed plenty of lovely complex flavours and drinks beautifully now. It has just got better and better with each vintage. The 1989 has all kinds of citrus flavours and good vanilla. The 1990 is top class, with fine nose and deep layers of flavour. It is full of fruit, with good oak and fresh finish, and is developing with great benefit. It is big, but beautifully elegant. The 1991 is full and rich, yet relatively soft, and good to drink now. It will develop with great benefit.

Kleindal Chardonnay ★★★ D

This is an unwooded Chardonnay with good cultivar character and nice clean finish. It is good to drink now but will develop with time.

Koelenhof Co-op Chardonnay ★★(★) C

The 1991 is easy-drinking wine with a pleasant flavour from fruit and wood. It is not for ageing, so drink it early. The 1992 is a bigger, better wine with good citrus flavour, some oak and a fresh finish.

La Cotte Chardonnay (Franschhoek Vineyards) ★★ B

The first release, from 1992, has faint varietal character and some wood.

La Couronne Chardonnay ★★★ D

The 1991 was a rather subdued but pleasantly drinkable wine, with lots of different nuances and flavours. The 1992 has more fruit and better oak. Given time, both releases could develop well.

Lanzerac Chardonnay ★★★(★) C

This is an unwooded wine with fine varietal character and lots of mouth-filling flavour. It is excellent value for money and a considerably better drink than many of the fancied names.

Le Bonheur Chardonnay ★★★ C

Early expectations that this could be one of South Africa's best Chardonnays have not been fulfilled. They are good wines, for sure, but not up to the standard usually associated with this cellar. They are fruity, soft and tasty, and developing age rather than character. There has been no release since 1989.

Lievland Chardonnay ★★★★ D

The 1992 is a well made wine, of fine style, with citrus flavours and good wood. It is developing well and becoming more complex.

Louisvale Chardonnay ★★★★ E

This is a beautiful wine from the 1989 vintage, especially for a first attempt. It has big, full flavour, yet is soft in the mouth with nice toasty butteryness and layers of citrus. It seemed to be losing it's tone in 1992, but has come back beautifully in 1993. The mark of a great wine. The 1990 is similar to the 1989, but with deeper toasty, and clean citrus-peach flavours. The 1991 continues the fine style, as does the 1992 which has a decided lemon tang and good oak. Lovely wine. It drinks well now but has everything to develop with benefit in the bottle.

Louisvale Chavant ★★★(★) D

Released early, after spending four months in oak, this is a blend of tank-fermented and cask-fermented wine. It has full varietal flavour, with good buttery and lemon tones, and light oak complexity. It has good, fresh, brisk finish.

L'Ormarins Chardonnay ★★★★ D

The first release from the 1987 vintage gave a hint of what was to come, although it didn't show so well at the start. It has now developed real substance in the bottle and subsequent vintages are on-going improvements. The 1988 has fruitier nose, fuller palate and is developing well. The 1989 is a wine to be respected: big, full wine with stylish character, and an intensity of lemon/lime character backed by oaky vanilla and firm tannin. It is developing very well in 1993. The 1990 shows that this cellar has established itself as one of the Cape's better Chardonnay producers. The 1991 is bright, fruity wine with all the best that Chardonnay can give. Another big attraction is the price.

87 ★★★(★) drink. 88 ★★★★ ready. 89 ★★★★(★) ready, will still develop. 90 ★★★★ ready, will still develop. 91 ★★★★ ready, will still develop.

Meerlust Chardonnay (no price or star rating available)

Only experimental amounts of this wine have been produced to date, but these are everything one would expect from Meerlust. It is not available commercially.

Mondial Chardonnay (Gilbeys) ★★★★ E

The first release from the 1990 vintage comes from grapes grown between Paarl and Durbanville, and the Stellenbosch side of Bottelary hills. This is a good, clean product with a most attractive nose and flavour. The 1991 release will be more complex, with components from throughout the winelands giving the most wide-ranging character of any Cape Chardonnay. Because the country's Wine of Origin laws will not allow vintage dating on wines made from grapes coming from different areas, and made in a central cellar, this lovely wine cannot be vintage dated. You will have to learn how to differentiate the unique pack each year. The crazy thing is that, when exported, the wine is allowed to carry a vintage date. Where's the logic?

Mont Blois Chardonnay ★★★ C

There are only two vintages, of which the second – from 1990 – is better, with good fruit and clean finish. The grapes are now being kept for bubbly production.

Morgenhof Chardonnay ★★★ D

The first release, from 1991, has good fruit but too much wood. The 1992 is an improvement, but the cellar samples of 1993 are altogether better.

Mouton Excelsior Le Moutonné Chardonnay ★★★ D

The first release from the 1991 vintage was a good attempt, with buttery, citrus flavours and background wood. But it was all a bit reserved. I look forward to future vintages.

Mulderbosch Chardonnay ★★★★ E

The first release, from 1992, is full of fruit in the style of this new, classy cellar. Future vintages are eagerly awaited.

Neethlingshof Chardonnay ★★★★ E

Neethlingshof delayed their entry into the fashionable field of Chardonnay to ensure they launched one of the best – an 'elegant, good varietal fruit, with a whisper of wood' (Brözel's words) – from five and six year-old vineyards. It is a blend of wooded and unwooded wine; the unwooded component a class winner in the 1990 SA Young Wine Show. This is a delicious wine in fine style and is developing well. The 1991 is a big, full-flavoured, fruity wine, with just the gentlest touch of oak.

Nederburg Auction Chardonnay ★★★★ D

Very little of this fine wine is available. Only 2 400 x 750 ml bottles of the 1984 vintage were sold at the 1987 Nederburg Auction and, according to Patrick Grubb, the auctioneer, it had superb palate, perfect balance and the potential to develop well over two to three years. It did. In 1988, the Decanter's panel rated it second only to the Mondavi Reserve 1985, against some of the world's greatest. Some of the 1985 vintage was chosen as the Wine of the Month on SAA's overseas flights during December 1987. The 1985 Special Auction Wine, of which there are only 3 300 bottles, is excellent but very expensive. The 1986 will need time to develop, but is showing very well. The 1987 was criticized on release but is beginning to show well; its faint flavours have developed more strongly and good nuances of citrus mingle with vanilla. The 1988 is altogether better, with its flowery nose and good depth of flavour. It is clean and stylish, and has developed beautifully in the bottle. The 1989 is positively exciting and is showing beautiful development. It is now well established as an Auction feature and a much admired wine.

84 ★★★★ needs drinking. 85 ★★★(★) needs drinking. 86 ★★★(★) ready. 87 ★★★ ready. 88 ★★★★ ready, but still developing. 89 ★★★★ ready, but still developing.

Nederburg Chardonnay ★★★★ D

Very different to the Auction wine, the first general release of this wine from the 1989 vintage was made at the 1991 Auction lunch. It is now a regular part of the Nederburg range. A portion is fermented in wood; the balance in stainless steel. The result is a complex, refreshing, limey wine with a buttery background, good fruit acid and the slightest touch of oak. The 1991 and 1992 show well-balanced, reliable style. It makes delicious drinking at the time of release and develops well over two to four years. It is good to have a classy Chardonnay at a reasonable price.

Neil Ellis Chardonnay ★★★★ E

First released from the 1990 vintage, this is a lovely, elegant wine with lots of citrus and vanilla flavours, in deep layers, backed by fine oak. Lots of lees contact and malolactic fermentation give great complexity. As good as it is to drink now, it will reward further ageing to the mid-nineties. The 1991 and 1992 follow in similar, good style, with rich complexity. They are truly elegant.

Onverwacht Chardonnay ★★ C

This wine is lightly flavoured and slightly too acidic. The first effort comes from the 1992 vintage.

Overgaauw Chardonnay ★★★(★) E

The 1986 was rich, full-flavoured wine, and the 1987 is even better, having a very good combination of cultivar and wood. It was the highest-priced white wine at the 1989 Nederburg Auction. The 1988 is five-star material – a big, full, fruit-flavoured, well-wooded wine in the New World style, that is developing well with time in the bottle. The elegant 1989, which has toffee and butterscotch flavours, is still developing well. The 1990 is the best balanced, is drinking very well now, but will probably be at its best earlier than the 1988 and 1989. The 1991 is just as flavourful, but a more gentle wine which is very satisfying. This is consistently one of the best.

Paul Cluver Chardonnay ★★★★ D

The first release from the 1991 vintage is an elegant, full, fruity wine with excellent oak backing. It has fine, fresh finish and could be one of the better Chardonnays in future vintages.

Pick 'n Pay Chardonnay ★★★★ C

Made by Backsberg from 1990 vintage. This is lightly wooded, medium-bodied wine with delicate citrus flavours and crisp, dry finish. It has developed with benefit and drinks well.

Rhebokskloof Chardonnay ★★★★ E

This is the first release from the 1991 vintage and comes from very young vines. It is light, elegant wine, with fine citrus tones backed by good wood, and a most encouraging start. It developed very well and was selected for the 1993 Nederburg Auction. The 1992 is very different in style and very drinkable at an early age.

Rietvallei Estate Chardonnay ★★★ D

The first release from the 1987 vintage was a somewhat stern and formal wine. It had very little nose and flavour, but what there was, was good cultivar. The 1988 is a far better wine with good cultivar character, and the 1989 better still – a big wine that is developing well. The 1990 is a four-star, elegant production with fine citrus character.

Robertson Co-op Chardonnay ★★★★ C

This prolific cellar produced two first-release Chardonnays out of the 1990 vintage. One is unwooded, medium-bodied, firm wine with good citrus character, the other, a barrel-fermented wine that spent four months on its lees and labelled 'Sur Lie'. The latter is a more complex wine that benefited with some age. Only the wooded style was released in 1991. This is one of the best Co-op Chardonnays and it is doing very well in tastings. The 1992 is in the same attractive style.

Romansrivier Chardonnay ★★ B

This cellar has produced two Chardonnays, one wooded and one unwooded. Both are promising, fruity wines. Be sure to watch out for future vintages.

Rooiberg Chardonnay ★★★ C

This is pleasant-flavoured, easy-drinking, unwooded, well-made wine.

Rooiberg Chardonnay Sur Lie ★★(★) C

The 1990 is an oak-fermented Chardonnay with more wood flavour than cultivar. It is soft and buttery, while the 1991 is big, full, robust wine with an almost Late Harvest, honey-like nose.

Ruiterbosch Mountain Cuvée Chardonnay ★★★(★) D

This is elegant, fine-flavoured wine from the cool mountain vineyards overlooking Mossel Bay. Cask-fermented oak is gentle and allows fresh fruit flavours to lead. The first release from the 1991 vintage has developed quietly. The 1992 is more generous in nose and flavour, and is showing good bottle development.

Rustenberg Chardonnay ★★★(★) D

The Estate's new wine is considered the regular release, while the existing wine becomes Chardonnay Reserve. The first release, from 1990, follows the trend to less wooded Chardonnay at a lower price. It is good, fruity, fresh on the palate and has good finish. The 1991 and 1992 are less wooded wines for easy drinking.

Rustenberg Chardonnay Reserve★★★★ E

The first limited release of this wine was in 1986. It was a good combination of fruit and wood, giving a softish wine, which developed elegance over four years. The 1987 was a great improvement, with good cultivar and nice wood. The 1988 is great, showing very good cultivar character with fine wood mingling into the flavour, giving a spicy tang to the taste. It developed with great style into 1993. The 1988 Chardonnay is now sold under the Rustenberg name, previously reserved for the Estate's red wines. (The whites of Rustenberg were previously sold under the name of its sister farm, Schoongezicht.) The 1989 is full, rich wine that is developing well. The 1990 is labelled 'Reserve', and deservedly so – it is full, complex, well-made wine, with good balance backed by fine wood. It is developing well. The 1991 continues in fine style with fresher fruit.

86 ★★★ drink. 87 ★★★(★) ready. 88 ★★★★ ready. 89 ★★★★ ready, will still develop. 90 ★★★★ ready, will still develop. 91 ★★★★ ready, will still develop further.

Simonsig Chardonnay ★★★★(★) E

After an indifferent start in 1980 and 1981, the 1982 vintage obtained Superior certification. With its very good nose and fair flavour, this wine gained acclaim at a tasting in Spain arranged by the world authority, Miguel Torres. It competed very successfully with good Chardonnays from around the world and was also a gold medal winner at the 1985 International Wine and Spirit Competition in Britain. The 1983 was a bigger, bolder wine which showed well in the bottle in 1987. The 1985 was certified Superior and developed well. The 1986 and 1987 are totally different wines with the big full character of the New World approach. The 1988 is a five-star wine with the toasty, buttery character associated with the world's greatest Chardonnays. The 1988 Reserve won a gold medal and the Cape Wine Academy Trophy for the best South African White Wine at the International Wine and Spirit Competition in Britain in 1990. The 1989 follows with good fruity nose and fine caramel and toffee flavours. The 1990 is a splendid wine which will develop well over five to seven years. The 1991 is even better than the great 1988, and well worth the money. Along with the cellar's Reserve, the wines are established as among the Cape's best.

82 ★★★★ drink. 83 ★★★★ drink. 84 no release. 85 ★★★★ drink. 86 ★★★★(★) ready. 87 ★★★★ ready. 88 ★★★★★ ready, will still improve. 89 ★★★★★ ready, will still improve. 90 ★★★★★ ready, will still develop. 91 ★★★★★ ready, will develop further.

Simonsvlei Co-op Chardonnay ★★★ D

The first release from the 1988 vintage was disappointing, but the 1989 was better, with some wood and lemony character. With the 1990 vintage came great improvement, good citrus, and nice fruit along the Chablis style. The 1991 is much bigger wine and will develop better than the 1990. The 1992 is a better balanced product.

Springlands Chardonnay (Drop Inn) ★★★ C

This is well made, light wine with a buttery character. It is also relatively woody.

Stellenryck Chardonnay ★★★(★)

The only release from 1989 is a well made yet somewhat subdued wine. It is not up to the usual high standard of this label.

Talana Hill Chardonnay ★★★★★ F

The introduction of this wine came with seventy cases of the 1988 vintage being sold at the 1990 New World Wine Auction. Made by Jan 'Boland' Coetzee from grapes grown on a small Stellenbosch property, this is wine that will need time to develop. It is well made, medium bodied and finely flavoured. The 1989 is a stylish wine which is developing well. The 1990 is elegant, with good citrusy flavours, is soft in the mouth and has fine oak backing. The 1991 has distinct fruity nose and flavour. This is lovely wine that should develop well. There was only a small production but it is well worth seeking out.

Thelema Chardonnay ★★★★★ D

The first release from the 1988 vintage is an elegant wine with a fine, fruity, pear-like nose and full, soft flavour backed by the fine use of good wood. It tasted good on release and developed beautifully. The 1989 is one of the Cape's best and is full of the intense flavours of citrus, lime, peach and toasty wood. The 1990 confirms this Thelema wine as among the best. It is a beautiful, elegant wine, full of fine, complex flavours, that is developing with great benefit. The 1991 is a stunner and keeps Thelema right up with the very best, if not leading the way. The 1992 confirms this cellar's greatness. It is very well priced for such super wine.

Tradouw Chardonnay (Barrydale Co-op) ★★★ D

A surprise from the 1989 vintage was Barrydale Co-op's first release of a wood-aged Chardonnay. Both the 1989 and the 1990 were good, early attempts. The 1991 has good citrus character, backed by lots of oak, and is a rich wine, with clean finish, that needs time to round out. The 1991 was the SA Young Wine Champion for a wood-matured white. Tradouw is the grapes' Wine of Origin Ward. Bottles are labelled 'Sur Lie' without mention of the Co-op. The 1992 is due for release late in 1993.

Uitkyk Chardonnay ★★★(★) D

The first release in the Estate's new livery came from the 1991 vintage and was a bit disappointing. The 1992 is far more appealing and is showing well in the bottle. Somehow one expects more from Uitkyk.

Van Loveren Chardonnay ★★★★ E

The first release, the 1987 vintage, was a very creditable first attempt and showed well at a number of tastings. The 1988 is a big wine with

14% alcohol. It was originally almost alcoholically bound, not yielding much nose or flavour, then bloomed, showing all kinds of citrus fruits, butterscotch and good wood characteristics. The 1989 is equally alcoholic but showed its form much earlier. It is consistently well rated in blind tastings and makes big, soft, easy drinking. The 1990 followed the same style. The 1991 is full of good cultivar flavour and is developing well in the bottle. The 1992 continues this cellar's very appealing style and is very good value for money.

Vergelegen Les Enfants Chardonnay ★★★★ D

This is a first-class first release from this spectacular cellar on the historic property. It is made from grapes from neighbouring vineyards and has good fruit, and good, light use of oak. The 500 ml bottles are developing well ahead of the 750 ml bottles. Well done Martin.

Villiersdorp Co-op Kroonland Chardonnay ★★★(★) C

The 1991 was big, full, yet soft in the mouth, and one of the best Co-op Chardonnays. The 1992 is bigger, better wine that is developing well in the bottle, and is excellent value for money.

Vlottenburg Co-op Chardonnay ★★★(★) D

The dramatic first release from the 1990 vintage attracted great attention. Elegant, complex wine with good citrus flavours backed by fine oaky toastiness, it was the 1990 SA Young Wine Show Champion wooded white. Regrettably, there was very limited production. The 1991 is not as showy, but is very drinkable – and there's more of it! The 1992 shows good, lively fruitiness and oak backing and makes easy, early drinking.

Vredendal Co-op Koekenaap Chardonnay ★★★ B

This wine was first made from only 10 tons of grapes, picked on 13 February 1989, on the second last block of the Olifants Rivier irrigation scheme, with the Atlantic Ocean less than a kilometre away. The cellar manager, Giel Swiegers, received advice from Imanuel Béné of Cave Cooperative de Vine. The result was very pleasing for a first attempt and won a silver medal at the International Wine and Spirit Competition in the UK in 1991. The 1990 is another good effort, though perhaps not quite the quality of the 1989, but very pleasant all the same. The 1991 is very pleasant, easy-drinking wine, best in its youth. The 1992 is a bit too woody. The 1993 is fruitier and far more pleasing.

Vriesenhof Chardonnay ★★★★(★) D

To date, very little of this wine has been available. The 1986 suggested that this was a cellar to keep an eye on. The 1987 was not exciting, but with the 1988, the wine really came into its own. Showing good flavours in the New World style, it developed with benefit in the bottle. The 1989 has the complexity one would expect from Jan 'Boland' Coetzee. It is big, rich, full-flavoured wine, with layers of fruit including lemon and lime, butterscotch and toasty wood. The 1990 is a delicious wine full of flavoury lime, lemon, vanilla, butteriness, and with good oak backing.

The 1991 is going to be stunning, while the 1992 sees new dimensions with more new-clone influence. The 1992 has not yet been released. These wines develop with great benefit.

86 ★★★(★) ready. 87 ★★★ ready. 88 ★★★★ ready. 89 ★★★★(★) ready, will still improve. 90 ★★★★★ ready, will still improve. 91 ★★★★★ good now, will develop.

Warwick Chardonnay ★★★★ (no price available)

This wine is not available commercially but rumours are that good red wine makers make good Chardonnays. Beg, borrow or steal – it's definitely worth a taste.

Welmoed Chardonnay ★★(★) C

The early releases of this wine lack fruit and style. Watch for future releases and improvement.

Weltevrede Estate Chardonnay ★★★★ D

The first release, from the 1989 vintage, has a decidedly citrus character. This was a good effort for a first release, and it is developing surprisingly well in the bottle. The 1990 is lovely wine and developed beautiful nose and flavour over two years. The 1991 is even better, and the best from this cellar. The 1992 continues the good quality. This wine deserves greater acclaim, especially at its low price.

Woolworths Chardonnay ★★★★ C

The 1991 from Vriesenhof cellars is an excellent follow-up on the fine 1990. It is well wood-aged, without wood dominating, and has attractive citrus nose with good buttery flavours. The 1992 maintains the quality. It is good for drinking now, and has lots of ageing potential.

Woolworths Chardonnay (unwooded) ★★★★ C

The 1991 from Neil Ellis is a blend of old South African clone with Davis (California) clone. It has good fruity flavours and is developing well in the bottle. The 1992 is fruity, full, mouth filling, and easy drinking wine.

Woolworths Klein Constantia Chardonnay ★★★(★)

This wine is a special selection for Woolworths with the Klein Constantia character and style.

Woolworths Chardonnay Magnum★★★(★) D

With Danie de Wet's move away from Bergkelder to doing his own labels, he has produced a series of magnums from 1991.

Zandwijk Chardonnay ★★★ E

The first release from this wine farm is one of its better products. The wine from the 1989 vintage was released in March 1990. It was immediately drinkable and much better tasting than most imported kosher wines. The 1991 and 1992 continue to be the best from this cellar.

Zevenwacht Chardonnay ★★★(★) D

The first release was from 1990 and had good citrus nose, nice buttery flavour, and good oak backing. It is developing well after three years. The 1991 is an improvement and shows promise for future vintages.

Zonnebloem Chardonnay (SFW) ★★★★ D

The first release from the 1989 vintage was very shy in character on release, although it developed very well in the bottle. The 1991 is among the best – medium-bodied with citrus-type flavours and a hint of oak in the background. The 1990 is a lovely, very friendly, wine with good nose and flavour. It drank well on release but has also developed well. In a very short time it has established itself as one of the better 'drinking Chardonnays' with excellent varietal character. Very affordable.

CHENEL

Andalusia Chenel (Vaalharts Co-op) ★ B

A clean, semi-sweet wine, and the only Chenel to survive!

Chenin Blanc/Steen – Dry

Aan-de-Doorns Chenin Blanc ★★★ A

This is a consistently good dry wine, a regular award winner at regional shows and good value for money. It has good cultivar character.

Backsberg Chenin Blanc ★★★ B

The 1991, 1992 and 1993 are lovely, fruity bright wines, full of varietal flavours. They are just off-dry and delightful drinking wines. Enjoy this wine in its youth.

Boland Co-op Chenin Blanc ★★★ A

The 1991 is a dry wine with good varietal character. It has good fruity finish when young.

Bottelary Co-op Chenin Blanc ★★(★) A

This cellar has a reputation for producing good dry white wine from this cultivar. It is delicate, fruity and clean, with fresh finish.

De Helderberg Co-op Chenin Blanc ★★(★) A

This is a delightful, light, easy-drinking dry wine, with Steen character.

Douglas Green Chenin Blanc (DGB) ★★★ B

This pleasant, dry wine with good cultivar nose and smooth palate, develops well in the bottle over a year or two.

Fairview Chenin Blanc ★★★(★) B

Originally this was a big, bold wine, but nowadays it is more elegant and very attractive, fruity wine with fresh finish. It is best enjoyed young.

Koelenhof Co-op Chenin Blanc ★★ B

This is a good, fresh, dry wine, with cultivar character which shows well when young.

Ladismith Co-op Chenin Blanc ★★ A

A light, dry wine with good cultivar character when young.

Landskroon Chenin Blanc ★★★ A

This mainly red-wine Estate has produced fairly ordinary Chenin Blancs, although the quality has improved with the 1990 and 1991 vintage.

Louwshoek-Voorsorg Co-op Chenin Blanc ★★ A

A dry Chenin Blanc, which has good fruit flavours and rare guava nose when young.

Mamreweg Co-op Dry Steen ★★ A

The 1989 is a great improvement on earlier vintages and the 1990 and 1991 continue the quality improvement. It has good cultivar nose and flavour, and is finished dry.

Onverwacht Chenin Blanc Dry ★★ B

This is an easy-drinking dry white wine. The latest release has good cultivar character.

Opstal Steen ★★(★) A

This Steen has very good cultivar nose and high acid. It is very dry.

Perdeberg Co-op Chenin Blanc Dry ★★★ A

This cellar produces a bright, semi-sweet wine, and a more serious, dry version which has been a consistent award winner. The 1988 was South Africa's champion dry white, but very little ever appeared in the bottle. Recent vintages are bigger and fuller.

Roodezandt Chenin Blanc ★★★ A

Always consistent, this dry wine has good cultivar character and is at its best when young.

Romansrivier Co-op Chenin Blanc ★★★ A

This is a delightful, fresh, fruity wine with lots of cultivar character.

Saxenberg Chenin Blanc ★★ B

One of the nice, fruity, dry wines with full flavour.

Simonsig Chenin Blanc ★★★ B

This is a very well-balanced dry wine with excellent varietal character. Recent vintages should be enjoyed in the bloom of their youth.

Simonsvlei Co-op Dry Steen ★★★ A

A gold medal winner at the South African Championship Wine Show, this is a well-made, dry wine with fine character.

Swartland Co-op Steen ★★★ A

This is a big, dry white with lots of cultivar character, and a wine well worth ageing for a year or so. One of the better Co-op Steens.

Vlottenburg Co-op Steen ★★★ A

This is a pleasing, fresh, dry Steen of good drinking quality, which has shown considerable improvement over the years.

Welmoed Co-op Dry Steen ★★★ A

A regular medal winner at regional and national shows, this Steen is always soft and dry, with good cultivar flavour. It makes easy-drinking.

Woolworths Chenin Blanc ★★★ A

From Rooiberg, comes this pleasant, dry Steen with nice, fruity finish, for easy drinking.

CHENIN BLANC/STEEN – OFF-DRY/SEMI-SWEET

Boschendal Chenin Blanc ★★★(★)C

Clean and fruity, this soft, tasty, off-dry wine ages particularly well, yet also drinks very nicely when fresh and young. Vintages of the 1990s are delightful wines with super cultivar character that is set off well by being finished off-dry. (It is used in my annual UK tasting as a particularly good example of Chenin Blanc and is very well received there.)

Botha Co-op Chenin Blanc ★★ A

Recent vintages are pleasant when fresh and young. They are just off-dry, have attractive, fruity nose, and are easy drinking.

Calitzdorp Co-op Chenin Blanc ★ A

A lightly flavoured, semi-sweet, white wine.

Cederberg Kelders Chenin Blanc ★★ A

This is an unusual, semi-sweet Steen. Since 1988 these have been full, soft, easy-drinking wines. The 1991 has a particularly good guava nose, as has the 1992, which is quite a lot sweeter.

Charles et Charles Steen ★★★ B

The label no longer exists, but this Steen, from 1992 vintage, is well made and developing well in the bottle.

Du Toitskloof Co-op Chenin Blanc ★★★(★) A

This off-dry wine with its fruity nose and good palate has improved over the vintages and is a regular winner at local shows. The 1988 has a beautiful, fruity nose and was delightful when young. It also developed in the bottle. The 1989 was not up to standard, but the vintages of the 1990s are delightful wines with good cultivar character. The 1991 received double gold Veritas and the 1992 is sweeter but delicious.

Du Toitskloof Co-op Vino Uno Amabile ★★(★) A

This is a pleasant, semi-sweet blend of mostly Muscat d'Alexandrie and some 20% Steen. It makes for easy drinking and comes in 500 ml screw-top bottles.

Eersterivier-Valleise Kelder Chenin Blanc ★★★ B

This is usually a consistently good dry wine that is frequently an award winner at regional and national shows. It has good cultivar nose and often the elusive guava character which is much sought after in Chenin Blanc. The 1988 was off-dry and out of character. The 1989 was back to the usual, good drinking quality, and the 1990 was particularly good. The 1991 is decidedly semi-sweet, but still a good drink, and value for money. The 1992 has returned to off-dry.

Goue Vallei Chenin Blanc ★★ A

This is a semi-sweet wine with good cultivar nose. The latest releases make very pleasant, easy-drinking wines.

Kleindal Chenin Blanc ★★★ B

This wine has a very nice fruit salad nose, is soft across the palate, yet has nice fresh finish – just off-dry.

KWV Chenin Blanc ★★★ (no price available)

This is an off-dry wine with attractive nose and pleasing flavour. It is one of KWV's best products and one of our better exports.

La Cotte Chenin Blanc (Franschhoek Vineyards) ★★(★) B

This is a pleasant, fruity, semi-sweet white wine, at a good price, and with a popular following.

Landskroon Chenin Blanc ★★★ B

The best Chenin Blanc ever from this Estate came from the 1990 vintage; semi-sweet, fresh, fruity, clean character wine. The 1991 is lighter but drinks well, and is most enjoyable when young, as is the 1992.

Les Chênes Chenin Blanc ★★★ A

This is one of a number of grape growers who have their wines made at the Co-op and then marketed under their own label. The wines are best when young.

Lutzville Co-op Chenin Blanc ★★ A

This is an off-dry, fruity white wine, that is best when young.

Mamreweg Co-op Chenin Blanc ★★ A

This is a pleasant, easy-drinking, off-dry wine. The latest releases are an improvement on those of the past. They have good flavour and fresh finish when young.

Matin Soleil Vin Bouquet Chenin Blanc ★★★ B

A very pleasant off-dry white wine, with good varietal character, makes this good, everyday drinking wine.

Merwida Co-op Chenin Blanc ★★ A

A semi-sweet wine with Late Harvest/Steen character.

Mon Don Chenin Blanc ★★★ A

This is a full, fruity, off-dry wine, with recent bottlings showing improved flavour and fresh finish.

Montagu Co-op Chenin Blanc ★★ A

The wines of the 1990s have good guava nose and are almost dryish.

Morgenhof Chenin Blanc ★★(★) B

This is a gentle, soft wine with fruity, off-dry finish. Recent bottlings have more character than previous releases.

Nuy Co-op Effesoet Steen ★★★ A

Slightly sweet and with a good cultivar character, this most agreeable, medium-bodied wine has been a champion at the South African Championship Wine Show and has also carried Superior certification.

Opstal Steen ★★★ A

This Estate produced two wines from the same cultivar. The off-dry Chenin Blanc was a light, easy-drinking, particularly good wine, but is no longer produced. The current Steen is big and bold wine.

Perdeberg Co-op Chenin Blanc Semi-sweet ★★★(★) A

This Co-op is a specialist Steen producer with more than half its receipts being this variety. The semi-sweet is a delightful, fruity wine that has its flavours enhanced by being finished with sweetness.

Pick 'n Pay Chenin Blanc ★★★ B

This is good, fruity wine with lots of guava and honey flavours. It is well-balanced, complex wine, from Swartland, and has a fresh, off-dry finish.

Riebeek Co-op Chenin Blanc ★★★ A

This particularly good wine is a consistent medal winner. In the past, it was finished semi-sweet but is now a very acceptable off-dry wine. It has subtle cultivar nose and soft palate, and must be enjoyed when young.

Rietrivier Co-op Chenin Blanc ★ A

A semi-sweet white wine.

Roodezandt Co-op Chenin Blanc Semi-sweet ★★★ A

The 1990 was a most attractive wine with lots of flavour and a remarkable 13,7% alcohol. Then the 1991 turned up with 14% alcohol! The 1992 is less challenging, with good, tropical fruity nose.

Rooiberg Co-op Vinkrivier Chenin Blanc ★★★(★) A

This delightful Chenin Blanc is made from grapes grown along the Vink River (hence Wine of Origin Vinkrivier). It has strong varietal nose, light acid, good, rounded taste, and is finished off-dry.

Simonsvlei Co-op Chenin Blanc ★★★ A

This wine is no longer produced but was one of the cellar's better products. It was a pleasant, off-dry wine, with slight spicey aroma and delicate but fresh flavour, and charming when young. An exception was the Superior 1977, which had developed beautifully when sold at the 1979 Nederburg Auction.

Slanghoek Chenin Blanc ★★★ B

This is a very good and attractive Chenin Blanc. Recent vintages have been fuller, fresh, fruity and sweetish. Very attractive.

Soetwynboere Co-op Chenin Blanc ★★★ A

An off-dry, easy-drinking wine with good varietal character.

Spruitdrift Co-op Chenin Blanc ★★★ A

This cellar is making particularly good off-dry wine from this cultivar.

Swartland Co-op Chenin Blanc ★★★ A

This is a well made, well-balanced, fruity, clean-tasting, semi-sweet wine for early drinking.

Tulbagh Co-op Chenin Blanc ★★★ A

This wine is off-dry, medium-bodied and has a light but fruity flavour.

Villiersdorp Co-op Chenin Blanc ★★★ A

A semi-sweet wine, with good cultivar character, which makes for easy drinking.

Vlottenburg Co-op Chenin Blanc ★★★ A

A well-balanced, off-dry wine with good cultivar character.

Vredendal Co-op Chenin Blanc ★★ A
This is a very pale Steen in all respects, with faint fruitiness, which is finished off-dry.
Waboomsrivier Co-op Chenin Blanc ★★ A
This is a well-made, easy-drinking wine, which is finished semi-sweet.
Welmoed Co-op Chenin Blanc ★★★ A
A very pleasant, off-dry wine, with good fruit and nice flavour.

CLAIRETTE BLANCHE

Aan-de-Doorns Clairette Blanche ★(★) A
Light in character, this wine is brisk and refreshing when young.
De Wet Co-op Clairette Blanche ★★(★) A
This is a fruity, dry white wine, with subtle nose and pleasant flavour. It makes easy and relaxed drinking.
Goudini Co-op Clairette Blanche ★★ A
This pleasant, dry, easy-drinking wine is a regular award winner at local and national shows. Those of the early 1990s are very pleasant and have tropical fruit nose. Easy drinking.
Overhex Co-op Clairette Blanche ★★ A
A pleasant, light, easy-drinking wine.

COLOMBAR(D)

Aan-de-Doorns Colombar ★★ A

This is an occasionally semi-sweet and sometimes off-dry wine with good cultivar character. It is a regular award winner at regional and national shows. There was no 1989 release, but the early 1990s are semi-sweet with little cultivar character.

Agterkliphoogte Co-op Colombar ★★★ A

This is a pleasant, light wine with good cultivar nose. The early 1990s are good and fruity, with clean, brisk finish. Best when young.

Andalusia Colombar (Vaalharts Co-op) ★★ B

A dry wine with some cultivar character. Ordinary, quaffing wine.

Ashton Co-op Colombar ★★ A

This is light-styled, fruity, dry wine of consistent quality.

Bakenskop Colombar (Jonkheer) ★★★ B

A good cultivar wine finished off-dry, making pleasant drinking.

Barrydale Co-op Colombar ★★ A

This Co-op used to produce both a dry and an off-dry Colombar. It now produces only a semi-sweet, low-alcohol wine.

Bonnievale Co-op Colombard ★★ A

This cellar offers two Colombars, one dry and the other off-dry. Both have good, fruity nose and full cultivar flavour.

Brandvlei Co-op Colombar ★★ A

A good, fresh, fruity, semi-sweet wine.

Calitzdorp Co-op Colombar ★★ A

The first release from 1991 was dry and pleasant. Best when young.

De Doorns Co-op Colombar ★ A

An off-dry, pleasant Colombar.

Douglas Co-op Colombar ★★ A

A dry white wine of medium body and faint varietal character.

Du Toitskloof Co-op Colombard ★★★ A

This was always a full-flavoured, off-dry wine that did well at young wine shows; consistently one of the better Colombars. Regrettably, it has now been discontinued.

Kango Co-op Colombar ★★ B

An off-dry, light-style wine, with little nose, but pleasant taste.

Klawer Co-op Colombar ★★★ A

This is usually a light, off-dry wine, but a semi-sweet version won a gold medal at the International Wine and Spirit Competition held in the UK in 1986. The early 1990s are easy-drinking, off-dry wines.

Langverwacht Co-op Colombar ★★ A

This cellar produces a pleasant, dry Colombar from regular gold medal wines at local young wine shows.

Louwshoek-Voorsorg Co-op Colombard ★★ A

An off-dry, pleasant, fruity wine.

Mamreweg Co-op Colombar ★★ A

A nice, fresh, off-dry wine with honey-like nose, for early drinking.

McGregor Co-op Colombar ★★ A

An off-dry, easy-drinking wine, which is best enjoyed when young.

Merwida Co-op Colombar ★★★ A

A delightful, off-dry wine with a full, fruity nose. Some of the 1978 vintage was certified Superior and sold at the 1979 Nederburg Auction. After a long absence this wine was re-introduced with the 1989. Since then it has been light and off-dry – not up to Auction standard.

Montagu Co-operative Colombar ★★ A

An off-dry wine with typical cultivar character.

Nordale Co-op Colombard ★★ A

A good wine with nice Colombar character. In the past it has been off-dry, dry and nowadays it is finished off-dry.

Nuy Co-op Colombard ★★★★ A

Nuy produces two Colombars: one dry and the other semi-sweet. The dry is fairly tart, with full cultivar nose and good full flavour. The semi-sweet is fuller in the mouth and usually the finer wine; it develops well in the bottle and is consistently one of the better Colombars. Both wines rank about the best in the Cape, and the best you can get.

Opstal Colombar ★★★ A

This is an off-dry white wine with clean nose and light flavour. Those of the early 1990s have fuller flavour but lighter fruit.

Oranjerivier Wynkelders Colombar ★★ A

Originally a full-flavoured, dry white wine, it is now finished off-dry.

Oude Rust Colombard (Mooiuitsig Wynkelders) ★★(★) B

This is a good, off-dry wine, with plenty of Colombar character.

Overhex Co-op Effesoet Colombard ★★(★) A

This full-bodied, semi-sweet wine is pleasant on the palate and has good fruit. It is best enjoyed when young.

Perdeberg Co-op Colombar ★★(★) A

This is not produced from every vintage; a wine finished dry and with soft cultivar character.

Riebeek Co-op Colombard ★★★ A

This is a light wine which has won regional and national awards. The latest releases are only just off-dry.

Rietrivier Co-op Colombar ★★ A

This is an off-dry wine and a regular regional champion.

Robertson Co-op Colombard ★★(★) B

The Robertson Co-operative is a consistent producer of top quality wines, and is justifiably regarded as the 'home' of Colombar. Latest releases are a little on the quiet side.

Romansrivier Co-op Colombard ★★★ A

This Co-operative bottles three Colombars (dry, off-dry and semi-sweet), all of which are very good. They have good cultivar character and do consistently well at the South African Championship Wine Show. The semi-sweet *(effesoet)*, frequently certified Superior, is usually one of the country's outstanding, quality Colombar wines.

Roodezandt Co-op Colombar ★★(★) A

A pleasant, easy-drinking wine with good Colombar nose. Those of the early 1990s are off-dry and have more complex character.

Rooiberg Co-op Colombard ★★★(★) B

One of the cellar's great successes, this Wine of Origin Vinkrivier has very good Colombar nose. Over the vintages the flavour has also developed well, with slight sweetness balancing well with the wine's relatively high acid. It regularly carried the old Superior rating. The 1983 was selected for sale at the New World Wine Auction in 1990. This is one of the few wines that develop well in the bottle.

Slanghoek Co-op Colombard ★★★ A

This is something special in the way of Colombars and is certainly one of the more interesting examples of the cultivar. All the vintages have outstanding cultivar character and good balance. It frequently gained Superior certification under the old system. Unfortunately, this is one that didn't show its best in 1992.

Soetwynboere Colombar ★★(★) A

An off-dry, very fruity wine, at a remarkably low price.

Spruitdrift Co-op Colombar ★★ A

An off-dry wine, with very little cultivar character.

Swartland Co-op Colombar Dry ★★★(★) B

A fruity, full-flavoured, dry wine with definite cultivar character. Those of the 1990s are very good quality and also good value for money.

Swartland Co-op Off-dry Colombar ★★★(★) B

A nice off-dry wine, which is not quite as light and fresh as the dry.

Van Loveren Colombar ★★★ A

This is a pleasant, semi-sweet wine with very good nose and full flavour.

Villiersdorp Co-op Colombar ★★★ A

An off-dry wine with good character, making nice, fruity, easy drinking.

Weltevrede Colombard ★★★(★) A

This Colombar has distinctive cultivar character and the unmistakable style of the wine maker, Lourens Jonker. An off-dry wine that, for Colombar, has reasonable ageing potential, it reaches its best in about two years from the date of vintage, though most will enjoy it young when it is full of cultivar character. It is a regular award winner. This is another wine which, in 1992, didn't come up to standard.

Woolworths Robertson Colombar ★★★ A

From Weltevrede. This is a good example of the cultivar finished off-dry.

FERNÃO PIRES

Anadalusia Fernão Pires (Vaalharts Co-op) ★★ B
A semi-sweet white wine with muscaty nose and pleasant flavour.

Bergsig Fernão Pires ★★★ B
This wine has definite cellar style yet retains the muscaty nose of the cultivar. It is finished off-dry and has relatively low alcohol.

Calitzdorp Fernão Pires ★★ B
New from the 1992 vintage, this is a full-bodied, muscat, semi-sweet white wine.

De Wet Co-op Fernão Pires ★★(★) A
Almost in the 'Light' category but with good flavour and pleasant semi-sweet finish. Not surprisingly, it is one of the cellar's most popular wines.

Douglas Co-op Fernão Pires ★ A
This wine has improved over the vintages, with the early 1990s being semi-sweet and low in alcohol. Pleasant drinking.

Nederburg Private Bin D207 ★★★★ B
This wine is 100% Fernão Pires, but is not certified as such. (*See* page 154 Blended/Non-varietal Dry White wines.)

Nuy Co-op Fernão Pires ★★★ B
This wine has less muscat character and is more distinctive than most wines from this cultivar. The good spicey nose, fine, fruity flavour and nice, long taste make for interesting drinking. Although semi-sweet, it finishes decidedly dry.

Swartland Co-op Fernão Pires ★★★ B
This wine from Swartland is in the 'Light' style, with pleasant flavour and an off-dry finish.

Van Loveren Fernão Pires ★★★ B
Van Loveren has probably produced a commercial wine from this cultivar through more vintages than any other cellar. Since 1987, production has been considerably good. It is off-dry wine with good, fruity nose, and tasty cultivar flavour. Previous vintages have been semi-sweet Late Harvests and the 1983 and 1984, produced as Perlé wines, were very good. Those of the early 1990s are well balanced, nice, fruity, off-dry wines, that are best in their youth.

Vredendal Co-op Fernão Pires ★★★(★) B
Giel Swiegers seems to be able to do unusual things with cultivars not noted for quality. With this wine he gets very good flavours and produces a good, easy-drinking, off-dry wine, which is value for money.

FURMINT

Bergsig Furmint ★★★ B
Launched as an easy-drinking off-dry wine with faint but fine flavour, it is becoming consistently good and one of the cellar's special products. The 1991 has delicate nose and pleasing palate; nice drinking wine and good value for money. The 1992 has an almost citrus character, with clean, brisk finish, and is best enjoyed while young.

GEWÜRZTRAMINER

Altydgedacht Gewürztraminer ★★★ B
This wine always has enticing nose and good fruity flavours, and is finished bone dry. This is a good example of a dry Gewürztraminer. The 1989 was labelled 'Masquerade'. The 1993 has developed dramatically.

Ashton Co-op Gewürztraminer ★★★ A
Improving by the vintage, this is an off-dry wine with tropical spice nose and brisk finish. Good value for money.

Backsberg Gewürztraminer
(See page 218, Noble Late Harvest)

Bergsig Gewürztraminer ★★★ B
A very pleasant off-dry wine with attractive nose. (See page 211, Special Late Harvest.)

Boschendal Jean Garde Gewürztraminer ★★★★ D
The first release comes from the 1986 vintage, from the Estate's single vineyard scheme. The 1987 was far better wine, in line with the quality expected of the Cape's better Gewürztraminers. The 1988 was a little light and lacked the concentration of the 1987. The 1989 was slightly disappointing, but the 1990 is dry, with fuller nose and better flavour. The 1990 was judged the best South African dry white wine at the International Wine and Spirit Competition and received the Cape Wine Academy trophy. The 1992 is somewhat subdued, but still attractive.

Bottelary Co-op Gewürztraminer ★★★ B
Throughout the 1980s this was a very good wine. Those of the 1990s are pleasant, but lack the concentration of the earlier wines.

Bovlei Co-op Gewürztraminer ★★★ B
A semi-sweet wine introduced from the 1991 vintage. A good start. The 1992 is a little quieter, but a very pleasant drink.

Danie de Wet Gewürztraminer ★★★(★) B
Dry wine in the style of Alsace, it has good rose petal nose, a nice, dry, herby flavour and clean finish. First release is from the 1991 vintage.

Delheim Gewürztraminer ★★★★(★) C
Always an interesting wine. This is one of the few South African Gewürztraminers which can deservedly be called Gewürztraminer. Super when young, it ages with benefit. All the 1980s were super. The 1990 was a more luscious and softer wine. The 1991 is one of the better, from consistently good vintages. The 1992 is a stunner with its beautiful rose petal nose, and lots of spicey and peach flavours. It has clean finish and big alcohol for good ageing. This is the best wine from this cultivar.

Die Krans Estate Gewürztraminer ★★★ B
The first release from 1989 vintage was very short on cultivar character. The 1990 was off-dry, lacked Gewürztraminer, but had pretty flowery

nose in its youth. The 1991 seems to have come of age, with good, rose petal nose and attractive, spicey flavour. It is finished off-dry.

Douglas Co-op Gewürztraminer ★★(★) A
The 1991 vintage was a semi-sweet, low-alcohol wine with nice floral character. This was followed by a similar 1992. Good price.

Fleur du Cap Gewürztraminer (Bergkelder) ★★★★ C
The first release from the 1984 vintage has lovely cultivar nose and delightful, semi-sweet, full-flavoured taste. The next release, from the 1990 vintage, is full of rose petal nose and nice spicey flavours. This is a lovely off-dry wine. The 1991 is also off-dry and ranks as one of the Cape's best – a four-star wine – with a nose full of flowery 'come-ons' and the taste a delight of fruits and spices, with long lingering finish.

Groot Constantia Gewürztraminer ★★★★ D
This is a very good off-dry version of the cultivar; it has full Gewürztraminer nose with plenty of flavour. The 1991 is great wine with all kinds of fruit flavours, made more complex by a touch of botrytis. It is consistently one of the country's best. The 1992 is along the same gorgeous lines.

Nederburg Gewürztraminer ★★★★★ C
This was originally sold at the annual Auction as a delicate, semi-sweet white with true rose petal nose. More recently, it has been released as a 'special'. Twice in succession it has been awarded the trophy for best Gewürztraminer on show at the Club Oenologique International Wine and Spirit Competition, first with the 1983 vintage at the 1984 event and then with the 1984 vintage at the 1985 event, helping Günter Brözel on his way to the Winemaker of the Year accolade. This wine has outstanding nose with full, rich flavour enhanced by the excellent sugar-acid balance. The 1985 vintage brought Günter his second Diners Club Award. The 1986 is one of the best ever – a beautiful wine. The powerful 1988 is developing very well. The 1989 is made in a slightly lighter style but has also developed with benefit. The 1990 and 1991 have it all – intense fruit and spice, floral nose with lots of rose petal, and is finished off-dry.

Nederburg Elgin Gewürztraminer ★★★★
This is a lovely, semi-sweet wine with enticing floral and spicey aromas and flavours.

Neil Ellis Gewürztraminer ★★★★ D
This is a beautiful, almost bone-dry wine in the style of the Alsace. It has wonderful rose petal scents and lots of Gewürztraminer. No more will be released under this label, but older vintages have developed beautifully.

Neethlingshof Gewürztraminer ★★★★ C
Originally one of the better dry versions of this cultivar in the Cape, it is now finished off-dry. The 1990 and 1991 vintages brings it into the ranks of the Cape's best. It is a complex wine, with full, rose petal bouquet, aromas and lots of lovely fruit salad flavour.

Roodezandt Co-op Gewürztraminer ★★★ **B/C**
This bone-dry wine, with good nose, full of flowery aromas and nice clean flavours, is briskly finished. The 1991 is softer and nicer.

Stellenryk Gewürztraminer ★★★★ **C**
Another of the Cape's fine Gewürztraminers. An off-dry wine, it sets off the cultivar at its best. It has lovely nose and good flavour. The first release from the 1984 vintage carried Superior Certification and aged dramatically. The next release, from 1990, is dry and wonderfully fragrant, with delicious flavours.

Theuniskraal Estate Gewürztraminer ★★★
This is a fairly ordinary, semi-sweet Gewürztraminer, not in keeping with the modern, bright styles. The 1988 is showing its age.

Van Loveren Gewürztraminer ★★★(★) **B**
The first release was from the 1987 vintage. This big, full-bodied wine has a high alcohol content, but is a little shy on cultivar character. With each vintage it has become progressively better.

Vlottenburg Co-op Gewürztraminer ★★★ **B**
The 1987 was beautiful, rich, sweet wine, certified Superior, and full of flavour and character. The inexpensive 1988 was less exciting but carried Superior; it appeared much sweeter, as did the 1990. The 1991 is much better wine, with lovely nose, good flavours and in a much better pack – four-star wine. The 1992 is not quite as good, but still very appealing.

Weltevrede Gewürztraminer ★★★★ **C**
This is consistently good wine, and the 1991 is one of the best. It has good rose petal nose, nice spicey flavour, and is finished off-dry, although it tastes much drier. Good, brisk finish. The 1992 is good, stylish and super, as well as excellent value.

Woolworths Le Quatrieme 914W ★★★★ **C**
This wine from Villiera is part of the Woolworths Vintage Collection. 91 indicates vintage; 4, fourth in the range; and W is for white. It is just off-dry but has enough acid to balance. Delicious wine.

Zevenwacht Gewürztraminer ★★★★ **C**
This wine is consistently top quality in a dry style. The 1991 has high alcohol, with lots of floral tones and spices, and a full, soft flavour. Delicious wine and one of the best. The 1992 continues the stylish quality.

Zonnebloem Gewürztraminer (SFW) ★★★ **C**
This wine has prominent spicey nose and good flavour. It is just off-dry and at its best when young and fresh.

HÁRSLEVELÜ

Lemberg (Hárslevelü) ★★★★ C
Previously called Hárslevelü, this wine is now called Lemberg. Hárslevelü has never been my favourite cultivar, yet the wines from this cellar's vintages of the early 1990s, have made me accept that wines that are not just good, but that really appeal to me, can be made from this Hungarian cultivar. The 1991 and 1992 are super, and elevate this label to a four-star wine – the Cape's best from this cultivar. It has lots of fruit on the nose, good full flavour, nice body and fresh finish. It will develop well with time.

Porterville Co-op Hárslevelü ★★ A
This is a new wine for this cellar, from the 1991 vintage. It is almost semi-sweet and is clean, fresh wine.

Swartland Co-op Hárslevelü ★★ A
The 1990 almost qualifies for the 'Light' category.

Van Loveren Hárslevelü ★★ A
This is one of the better examples of this variety, which first appeared with the 1982 vintage. It is consistently good each vintage. Nowadays it is finished just off-dry, and is reliable, good drinking wine.

Vredendal Co-op Hárslevelü ★★(★) A
One of the better efforts with this variety from a Co-op, this dry wine has full flavour and a somewhat sharp finish. Latest releases of this wine have good nose, herby flavour, and are soft and easy-drinking.

LATE HARVEST

Aan-de-Doorns Co-op Laatoes Steen ★★(★) A
A honey-nosed wine in Late Harvest style.

Andalusia Late Vintage (Vaalharts Co-op) ★(★) B
A semi-sweet Colombar and Chenel blend.

Ashton Co-op Laatoes ★★(★) A
This wine has a Colombar base, with other varieties giving a fruity-nosed, light bodied, semi-sweet, gentle wine.

Autumn Harvest Late Vintage ★★ A
A semi-sweet blend with clean, honeyed nose and soft, fruity flavour.

Badsberg Co-op Late Harvest ★★ A
A delicate semi-sweet wine, sometimes made from Steen, but more recently from Colombar and Hanepoot.

Bakenskop Late Harvest (Jonkheer)★★ A
A good, semi-sweet white made from clean, fruity Colombar.

Barrydale Late Harvest ★★ A
A semi-sweet wine with nice, fruity nose.

Beaufort Late Harvest (Solly Kramer) ★★(★) A
This is a typical example of a semi-sweet, honeyed nose Late Harvest. Like all the products in the range, it is excellent value for money.

Bergendal Late Harvest ★★★ B
This semi-sweet multiple blend has clean style and fresh finish.

Bolandse Co-op Late Vintage ★★(★)A
A Chenin Blanc-based, semi-sweet wine, with honeyed nose.

Bon Courage Kerner Late Harvest ★★★ B
This is a rich, semi-sweet white, with lovely flavour and soft mellow taste.

Boplaas Late Harvest ★★(★)B
This reliable, semi-sweet wine has attractive nose and good flavour; usually from Colombar and Muscat.

Botha Co-op Chenin Blanc Late Harvest ★★ A
A semi-sweet, Late Harvest-style wine from Chenin Blanc.

Bottelary Co-op Late Harvest ★★ A
A semi-sweet white, which is fairly full-flavoured and has honeyed nose.

Brandvlei Co-op Laat Oes ★★ A
Made from Steen, this is pleasant, fruity, semi-sweet wine.

Breughel Late Harvest (Aroma Group) ★★ A
A semi-sweet wine with a slightly honeyed nose and flavour from Steen.

Carnival Late Harvest (Spar) ★★(★) A
A pleasant semi-sweet wine from Colombar and Steen.

Cellar Cask Premier Late Harvest (Castle Wine and EK Green) ★★ A
A good, rich-flavoured, semi-sweet wine from Steen. Originally it was only available in a box, but it now comes in cork-closed bottles.

Cellar Reserve Late Harvest (Hyperama) ★★ A

A semi-sweet, fresh, fruity wine.

Checkers Yellow Label Late Harvest ★★(★) A

This is a multiple blend, with fruity nose, and is finished semi-sweet.

Clairvaux Late Harvest ★★ A

A soft, semi-sweet wine from Rhine Riesling.

Culemborg Late Harvest (Douglas Green Bellingham) ★★★ B

This is an ever-improving wine, with good sweetness and acid balance.

De Doorns Co-op Laatoes ★ A

A pleasant, semi-sweet wine.

De Leuwen Jagt Late Harvest ★★★ B

This wine has attractive nose and good flavour in which the small percentage of Chardonnay in the mainly Chenin Blanc blend stands out. It is not too sweet, well-made, good drinking wine.

Delheim Spatzendreck Late Harvest ★★★(★) B

This is a semi-sweet wine which is labelled 'Late Harvest'. The name and the cheeky sparrow featured on the label reflect the lively nature of its wine maker, Michael 'Spatz' Sperling. A sample of one of his first efforts, produced when he was struggling with the techniques of wine-making, was given to a friend – and promptly evoked a simple, four-letter, agricultural assessment. Sperling vowed to make the man eat his words and, eventually, after years of doggedly determined experiment, produced this splendid Late Harvest. The name he gave it is a whimsical play on words: both Michael's surname and nickname mean 'sparrow' in German; 'spatzendreck' literally translates as 'sparrow droppings' – an appropriate, if not entirely sophisticated, allusion to the original trial sampling. It is a semi-sweet, full-bodied wine, nowadays based on Steen, with good Late Harvest qualities. In 1986, the wine celebrated its 25th anniversary, with an excellent 1985 vintage carrying Superior certification. All recent vintages are very good, luscious, full-flavoured wines. The 1991 is splendid, and the 1992 has distinct muscat nose.

Die Krans Late Harvest ★★(★)A

This is a multiple blend of Colombar and Steen, and a touch of Muscat, which gives a lovely flavour and fresh, fruity nose.

Douglas Co-op Late Harvest ★(★)A

A wine from Colombar, with Steen and Hanepoot, finished semi-sweet.

Douglas Green Late Harvest ★★(★)B

A clean, well-made, light-style Late Harvest.

Drostdy-Hof Late Harvest (Cape Wine) ★★ B

A nice, fruity, clean, semi-sweet wine.

Edelkeller Late Harvest ★★★ B

Well-made, good-tasting, sweet white wine.

Goudini Co-op Steen Late Harvest ★★(★) A

A good semi-sweet white with pleasant flavour and fruity nose.

Goue Vallei Late Harvest (Citrusdal Co-op)★★★ A

Based on Steen, with some Sauvignon Blanc and a touch of Muscat, the result is pleasant, fruity wine, with attractive nose and fresh finish.

Groot Eiland Co-op Laat-Oes Steen ★★(★)

This is an attractive, honey-flavoured, semi-sweet wine.

Helderberg Co-op Late Vintage ★★(★) B

A well-made wine where Steen dominates in its own Late Harvest style.

Huguenot Late Harvest ★★(★)A

A nice, fresh, fruity, simple Late Harvest, with clean finish.

Jonkerskloof Late Harvest (OK) ★★ A

This is a well made, semi-sweet wine, based on Steen and Colombar.

Kellerprinz Late Harvest (SFW)★★ A

This is a remarkable wine, not only in terms of the volume of its sales but also because of its surprisingly good Late Harvest character.

Klawer Co-op Late Vintage ★ A

A semi-sweet Steen and Colombar blend that is pleasant tasting but lacks nose.

Kleindal Late Harvest ★★★ B

A pleasant, honey-nosed, semi-sweet wine from the 1989 vintage.

Kupferberger Auslese (Bergkelder)★★★ C

Basically a Late Harvest Steen, this wine has improved in quality in recent years and now shows very good Late Harvest character.

KWV Late Harvest ★★★ (no price available)

An easy-drinking semi-sweet wine with appealing flavour.

Landzicht Late Harvest ★★(★) A

This is a multiple blend with an attractive nose.

Langverwacht Co-op Late Harvest ★★ A

A light, fruity, semi-sweet Steen.

Loopspruit Late Vintage ★★★ B

This is good, fruity, semi-sweet white wine.

Louwshoek-Voorsorg Co-op Laatoes ★★(★) A

A very sweet, full-bodied wine from Chenin Blanc.

Lutzville Co-op Laatoes ★ A

A fruity-nosed, semi-sweet wine, usually from Steen, sometimes Colombar.

Mamreweg Co-op Late Harvest ★★ B

A semi-sweet Steen with good cultivar character.

McGregor Co-op Laatoes Steen ★★ A

This was one of the more interesting Co-op semi-sweet Steens, that had some Late Harvest character. Nowadays it is from Weisser Riesling.

Merwespont Co-op Late Vintage ★★ A

A blend of equal proportions of Steen and Colombar, with good, fruity nose and pleasant flavour.

Monterey Late Harvest (Western Province Cellars) ★ A

A soft, full, semi-sweet wine.

Montpellier Late Harvest ★★(★) B

The blend varies vintage by vintage, but it is always pleasing, light and fresh wine, with fruity nose and appealing flavour.

Nordale Co-op Late Harvest ★★ A

A semi-sweet wine made from Steen, with fine, fruity flavour.

Nuy Steen Late Harvest ★★★★ B

A well-made, good-flavoured wine, full of fruit and very well balanced. It makes lovely easy drinking, and is best enjoyed when young. It stands out in the wide range of wines labelled Late Harvest.

Oranjerivier Wynkelder Late Harvest ★ A

A Sultana-Colombar blend, finished semi-sweet.

Overhex Bukettraube Late Harvest ★★(★)B

A gentle, semi-sweet wine, with flowery nose and soft flavour.

Overmeer Laatoes ★★(★) A

A consistently good, clean-flavoured, semi-sweet white wine, which makes pleasant, easy drinking.

Overvaal Late Harvest (Vaalharts Co-op)★★ A

A semi-sweet blend of Chenel and sometimes Steen, or Colombar.

Party Pack Late Harvest ★★

A semi-sweet, fruity-nosed bag-in-the-box wine.

Perdeberg Co-op Late Vintage ★★ A

This is a semi-sweet wine, with attractive fruity nose and pleasing flavour.

Porterville Co-op Late Vintage ★ A

A semi-sweet Steen with full flavour.

Ravenswood Late Harvest (Pick 'n Pay) ★★ A

A semi-sweet, low-alcohol wine, with clean finish.

Rebel Late Harvest ★★ A

A full, semi-sweet wine.

Rendition Late Vintage (Welmoed Co-op) ★★ A

A good, fruity Steen with nice, full flavour.

Riebeek Co-op Late Harvest ★★★ A

A well-made, semi-sweet wine from Steen and Rhine Riesling with lots of flavour and well-balanced fruit.

Rietrivier Co-op Late Harvest ★★ A

An interesting, semi-sweet Late Harvest, blended from varying cultivars, vintage to vintage. Usually Colombar, with Steen and Sauvignon Blanc.

Robertson Co-op Steen Late Vintage ★★★ A

Although named 'Steen', recent vintages contain 25% Rhine Riesling, giving a very pleasant, easy-drinking wine with a clean, fresh finish.

Romansrivier Co-op Late Harvest ★★(★)A

This is a well-made, good-flavoured, clean, semi-sweet wine.

Roodezandt Co-op Late Harvest ★★(★)B

A full-flavoured wine of reasonable body and clean, clear finish. Previously of Steen, but now from Colombar.

Rooiberg Co-op Late Vintage ★★★ B
The Vinkrivier Ward provided the grapes for this semi-sweet wine. It has full nose and flavour, and a little Muscat on the nose. It is well made wine, with good Late Vintage character.

Rusthof Late Harvest (Mooiuitsig)★★ A
A semi-sweet white wine with attractive Muscat nose.

Simondium Wines Co-op Late Harvest ★★ A
A semi-sweet, Colombar-based wine with some Muscat.

Simonsvlei Co-op Late Vintage ★★ B
An honest, semi-sweet Steen of medium body.

Slanghoek Co-op Late Harvest ★★ A
A good wine, with good fruity flavour.

Soetwynboere Late Harvest ★★ A
This is a nice flavoured wine which is finished semi-sweet.

Spruitdrift Co-op Late Harvest ★★★ A
A semi-sweet wine with far more Late Harvest character than most in this category. It is full-flavoured and ages reasonably well.

Swartland Co-op Late Vintage ★★ A
This is a blend which has varied unbelievably over the years, but is ordinary, easy-drinking Steen.

Trawal Co-op Late Harvest ★★
A complex semi-sweet, Steen-based blend with spicy nose.

Tulbagh Co-op Late Harvest ★★ A
A semi-sweet white with soft feel and pleasant flavour, from Steen, Colombar and Sauvignon Blanc.

Twee Jongegezellen Night Harvest ★★★(★) C
This Late Harvest-style wine is made from grapes picked in the cool of the night, thereby retaining the delicate nuances of the grape. The multiple blend varies with the year, and can contain Steen, Sauvignon Blanc, Gewürztraminer, Rhine Riesling and even Furmint, giving a rich, yet delicately flavoured, semi-sweet wine, with a touch of botrytis.

Valley Late Harvest (Gilbeys) ★(★) B
A full-flavoured, semi-sweet wine, with Muscat which adds to its attraction.

Villiersdorp Co-op Late Vintage ★★★ A
Clean, fresh wine, with brisk finish.

Vinovat Late Harvest (Marcows) ★ A
A semi-sweet blend.

Vintner's Choice (Drop Inn) Late Harvest ★★ A
This is pleasant, semi-sweet wine, with flowery nose and brisk finish.

Vredendal Co-op Late Harvest ★★★ A
A nice Steen-based wine with varying blending partners (recently Sauvignon Blanc and Hárslevelü), giving fresh fruity wine.

Vredenheim Late Harvest ★★ C
From 1991 comes a Steen with fruity, honey nose and gentle flavour.

Wamakersvallei Laat Oes ★★ A

This semi-sweet wine has a fruity, spicey nose with good flavour.

Wellington Wynboere Late Vintage ★★ A

A pleasant, light-bodied, semi-sweet wine, with a bit of Muscat nose.

Weltevrede Therona Late Harvest ★★★ B

This Late Harvest is made from a locally-developed grape variety, and makes for easy drinking. It is clean, well-made and fruity.

Witzenberg Late Harvest Edelgoud (Cape Wine) ★★(★) A

A semi-sweet, soft, white wine with honeyed nose.

Woolworths Late Harvest ★★(★) A

A good, semi-sweet wine, which drinks easily.

Woolworths Petit Vin Late Harvest ★★ B

A semi-sweet, white wine, available in 250 ml Tetrapak.

SPECIAL LATE HARVEST

Aan-de-Doorns Co-op Spesiale Laatoes Steen ★★ A

This wine was introduced with the 1987 vintage, and was regarded as light, delicate and easy-drinking. The 1989 had more botrytis than usual. The 1991 was somewhat delicate, but the 1992 is full of fresh scents and flavours, without botrytis.

Ashton Co-op Special Late Harvest ★★★ A

The 1991 was a most attractive wine from Muscat de Frontignan, and remarkable value. The 1992 is a disappointment.

Backsberg Special Late Harvest ★★★★ B

A luscious, full-flavoured, rich wine, with a honeyed Steen taste that is soft and smooth across the palate. This wine has always been good and is now making the most of the more recent laws allowing higher sugar levels. It used to carry Superior certification. It is usually a blend of Steen, Muscat and Gewürztraminer, with the latter consistently good and giving a flowery lift to the nose.

Barrydale Co-op Special Late Harvest ★★★ B

The 1992 is fresh-flavoured wine, with nice smoothness.

Bellingham Special Late Harvest ★★(★) C

The recent releases are Steen-based, with Rhine Riesling and Sauvignon Blanc. They are clean tasting, brisk finish, semi-sweet wines, and not the botrytis wines of the middle 1980s.

Bergsig Chenin Blanc Special Late Harvest ★★★ B

A good, golden, rich, sweet wine, which is consistently good. The 1991 and 1992 are good, fruity wines, with satisfying flavour and fresh finish.

Bergsig Gewürztraminer Special Late Harvest ★★★★ B

This wine is well made, with intense flavours of peaches and tropical fruits. It has great complexity, is lovely young and develops well.

Bergsig Weisser Riesling Special Late Harvest ★★★ B

From the 1989 vintage came this good, semi-sweet wine with definite cultivar character. It has developed well and should be consumed now.

Blaauwklippen Special Late Vintage ★★★(★) B

This is a wine with a long history of success, of which 1990 seems to be the last release. The cellar is now opting for the Natural Sweet route. The 1990 is developing well. Blaauwklippen suggests serving this wine in summer, poured over crushed ice.

Bon Courage Gewürztraminer Special Late Harvest ★★★★ C

André Bruwer has a string of awards to his name, but the one he probably takes most delight in was the 1991 Diners Club Award for his 1989 Gewürztraminer Special Late Harvest. When the quality of Cape Special Late Harvests is so high, to be judged the best is no mean accolade. With its 11,6% alcohol and 48 g/l sugar balanced with 6,6 g/l acid, the wine has good botrytis character, yet enough fruit flavour to be very attractive. The 1990 is more elegant, with citrus and tropical fruit flavours, and the 1991 has the most enticing floral nose. It is developing layers of lovely flavour in the bottle. Delicious wine.

Bon Courage Kerner Special Late Harvest ★★★(★) B

This is usually a good, full-flavoured wine, which has had a surprising lack of aroma, but is well balanced. The 1986 had good botrytis, which added much-needed complexity. This wine is ageing with interest.

Boplaas Special Late Harvest ★★★(★) B

Usually blended from late-harvested Colombar, Muscat d'Alexandrie and a little Weisser Riesling, this combination results in a most attractive nose, touched out with enough botrytis to give a fascinating complexity, although the wine still has good, clean freshness. The 1990 was Steen and Muscat, and appears slightly less sweet than usual, giving better elegance. This is a lovely, fragrant wine.

Bovlei Co-op Special Late Harvest ★★ A

A pleasant semi-sweet wine with lots of bottle age.

Clairvaux Co-op Special Late Harvest ★★(★) B

This Steen-based, well balanced wine has light, but most attractive, fruity nose. The pleasing flavour makes for easy drinking.

Delaire Special Late Harvest ★★★★ C

This is a delicious, full, fruity wine from the 1989 vintage. It has good botrytis with citrus and tropical fruit tones. Lovely as it is when young, it has developed beautifully in the bottle.

Delheim Special Late Harvest ★★★★ B

This was excellent wine throughout the 1980s and regularly certified Superior. The 1989 was tremendous and developed with benefit. The 1990 is a slightly lesser wine, although it continues to be one of the Cape's best. The 1991 is a stunner and the 1992 continues the delicious style.

De Wet Co-op Special Late Harvest ★★★ B

Based on Chenin Blanc, sometime with a bit of Bukettraube for spiciness and other times Colombar, this is semi-sweet wine with enough acidity to have a brisk finish.

Die Krans Special Late Harvest ★★★ A

Not too sweet, with slight botrytis character, this wine is most recently blended from Steen and some Hanepoot.

Drostdy Hof Adelpracht Special Late Harvest (Cape Wine) ★★★ B

This is a good example of a well-made Late Harvest Steen, which regularly carried Superior certification. It is always good quality and good value.

Du Toitskloof Co-op Special Late Harvest ★★★★ B

Established as one of the consistently better Special Late Harvests, this is good, full-flavoured wine that is a regular award winner. The 1988 was particularly good, with lots of flavour and a little botrytis, and is developing well. The 1989 has also developed well and now needs drinking. The 1990 has better botrytis, with good fruit acid. The 1991 is fresh, clean wine, without botrytis, and drinks well in 1993. The 1992 is more muscaty and not quite up to the standard of previous vintages.

Edward Snell Special Late Vintage ★★★ B

A good, clean, well-made wine, with fruity nose and rich flavour.

Eersterivier-Valleise Kelder Special Late Harvest ★★★ B

A fine Late Harvest, with particularly pleasing nose, which ages well in the bottle. The 1987 is from Steen, the 1988 from Sauvignon Blanc and the more recent releases have a very attractive, Gewürztraminer character.

Eikendal Special Late Harvest ★★★★ C

The first release, from the 1986 vintage, has established itself as one of the better Special Late Harvest wines. The 1990 was bigger and better in every way – more botrytis, more nose, more flavour. It is developing with great benefit. The 1991 is attractive, but without the botrytis it doesn't have the complexity of the 1990. The 1992 shows more botrytis.

Fairview Special Late Harvest ★★★(★) C

This is a good wine which has varied in taste over the past few vintages, but is always full of fine, fresh flavour at the time of release. Nowadays it is usually made from Steen, with an occasional touch of Bukettraube. It often carried Superior. The 1991 and 1992 are super, four-star wines.

Fleermuisklip Spesiale Laatoes (Lutzville Co-op) ★★ A

From Colombar, comes this simple, semi-sweet wine, which is ready for early consumption.

Fleur Du Cap Special Late Harvest (Bergkelder) ★★★★ C

A lovely wine with enticing botrytis character. It usually carried Superior certification and develops beautifully in the bottle. The 1983 won the Cape Wine Academy Trophy for the highest scoring Cape white wine at the 1988 International Wine and Spirit Competition. In 1988 and 1989 it was awarded the Mondé Selection trophy, and in 1991 it gained Double Gold Veritas. The 1989 is developing nicely in the bottle and is a lovely, stylish, elegant wine. The 1990 continues the elegant style.

Goue Vallei Special Late Harvest (Citrusdal Co-op) ★★(★) A

A respectable, well-balanced wine, with tropical fruit and nice smooth texture is now being produced in an effort to improve the cellar's quality.

Hartenberg L'Estreux ★★★★ C

L'Estreux is only bottled in vintages when the cellar believes that nature has provided the style of wine that fits their quality requirement. There was no 1986, owing to a lack of botrytis. The 1987 is made from Steen that was harvested at about 30 Balling and some 30% botrytis-infested, giving delightfully attractive nose and complex flavour. It is about at its best now. The 1989 is 40% Steen, with the balance made up of Gewürztraminer, Morio Muscat and others. It has a nice touch of botrytis, but not enough to cover the fresh, fruity, Muscat character. Although included in this section, it is not certified Special Late Harvest. The 1990 continues the same enticing quality. The 1991 is, to my taste, the best so far – made from no fewer than five cultivars, including some botrytized Gewürztraminer, giving a full range of perfumes, luscious feel and fresh finish. The 1992 is a blend of Gewürztraminer and Morio Muscat, made more complex with botrytis. A delicious wine.

Hazendal Freudenlese ★★★ C

This Special Late Harvest was first released from the 1982 vintage with 44 g/l residual sugar. Fresh and fruity when first released, it has developed well in the bottle. It carried Superior certification. The 1987 was a full-bodied wine with a hint of botrytis, and although the 1988 is a full, sweet wine, it has a rather dull nose. The 1990 is a fresher, better wine with a honey-like character.

Huguenot Special Late Harvest ★★ B

A semi-sweet wine with honey hints and good balance; best when young.

Kaapzicht Weisser Riesling Special Late Harvest ★★★ B

This wine has an attractive nose, soft texture and a clean, sharp finish.

Klawer Co-op Special Late Vintage ★★ A

A full-flavoured, sweet wine made from Steen. Some years it has botrytis nose, and in others, not.

Koelenhof Co-op Chenin Blanc Spesiale Laatoes ★★(★) B

A well-balanced, good-value-for-money wine, which is not too sweet, yet has a nice touch of botrytis.

Lievland Kerner Special Late Harvest ★★★ D

Released from the 1985 vintage, this wine had a strange but not unattractive nose and good, full flavour, which is developing well in the bottle. The 1987 is a good, full-flavoured wine, with a distinctive nose, and carries Superior certification. The 1989 has a full, fruity nose and good flavour, which should bottle-age with benefit.

Lievland Special Late Harvest ★★★ B

A blend of varieties, including Weisser Riesling and Kerner, with some botrytis and good fruit on the nose, makes this wine smooth in the mouth with ripe flavours. Lovely wine.

L'Ormarins Guldenpfennig ★★★(★) C

A lovely, fresh-flavoured, Late Harvest-style wine, full of attractive nose and complex flavour.

Lutzville Co-op Spesiale Laatoes ★★ A

A semi-sweet wine from Colombar.

Mamreweg Co-op Special Late Harvest ★★(★) B

Made from Steen, this wine has reasonable Late Harvest character, and nice softness in the mouth.

Montpellier Special Late Harvest ★★★(★) B

The first release, from the 1985 vintage, was very good wine. It had good botrytis nose and lovely, fruity, semi-sweet taste from Hárslevelü. The

1989 is a blend of Chenin Blanc, Hárslevelü and Rhine Riesling. The blend of 1990 changes again to Bukettraube, Riesling, Sauvignon Blanc and Steen, which has a honey-like character, and is rich in the mouth, with a fresh finish.

Nederburg Special Late Harvest ★★★★ C

This is South Africa's leading Late Harvest wine which has enjoyed many, many years of acclaim for its high quality. This Wine of Origin Paarl is full of sweet richness, developed from grapes allowed to age on the vine prior to pressing. In recent years it has had very good botrytis, or noble rot, character which places it in a class of its own. With the most recent definitions of sweetness legally classifying Late Harvest wines, the Nederburg is automatically classed as Special Late Harvest and was almost always certified Superior. When allowed to age for three to four years, a luscious wine of intense depth develops – an outstanding example of an elegant and gentle botrytis wine. Eight successive vintages carried Superior before this certification was dropped. Latest releases are more complex blends of Sauvignon Blanc and Steen, topped with Gewürztraminer. The 1990 is a show-stopper!

Nederburg Weisser Riesling Special Late Harvest ★★★★ D

The first release of this elegant, rich, golden-textured wine came from an almost perfect 1982 vintage. This yielded a beautiful wine, released only at the annual Nederburg Auction. The 1986 vintage was sold at the 1988 Auction and the 1987 sold at the 1989 and 1990 Auctions. It is probably the best so far, but all are developing with great distinction.

Vintage	Alcohol	Sugar g/l	Acid g/l
1982	14,29	26,4	7,0
1986	11,6	40,9	6,1
1987	13,6	45,6	6,8

Neethlingshof Gewürztraminer Special Late Harvest ★★★★ B

A well-made wine from the 1984 vintage, with excellent cultivar character. It has developed beautifully in the bottle, but has given way to the Noble Late Harvests.

Neethlingshof Weisser Riesling Special Late Harvest ★★★★ C

The maiden vintage of 1983 was a beautiful wine, with complexity which can only come from botrytis and good wine-making. It has been awarded Superior certification and is developing beautifully in the bottle. It has also given way to the Noble Late Harvests.

Overhex Spesiale Laatoes ★★★ A

A Late Harvest Steen with full flavour, available in screw-top bottles.

Pick 'n Pay Special Late Harvest ★★★

A lovely floral wine that makes very easy drinking.

Rendition Special Late Harvest (Welmoed Co-op) ★★(★) A

A good, full, Late Harvest wine. The 1992, from Steen, has very little nose but nice flavour, and is for early drinking.

Rhebokskloof Special Late Vintage ★★★(★) C

This wine is not available on a regular basis. The 1990 was most attractive and has developed well in the bottle. The 1992 is particularly good.

Riebeek Co-op Special Late Harvest ★★★(★) A

The 1991 is a big wine, from Rhine Riesling, with good fruit. It has not developed as well as anticipated.

Robertson Co-op Special Late Harvest ★★★(★) B

Since 1989 it has been certified Gewürztraminer. The 1990 lacked 'gewürz', but the 1991 has good rose petal nose and is not too sweet.

Romansrivier Co-op Special Late Harvest ★★★ A

Recent vintages are very good, Steen-based wines with good botrytis character. They are full-flavoured wines that are best enjoyed young.

Roodezandt Co-op Special Late Harvest ★★★ A

The varietal has varied over the years from Steen, Colombar and lately Gewürztraminer. This wine is always good.

Rooiberg Co-op Spesiale Laat Oes ★★★ A

The earlier vintages made from Colombar were most unusual wines. The 1988, from Steen, had lots of good, rich flavour, but no botrytis. The 1989 was made from Steen with 20% Gewürztraminer, giving good spicey/fruity flavours. It was a four-star product. The 1990 was the same blend, but not quite as good, and the 1991 was much the same.

Saxenheim Special Late Harvest ★★★(★) B

The 1985 was the first release and was followed by the Superior 1986. The 1987 had good botrytis character, is not too sweet and has developed well. The 1991 follows in the same character.

Simonsig Franciskaner Special Late Harvest ★★★(★) B

Generally a good, Steen-based, late-harvested wine with medium body and rich sweetness. All vintages have been good and have aged well.

Simonsig Gewürztraminer Special Late Harvest ★★★★ C

This wine is always good, and the 1991 is delicious wine with good varietal flavours, made more complex with light botrytis.

Simonsvlei Co-op Special Late Harvest ★★(★) B

The 1990 and 1991 are good wines, with botrytis influence, and good, brisk, fresh finish. The 1992 lacks botrytis, but is a very pleasant wine.

Spruitdrift Co-op Special Late Harvest ★★★(★) A

The original release was the 1982, and it had the distinction of being the first Olifants River wine to gain Superior certification. The 1990, from Sauvignon Blanc, is nice and fruity.

Swartland Co-op Special Late Harvest ★★★ B

This is a full-flavoured, semi-sweet wine made from Steen. The 1992 has retained good Steen flavour with hints of honey.

Thelema Special Late Harvest ★★★★

This is a wood-aged blend of nearly two-thirds Rhine Riesling and a third Sauvignon Blanc, with a touch of muscat. It is not too sweet.

Trawal Wynkelder Co-op ★★

This pleasant, semi-sweet, Steen-based wine has some Colombar and a touch of muscat.

Van Loveren Special Late Harvest ★★★(★) B

This is consistently good wine, with recent vintages showing good Gewürztraminer. The 1991 contains a massive 14,5% alcohol and will develop as well as all the previous vintages. The 1992 also shows Gewürztraminer, but is much more delicate.

Villiera Garonne Special Late Harvest ★★★★ B

Consistently pleasant, full-bodied, Steen-based wine with an attractive complexity that develops well over a year or two. This is one of the best.

Vlottenburg Co-op Special Late Harvest ★★★ A

This is usually a sprightly, fruity wine with enough acid to balance the sweetness. It occasionally carried Superior certification when this still existed. The 1990 and 1991 are delicious, elegant wines.

Vredendal Co-op Special Late Harvest ★★ A

A soft, well-flavoured wine in Late Harvest style.

Vredenheim Special Late Harvest ★★(★) B

This is a wine with full flavour and pleasant nose, which is showing some bottle age.

Weltevrede Special Late Harvest ★★★(★) B

Weltevrede's strength lies in their Superior liqueur wines, and clearly this rich, semi-sweet Late Harvest shows that the wine maker has a feel for sweeter wines. It is a very good example of a Chenin Blanc in Late Harvest style, often touched with Gewürztraminer.

Zevenwacht Special Late Harvest ★★★ C

The 1988 can still be found on the shelves. It is showing lots of bottle age, but is still attractive.

Zonnebloem Special Late Harvest (SFW) ★★★(★) C

The successor to the popular Zonnebloem Late Harvest, the Special Late Harvest, was launched with the 1982 vintage and carried Superior certification. The 1989 and 1990 are complex, quiet wines.

NOBLE LATE HARVEST

Backsberg Noble Late Harvest ★★★★ E

To my knowledge this was the earliest Gewürztraminer made in Noble Late Harvest style. First made from the 1987 vintage, it is full-flavoured, light-coloured and packed with good character, and is one of the more elegant wines. It has developed very well. In spite of the botrytis, the 1988 still has very good varietal character; it has developed beautifully and is a lovely wine.

Bellingham Noble Late Harvest (DGB) ★★★★ D

The first of Bellingham's limited-release wines was a 1987 Noble Late Harvest. It is a lovely botrytised wine, with good raisin character, and has developed beautifully. The 1991 vintage is full of floral fragrance from Gewürztraminer and forms part of Bellingham's French theme. The 1992 is along the same lines and has good rose petal character.

Bergsig Edel Laatoes ★★★(★) D

This good, Steen-based wine, with its attractive nose and luscious palate, celebrated its maiden vintage in 1982. The 1983 vintage had 12% Bukettraube and 8% Chenel added to the blend, giving a fuller wine with more complex nose and rich flavour. Both were awarded Superior certification. The 1984, made from Chenin Blanc, has good botrytis, complexity, and crisp finish, which is developing well.

Blaauwklippen Noble Late Vintage ★★★★(★) C

A powerfully flavoured wine with botrytis character. It is ageing beautifully. Like most Noble Late Harvests, it is not available on a regular basis.

Boland Co-op Noble Late Harvest ★★★★ D

The first release from 1992 is deep, intense, and from Chenin Blanc.

Bon Courage Noble Late Harvest ★★★(★) E

A very good, delicate Noble Late Harvest made from Bukettraube of the 1985 vintage. Its citrus nose has a vague resemblance to Sauternes. It needs to be consumed. The next release, from the 1991 vintage, has prominent botrytis and high acids, and should develop with interest.

Boschendal Vin d'Or ★★★★ E

The first vintage, from 1979, came from Riesling and Steen, and was a rich, smooth wine with plenty of sugar (170 g/l) and good acid. It is past its best. There is now a very limited quantity of 1990 from Pinot Gris. It is unusual wine, with enticing nose and full flavour. The 1991 is from Bukettraube, and the 1992, from Chardonnay, is fuller in all respects.

Bottelary Co-op Noble Late Harvest ★★★(★) D

The first release, from the 1983 vintage, had plenty of sweetness, botrytis character and honeyed flavour, making more than just pleasant sipping. It developed well over five years. The 1985 is probably at its best now and should be drunk up and enjoyed. The 1989 is, to date, the best produced and, in fact, the best wine from this cellar. It is made from Bukettraube and packed with fruit and botrytis. Definitely a four-star wine.

Buitenverwachting Noblesse ★★★★ E

This release, from the 1987 vintage, has a sugar content of 136 g/l, total acid of 10,3 g/l and alcohol of 12,3%. It is well-balanced with good botrytis and is developing well in the bottle. It won a gold medal at the International Wine and Spirit Competition in 1989. The 1991 is gorgeous wine, from Rhine Riesling, with botrytis and oak.

Chapelle d'Or Belcher Noble Late Harvest ★★★ D

From the 1992 vintage comes this good botrytis Steen, with a touch of oak, and a fresh clean flavour.

Delheim Edelspatz Noble Late Harvest ★★★★★ E

Vintages tasted to date include the 1979, 1980, 1981, 1982, 1984, 1987, 1988, 1989, 1990 and 1991. All were recognizable as coming from the same cellar, but each had its own special point of distinction. All have definite botrytis character and occasionally have small amounts of Bukettraube and Kerner added to the blend. The 1987 was more along the lines of a Sauternes than ever before. The 1988 and 1989 follow this line of lower sugar, resulting in a very attractive wine with good acid balance, making an excellent digestif. The 1990 is a more concentrated, very rich wine, from Bukettraube, with some Steen and Rhine Riesling offering great depth of flavour. The 1991 is made from Rhine Riesling, Bukettraube with touches of Steen, Muscat and Sauvignon Blanc, and is as good as ever. Truly delicious wine. The 1992 is Bukettraube-based with Chenin Blanc and Rhine Riesling. Another delicious wine.

De Wetshof Edeloes ★★★★ E

Small quantity were produced from 1991 from botritized Rhine Riesling. This is lovely wine.

Die Krans Noble Late Harvest ★★★(★)C

This wine was first released from the 1988 vintage. The low sugar content (60 g/l) makes a soft, silky wine, with good fruit and botrytis layers. This is the best wine from this cellar. Plans for 1990 were thwarted by Mother Nature when the grapes that had hung on the vines for weeks after normal riching for concentrate, were blown off by strong wind before they could be picked. There has been no subsequent release.

Du Toitskloof Co-op Noble Late Harvest ★★(★) E

Packed in 375 ml bottles, this wine has distinct pineapple nose, honey-like flavour and sweet finish.

Eikendal Noble Late Harvest ★★★★ E

This is a delicious Steen, from the 1992 vintage, with rich flavours and a touch of oak. It comes in 375 ml bottles.

Fleur du Cap Noble Late Harvest ★★★★ D

A lovely Steen, along Sauternes lines, available in 500 ml Bordeaux bottles. This is delicious wine at a reasonable price.

Goudini Co-op Steen Noble Late Harvest ★★★(★) C

The cellar's first Superior, from the 1987 vintage, is a light, fruity wine with good acid balance.

Groot Constantia Noble Late Harvest ★★★ D

The 1984 was Groot Constantia's first attempt at this type of wine and contained 270 g/l sugar. The 1986 is a much better, with 180 g/l; it is better balanced and has good flavour. Two wines were produced in 1990, one from a Rhine Riesling-Chenin Blanc blend, and a Gewürztraminer-Muscat blend. Both are very attractive wines. The 1991 was used to celebrate the 200-year anniversary of the pediment at the Groot Constantia Wine Cellar. It is a lovely wine from Sauvignon Blanc, Rhine Riesling and Chenin Blanc. At the celebratory function, Mrs Marike de Klerk, wife of the State President, was presented with a numbered bottle, number one. I had the honour of representing the SA Wine writers and was presented with bottle number two! Plans are afoot for a special release of 1992.

KWV Noble Late Harvest ★★★★(★) (no price available)

This is one of KWV's best products from the 1984 vintage. It is full of botrytis but still has good, fruity flavours. The 1987 became the Cathedral Cellars export brand. This is beautiful wine, as is the 1988.

La Dorée Noble Late Harvest (Delaire) ★★★★ E

This wine is made from Weisser Riesling, from the 1992 vintage. It gets its name 'the golden one' from its colour. It is a good, rich mix of varietal character and botrytis.

Lievland Noble Late Harvest ★★★★ D

The first attempt, from the 1986 vintage, had faint botrytis nose and full, sweet flavour, but lacked finesse. The 1987 is in a totally different class, with lovely fruity flavours, not too much sweetness and of a more delicate style. It is good, four-star wine. A wood-matured variation was bottled for Lievland and first shown at the Cape Winemakers' Guild Auction where it realized an average price of R125 per case of 12 x 375 ml bottles. The 1988 is a deep, rich wine. The 1989 has a much higher sugar content, with full botrytis and lots of fruit, and was awarded a gold medal at the International Wine and Spirit Competition. The 1990 maintains the same high standard. The 1991 is more along the style of Sauternes with lower sugar, gentle botrytis, and is wood-aged. The high alcohol of 14% gives beautiful glycerine sweetness. Definitely a four-star, wine.

L'Ormarins Noble Late Harvest ★★★★ C

Usually sold through the Bergkelder Vinotèque scheme. The cellar contains botrytised Steens, Rhine Rieslings and Bukettraubes from various vintages. Eventually, more of these palate-confusing wines will be launched as prestige products.

Louwshoek-Voorsorg Co-op Noble Late Harvest ★★ A

The 1986 vintage was made from Steen with good, clean, botrytis character. The 1989 won a gold medal at the SA Show.

Nederburg Bukettraube Edelkeur ★★★★ D

The first vintage was the 1979, which had a very low alcohol content of only 7%, acid of 10,3 g/l, and incredible sugar of 258,4 g/l.

Nederburg Bukettraube Noble Late Harvest ★★★★ D

The word Edelkeur was dropped from the name for the 1983 vintage. The alcohol content is 12,3%, acid 10,6 g/l and sugar 152,3 g/l. This is beautiful wine which fills the mouth with the smallest sip. It is released only at the annual Nederburg Auction. The 1986 vintage has an analysis very similar to the 1983, and was sold at the 1988 and 1989 Auctions.

Nederburg Chardonnay Noble Late Harvest ★★★★(★)

A one-off allowed the production of only 54 cases of half-bottles from the 1987 vintage, containing 12% alcohol, 158 g/l residual sugar, and 9,7 g/l acid. This is unique wine, full of most unusual flavours, and is developing with great distinction.

Nederburg Edelkeur ★★★★★ D

Edelkeur cannot be adequately described – it must be tasted. A half-bottle costs a lot of money, but offers wine-lovers an experience never to be forgotten. Moreover, half a bottle is enough for six to eight people to sip in liqueur fashion at the end of the meal. Made in extremely small quantities, this incomparable botrytis wine varies greatly from vintage to vintage: there is no guarantee that the elements conducive to noble rot will occur each year. Except for the very first vintage (1969), which was sold by postal auction, it is available to retailers only at the annual Nederburg Auction. It will age for many years. In accordance with the Wine and Spirit Board's regulations, special permission and supervision is required each time the wine is made. The 1987 is considered by overseas fundis to be the best ever produced. The approximate figures for the vintages are:

Vintage	Alcohol%	Sugar g/l	Acid g/l
1974	11,0	183	8,7
1975	12,1	133	8,9
1976	9,1	212	11,7
1977	13,1	159	10,9
1978	10,9	193	8,9
1979	10,4	190	12,5
1980	10,9	184	13,1
1981	11,5	165	12,4
1982	10,5	183	12,2
1983	11,2	195	11,1
1984	12,2	162	9,9
1985	11,6	145	10,4
1986	12,2	151	10,5
1987	11,4	159	9,1
1988	11,7	180	9,5
1989	10,0	178	11,9

Nederburg Eminence Noble Late Harvest ★★★★★ E

The maiden vintage of this remarkable wine was the 1983. It was made from the historic White Muscadel grapes, known variously as Muscat de Frontignan (in France), Muscat Canelli (in California) and Gelber Muskateller (in Germany). The grapes were allowed to ripen to a raisin-like stage, yielding a very aromatic wine with luscious sweetness and magnificent Muscadel characteristics, totally free of botrytis. It has been produced regularly since then. These later vintages show a little botrytis which adds to this fine and very attractive wine. The wine is an instant show-stopper at its pre-Auction tastings, and is sold only at the annual Nederburg Auction.

Vintage	Alcohol%	Sugar g/l	Acid g/l
1983	12,7	107	8,4
1984	13,2	109	7,4
1985	13,5	117	9,0
1986	13,8	101	8,1
1987	12,5	119	8,1
1988	12,5	112	7,7
1989	11,2	102	8,8
1990	12,7	115	6,8

Nederburg Noble Late Harvest ★★★★ D

Three vintages of this delightful wine were packed in 250 ml bottles with screw-tops. This is a super idea as the concentrated wine is an ideal amount to be shared by two. Since 1988 it has been produced in cork-closed 375 ml bottles. The 1990 is a delicious blend of two-thirds Steen, with the balance made up of Rhine Riesling and Muscat de Frontignan.

Nederburg Riesling Edelkeur ★★★★ D

First produced in 1979, this wine has an alcohol content of 10,3%, acid 10,6 g/l, and sugar 162,5 g/l. It has a fruit-filled nose combined with botrytis, and lovely mouth-filling flavour, well-balanced with good fruit acid. It is just for sipping and released only at the annual Nederburg Auctions. It is now dark mahogany in colour.

Nederburg Steen Noble Late Harvest ★★★★(★) C

This is a truly great South African wine, which was first produced from the 1980 vintage, and was followed by the 1981 and 1982 vintages. It was one of the earliest wines to make use of the new Late Vintage epithet of 'noble', and its availability is limited. It has wonderful depth of complexity and lusciousness seldom achieved in a South African wine. It ages with great merit. The latest vintage is the 1986, which can only be described as truly magnificent.

Nederburg Weisser Riesling Noble Late Harvest ★★★★★ D

This is a distinctive wine showing clean cultivar characteristics. As with all the Nederburg Noble Late Harvests, this one is superb. It is released only at the annual Nederburg Auction.

Vintage	Alcohol%	Sugar g/l	Acid g/l
1986	13,4	139	11,8
1987	13,4	117	9,6
1989	10,0	131	10,3

Neethlingshof Rhine Riesling Noble Late Harvest ★★★★ D

The first vintage from the 1990 won the General Smuts trophy for South African Champion wine at the 1990 SA Championship Young Wine Show. It is full of super citrusy and tropical fruit fragrances and flavours, all mingled with botrytis, and contains 166 g/l residual sugar. In 1991 the awards were reversed – the Rhine Riesling following the Sauvignon Blanc – but once again super wine. The 1992 is in the same super style.

Neethlingshof Sauvignon Blanc Noble Late Harvest ★★★★ D

To highlight the master's ability, this 1990 wine was the Reserve champion at the 1990 SA Championship Young Wine Show. It has a lot of sugar at 224 g/l, and a decidedly peachy nose with fruit salad flavours in the mouth. The 1991 SA Champion is packed with fruit and botrytis. It is a beautiful wine which should age with considerable interest. The 1992 is in the same super style.

Perdeberg Co-op Noble Late Harvest ★★★★ D

To celebrate the Co-op's 50th anniversary, comes the first botrytis wine from 1991 vintage. This is lively botrytis Steen in half bottles.

Pick 'n Pay Noble Late Harvest ★★★★ D

This wine, made under the masterful eye of Günter Brözel in the Stellenzicht cellars, comes from Rhine Riesling of the 1991 vintage. It is definitely South African Championship material, and super after-dinner sipping at 16,5 g/l.

Romansrivier Co-op Edel Laatoes ★★★(★) B

A very good botrytis wine, made in 1984, from Steen. It has developed well and is well worth seeking out.

Roodezandt Co-op Le Grand Deluge Noble Late Harvest ★★★ E

This is a rich botrytis wine named in memory of the 1981 floods which wrought havoc along the Breede River. Ironically, however, the floods also produced conditions conducive to noble rot, enabling this wine to be produced. It should be drunk now. The 1991 was produced 10 years after the deluge. It is rich, full wine, with botrytis and apricot flavours, and comes in sensible 250 ml bottles.

Rooiberg Edel Laatoes ★★★★ C

My introduction to this wine was from an amazing magnum (this kind of wine is usually bottled in 375 ml units). It was from the 1986 vintage and made from Muscat de Frontignan, which shows well, and has complexity coming from some botrytis. It is not all that rich and has good acid balance. The 1988 and 1989 are lovely wines, the latter a blend of 60% Steen and 40% Rhine Riesling. The 1991 is from Chardonnay, with lots of botrytis and good fruit.

Saxenburg Noble Late Harvest ★★★(★) D

A full, fruity-flavoured wine, with good acid balance and most attractive nose. The 1990 vintage comes from three varieties: Chenin Blanc, Sauvignon Blanc and Weisser Riesling, and has a honeyed character with some botrytis. It was followed by an over-sweet 1991 from Rhine Riesling and Sauvignon Blanc.

Simonsig Noble Late Harvest ★★★★ D

Simonsig was once a regular producer of very good Noble Late Harvest and now, after a long break, has bottled 750 ml and 375 ml of 1990 vintage from Gewürztraminer. It is a stunning wine, full of enticing aromas and wonderful flavours.

Simonsvlei Co-op Noble Late Harvest ★★★(★) C

The first release came from Bukettraube, out of the 1989 vintage, and is one of the cellar's best-ever wines. It is full of fruit, spice and sweetness, and is well balanced with good acid. The 1992 is a lovely, light, fruity wine with some botrytis.

Twee Jongegezellen Engeltjepipi Noble Late Harvest ★★★★ C

Over the years, Twee Jongegezellen has produced some remarkable Late Harvests. These were shared with friends only and not for sale. The 1982 vintage was certified Superior and is a well-made, fine, gentle wine. Then, at last, a small quantity of the 1983 was released to the public, followed by the 1987 vintage, made in a light style, with less sugar than many others. This is a wine very much along the lines of a Sauternes.

Stellenzicht Noble Late Harvest ★★★★ E

The first release, from 1991, is made from Rhine Riesling and has concentrated flavours, almost sweet-sour character, and clean fresh finish. The 1992 is very similar. Both will develop well.

Van Loveren Noble Late Harvest ★★★(★) B

A well-balanced, complex wine made predominantly from Weisser Riesling, with a lesser amount of Steen from the 1985 vintage. This was followed by a similar wine from the 1990 vintage.

Vredendal Co-op Noble Late Harvest ★★★★ C

This wine is a very good attempt with Steen from the 1989 vintage. It is a soft wine with fruit salad flavours.

Weltevrede Noble Late Harvest ★★★(★) C

The first release from the 1981 vintage was a most unusual wine with deep colour and good botrytis character. It had a low alcohol content and now needs to be drunk. The 1988 release from Muscat de Frontignan has 13% alcohol and about 100 g/l sugar. Its characteristics include good botrytis and nice fruit. It continues to develop well.

Woolworths Noble Late Harvest ★★★★(★)

This is a delightful wine, made by Klein Constantia for Woolworths, out of the 1990 vintage, from Sauvignon Blanc. The 120 g of sugar is balanced with fruit acid and good botrytis character. Nectar in 375 ml bottles!

Zonnebloem Noble Late Harvest (SFW) ★★★★★ E
The most appealing pack contains a beautifully balanced botrytis wine, which is a departure in style for Cape Noble Late Harvests. It is more along the style of Bordeaux than of Germany. Light, fresh flavour, led by inviting fruity aroma, gives a wine which can be drunk and not simply sipped like most Noble Late Harvests. The 1983, in a gold pack, was made from Steen. The 1987, in a green pack, is certified Sauvignon Blanc. Overseas fundis believe this to be one of the Cape's best Noble Late Harvests and it is very much a five-star wine. The 1989 is again a gold label wine, made from Steen, and a lovely, luscious wine which is not quite up to the 1987 standard. The 1990 is lovely wine.

MÜLLER-THURGAU

Uiterwyk Müller-Thurgau ★★(★) B
From the 1985 vintage came an interesting first-release of Müller-Thurgau in the Cape – a delicate, dry wine with good potential. The 1986 was a good, dry white with attractive, fruity nose. The 1987 had good, fruity nose and fresh, zesty taste, which has now toned down. The 1988 was a delightful off-dry wine with fruity, almost apple-like nose, and very pleasing flavour. The 1989 was made along the same lines. The 1990 showed improved quality – nice and fruity, yet soft on the palate. The 1991 was a fresh, off-dry wine. The 1992 continues the pleasant, soft style. Definitely best enjoyed when young.

MUSCAT WINES

Blaauwklippen Muscat Ottonel ★★★ B
This popular semi-sweet wine is most attractive and full of flavour. The 1991 appeared drier, low in alcohol, and made very easy drinking. The 1992 follows a similar easy and attractive style.

Die Krans Muscat d'Alexandrie ★★★(★) A
A delightful, semi-sweet wine with very pleasant nose and flavour. The early nineties are attractive, fruity wines with lots of cultivar character, and most suitable for youthful drinking. This is one of the cellar's better natural wines.

Du Toitskloof Co-op Muscat d'Alexandrie ★★★ B
This was a very pleasant semi-sweet wine, with good cultivar nose and pleasing flavour, but regrettably not produced in latest vintages.

Eersterivier-Valleise Kelder Muscat d'Alexandrie ★★(★) B
This is a very good Muscat, unusual in that it is bone-dry, yet has all the attractive Muscat aromas and taste. Best when young.

Nederburg Muscat de Frontignan ★★★(★) C
Sold only at the Nederburg Auction, this Late Harvest-style wine was a most attractive, fine Muscat. The last vintage to be released, the 1980, was a beautiful wine and was sold at the 1987 Nederburg Auction. At twelve years of age it had developed remarkable bottle age character.

Pick 'n Pay Bouquet Blanc ★★★ B
Delightful wine, similar to 'Fragrance' and produced by the same cellar – Stellenzicht. It has enticing nose, is off-dry, and has fine Muscat flavour.

Soetwynboere Co-op Muscat d'Alexandrie ★★ A
A semi-sweet, lightish wine, with acceptable nose and flavour.

Spruitdrift Co-op Mario Muskaat ★★(★) A
New from 1991, this is an off-dry wine with floral nose and soft palate.

Stellenzicht Fragrance ★★★ B
This is a delightful, light, dry wine with most attractive Muscat nose. It contains less than 10% alcohol and is made from the table grape variety Erlihane, which is a type of Hanepoot. Lovely, easy drinking.

Thelema Muscat de Frontignan ★★★★ B
A delightful, off-dry wine, with a most attractive nose and good acid balance. This is a lovely, refreshing drink.

Natural Sweet

Avontuur Above Royalty ★★(★) B
A sweet wine of nearly 60 g/l with citrus flavours, it is named after one of the Estate's thoroughbred race horses.

Belcher Grand Vin Doux ★★★
The first release from 1992 has 36 g/l sugar and is made from Steen. It has good, rich sweetness with fresh finish.

Blaauwklippen Natural Sweet ★★★ B
With just over 50 g/l sugar and high alcohol of 13,7% this is an interesting first from the cellar in this new category. It comes from the 1991 vintage and is good, fruity, clean, sweet wine.

Bovlei Co-op Natural Sweet ★★ A
This wine is not certified so it carries no vintage. It is very similar to the cellar's Special Late Harvest, and contains close to 50 g/l sugar, but not much fruit acid. It is showing bottle age very early.

Dwarsrivier Cederberger (Cederberg Cellars) ★★ B
This is a full-flavoured Steen with lots of cultivar character and some 75 g/l sugar.

Domein Doornkraal Kuierwyn Sweet Natural ★★ B
A lowish-alcohol wine and only 40 g/l sugar. Several varieties of grape are used in its production, and it has pleasant Muscat nose.

Goudini Co-op K'Gou Dani ★★★ A
Using the Hottentot name for Goudini on this first entry into the new category from the 1991 vintage, this is a semi-sweet, honey-nosed wine from Steen, with delicate flavours. It comes in 250 ml bottles.

La Cotte Natural Sweet (Franschhoek Co-op) ★★★
A good, sweet wine with some botrytis, high alcohol of 13,5%, and sugar at 90g/l. It is easy to drink and one of the cellar's best wines.

Klein Constantia Vin de Constance Noble Late Harvest ★★★★★ E
When Duggie Jooste bought Klein Constantia in June 1980, it was his intention to reproduce the great wines that made Constantia famous around the world during the 18th and 19th centuries. Muscat de Frontignan was planted specifically to try and reproduce the great wine. Five years after the first harvest and four years after Vin de Constance was put into wood, wine maker Ross Gower released the magnificent 1986 wine bottled in replica antique bottles. It contains 13,7% alcohol and 95 g/l residual sugar, and tastes unreal. The next release, from 1987, is along the same lines, with slightly higher alcohol at 15%, and much more flavour and complexity. Delicious.

Loopspruit Goldenes Fest ★★★ B
Mainly from Steen, but with Muscat showing on the nose, this wine has a vague hint of botrytis, and nice, clean finish.

Nederburg Sauvignon Blanc Natural Sweet ★★★★ C

This is the first wine in this new category to be made at Nederburg from the 1989 vintage. It is an elegant wine, with good fruitiness and lovely flavours, free of botrytis. Alcohol is 12,2%. Residual sugar is 76 g/l and total acid is 6,6 g/l. This one is in a class of its own in this category. Two-hundred cases of 12 x 375 ml were sold at the 1992 Nederburg Auction, and another 440 cases, from the 1990 vintage, which were sold at the 1993 auction had a very similar analysis.

Overvaal Natural Sweet Table Wine (Vaalharts Co-op) ★★ B

This is non-vintaged wine, from 1991, blended from Colombar and Chenel. It has an odd herby nose, but a pleasant, soft flavour, and contains 40 g/l sugar and 6 g/l acid.

PINOT BLANC

Landskroon Pinot Blanc ★★ B

The first and only release from 1990, was a light-flavoured, dry white that now needs to be drunk.

Van Loveren Pinot Blanc ★★★ C

This wine, made from Pinot Blanc, has some 20 to 25% Chardonnay blended into it and is nicely oaked. It is very good value for money and lovely drinking with lots of flavour. It will develop well over two to three years and has high alcohol of 13 to 14%.

Nederburg Pinot Blanc ★★★(★) D

The first release from the 1989 vintage was easy-drinking, uncomplicated wine, with attractive nose and pleasant flavour. The 1991 and 1992 have been fuller and just off-dry, but with enough acid to appear dryish. It is lively on the palate, with crisp, fresh finish. This is lovely summer drinking wine at a very affordable price.

PINOT GRIS

Buitenverwachting Pinot Gris Reserve ★★★ D
Wine from the 1989 vintage is still available with lots of bottle age.

Cederberg Cellars Pinot Gris ★★(★) A
An off-dry white wine, with a slightly perfumed nose and sweet, spicey flavour, from the 1991 vintage.

Drostdy-Hof Pinot Gris ★★★ B
The original release was fairly lacking in nose, but had a pleasant flavour. The 1990 is much better, and is dry with a good, fresh finish.

Fairview Pinot Gris ★★★(★) B
This is one of the better efforts with the cultivar. The 1992 is a lovely full-flavoured wine with a brisk finish. A good wine at an affordable price.

Goue Vallei Pinot Gris ★★★
The first release from 1992 is dry, full flavoured, and soft in the mouth.

Groot Eiland Co-op Pinot Gris ★★ A
A dry white wine, with the first release from the 1990 vintage. The 1991 was released as Nouveau. This is a pleasant-tasting, medium-bodied wine, with some spice on the nose, and best when young.

Landskroon Pinot Gris ★★★ B
The first release, from 1990, was dry and had an unusual flavour, almost like basil and thyme. The 1991 and 1992 are good for early drinking.

L'Ormarins Pinot Gris ★★★ C
The first vintage (1985) gave a full-flavoured, off-dry wine with sufficient acid to make it taste drier. The second vintage (1986) had much the same chemical make-up with perhaps better flavours. The well-balanced 1987 was full of character. The dry 1988 was best to date, with good flavour and a hint of wood, which made an easy-drinking wine. The 1989 had good flavour. The wines of the early 1990s are much the same.

Roodezandt Co-op Pinot Gris ★★(★) B
The first release was from the 1989 vintage and a first for the Co-op. The 1990 had better flavour, fruitier nose and is a pleasant, gentle, dry wine. The 1991 is bigger, bolder wine, and an improvement on earlier vintages.

Uitkyk Pinot Gris ★★★ C
The first release from the 1991 vintage came in new-style packaging. It has a nice spicey flavour, a touch of wood, and more body than most. The 1992 is much along the same lines.

Van Loveren Pinot Gris ★★★ B
The 1986 was a pleasant off-dry wine which developed well. The 1987 had far better cultivar character and was finished off-dry. The 1989 was a full-flavoured, well-wooded wine. In blind tastings it was mistaken for Chardonnay! The 1990 was bone-dry. The 1991 has massive 14,5% alcohol but is lacking in character, and the 1992 is fruitier and better.

Premier Grand Crû

Aan-de-Doorns Co-op Premier Grand Crû ★★ A
This wine is not produced with every vintage, and its composition has varied with each production, but it is always dry, with a fresh, appealing nose when young.

Autumn Harvest Grand Crû (SFW) ★★(★) A
This is a blended dry wine containing Colombar. Its good, vinous character and crisp freshness have made it a favourite of Grand Crû devotees and it is an award winner in international competitions.

Bakenskop Grand Crû (Jonkheer)★★ A
A pleasant, fruity, dry blend of Colombar and Steen.

Bellingham Premier Grand Crû (DGB) ★★★ C
This is the wine which gave South Africa the term 'Premier Grand Crû' some 40 years ago, and has shown great variation of character over the decades. In line with Bellingham's entry into the top quality market, this wine has improved in character and consistency. Today it is blended from Riesling and Steen, with a touch of Colombar, to give good nose and flavour. It is still the biggest seller under the Premier Grand Crû title, and is good drinking wine.

Bovlei Co-op Grand Crû ★★(★) A
An attractive, dry, refreshing wine.

Brandvlei Grand Crû ★★ A
An easy-drinking wine, dry yet soft, and with less acid than most.

Breughel Wines Grand Crû (Aroma Group) ★★ A
A light, easy, dry wine from Steen and Colombar.

Carnival Grand Crû (Spar) ★★(★) A
Nice flavoured, good fresh wine, and best when young.

Cellar Cask Premier Grand Crû (Castle Wines) ★★ A
A dry wine which is good value for money. It is now available in cork-closed bottles.

Cellar Reserve Premier Grand Crû (Hyperama) ★★ A
A pleasant enough, dry, white wine.

Checkers Yellow Label Premier Grand Crû ★★(★) B
This is a dry white wine with Colombar-Steen, guava nose.

Culemborg Grand Crû ★★ A
A good value for money, dry wine, with good, fresh, fruity character.

De Doorns Co-op Grand Crû ★★ A
A dry blend of Steen and Colombar.

Die Poort Premier Grand Crû ★★ A
A low-alcohol Colombar for early drinking.

Douglas Green Premier Grand Crû ★★ C
A pleasant dry white wine, at its best in its youth.

Drostdy-Hof Premier Grand Crû (Cape Wine) ★★ B

A consistent, pleasant, fruity, dry wine with more complexity than most.

Fleur Du Cap Premier Grand Crû (Castle Wine and EK Green) ★★★ B

A good, Steen-based, crisp, dry wine, recent blends of which are being improved in complexity with Sauvignon Blanc. A good aperitif.

Huguenot Premier Grand Crû ★★ A

A nondescript dry blend that needs early drinking.

Jonkerskloof Premier Grand Crû ★★★ B

This is a well made, multiple dry white blend with good, fresh finish.

Kellerprinz Grand Crû (SFW) ★★(★) A

A consistently sound, dry white, with subtle flavour, which makes a good quaffing wine. It is best enjoyed when young.

Klawer Co-op Grand Crû ★★ A

This is always a pleasant, dry, inexpensive product. The blend varies from vintage to vintage.

Landzicht Premier Grand Crû ★★ A

This wine is predominantly Colombar, with blending partners selected from Chenel, Hanepoot and Steen. Pleasant when young.

Louwshoek-Voorsorg Co-op Premier Grand Crû ★★ A

The cellar's best seller. It is a dry blend based on Colombar and Steen, with some Clairette Blanche.

Lutzville Grand Crû ★★★ A

Screw-capped for low price, this is a nice dry wine from Steen and Colombar, which is good for early drinking.

Monterey Premier Grand Crû (Western Province Cellars) ★ A

A crisp, bone-dry, white wine.

Nederburg Premier Grand Crû ★★★(★) C

A delightfully light, crisp, dry wine showing that character is attainable in this style. The latest releases are particularly good wines. When well chilled, it is the ideal partner for oysters and other flavoured seafoods.

Oranjerivier Wynkelders Grand Crû ★ A

This is one of the better dry wines from these cellars, and shows good Colombar character.

Overmeer Premier Grand Crû ★★(★) A

Only available in boxes, this is consistently good, crisp, quaffing wine.

Overvaal Grand Crû (Vaalharts Co-op) ★ A

A dry white wine with little character.

Party Pack Premier Grand Crû (Drop Inn) ★★ B

A clean but neutral product for ready quaffing.

Porterville Co-op Grand Crû ★★ A

The dry blend varies but is usually from Colombar and Steen. It is fruity when fresh.

Ravenswood Premier Grand Crû (Pick 'n Pay) ★★★ B

A well made dry white wine, with good, fruity nose and crisp finish.

Rebel Premier Grand Crû ★ A

A brisk, blended, dry white.

Riebeek Wine Farmers' Co-op Grand Crû ★★★ A

This is one of the lighter-styled Premier Grand Crûs, and is better than many others.

Romansrivier Co-op Grand Crû ★★★ A

A pleasant, soft-drinking wine, blended from Steen, Colombar and Clairette Blanche.

Roodezandt Co-op Premier Grand Crû ★★ A

The latest releases of this wine are fresh and fruity when young.

Rooiberg Co-op Premier Grand Crû ★★★ B

A dry white blend, that is full-bodied and bold, and best when young.

Rusthof Premier Grand Crû (Mooiuitsig) ★★ A

A typical, dry, Steen/Colombar blend, touched out with some Muscat on the nose.

Simondium Co-op Grand Crû ★★ A

New from 1991 comes a big, strong Steen.

Simonsvlei Co-op Premier Grand Crû ★★(★) A

Originally this was a light wine with a slightly fruity nose. The blend has varied over the years but is usually from Steen, and is now a full bodied, generally good, easy-drinking wine.

Slanghoek Co-op Premier Grand Crû ★★ A

This is a blend of a number of varieties, including Steen, Colombar and others. Recent vintages are possibly the most delicate of all the Premier Grand Crû wines from the Co-ops.

Soetwynboere Co-op Grand Crû ★★ A

This wine has vague Sauvignon Blanc character.

Spruitdrift Co-op Premier Grand Crû ★★ A

Recent vintages are dry, Steen/Colombar blends, with good fruit and pleasant flavour. They are good value for money and available in screw-top bottles.

Swartland Co-op Premier Grand Crû ★★(★) A

This is a surprisingly light, smooth wine, usually Steen-based, but also containing other varieties such as Clairette Blanche and Colombar. It is always fruity, soft and dry across the palate, making for easy drinking.

Trawal Wynkelders Co-op Premier Grand Crû ★★ A

A triple component blend of mainly Steen with one-third Hárslevelü and 10% Colombar. A pleasant dry white when young.

Valley Premier Grand Crû (Gilbeys) ★★(★) A

A dry blend featuring Colombar, Sémillon and Steen, giving attractive nose as well as good fruit.

Van Loveren Premier Grand Crû ★★★ B

A very pleasant, light, dry blend of numerous cultivars, with a touch of Muscat on the nose, giving an above-average Premier Grand Crû.

Villiersdorp Co-op Grand Crû ★★ A

A bone-dry Grand Crû, with nice fruity nose when young.

Vinovat Premier Grand Crû (Marcows) ★ A

A dry white vin ordinaire.

Vintner's Choice Premier Grand Crû (Drop Inn) ★ A

A pleasant, dry white wine with refreshing crispness.

Vredendal Grand Crû ★★★ A

A Steen/Sauvignon Blanc blend results in this easy-drinking dry wine.

Waboomsrivier Co-op Grand Crû ★★ A

A well-made, clean, dry wine, based on Colombar with some Steen.

Wamakersvallei Co-op Premier Grand Crû ★★★ A

An unusually good Co-op Premier Grand Crû, this is a light, uncompli-cated blend with a pleasant flavour.

Welmoed Co-op Grand Crû ★★(★) A

A good, clean, dry blend of mainly Steen, giving ample flavour and bal-ance. This is another cellar to drop 'Premier' from its label.

Woolworths Premier Grand Crû ★★ B

From Gilbeys. A pleasant, fresh, easy-drinking, dry wine.

Zellerhof Premier Grand Crû (Huguenot) ★★(★) B

This wine is showing some bottle age and has developed a typical, honey-like nose of older Steen.

Zonnebloem Premier Grand Crû (SFW)★★★(★) C

It took many years before Zonnebloem joined the ranks of Premier Grand Crû producers, but when it did it was with an outstanding wine, full of flavour from the fruit of its Steen and Colombar blend. Delightful and refreshing when young, it ages with interest over two or three years. The latest releases are amazingly good quality for this category of wine.

Riesling – Cape

Aan-de-Doorns Co-op Riesling ★★ A
The Co-op's Riesling, from the 1988 vintage, is a good addition to the range, with fruity nose and good, dry flavour. The early 1990 vintages are fuller-bodied, but best when young. Good value.

Ashton Co-op Riesling ★★ A
This wine often features well on local young wine shows. Recent vintages offer delicate flavours and brisk finish.

Avontuur Cape Riesling ★★★ B
Unusual character, big, full wine, with lots of life, which is best in its youth. There was no 1992.

Badsberg Co-op Riesling ★★ A
This wine is dry and has fair cultivar character.

Bakenskop Riesling (Jonkheer) ★★★ A
A nice, crisp, dry white for easy drinking.

Barrydale Co-op Riesling ★★(★) A
Usually a fresh, fruity wine, with good clean flavour.

Belcher Riesling Special Reserve ★★★
This is a very different wine for this cultivar, which has been fermented and aged for six months in oak. It has good fruit and vanilla flavours which are developing in the bottle. Well worth a try.

Bellingham Paarl Riesling ★★★ C
A vast improvement on the old type of Bellingham Riesling. This is an off-dry wine with strong cultivar character, and it drinks very well.

Bergsig Riesling ★★★ B
This is a good, dry Riesling, with softness on the palate and distinct cellar character. It is good-value, easy-drinking wine.

Bolandse Co-op Riesling ★★★ B
This is a regular gold medal winner at the regional shows, and good value for money. It is best enjoyed young. Recent vintages are fresh and fruity.

Bon Courage Cape Riesling ★★★(★) B
A soundly made wine with good, fruity, Riesling character. It is best enjoyed when young to savour its good, fresh flavour. It is finished fractionally off-dry, and is always an easy-drinking wine.

Boschendal Riesling ★★★ C
Boschendal entered the wine-making industry in 1976 with some wines of rather dubious quality, so it is pleasing to see such a dramatic improvement. The Riesling has not been one of the Estate's fashionable wines, yet it is consistently very good. Recent releases are lovely wines, and the addition of some Rhine Riesling gives considerable complexity.

Botha Co-op Riesling ★★ B
A big, dry wine, with good cultivar nose.

Bottelary Co-op Riesling ★★★(★) B

This Co-op has developed into a producer of good white wines, and the Riesling in particular has become a delightful wine with pleasing cultivar character. A friendly, easy-drinking wine, it was a regular award winner both regionally and nationally. Recent vintages are lighter-bodied, fresh and lively, and best enjoyed when young.

Bovlei Co-op Riesling ★★ A

Recent vintages have full varietal nose and crisp finish.

Cape Vintners Members Only Riesling ★★★ B

This is well-made dry wine from Welmoed, with good, brisk finish.

De Helderberg Co-op Cape Riesling ★★ A

Recent vintages are well-made, dry wines with fine, fruity, fresh finish.

De Leuwen Jagt Paarl Riesling ★★★ B

This wine has good cultivar character, lots of fruit, is soft in the mouth, and has a crisp finish.

De Wet Co-op Cape Riesling ★★★ A

The first release came from the 1986 vintage. It is a regular class winner at the Worcester show, and is always good, easy-drinking wine. It is probably this cellar's best natural wine, and best enjoyed when young.

Douglas Green Paarl Riesling (DGB) ★★(★) C

Although this is never one of the better wines from this merchant, recent releases have improved considerably. The latest vintages show more character and are soft, easy-drinking wines.

Du Toitskloof Co-op Riesling ★★★ B

The cellar has improved the quality of its white wines over recent years and its Riesling has become a regular award winner at the Worcester show. Recent vintages are soft, not totally dry, easy-drinking wines.

Edelkeller Riesling ★★★ B

Well-made Cape Riesling. Good, easy drinking.

Edward Snell Cape Riesling ★★(★) B

A non-vintaged, fresh, dry white wine, with brisk finish, which is at its best when young.

Eersterivier Valleise Kelder Riesling ★★★(★) B

This cellar consistently produces Rieslings of good value. Recent vintages are big, full wines with lots of flavour. They should age well if left to develop over the next three to four years.

Fleur Du Cap Riesling (Bergkelder) ★★★(★) C

A delightful Cape Riesling of sparkling, fresh fruitiness. Always good, occasionally superb, it develops well in the bottle. It is delightful when young, yet one of the few Cape Rieslings that improves with age. It is made very drinkable by being finished fractionally off-dry.

Franschhoek Vineyards Co-op Cape Riesling ★★ B

This is a light-bodied, well made, fresh, fruity dry white, which used to be bottled under the La Cotte label.

Goudini Co-op Riesling ★★★ A

This wine does well at local shows. It has good cultivar character and is bottled dry. Enjoy when young.

Goue Vallei Riesling (Citrusdal Co-op) ★★★ A

A good, easy-drinking, fruity, dry white, which is better than most, and very good value.

Groot Eiland Co-op Riesling ★★ A

A pleasant, dry, medium-bodied wine, for easy drinking.

Huguenot Cape Riesling ★★ A

Nice, easy-drinking wine, which is best when young.

Kleindal Cape Riesling ★★★ B

A good, dry, reliable wine with attractive cultivar character.

Koelenhof Co-op Riesling ★★★ B

A consistently good wine with definite cultivar nose.

KWV Riesling ★★★

A consistent dry wine with somewhat delicate features. It is best enjoyed when young and fresh, or after four to six years when it develops an unusually deep bottle-age character.

L'Ormarins Franschhoek Riesling ★★★★ C

A prolific gold medal winner, both regionally and nationally, this is a very well-made, big wine, and one of the Cape's best representatives of the cultivar. The 1983 was labelled Cape Riesling; from 1986 on it is certified Franschhoek Riesling. The lovely 1989 is not quite dry. The 1990s are fresh, fruity, substantial wines – lovely when young, yet develop well with a few years in the bottle.

Louwshoek-Voorsorg Co-op Riesling ★★ A

A light, dry wine.

Mamreweg Co-op Riesling ★★★ B

Fruity, attractive wine, with good flavour and brisk finish. Best when young. Current production is a big improvement on earlier releases.

Merwespont Co-op Riesling ★ A

A dry white with reasonable cultivar character. Best when young.

Merwida Co-op Riesling ★★ A

A fairly consistent wine of pleasing style.

Nederburg Paarl Riesling ★★★ C

This is the successor to the wine which introduced South Africans to Rieslings of fine quality. It is usually characterized by a good varietal aroma and clean, dry finish. The various vintages are notably consistent: the firm teutonic influence ensures a stable wine which ages with beautiful results. Always good, it has flowery nose, excellent varietal character and dry finish. Like all the Nederburg products, this is not a simple wine. It has good depth of character and, as excellent as it is on release, will age with interest for a couple of years, developing remarkable bottle bouquet. It has confounded many an expert when used in blind tastings.

Neethlingshof Cape Riesling ★★★ C

The latest releases are clean, fresh, medium-bodied wines that drink well.

Nuy Co-op Riesling ★★★(★) B

This is a consistently good dry wine with more complex nose than a lot of other Cape Rieslings. The 1991 is outstanding and will age with benefit. Excellent value for money. The 1992 is fresh and fruity, and a very good drinking wine.

Oude Rust Riesling (Mooiuitsig) ★★ A

A crisp, light, clean, easy-drinking wine.

Overhex Co-op Riesling ★★ B

Usually a pleasant, light, delicate dry wine, best enjoyed when young.

Perdeberg Co-op Riesling ★★ A

The 1990 was for early drinking. Now tired.

Pick 'n Pay Cape Riesling ★★★ B

Bone-dry, well made wine with fresh finish.

Rendition Riesling (Welmoed Co-op) ★★★ B

A regular award winner, this is a most attractive dry wine with delicate Riesling cultivar character. It is regularly one of the better Rieslings from the Co-op.

Riebeek Wine Farmers' Co-op Cape Riesling ★★ A

A good, dry wine with sound cultivar character.

Romansrivier Co-op Riesling ★★(★) A

A medal-winning wine, recent vintages of which are showing very well. It is zesty, fresh and attractive, especially when young.

Roodezandt Co-op Cape Riesling ★★ B

This is a fuller, fruitier wine that makes good, early drinking. The cellar offers them with a bit of age and there are usually a few vintages available. I still prefer the most recent.

Rooiberg Co-op Vinkrivier Riesling ★★★(★) B

A Wine of Origin Vinkrivier, Rooiberg Riesling has good cultivar character and, because of its high acid content, ages into a most attractive wine.

Simondium Winery Co-op Riesling ★★ A

A dry white wine with honey-like nose and some bottle age.

Simonsig Riesling ★★★ B

Frans Malan, the owner of Simonsig, took the Wine and Spirit Board to court to defend his right to state '100% varietal' on his labels. He won his case and his Riesling was thus presented, but the law was subsequently changed, not allowing percentage contents to appear on labels. This law, however, changed in 1990 to permit more informative labelling. Recent vintages are dry and delicate, and develop well in the bottle, as have previous vintages.

Simonsvlei Co-op Riesling ★★(★) B

This light, dry wine, with its good aroma, has varied over the years. Recent vintages are fresh and attractive, and make good, early drinking.

Slanghoek Co-op Riesling ★★(★) A

This is good, dry wine, with honest cultivar character, brisk finish, and regarded as pleasant, easy drinking.

Spier Riesling ★★★ B

Blended with 25% Rhine Riesling, this is good, well-flavoured dry wine.

Spruitdrift Co-op Riesling ★★ A

This is light bodied, fairly fruity dry wine, that is at its best when young.

Swartland Co-op Riesling ★★★ B

This is a wine that has improved over recent vintages. It is full-bodied, yet elegant, with good flavour and fresh finish.

Theuniskraal Riesling ★★★ C

A Riesling of remarkably consistent quality – it is pleasant, dry and light.

Tulbagh Co-op Riesling ★★ A

Delicate, easy-drinking, dry white wine.

Uiterwyk Riesling ★★★ C

This wine was consistently good during the 1980s, and the 1990s continue the quality. It is dry, full-flavoured, with good style, and develops well.

Uitkyk Riesling ★★★ C

A good, dry Riesling, which has a subtle, sometimes elusive fragrance. It is best in the bloom of youth, but also ages with elegance. The vintages of the 1990s are fine, fresh, well-made wines, with good, long finish.

Van Loveren Cape Riesling ★★★ B

A well-made, dry wine, with good fruity nose and pleasant flavour. This is one of the cellar's lighter wines and best when young.

Villiersdorp Co-op Riesling ★★(★) A

New from 1992, this wine is full of varietal nose, but not a lot of flavour.

Vlottenburg Co-op Riesling ★★★ A

This is always a reliable dry white and frequent champion of the district. It has good varietal character and develops well.

Vredendal Co-op Riesling ★★★ A

This wine has light varietal nose and nice, soft feel in the mouth.

Waboomsrivier Co-op Riesling ★★ A

This is a dry wine which needs to be drunk early.

Wellington Wynboere Co-op Riesling ★★ A

A light-style Riesling, which is fresh and fruity with brisk finish.

Weltevrede Cape Riesling ★★★★ B

A dry, full-flavoured wine that is one of this cellar's most attractive products and consistently one of the Cape's better wines from this cultivar.

Woolworths Cape Riesling ★★★ B

From Weltevrede. This is a good example of the cultivar, which drinks well when young, although recent releases can develop with benefit.

Zonnebloem Riesling (SFW) ★★★ C

A reliable dry wine with a touch of Sauvignon Blanc adding to the fruity nose. It develops with interest but is best as a young, fresh wine.

RIESLING – EMERALD

Andalusia Emerald Riesling (Vaalharts Co-op) ★★ B
A fairly neutral, off-dry white wine that is best enjoyed when young.

Porterville Emerald Riesling ★★ A
Light, pleasant, good quality, dry wine.

Roodezandt Co-op Emerald Riesling ★★★ A
This is an interesting dry wine, with fruity nose and firm flavour.

RIESLING – RHINE/WEISSER

Alphen De Gruchy Rhine Riesling ★★★ B
The first release from the 1990 vintage was highly successful and well received. Subsequent vintages are also just off-dry, with good cultivar character and a touch of Gewürztraminer, making a delightful, good drinking wine.

Ashton Co-op Weisser Riesling ★★★ A
This is a consistently good, semi-sweet white and a regular prize winner.

Avontuur Weisser Riesling ★★(★) B
The first release from 1990 vintage was dry with a sharp finish. The 1991 is a better effort and drinks well.

Backsberg Rhine Riesling ★★★(★) B
This is one of the easiest, pleasant-drinking Rhine Rieslings available at a good price, and capable of developing in the bottle over a year or two.

Bergsig Weisser Riesling ★★★ B
The 1987 has aged into deep-flavoured intriguing wine in 1993. The 1990 and 1991 are lighter, off-dry wines with good flavour and clean finish. They are probably at their best while young.

Blaauwklippen Rhine Riesling ★★★ C
This wine was first introduced in 1981 and became a regular award winner. The finish varies between just off-dry to dry. It is consistently one of the best wines from the cultivar. The latest releases are very attractive, with lovely bouquet and full flavour. The 1991 and 1992 are finished just off-dry. They drink well when young, and develop well over two to three years.

Bon Courage Rhine Riesling ★★★ B
The 1987 was an attractive off-dry wine. It developed beautifully, but needs to be drunk. The 1988 was not released. The 1991 is fruity and off-dry. The 1992 is a well-balanced, flowery, fruity wine.

Boschendal Rachelsfontein Rhine Riesling ★★★(★) C

This was one of the wines launched in 1987 with the Estate's single vineyard concept. Although it had only a little cultivar character at the time of the launch, a year later it developed much more flavour. The 1988 was a drier wine, but had more cultivar character. It developed a considerable richness, seldom found in Cape Rhine Rieslings. The 1989 and 1990 releases are showing good bottle development. The 1992 is drier. No 1991 was bottled.

Bottelary Weisser Riesling ★★(★) B

This is usually one of the better Weisser Rieslings. The 1981 vintage was excellent, as was the 1984, although the 1983, 1986 and 1988 were also good. All developed well over two to three years. Recent vintages are off-dry, much lighter in style, and are best enjoyed in their youth.

Bovlei Co-op Weisser Riesling ★★(★) A

A full-flavoured, off-dry wine for easy, early drinking.

Buitenverwachting Rhine Riesling ★★★(★) C

The 1989 is a four-star wine with full flavour, and lots of spice and fruit, all on a bone-drybackground. The 1989 is still available and one of the Cape's best.

Cape Vintners Members Only Rhine Riesling ★★★ B

An easy-drinking, off-dry wine, with attractive nose and fresh finish.

Clairvaux Co-op Rhine Riesling ★★ B

The 1992 is bone-dry, like the earlier vintages, and best when young.

Danie de Wet Rhine Riesling ★★★★ C

Danie produces a couple of labels made from Rhine Riesling. One is low alcohol and sweet in the Rhine style. The other is very much Late Harvest with delicious flavours.

De Helderberg Co-op Weisser Riesling ★★ A

The early 1990s are pleasant, light, off-dry, delicate wines, and best within two years of age.

Delaire Weisser Riesling ★★★★ C

An attractive wine, fractionally off-dry, with good cultivar character that is developing well. The 1989 is delightful, has developed well over three years and will still go more. The 1990 ranks as one of the Cape's best: drier than before, with full cultivar character that will also develop well in the bottle. The 1991 and 1992 continue the fine style.

Delheim Rhine Riesling ★★★★ C

This is a wine with a good history of being one of the Cape's best Rhine Rieslings on a regular basis. The 1991 is excellent, with very complex nose, and lots of layers of deep flavours. It is rich without being too sweet. Delicious wine. The 1992 is slightly drier but another stunner.

De Wetshof Rhine Riesling ★★★(★) C

First produced in 1981, this was a most impressive wine, as have been all subsequent vintages.

Douglas Green Rhine Riesling ★★★(★) C

A special release of the 1982 vintage was a delightful off-dry Superior. The 1983 was fuller and developed a distinct terpene nose within the year. Both wines developed with benefit and showed considerable complexity. They should now be drunk up. The 1984 is probably the best and has developed beautifully in the bottle. The 1986 carries Superior certification and is one of the best examples of the cultivar. A lighter wine, it is probably past its best now. The late 1980s were drier and not as attractive. The 1991 is a big, rich, off-dry wine in much the same style as the mid-1980s.

Du Toitskloof Co-op Weisser Riesling ★★(★) A

The first release, the 1989 vintage, came from very young vines. It was off-dry and had more Muscat character than real Weisser Riesling, but did well at local shows. The 1990 and 1991 are good, off-dry white wines. The 1992 is off-dry, but the high acid gives a dry impression.

Eersterivier-Valleise Kelder Weisser Riesling ★★★ B

This wine is a pleasant example of this cultivar, finished off-dry. It makes good drinking wine, especially when young.

Fairview Weisser Riesling ★★★★ B

This is usually a slightly off-dry wine, with aromatic nose and pleasant flavour, that develops well in the bottle over a year or three. The 1991 is a lovely, aromatic, off-dry wine, and the 1992 appears even drier, with a clean, brisk finish. (Limited supply.)

Goue Vallei Weisser Riesling (Citrusdal Co-op) ★★★ A

The first release from the 1988 vintage was semi-sweet with good fruity nose. Since then, it has improved vintage by vintage. In keeping with the cellar's determined effort to improve its quality and image, it has produced a lovely, fruity, semi-sweet wine with good flavour. The label depicts a gousblom. All the 1990s have been attractive wines at good-value prices.

Groot Constantia Weisser Riesling ★★★★ C

I thought this wine was first produced in 1977 and that it was the best example of Weisser Riesling yet made in the Cape. In 1987, however, I was given a 1976 to taste and now must accept that it was as good as the 1977. The wines were dry, yet full-bodied, and five-star material. The 1976 matured majestically. These earlier vintages aged magnificently over ten or more years. Subsequent vintages were semi-sweet and pleasing, with the 1984 carrying Superior certification. The 1985 was a little subdued when released but showed very well three years later. I doubt very much that the recent wines will age as well over ten or more years, but over two to three years they have lovely cultivar character. In 1988, the 1986 showed very well. The 1987 and 1988 are very good examples, with 1987 being selected by Alphen Wine of the Month Club as the best wine in its category. The 1989 is a super, off-dry Weisser Riesling, full of spice, fruit and a lovely penetrating flavour that has developed with great benefit. The 1990 continued the lovely off-dry style and full character. The 1991 is low in alcohol (under 11%) but has good acid and off-dry finish, with delightful nose and flavours, as does the 1992. The 1990s are probably at their best when young and fresh.

Hartenberg Weisser Riesling ★★★★ B

A wine that seems to have got better vintage by vintage and is nowadays finished off-dry with a hint of botrytis among the fruity, flowery aromas and good flavours. Each vintage appears to have the ability to age well over about four years. The 1992 is particularly pleasing.

Kaapzicht Weisser Riesling ★★★ B

The 1989 is off-dry, with good nose and fruity flavours, and has developed well in the bottle. The 1991 is off-dry and very attractive.

Klein Constantia Rhine Riesling ★★★★ C

The 1986 is the first vintage released from this restored and expanded Estate. Each vintage released has had grand style and great complexity. The 1990 is stunning wine, finished off-dry and packed with deep rich flavours. There was no release from 1991. The 1992 is fractionally drier but equally delicious. These wines all develop remarkably well. Absolutely super wine and definitely Constantia at its best.

Koopmanskloof Rhine Riesling ★★★ C

First released from the 1984 vintage. The 1986 was released in numbered bottles carrying a neck label depicting *Erica mammosa* drawn by the Cape artist, Drexler Kyzer. It was good, off-dry, pleasing wine, with honest cultivar character. It is no longer produced. Latter vintages have developed good bottle-age, but now need drinking.

KWV Weisser Riesling ★★★(★)

Consistently one of the Cape's better wines from this cultivar, it is finished off-dry and develops good bottle character over the years.

La Bri Weisser La Bri ★★★ C

The first release of this attractive wine came from the 1986 vintage. It is very pleasant and easy drinking. It is marketed in an eye-catching pack, similar to that of German wines, but which fairly and boldly states on the front label 'Wine of Origin Franschhoek'. It has improved vintage by vintage, with the 1991 a decided step-up in overall quality, and should develop well over two to three years.

Lebensraum Weisser Riesling ★★(★) B

The first release, from 1987, is off-dry and has good cultivar character. The 1989 is considerably better and is also off-dry. Both are developing with interest. The next release, from 1992, is along the same lines.

Lievland Weisser Riesling ★★★★ C

A well-made, off-dry wine with good cultivar character, the 1986 was tremendous and recognized at the Wine Olympiad in Paris. The extremely pungent terpene nose of this extraordinary wine developed remarkable intensity – to the dislike of some people and the delight of others. The 1988 is a full-bodied and -flavoured off-dry wine, packed with a complexity that has developed with benefit over the years. The 1989 is lighter than usual but a delightful product. Apparently drier, it has lots of fine flavour and good spicey-citrus nose. The 1990 is along the same lines. The 1991 and 1992 are wines well worth waiting for. This is continually one of the Cape's more unusual, but better, Rhine Rieslings.

L'Ormarins Rhine Riesling ★★★(★) C

This is an award-winning wine which develops well in the bottle. The 1986 was off-dry and a fine example of the fullness of flavour this cultivar can produce. The 1988, 1989 and 1990 are along the same lines, with good fruit and fine flavour. They will develop well over two to four years. There was no release from 1991.

Mon Don Rhine Riesling ★★★ B

Clean, fruity, well made, off-dry, easy-drinking wine came with the first release from 1991 vintage.

Montpellier Tuinwingerd ★★ A

The wine is simply labelled 'Tuinwingerd' with no mention of the cultivar. There is no doubt, however, that this wine is made from Weisser Riesling. The 1989 is light, off-dry, and better than usual.

Morgenhof Rhine Riesling ★★★ C

The 1991 and 1992 are big, full-flavoured wines with high alcohols that might age well. The first release, from the 1987 vintage, was off-dry, but with such high acid that it needed years to soften. The 1988 and 1989 have developed good terpene but is now a little tired. The 1989 and 1990 were firmer, fuller, fruity wines that now need drinking.

Nederburg Elgin Weisser Riesling ★★★★ D

This wine, released from 1990 vintage under the cellar's 'Limited Vintage' label, comes from grapes grown in the cooler Elgin area. This is lovely wine, full of enticing aromas and deep layers of flavour. It was good when young and has developed well in the bottle.

Nederburg Rhine Riesling ★★★★ C

A welcome addition (in 1981) to the cellar's range, this wine has been tremendously successful in terms of public acceptance, awards and Superior certification. It was winner of the 1983 Diners Club award, and a regular carrier of Superior certification. The 1988 was selected for SAA in 1989. An off-dry, well-flavoured wine with good cultivar character, it has enough acid to be attractive when young, yet is able to age with benefit. Vintages of the early 1990s show even better vinous qualities, and the high quality of wine produced in this quantity is remarkable.

Nederburg Weisser Riesling ★★★★ D

This wine occasionally appears on the Nederburg Auction, and is very different to the regular range wine. Decidedly dry, full of good nose and flavour, it ages with great benefit over five years.

Neethlingshof Weisser Riesling ★★★★ C/D

This is consistently one of the Estate's better wines. The 1990 and 1991 are well-balanced, well made, off-dry wines that will repay two or three years in the bottle. The 1992 is decidedly dry.

Neil Ellis Rhine Riesling ★★★★ C

The first release, from the 1986 vintage, was a very good example of this cultivar in a dry style. It has developed very well. The 1987 is off-dry and was drinking earlier and more easily than the previous vintage. The 1988 has good character intensity, in line with previous releases, and is also not quite dry. The 1989 is much drier, but just as good. Each release has developed well in the bottle. Wine is no longer bottled under this label, but the latter vintages are still full of life.

Onverwacht Weisser Riesling ★★ B

The 1991 and 1992 are better than earlier vintages. Finished off-dry, these are pleasant, lightly flavoured wines.

Paul Cluver Weisser Riesling ★★★ D

From the 1991 vintage comes a delightful, off-dry wine with good acid balance and fresh, elegant finish.

Rhebokskloof Weisser Riesling ★★★★ B

A first release from the 1991 vintage is a delightfully fragrant wine, finished off-dry. This is an excellent start with the cultivar. The 1992 is a good follow-up.

Riebeek Wine Farmers' Co-op Weisser Riesling ★★★ A

Recent vintages are somewhat toned-down compared to those of the late 1980s. They are off-dry, pleasant flavoured wines, for early drinking.

Rietvallei Estate Rhine Riesling Dry ★★★ C

A dry, fruity wine with good cultivar character and fresh finish.

Rooiberg Co-op Rhine Riesling ★★ B

This was a dry wine with good cultivar nose and full flavour, but, with the change of name from Weisser to Rhine, it has become off-dry. Despite this, the wines of the early 1990s have a relatively hard finish.

Ruiterbosch Mountain Cuvée-Rhine Riesling ★★★(★) C

The first release from 1989 vintage was dry and developed well into early 1993. The 1990 is off-dry but with the same depth of fruit and flavour. The 1991 is a fine wine, with a good flowery nose.

Simonsig Dry Weisser Riesling ★★★★ C

Weisser Riesling has become one of the specialities of this Estate. It appeared for the first time with the 1977 vintage and was sold as a rare wine at the 1978 Nederburg Auction. It has developed with subsequent vintages – the 1979 had a good, distinct, spicy nose and slightly sweet, medium body, and aged well. It used to be available as a dry or semi-sweet wine. The latter accumulated a number of Superior certifications and had a good varietal nose followed by complex taste. It has now been discontinued. The dry was certified Superior in 1983 while both sweet and dry versions, from the 1985 vintage, carried Superior certification. The 1983 won a gold medal at the Club Oenologique International Wine and Spirit Competition in 1985. It developed beautifully in the bottle. The 1984 (dry) was Superior and featured at the 1987 Nederburg Auction. The 1983 and the 1985 (dry) featured at the 1988 Nederburg Auction. The 1986 and 1987 vintages are both Superior. The 1988 is not as big as 1987 but has developed well. The 1989 continued the high quality style, with 1990 particularly full-flavoured and fruity. It is developing into a beautiful wine. The 1991 has a hard act to follow, but is also very good.

Simonsvlei Co-op Rhine Riesling ★★★ B/C
An off-dry wine with fine flavour and good cultivar nose. Excellent value for money.

Spier Weisser Riesling ★★★ B
From the 1989 vintage. This wine is showing some age, but has developed flavours that are very pleasant.

Spruitdrift Weisser Riesling ★★ B
The first release, from 1991, is off-dry with an attractive flowery nose.

Stellenryck Collection Rhine Riesling (Bergkelder) ★★★★ C
This is an excellent example of this cultivar, with the typically flowery yet spicey nose which distinguishes the Rhine Riesling grape. These old vintages are all developing amazingly well in the bottle, but reaching the time that they should be drunk up. There have been no recent bottlings.

Stellenzicht Vineyards Weisser Riesling ★★★ E
The first release from the 1989 vintage has developed beautifully. The 1990 is full of varietal character, as is the 1991. The name has changed from Rhine Riesling to Weisser Riesling. These are fine, off-dry, elegant wines that are super when young, but have the potential to develop well.

Thelema Rhine Riesling ★★★★ B
The first release, from the 1988 vintage, was an excellent start. It was only fractionally off-dry and full of attractive cultivar character. It drank delightfully while fresh and zesty, and has aged with benefit. The 1989 is most attractive, with full flavour, good cultivar, and distinct classy style. The 1990 is as near to dry as one can get. The 1991 is well made, well-balanced, off-dry wine. The 1992 is finished dry. These are lovely wines that develop well, but are very good drinking when young.

Uiterwyk Rhine Riesling ★★(★) C
Originally a good, brisk, dry wine, with later vintages slightly off-dry. These are clean wines with good cultivar character.

Van Loveren Rhine Riesling ★★★ B
This is a fuller-bodied wine than most, and finished off-dry. The 1987 developed beautifully into 1993, and the early 1990s are all good.

Villiera Rhine Riesling ★★★★ B/C
This wine has improved over the years; the later vintages are delightfully dry, full and fragrant. The 1984 was a winner at the 1988 Paris Wine

Olympiad. The 1985 was particularly good and developed beautifully in the bottle. The 1987 is a delightful, off-dry wine and still ageing well. The 1988, 1989 and 1990 are finished dry and are superb wines that are developing with distinction. The 1991 and 1992 are off-dry, adding complexity to the wines, which will develop with great distinction. The cellar is firmly established as one of the most consistent producers of fine wines from this cultivar.

Vlottenburg Co-op Weisser Riesling ★★★ A

This is a consistently good, off-dry wine, with attractive nose and true cultivar character.

Legend Weisser Riesling (Welmoed Co-op) ★★★ A

This is another very good wine which celebrated its maiden vintage in 1981. Modern vintages are off-dry, fruity wines that make good drinking.

Weltevrede Rhine Riesling ★★★★ B

This is an off-dry wine with good nose, touched out with a hint of botrytis. The Superior 1985 developed beautifully over four to five years. The 1989 was fresh, fruity, off-dry wine with good cultivar character, and was an Alphen Wine of the Month selection. The 1990 is almost dry, lovely wine. The 1991 was not as attractive when young, but it is developing well. The 1992 is following the same pattern, and both are developing well. This wine is established as one of the best of the area.

Woolworths Rhine Riesling ★★★★ C

The 1989, 1990 and 1991 from Simonsig were super wines. There is another 1991 available, but this comes from Klein Constantia. It is a deep, beautiful wine, that is finished off-dry.

Zandwijk Weisser Riesling ★★ C

The first release, from the 1989 vintage, is a somewhat neutral, off-dry wine. Considering that to make kosher wine the wine maker has to pasteurize the fresh juice before fermentation, the result is surprisingly acceptable. The 1990 is finished dry and the 1992, off-dry.

Zevenwacht Rhine Riesling ★★★(★) B

This is a delightful wine with excellent nose and fresh, off-dry taste. It fully deserved its Superior rating. The 1985 and 1986 were made dry and took time to show their best. The Superior 1985 was selected for the 1988 Nederburg Auction. The 1987 was off-dry and has developed well. The attractive 1989 is full of flavour and only just off-dry. The 1990 is the best release to date. As one of the cellar's best products, it will develop well. There was no 1991 release, but the 1992 is dry and delicious.

Zonnebloem Rhine Riesling (SFW) ★★★ C

Limited quantities were released from the 1984 and 1985 vintages. Both were pleasant, off-dry wines, but neither were great examples of the cultivar. Now a regular member of the range in an off-dry form, this is a reliable wine with good cultivar character. The recent vintages are good examples of well-made, true-to-cultivar wines with no dramatics.

Sauvignon Blanc

Aan-de-Doorns Co-op Sauvignon Blanc ★★ B
A light-flavoured, smooth, dry wine that makes pleasant drinking.

Aan de Wagenweg Blanc Fumé (Bergkelder) ★★★★ E
This wine has been produced in very small quantities. The first release came from the 1989 vintage and was launched early in 1990. It was made from grapes grown in the Stellenbosch district and aged for six months in small oak, and then in the bottle for another six months, before release. It is pale in colour, with good varietal nose, and backed by nice oak. The 1990 was the next release. It has now been discontinued.

Alphen Le Fevre ★★★★ C
First release came from 1990 vintage as part of the revamped Alphen range and was produced in the Kleine Zalze cellar from grapes grown in Stellenbosch and the Somerset West area. Part of the blend is wood-fermented producing fine, well-flavoured wine that has been successful in tastings, including the SAA selection. The 1992 and 1993 are delicious.

Altydgedacht Estate Sauvignon Blanc ★★★ C
The Estate introduced this wine to their range from the 1988 vintage. There was no 1989, but the 1990 was a good, grassy, unwooded wine with fine, brisk finish, as was the 1991. The 1992 has almost fierce, gooseberry-like aromas that I find very attractive. It will develop well.

Arthur Freedburg Selection Sauvignon Blanc (Rebel) ★★★ B
A well-balanced, steely, dry white wine with good cultivar character.

Ashton Co-op Blanc Fumé ★★★ B
A slightly wood-aged wine with good fruit.

Ashton Co-op Sauvignon Blanc ★★★ B
Full-flavoured unwooded wine.

Avontuur Blanc Fumé ★★★ C
The first release from 1992 is a good drinking wine with a nice balance of fruit and wood.

Avontuur Sauvignon Blanc ★★(★) C
A dry, wood-fermented wine with attractive nose and flavour. While young, however, it is not showing much cultivar character.

Backsberg John Martin ★★★★ C
This wine is made from Sauvignon Blanc and named after the Estate's late administrator, bottling man and even wine maker on occasion – indisputably a character and persuasive salesman. John was always against wood-aged or wood-treated white wine and Sydney Back quirkily named this wood-fermented and further wood-aged wine after him. It appears that John had no choice but to learn to appreciate this massive, full-flavoured, complex wine. The first release, from the 1985 vintage, was a stunning wine at the time. It has aged with great interest and in

1993 was still full of life. The 1986 was much the same, while the 1987 was as good but has developed far greater complexity much sooner. The 1988 is great, and about at its best now. The 1989 is not quite in style, but the 1990 is really super and developing well. The 1991 will be a stunner. Although there is no mention of the cultivar on the label, it has been included here as it is obviously Sauvignon Blanc. .

85 ★★★★ drink. 86 ★★★★(★) ready. 87 ★★★★ drink. 88 ★★★★(★) ready. 89 ★★★(★) ready. 90 ★★★★ ready, will still develop. 91 ★★★★(★) ready, will still develop.

Backsberg Sauvignon Blanc ★★★(★) B

This dry, medium-bodied wine with good varietal character was one of the earliest, if not the first, of the modern string of wines made from this cultivar. It was the South African white wine champion at the South African Championship Wine Show in 1982, and the regional champion white in 1984. The amount of wood treatment has varied over the years, but the experience gained shows in the 1985 release, which is probably one of South Africa's best examples of this cultivar, and it deserved five stars. The 1986 has pleasant nose and attractive flavour. The 1987 was a good dry white but lacked a little in cultivar character. The 1988 has more to offer and drank very easily when young. The unwooded 1989 is full of cultivar character and lovely wine, as are all those of the 1990s.

82 ★★★★ past its best. 83 ★★★★ drink. 84 ★★★★ drink. 85 ★★★★★ drink. 86 ★★★(★) drink. 87 ★★★ drink. 88 ★★★(★) drink. 89 ★★★(★) ready. 90 ★★★(★) ready. 91 ★★★(★) ready. 92 ★★★ ready.

Badsberg Co-op Sauvignon Blanc ★★ A

The first release from the 1989 vintage is a pleasant enough example of this variety; subsequent vintages show improvement. Unlike other wines of the cellar, it is closed with a cork and not a screw-top.

Barrydale Blanc Fumé ★★★ B/C

The 1991, made from Tradouw Valley grapes, has good cultivar character and a touch of oak background. The 1992 is well wooded and pleasant.

Barrydale Co-op Sauvignon Blanc ★★ B

The first release from the 1988 vintage was a fraction off-dry with very faint nose but pleasant enough taste. The 1989 is a massive wine with lots of flavour and alcohol. It is much better than the first release. The 1991 vintages are clean, fresh, well-made wines.

Bay View Sauvignon Blanc (Du Preez and Laubser) ★★★ B

The first release from 1992 has a medium bodied, grassy character, with a dry, clean finish.

Bellingham Blanc Fumé ★★★ C

This was a new wine for this cellar, from the 1991 vintage, of which about 20% spent some time in small oak. It is big wine with lots of cultivar character and fresh finish. The 1992 is made along the same lines. It has slight peppery nose, grassy flavours and fresh finish.

Bergsig Sauvignon Blanc ★★ B

The 1987 lacked the sharpness of the 1986, but it still made pleasant drinking and was best enjoyed young. The same goes for the 1988, which was very light in character. The 1989 was much the same. There was no release in 1990, but the 1991 was a light, soft wine for early, easy drinking. The 1992 is along the same lines.

Blaauwklippen Sauvignon Blanc ★★★(★) C

This is consistently good wine, and the 1991 was outstanding – the best since the first release from 1982 vintage. It is dry, full-flavoured, and has lots of cultivar character, without any oak influence. It drinks well now but has plenty of potential for ageing. The 1992 is again unwooded, with a very agreeable character, and is easy to drink.

Bloemendal Estate Sauvignon Blanc ★★★(★) B

The original vintage from 1987 was very light in character. Each subsequent vintage has shown improvement, with the 1991 being full-flavoured dry wine with fig and grassy characters. The 1992 is very aromatic and full of soft flavour. It is a very good four-star wine.

Bolandse Co-op Sauvignon Blanc ★★ B

This first and very creditable release from the 1985 vintage was dry and had a touch of wood highlighting the cultivar character. Subsequent vintages were decidedly odd, but the 1991 is lovely crisp, clean, unwooded dry wine, worthy of three stars. The 1992 follow-up is similar.

Bon Courage Sauvignon Blanc ★★★ B

After skipping a few vintages, a fresh, clean release came from 1991. It has flowery nose and distinct asparagus flavour. The 1992 was not available at the time of writing, but should be similar to the 1991.

Boplaas Blanc Fumé ★★★ B

Those of the early 1990s are pleasant, easy-drinking wines with good but light oak backing.

Boplaas Sauvignon Blanc ★★★ B

This is a nice, fresh wine with good cultivar character of a grassy style. It is an easy-drinking wine which is good value for money. From 1992 comes a crisp, fresh wine with good cultivar character.

Boschendal Sauvignon Blanc ★★★(★) D

The 1987 is an unwooded wine which was launched with the concept of making separate wines from individual vineyards. This release, from the Pierre Simon Vineyard, is a wine that develops well over two years in the bottle. The 1990 is a bone-dry, unwooded, flinty-type wine with a brisk finish. The 1991 reflects the quality of the vintage for this cultivar and is much better than earlier vintages. A touch of wood adds extra complexity. Definitely a four-star wine. The 1992 is a softer, quieter wine.

Bottelary Co-op Sauvignon Blanc ★★★ B

The first bottling, in 1982, showed plenty of promise, confirmed by numerous awards at the Stellenbosch show, as well as regional and bottled wine shows. The wines have developed a continuity of style, with lovely fresh character that is best enjoyed when young.

Bouchard Finlayson Sauvignon Blanc ★★★ D

The first release, from 1991, from the new cellar in the Hemel en Aarde Valley, Walker Bay, was made from grapes grown at Bot Rivier. This creditable start was gentle, soft, unwooded, dry wine. The 1992 is a much bigger, bolder wine, full of strong flavour and still unwooded. It has a high alcohol content of 13%, yet is easy to drink, and will develop well.

Bovlei Co-op Sauvignon Blanc ★★★ A

Although there is considerable variation vintage by vintage, this wine is usually big-bodied, bold, and better in its youth. The 1992 is better.

Buitenverwachting Blanc Fumé ★★★★ E

The 1986 vintage produced only 8 000 bottles of this beautiful wine. Big, rich and complex when launched, it has developed beautifully. The 1987 has been fermented and aged in good French oak, and is proving to be even better than the 1986. The 1988 is made from high-sugar, almost Late Harvest grapes. It is a big, complex wine without the charm of the 1987. The 1989 is also a beautiful, complex wine which is full of cultivar character, highlighted by good wood. It is developing with great benefit. The 1990, 1991 and 1992 continue the impressive style. It is well worth ageing this wine. It could become a collector's item.

Buitenverwachting Sauvignon Blanc ★★★★ D

The 1988 shows a change in style for the better. It has good cultivar nose with lots of penetrating clean flavour, and tasted very good on release. With time it has developed into a fine drinking wine. The 1989 is bigger in all respects – nose, flavour and alcohol – with a tremendous intensity of cultivar character. The 1990 is another fine wine, but the 1991 is outstanding. The 1992 is a little less showy but good all the same.

Cape Vintners Members Only Blanc Fumé ★★★ C

This is a blend of 70% wooded and 30% unwooded Sauvignon Blanc, from Welmoed, out of 1991 vintage. A satisfying, good drinking wine.

Cape Vintners Members Only Sauvignon Blanc ★★★ B

This is a full-flavoured, unwooded Sauvignon Blanc from Welmoed, with attractive nose, good flavour and brisk finish.

Cederberg Kelders Sauvignon Blanc ★★★ B

This is the best wine from this remote cellar. It has good, fruity nose, good-flavoured taste and makes pleasant drinking. Recent vintages have good steely touch, good fruit and brisk finish.

Danie de Wet Sauvignon Blanc ★★★(★) B

Although made by Danie de Wet, this range is not to be confused with the De Wetshof range. The 1991 is lovely, dry, fresh, fruity wine.

De Doorns Co-op Sauvignon Blanc ★ A

This cellar produces an off-dry wine that is unmistakably Sauvignon Blanc and needs a year to soften.

Delaire Blanc Fumé ★★★★ C

This is a consistently good dry wine with complex character that develops over time. The 1992 has fine fruit and wood.

Delaire Sauvignon Blanc ★★★(★) B

This wine has good, clean cultivar character that develops well in the bottle, although it is still a nice, easy drink when young. The unwooded freshness in the 1992 is delightful.

Delheim Blanc Fumé ★★★(★) B

This is an ever-improving wine, with the 1991 partially fermented in French oak, making it more complex than previous vintages. It is a four-star wine, and although it makes good drinking now, it has the potential to benefit with time in the bottle. The 1992 has fine cultivar character with light oak, but big alcohol content of 13%.

De Wet Co-op Blanc Fumé ★★★ B

This is fairly well-wooded, full-flavoured wine, with distinct cultivar showing above the wood.

De Wet Co-op Sauvignon Blanc ★★ A

A dry and light-bodied wine with pleasant but sharp cultivar character. It softens after about a year in the bottle. The 1991 has a hefty 13,5% alcohol. The 1992 is quieter, easier drinking.

De Wetshof Blanc Fumé ★★★(★) C

A delightfully different South African white wine: big in structure, it commands attention with a very definite character and style, although it is undeniably a Sauvignon Blanc. The more recent vintages are particularly appealing, especially the 1992. This wine is very different from the Sauvignon Blancs of Constantia, Stellenbosch or Franschhoek.

Die Krans Sauvignon Blanc ★★★ A

The first release from the 1990 vintage was a very good effort. It had a nice gooseberry character which developed over the year. The 1991 is fuller flavoured with long finish.

Dieu Donné Sauvignon Blanc ★★★ B

The 1990 is a great improvement on previous releases and is a big, high-alcohol wine. No 1991 was released, but the 1992 is dry and fruity, with a clean, sharp finish.

Douglas Green Sauvignon Blanc ★★★ C

The 1990 vintage spent three months in new French oak. It is easy-drinking wine that is now showing lots of bottle age.

Du Toitskloof Co-op Sauvignon Blanc ★★(★) B

This is a consistently good, gentle wine that is at its best in its youth.

Edelkeller Sauvignon Blanc (Marcows) ★★★ B

This is a well made, good cultivar wine, that is dry on the palate and freshly finished.

Edward Snell Sauvignon Blanc ★★★ B

A non-vintaged, good, dry, cultivar character wine in the grassy style.

Eersterivier Valleise Kelder Sauvignon Blanc ★★★(★) B

The surprise of 1984 must have been wine maker Manie Rossouw's Diners Club Award for this Sauvignon Blanc. It was a good dry wine with true Sauvignon Blanc cultivar character. The 1985 had attractive cultivar nose and good flavour, and the 1986 was a gold medal winner at the Stellenbosch show. In 1987 I said I preferred these wines when they are young. If, however, they age as well as the 1984, which was at the 1988 Nederburg Auction, then it is worth keeping a few bottles for four years. The 1984 developed a magnificence difficult to believe unless experienced. The 1988 had big pungent cultivar character that has developed well with time. Seventy cases were selected for the 1991 Nederburg Auction. The 1989 seems to have suffered along with many others with the vintage, but this could be one of the better efforts. The 1990 is very good and developing well in the bottle. The 1991 was great as a young wine, but seems to be going through a dip in early 1993. Hopefully it will recover and develop as well as the earlier vintages. The 1992 is a super wine and four-star material; very good value for money.

Eikendal Sauvignon Blanc ★★★(★) C

This cellar is producing better and better wine. The Sauvignon Blanc has settled into a good substantial style with full body, distinctive nose and an easy drinkability. The 1992 is steely with a fresh finish.

Fairview Sauvignon Blanc Fumé ★★★ B

The first release, from the 1989 vintage, is a good combination of wood and cultivar. Actually wood-fermented, it is dry and has good potential. There has been no release since the 1989.

Fleur Du Cap Blanc Fumé (Bergkelder) ★★★(★) C

The 1987 is big, serious, bone-dry, well-wooded wine, full of cultivar and complexity. It is developing well in the bottle and is packaged in the new style, similar to the Chardonnay. The 1989 is very good considering the generally poor year for Sauvignon Blanc. The 1990 is a good, clean cultivar with nice oak backing, and is developing well in the bottle. There was no 1991 or 1992.

Goedvertrouw Estate Sauvignon Blanc ★★★

The first release from this new Botrivier cellar came from 1991 vintage. It is good, fruity, unwooded, dry white wine with pale cultivar character and clean, fresh finish. The 1992 is big and full.

Goue Vallei Sauvignon Blanc (Citrusdal Co-op) ★★ B

A good example of clean cultivar character. The 1992 is off-dry and fruity.

Groot Constantia Sauvignon Blanc ★★★(★) B/C

Since the first release in 1982, this wine has varied in type, style and quality. The 1987 was outstanding and is still a fine wine. From 1989 the wines have settled into a consistent style: big, full, unwooded, generous wine, which is exciting when young, but with every potential to age. The 1992 is a four-star wine with good fruit and nuances of herbs.

Hamilton Russell Vineyards Sauvignon Blanc ★★★★ D

Originally marketed under the Grand Vin Blanc label, the 1983 is a good representative of a well-wooded Sauvignon Blanc. It is a more complex wine than the 1982. The 1984 is a lovely, light, dry example of the cultivar, while the 1985 was the best to date when released. But the 1986 proved to be even better! Forty per cent of this vintage spent three months in small French oak, giving a complexity which is developing well with time. The 1987 is yet another improvement, in a very good year for Sauvignon Blanc. The vines, which were between six and nine years of age, yielded very good fruit and a wine, rare both in quality and quantity, of which only 1 500 bottles were produced. The 1988 reflects the vintage, yet it is still one of the best, with good fruit flavour but no wood. The 1989 is lovely wine, but not quite up to the standard of the 1988. The 1990 is very good and will develop well. The 1991 could well be the best to date, and a beautiful wine which will develop with great distinction. Definitely one of the Cape's best. The 1991 was the last to be released – the Sauvignon Blanc is now blended to produce a Chardonnay/Sauvignon Blanc blend.

82 ★★★★ ready. 83 ★★★★ ready. 84 ★★★★ ready. 85 ★★★★★ ready. 86 ★★★★★ ready. 87 ★★★★★ ready, will still improve. 88 ★★★★(★) ready, will still improve. 89 ★★★★ ready. 90 ★★★★ ready, will still improve. 91 ★★★★(★) ready, will improve.

Hartenberg Sauvignon Blanc ★★★ C

The wine from the 1987 vintage had good cultivar character, but rather hard acidic finish, which softened with age. The 1988 is better. The 1989 is very good, with lots of complex character, and is ageing with benefit. The 1990 is very attractive and will probably improve in the bottle, although it is not quite up to the 1989. The 1991 is big in every way, and the 1992 not quite as promising.

Haute Provence Blanc Fumé ★★★ C

The first release, from the 1989 vintage, was a very good effort, with the cultivar character marrying well with the wood. The 1990 is not quite as good as the 1989, but very acceptable, while the 1991 is disappointing for a year so good (in general) for Sauvignon Blanc. It has not shown signs of good development.

Hazendal Blanc Fumé ★★★ C

The first release from the 1989 vintage was fairly ordinary, but the 1990 was much better, with good cultivar character and a much brisker feel. The 1991 is still to be released.

Helderberg Co-op Sauvignon Blanc ★★ B

The wines of the 1990s are good, clean, refreshing wines, best enjoyed in their youth. The 500 ml bottle is a very good idea.

Huguenot Sauvignon Blanc ★(★) B

A soft, light wine, with little flavour.

Kaapzicht Estate Sauvignon Blanc ★★★(★) B

This is a very good value for money wine. The 1991 has fine cultivar character and is full of rich aromas and flavours. The 1992 is dry and unwooded, with good fruits, acid, and a fresh finish.

Kango Co-op Sauvignon Blanc ★ A

A dry, simple wine with very little cultivar character.

Klawer Co-op Sauvignon Blanc ★★ A

A soft, well-rounded wine in which the cultivar character is recognizable, but certainly not a great feature.

Klein Constantia Sauvignon Blanc ★★★★★ D

New Zealand is supposed to be making the best Sauvignon Blancs in the world and Ross Gower, the wine maker at Klein Constantia, spent a few years working there after leaving Nederburg. No doubt the experience he gained, together with the magnificent fruit from this Estate, has enabled this talented man to produce such a tremendous Sauvignon Blanc. Like so many South African wines of great character, it has a high alcohol content of almost 13%, and is undoubtedly one of the Cape's great wines. The wine, which won the white wine championship at the 1986 Young Wine Show, was also a Sauvignon Blanc from this cellar, but it has been kept for special releases, for example, the New World Wine Auction. Neither wine has had any wood-ageing as the wine maker believes that wood would detract from rather than enhance it. There was no bottling of the 1987 vintage as it was not considered up to standard. Instead, it was blended into the Blanc de Blanc. The 1988 is an even bigger wine than the 1986. It has astonishing character and is developing well into 1993. The 1989 and 1990 continue the great quality. The 1989, tested by British critics in the United Kingdom in 1990, was rated above the same vintage of the fabled New Zealand Cloudy Bay Sauvignon Blanc. The 1991 reflects the quality of vintage better than almost any other cellar. The 1992 is big, full, bold and delicious.

Kleindal Sauvignon Blanc ★★★ B

A well-made dry wine with good cultivar character. The 1991 and 1992 are good drinking wines.

Koopmanskloof Marbonne Sauvignon Blanc ★★★ C

The 1990 was Sauvignon Blanc with 30% Sémillon. The 1991 is all Sauvignon Blanc. It has good varietal flavour and dry, flinty finish.

KWV Sauvignon Blanc ★★★

Until the 1988 vintage the wines were lacking in cultivar character. From then on, there was a great improvement, with good nose and pleasant taste. It is now a regular, good quality wine.

La Bri Sauvage de La Bri ★★★(★) C

The 1987 release was outstanding. Made at the Franschhoek Vineyards Co-op from grapes grown by Michael Trull at La Bri, this wine had intense character on the nose and full-flavoured palate. Sauvage de La

Bri must be the most outstanding wine to have ever come out of this Co-op. The 1988 was also good, but the 1989 was not quite up to scratch. It was better, however, than many wines produced during what was a poor year for this cultivar. The 1990 was an improvement and has developed well. The 1991 is a good four-star wine with lots of fruit, good palate and long, fresh finish. The 1992 is a little off the pace, and somewhat high acid counters the usual smoothing, off-dry finish.

La Cotte Sauvignon Blanc (Franschhoek Vineyards) ★★(★) B

The first release, from the 1983 vintage, was an excellent wine when young. Subsequent vintages have not been quite as arresting, but the 1990, 1991 and 1992 are much better wines.

La Couronne Blanc Fumé ★★★ C

The first release comes from the 1991 vintage. Highly alcoholic. This is a barrel-fermented wine, strongly flavoured with lots of oak. The 1992 is much better, with good fruit and a brisk finish.

La Couronne Sauvignon Blanc ★★★ B

This unwooded wine was first released with the 1989 vintage; it had good cultivar character and fruitiness in its youth. The 1990 was along the same lines, with the 1992 being much better with good clean fruit.

La Couronne Sauvignon Blanc Reserve ★★★(★) C

The 1990 has good cultivar character. It is a clean, dry wine that could develop well in the bottle. The 1991 is much better.

La Motte Blanc Fumé ★★★★ C

The first release from the 1989 vintage was a beautiful, elegant wine, with good cultivar character and fine oak; very soft in the mouth. The 1990 was even more complex and appealing, with good texture, and has developed well into 1993. The 1991 is a very fine wine and close to five stars. It is beautifully balanced, delicious, full flavoured, and slides gently across the palate. These wines drink very well young, yet the earlier ones are developing in the bottle with great benefit.

La Motte Sauvignon Blanc ★★★★ C

This is a really super Sauvignon Blanc in the bold, high fruit style. The first release, from 1989, has shown good development in the bottle. The 1990 has everything of the first release and will develop with the same distinction. The 1991 is even better, and the 1992 is more complex without the pungent youthful nose. These wines will develop with great benefit.

Landskroon Sauvignon Blanc ★★★ C

The wines of the 1990s are very attractive and good drinking products, with good cultivar and cellar character.

La Provence Blanc Fumé ★★★ C

This was originally named Blanc Fleuri, but was forced to change to Blanc Fumé by the owners of the Fleur label. The 1990 vintage is a good, unwooded (despite the name) Sauvignon Blanc. The 1991 is a big, full, alcoholic wine with a hard, dry finish.

Le Bonheur Blanc Fumé ★★★★ C

Despite the name, this was an unwooded wine. It is a pity that a cellar that has produced such a good Sauvignon Blanc has not had any releases since 1990. The 1989 was good considering the poor vintage and the 1990 was as good as ever, with full, intense cultivar character.

Lemberg Aimée ★★★★ C

I thought that the 1991 was possibly the best-ever, and was full-flavoured at an early stage. It developed with great benefit. The label does not carry the name 'Sauvignon Blanc', but the leaf depicted is one from the cultivar. The 1992 is one of the best well-oaked, fruity Sauvignon Blancs produced in the Cape for the year.

Les Monts Malverne Sauvignon Blanc (Clos Malverne) ★★★ C

This cellar's first white is from 1993, and ready to drink on release. Good and fruity wine.

Lievland Sauvignon Blanc ★★★ C

This is a good, easy-drinking wine, with attractive Sauvignon Blanc character. It is always interesting. Recent vintages have good cultivar character and drink well. The 1992 has an attractive mushroom character.

L'Ormarins Blanc Fumé ★★★★(★) C

This is a wine packed with powerful cultivar nose and flavour, touched out beautifully with good oak. The cellar has an incredibly good record for well made wine since the first release in 1982, and this Blanc Fumé is consistently one of South Africa's best. The 1989 is in the same, big style, as is the 1990. The 1992 is big and bold.

L'Ormarins Sauvignon Blanc ★★★★ C

The Estate's Sauvignon Blanc was the 1983 South African white wine champion. The 1984 had even more piercing character and, in early 1986, was showing very well with some bottle age. The 1988 was a delightfully fruity wine, and thoroughly enjoyable when young. The 1989 was more reserved; dry and unwooded, and a very good example of the cultivar. Not so the 1990 – a full flavoured, great wine, with a strong, varietal nose. The 1991 continues the big bold style, as does the 1992.

Lutzville Co-op Fleermuisklip Sauvignon Blanc ★★ A

This is early drinking, fruity, soft wine with brisk finish.

Matin Soleil Sauvignon Blanc ★★★ C

The first release from the 1991 vintage is a reasonable effort and, although without much cultivar character, a pleasant drink. The 1992 was a much improved, good drinking wine.

Mont Blois Blanc Fumé ★★ C

The first release from the 1989 vintage has little fruit character. The wood shows through.

Morgenhof Sauvignon Blanc ★★★ C

The 1986 vintage was a good first attempt giving a fresh wine with a hint of wood and reasonable cultivar character. Subsequent vintages have varied, with the 1991 showing well, with crisp, fresh finish. The 1992 is fuller, with good, clean finish.

Mulderbosch Blanc Fumé ★★★★ D

The first release from this new cellar, on the Koelenhof side of the Bottelary range, came from the 1991 vintage. A portion of the wine was oak-fermented and the lot matured in various oaks, including some American. This is a fine first effort, and comes in eye-catching, strip-label bottles. It augurs well for the future. The 1992 is a bold wine, with a piercing nose and strong, fruity flavours.

Mulderbosch Sauvignon Blanc ★★★★ C

This wine is full of exciting cultivar character. The first release, from the 1992 vintage, is big in all respects, has 14% alcohol, is bounding with aroma and flavour, and has developed well. The 1993 follows in the same impressive style.

Nederburg Private Bin D229 ★★★(★) E

The first release came from the 1985 vintage, and there has been one from each vintage through to the most recent 1990. All are big, full, unwooded wines with excellent fresh acidity, which gives this predominantly Sauvignon Blanc blend good fruitiness and character, without any wood influence. It is released only at the annual Nederburg Auction.

Nederburg Private Bin D234 ★★★ E

This is a wood-aged Sauvignon Blanc that spent nine months in small French oak, developing a strong vanilla and cultivar nose, an attractive dry flavour, and deep character. It should develop well over two to three years. The 1988, 1989 and 1990 vintages have been sold to the trade at the Auction.

Nederburg Sauvignon Blanc ★★★★ C

The first release in the regular line, from the 1991 vintage, has been a very good, clean varietal, made in a decidedly drinkable style.

Nederburg Sauvignon Blanc (Limited Release) ★★★ C

To date there have been limited releases of two vintages: the 1982 and the 1984. The wine is offered in a clear, Bordeaux-type bottle and is very much in the style of coastal Sauvignon Blancs. It is dry, fresh and finely flavoured, the cultivar true, and without wood influence. There was also a 1980 Sauvignon Blanc, which was offered at the 1983 Nederburg Auction: a fine, steely wine which drank well when young. It has now given way to the 1991, which has been released in the regular range.

Neethlingshof Sauvignon Blanc ★★ C

Nowadays this is a consistently good wine, with crisp, appealing, varietal character. It is well made, soundly balanced, and the 1991 and 1992 are particularly good.

Neil Ellis Blanc Fumé ★★★★ C

From the 1988 vintage came a big, rich wine with full flavour and lots of complexity of cultivar and wood. One of the Cape's best Sauvignon

Blancs, it is very good and developing beautifully. The 1990 is a beautiful wine, and also one of the best. Although it is no longer produced, previous bottlings are still developing well.

Neil Ellis Sauvignon Blanc ★★★(★) C

The first release from the 1986 vintage had good cultivar character and has developed well over the years. The 1987 was a more complex wine with 25% having been fermented and matured in wood. It developed well in the bottle and is four-star material. The 1988 and 1989 are showing well now. (Replaced by Whitehall.)

Neil Ellis Whitehall Sauvignon Blanc ★★★★(★) C

The first release from the 1990 vintage comes from Elgin and is a magnificent wine. It is a bright, brisk, flinty style wine, with great fruit intensity. Tremendous to drink in its youth, it is certainly developing with great distinction. The 1991 is an exciting wine and set a new standard for this varietal. The 1992, with its 13% alcohol, is certainly proof of the quality of the region and the wine maker.

Nordale Co-op Sauvignon Blanc ★★ A

A light, dry white wine for easy drinking.

Nuy Sauvignon Blanc ★★★ B

A good introduction from the 1991 vintage was followed by a nice, fruity 1992. Both have fine varietal flavour, are dry, and very drinkable.

Oude Nektar Sauvignon Blanc ★★★ B

The first release came from the 1992 vintage. It has an odd, but pleasant, grassy character.

Overgaauw Sauvignon Blanc ★★★(★) C

This is consistently good, regular drinking wine, with lots of cultivar character. Recent vintages are good, clean and well-balanced.

Overhex Co-op Sauvignon Blanc ★★ A

A light, easy-drinking, dry white, first released from the 1991 vintage.

Paul Cluver Sauvignon Blanc ★★★★ C

The first release, from the 1991 vintage, was made from Cluver grown Elgin grapes in the Nederburg cellars. It is fresh, fruity and peppery.

Pick 'n Pay Sauvignon Blanc ★★★ C

Made by Simonsig. This is an unwooded, big, full, New World-style wine. It has good varietal nose, lots of flavour and good, fresh, crisp finish. From 1989 vintage, this wine is showing good bottle age.

Pieter Cruythoff Sauvignon Blanc Reserve ★★★ B

The 1991 vintage is good, full-flavoured wine, with steely character and fresh finish. Good value for money.

Porterville Co-op Sauvignon Blanc ★★ A

A dry, unwooded, lightly flavoured but full-bodied wine.

Rhebokskloof Blanc Fumé ★★★(★) C

A well made, dry, crisp and easy-drinking wine, with good cultivar character. A touch of oak helps its complexity.

Robertson Co-op Sauvignon Blanc ★★★ B

This is regular quality, easy-drinking dry wine.

Romansrivier Co-op ★★ A/B

The 1992 is a good dry white wine with some varietal character.

Roodezandt Co-op Sauvignon Blanc ★★ B

A two-time first for this Co-op. Their 1987 vintage was their first Sauvignon Blanc, and their first white wine to be wooded. It reached its best two years after being released. The 1990 is a well-balanced wine for early drinking. The 1992 is an unwooded, simple dry white.

Rooiberg Co-op Blanc Fumé Sur Lie ★★★(★) B

To my taste, the best Sauvignon Blanc from over the mountains was the 1987 vintage of this wine. It was cask fermented and left on its lees for five months, and then the clear wine was drawn off and bottled unfiltered. Packed with cultivar character, it showed good, tasty wood and other flavours that enabled it to develop with spectacular results. The 1989 is not as good, but the 1990 has good cultivar character backed by good wood. The 1991 is a little subdued.

Rooiberg Co-op Sauvignon Blanc ★★ B

This is a full-flavoured wine, with the 1992 having good cultivar character.

Ruiterbosch Mountain Vineyard Sauvignon Blanc ★★★★ C

A very good first attempt from the 1989 vintage came from the cool mountain-side vineyard overlooking Mossel Bay. The 1990 was fine wine but the 1991 was a great improvement; a crisp, clean cultivar which is developing well. The 1992 is a fine wine that will need time to develop.

Saxenburg Sauvignon Blanc ★★★ C

The 1991 is good fruity wine. The 1990 developed very quickly, and the 1992 is a little reserved and lacking in fruit.

Saxenburg Private Collection Sauvignon Blanc ★★★ C+

This is good cultivar wine backed with good, clean wood.

Simonsig Sauvignon Blanc ★★★(★) C

While always good, recent vintages have had touches of class. These are big, bold, flavourful wines that can be relied on to satisfy.

Simonsvlei Co-op Blanc Fumé ★★★ C

A full-flavoured, well-oaked Sauvignon Blanc with a slight, smokey tone.

Simonsvlei Co-op Sauvignon Blanc ★★★ B

This cellar must be pleased at having achieved such good wine on a regular basis. Those of the early 1990s are not totally dry, which gives added smoothness. A very satisfying drink.

Slanghoek Co-op Sauvignon Blanc ★★ A

A dry wine, with reasonable cultivar character, making easy-drinking. The 1992 has good varietal character.

Spier Sauvignon Blanc ★★ B

The first release from the 1984 vintage was very light wine. The 1985 was better, and the 1987 was a gold medallist at the Stellenbosch show. The

1988 is a soundly-made dry white wine, and the 1989 is light and pleasant, with good cultivar character. There have been no recent releases.

Spruitdrift Co-op Sauvignon Blanc ★★ A

A regular medal winner at local shows, this is pleasant wine which is best enjoyed in its youth.

Stellenryck Blanc Fumé ★★★★ D

This is an extremely good, unwooded wine which develops beautifully with two to three years of bottle-ageing. It is dry, with high natural acidity and the distinctive flavour of grassiness and gunflint, typical of wine made from Sauvignon Blanc in the Sancerre style. The 1984 vintage was magnificent and has developed beautifully in the bottle. The 1985 also showed well. The 1987 was a lesser wine, but developed well into 1993. The 1988 was selected for the 1989 SAA wine list. The 1989 and 1990 are super wines that have developed well and are now at their best.

Stellenzicht Sauvignon Blanc ★★★★ D

The 1992 release is a beautiful, big, dry wine packed with fresh cultivar character, and has long lingering finish. Super. The 1992 is equally good.

Swartland Sauvignon Blanc ★★★ B

Introduced with the 1985 vintage, this wine showed distinct cultivar nose, but had a somewhat flat flavour. It has improved since then. The 1988 was a good example of how good a Co-op can be with this cultivar, combining penetrating nose and intense flavour with medium body. The 1989 was not as good, and the 1990 was not up to standard. The 1991 is back to being a good quality wine. The 1992 is very good. This wine is best enjoyed in its youth to capture its good character.

Thelema Blanc Fumé ★★★★ C

The 1989 bottling for the 1990 Cape Independent Winemakers' Guild and Auction was a spectacular wine. The 1990 regular release is not quite as great, but very good all the same. The 1991 is the last release, to allow the grapes to be used for very good, and very popular, Sauvignon Blanc.

Thelema Sauvignon Blanc ★★★★ C

The first vintage from 1987 was remarkable for the intensity achieved from such young vines on this farm. The 1988, released for sale just after the 1989 vintage was in the cellar, is opening up into a bright, fresh, dry wine with good cultivar nose and fine flavour in the mouth. The 1989 is a super wine with very good cultivar character. Lovely as a young wine, it is developing with benefit. The 1990 is superb, and the 1991 and 1992 are excellent in all respects – among the Cape's best. It is full of lovely fruit and lots of flavour that will develop with great distinction.

Uiterwyk Estate Sauvignon Blanc ★★★ D

The first release from the 1988 vintage was a good example of young Sauvignon Blanc and made pleasant meal-time drinking. The 1989 was altogether better, with attractive nose and good flavour. The 1990, 1991 and 1992 are good, steely wines.

Uitkyk Estate Sauvignon Blanc ★★★★ C
Throughout the 1970s this was a pleasant, off-dry, Steen-based blend. In 1981, however, a considerable amount of Sauvignon Blanc was introduced, producing a delightfully dry wine. The 1986, a strict, more formal wine, carried Sauvignon Blanc on the label. With the 1991 release the 'Carlsheim' has been dropped and it is now labelled as Sauvignon Blanc. It is strong, full, beautiful wine with lots of development potential. The 1992 is a full, dry, unwooded wine.

Van Loveren Sauvignon Blanc ★★ B
The first release came from the 1983 vintage. Nowadays this is a big wine with better cultivar character and full flavour.

Vergelegen Les Enfants ★★★ B
The first release, from the 1992 vintage, is a very creditable effort. It is very good as an early drinker and is developing quickly.

Villiera Cru Monro Blanc Fumé ★★★★ C
A beautiful Sauvignon Blanc with good oak influence, this is a well-rounded, complex wine, that taste good on release and should develop well with time. The 1991 and 1992 are stunning wines.

Villiera Sauvignon Blanc ★★★★(★) C
The 1980 vintage was a delightful, off-dry wine with clear varietal character, and drank very well when young. Subsequent vintages have been bone-dry, with good cultivar character. The latest vintages have some wood influence, which adds a little more complexity. The 1985 was a lovely, light wine with fine flavour, and the 1986 has freshness and good character. The 1987 was delicate with a pleasant, fragrant bouquet and nice, dry flavour. It developed well over two years. The 1988 and 1989 have good character, the 1988 being the best and worthy of four stars. The same can be said for the 1990. These wines are characterized by a touch of lightness seldom found in South African Sauvignon Blancs – a delightful difference. The 1991 is one of the Cape's best, as is the unwooded 1992.

Villiersdorp Co-op Sauvignon Blanc ★★ A
The first release, from the 1988 vintage, was a dry white wine with reasonable cultivar nose and flavour. The next vintage was the 1990, a good, easy-drinking wine. The same could be said of the 1991. The 1992 is a little disappointing.

Vlottenburg Co-op Sauvignon Blanc ★★ A
A good, regular-drinking wine with brisk finish.

Vredendal Co-op Sauvignon Blanc ★★★ A
This may not be a 'purist's' wine but it is remarkable considering its origin. A good wine and excellent value for money. The 1990 and 1991 are lighter, but still have an attractive flavour. The 1992 has good varietal character and makes easy, good drinking. It always amazes me how Giel Swiegers pays attention to these smaller productions, despite the massive quantities this Co-op handles.

Welmoed Co-op Sauvignon Blanc ★★★ C

The maiden vintage was the 1981 and contained a little of everything that a wine from the Sauvignon Blanc cultivar should. Subsequent vintages have not been quite as exciting, although the mid-1980s showed an improvement. The 1990 and 1991 were good, the 1992 similar, and all at their best when young.

Weltevrede Estate Blanc Fumé ★★★ C

Oak-ageing has helped this wine develop a better complexity of character than its unwooded partner. It is dry and tasty. The 1990 was the first release since 1987, and is followed by a very acceptable 1991.

Weltevrede Estate Sauvignon Blanc ★★★ B

1986 provided the first vintage of this cultivar from this Estate. Latest vintages, especially the 1992, are well flavoured and good drinking.

Woolworths Blanc Fumé ★★★★ B

Produced by Neil Ellis. This is an excellent buy, and beautiful wine, with plenty of cultivar character, out of the 1990 vintage. It has developed very well. The 1992 is great, slightly wooded, drinking wine.

Woolworths Sauvignon Blanc ★★★(★) B

Produced by Robertson Co-op. An attractive Sauvignon Blanc ready for drinking. Fresh and fruity when young, it is worth ageing at the price.

Woolworths Sauvignon Blanc Reserve ★★★★ D

An excellent wine from Klein Constantia specially blended for Woolworths out of 1989 vintage. It is less alcoholic than the Estate's label, but has attractive nose, good flavour. It was followed by a four-star-plus 1991, with big alcohol (14%) and lots of fine, full flavours.

Zandwijk Sauvignon Blanc ★★ D

The 1989 vintage was the first release. It did not have much cultivar character, but was sound and pleasant. The 1990 was an improved product, with better cultivar character, and the 1992 is good and fruity.

Zevenwacht Blanc Fumé ★★★★ C

The first release came from the 1992 vintage, with good gooseberry nose and flavour, and subtle wood backing.

Zevenwacht Sauvignon Blanc ★★★★ C

The 1989, 1990 and 1991 are big, full wines packed with cultivar character and should all develop as well as the 1989 is now showing. The 1992 is the best to date and a good, four-star, complex wine.

Zonnebloem Sauvignon Blanc (SFW) ★★★ C

Made in the Loire style, this wine develops well in the bottle but is also good when young. It is one of the best-drinking, dry Sauvignon Blancs in the Cape. During its relatively short career it has been selected by SAA for its wine list, and picked up a number of overseas awards. It is consistently reliable. The 1990 was a bigger, bolder product, with good cultivar character. The 1991 has developed well in the bottle. The 1992 is a fruity, full flavoured, soft on the palate, easy drinker.

Sémillon

Belcher Sémillon ★★★
A pleasant, light, easy-drinking wine from the 1992 vintage.

Boschendal Sémillon
Still to be released; full-flavoured, oaky wine.

Delheim/Lloyd Sémillon ★★★
A small amount was produced from 1989 – a good attempt with this wine, which proves that there is a place for a well-made Sémillon.

Eikenhof Sémillon ★★★ D
A small quantity was made from 90 year-old vines and matured for two months in small wood. It is good, dry wine with citrus nose and flavour.

Fairview Sémillon Reserve ★★★★ D
The first from 1992 is big, alcoholic, wood-fermented wine with a strong, fresh finish.

La Bourgogne Joie de Vivre Sémillon ★★(★) B
Dry, fruity wine with flowery tones.

La Cotte Sémillon (Franschhoek Vineyards Co-op) ★★(★) B
Consistently one of the cellar's better, well-flavoured, dry wines. The 1990, 1991 and 1992 are easy-drinking, fresh and fruity wines.

Les Chênes Sémillon ★★(★) B
The first release, from the 1986 vintage, was a dry white with good, clean character. The 1987 was much better wine, with good fruit and flavour.

Mouton Excelsior Le Moutonné Sémillon ★★(★) B
A dry, crisp wine with good cultivar character. The 1985 vintage was the first to be released, and the 1986 has developed well in the bottle. The 1987 is showing good bottle development and should be consumed.

Sylvaner

Overgaauw Sylvaner ★★★(★) B
This is a speciality of this cellar, and is always good, interesting wine with a fresh and fine Sylvaner bouquet. It is of consistent quality, and matures very well in the bottle. The 1986 was very fruity on release and in excellent condition in 1992. The 1987 and 1988 are not developing as well as the 1986 and need to be drunk up. The 1989 and 1990 are both delightful in 1993. The 1991 seems to be slightly sweeter than previous vintages, but still only off-dry, lovely fresh, fruity wine that is delightful in its youth. The 1992 is a dry, delightful, fine flavoured wine.

Blanc de Noir

Aan-de-Doorns Co-op Blanc de Noir ★★ A

A semi-sweet wine made from Pinotage.

Alphen Deliana Blanc de Noir ★★★ C

This is a blend of Pinotage and Zinfandel. Latest bottlings are finished dry and have good, fruity nose and fresh finish. The wine is part of the revamped Alphen range, made in the Kleine Zalze cellar.

Avontuur Blanc de Noir ★★★ B

Originally this wine was made from Pinotage; the 1991 is Pinotage-Merlot and 1992, Pinotage-Cabernet. Both are good, fruity, and finished off-dry. Delightful wine, especially when served chilled.

Barrydale Co-op Blanc de Noir ★★ A

This interesting orange/pink wine made from Red Muscadel has a pretty nose and pleasant, semi-sweet flavour. It is best enjoyed in its youth.

Beaufort Blanc de Noir (Solly Kramer) ★★ A

A pleasant, easy-drinking off-dry wine from Pinotage.

Bon Courage Blanc de Noir ★★★ B

A light, easy-drinking wine from Shiraz and Muscat, with the latter present in sufficiently small quantities to add interest without being obtrusive. The wine is off-dry and well balanced with the fresh, fruity finish.

Boplaas Blanc de Noir ★★★ B

A blend of predominantly Pinotage with small amounts of Cabernet and Tinta Barocca which give intriguing nose and flavour. It is finished off-dry and, with a lowish alcohol content of 10%, it makes very easy and pleasant drinking.

Boschendal Blanc de Noir ★★★(★) C

This was the first Blanc de Noir to be marketed under this name in South Africa. The maiden vintage, 1981, was an instant success and became the drink of the fashion-conscious. The blend has varied and improved over the years, and now has good complex character owing to the combination of Cabernet, Pinotage, Shiraz and Tinta Barocca. Usually finished off-dry (but tastes dryish), it makes very easy drinking.

Botha Co-op Blanc de Noir ★★ A

This wine is made from Cabernet and finished off-dry, with some 10 g/l sugar content. It is pale in colour, but strong in alcohol, and best enjoyed while young.

Bottelary Co-op Blanc de Noir ★★(★) A

This is usually a very pleasant, crisp, off-dry wine, and like most wines of this type, is best enjoyed while young.

Calitzdorp Co-op Blanc de Noir ★ A

Fruity and semi-sweet, this Blanc de Noir has definite Pinotage nose. The latest apparently contains some Merlot.

Cederberg Kelders Blanc de Noir ★★★ B

From Pinotage, this wine has lovely colour, fruity nose, plenty of off-dry taste, and good, sharp finish.

Culemborg Blanc de Noir ★★★ B

This is an attractive, off-dry wine with young, fruity, Pinotage character. It is excellent value for a vintage-dated wine.

De Helderberg Co-op Blanc de Noir ★★(★) A

The first release, from the 1989 vintage, has attractive colour and nose, with good Cabernet flavour. It is finished off-dry. Latest vintages have a decided cherry character.

De Wet Co-op Blanc de Noir ★★ A

Finished semi-sweet, this Blanc de Noir is unusual in that it is normally a blend of Cabernet Franc and Cinsaut. It was a class winner at the South African Championship Wine Show.

Die Krans Blanc de Noir ★★(★) A

A semi-sweet wine, with unusual nose, from Pinotage.

Domein Doornkraal Tinta Bianca ★★ A

The first release, from the 1988 vintage, is an interesting blend of 45% Pinotage, 40% Tinta Barocca and 15% Red Muscadel, all pressed and fermented together. The 1989 was made the same way and has a most attractive orange colour. It is finished off-dry, with a white capsule, and semi-sweet, with a red capsule. Both are pale, coppery-coloured wines and make easy drinking.

Douglas Co-op Blanc de Noir ★★ B

A very pink, easy-drinking wine made from Pinotage and finished off-dry.

Du Toitskloof Co-op Blanc de Noir ★★★ A

This is a blend that usually contains Cinsaut and Ruby Cabernet and, most recently, Pinotage. Finished off dry, this attractive, fruity wine is best enjoyed when young.

Edward Snell Blanc de Noir ★★★ B

A non-vintage, off-dry wine from Pinotage.

Goudini Co-op Blanc de Noir ★★ A

An easy-drinking, off-dry wine from Cinsaut.

Goue Vallei Blanc de Noir (Citrusdal Co-op) ★★ A

This is an unusual example in the Blanc de Noir line-up as it is made from Grenache. It is sharp-flavoured and has a fairly sharp finish, which is balanced by being off-dry.

Hartenberg Blanc de Noir ★★★ C

Earlier wines were a blend of Cabernet and Shiraz, and finished dry and crisp. Later vintage-dated releases are most attractive wines, mainly Shiraz, with around 20% Zinfandel. It was last produced in 1991.

Helderberg Co-op Blanc de Noir ★★(★) A

This wine has an attractive colour and nose with good Cabernet flavour, and is finished off-dry.

Huguenot Blanc de Noir ★★ A

This is a big, strong, bright, semi-sweet Pinotage.

Kango Co-op Blanc de Noir ★★ A

This is sometimes a blend of Pinotage and Muscadel, with an off-dry finish. The latest is a light Pinotage.

Klawer Co-op Blanc de Noir ★★ A

A low-alcohol, semi-sweet wine from Grenache.

La Cotte Pinotage Blanc de Noir ★(★) B

A pretty, pale wine with full Pinotage nose, finished off-dry.

Landskroon Blanc de Noir ★★ B

The varying characteristics of the vintages have made this an interesting wine. It was previously made from Pinot Noir, but the latest vintages are from Pinotage and finished off-dry.

Les Monts Malverne (Clos Malverne) ★★★ C

The 1993 is the first Blanc de Noir from this cellar, made from Pinotage. It is eye-catching, dry wine with good nose.

Loopspruit Noorderkeur Vin Blanc de Noir ★ A

In the past, this wine was made from Red Hanepoot; nowadays it is made from Cinsaut.

Lutzville Co-op Blanc de Noir ★ A

This full-flavoured wine was made from Grenache and Carignan, and now Grenache alone. It is finished semi-sweet.

Mamreweg Co-op Blanc de Noir ★★ B

Recent vintages, from Cinsaut, are pleasant, fruity, semi-sweet wines.

Morgenhof Blanc de Noir ★★(★) C

Originally a light, dry wine, with high acid, good Cabernet flavour and most attractive colour, it is now made from Pinotage and finished off-dry. The 1991 has a powerful 13% alcohol. The 1992 is more agreeable.

Nederburg Cabernet Sauvignon Blanc de Noir ★★★★ C

Initially produced from the 1982 vintage, this was the first Blanc de Noir to carry a cultivar claim and to achieve Superior certification. Each subsequent vintage has been dry, elegant and gentle, yet persistent, with a most attractive aroma and a light but fine flavour. It is best when young.

Neethlingshof Blanc de Noir ★★★★ C

Made from Cabernet, this wine is a touch of class, with good cultivar character. It is finished dry.

Opstal Blanc de Noir ★★★ B

The 1992 is made from Cabernet Sauvignon, is finished off-dry, and makes for easy drinking.

Rendition Blanc de Noir (Welmoed Co-op) ★★★ B

This is an off-dry Pinotage wine of consistently good character. It is well balanced and, although semi-sweet, appears drier.

Riebeek Co-op Blanc de Noir ★★★ A

Usually from Pinotage, this is an easy-drinking, pleasant off-dry wine.

Roodezandt Co-op Blanc de Noir Muscat de Frontignan ★★ A

A pale wine with lovely nose and good flavour; dry or off-dry.

Rooiberg Co-op Blanc de Noir ★★★ B

The 1983 vintage was judged champion Blanc de Noir at the South African Championship Wine Show. Made from Pinotage, it carried Superior certification. Various blends (including Cabernet, Cinsaut and Pinotage) have been made over the years. It is finished off-dry and makes pleasant drinking.

Saxenburg Blanc de Noir ★★(★) B

The first release was a fairly ordinary dry wine from Cinsaut. Subsequent releases have been much better. It is now a Cinsaut/Pinotage blend, with good fruity nose and nice dry finish.

Simonsig Blanc de Noir ★★★ B

A very pale-coloured, but fruity, dry wine from Pinotage.

Simonsvlei Co-op Blanc de Noir ★★ A

An off-dry wine from Pinotage, with good flavour, it is at its best when young and chilled.

Spier Blanc de Noir ★★ B

A dry, easy-drinking, light-bodied wine from Pinotage.

Spruitdrift Co-op Blanc de Noir ★★ A

An easy-drinking, off-dry wine from Pinotage.

Swartland Co-op Blanc de Noir ★★★ B

Originally a blend of Tinta Barocca and Pinotage, this wine is currently made only from the latter. It shows well on the nose, is finished off-dry and excellent value for money.

Van Loveren Blanc de Noir Muscat de Frontignan ★★(★) B

This wine has a strong Muscat nose and good semi-sweet flavour. Each vintage drinks well when young.

Van Loveren Blanc de Noir Shiraz ★★ B

Made from Shiraz, this very pale-coloured wine has an unusual character, and when chilled, makes an excellent aperitif.

Villiera Gavotte ★★★(★) B

Mainly from Cabernet and some Shiraz. This is a delightful, off-dry, well-flavoured wine, that is regularly selected by the Wine of the Month Club. To my mind, this cellar consistently produces one of the most attractive Blanc de Noirs available. Regrettably it is no longer available.

Villiersdorp Co-op Blanc de Noir ★★(★) B

This is a pleasant, easy-drinking, semi-sweet wine from Pinotage.

Vintner's Choice Blanc de Noir (Drop Inn) ★★ A

This is a very pleasant, off-dry, salmon-coloured wine, with good vinous nose and fresh flavour.

Weltevrede Blanc de Noir ★★★ B

This is one of the more interesting Blanc de Noir wines. It has a fine, off-dry flavour and Muscat nose.

Woolworths Blanc de Noir ★★★ B

From Rustenberg. A very pleasant off-dry wine with more complex flavours than one would expect from a Blanc de Noir.

Zevenwacht Blanc de Noir ★★★ C

This is an attractive Pinotage, Shiraz and Cabernet blend that is finished off-dry.

Zonnebloem Cabernet Sauvignon Blanc de Noir (SFW) ★★★ C

Recent vintages are lovely when released, off-dry, and best when young. It is certified Cabernet Sauvignon.

Rosé

Autumn Harvest Rosé ★★ B

A pleasant, easy-drinking, semi-sweet wine that has more body than most Rosés.

Backsberg Rosé ★★★ B

A consistently delightful, semi-sweet Rosé, made from Pinotage, and designed for early drinking.

Bellingham Almeida Rosé (DGB) ★★★ B

An attractive, semi-sweet Rosé from Pinotage.

Bellingham Rosé Sec ★★★ A

In keeping with the upgrading of Bellingham products, the cellar's Rosé Sec is a good, light, fresh, fruity wine from Pinotage. Best enjoyed young.

Delheim Pinotage Rosé ★★★★ B

It used to be released annually alongside the Nouveau wines of that year, but not any longer. In the pink of its youth it is delightful wine, yet it has enough body to sustain its attractiveness 12 to 18 months later. It is finished off-dry, and is one of my favourites. Very easy drinking.

De Zoete Inval Rosé Sec ★ B

Anything but dry, this deep-coloured wine has an unusual nose and, although soft in the mouth, leaves a strange aftertaste.

Douglas Co-op Rosé ★★ A

This wine seems to vary with each release. It has been an off-dry Rosé from Pinotage and Tinta Barocca, and the last was a semi-sweet from Pinotage, Cabernet and Steen.

Douglas Green St Clare (DGB) ★★★ B

A Rosé mainly from Pinotage.

Fairview Rosé D'Une Nuit ★★★ B

A vintage-dated wine made from Pinotage. The skins are left in contact under refrigeration – to prevent fermentation – for one night, and the result is a very pleasant, fragrant, fruity, semi-sweet wine.

Kellerprinz Rosanne (SFW) ★★ A

A well-made, semi-sweet blend, with attractive, fruity nose.

Koelenhof Co-op Pinotage Rosé ★★ A

This wine is not produced with every vintage, but when it does appear, it has deep colour, is usually semi-sweet and makes for easy drinking.

Landzicht Bloemdal Rosé ★★ A

A semi-sweet wine from Pinotage, with a Muscat nose.

Lanzerac Rosé ★★★ B

A lovely, semi-sweet Rosé, full of flavour and presented most attractively in its dewdrop-shaped bottle.

Loopspruit Noorderkeur Rosé ★★ B

The 1990, from Cabernet, Steen and Muscat, is showing age.

Nederburg Rosé ★★★ B

This is one of South Africa's earliest Rosés and a long-time favourite. It is sold in an attractive Italian-style bottle, the cross-hatching of which shows off its pink colour to perfection. It is Pinotage-based, with the latest blends containing Gamay. It is a semi-sweet and well-flavoured wine that is best consumed in its vibrant youth. It is vintage-dated.

Nederburg Rosé Sec ★★★ C

This was the first really successful dry Rosé, of good quality, to gain popularity in South Africa. It has always had a hint of Cabernet, but is now a Cinsaut-Gamay blend. Delightful when young, this vintage-dated Rosé ages into a most intriguing wine over two to three years.

Noorderkeur Rosé ★★ B

The 1990 is a semi-sweet wine from Cabernet, Steen and Muscat. It is showing age.

Oranjerivier Wynkelders Rosé ★★ A

A pleasantly flavoured, dry Rosé, originally from Pinotage and Colombar, but now only from Pinotage.

Simonsig Rosé ★★ B

A semi-sweet, vintage-dated Rosé that is always reliable.

Simonsvlei Co-op Rosé ★★ A

A fruity, semi-sweet Rosé from Pinotage and Chenin Blanc.

Swartland Co-op Rosé ★★ B

An easy-drinking semi-sweet wine from Pinotage and Steen.

Valley Rosé (Gilbeys) ★★ A

A pleasant, non-vintaged, semi-sweet Rosé.

Woolworths Rosé ★★ B

From Simonsig. Almost crimson in colour, this Rosé wine has a pleasant fruity nose and a semi-sweet taste. It is made from a number of red and white varietals.

MÉTHODE CAP CLASSIQUE
SPARKLING WINES

Avontuur Cordon D'Or

A classic blend of 80% Chardonnay and 20% Pinot Noir, it has a fruity nose with apple flavour and sharp, firm finish.

Backsberg Cap Classique ★★★★ E

Made by the Méthode Cap Classique and clearly labelled 'fermented in the bottle', this sparkling wine was launched in 1988, coinciding with Sydney Back's 50th anniversary of wine making on the property which now forms the Backsberg Estate. Showing the exceptional quality which only time can give, the 1985 vintage was made from equal portions of Pinot Noir and Chardonnay, resulting in a very good wine. The 1986 was of the same quality and developed well in the bottle. The 1987 and 1988 are 40% Pinot Noir and the balance Chardonnay, making nice, easy drinking. These wines develop in the bottle over two or so years.

Backsberg Rosé ★★★(★) C

An off-dry Méthode Cap Classique wine made entirely from Pinot Noir. It has attractive colour, and very appealing fruity nose, with lovely deep flavour. It was released earlier than the white and is a delightful wine.

Barrydale Co-op Cap Classique Chardonnay

This bubbly is yet to be released so there is no price or rating available. On the lees, in bottle, is a Méthode Cap Classique from Chardonnay.

Blaauwklippen Barouche ★★★(★) D

The first release was a blend of 90% Pinot Noir and 10% Chardonnay, resulting in a pink sparkling wine, with beautiful nose and fine flavour. It is a first from the 1984 vintage and has developed well in the bottle. The 1985 was made only from Pinot Noir and developed lovely nose and good, full, lively flavour. The 1987 is all Pinot Noir, has good flavour and has developed beautifully. The 1988 is full flavoured and very good. It is up there with the best of them.

Boplaas Pinot Noir Sparkling Wine ★★★ B/C

This is made from Pinot Noir. The 1986 had a full, strong flavour and good mousse. The 1988 was a vast improvement, then there was a gap in production. The 1991 is a fresh, lively product, with good character.

Boschendal Brut ★★★★ F

The first release of this decidedly dry wine was from the 1979 vintage by the Méthode Cap Classique. It was basically a Riesling but had good, bottle aged character and incredibly lively, fine bubbles, which gave an excellent nose. Thereafter the blend became much more interesting and, over the years, has contained Pinot Blanc, Pinot Gris and Pinot Noir. A limited amount of the 1980 vintage was released in numbered magnums to celebrate the 300-year anniversary of the arrival of the Huguenots at the

Cape. The 1984 contained Pinot Noir and a high percentage of Chardonnay. It is now more or less a 50/50 blend, with a leap in quality since the 1986 vintage. Latest productions also carry a degorgement date.

Boschendal Brut ★★★★ E

This is no longer produced, but the old bottles are delicious if you can find them.

Boschendal Grande Reserve ★★★★ D

A limited amount of this fine wine was produced to commemorate the tercentenary of the Huguenots' arrival in Franschhoek. It has developed a very attractive nose and flavour.

Boschendal Le Grande Pavillion Blanc de Blancs ★★★(★) E

The first release in 1991 was a blend of Chardonnay, Riesling and Sémillon. It is a delightful bubbly, not entirely dry, with decided apple character. The subsequent release was 100% Chardonnay. It is attractively packed with a label covering almost every description option: 'Méthode Champenoise', 'Fermente en Bouteille' and 'Sparkling Wine' plus 'Cuvée Brut' and 'Blanc de Blancs'.

Buitenverwachting Brut ★★★★ F

The first release from 1988 was vintage-dated, and a blend of Pinot Noir and Pinot Gris. The next release is an improvement with the addition of Chardonnay. In future, the white components will be barrel-fermented.

Clos Cabrière Pierre Jourdan Cuvée Belle Rosé ★★★★ F

Made from Pinot Noir, it has lovely orange colour that comes from the initial carbonic maceration, with distinct Méthode Cap Classique character and good, steady, fine bubbles. Complex and delicious.

Clos Cabrière Pierre Jourdan Brut ★★★★ (★)E

Clos Cabrière's original Méthode Cap Classique has the traditional champagne combination of Pinot Noir and Chardonnay. This wine was released late in 1985 and very good, commanding a grand price. Of the number of Pierre Jourdans, this one has the original blue-green label, although it does not carry a vintage date. The punt of each bottle also has a colour code: the yellow stripe indicates the 1984 Reserve vintage, the red and white stripe the 1985, and the white stripe the 1986. The 1987 has a single red mark on the edge of the punt. The 1988 and 1989 have strip labels which disappear under the punt and the 1989 vintage carries a big star on the back label, also showing the bar code. All these wines are developing beautifully and there is no doubt that specializing is worthwhile. The Brut is also available in magnum bottles.

Clos Cabrière Pierre Jourdan Blanc de Blancs ★★★★ F

This wine is made from Chardonnay and is a delightfully light and frothy, with crisp, fresh flavour. It is not produced every vintage.

Clos Cabrière Pierre Jourdan Cuvée Reserve ★★★★ F

The yellow label is of the same blend as the blue-green label, although it spends three years or more, on the lees, in the bottle before being disgorged. This gives it a more complex character and deeper flavours. A super wine.

Clos Cabrière Pierre Jourdan Brut Sauvage ★★★★ F

This is the one with the paler blue label. The good bottles are stunning. It is produced solely from selected Cuvée juice. It is not everybody's taste, but for those who like their bubblies from the first pressing and finished bone-biting dry, this is the one.

Douglas Green Blanc de Noir (DGB) ★★(★) D

A very pale, bottle-fermented wine, with good acid and fine, but subdued, flavour. It does not age well, so enjoy it while young.

Fairview Charles Gerard Brut ★★★(★) D

The original production from the 1987 vintage was so successful that twice the amount has been produced from the 1989 vintage. This wine is made from red grapes using the Méthode Cap Classique, the combination of which gives good character wine with fine bubbles.

Graham Beck Brut Cap Classique ★★★★(★) E

This wine is made from equal quantities of Pinot Noir and Chardonnay. This is a non-vintaged wine, but the first release from 1991 had 18 months on the lees and six months on the cork before release. It has a good creamy texture and elegant mousse. It is very well priced.

Grand Mousseux Blanc de Blanc Chardonnay ★★★★ E

The first release came from the 1989 vintage. It is a fine flavoured bubbly with good zesty finish. Good stuff.

Grand Mousseux Grand Cuvée (SFW) ★★★ E

The first commercial release of a vintage-dated Méthode Cap Classique from this long-time favourite brand name, came from the 1986 vintage, after three years on the lees. There was no 1987. The next release from 1988 has a lovely, yeasty aroma with fine, sustained mousse.

Here XVII Grand Cuvée (Bergkelder) ★★★★ E

This was launched late in 1988 as a non-vintage, bottle-fermented bubbly with good character. It is made from Pinot Noir in the Méthode Cap Classique. Spending two years on the lees gives this wine a special quality. Since the release of the 1987 it is certified for vintage.

JC le Roux Chardonnay ★★★(★) E

The 1984 was released possibly a little too early, but it developed into a fine wine over the years. After six years of ageing, the Chardonnay character had developed very well, and has probably reached its limit. The 1988 is very good.

JC le Roux Pinot Noir ★★★★ D

Originally made from Pinot Noir of the 1984 vintage (grown on the Alto and Meerlust Estates) and fermented in the bottle, it was almost water-white, but with good flavour that developed in the bottle. The 1986 was released in 1990, after four years on its lees. Definitely a delicious Méthode Cap Classique wine. In 1991 it won the Schramsberg Trophy for the best bottle-fermented sparkling wine entered in the International Wine and Spirit Competition.

L'Ormarins Jean Roi ★★★★ (no price available)

From the 1987 vintage comes this classic Pinot Noir-Chardonnay blend. It is among the growing number of wines that have been slightly oaked before bottling. A delicious bubbly.

Nederburg Blanquette ★★★★ E

Released at the 1992 Auction from Chardonnay harvested in 1990. It is lovely, full-flavoured wine, that is delightfully light on the palate. This is one of the products used to mark Nederburg's bicentenery.

Onverwacht Laurent ★★ F+

Only 500 bottles of this bubbly were produced, the cheeky labels numbered and signed by the artist André Naudé.

Pick 'n Pay Crémant ★★★(★) D

A very good value bubbly made by Villiera. It has a distinct, youthful character and is very refreshing. It will benefit with an extra year of ageing before drinking.

Pongrácz (Bergkelder) ★★★★ E

Named after Desiderius Pongrácz, a Hungarian aristocrat who settled in the Cape after fleeing his country of birth when it was overrun by the Bolsheviks. He was a viticulturist who produced two books on the subject and, although a controversial personality, was always an absolute gentleman. He died after a tragic motor accident in 1985. The wine, a Méthode Cap Classique, was specially prepared by countryman and colleague Julius Lazlo and is a classic blend of 75% Pinot Noir and 25% Chardonnay. It is a fraction off-dry, with a most attractive 'French' nose, making light, easy drinking. It is a well-flavoured bubbly with fine creamy mousse. It is splendidly packaged and there's no mistaking the value for money price.

Simonsig Kaapse Vonkel ★★★★ E

This sparkling wine is made by the Méthode Cap Classique, which was reintroduced to the Cape by the wine maker, Frans Malan, with the first vintage in 1971. Originally a Steen-based wine, which was produced each alternate vintage, it is currently produced each year. It has grown in character and the blend varies, but recent wines are mainly Pinot Noir with some Chardonnay. There was no 1986, but the 1987 represents a total change of style in that it used just the classic Champagne grapes – Pinot Noir and Chardonnay. This resulted in a good, mouth-filling wine with creamy mousse and yeasty character. It developed very well, as has the 1988. The 1989 is very fine, with perhaps the best potential so far. The 1990 is much the same.

Twee Jongegezellen Krone Borealis ★★★★ F

This bubbly has been produced in the most attractive custom-built cellars. The original release was 40% Chardonnay, 40% Pinot Blanc and

20% Pinot Noir. Nowadays it is more or less made from equal quantities of Chardonnay and Pinot Noir, on lees for three years. No sulphur has been used in its production. It has lovely soft mousse and fine flavours backed with full yeast aromas. An attractively packaged sparkling wine.

Villiera Tradition de Charles de Fère ★★★★ D

An unusual partnership – between Villiera Estate and the Frenchman, Jean Louis Denois – led to the creation of this sparkling wine. Both red and white grapes were used in its production, the result of which is a splendid, refreshing wine which is improving all the time. It is excellent value for money, and constantly one of South Africa's better Méthode Cap Classique wines. The latest releases contain 45% Pinot Noir, the balance Chenin Blanc. In keeping with the traditions of Champagne, this cellar's main production is not vintage-dated. However, to give an indication of age, the 1985 release has an unmarked punt, the 1986 has a round red sticker, the 1987 yellow, the 1988 blue, the 1989 orange and 1990 red. This is one of my favourites.

Villiera Tradition de Charles de Fère Reserve ★★★★ (★) E

Some 50 cases are sold occasionally at the annual Cape Independent Winemakers' Guild Auctions. The wine is never less than three years on its lees and is disgorged just shortly before the Auction. This is a delicious bubbly that improves with each release as the cellar perfects its techniques and introduces more of the classic varieties to the blend. It is a bubbly well worth seeking out.

Villiera Tradition Prestige Cuvée

Yet to be released, but the chances are that it will be South Africa's best Méthode Cap Classique.

Villiera Tradition Rosé ★★★(★) C

A dry Rosé made from Pinot Noir in the Méthode Cap Classique. Two and a half years on the lees, and three months on the cork before release, gives this pink-coloured bubbly a full flavour and aftertaste.

Woolworths Méthode Cap Classique ★★★★ C

From Villiera. This is unbelievably good value for money and a fine Méthode Cap Classique wine.

Non-Méthode Cap Classique Sparkling Wines

Aan-de-Doorns Co-op Sparkling Wine ★★ A

This is a blend of Pinotage and Chenin Blanc resulting in a pink semi-sweet wine.

Badsberg Co-op Sparkling Wine ★★ B

A bubbly, predominantly from Steen, with fruity, foamy mousse.

Barrydale Co-op Demi-sec Sparkling Wine ★★ B

The original blend had nice nose and pleasant flavour from Hanepoot and Sauvignon Blanc. Since the 1990 vintage it has 60% Colombar and 20% each Sauvignon Blanc and Muscat, with enough acid to counter the sweetness. It is tank-produced and has good, consistent bubble.

Beaufort Cuvée Brut (Solly Kramer) ★★ B

A good, value for money bubbly with pleasant nose and light flavour.

Beaufort Cuvée Doux (Solly Kramer) ★★ B

This is a sweet bubbly that will appeal to wedding-reception caterers.

Belcher Vin Sec ★★

A Steen/Colombar blend finished off dry.

Bellingham Blanc de Noir Sparkling Wine (DGB) ★★★ C

A pleasant, pale-pink, dry sparkling wine which has improved since it was launched. Although culled, the older bottles are rather nice.

Bellingham Brut (DGB) ★★★ C

An extra-dry wine which usually has good bottle-age on the nose. The latest blends are mainly Chardonnay.

Bellingham Brut Vintage Rosé (DGB) ★★★★ C

The 1989 vintage of this Pinotage-based wine was launched late in 1990 in its own specially-produced bottle. It has attractive, fruity nose, is full-flavoured with a hint of sweetness on the palate, yet finishes nice and dry. The 1990 has a decided strawberry flavour and appears drier. It is beginning to show full bottle age.

Bellingham Gold (DGB) ★★★ C

A delicious and most unusual Special Late Harvest from Chenin Blanc with a fine foamy mousse. Full of flavour, it would appeal to the sweet-toothed, although the bubbles tend to hide the sweetness. A well-chilled glass or two makes an excellent aperitif.

Bergsig Painted Lady ★★★ B

The bright pink label depicts the *Gladiolus carneus*, commonly known as the Painted Lady. This is a peach-coloured, semi-sweet Blanc de Noir made from Pinotage.

Bolandse Co-op Demi-sec Sparkling Wine ★★ B

This is a tank-produced bubbly from Sauvignon Blanc. It is sweet but still has good cultivar character.

Bon Courage Blush Vonkelwyn ★★(★) C

With the success of their Chardonnay bubbly, this one comes from 1992 Pinot Noir. Sweetness is covered by the good fruit flavours. This is a nice drink when chilled.

Bon Courage Chardonnay Vin Sec ★★(★) C

A well-balanced, off-dry bubbly with good cultivar character.

Boplaas Sparkling Wine (Sweet) ★★ B

A pleasant-flavoured sweet wine, with good muscat nose and a consistent stream of bubbles for easy drinking.

Botha Co-op Sparkling Wine ★★ B

A Steen-based, semi-sweet bubbly with clear finish.

Bottelary Co-op Vin Sec ★★(★) B

This is a tank-produced bubbly from equal quantities of Sauvignon Blanc and Steen. It tastes drier than most of the Co-op bubblies.

Bovlei Co-op Dry Sparkling Wine ★★ B

A carbonated bubbly with the blend changing over the years. The latest production is mainly Steen with honeyed nose.

Bovlei Co-op Semi-sweet Sparkling Wine ★ B

A carbonated, sweet Chenin Blanc.

Calitzdorp Co-op Vin Doux ★★ B

A semi-sweet bubbly with good muscat flavour.

Carnival Vin Sec/Vin Doux (Spar) ★★ B

This is a multiple blend in which Muscat shows on the nose. It has good mousse. Sec is off-dry; Doux is sweet.

Chamonix Courchevel Cuvée Brut ★★ C

This sparkling wine is produced by the tank method, using the traditional South African blends of Steen and Clairette Blanche. The label bears a remarkable resemblance to the famous Korbel Natural of California.

Chamonix Courchevel Demi-sec ★★ C

A sweeter version of the above.

Checkers Semi-sweet Sparkling Wine ★★ B

A sweetish blend of a number of cultivars, giving attractive fruity nose and full flavour.

Cinzano Spumante (Gilbeys) ★★★ C

A very popular, sweet, sparkling wine with Muscat nose and good flavour. It deserves to be the biggest single brand on the market.

Cinzano Tiziano (Gilbeys) ★★★ C

Cinzano's entry into the sweet red bubbly segment. This is delightful, easy-drinking wine, full of flavour. It is attractively packaged.

Cinzano Vittoria ★★★ C

A first from the 1992 vintage with fresh, fruity Sauvignon Blanc character and finished dry. Good value.

De Doorns Co-op Sparkling Wine ★ B

A semi-sweet, tank-produced bubbly from Sauvignon Blanc.

De Helderberg Co-op De Heldere Vonkel Brut ★★(★) B
This pale-pink, off-dry wine is made from Pinot Noir. It has a good flavour is light-bodied, low in alcohol and crisply finished.

De Helderberg Co-op De Heldere Vonkel Demi-sec ★★(★) B
Following the success of their Brut, the cellar introduced this Sauvignon Blanc-based bubbly. It is not too sweet nor over-gassy, but a soft, pleasant, uncomplicated, low-alcohol wine.

Delaire Joie de l'Air ★★★ D
This was a semi-sweet (now off-dry) fruity, tank-produced bubbly made from Weisser Riesling. It has attractive nose and good flavour.

Delheim Pinot Noir Rosé Brute ★★★ B
The first release from the 1986 vintage was a bright-coloured wine with lots of fresh fruit and full flavour. The 1988 was a better wine, with good yeasty character complementing the fruit of the cultivar. Since 1989 it has settled into a consistently good character bubbly.

De Wet Co-op Cuvée Brut ★★★ B
Made from Sauvignon Blanc, this bubbly is dry and refreshing.

De Wet Co-op Vin Doux ★★ B
A low-alcohol, semi-sweet wine with pleasant muscat nose and flavour.

Die Krans L'Enchanté ★★★ B
This is an off-dry, pretty pink wine from Pinotage. Served chilled, it makes pleasant, easy drinking.

Die Krans Skrikkelwyn ★★★ B
A one-off fun product blended by friends of Die Krans on 29 February 1992 to celebrate leap year. It comprises mainly Muscat and some Colombar, and is finished off-dry. Rather pleasant.

Die Krans Spumante ★★★ B
An off-dry addition to the Muscat-flavoured bubblies, with good, crisp, clear finish.

Die Poort Vin Doux ★★ B
A sweet Muscat bubbly.

Domein Doornkraal Tickled Pink Vonkelwyn ★★★ B
This is a Blanc de Noir sparkling wine from Red Muscadel, Tinta Barocca and Pinotage, with a very pleasant nose and satisfying, semi-sweet taste. For an extra R2,00 you can have the bottle gift-wrapped with a pink ostrich feather.

Douglas Green Cuvée Brut (DGB) ★★(★) C
A refreshing, sparkling wine which is not as dry as the label suggests.

Douglas Green Demi-sec Sparkling ★★ C
A semi-sweet and fruity-flavoured sparkling wine.

Du Toitskloof Sparkle ★★★ B
A semi-sweet bubbly with a better balance of acid than most Co-op bubblies. Made from Muscat varieties, it is an attractive wine in an attractive pack. Sparkle replaces Dagbreek.

Edward Snell Brut ★★ B
A Steen-based, dry, easy-drinking, fruity bubbly.

Edward Snell Vin Doux ★★ B
A semi-sweet Steen.

Eikendal Vineyards Duc de Berry C'est si Blanc Brut ★★ C
A non-vintaged, off-dry, tank-produced bubbly from Steen and Sauvignon Blanc, with pleasant fruitiness, making for easy drinking. Good value for money.

Eikendal Vineyards Duc de Berry C'est si Blanc Demi-sec ★★ C
The same wine as above, but with a semi-sweet finish.

Enchanté Brut ★★(★) B
This is a dry bubbly from Sauvignon Blanc.

Enchanté Sparkling Demi-Sec Wine (Heritage Wines) ★★(★) B
An off-dry bubbly with Muscat nose that tastes sweeter than the analysis would suggest. It should not to be confused with the established pink bubbly produced by Die Krans.

Fifth Avenue Cold Duck (SFW) ★★★ C
Another very popular, medium-sweet pink bubbly with an intriguing flavour not found in any other South African sparkling wine.

Franschhoek Vineyards Co-op Sauvignon Blanc Brut ★★(★) B
This Sauvignon Blanc is better than most from this variety. It is dry, yet fruity, and is highly alcoholic (nearly 13%).

Franschhoek Vineyards Co-op Sparkling Wine ★★ B
The composition varies with the vintage. Originally a semi-sweet wine, highly acidic Colombar, then a toned-down blend of Chenin Blanc and Weisser Riesling, it is now a pleasant, fruity wine from Sémillon and Colombar. It is tank-produced wine.

Frère Jacques Sparklers (OK Bazaars) ★★(★) B
A Vin Sec and Vin Doux are available, and both are pleasant, well-made products.

Goue Vallei Rosé Sparkling Wine ★★★ B
A light-hearted, sweetish sparkling wine with good flavour and pink colour, from Grenache.

Goue Vallei Vin Doux (Citrusdal Co-op) ★★ B
This wine is a blend of Sauvignon Blanc, Hanepoot and Steen, which is produced in the tank and finished semi-sweet. It has a softer bubble than other Co-op sparklers.

Grand Mousseux Extra Brut (SFW) ★★★ C
This is a good, quality product, which is drier than most popular South African sparkling wines. It has become even drier in recent years but has kept its good flavour. Its quality is reflected by consistent success in overseas competitions, including the annual Club Oenologique International Wine and Spirit Competition. If you can find any – buy and enjoy, as it has been discontinued.

Grand Mousseux Grand Rouge (SFW) ★★★ C

This semi-sweet bubbly was originally Cabernet-based, but now contains various red cultivars. It was launched in 1990, and has developed a popular following. It is a good wine to accompany a sweet course at the end of a meal.

Grand Mousseux Spumante (SFW) ★★★ C

This sparkling wine has good Muscat nose and decidedly fresh flavour. Sufficient acid ensures that it does not taste as sweet as it really is.

Grand Mousseux Vin Doux (SFW) ★★(★) B/C

At one time this was South Africa's favourite bubbly, and it is still very popular. It is a well-made, medium-sweet wine that is full of flavour.

Grand Mousseux Vin Sec (SFW) ★★(★) B/C

An off-dry sparkling wine with good flavour.

Grand Provence Cuvée Doux (Douglas Green Bellingham) ★★★ B/C

A semi-sweet sparkling wine with attractive character.

Haute Provence Brut ★★(★) B

This is a dry bubbly from a blend of Sauvignon Blanc and Sémillon. It is very fizzy with a nice nose, although it is a little neutral on the palate.

Here XVII Souverein (Bergkelder) ★★★ C

Regarded as one of South Africa's prestige sparkling wines, Here XVII's character has improved in recent times, giving it a good nose and an off-dry taste.

Huguenot Wine Farmers Valentine Cerise ★★ B

A sweetish red bubbly, with attractive nose and pleasant flavour.

Huguenot Wine Farmers Valentine Vin Doux ★★ B

A pleasant, semi-sweet, white bubbly.

Jac Canard Spumante (OK House brand) ★★★ B

A lovely, fresh, sweet bubbly with good Muscat nose, blended from Colombar, Steen and White Muscadel.

Jac Canard Vin Sec (OK House brand)★★ B

An off-dry blend of Cape Riesling, Chenin Blanc and Sauvignon Blanc; none show on the nose or palate. It has full and vigorous bubble.

Jac Canard Vin Doux (OK House brand)★★ B

A semi-sweet Steen with fruity nose, good clean flavour, and very vigorous bubble.

JC le Roux La Chanson (Bergkelder) ★★★ C

A ruby-red bubbly that is sweet, but with enough acid not to be cloying, and a low alcohol level of only 8,2%. It makes very easy drinking, with good bubbles, attractive fruity nose and full, satisfying flavour. Like all the JC le Roux wines, it is most attractively packaged.

JC le Roux Le Domaine (Bergkelder) ★★★ C

A lovely flavoured, Spumante-style wine made from Muscadel and Sauvignon Blanc. It has fine bubbles and good, clean character, with very low alcohol of only 7,5%. Very popular.

JC le Roux Sauvignon Blanc (Bergkelder) ★★★ C

A most unusual, dry sparkling wine made from Sauvignon Blanc. It might not be everyone's idea of flavour, but it certainly is a good wine and adds an extra dimension to the market. The wine is vintage-dated.

Jean Pierre Marcé (Gilbeys) ★★★ C

A most attractively packaged, off-dry bubbly which has very good mousse and pleasing flavour, and drinks very easily.

Klawer Co-op Vonkelwyn Demi-sec ★★(★) B

This sweet, tank-produced bubbly is made from Muscat Ottonel in the Spumante style.

Klawer Co-op Michelle Vin Doux ★★ B

This is a light-coloured, red bubbly, mainly from Red Muscadel, with a touch of Colombar. A nice one for the sweet palate.

Klawer Co-op Vonkelwyn Sec ★★ B

A dry, gassy, tank-fermented wine, from Sauvignon Blanc.

KWV Mousseux ★★(★)

KWV produce a Blanc Brut, Blanc Demi-sec and a Rouge. They are all pleasant wines and match most commercial products.

KWV Cuvée Brut ★★(★)

The pack bears a strong resemblance to a commercially-available product but the content is a give-away. Not quite a Brut but with a sweetish aftertaste, it is easy-drinking, uncomplicated wine.

Laborie Sparkling Blanc de Noir (KWV) ★★★ C

A sparkling wine made by the tank method. It is usually lively and refreshing when young. The 1989 is showing bottle age.

La Valle Vin Doux (Reserve) (SFW) ★★★ C

An inexpensive, but soundly-produced bubbly, with pleasant nose and sweet taste.

Le Phantom Saxenburg ★★★

This is a blend of Sauvignon Blanc and Cape Riesling, with fresh, bright flavours and aromas.

Loopspruit Winery Demi Sec Rosé ★★ B

In 1989 this cellar introduced two bubblies named Bosveldvonkel. Nowadays it is using more conventional names. The Demi-dec Rosé is off-dry and pale pink, from Hanepoot and Steen, and is coloured with Cinsaut. The Vin Doux is semi-sweet.

McGregor Co-op Demi-sec ★★★ B

This is a tank-produced bubbly, from Rhine Riesling, which is fruity and fresh, and has consistent bubble.

Merwida Co-op Cuvée Brut ★ B

This is an off-dry, tank-produced bubbly from Sauvignon Blanc.

Montagu Muscadelboere Sparkling ★★ B

An unusual bubbly from White Muscadel, which was produced to commemorate the cellar's 50th anniversary.

Mont D'Or (Drop Inn) ★★(★) B

The Mont D'Or name was originally a Benny Goldberg house brand. Now it is available throughout the Drop Inn group in the Cape. The bubblies are made by Rooiberg Co-op.

Brut: a good, clean wine made from Sauvignon Blanc.

Vin Sec: an off-dry, fuller wine from Rhine Riesling.

Vin Brut: a semi-sweet with lots of flowery nose.

Nederburg Kap Sekt ★★★★ C

Originally produced for export to Germany where, to qualify for the appellation 'Sekt', this wine has to be aged for at least one year. In 1993, the 1987 vintage is still available, indicating that this wine has good bottle bouquet, especially after having at least six to nine months lees contact before bottling. It does not appear to be dry, but has sugar of less than 10 g/l. The 1981 vintage was introduced to the local market in 1982 and showed excellent character after bottle-ageing. In fact, all the vintages have been good and develop beautifully. While it existed, at least one bottling of each vintage carried Superior certification. The 1986 was very good, the 1987 is developing well, and the 1988 is very good. The 'German' style will begin to disappear as small quantities of Chardonnay are introduced.

Nederburg Première Cuvée Brut ★★★(★) C/D

This is South Africa's most outstanding sparkling wine made by tank~fermentation. When young and fresh, it has a vitality and appeal all of its own. Its high acid is refreshing and allows ageing with great attraction. It has a character seldom obtained in South African sparkling wines.

Nederburg Première Cuvée Doux ★★★(★) C

Produced originally for export, and now available locally, this is an absolute delight for those with a sweet tooth.

Nuy Co-op Sparkling ★★★ B

A delightful, fresh, off-dry bubbly made from Sauvignon Blanc.

Onverwacht Savoire Brut ★★(★) B

A dry sparkler without much finesse.

Onverwacht Cloche Demi Sec

This new bubbly is a three-way blend of Colombar, Rhine Riesling and Steen, and is finished off dry.

Overhex Demi-Sec ★★(★) B

This is a good first attempt at a sweet, carbonated Sauvignon Blanc.

Paul Bonnay Rouge (Pick 'n Pay) ★★ B

This is an easy-drinking, good-flavoured, sweet bubbly, made from good red varietals.

Paul Bonnay Vin Sec (Pick 'n Pay) ★★ B

This is a complex blend giving a fruity, off-dry sparkler.

Paul Bonnay Vin Doux (Pick 'n Pay) ★★ B

A semi-sweet, Steen-based bubbly.

Renee Charbon (Marcows) ★★ **B**
A Vin Sec and a Vin Doux for the Marcows chain.

Rhebokskloof St Felix Vineyards Tamay ★★★★ **C**
A light, pleasant, easy-drinking, off-dry bubbly. The fruity nose suggests a much sweeter wine, although the finish is pleasantly dry.

Riebeek Co-op Sparkling Brut ★★★ **B**
An off-dry bubbly from Sauvignon Blanc with good, brisk mousse.

Riebeek Co-op Sparkling Demi-sec ★★★ **B**
A semi-sweet bubbly from a multiple blend of Muscat-flavoured wines. It makes pleasant and easy drinking for the sweet palate.

Rietrivier Co-op Vonkelwyn ★★ **B**
An easy-drinking, sweet wine, from Sauvignon Blanc and Colombar.

Robertson Co-op Santino Spumante ★★★ **B**
A triple blend in which the Muscat shows well on the nose, this is a semi-sweet bubbly, full of nice fruity flavour.

Romansrivier Co-op Vin Doux ★★ **B**
A well-made, semi-sweet wine with good clean character.

Romansrivier Co-op Vin Sec ★★ **B**
It seems sweeter than the name would suggest and is made from Sauvignon Blanc.

Roodezandt Co-op Sparkling Wine Brut ★★ **B**
A dryish blend of Sauvignon Blanc, Pinot Gris and Gewürztraminer, with a fresh flavour heightened by the bubbles.

Roodezandt Co-op Sparkling Wine Demi-sec ★★(★) **B**
The same as above, but finished as a semi-sweet bubbly.

Rooiberg Co-op Brut ★★★ **B**
This is another dryish Sauvignon Blanc-based sparkling wine, with good fruit and massive mousse.

Rooiberg Co-op Chardonnay Brut ★★★★ **B**
This is probably South Africa's first carbonated Chardonnay. It is very acceptable, with lots of bubble and good flavour. It is no longer produced.

Rooiberg Co-op Chardonnay Demi-sec ★★★(★) **B**
This one is not as flavourful as the above, but just as bubbly. It is finished semi-sweet. It is no longer produced but is ageing with attraction.

Rooiberg Co-op Vin Doux ★★★★ **B**
This rich, fruity wine, with soft, slow bubbles, has a very attractive nose, mainly from Gewürztraminer.

Rooiberg Co-op Demi-sec ★★(★) **B**
A semi-sweet sparkling wine with fine bubble, rather pleasant nose and good, clean taste.

Santino Sparkling Wine (Robertson Co-op) ★★(★) **B**
The Vin Doux and Vin Sec produced are both pleasant, fruity bubblies.

Santino Rosé (Robertson Co-op)
This multiple blend of various reds gives a sweet, pink sparkler.

Simonsig Jean Le Riche Vin Doux ★★★ B

This is a non-vintaged, inexpensive, semi-sweet bubbly which was launched in 1990. It is a blend of four varieties, of which the Muscat gives attractive nose. It is a fresh, clean wine with good, lively bubble.

Simonsig Jean Le Riche Vin Sec ★★★ B

A drier version of the above wine.

Simonsvlei Rouge Classique ★★(★) B

This sweet red bubbly is a new release and comes from Pinotage and Pinot Noir.

Simonsvlei Co-op Vin Sec ★★★ B

An off-dry bubbly with good, clean nose, fine bubble and satisfying flavour.

Simonsvlei Co-op Vin Doux ★★★ B

This is very definitely a Muscat in the semi-sweet, Spumante style, with good, fine bubble and clean finish.

Slanghoek Co-op Vonkelwyn ★★★ B

Produced to celebrate the Co-op's new cellar, this is a clean, semi-sweet wine with decided Sauvignon Blanc nose and good flavour.

Soetwynboere Vin Doux ★★ B

A sweet, carbonated Sauvignon Blanc.

Soetwynboere Vin Sec ★ B

This carbonated, semi-sweet bubbly contains a strange blend of Sauvignon Blanc and Hanepoot, giving it a pleasing fizz.

Spruitdrift Co-op Demi-sec ★★★ B

A blend of three cultivars – Colombar, Hanepoot and Steen – make up this semi-sweet sparkler, with citrusy flavours and lots of bubble.

St Louis Cold Duck (Gilbeys) ★★ C

An interesting, sweetish Rosé bubbly with good flavour.

St Pierre (Vinimark) ★★ B

The Vin Sec and a Vin Doux are well-made products with plenty fizz.

Swartland Co-op Cuvée Brut ★★★ B

This is a dry, tank-produced sparkler from Sauvignon Blanc.

Swartland Co-op Demi-sec ★★(★) C

An inexpensive, semi-sweet bubbly with pleasant nose and flavour.

Swartland Co-op Vin Doux ★★ B

This is a Muscat-nosed, sweet, well-made bubbly, with good fizz.

Symphony (Gilbeys) ★★★ C

This is a very pale pink bubbly for those with a sweeter tooth. It has been discontinued, but odd bottles can still be found. It has developed a most attractive flavour.

Toujours ★★(★) B

A Brut, Vin Sec and Vin Doux are produced under this label for Rebel.

Tulbagh Co-op Demi-sec ★★ B

This used to be a fresh, sweet, pink bubbly made from Pinotage, but is now a sweet Sauvignon Blanc.

Tulbagh Co-op Vin Sec ★★ B
A pleasant, off-dry sparkler.

Val du Charron (Wamakersvallei Co-op) ★★ B
The Mousseux Blanc is dryish, and the Val du Charron Demi-sec a sweeter version, from Sauvignon Blanc.

Vaalharts Co-op Overvaal Doux ★★★ B
A semi-sweet bubbly from Colombar and Hanepoot.

Van Loveren Papillon Brut ★★★ B
Of the three Papillons, the Brut has the most enticing nose. It is made in tank from Sauvignon Blanc and Muscat de Frontignan, with the latter showing well on the nose. The bottle has an attractive butterfly label.

Van Loveren Papillon Demi-sec ★★(★) B
This is a multiple blend that has included Fernão Pires, Colombar, Pinot Blanc and Muscat de Frontignan. The almost guava-like nose is attractive, and the flavour is drier than most labelled Demi-secs.

Van Loveren Papillon Doux ★★ B
This is a sparkling wine of orange-pink colour with tropical nose. It's semi-sweet taste hints of Muscat.

Villiersdorp Co-op Demi-Sec Sparkling wine ★★★ B
A semi-sweet white, from Colombar and Hanepoot, with good bubble.

Vredendal Co-op Vonkelwyn Blanc Fumé ★★★ B
The strong cultivar character and vigorous bubbles make this semi-sweet carbonated wine taste drier than it actually is. It is no longer produced.

Vredendal Co-op Vonkelwyn ★★(★) B
A three-way blend of Sauvignon Blanc, Chardonnay and Chenin Blanc. The Demi-sec is finished semi-sweet, and the Sec, off-dry.

Waboomsriver Co-op Rubele Demi-sec ★★★ B
A semi-sweet, pink bubbly from Pinotage and Cinsaut.

Wamakersvallei Co-op Val du Charron Brut ★★ B
A clear, well made, dryish, vintage-dated bubbly.

Welmoed Co-op Cuvée Brut ★★★ B
A dry bubbly with packaging that makes you suspect that you've seen it somewhere before.

Welmoed Co-op Sec ★★★ B
An off-dry bubbly made from Steen, Clairette Blanche and Hanepoot.

Woolworths Vivezza Brut ★★★ B
A good, clean, finely-bubbled sparkler from Douglas Green Bellingham.

Woolworths Vivezza Dry ★★★ B
From Gilbeys. This is a pleasant, well-made, off-dry bubbly with good fruity flavour, which drinks very easily.

Woolworths Vivezza Sweet ★★★ B
From Gilbeys. This is a good, semi-sweet, Spumante-style bubbly.

Woolworths Vivezza Blanc de Noir ★★★ C
From Douglas Green Bellingham. A fruity, dry wine, with fine bubbles.

PERLÉ WINES

Ashton Co-op Pétillant Blanc ★★(★) A

A semi-sweet white blend, of predominantly Colombar, with a nice attractive nose coming from small amounts of Bukettraube, Gewürztraminer and Weisser Riesling. This seems rather a lot to go into a relatively inexpensive wine, but it has obviously worked, as it is the cellar's best seller!

Autumn Harvest Crackling (SFW) ★★(★) A

An enormously popular, semi-sweet Perlé which, when chilled, has a very pleasant, fruity nose accentuated by the pétillance. It is a refreshing, lively wine that has gathered a string of international awards, including gold medals at The Monde Selection and the Club Oenologique International Wine and Spirit Competition.

Botha Co-op Perlé ★★ A

A blend, with Colombar, finished semi-sweet, that has gentle bubbles.

Capenheimer (SFW) ★★★ A

This is the oldest Perlé on the market and holds premier position. With its off-dry effervescence and clean, fruity flavour, it makes a very refreshing wine. It is also a winner of international awards.

Culemborg Diamanté Crystal Blanc Perlé ★★★ A

This is a semi-sweet Perlé, with good Muscat nose and Steen flavour.

Culemborg Diamanté Perlé Blanc de Noir ★★★ A

This Perlé has a pretty pink colour and gives a nice fresh bubble. It is made from Pinotage from which it gets slightly more flavour than most.

De Doorns Co-op Perlé Blanc ★ A

A somewhat ordinary semi-sweet wine from Chenin Blanc and Colombar.

Groot Eiland Co-op Perlé Dali ★★ A

The same blend as Honigtraube, which is Bukettraube and Ferdinand de Lesseps, which is very apparent with the bubbles. It is named after the painter and has a label to match.

Grünberger Spritziger (Bergkelder) ★★★ B

This Perlé wine, attractively presented in a green, tower-type bottle, is, according to the label, produced by the charmat process, which is usually associated with the more expensive sparkling wines. It has excellent, fine bubbles. It has a very refreshing, off-dry finish and a slight Muscat nose, with lovely Steen flavours.

KWV Musanté ★★(★)

A semi-sweet Perlé wine with Muscat nose.

KWV Pétillant Blanc ★★

A pleasant, clean, off-dry wine, with a fresh finish.

KWV Pétillant Rosé ★★

This wine always seems to have more bubbles, than most Perlés. It is a very pleasant, off-dry wine.

Loopspruit Muxandre ★★ A

Under its new name, which comes from Muscat d'Alexandrie, this wine is an improvement on the previous Perlé. It is light in flavour and bubbles, and makes a pleasant off-dry drinking in comparison with the previous semi-sweet and very ordinary product.

Merwespont Co-op Morlé ★★★ A

This Co-op has produced some interesting Perlés in the past, and this latest addition maintains the interest. One-third Mario Muscat and the balance Sauvignon Blanc gives most attractive nose to this full-flavoured, semi-sweet wine. It is not too fizzy.

Merwespont Co-op Vin Rosé ★★ A

A semi-sweet, Pinotage, pink Perlé.

Mooiuitsig Bonperlé ★ A

This is a semi-sweet, white Perlé.

Original Paarl Perlé (SFW) ★★ A

This wine does not necessarily come from the Paarl region, but is a very popular, semi-sweet, white Perlé.

Perlino Perlé ★★ A

Popular in parts of the country, this wine has an attractive Muscat nose and is finished semi-sweet.

Romansrivier Co-op Rosé Perlé ★★ A

A semi-sweet, pink Perlé.

Sprizzo (DGB) ★★ A

A delightful, semi-sweet Muscat with soft bubbles.

Valley Frizzanté (Gilbeys) ★★★ A

A well-packaged Perlé with good flavour from the Chenin Blanc and Clairette Blanche blend. It has refreshing appeal when well chilled.

Waboomsrivier Co-op Wagenboom Perlé ★★(★) B

A semi-sweet, white Perlé from Steen, with lots of bubble and better taste than nose.

MUSCAT WINES

Aan-de-Doorns Co-op Muscat d'Alexandrie ★★★ B
A reliable, rich, full, sweet dessert wine. The 1977 vintage was outstanding, though subsequent vintages have been lighter-bodied and more delicate – something apparent in all recent releases. The 1991 is spirity, light and delicate, but well flavoured. These wines are enjoyable when released.

Aan-de-Doorns Co-op Muskadel ★★★ B
The first release, from 1990, is a full-flavoured, rather spirity product.

Agterkliphoogte Co-op Muscadel/Jerepigo ★★ A
This is the same wine which is produced under different labels to suit the market. It is spirity wine, yet light in character, with amazing colour.

Apex (Cape Wine) ★★(★) B
Falling under this label are various well-made fortifieds including Mustelle. Good, inexpensive Muscadels.

Ashton Co-op Hanepoot ★★ A
A light, sweet wine with good flavour.

Ashton Co-op Rooi Muskadel ★★★★ A
This is a bright red, full-flavoured, fruity wine that tastes like raisins. Delicious when released.

Ashton Co-op Wit Muskadel ★★★(★) A
A golden-coloured, smooth, good Muscat, with fresh finish. This is well-made, lightish wine with clean flavours.

Backsberg Hanepoot ★★★ C
This vintage-dated wine is a delicious, fresh, full, sweet Hanepoot with a hint of tropical fruit in the nose. The 1987 and 1989 had the most attractive nose and very good flavour, and have developed beautifully into 1993. The consistency continues with the 1990 and 1991. They will develop well with time, but are good when fresh and young.

Badsberg Hanepoot ★★★★ C
This cellar produces an excellent, full, sweet and golden Hanepoot: a remarkable wine that has gained numerous awards at regional and national shows. It is also a consistent gold medal and trophy winner at the South African Championship Wine Show, and carried Superior certification for almost every vintage since 1974.

Barrydale Co-op Hanepoot Jerepiko ★★(★) B
A full-flavoured, medium-bodied Hanepoot from 1991.

Barrydale Co-op Red Muscadel Jerepiko ★★ B
From 1991 comes a pale-coloured, full, sweet wine of subdued character.

Bergsig Sweet Hanepoot ★★★ B
This has a strong Hanepoot nose, with full, sweet, Muscat flavour. The 1991 is a lovely wine and sports an original label in an otherwise very boringly labelled area.

Bolandse Co-op Hanepoot Jerepiko ★★ B

A good, sweet, full, alcoholic Hanepoot.

Bolandse Co-op Muscadel ★★★ B

This is a pale-coloured wine, with good Muscat flavours, which is smoothly sweet.

Bon Courage Red Muscadel Jerepiko ★★★★ B

The 1984 carried Superior certification and was a clean, full-flavoured Muscadel. The next release, from the 1988 vintage, was delicate in style yet intense in flavour. It was followed by a beautiful 1989. The 1990 continues the gentle but full-flavoured and complex style.

Bonnievale Co-op Hanepoot Jerepigo ★★★ B

Light bodied, fruity nosed, bright, golden, sweet wine.

Boplaas Bonaparte Red Dessert ★★★(★) B

This is a Tinta Barocca/Muscadel blend but not quite as sweet as the Red Dessert. There has been no recent release.

Boplaas Red Dessert ★★★ B

A delicious, portish wine with Muscat. It is a fortified blend of Tinta Barocca and Muscadel.

Boplaas Sweet Hanepoot ★★ B

The 1987 was a full, sweet wine but lacked fruit. The 1988 has a good Muscat nose and a full, sweet flavour. The 1990 is considered the best from the past ten years, although the 1991 is deeper and fuller.

Boplaas Muscadel ★★★★ B

This Wine of Origin Klein Karoo is a deep yellow, full-bodied, sweet wine with lots of intense Muscadel character. The 1991 is splendid.

Botha Co-op Soet Hanepoot ★★★ A

A full, sweet, award-winning Hanepoot.

Bottelary Co-op Goue Muskaat ★★★ B

Golden, delicious, light bodied wine.

Bovlei Co-op Soet Hanepoot ★★★ A

This Co-op produces good quality, red and white, sweet Hanepoots.

Brandvlei Co-op Soet Hanepoot ★★ A

A full-bodied Hanepoot and a consistent gold medal winner.

Calitzdorp Co-op Hanepoot ★★★ A

A dark-coloured, full-bodied dessert wine.

Calitzdorp Co-op Jeripiko ★★ A

This wine is similar to the Hanepoot but is not certified.

Calitzdorp Co-op Muskadel ★★ A

This Co-op produces both Red and White Muscadels which are deep-coloured, full, sweet dessert wines.

Clairvaux Co-op ★★ A

The Co-op produces both red and white Jerepigos. Early vintages had substantial wood character, but the more recent ones are somewhat lighter and not wooded.

De Doorns Co-op Hanepoot ★★★ B
A full-flavoured Hanepoot
De Leuwen Jagt Muscadel ★★★(★) C
The 1990 and 1991 are good, old-style, sweet and delicious wines.
De Wet Co-op Muscats ★★(★) B
This Co-op produces good, full, sweet Hanepoot and white Muscadel, and a lighter-styled, sweet Red Muscadel.
Die Krans Estate ★★★(★) B
This cellar produces a good, honest range of vintage-dated fortified wines including the 'Heritage' collection.
Die Poort ★★ A
The cellar produces good Hanepoots, Muscadels and an interesting White Port made from Muscat de Hambourg. It also has well-aged white and red Jerepigos under 'Limited Release' labels.
Domein Doornkraal Hanepoot ★★★ A
The 1989 has a smooth, light, raisin character.
Domein Doornkraal Muscadel ★★(★) A
The 1989 release is garnet-coloured, with a somewhat alcoholic character and good Muscat fruit and raisin character. The 1990 is soft and rich.
Domein Doornkraal Pinta ★★★ B
This wine takes its name from its blend of Pinotage and Tinta Barocca, and is a rich, sweet dessert wine.
Douglas Co-op ★★ A
The Co-op produces fortified Muscat d'Alexandrie, Rooi Muskadel and Sultana.
Durham (DGB) ★★ C
There are three wines available: Hanepoot, Marsala and Sultana.
Du Toitskloof Co-op Red Jerepigo ★★★(★) B
This is an unusual, very sweet red, raisin-like wine made from Cinsaut.
Du Toitskloof Co-op Hanepoot Jerepigo ★★★★ B
The 1985 vintage carried Superior certification and 27 cases were offered at the 1988 Nederburg Auction. It was the Worcester Show Champion Hanepoot and won a gold medal at the South African Championship show. It is a very sweet, full-flavoured wine with plenty of fruit. The 1986 carried Superior certification. The 1990 is excellent.
Dwarsrivier Wit Jerepiko (Cederberg Kelders) ★★★ B
This new release is a full, sweet, white Jerepiko.
Eersterivier-Valleise Kelder Hanepoot ★★★ B
A light-styled, grape-flavoured, sweet aperitif.
Fairview Sweet Red ★★★(★) C
This is a good value, fortified Shiraz which is deep, rich and lovely.
Goudini Co-op Soet Hanepoot ★★★★ B
Previously called Muscat d'Alexandrie. A regular medal and trophy winner at local and national shows, it is always full and sweet, with plenty of

fruit flavour. Wines such as this one deserve to be better known. The 1988, 1989, 1990 and 1991 are all very good. The latest release has far more complexity than earlier ones.

Goudveld Goue Nektar ★★ A
A sweet fortified white Hanepoot.

Goudveld Rooi Robyn ★★(★) A
A super, attractive Red Muscadel.

Goue Vallei (Citrusdal Co-op) ★★ B
The Co-op produces full, sweet dessert wines ranging from Hanepoot Jerepigo through full, sweet Steen Jerepigo to sweet red wine. The Hanepoot Jerepigo carries the Gousblom on its label. The Wit Jerepiko is a local show award winner. The Rooi Jcrepiko is made from Pinotage. The three-star 1988 (South African Champion Non-Muscat Jerepigo) was a beautiful, deep wine; the 1989 much lighter. The Wit Muskadel is pale in colour and lighter in style, but still a lovely wine.

Groot Eiland Co-op Hanepoot Soetwyn ★★(★) B
This regular medal winner at local shows, and occasionally at national shows, is a good, smooth wine with a fair amount of Hanepoot flavour.

Groot Trek Red Jeripigo (Vredendal Co-op) ★★★★ B
Excellent wine from Tinta Barocca. Rich, red and fruity.

Huguenot Wines ★★(★) A
This cellar sells very acceptable Soet Hanepoot, Wit Muskadel and Wit and Rooi Jeripiko.

Huguenot Wines ★★(★) B
This cellar produces a Nagmaalwyn and a Nektar which are good, clean, well-flavoured fortified wines.

Jonkheer Farmers' Winery ★★ A
This winery markets a range of good fortified Muscats under the brand names of Melita and Myrtella, of which the Red Muscadel is perhaps the best. Their 1985 White Muscadel was the South African Championship Fortified Muscat.

Kaapzicht Hanepoot Jerepigo ★★★(★) C
This Jerepigo is light gold, has a clear muscat nose, is medium bodied, super smooth and has a crisp finish. It is very different to those from over the mountains.

Kango Co-op ★★★ A
This Co-op makes a good range of Muscadels and Hanepoots.

Klawer Co-op ★★ B
The Co-op produces Muscadels and a good Halfsoet Hanepoot.

Koelenhof Co-op Hanepoot ★★ B
A good, golden Hanepoot.

KWV ★★★★(★) D
Releases include the 1953 Muscadel Jerepigo, 1963 White Muscadel Jerepigo, 1969 Hanepoot Jerepigo and 1968 Jerepigo Liqueur wine. In

1987 the KWV released the 1973 Hanepoot Jerepigo to succeed the 1969. It was a Wine of Origin Breede River, full, luscious and very satisfying. All are Superior.

KWV 75 ★★★★(★)

This is a Red Muscadel from the 1975 vintage, released in 1993 to celebrate the KWV's 75th anniversary. It comes in a tall, slim-line bottle with a distinctive label – a large 75 covers the anniversary and the vintage!

Landzicht ★★ A

The Co-op produces a full, sweet Hanepoot and a fortified Sultana. It also makes a less sweet Hanepoot called Morddré.

Langverwacht Co-op Hanepoot Jerepiko ★★★(★) A

The 1991 is beautiful and packed with golden sunshine.

Libertas White Muscadel (SFW) ★★(★) A

A consistently good, full, sweet, inexpensive wine.

Lombards Sweet Hanepoot (Castle Wine and EK Green) ★★ A

A very popular, good, golden Hanepoot.

Loopspruit Winery ★ B

Fortified Hanepoots are produced at this winery in the Transvaal.

Louwshoek-Voorsorg Co-op Muscat d'Alexandrie ★★★★ B

Consistently and deservedly certified Superior, this full, sweet Hanepoot is well worth locating.

Lutzville Co-op Hanepoot ★ A

A full-bodied, smooth, very sweet, fortified Hanepoot.

McGregor Co-op Muscadel ★★★ A

This Co-op produces both red and white Muscadels. The red is remarkable wine with deep flavours and an amazing amber colour.

Mamreweg Co-op Hanepoot ★★ A

A deep, dark, rich, sugary wine with full Hanepoot flavour.

Merwida Co-op Hanepoot ★ B

A full, sweet, dessert wine.

Monis Moscato ★★★(★) C

Everything a good, clean, red Muscat should be, this is a Wine of Origin Breede River Valley which is invariably Superior.

Mons Ruber Hanepoot Jerepigo ★★(★) B

The local young wine champion: a strong, big, sweet wine.

Mons Ruber Muscadel Jerepigo ★★★ A

This is a light-style wine with lovely Muscat nose and delicious flavour.

Mons Ruber Red Jerepigo ★★★(★) B

From this tiny Klein Karoo Estate comes a deep, rich wine. Muscat whiffs arise from the nose and although the full, sweet flavour is complex it is not dominated by Muscat. The 1991 is a great, four star wine.

Montagu Muskadelboere Co-op Rooi Muskadel ★★★ A

A good example of a full, sweet Red Muscadel. Bottled young, it has a delightful nose and fresh flavour.

Mont Blois White Muscadel ★★★★(★) C

A consistent award winner at home and abroad, this rich, delicious, golden coloured dessert wine is the classic of Robertson Muscadels. It might develop in the bottle, but is so good when released that I think that's the time to enjoy it. The 1985, 1987 and 1988 are classics.

Mooiuitsig Wynkelders ★★★ A

In the true tradition of the Bonnievale Ward, this cellar produces a range of good fortified wines: White Muscadels, Hanepoots, Jerepigos, Marsalas, and Bonwins (Muscadel liqueur wines).

Multana (Cape Wine) ★★★ B

A red and a white Muscadel are produced under this label, with well-made, clean, good Muscat flavours. This is considered to be the largest selling Muscadel in South Africa.

Muratie Amber ★★★ D

This is a vintage-dated, fortified Hanepoot which has a considerable following. The latest releases are very good.

Nordale Co-op Red Muscadel Jerepigo ★★★★ A

A beautiful, rich wine, full of raisins on the nose.

Nuy Co-op Red Muscadel ★★★★★ C

This is one of the best sweet Red Muscadels made in South Africa: light, not full, sweet, and showing the Hanepoot character at its best. A consistent award winner at regional and national shows, it has twice been judged champion Muscat at the South African Championship Wine Show and every vintage carried Superior certification. It is regularly sold at the Nederburg Auction.

Nuy Co-op White Muscadel ★★★★ C

This wine is of the same high quality as the Nuy Red, but it does not quite achieve the latter's peak. Nevertheless, it is a regular medal and class winner at regional and national shows. It was not only winner of the 1988 Diners Club Award with the 1985 vintage, but runner-up with the 1983. It is regularly sold at the Nederburg Auction.

Opstal Volsoet Hanepoot ★★(★) A

A golden, rich, full-sweet Hanepoot of very good character.

Oranjerivier Wynkelders ★★ A

The cellar produces a range of Hanepoots, Jerepigos and Muscadels.

Overhex Co-op Muscadels ★★★ B

This Co-op has pleasant, light-styled red and white Muscadels.

Overvaal (Vaalharts Co-op) ★★(★) B

Some very acceptable Jeripigos and Hanepoots have been known to come from this Co-op.

Paddagang Vignerons Paddapoot ★★ C

A full, sweet, fortified Hanepoot, which makes for easy sipping.

Perdeberg Muscat d'Alexandrie ★★ A

Full, sweet, Muscat fortified wine.

Porterville Co-op Jerepigos ★ A

Good, sweet, white and red Hanepoots.

Riebeek Wine Farmers' Co-op ★★ A

This Co-op makes two Jerepigos: a red from Pinotage and a full, sweet Hanepoot, which is the better of these two fine wines.

Rietvallei Rooi Muskadel ★★★★(★) B

A sweet fortified wine of the kind every person should try as an alternative to after-dinner Port. It's excellent. The wine is vintage-dated and a Wine of Origin Robertson. The 1985, 1987 and 1988 are particularly attractive. It was always Superior and really what this cellar does best.

Robertson Co-op Baron Du Pon Red Muscadel ★★★★ B

The 1986 Red Muscadel is bottled in magnums and carries Superior certification. Next is a lovely 1988 smooth Red Muscadel. Only when this cellar produces an exceptional wine will it carry the Baron Du Pon label.

Robertson Co-op Soet Muskadel ★★★★ A

This is a different kind of Muscadel, and is delicate, soft and very well-balanced. It deserves to be better known.

Roodezandt Co-op ★★★★ B

This Co-op excels in its fortified Hanepoots and Muscadels. Its Muscat d'Alexandrie, Soet Hanepoot and White Muscadel are all outstanding examples of four-star wines: all regularly carried Superior certification.

Roodezandt Co-op Hoopsrivier Red Muscadelle ★★★ B

This vineyard's fine, full, sweet, red dessert wine achieved Superior certification with its 1981, 1982 and 1984 vintages. The 1986 is just as good, while the 1987 and 1989 are a little lighter.

Rooiberg Co-op Jerepiko Red Muscadel ★★★★ B

A deep-red Muscadel which is always reliable. It is a regular gold medal winner at local and national shows. The 1986, 1989 and 1990 are outstanding products.

Rooiberg Co-op White Hanepoot ★★★ B

A delightful, golden dessert wine with very good Hanepoot character. It is a consistent award winner and was frequently certified Superior.

Rooiberg Co-op White Jerepiko ★★★(★) B

The 1986 is a big, full, sweet, Muscat-flavoured wine. The 1987 and 1988 are not of the same quality, but the 1989 is Superior. The 1990 is the best for several years.

Rooiberg Muscadel ★★★(★) B

The 1989 Red Muscadel was a stunner. The 1990 and 1991 are a little quieter in flavour and harder in spirit.

Simondium Hanepoot ★★ B

Good flavoured, full, sweet wine.

Simonsvlei Co-op Hanepoot ★★★ B

The Co-op is a regular award winner with this full, sweet, pale gold Hanepoot. It regularly carried Superior certification.

Simonsvlei Co-op Humbro ★★★ B

Made from Muscat de Hambourg grapes, this full, sweet red dessert wine
has very good Muscat flavour and is a regular award winner at the South
African Championship Wine Show.

Simonsvlei Co-op Muscadel ★★★(★) B

This Co-op makes consistently good quality red and white Muscadels.

Slanghoek Co-op Soet Hanepoot Jerepigo ★★★(★) B

This is a dessert wine with very good Hanepoot character and golden
colour. The 1980, 1982 and 1984 vintages carried Superior certification.
The first bottling from 1988 was certified Superior; at subsequent bottlings the Superior was dropped. The 1990 is among the best.

Soetwynboere Co-op ★★★(★) B

Situated in the Montagu region, this Co-op specializes in making rich,
fruity, fortified wines, including Muscadels, Hanepoots and Jerepigos.

Southern Cape Cellars ★★★(★) (various prices)

This is a wholesale operation set up by Boplaas to market a range of
select and rare Cape wines. Initial releases are various Muscats carrying
the label adorned with the rare mountain flower, Golden Mimetes.

Spruitdrift Co-op Muskadel Jerepiko ★★★(★) A

An award-winning, full-flavoured wine.

Spruitdrift Co-op Sweet Hanepoot ★★★(★) A

Sampling is like eating raisins. This is a regular award winner.

Swartland Co-op ★★★ B

The Co-op makes a range of award-winning fortified wines, including
Hanepoots, Jerepigos and Ports.

Tulbagh Co-op ★★ B

This cellar produces good Hanepoots and Jerepigos.

Van Loveren Red Muscadel ★★★(★) B

A delicious, well-made Muscadel with attractive, almost rose, colour. It is
a regular winner of local awards and an Oaks Club selection.

Villiersdorp Co-op Hanepoot Jerepigo ★★ B

A full, sweet, golden dessert wine.

Vlottenburg Co-op Hanepoot ★★(★) B

A full, sweet, fortified wine with good cultivar character. The 1983 was a
super four-star wine. Recent vintages are good (uncertified) wines in
screw-top bottles.

Vlottenburg Co-op Muscat de Hambourg ★★(★) B

Previously called Vin Doux Noir, this is an unusual, full, sweet, red
dessert wine made from Muscat de Hambourg.

Vredendal Co-op ★★★(★) A

The Co-op makes a very good range of full-bodied, fortified wines, including Muscadels, Hanepoots, Marsalas and Jerepigos.

Waboomsrivier Co-op Hanepoot ★★★ A

A full, sweet Hanepoot.

Wamakersvallei Co-op Hanepoot Jerepigo ★★ A

A full, sweet, white Hanepoot.

Wellington Wynboere Co-op Hanepoot Jerepigo ★★ A

A full, sweet, white Hanepoot.

Welmoed Co-op ★★★ A

This is another Co-op which makes a range of good fortified wines, including sweet Hanepoot and excellent Red Jerepigo.

Weltevrede Muscat de Hambourg ★★★★ C

This is a beautiful, light, red dessert wine with fine cultivar character. It regularly carried Superior certification.

Weltevrede Rooi and Wit Muskadel ★★★ C

These are delicate fortified wines with good cultivar character.

Weltevrede Oupa se Wingerd Red Muscadel ★★★★ C

To my knowledge this is the only 'single vineyard' fortified wine in the Cape. The label honours Weltevrede's founder, Klaas Jonker. This is a deep, rich, red wine which was SA Champion Muscat at the National Young Wine Show.

PORTS

Aan-de-Doorns Co-op Port ★★ B

This is usually made from Tinta Barocca, without any wood influence, but the 1990 was from Cabernet. It is not suitable for ageing.

Allesverloren Port ★★★★ D

This is a consistently and highly successful Port with many Superior certifications and young wine show medals and trophies to its credit. It is made predominantly of Tinta Barocca, with the balance comprising Souzão, giving a deep, rich, Ruby Port which ranks among the best in the Cape. It usually carried Superior. It is vintage-dated, with the latest from 1984 and 1986.

Apex Port (Cape Wine) ★★(★) B

A pleasant, inexpensive, ruby-type Port.

Bergsig Port ★★ B

A young Port made from the fruit of old vines, including Cinsaut and various Port varieties and sometimes Cabernet, which all contribute to the good flavour. The 1989 is followed by a 1991; there was no 1990.

Bertrams Ruby Port ★★★ C

A Wine of Origin Boberg Port which drinks very easily and carried Superior certification. It is closed with a cork.

Blaauwklippen Port ★★★(★) D

The 1982 release had good Pontac content, in contrast to its Zinfandel-based predecessors. There is great depth of colour and good flavour, from the blend and from wood-ageing. The 1983 and the 1984 are both wines of interest. The 1985 and 1986 are apparently less alcoholic than the previous vintages and are made in the old style, with Zinfandel and Pontac from bush vines. The 1987 and 1988 are slightly drier, and the 1989 is decidedly drier and less alcoholic, but again from Zinfandel and Pontac. All vintages are developing well and are worth laying down.

Bolandse Co-op Port ★★(★) B

The 1986 is the first release of a vintage Port from Pinotage. It is a good, rich wine with a nice, dry finish. A quantity was held back for release in magnums in 1990. The slightly drier 1988 is good and fruity, with berry flavour – a nice attempt. The 1989 SA Champion Non-Muscat is made from Pinotage and Tinta Barocca, as are the 1990 and 1991, which are good and smooth, but not too sweet.

Boplaas Ruby Port ★★★ C

A very pleasant young Port with good, full flavour and character.

Boplaas Vintage Reserve Port ★★★★(★) E

This cellar has produced excellent Ports over a number of years and, after a good run of medals and awards, achieved South African Champion status in 1986. The flagship wine comes from selected barrels and is now bottled with a distinctly Portuguese-style label in an imported Portuguese Port bottle. It is only available from the Estate. The 1987 was again the SA Champion and considered to be one of the finest Ports ever produced at Boplaas, if not in South Africa. There will be no release of the 1988, but the 1989 is the best ever and is the first Port to which I have given five stars. Sales are limited to six bottles per person.

Boplaas Vintage Port ★★★★ D

This Port is sold with the traditional Boplaas label, and has the Boplaas pedigree of awards behind it. Since 1988 it has been bottled at under two years of age and will benefit from long ageing (ten years or more). The 1989 and 1990 are gorgeous examples of Port.

Boplaas White Port ★★★ B

An off-dry Port with good flavour and a pleasant aperitif when chilled.

Botha Co-op Portwyn ★★ A

A well-wooded Port made entirely from Cabernet.

Bottelary Co-op Port ★★ B

Made from Pinotage, this Port has good fruity nose and sweet finish.

Bovlei Co-op Port ★★★

This Port is made from Tinta Barocca and very drinkable.

Brandvlei Co-op Port ★★ A

A well-made wine from Cinsaut.

Calitzdorp Co-op Port ★★ A

This used to be a young fortified wine from Shiraz and Pinotage, but the 1988 was from Cabernet. It has no wood influence and needs time to develop. The 1990 is a Pinotage/Cabernet blend and the 1991 a Merlot/Pinotage blend. Next a Cabernet/Merlot?

Clairvaux Co-op Port ★★ B

Made from Tinta Barocca, and certified as such, this Port is intended for relatively early consumption.

De Helderberg Co-op ★★★ B

This wine, from the 1989 vintage, won the Young Wine Show Gold Medal. The 1990 also received gold awards. It will age well, and is a blend of Tinta Barocca and Cinsaut.

Die Krans Port ★★★(★) B

This is a blend in which Pinotage used to dominat, giving a light, fruity Port with good wood character. Nowadays it is a more typical Port made with a higher percentage of Tinta Barocca and then aged in wood for a year before bottling. The 1986 has good character and is not as sweet as many other Ports. The 1988 is predominantly Tinta Barocca, with 20% Pinotage, and a very good wine. The 1990 and 1991 are decidedly better efforts, from Tinta Barocca.

Die Krans Vintage Reserve Port ★★★★ C

The 1990 was so good, a selection of the best was bottled as 'Reserve'. Only Tinta Barocca was used.

Die Poort Port ★★★ A

A wood-matured Port from Pinotage.

Domein Doornkraal Port ★★ A

The first release came from the 1987 vintage. It is a good, strong, yet complex wine that could develop well. The 1988 was a gold medal winner at the South African Championship Wine Show. The 1989 and 1990 are full-flavoured, fruity and dryish. Like all the wines of Domein Doornkraal, this one has an innovative label: all the pertinent information is silk-screened directly onto the bottle, which causes some frustration for label collectors like me!

Douglas Green Ports (DGB) ★★★ C

Douglas Green produce a range of inexpensive, good-value-for-money Ports. Their 1963 Port, however, was in a different class altogether. It had good, tawny, wood-aged character and is a four-star wine. In 1988 they introduced a non-vintage white Port which, when chilled, makes a good aperitif. The current Ruby is delightful.

Durhams Finest Old Port (DGB)★★ C

A lightish, sweet wine, which is on the dry side, from Tinta Barocca.

Du Toitskloof Co-op Port ★★★ B

This is a pleasant, light-bodied wine made from Cinsaut. The 1986, however, is a wood-matured wine with good Port character. The 1990 shows some potential after a year in wood and could develop well. A Wine of Origin Goudini, it was an award winner at the local show. The 1989 is ageing well.

Goue Vallei (Calitzdorp Co-op) ★★★ B

A good, tawny-type Port, which is not as sweet as most.

Groot Constantia Port ★★★(★) C

The first release from 1984 is not too sweet, and comes from Tinta Barocca and Shiraz. It is developing well in the bottle, as is the 1986.

Huguenot Port ★★(★) A

Two nice ports – one labeled 'Invalid' and the other 'Tawny'.

Jonkheer Farmers' Winery★★ B

This cellar produces a fresh, young Invalid Port, and a nutty, wood-aged Old Port.

Kango Co-op Port ★★ A

Made from Tinta Barocca and Cabernet, this is a dryish, spirity wine. The 1990 is entirely from Tinta Barocca.

Koelenhof Co-op Port ★★ B

A full, sweet, spirity Pinotage Port, aged in oak.

KWV 1948 Port ★★★★ D

Released in 1987 in 750 ml bottles and in magnums, this Wine of Origin Boberg is a tawny, wood-aged Port, bottled to celebrate Paarl's tercentenary. The 750 ml bottle is a unique, oval shape, specially designed for the occasion. It is ready for drinking now.

KWV Bartolomeu Dias 1963 Port ★★★★ D

To commemorate the rounding of the Cape 500 years before, the KWV launched a 1963 wood-aged Port, early in 1988. Available in magnums, this flavourful wine drinks well now, but has the potential to develop further in the bottle.

KWV Crusted Vintage Port ★★★★(★)

A bottling from the 1963 vintage was matured in the bottle for 16 years to enable the crust to form. In 1993 it has developed extremely well and it is a pity that this has not been done more often.

KWV Tawny 1956 Port ★★★(★) D

A Wine of Origin Boberg. This Port, certified Superior, is smooth across the palate and full of wood-aged flavour. However, it lacks the complexity of a bottle-aged Port. It drinks very easily.

La Cotte Red Port (Franschhoek Vineyards Co-op) ★★ B

A fairly ordinary Port made from Tinta Barocca and Cinsaut.

Landskroon Port ★★★★ C

A regular medal and trophy winner at regional and national shows, this distinctive wine was, in its earlier vintages, made from Tinta Barocca, Cinsaut and Alicante Bouschet. It is not as sweet as most local Ports and is a little more chewy than most. It is vintage-dated. The 1978 developed with interest in the bottle over five years, and other vintages should do the same. The 1983 is worth trying, and the 1985 promises to be good. The 1986, however, could be the best. Since 1988, Cinsaut has been dropped from the blend and it now comes in a dumpy Port bottle. It is a good wine that will develop well.

Merwida Co-op Port ★ B

Equal proportions of Cabernet and Pinotage make up this full-bodied dessert wine.

Monis Collector's Port ★★★★ C

Excellent, old, wood-aged Port, vintage-dated 1948, of which three issues have been released. Their labels reproduce rare old South African stamps. A special edition was produced for the Johannesburg centenary. The last release is from the 1961 vintage and features six different labels, each showing pieces of artillery used by both sides in the South African War. The Superior Tawny Port was made from Souzão, Cinsaut, Tinta Barocca and Cabernet Sauvignon.

Monis Special Reserve Port ★★★(★) C

A dry, ruby-styled Port from Cabernet, Cinsaut and Tinta Barocca.

Monis Very Old Mature Port ★★★(★) C

This is one of the most respected and oldest names in fortified wines. For years Monis have sold a product called Vintage Port, which, as good as it was, was certainly not a Vintage Port. It has been renamed Very Old Mature Port, which describes more accurately this 10 to 15 year old, wood-matured Port which has good character and is excellent value.

Mons Ruber Port ★★★ **B**
Good, dryish Ports from the 1990s, made from Cabernet.

Mooiuitsig Wynkelders ★★ **A/B**
This cellar produces a range of Ports under various names such as Fine Old, Old Tawny and Old White.

Morganhof Port ★★★(★) **C**
From 1988 comes a good attempt from Pinotage and Tinta Barocca, which has good fruit and a dryish aftertaste.

Muratie Port ★★★ **E**
This blend of Cinsaut and various Port varieties is in line with the cellar's style. The 1990 and 1991 are of a totally different style, made from Port varieties, and bottled early. Both should develop well.

Nederburg Port ★★★★★ **(no price available)**
This is a very rare wine which is always given away and never sold. It is light and fruity, and completely different from any other South African wine. Beg, borrow or steal a bottle – it'll be worth the experience.

Overgaauw Port ★★★★ **E**
This Port, made from various cultivars, has been wood-aged for two years and then bottled in the true Vintage Port style. It develops well, but needs many years in the bottle to reach its full potential. The 1976 is good in 1993. The 1981 is similar and keeps Overgaauw among the fore-runners in South African Vintage Port production. The 1983 is very Por-tuguese in style.

Riebeek Co-op Port ★★★ **B**
A light but attractive Port made in 1982 from a number of Port varieties. It was reserved for release in 1992 to celebrate the cellar's golden anniversary. The cellar also makes a regular Port, and the 1987 and 1989 are from Shiraz.

Romansrivier Co-op Port ★★(★) **B**
This limited release in magnums is a blend of vintages from 1981 and 1984, made from a number of varieties including Cabernet, Pinotage and Tinta Barocca. It is a Wine of Origin Breede River. The 1987, from Tinta Barocca, is pale, light, oaky and dryish.

Rooiberg Co-op Port ★★★(★) **A**
This 1985 Port replaces the previous Pinotage-based Port. Made from equal portions of Tinta Barocca and Souzão, and fortified with three-year-old Brandy, it was wood-aged in small oak for a year. The result is a good, rich, concentrated wine with lots of fruit and a firm, dry finish. The 1986 and 1987 were made along similar lines. The 1988 had 20% Caber-net Franc added to give an unusual dimension.

Rustenberg Port ★★★(★) **C**
The 1984 was the first release of this Port, of predominantly Souzão with some Cabernet. It is a big, rich Port that is developing beautifully in the bottle. The next release, from the 1987 vintage, follows the same style.

Santys Invalid Port ★★ B
A good, inexpensive, tawny Port.

Santys Old Ruby Port ★★★(★) B
A fruity, flavourful, wood-aged Port from Port varieties and Cinsaut.

Sedgwicks Government House Port ★★★ B
One of South Africa's oldest Port labels. It is much respected, popular and inexpensive, and has good character.

Simonsvlei Co-op Port ★★★(★) E
A limited release came from 1983, blended from Cinsaut, Shiraz and Tinta Barocca. It was aged for a year in small wood and will need a further five to seven years in the bottle to smooth out. A good attempt. The next release, from the 1986 vintage, is much better.

Spier Port ★★ C
The 1983 Pinotage Port is a great improvement on earlier releases and the powerful 1984 continues the trend. The 1986 and 1987 are now available.

Swartland Co-op Port ★★(★) A
A very young, full, grape-flavoured Port. Mixed with lemonade, it makes a delicious summer drink.

Vergenoegd Estate Port ★★★ C
Although it was made from Tinta Barocca, this wine is not as big and rich as most South African Ports. The 1986 was the first release. The 1987 is sold in tall, high-shouldered bottles, and comes with a separate stopper cork so that once you have pulled the cork you can reseal the bottle. The next release was from the 1988 vintage and will be followed by the 1989.

Villiersdorp Co-op Port ★★(★) B
A blend of Pinotage and Tinta Barocca giving full, sweet wine with a pleasant flavour.

Vredendal Co-op Port ★★★ A
An interesting young Port made from almost equal parts of Carignan, Cinsaut, Grenache, Pinotage and Tinta Barocca, all of which produce a most unusual nose and character. It will need time to integrate, and should develop depth of complexity.

Waboomsrivier Co-op Port ★★(★) A
This is a blend of Cinsaut and Tinta Barocca, aged for two years in wood and then kept for two years in the bottle before being released. This produces a good, rich flavour that could develop with age.

Welmoed Co-op Vintage Port ★★★ C
The wood-aged 1983 Port, made from Tinta Barocca, has developed well in the bottle. The 1985 is similar. The 1989 is the next release.

SHERRIES

South Africa produces very good Sherries, the more expensive brands being very similar in quality, varying only in name, through a range of styles and sweetness, for example:

Dry: Often termed 'pale dry', because these are the lightest of the Sherries in terms of colour. These are usually bone-dry, in the tradition of the Spanish finos, or have, at the most, the smallest fraction of sweetness. Delicately flavoured, these Sherries make the best aperitifs.

Medium, Medium-dry, or Medium-sweet: Sherries thus labelled vary widely in degree of sweetness, depending on the individual brand name's particular market. Usually they are of the Spanish oloroso style: golden, with good bouquet and lovely flavour.

Full Cream: Usually the darkest-coloured and the sweetest of the finer Sherries, they are of the Spanish amoroso style and at one stage were known as 'East Indian Walnut' or 'Old Brown'.

Old Brown: In South Africa, Old Brown Sherries are in a category of their own, and are usually inexpensive, deep in colour and full of flavour.

Golden Sherries: This is another category peculiar to South Africa. Such wines are usually sweet and full of flavour, but bear very little resemblance to the classic Sherry. They are survivors of a bygone age in this country when fortified wines ruled supreme and unfortified wines were hardly known.

Owing to these broad similarities, I have not described individual wines in any detail, except in a few instances where some outstanding or unusual aspect has invited further comment. The following list does not reflect the full range of Sherries on the market and relates only to those I have tasted during the past two years.

Bertrams (Gilbeys) ★★★★ C

The range of Sherries from this merchant include Santa Petra Pale Dry, Medium Dry, Medium Cream and Full Cream, and Premier Reserve Fine Old Pale Cream.

Boschendal 'Ronnie van Rooyen' Vintage Sherry (1977) ★★ C

This Wine of Origin Paarl was made by Ronnie van Rooyen in 1977; none has been made since. It is something of a curiosity as Sherries are not normally vintage-dated; the method of Sherry making in a solera involves the slow blending of many vintages. This is a collector's item.

Douglas Green (DGB) ★★★★ B

The 'Flor' Sherries from Douglas Green are well known and include the Extra Dry (No 1), Medium (No 3) and a Full Cream.

Drostdy ★★★(★) B

The Drostdy Sherries are all Wine of Origin Tulbagh, and were certified Superior. The range includes Pale Dry, Medium and Full Cream.

Eekay Old Brown (EK Green) ★★ A

Inexpensive, sweet, Old Brown-style Sherry.

Goue Vallei (Citrusdal Co-op) ★★★ B

This Co-op markets Pale Dry, Medium Cream and Old Brown Sherries.

KWV Very Old Medium Dry and Medium Cream ★★★★ C

This is Wine of Origin Boberg and certified Superior.

KWV Very Old Sherry ★★★ C

Sold in the KWV's long-necked bottle, this Medium Cream Sherry was released in 1988. A very good wine, it carries Superior.

Monis ★★★★ C

Monis Sherries are certified Superior. The range is Pale Dry, Medium Cream and Full Cream.

Monte Vista (Mooiuitsig) ★★ B

In addition to the popular Old Brown Sherry this merchant also makes Pale Dry, Medium Dry and Medium Cream Sherries.

Santys Walnut Old Brown (Gilbeys) ★★ A

A good quality, Old Brown-style Sherry.

Sedgwicks Old Brown ★★★ A

This is by far the market leader in terms of the Old Browns.

Ship Sherry (SFW) ★★ A

This is a surprisingly good product that is the friend of many of South Africa's commercial deep-sea fisherfolk. In Port Elizabeth alone, more than a million cases are sold each year.

Van der Stel Club Sherry ★★ A

Inexpensive, well-made, sweetish Sherry.

OTHER FORTIFIED WINES

Die Krans La Difference ★★★ B
This is a good-flavoured, fortified Steen.

Domein Doornkraal Kaptein ★★★ A
A blend of Pinta (Pinotage and Tinta Barocca) and Muscadel produces a most unusual wine that is full of flavour and character.

Domein Doornkraal Majoor ★(★) A
A full-flavoured Steen Jerepigo.

Fairview Full Sweet Sémillon ★★★ B
This is an unusual fortified wine made from Sémillon. Served ice-cold, it makes a fine substitute for a sorbet between dinner courses. The 1980 vintage has a most attractive grapey character.

Goudini Co-op Red Dessert ★(★) A
A 1987, fortified, sweet Pinotage which has an attractive nose, but lacks flavour, and is a little watery in the mouth.

Goue Vallei Jerepigo (Citrusdal) ★★★ A
This national champion from the 1988 vintage has good, clean aroma and fine flavour. Made from very ripe Pinotage and fortified with wine spirit, it should develop with time in the bottle.

Kango Co-op Golden Jerepiko ★★★★ B
A super fortified Steen and a regular award winner. This is one of the best non-Muscat fortifieds.

Kango Co-op Red Jerepigo ★★ A
Made from Tinta Barocca, and an interesting variation.

Louwshoek-Voorsorg Co-op Nectar de Provision ★★★ B
A first release came from the 1987 vintage. This Co-op produced a fortified wine typical of the Cognac region where it is called Pineau des Charentes. In other parts of France similar products are called Amistelle. This one is made from fully-ripe Colombar and fortified with Brandy. It is aged for two years in oak and should be served chilled. The next release comes from the 1991 vintage.

Mons Ruber Bonitas ★★ A
This is a white dessert wine that is somewhat smoother than the Regalis.

Mons Ruber Elegantia ★★ B
A full-flavoured, red dessert wine.

Mons Ruber Regalis ★★ B
Initially this was a spirity, hot, white dessert wine, with definite character. It has developed into a smooth, easier-drinking wine with unmistakable Hanepoot character.

Paddagang Vignerons Brulpadda ★★ D
This sweet, porty wine carries my favourite label in the Paddagang range. Very pleasant young, although it will no doubt improve with time.

Perdeberg Co-op Cinsaut Liqueur Wine ★★ A

A good, light, Port-style, fortified wine, made from Cinsaut.

Vaalharts Co-op ★★ A

Interesting fortified wines from this Co-op include Andalusia Jerepigo from Pinotage, and Andalusia Erlihane, which is the first fortified wine from the cross between Hanepoot and Queen of the Vineyards table grape varieties.

Welmoed Co-op ★★★(★) B

This Co-op produces interesting red dessert wines. Previously, they were made from Shiraz, but more recently from Tinta Barocca.

Nouveau Wines

The wines below have not been star-rated as they are designed for early consumption and not for ageing, although some of the reds do develop with interest over a year or so.

Altydgedacht Nouveau

1992 saw the first production of Nouveau from this cellar. A small quantity is produced annuallt for De Oude Welgemoed Restaurant Nouveau Wine Festival.

Backsberg Nouveau Rouge

Produced annually from Pinot Noir, although it is not certified as such. It is made by carbonic maceration giving a most attractive, easy-drinking wine in real Nouveau style. It is finished dry.

Boland Wineries Nouveau

Produced each year for the Paarl Nouveau Festival.

Buitenverwachting L'Arrivée

This is one of the more interesting Nouveaus, first released in 1986 and now released each year at a fun-filled festival day at Buitenverwachting which is combined with a very worthwhile charity auction. Always good tasting and made in the traditional way using Gamay.

De Leuwen Jagt Nouveau

Always interesting and produced for the Paarl Nouveau Festival.

De Wet Co-op Fronté Pétillant

A bubbly, semi-sweet Muscat de Frontignan made as a Nouveau, with low alcohol.

Diemersdal Nouveau

This comes with the same attractive and colourful label as used on Bloemendal and Altydgedacht Nouveaus produced for the Welgemoed Nouveau Festival.

Eikendal Nouveau

Produced for this cellar's annual Weintaufe, where each year a celebrity names the new young wine 'Jung Frau' after the mountains in Switzerland, the home of the owner's of this cellar.

Fairview Gamay Noir

One of the earliest Nouveau wines made from Gamay along the lines of a Beaujolais, using the traditional method of carbonic maceration. It is dry and full of flavour, and although made for early drinking, it is more of a serious red that develops well with a year or two in the bottle. The attractive label shows Adam and Eve being led astray by a serpant with a glass of wine rather than an apple.

KWV Nouveau

KWV produce red and white Nouveaus for the overseas market, where they cause considerable interest as they are available outside the northern hemisphere's 'Nouveau season'. The white is from Steen and the good, fruity red is from Pinotage.

Landskroon Nouveau Rouge

A dry red made for the Paarl Mountain Festival.

Nederburg Nouveau

A token quantity was produced for the Paarl Mountain Festival.

Romansrivier Co-op Nouveau

A dry red Nouveau which is produced annually.

Simondium Co-op Nouveau

Made for the Paarl Mountain Festival.

Simonsvlei Co-op Nouveau

From Pinot Noir, with good, fresh flavours. It can be found at the Paarl Mountain Festival.

Vredendal Co-op Goiya Kgeisje

Again the first to be certified and this year made from Sauvignon Blanc and Chardonnay and labelled as such – this year with a stylised ostrich.

Woolworths Jeune Blanc

From Villiera. An elegant dry wine with lively crispness and attractive fruity nose. A blend of 25% Gewürztraminer, 35% Chenin Blanc and 40% Muscat Ottonel.

Woolworths Jeune Rosé

From Villiera. A very attractive rose coloured wine with fruity nose and good floral flavour, finished off-dry. A blend of 44% Gewürztraminer, 36% Chenin Blanc and 20% Gamay.

Woolworths Jeunesse

From Villiera. A classic Nouveau made form Gamay using the traditional carbonic maceration method. Brilliant red colour with striking fresh fruitiness and lovely strawberry and raspberry flavours, finished bone dry. Best enjoyed young and slightly chilled.

STOP PRESS

Alphen Noble Late Harvest ★★★ D
This wine is from the 1987 vintage, and was bottled in 1988, so it is now showing good bottle age and deep, golden colour. It is 100% Chenin Blanc, with good honeyed nose and spicey flavours.

Craighall Cabernet/Merlot ★★★(★) C
A delightful, modern, international, fruity-type wine. It has gorgeous bright-red colour and deep, berry flavours. It is made up of 60% Cabernet Sauvignon, 35% Merlot and 5% Cabernet Franc. The first release from the 1991 vintage is a Wine of Origin Stellenbosch. Twenty per cent of the blend has been wood-aged. Excellent value for money.

Le Pavillon Rouge (Boschendal) ★★★ C
A delightful, unassuming wine, blended from classic red varietals, of which the Pinot Noir and Merlot gives the wine the soft fruitiness of ripe raspberries and cherries. The varietals are not mentioned on the label. Sixty per cent of the wine was matured in large oak for a year. This gentle wooding has ensured no wood flavour which could detract from the wine's inherent fruit flavours. Very affordable.

LISTING OF WINES
ACCORDING TO STAR RATING

Bordeaux Blends
★★★★★
Delheim Grand Reserve F
Fairview Merlot Reserve E
Glen Carlou Grande
  Classique F
Kanonkop Auction Reserve F
Kanonkop Paul Sauer F
Klein Constantia Marlbrook
Meerlust Rubicon E/F
Overgaauw Tria Corda E
Rozendal C
Rustenberg Gold E/F
Rust-en-Vrede E
Simonsig Tiara F
Villiera Crû Monro D
Warwick Trilogy F
Welgemeend E
★★★★(★)
Backsberg Klein
  Babylonstoren D
Bertrams Robert Fuller E
Clos Malverne Auret Reserve
Glen Carlou Les Trois E
La Motte Millenium D
L'Ormarins Optima Reserve
Meinert Blend D
Neil Ellis Cabernet E
Vriesenhof Kallista E
Woolworths Cabernet
  Sauvignon-Merlot D
Zevenwacht E
★★★★
Avontuur Avon Rouge B
Avontuur Baccarat D
Barrydale Co-op Tradeaux
  Reserve C
Boplaas Grand Vin Rouge
Buitenverwachting Grand
  Vin E
Cape Vintners Members
  Only Grand Reserve D
Claridge Red Wellington D
Clos Malverne Auret E
Delaire Barrique E
Eikendal Classique E
Fairview Charles Gerard
  Reserve C
Groot Constantia
  Gouverneurs Reserve F
Hamilton Russell Vineyards
  Premier Reserve E
Kloofzicht Alter Ego E
Le Bonheur Blend D
Meerlust Red D
Nederburg Private Bin R109

Neil Ellis Reserve Selection
Overgaauw DC Classic D
Talana Hill Royale E
Vergenoegd Reserve E
Welgemeend Douelle C
Woolworths Grand Rouge C
Woolworths Le Cinquieme
  895R D
Woolworths Le Premier 881R
Zonnebloem Lauréat D/E

Cape Traditional Blends
★★★★★
Nederburg Private Bin R103
★★★★(★)
Nederburg Private Bin R115
Rustenberg Dry Red D
★★★★
Nederburg Edelrood D/E
Roodendal Reserve (SFW) C
Rozendal E/F
Vaughan Johnson's House
  Red C
Warwick Femme Bleu E

Dry Red Blends
★★★★
Altydgedacht Tintoretto C
Hemel-en-Aarde Valley Vin
  Rouge C
Overgaauw Overtinto B
Vin Rouge (Picardi) C

Cabernet Sauvignon
★★★★★
Cellarmaster's Choice F
Beyerskloof F
Blaauwklippen Reserve D
Kanonkop F
Klein Constantia E
Meerlust E
Nederburg Auction E
Stellenryck Collection E
Thelema E
Vriesenhof E
★★★★(★)
Backsberg D
Bellingham E
Blaauwklippen E
Fleur Du Cap D
Glen Carlou E
Le Bonheur F
Middelvlei E
Nederburg Paarl D/E
Overgaauw E
Rustenberg E

Uitkyk Carlonet F
Vergenoegd D
Warwick E
Woolworths E
Zonnebloem (SFW) D
★★★★
Allesverloren D/E
Alphen C
Alto F
Bertrams F
Bloemendal E
Clos Malverne E
Delheim D
Fairview Reserve D
Fleur Du Cap Oak Collection
Goedvertrou E
Groot Constantia D
La Motte E
Landskroon D
Lievland E
L'Ormarins E
Neil Ellis C
Oude Libertas (SFW) B
Rhebokskloof D
Rozendal Magnums D
Rustenberg Reserve E/F
Rust-en-Vrede E
Simonsig D/E
Stellenzicht E
Welgemeend C
Woolworths C
Zevenwacht E

Merlot
★★★★(★)
Villiera D
★★★★
Boschendal Jean de Long E
Bouchard Finlayson E
Buitenverwachting Auction
  Reserve E
Cape Vintners D
Delheim C
Eikendal D
Fairview Reserve D
Fleur Du Cap D
Glen Carlou E/F
Meerlust E/F
Overgaauw C
Rustenberg E
Warwick E
Warwick Special Reserve
Woolworths Elgin E
Woolworths Le Deuxieme
  902R E
Zonnebloem D

Pinotage
★★★★★
Kanonkop CIWG E
★★★★(★)
Simonsig Reserve E
★★★★
Fairview Reserve C
Fleur Du Cap C
Kanonkop E
Meerendal D
Meinert Winery Devon Crest
Nederburg Auction E
Oude Libertas (SFW) F
Rhebokskloof D
Simonsvlei Co-op B
Zonnebloem (SFW) C

Pinot Noir
★★★★★
Hamilton Russell F
★★★★
Blaauwklippen D
Bouchard Finlayson E
Glen Carlou E
Nederburg D
Rustenberg E
Woolworths C

Shiraz
★★★★(★)
Nederburg C
★★★★
Allesverloren D/E
Backsberg D
Bellingham D
Bertrams E
Delheim C
Fairview Reserve B/C
Groot Constantia C
Hartenberg E
Klein Constantia D
La Motte D
Landskroon C
Lievland D
L'Ormarins F
Pick 'n Pay C
Rust-en-Vrede E/F
Simonsig D
Vergenoegd C
Zonnebloem (SFW) D

Blended/Non-varietal Dry White Wine
★★★★(★)
Fairview Charles Gerard
  Reserve C
★★★★
Chant de Nuit B
Klein Constantia Blanc de
  Blanc C
Landskroon Premier Blanc
Nederburg Prelude C

Nederburg Private Bin D207
Simonsig Vin Fumé C
Stellenzicht Grand Vin Blanc
Stellenzicht Heerenblanc B
Weltevrede Privé de Bois C
Woolworths Le Troisieme
  913W
Zonnebloem Grand Soleil C

Blended/Non-varietal Off-dry/Semi-sweet White
★★★★(★)
Nederburg Private Bin S354
★★★★
Fairview Bouquet Fair C
Nederburg Private Bin S312
Nederburg Private Bin S333
Twee Jongegezellen
  Schanderl C

Chardonnay
★★★★★
Hamilton Russell Reserve F
Klein Constantia F
Talana Hill F
Thelema D
★★★★(★)
Backsberg D
Glen Carlou E
Hamilton Russell E
Overgaauw E
Simonsig E
Vriesenhof D
★★★★
Aan de Wagenweg E
Altydgedacht D
Avontuur Le Chardon E
Bellingham Reserve E
Bon Courage E
Boschendal C
Bouchard Finlayson E
Buitenverwachting E
Danie de Wet E
Delaire E
Delheim D
De Wetshof Estate Finesse
Eikendal D
Fairview D
Fleur Du Cap C
Graham Beck Lone Hill C
Groot Constantia E
John Platter D
Lievland D
Louisvale E
L'Ormarins D
Mondial (Gilbeys) E
Mulderbosch E
Neethlingshof E
Nederburg D
Neil Ellis E
Paul Cluver D
Rhebokskloof E

Robertson Co-op C
Rustenberg Reserve E
Van Loveren E
Vergelegen Les Enfants D
Warwick
Weltevrede Estate D
Woolworths C
Zonnebloem D

Colombard
★★★★
Nuy Co-op A
Nederburg Private Bin D207

Gewürztraminer
★★★★★
Nederburg C
★★★★(★)
Delheim C
★★★★
Boschendal Jean Garde D
Fleur du Cap C
Groot Constantia D
Nederburg Elgin
Neil Ellis D
Neethlingshof C
Stellenryk C
Weltevrede C
Woolworths C
Zevenwacht C

Special Late Harvest
★★★★
Backsberg B
Bergsig Gewürztraminer B
Bon Courage
  Gewürztraminer C
Delaire C
Delheim B
Du Toitskloof Co-op B
Eikendal C
Fleur Du Cap C
Hartenberg L'Estreux C
Nederburg C
Nederburg Weisser Riesling
Neethlingshof
  Gewürztraminer B
Neethlingshof Weisser
  Riesling C
Simonsig Gewürztraminer
Thelema
Villiera Garonne B

Noble Late Harvest
★★★★★
Delheim Edelspatz E
Nederburg Edelkeur D
Nederburg Eminence E
Nederburg Weisser Riesling
Neethlingshof Rhine
  Riesling D
Zonnebloem E

★★★★(★)
Blaauwklippen C
KWV
Nederburg Chardonnay
Nederburg Steen C
Woolworths
★★★★
Backsberg E
Bellingham (DGB) D
Boland Co-op D
Boschendal Vin d'Or E
Buitenverwachting
Noblesse E
De Wetshof Edeloes E
Eikendal E
Fleur du Cap D
La Dorée (Delaire) E
Lievland D
L'Ormarins C
Nederburg Bukettraube
Edelkeur D
Nederburg D
Neethlingshof Sauvignon
Blanc D
Perdeberg Co-op D
Rooiberg Edel Laatoes C
Simonsig D
TJ Engeltjepipi C
Stellenzicht E
Vredendal Co-op C

Natural Sweet
★★★★★
Klein Constantia E
★★★★
Nederburg Sauvignon Blanc

Riesling – Cape
★★★★
L'Ormarins Franschhoek C
Weltevrede B

Riesling – Rhine/Weisser
★★★★
Danie de Wet C
Delaire C
Delheim C
Fairview B
Groot Constantia C
Hartenberg B
Klein Constantia C
Lievland C
Nederburg D
Neethlingshof C/D
Neil Ellis C
Rhebokskloof B
Simonsig Dry C
Stellenryck Collection C
Thelema B
Villiera B/C
Weltevrede B
Woolworths C

Sauvignon Blanc
★★★★★
Klein Constantia D
★★★★(★)
L'Ormarins Blanc Fumé C
Neil Ellis Whitehall C
Villiera C
★★★★
Aan de Wagenweg Blanc
Fumé (Bergkelder) E
Alphen Le Fevre C
Backsberg John Martin C
Buitenverwachting Blanc
Fumé E
Buitenverwachting D
Delaire Blanc Fumé C
Hamilton Russell D
La Motte Blanc Fumé C
La Motte
Le Bonheur Blanc Fumé C
Lemberg Aimée C
L'Ormarins
Mulderbosch Blanc Fumé
Mulderbosch C
Nederburg
Neil Ellis Blanc Fumé C
Paul Cluver C
Ruiterbosch C
Stellenryck Blanc Fumé D
Stellenzicht D
Thelema C
Uitkyk C
Villiera Cru Monro Blanc
Fumé C
Woolworths D
Zevenwacht Blanc Fumé C
Zevenwacht C

Blanc de Noir
★★★★
Nederburg Cabernet Sauvi-
gnon Blanc de Noir C
Neethlingshof C

Méthode Cap Classique
★★★★(★)
Clos Cabrière Pierre
Jourdan Brut E
Graham Beck Brut E
Villiera Tradition de
Charles de Fère Reserve E
★★★★
Backsberg E
Boschendal Brut E
Boschendal Grande Reserve
Buitenverwachting Brut F
Clos Cabrière Pierre
Jourdan F
Grand Mousseaux Blanc de
Blanc Chardonnay E
Here XVII Grand Cuvée E
JC le Roux Pinot Noir D

L'Ormarins Jean Roi
Nederburg Blanquette E
Pongràcz (Bergkelder) E
Simonsig Kaapse Vonkel E
TJ Krone Borealis F
Villiera Tradition de
Charles de Fère D
Woolworths Méthode C

**Non-méthode
Cap Classique**
★★★★
Bellingham
Nederburg Kap Sekt C
Rhebokskloof C
Rooiberg Chardonnay Brut
Rooiberg Co-op Vin Doux B

Muscat
★★★★★
Nuy Co-op Red Muscadel C
★★★★(★)
KWV D
Mont Blois White Muscadel
Rietvallei Rooi Muskadel B
★★★★
Ashton A
Badsberg C
Bon Courage B
Boplaas B
Du Toitskloof B
Goudini B
Groot Trek B
Louwshoek-Voorsorg B
Nordale A
Nuy
Robertson B
Roodezandt B
Rooiberg B
Weltevrede C

Port
★★★★★
Nederburg
★★★★(★)
Boplaas Vintage Reserve E
KWV Crusted Vintage
★★★★
Allesverloren D
Boplaas Vintage D
Die Krans Vintage Reserve
KWV D
Landskroon C
Monis Collector's C
Overgaauw E

Sherry
★★★★
Bertrams C
Douglas Green B
KWV C
Monis C

INDEX

Wines printed in italics are available but have not been assessed.
(npa) = no price available

324

THE WAYS OF THE WORLD

THE WAYS OF THE WORLD

Robert Goddard

BANTAM PRESS

LONDON · TORONTO · SYDNEY · AUCKLAND · JOHANNESBURG

TRANSWORLD PUBLISHERS
61–63 Uxbridge Road, London W5 5SA
A Random House Group Company
www.transworldbooks.co.uk

First published in Great Britain
in 2013 by Bantam Press
an imprint of Transworld Publishers

A CIP catalogue record for this book
is available from the British Library.

ISBNs 9780593069738 (cased)
9780593069745 (tpb)

Addresses for Random House Group Ltd companies outside the UK
can be found at: www.randomhouse.co.uk
The Random House Group Ltd Reg. No. 954009

The Random House Group Limited supports the Forest Stewardship Council®
(FSC®), the leading international forest-certification organisation. Our books
carrying the FSC label are printed on FSC®-certified paper. FSC is the
only forest-certification scheme supported by the leading environmental
organisations, including Greenpeace. Our paper procurement policy
can be found at www.randomhouse.co.uk/environment

Typeset in 11/14.25pt Times New Roman
by Falcon Oast Graphic Art Ltd.
Printed and bound in Great Britain
by Clays Ltd, Bungay, Suffolk

2 4 6 8 10 9 7 5 3 1

THE WAYS OF THE WORLD

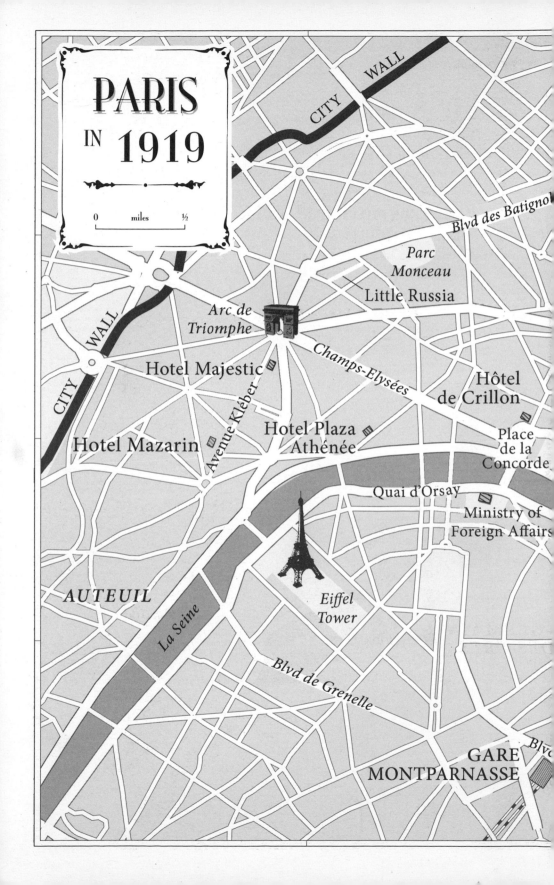

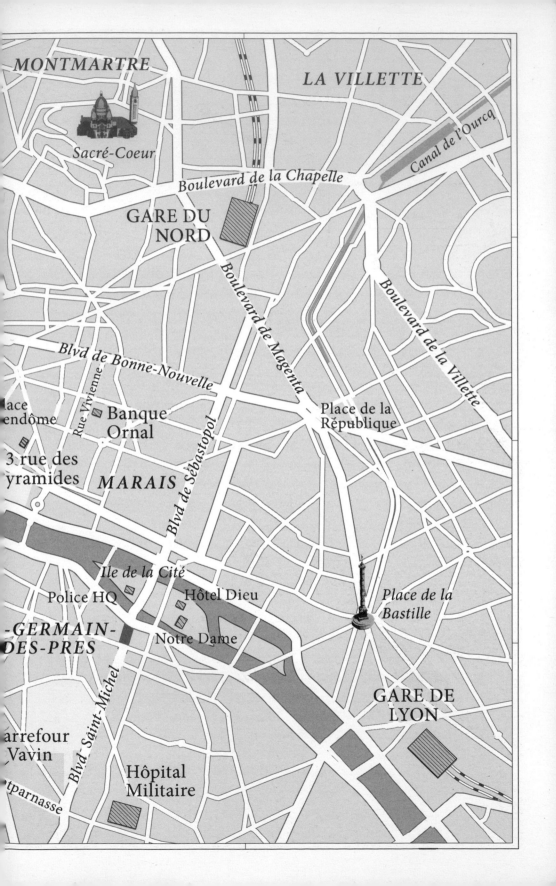

SPRING, 1919

THEY COULD IGNORE THE TELEPHONE. THAT WAS ONE OF the unwritten clauses of the Armistice. No telephone would have rung unanswered for long at the squadron base in France where their paths had first crossed in the summer of 1915. But they were not in France. And the war was over. So there they stood, side by side, aware of the importunate ringing in the unattended office in the corner of the hangar, but unmoved by it, lulled by the scent of oil and varnish and the fluttering of a pigeon in the rafters and the vernal brightness of the light flooding in around them.

It was a silvery late-morning light that gleamed on the fuselages of an array of aircraft that had never strained through dives or loops in combat, or been strafed by enemy fire, because they had been constructed just as the war was ending and were now as redundant, for all their elegance and cunning of design, as the pair of youthful Royal Flying Corps veterans who were admiring them.

Even at a glance the two men would have struck an observer as dissimilar, so dissimilar that probably only the war could account for their ease in each other's company. The taller and slimmer of them was James Maxted, former lieutenant, known to all but his family as Max. He had a good-looking face that held a promise of rugged handsomeness in middle age, boyishly flopping fair hair, pale-blue eyes and an ironic tilt to his mouth that hinted at cynicism. His companion, a shorter, bulkier figure, was Sam Twentyman, former sergeant. Max had served in the RFC as a pilot and known Sam as the most reliable and resourceful of the engineers who kept his plane in the air. Sam was five years older

3

than Max, but looked younger, despite some greying of his curly brown hair, thanks to his round, rosy-cheeked face and general air of terrier-like eagerness.

'You're sure Bristols are the ones to go for?' Max asked, arching a sceptical eyebrow. 'Some of the lads who flew them said they preferred the Sopwiths.'

'They did at first, sir,' Sam replied. He still addressed Max as an NCO would an officer and showed no sign of breaking the habit. 'But after all the modifications we made the Bristol was the best two-seater by a long chalk. You were out of circulation by then, of course.'

By 'out of circulation' Sam meant held for the duration in a prisoner of war camp in Silesia. Max smiled at the euphemism and stepped close enough to the nearest plane to run an appreciative hand over the burnished wood of its propeller vanes.

'Well, you're the boss, Sam.'

Now it was Sam's turn to smile. They were spending Max's money, not his. He had no illusions about who would be calling the tune in their future enterprise. 'Will the budget stretch to a couple of SE5s, then? Beautiful machines, they are. Ten quid the pair. A real bargain.'

'Is that what Miller said?' Max nodded towards a scurrying, overalled figure who had just entered the hangar by a side-door and was heading towards the still-ringing telephone in the office. He wore an irritated frown on his thin, oil-smudged face. 'The air-worthiness certificates will treble that price, remember.'

'You're right. They will. But . . .'

'But?' Max turned and gazed at Sam expectantly.

'Our customers will want to fly solo eventually.'

'If I teach them well enough?'

Sam grinned. 'You're a natural, sir. You gave quite a few of the Hun a flying lesson, as I remember.'

The telephone had stopped ringing. Miller had finally answered it. In the welcome silence Max recalled the intoxicating pleasure of his first flight, a joy-ride from this very aerodrome eight years before, in the summer of 1911. Was it only eight years? It seemed longer, so very much longer, in so very many ways. Cambridge.

4

Farnborough Flying School. The Western Front: those crazy days of scouting above the trenches, nerves stretched as taut as the rigging of his plane, ending in a crash behind enemy lines he had been lucky to survive – doubly so, given the rapidly declining life expectancy of pilots as the war advanced. Then eighteen months of tedium and privation in the POW camp. And now, here he was, back at Hendon, birthplace of his passion for flying, about to acquire a training squadron of his own at a knock-down price.

'Miller would let you take one of the SE5s for a spin,' Sam continued, 'if that's what you need to make your mind up.'

'I'm sure he would. And I'm sure you reckon it *would* make my mind up.'

'They're sweet as honey, sir.'

'And we deserve some honey, don't we, Sam, you and I?' Max clapped his friend on the shoulder and was suddenly overtaken by a surge of optimism about their joint venture. He planned to call the flying school Surrey Wings. He had the perfect partner in Sam. He had the site, courtesy of his father. And soon, after a little horse-trading with Miller, he would have the planes. Flying was the future. For the first time in years, the sky was wide and blue and full of promise.

'*Mr Maxted.*'

'What?' Max emerged from his fleeting reverie to find Miller looking towards him from the doorway of the office. 'What is it?'

'This call's for you.'

'For me? Impossible. No one knows I'm here.'

'Well, evidently your mother knows. And she wants to speak to you. She says it's urgent.'

'My mother? Confound it all.' Max glanced at Sam and shrugged helplessly, then hurried towards the office.

In the twenty seconds or so it took him to reach the telephone, Max concluded that the only way his mother could have tracked him to Hendon Aerodrome was first to have telephoned the flat. Saturday was one of Mrs Harrison's cleaning mornings. He had mentioned his destination to her on his way out. She must still have been there when Lady Maxted rang. But as explanations went it did not go far. Lady Maxted was of a generation that scarcely

made habitual use of the telephone. Off-hand he could not recall her ever calling him before.

He grasped the receiver. 'Mother?'

'James?' No telephone line could drain from her voice the querulousness that always seemed to attach itself to her pronunciation of his name.

'Yes. I'm here.'

'I think you should come home at once.' By home she meant Gresscombe Place, the house in Surrey where Max had spent a sizeable portion of his childhood and youth without ever quite thinking of it as home. 'There's been . . . an accident.'

'What sort of accident?' Max felt the mildest tug of anxiety, but nothing more. Surviving the aerial war in France had inured him to most of the calamities of everyday existence. Whatever his mother might be about to say, it surely did not represent a turning point in his life.

But such moments come when fate decrees. And this was such a moment. 'It's your father, James,' said Lady Maxted. 'He's been killed, I'm afraid.'

MAX USED TO TELL ANY FRIENDS WHO ASKED ABOUT HIS father that they could know him as well as he did simply by studying his entry in the Foreign Office List. He was only half-joking.

MAXTED, Sir Henry, 2nd Baronet, born 1853. Educated Eton and Trinity College, Cambridge. Clerkship in the Foreign Office, 1875. Assistant Private Secretary to Lord Granville, 1880–82. 3rd Secretary, Vienna, 1882–86. Vice-Consul, Budapest, 1886–89. 2nd Secretary, Tokyo, 1889–91. Home attachment, London, 1891–92. 2nd Secretary, Constantinople, 1892–96. 1st Secretary, later Chargé d'Affaires, Rio de Janeiro, 1896–1910. (Succeeded as 2nd Baronet, 1897.) Consular Counsellor, St Petersburg (later Petrograd) 1910–18.

That was as much as the latest edition revealed. There was no mention of Sir Henry's father, Sir Charles Maxted, a diplomat in his own right as well as a noted Assyriologist, who had earned the baronetcy his son inherited through his negotiation of the route of the Odessa–Tehran telegraph in the 1860s. Nor was his marriage to Winifred Clissold, the future Lady Maxted, alluded to. Their eldest son, Ashley, was born in 1882, Max's senior by nine years. Max was born in Tokyo, during the last posting on which his mother accompanied his father. She professed a dread of Turkish sanitation and sent her husband off to Constantinople alone. The threat of yellow fever precluded her joining him in Rio de Janeiro and by then the

7

pattern was set. Lady Maxted led a contented life in Surrey with little thought (as far as Max could tell) for Sir Henry's activities a continent or half a world away.

So it was that Max knew his father merely as an occasional visitor during periods of leave, which often coincided with his school or university terms, thereby limiting their contact to a stilted conversation in an Eton or Cambridge tea-room. Sir Henry struck the young Max as a gruff, stiff, emotionally restrained man, the archetypal diplomat in that sense, who conversed with his son about as freely as he might with an official of a foreign government. But perhaps he was too gruff and stiff for his own good. Rio de Janeiro was far from the diplomatic high road and St Petersburg was no place for him to spend the concluding years of his career. Lady Maxted sometimes referred to him 'losing his way', though precisely how he had done so she never specified.

Retirement was bound to reunite Sir Henry and Lady Maxted in due and problematical course. It came while the Great War was in its final months and Max was still a prisoner of the Germans. But by the time he was repatriated, in January 1919, Sir Henry was abroad on government business again. The British delegation to the Paris Peace Conference required the services of expert advisers in numerous fields. Sir Henry was asked to be one of them. He departed with what Lady Maxted later described as 'alacrity'.

Who, in the circumstances, could blame him? Paris, even in the aftermath of the war to end all wars, was still Paris. He was hardly to know that death lay in wait for him there.

After a hurried explanation, Max left Sam to stall Miller as best he could and set off for Surrey.

He and his mother had never enjoyed the warmest of relationships. There were reasons for that they had never spoken of and probably never would. He was not her idea of what a son should be. Nor was she his idea of a good mother. Still, Sir Henry's sudden death was an event which even Max acknowledged as a family emergency. His place, now if hardly ever, was at home. So, home he went.

The journey took longer than he would have wished, involving a

8

forced march to Hendon station, a train to St Pancras, a hectic
crossing of London by Tube and another train from Waterloo to
Epsom. The Tube he particularly loathed. The horror of confinement he carried with him from the camp meant his nerves were
tested whenever he descended into the Underground's malodorous
depths. The services were busy that day, reminding him how
uncomfortable he now was amidst any mass of humanity.

He was, of course, unduly familiar with death in numerous
forms and disguises, thanks to the swathe it had cut through his
squadron in France. But there were many men of his age carrying
gruesome memories with them into the genteel peacetime world.
He would have claimed no distinction on that account. He had
fully expected to die himself. The expectation had aged him, he
suspected. He was young, in the veritable prime of his life. But
he did not always feel so.

Yet the depression that had claimed some had never
touched him. 'You're a tough 'un and no mistake,' Sam had once
said to him, in the wake of a particularly heavy day of losses, when
Max had been keener to discuss minor adjustments to the gun-
mounting on his plane than mourn the comrades he had seen shot
down in flames. But toughness was not quite it. Max knew that to
allow himself to care would be fatal. 'This is all just a joke we can't
quite see the funny side of, Twentyman,' he had replied. And he had
believed it. That was why he had laughed the afternoon his luck
had run out behind German lines and, with a failed engine and a
jammed gun, he had gone down like a falling leaf spiralling
through the Flanders sky.

But his luck had not quite run out, not to the last morsel. The
shots that had stopped his engine had missed his fuel tank by a
matter of inches. And the ground was flat and soft enough to make
some kind of a landing. He had emerged, to his own astonishment,
in one piece.

And that astonishment stayed with him to this day, as an unsmiling light-heartedness, a blithe disregard for how others
expected him to lead his life. It meant the news of his father's death,
though surprising, had not shocked him. He was not indifferent to
such things, but he was well accustomed to them.

9

His mother had supplied little in the way of concrete information. Sir Henry had died in a fall from a roof, apparently. It was, Lady Maxted had emphasized, an accident. 'A tragic and dreadful accident.' How she could be sure of that she did not say and Max had known better than to ask. He would attempt to elicit more details when he reached Gresscombe. His brother would be there. He might be in possession of the facts. When it came to facts, Ashley could generally be relied upon. *Sir* Ashley, as he was now, of course. Max was going to find it hard to think of him as such, but he supposed he would grow used to it. Ashley himself would relish the status of the baronetcy, though perhaps not as much as his wife. Lydia had the prize for which Max suspected she had married his brother – and many years earlier than she could have expected. She would be mourning her father-in-law, but with secret satisfaction.

All in all, Sir Henry Maxted's passing was unlikely to prompt an outpouring of grief among his relatives. For the last twenty years and more he had been largely absent from their lives. He attributed this, in one of his typically lofty phrases, to 'the exigencies of the service', and Lady Maxted never suggested it was otherwise. To Max, however, it seemed an arrangement that suited both parties to the marriage. How Sir Henry filled the waking hours not given over to the tireless and patriotic pursuit of British interests in foreign parts Max could only imagine. As for his mother, good works, Surrey society and occasional forays to London appeared to content her, though Max had cause to believe that had not always been the case, if indeed it was now.

Sir Henry's death raised a delicate issue, however, one which Max turned over uneasily in his mind as the train steamed slowly through the countryside south of Wimbledon. He had not yet told Ashley of the agreement he had reached with their father and he doubted if Sir Henry had either, since there would surely have been some reaction to the news from his brother. The question now – the devilishly tricky question – was whether Ashley would honour the agreement, as the new owner of the Gresscombe estate. If not, Max's plans for the future, along with Sam's, would go badly awry. He had not mentioned this disturbing possibility to Sam. It had not

actually occurred to him until after he had left Hendon. Without the land his father had promised him, there could be no flying school. And the land was now in his brother's gift.

'Damn it all to hell, Pa,' Max murmured under his breath as he gazed out through the window of the train. 'Why'd you have to go and die on me?'

S IR CHARLES MAXTED, MAX'S GRANDFATHER, BOUGHT THE Gresscombe estate following an early retirement from the diplomatic service funded by his prudent investments in mining and railway stock. The estate had suffered from decades of neglect. But Sir Charles had a keen eye for a bargain. He re-tenanted Gresscombe Farm and demolished the tumbledown Georgian manor house to make way for an Arts and Craft mansion of his own commissioning. Gresscombe Place was a red-brick house of multiple gables and parapeted bays, with high windows to admit as much light as possible in a vain attempt to recreate the dazzling brilliance of Mesopotamia, where he had served as consul for fifteen years. An abundance of Middle Eastern rugs and beaten copper were nods in the same direction, overwhelmed since his death by the more cluttered and heavier-curtained tastes of his daughter-in-law.

Max barely remembered his grandfather. He was only six when the old man died. Sir Charles's greatest claim to fame was to have assisted Henry Rawlinson, his predecessor as consul in Baghdad, in his pioneering translation of cuneiform script. Max's father was named in honour of Rawlinson and Sir Charles pursued his interest in Sumero-Babylonian languages to the end of his days.

Haskins, the chauffeur, had been sent to meet Max at Epsom station. He was a taciturn fellow at the best of times and Max knew better than to seek his views on what he described, uncontroversially, as 'a bad business'. He would doubtless have said the

12

same, in the same neutral tone, if Max had been killed in the war. He was more sentimental about the internal combustion engine than the crazed doings of humankind.

Accordingly, there was nothing in the way of idle conversation to distract Max as they passed the flat quartet of fields west of the town where he planned to open his flying school. Sir Henry had agreed to their use for the purpose with disarming readiness. 'Gladly, my boy,' had been his exact words. But gladness was likely to be in short supply now at Gresscombe Place.

And so it proved. The family had gathered to discuss the sad news from France. None of the early-spring sunshine penetrated to the drawing-room where they were assembled: Lady Maxted, the Dowager Lady Maxted as she now was, with Ashley and Lydia, as well as Uncle George, Lady Maxted's brother. There was a notable dearth of tears, though Max would not have expected his mother to be prostrated by grief, even if she felt it. She was rigidly self-controlled at all times. She considered any display of emotion to be an admission of weakness. And she was not weak. Nor was her daughter-in-law. Lydia was a woman of hard features and firm opinions, who spoke to her husband, her children and indeed her brother-in-law in the same tone she used to instruct her several dogs and horses.

Ashley was predictably subdued in the presence of the two women who dominated his life. He was shorter and bulkier than Max, with darker hair, a puffier face and a ruddier complexion. A knee mangled in a hunting accident ten years before had left him with a slight limp that had spared him frontline service in the war. Somehow he had acquired a captaincy by sitting behind a desk in Aldershot for the duration. He never referred to the contrast with Max's aerial derring-do and nor did Max, but that did not mean either of them was heedless of it.

George Clissold had arrived hotfoot from an undemanding half-day in the City, where he was something (probably superfluous) in marine insurance. He was, as usual, not entirely sober, but sobriety had never suited him. Lady Maxted claimed to rely on him for advice in financial matters. For his part, Max would have

relied on him for nothing beyond the recommendation of a good malt whisky. But he was a genial and unobjectionable presence. And he did at least raise a smile at his nephew's arrival.

'Bit of a facer, what, James my lad?' he said in his rumbling voice as he clasped Max's hand.

'A terrible shock, Uncle, yes.' He turned to Lady Maxted. 'How are you, Mother?'

'It is a fearful blow, James,' she responded. 'But we must bear it.'

'That's the spirit, old girl,' said George.

Tea was served. Lydia plied Max with an unsought account of how bravely little Hetty had taken the news of her grandfather's death and the arrangement she had made for Giles's housemaster to inform him of the sad event. Max knew convention demanded that he display some interest in the welfare of his brother's children, but he felt even less able than usual to express any. Besides, Lydia was clearly only filling in until the maid left them to it.

'I shall tell you what Mr Fradgley from the embassy in Paris told me, James,' said Lady Maxted as soon as privacy was restored. 'Heaven knows, it leaves much unexplained, but I do implore you all to guard against unwarranted speculation.' She paused to let her request, which was more in the way of an instruction, sink in. There was already an implication that they should be guarding her good name as well as her late husband's. 'Some time last night, Henry fell from the roof of an apartment building in Montparnasse. Precisely when this occurred is unclear. No one seems to have seen him fall – that is, no one has yet come forward to say they did. He was found . . . in the early hours of the morning . . . by a group of people leaving a . . . well, some place of amusement. According to Mr Fradgley, there can be no doubt the fall killed him instantly, which is a blessing, I suppose. Mr Fradgley had already spoken to the police. They were satisfied the fall had been . . . accidental.'

Max assumed he was not alone in wondering how the police could be so swiftly satisfied on such a point. In the circumstances, suicide was surely a possibility, although not a likely one in his opinion. Sir Henry was hardly the self-destructive type and had been in notably good spirits when Max had visited him in Paris two weeks before. There was, of course, a third possibility. But he was

not about to mention it. Still, there was one obvious question he reckoned he could risk asking. 'How can the police know Pa fell from the roof rather than a window on one of the upper floors, Mother?'

'I don't know, James. There must be . . . evidence pointing to that.'

'But Mr Fradgley didn't say what the evidence was.'

'I'm sure the poor man didn't want to burden your mother with the particulars,' said Lydia.

'But he was definite this occurred in . . . Montparnasse?'

'Are you familiar with the area?' Lydia asked sharply, as if unfamiliarity with Montparnasse would somehow disqualify Max from querying the point.

'No, I'm not. But . . . his hotel was off the Champs-Elysées. That's a long way from Montparnasse.'

'Is it?'

'You know he was always very keen on astronomy,' said George. 'That'll be what got him up there. Someone offered him the use of their roof to admire the night sky. It was the equinox, wasn't it?'

Into Max's mind came a memory of his father instructing him in the distribution of the constellations one clear summer night around the turn of the century, when his home leave had briefly intersected with Max's school holiday. Sir Henry had given him a cardboard-mounted chart of the heavens – a planisphere – as a late birthday present and shown him how to identify Perseus and Orion and the Great Bear. On the reverse was a chart of the southern sky, the one Sir Henry saw from his residence in Rio. Max had looked long and often at it after Sir Henry's departure, imagining what it was like to be so far away that even the stars were different.

'Please, George,' said his mother, her words cutting through the memory. 'This is exactly the sort of futile supposition I wish to avoid.' She allowed herself a sigh of exasperation. 'And it is why I want you and Ashley to go to Paris as soon as possible, James, to clarify the circumstances of your father's death and to arrange for his body to be brought home for a funeral here in Surrey at the earliest opportunity.'

'Really?'

'I can't see why we both need to go,' said Ashley in his first contribution to the discussion. 'I can perfectly well deal with . . . whatever needs dealing with.'

'You must both go,' said Lady Maxted, in a tone Max recognized as brooking no contradiction. 'It is only fitting that his two sons should accompany him . . . on his final return to these shores.'

'Well . . .'

'You will do this for your father, won't you, James?' His mother stared expectantly at him.

'Of course, Mother.' He glanced at Ashley, who was frowning dubiously. The arrangement evidently did not suit him, nor in all likelihood Lydia, which was something to commend it from Max's point of view. 'Of course I'll go.'

AFTER TEA, ASHLEY SUGGESTED MAX ACCOMPANY HIM TO HIS study, so that they might consult *Bradshaw* and plan their journey. Max suspected he also wanted a word alone with him, out of their mother's – and his wife's – earshot.

Certainly planning the journey did not occupy them for long. 'We can have Haskins run us up to town first thing in the morning and catch the eleven o'clock train from Victoria. Where did you stay when you went over?'

'The Mazarin. Pa booked it for me. He said it was one of the few places not overrun by delegates to the peace conference.'

'Conveniently located?'

'I should say. Halfway between the Arc de Triomphe and the Eiffel Tower.'

'We'll cable them, then. We shan't need to stay for more than a couple of days.'

'You don't think so?'

'You heard Mother. Sort out the paperwork and ship Pa home p.d.q. That's what she wants. So, that's what she must have.'

'But we don't know what we'll find out when we get there, Ashley.'

Ashley hurrumphed at that and subsided into the chair behind his desk. Above him hung, as it always had, a large framed map of Mesopotamia circa 1850. The study had originally been their grandfather's and was furnished much as he had left it. The clay jar on the desk that served as a pencil-pot could easily have been thousands of years old, chanced upon in one of the places marked

17

on the map. Max had been angling for a transfer to the Mesopotamian Front in the months before he was shot down. He had dreamt of flying over the sun-baked remains of the ancient civilization whose language his grandfather had helped to translate. But a dream was all it had been.

Ashley flicked open the silver cigarette-box that stood beside the pencil-pot, took out a cigarette, tamped it on the blotter and lit up. Max sat down and lit one for himself. A short interlude of fraternal understanding elapsed as smoke curled into the air between them. Then Ashley said, 'Unless you credit Uncle George's hare-brained idea about star-gazing, it's hard to imagine anything reputable lying behind this . . . accident.'

'What are you suggesting?'

'You saw Pa more recently than I did. How would you describe his . . . state of mind?'

'Cheerful. Optimistic. Rather more so than I'd have expected.'

'Retirement didn't suit him, you know. He prowled round here like a caged lion. He greeted the summons to join our delegation in Paris as a gift from the gods. "I'm back in the saddle," he said to me.'

'He said the government wanted someone with knowledge of Brazilian politics to advise them on how to respond to Brazil's claims at the peace conference. Something to do with confiscated German ships and impounded cargoes of coffee.'

'Coffee? Small beer, more like. I can't believe his expertise has been in high demand. And given that, he's probably not been kept very busy . . .'

'Yes?'

'An accident pure and simple's highly unlikely, James. You know that as well as I do. And suicide's out of the question, I think we can agree. Montparnasse is a long way from the Champs-Elysées, as you yourself pointed out. I believe it has a somewhat . . . dissolute reputation.'

Max shrugged. 'I bow to your superior knowledge.'

'Well, it's full of artists, isn't it?'

'I believe so.'

'There you are, then. Models *au naturel*. Drugs. Drink. Debauchery of all kinds.'

'I'm sure that's a—'

'The point is, Pa probably started mixing in circles he shouldn't have and ended up dead. How exactly, we may never know. And perhaps we *needn't* know. If the French police are happy to write it off as an accident, there's no sense our raising a stink, is there?'

'Well, Mother wouldn't want us to, it's true.'

'She certainly wouldn't.' Ashley regarded Max studiously through a slowly exhaled plume of smoke. 'We're of one mind on this, are we?'

'I won't do anything that risks . . . embarrassing our family, if that's what you mean.'

'Good.'

1042 516/AFP

'Though—'

'Why did you go and see him, by the way?'

'Pa?'

'Yes. Why did you go and see him?'

Max was damned if he would pretend this was anything but a strange question, even though it was not quite as strange as he meant to imply. 'I hadn't seen him in nearly five years, Ashley. Even by our standards, that's a long gap.'

'You'll have noticed how his time in Russia aged him.'

'He *was* five years older. Like me. I dare say I'm not as twinkle-eyed and clear-browed as I was in 1914. Actually, I thought he was . . . surprisingly invigorated.'

'And receptive?'

'If you like.'

'You had no other reason for going, then? No . . . proposal to put to him?'

So, now they had come to it. Sir Henry had promised he would write to Ashley, telling him of his agreement to let Max open his flying school on part of the estate. Max had expected to hear from Ashley once he had received the letter. He had heard nothing. Until now. 'Did he write to you?'

'Yes.' Ashley opened the desk drawer and pulled out a letter, still in its envelope. The stamp was French and Max recognized the handwriting as his father's. 'A flying school, eh? Well, well. That's your plan for the future, is it, James?'

'Pa liked the sound of it.'

'I doubt Barratt will.'

Barratt was the tenant at Gresscombe Farm. According to Sir Henry, he had no legal right to object and Max had confidently assumed that was true. 'He doesn't seem to be making much use of the fields.'

'Appearances can be deceptive in farming, as you'd know if you'd ever taken an interest in the estate. I've had to manage the place in Pa's absence. You may be surprised to learn it doesn't run itself.'

'Are you going to let me open the flying school, Ashley?' The moment had come to pose the question directly.

'Do you really think you can make a success of it?'

'Certainly.'

'These are straitened times. Who's going to have money to throw away on flying lessons?'

'People who see the commercial potential in becoming a pilot and consequently *won't* be throwing their money away.'

'And what is the commercial potential? No, no.' Ashley held up his hand. 'We can save this for the trip. Make a good enough case, James, and, who knows, I might let you go ahead.'

'I was hoping you'd honour Pa's agreement.'

'I'd like to, obviously.' Ashley smiled, but his smile in fact made nothing obvious. 'I have to consider the financial security of the estate as a whole. I wasn't going to mention it, but Lydia's expecting another child. And there'll be no easy money for anyone while the nation pays off its war debts. Pa may not have thought this through properly.' His smile broadened. 'I owe it to the family to be sure that I do.'

WINIFRED, THE DOWAGER LADY MAXTED, HAD ANNOUNCED that she would rest before dinner. She had retired to her room, where she lay on her bed and contemplated the slow advance of twilight through the half-curtained windows.

Sir Henry's retirement from the diplomatic service had hung over her head for a decade or more as an unwelcome but unavoidable end to a long separation both had found increasingly congenial. Strictly speaking, she could not be sure Sir Henry had found it congenial, but he had never given her cause to doubt it. She assumed and rather hoped he had found some discreet companionship along the way. She bore him no ill will. And certainly she would not have wished him dead in this sudden, strange and possibly scandalous manner. A fall from a roof in Paris, indeed. She shook her head at the tragic inappropriateness of it all. This was not how Sir Henry Maxted should have ended his days – though, to be sure, precisely how he had ended them she did not know.

She thought for a moment of how close they had been at the loving outset of their marriage, of the lengths she had been prepared to go to to ensure his happiness and to protect his good name. Tears came into her eyes for the first time since she had heard of his death. 'My poor dear Henry,' she murmured. 'Who would have predicted this?'

There came a knock at the door. She dabbed her eyes with her handkerchief and was instantly composed. 'Come in,' she called. She did not sit up, for she knew who her visitor was. And he would take her as he found her. He always had.

'You wanted a word, Win,' said George Clissold, stepping quietly into the room. There was something in his tone and bearing that was fractionally different from the buffoonish uncle he had presented himself as in the drawing-room. 'Is this a good time? If you really do need to rest . . .'

'Sit down and tell me how I'm placed.'

George conveyed an armchair to the foot of the bed and eased himself into it. The evening light fell obliquely on his silvery hair and handsome man-of-the-world features and Winifred smiled affectionately at him.

'Why did you never marry, George?'

'Who'd have had me?'

'There were quite a few who were willing, as I recall.'

'But I always played fair by letting them glimpse the depraved core of my being before I popped the question. That generally settled it.'

'What nonsense you do talk.'

'Yes. I'm known for it. And nonsense is what I may have been talking when I said I thought I'd seen Henry last week. I was probably mistaken. Chance resemblances are common enough. He was out of sight before I could get a proper look at him.'

'It was Henry you saw.'

'A few days ago you were sceptical, to say the least. What's changed your mind?'

'A letter from the curator of the county museum.'

'What has he to do with it?'

'Some years ago – many years ago, in fact – Henry's father presented to the museum a small collection of what the curator tells me are Sumerian cylinder-seals. I've never actually seen them. I'm not even sure they've been on display recently. He didn't say.'

'And you don't visit the museum often.'

'No. Nor had Henry ever interested himself in the seals, as far as I know. Until last week. They were only on loan, it seems, albeit indefinitely extended. But last week, on the very day you thought you saw him in Lombard Street, he went to the museum and reclaimed them.'

'Did he, now?'

'Yes. The curator wasn't there. He wrote to me asking for an address where he could contact Henry, in order to ascertain whether their removal was permanent. He mentioned that the seals are probably . . . quite valuable.'

'Really?'

'It's clear to me Henry told no one he was in England because he didn't want to have to explain the purpose of his visit. What could have taken him to Lombard Street, George?'

'His bank.'

'Money, in other words.'

George shrugged. 'Probably.'

'And I think we can assume he didn't want the Sumerian cylinder-seals to decorate his hotel room in Paris.'

'I admit it sounds as though he was . . . raising funds.'

'I don't care about ancient Mesopotamian knick-knackery. But I do care about this house and the estate. Ashley has his children to consider. Lydia's expecting again, you know.'

'You always said she was good breeding stock.'

'I'm sure I never said anything so indelicate.'

'Perhaps I said it, then.'

'My concern is that if Henry was so desperate for cash that he resorted to pillaging the county museum, might he have mortgaged the estate?'

'We'll know soon enough if he did. Once the boys return from Paris with a death certificate, we can make the necessary enquiries.'

'And learn the worst.'

'Mortgages aren't agreed and paid overnight, old girl. Even if he was in London to negotiate one, it's highly unlikely the capital will have been released yet.'

'Let's hope not.' Winifred sighed. 'What can he have got himself mixed up in, George?'

'It may be better for you never to know.'

'Papa was so pleased when I told him Henry would be asking for my hand in marriage. "You can't go wrong with a Foreign Office wallah, Winifred," he said. And I believed him. I believed him absolutely.'

'Why wouldn't you? Henry always seemed such a fine fellow.'

'He was. In his way.'

'Brigham's in Paris, isn't he?'

Winifred propped herself up and frowned at her brother. 'Half the Foreign Office is in Paris. What are you implying?'

'Nothing. But if he crosses Ashley's and James's path . . .'

'There's no reason why he should. He may write to me, of course, offering his condolences. I'm sure many people will write to me. Henry was well liked wherever he went.'

'Are you sure Ashley *and* James is a good idea? They always tend to rub each other up the wrong way.'

'It's time they learnt to cooperate. I don't want their . . . temperamental differences . . . to fester into some kind of feud.'

'An admirable sentiment, I'm sure.'

'But a foolish one, in your opinion?'

'Not at all. You know them better than I do. They're *your* sons.'

'Hah!' Winfred laid her head back on the pillow. 'Only someone with no children could suppose that having them means you understand them. You never do, George, believe me, you never do. Ashley and James are grown men, and Henry was their father. They must do their best for him. And I must let them.'

MAX TOOK A SIP OF WHISKY AND REPLACED THE GLASS ON the chair beside his towel, then lay back in the bath and let the heat of the water ease some of the stresses and anxieties of the day. He had returned from Germany ten weeks before – ten weeks that sometimes felt much longer than that and sometimes much less – determined to live his life henceforth on his own terms. Being alive at all was so outrageous a piece of good fortune that he had no intention of squandering his existence on dull pursuits and workaday routine.

So much for intentions. They did not trump circumstances. The flying school was such a good idea. He did not want to abandon it. He knew Sam was pinning his hopes of liberation from the family bakery business on it. He was pinning a good many hopes on it himself. And the last thing he wanted to do was to let Sam down. But could he trust himself to dance obediently to Ashley's tune in order to pursue it?

Everything had seemed so much simpler a fortnight ago. He had travelled to Paris, wondering how his father would react to his request. His memories of their meeting were confused by a growing suspicion that he had overlooked abundant evidence that all was not well in his father's world, so preoccupied was he with the question of the flying school. To be sure, Sir Henry had been cheery and welcoming. But in retrospect his exuberance had been unnatural. He too had been preoccupied, happy to let Max do whatever he wanted with a portion of the Gresscombe estate, perhaps because he was caught up in matters which made the fate

25

of four fields west of Epsom seem as distant as it was insignificant.

But what might those matters have been? And did they have any bearing on Sir Henry's death? Max took another sip of whisky, rested his neck against the rim of the bath and tried to force his brain to reconstruct the details of their final encounter in search of the answers.

The journey from London to Paris was supposed to take seven hours, but there were delays all along the line in France and Max's train eventually pulled into the Gare du Nord three hours late. He went straight to the hotel Sir Henry had booked for him, the Mazarin, in Rue Coligny. There was a note waiting for him there on Hotel Majestic writing paper.

5.iii.19

Dear boy,
Welcome to Paris. I am so sorry about this, but I have to cancel our luncheon engagement for tomorrow. I am not my own master during this damned conference. But dine with me instead. The Ritz at eight. It will be a grand evening.
Affectionately,
Your father

There they were again, Max, supposed: those famous exigencies of the service. The peace conference was important. No one who had fought in the war could doubt that. It was a re-ordering of the world map – the creation of new countries and boundaries intended to heal the old divisions. It was the shaping of a future that would be safe for all to live in.

Still, his father's postponement of their reunion seemed odd, not to say unfeeling. As he unpacked, Max decided he would not simply wait for their dinner date at the Ritz. The Majestic was only a shortish walk away. Armed with directions from the concierge, he set off into the Paris evening. His hopes for a touch of spring were misplaced.

A fellow looking remarkably unlike a Parisian hotel doorman was guarding the entrance to the Majestic. He was, in fact, as he

swiftly revealed, a Scotland Yard detective. No chances were being taken with security at the headquarters of the British delegation. Without a pass, or someone to vouch for him, Max was not going to gain admittance.

He was escorted as far as the reception desk, however. But Sir Henry Maxted was out. 'He generally leaves very early and returns very late,' the clerk informed him, discouragingly. The clerk, like the policeman, was English. 'I've been imported from the Grand in Birmingham, sir,' he explained, noting Max's puzzlement. 'The gentlemen from the Foreign Office wouldn't be happy with French staff. They want people they can rely on. So, here we all are.'

'Would you tell Sir Henry when he gets in that his son called to see him?'

'Certainly, but I wouldn't like to say when that might be, if you know what I mean.'

Max was far from sure he did know what the man meant, but he left it at that. He felt a sudden desire for life, colour and entertainment. He hopped into a cab and named the Folies Bergères as his destination.

Max rose late the following morning and treated himself to a gentle day. He walked down to the Seine and crossed to the Quai d'Orsay, briefly joining the small band of onlookers outside the French Foreign Ministry, hoping for a glimpse of someone notable – Lloyd George, perhaps, or President Wilson – coming or going. But those who came and went were anonymous functionaries to a man. He returned to the Right Bank and wandered east, noting the captured German cannons in the Place de la Concorde and the enormous bomb crater in the Tuileries rose garden. There were refugees everywhere from the war zones and disabled ex-servicemen begging at street corners. He rewarded them with cigarettes, which he suspected were more valuable than the sous and centimes in his pockets. The war was over. But in Paris it could not be said to have ended. It was settling around him: the dust of a vast upheaval falling slowly to earth.

*

27

The Ritz was as glittering an oasis of opulence as Max had hoped. There were no doorkeepers from Scotland Yard to be braved. It was open house for those with money and fine clothes, many of whom were laughing and flirting over cocktails in the bar. It was there that Max waited for his father, after leaving word for him with the maître d' of the restaurant. To Max's no very great surprise, Sir Henry was late.

'Dear boy,' were Sir Henry's first words to his son, before astonishing him with a hug. Stiff handshakes had been their usual greeting, but Sir Henry was in an expansive, expressive mood. He looked older than when they had last met because he was. His dress and appearance were those of a senior civil servant of a bygone era: bow-tied, starch-collared, frock-coated and Edwardianly bewhiskered. But that, Max instantly sensed, was not the whole story. There was a sparkle in his pale-blue eyes, a warmth to his smile and something Max could only have described as a bounce in his bearing. He was not as stout as he had been either. He looked like a man with plenty on his mind, but uplifted because of it.

Champagne was ordered and Max soon found himself infected with some of his father's unwonted good cheer. They moved into the restaurant and were plied with fine food and wine by waiters gliding to and fro beneath glistening chandeliers. Max was persuaded to describe a few of his more hair-raising exploits with the RFC and to recount some of his experiences as a prisoner of war. Sir Henry could hardly be said to have had a quiet war himself. From his post at the British Embassy in St Petersburg, he had had a ringside seat during the upheavals of the Russian revolution. 'They were dangerous days, my boy. I could easily have got in the way of a Bolshevik bullet if my luck had been out. Fortunately, the Ambassador took pity on the older members of staff and took us with him when he was evacuated. The people we left behind had a very rough time of it, I can tell you.'

And what of his activities in Paris, which were evidently keeping him so busy? Officially, he explained, he was there to give advice to the leaders of the British delegation, as and when required, about the demands and expectations of the Brazilian delegation in

respect of German merchant ships held in Brazilian ports and cargoes of Brazilian coffee the Germans had never paid for. 'It shouldn't matter a damn to LG.' (Sir Henry referred to the Prime Minister so casually Max assumed they were on familiar terms.) 'But our American cousins want to be seen to be doing their continental neighbours a few favours, so we have to be on our guard. And fourteen years in Rio de Janeiro made me the closest to an expert the FO could find. Most of the time, though, I just make myself useful. And when that fails I try to enjoy myself. I always wanted a posting to the Paris embassy, but I never got it. This is the next best thing.'

It was over Tokay and crêpes Suzette that Max finally unveiled his plans for a post-war career as a flying instructor. By then he was optimistic that his father would give him the use of the land he needed at Gresscombe. And his optimism was not misplaced. 'You shall have it, James, you shall indeed. I'll write to Ashley and have him tell Barratt to grub up whatever miserable crop he's planted and make way for you. It's the least I can do – the least *he* can do – after what you flyers endured in the service of your country.'

The discussion could hardly have gone better. And in the circumstances it seemed fitting to return to the bar after their meal to toast Max's airborne future with the Ritz's finest cognac. It was there that the evening took a faintly puzzling turn, when a man detached himself from a party in the farthest corner of the room and came across to greet Sir Henry as a close, if not necessarily cordial, acquaintance.

He was tall, lean and slightly crooked in his posture, immaculately dressed and groomed, but with rugged features bordering on rough and a scar, partially concealed by a pencil moustache, that distorted his left nostril. He had dark, wary eyes and a fine head of grey-flecked hair. He was not the sort of man it was easy to place at a glance, either as to nationality or profession, although, as soon as he spoke, it was obvious he was an American.

'Good to see you, Henry,' he drawled. 'Who's your young friend?'

'My son, James. James, this is Travis Ireton.'

Max rose to shake Ireton's hand. His grip was firm and cool, his

gaze likewise. Max had the disquieting impression that he was being treated to swift but skilful scrutiny.

'Are you with the US delegation, Mr Ireton?'

'Sometimes. With but not of, that is. More often neither. I'm here in a freelance capacity. And you?'

'Visiting my father.'

'Ah, you'll be the pilot. Henry's mentioned you. Congratulations.'

'For what?'

'Surviving. Not many did, did they?'

'I was lucky.'

'Aren't we all? To be here in Paris, having a swell time of it, while gatherings of old men in smoke-filled committee-rooms decide the fate of the world.'

'If you take a look at Travis's passport, you'll see he records his occupation as cynic,' Sir Henry remarked affably. 'Who are you with, Travis?'

'Rumanians.' Ireton glanced back over his shoulder. 'I'd better not leave them too long. Patience isn't one of their strengths.' Max glanced in the same direction and saw several dramatically moustachioed men glaring towards him. 'But we need to talk, Henry, you and I. You've been . . . elusive . . . recently.'

'Elusive? No, no, merely busy, I assure you.'

'But busy with what? That's the question. There are quite a few people who—' Ireton cut himself off with a strange little half-smile of self-reproval. 'We do need to talk.'

'Then we will.' Sir Henry grinned. 'Those Rumanians are looking restive, Travis.'

'Good of you to point that out to me, Henry. Excuse me, will you?'

As soon as Ireton was safely back on the far side of the room, Max sat down and asked his father, 'Who's he, exactly?'

'He's a man who talks to everybody and tells them nothing,' Sir Henry replied. 'He's never been inside one of those smoke-filled committee-rooms he referred to. But he knows what's said in them. Often word for word.'

'How does he manage that?'

30

'By persuading people like me to be indiscreet.'

'You'd never be indiscreet, Pa. It's against your nature.'

'I'll accept that as a compliment, my boy. You're right, I'm glad to say. I'm impervious to the wiles of Travis Ireton. But he never gives up, even when he should. And now . . . I think this may be the moment for me to give up, before I have one cognac too many.'

They walked back to their hotels together along the Champs-Elysées. Sir Henry puffed at a cigar and listened with occasional nods of encouragement as Max expounded his case for the air as the universal medium of transport in the future. 'Roads and railways are old hat, Pa. One day you'll be able to fly across the Atlantic – or round the world – as a fare-paying passenger. The war did aircraft design a big favour.'

'I'm glad it achieved something, James. And that you may benefit from it.'

'It'll happen, Pa. Believe me.'

'I'm sure it will. I wonder if I'll live to see any of it come to pass, though.'

'I should jolly well hope so. Why don't you take a maiden flight with me once we have the flying school ready?'

'I should like that.'

'Consider yourself booked in.'

Sir Henry pulled up and turned to his son with a smile. 'Capital, my boy.' He clapped Max on the shoulder. 'Capital.'

They parted at the door of the Majestic. Sir Henry did not look back as he went in. And it did not cross Max's mind even as a remote possibility that he would never see his father again.

MAX STEPPED OUT EARLY FROM GRESSCOMBE PLACE ON Sunday morning to post a letter in the box at the end of the drive. He had written to Sam, explaining that he would be out of the country for a few days, but that they should be able to complete the purchase of the aircraft they had their eyes on as soon as he returned. He said nothing in the letter about the possibility that the land for their flying school might no longer be available. There was nothing to be gained by worrying Sam at this stage.

Why he did not simply leave the letter for one of the servants to post he would have been hard-pressed to explain. But the war had taught him to bestow his trust sparingly. Self-reliance was his unspoken watchword.

Max's progress back up the drive was observed by Lydia from her bedroom window, as she sat brushing her hair at the dressing-table. There he was, that strange brother-in-law of hers she had never understood nor greatly liked. She could not help reflecting how much more convenient it would have been if he had died in the war. Lydia would have been happy to pay tribute to him then. James valiantly deceased would have earned her fond praises. James stubbornly and inconsiderately alive was a beast of quite a different stripe.

She turned at the sound of the door opening behind her. Ashley, shaved and washed, had returned from the bathroom, ready for his early start for Paris – *their* early start, that was, his and James's.

'Your brother's already been out,' she said, signalling with a

32

twitch of her eyebrows her bemusement at the doings and purposes of James Maxted. 'I've just seen him coming back – from a walk, presumably.'

'Perhaps he couldn't sleep,' said Ashley. 'I didn't have a restful night myself.'

'Are you worried, darling?'

'I wouldn't be, if Mother had had the good sense to send me alone.'

'What is she thinking of by involving James?'

'What is she *ever* thinking of?' Ashley sighed and patted Lydia's shoulder. 'I wish I knew.'

'You must keep James on a tight rein in Paris, darling. We don't want him . . . stirring anything up.'

'Indeed we don't. But I believe I have the means to ensure he doesn't.'

'You're not seriously considering letting him proceed with this flying school nonsense?'

'Good God, no. Pa should never have agreed to such a half-baked proposal. I haven't the least intention of allowing James to turn good agricultural land into an aerodrome. But nor do I intend to tell him that – just yet.'

'After the funeral, perhaps?'

'Yes. That's exactly what I was thinking. After we've brought Pa home and buried him. That'll be the time to tell James how matters stand. Until then, I'm hopeful he'll be on his . . . best behaviour.'

'You are clever, darling.'

'Not clever, my dear. Merely . . . practical.'

As Max crossed the hall, bound for the dining-room, where he supposed breakfast would be waiting for him, he noticed that the door to the library was open. His mother stepped out through it to greet him.

'Good morning, James,' she said quietly. 'Do you have a moment?'

'Of course, Mother.'

He followed her into the library. The room faced east and was

33

normally one of the darkest in the house. Only at this hour was sunlight, albeit of a watery variety, flooding through the high bay window at the far end. Lady Maxted walked towards it and came to a halt by the massive floor-standing globe that was one of the more memorable fixtures of Gresscombe Place.

'When you were a child, the globe was always at this angle,' she said, laying her hand on a gleaming curve of the north-western Pacific Ocean.

'Really?' Max joined her beside it and realized that it was true. He had regularly turned the globe and peered at the islands of the Japanese archipelago and wondered what his birthplace was like. He shrugged. 'Well, it's strange to have been born somewhere one has no memory or knowledge of.'

'We lived in Japan for two years. I assure you I had little more knowledge of the country at the end of that time than I had at the beginning.'

'But you remember it.'

'Increasingly, my memories seem like recollected dreams. Spring blossom so bright it hurt my eyes. A deafening chorus of frogs after heavy rain. Junks bobbing on the water. Winking cages of fireflies on a market stall. Ghost-moths thumping against the window-screens on hot summer nights. Really, what does any of that amount to? Impressions, nothing more. And even they are fading.'

'I should like to go there one day.'

'Then I'm sure you will. You do as you please, James. You always have.'

'Are you praising me or rebuking me, Mother?'

'Neither. I am quite reconciled to the fact that you have never been what might be termed an obedient son.'

'Perhaps Ashley does enough obeying for both of us.'

'Perhaps he does. I know I can rely on him to protect your father's memory at all costs. Whereas you . . .'

'Whereas I?'

'Will go in search of the truth . . . wherever it is to be found.'

'Would you prefer me not to?'

'No one should act against their nature. I'm confident you won't. All I ask is this: if you discover your father was the victim of

something other than an accident and if you discover what that something other was . . .'

'Yes?'

'I should like to hear of it before you proclaim it to the world.'

Max felt the full force of his mother's gaze as he stood before her. He had supposed she wanted him to support his brother loyally in suppressing any scandal they came across in Paris. But it appeared she did not believe him capable of fulfilling such a role. Nor did she want him to. She had something altogether more subversive in mind. 'I suspect Ashley would be more than a little alarmed by this conversation,' he said.

'Then don't mention it to him. I certainly won't.'

'Very well.'

'Do I have your word?'

'That I will tell you the truth – if I uncover it – before I tell anyone else?'

'Precisely.'

It was a safe enough bargain, Max thought. He could follow Ashley's lead and assure his mother there was no sinister explanation for Sir Henry's death. He had ample room for manoeuvre. Troublingly, though, he was beginning to believe he would need all of it. 'You have my word, Mother.'

She stepped forward and kissed him on the cheek. 'Thank you, James. I know you will keep it. Tread carefully in Paris, won't you?'

'But not *too* carefully?'

She smiled at him. 'There is no danger of you doing that.'

An hour later, after hurried breakfasts and equally hurried farewells, Max and his brother set off.

MAX SURPRISED HIMSELF BY MAINTAINING AN EVEN TEMPER and a flow of uncontroversial conversation as the journey proceeded. His brother Ashley – *Sir* Ashley now, as Max felt sure he would not be allowed to forget – expatiated, with no apparent sense of irony, on the challenges of managing the military supply chain in time of war. Aldershot sounded positively perilous in his version of events.

He had never been as near the Front as he was now going, however. The devastation to be seen from the train near Amiens, stretching around them, had a noticeable effect on him. Perhaps, Max thought, he could dimly imagine the horror buried not so deep beneath the mangled earth. It shamed him, though he hid the emotion as best he could. Ashley was not about to admit that Max had been one of those braving the hazards his crocked knee had spared him.

Ashley had cabled Fradgley at the embassy in Paris telling him of their travel plans. A note from him was waiting for them at the Hotel Mazarin on Lion-&-Unicorn-crested paper.

> March 23, 1919
>
> Dear Sir Ashley,
> Thank you for your cable. I hope it will be convenient if I
> call at your hotel at 9.30 on Monday morning to discuss
> with you and your brother the circumstances of your father's
> regrettable demise and the procedures it is necessary to

36

follow in order to repatriate the body. I will be accompanied
by Mr Appleby of the security detail to the British
delegation to the peace conference. I trust this will be
satisfactory.
Respectfully yours,
W. H. Fradgley

'It's dated today,' was Ashley's first reaction.

'What of it?' Max asked, feeling vaguely curious about his
brother's thought processes.

'A civil servant bestirring himself on a Sunday suggests our visit
is being taken seriously. It's an indication that they mean to show
us every consideration. As they should.'

A more sinister possibility had occurred to Max. The attention
they were receiving suggested to him that Sir Henry's death was a
problem the likes of Fradgley wanted to solve as quickly and easily
as possible. And that did not necessarily involve establishing the
truth of what had happened to him. 'How very reassuring.'

Ashley nodded in agreement, apparently believing Max meant
what he had said. 'It is, isn't it?'

A desolate Sunday evening stretched ahead. Max had no intention
of spending it dining with Ashley and enduring another
outbreak of Aldershotian reminiscence. He said he was in need of
an early night and went up to his room; then, as soon as the coast
was clear, he took himself off in search of entertainment.

The ringing of the telephone roused him the following morning.
Being jolted awake always had the same effect on him. He believed
for a moment that he was back with his squadron and his first
thought was the thought that greeted him unfailingly in those
wartime dawns. *I'm damned if this will be the day I die.*

Then the gloomy furnishings of his hotel room came into focus
around him. He fumbled for the telephone.

'James?' It was his brother. And he did not sound happy.

'Yes . . . Ashley.' Max covered the receiver and cleared his throat.
'Good morning.'

37

'Fradgley and Appleby will be here in fifteen minutes. I thought I ought to check with you that you'll be ready.'

'Oh, yes, yes. I'll, er . . . be down directly.'

'Did I wake you?'

'No, no. Of course not.'

'Mmm. I'll see you shortly, then.'

Max was no stranger to washing and shaving against the clock. He reached the lobby with one of the fifteen minutes remaining and spotted Ashley grumpily perusing a newspaper in the writing-room.

'How goes the world?' Max ventured by way of greeting.

'Badly.' Ashley folded up his newspaper in an explosion of rustling. 'The Reds are running amok in Budapest.'

'I had no idea.'

'Don't you follow the news?'

'Would it benefit me if I did?'

Ashley frowned at him, uncertain, as so often, whether to take Max's remarks seriously. 'That early night doesn't seem to have done you a lot of good.'

'Sometimes you can have too much sleep.'

'Symptoms of which are bags under the eyes and a deathly pallor, I assume.'

'The lighting in here isn't catching me at my best.'

'Flippancy isn't likely to serve us well today, James.' Ashley tossed the newspaper aside and stood up. 'I believe our visitors have arrived.' He nodded towards the lobby.

It was easy for Max to tell which of the two was Fradgley and which was Appleby. He took the short, thin, pale-faced man with a tight little mouth to be Fradgley, every inch the self-effacing minor diplomat, and his bulky, balding, jowly companion of the far-seeing gaze and self-possessed smile was surely Appleby.

Introductions swiftly confirmed Max's surmise. Appleby, he noted, was plain Mr Appleby, though an admission to high police rank would have been no surprise. He had the cautious, watchful demeanour of some kind of detective, combined with an air of authority.

38

He and Fradgley expressed brisk condolences before explaining what assistance they could offer. 'Your father's body was removed to the mortuary of the military hospital at Port-Royal,' he said. 'I assume you'd like to satisfy yourselves as to his identity.'

Ashley appeared taken aback by the possibility that it could be in doubt. 'Surely you've established that.'

'Of course, Sir Ashley,' said Fradgley, suddenly all of a flutter. 'It's merely a formality.'

'We would like to view the body,' said Max.

'Naturally.' Appleby eyed Max as if it was now obvious to him which of the brothers he should pay attention to. 'And then the address where the fall occurred?'

'Yes.'

'Then let's proceed. We have a car waiting.'

They were driven across the Seine by the Pont de l'Alma, then along the quais as far as the National Assembly, before heading south towards Montparnasse. Fradgley set out in exhaustive detail the procedures that would have to be followed to permit the removal of Sir Henry's body from France, assuring them through-out that he would personally attend to such matters and that he hoped to complete them within twenty-four hours. His purpose seemed to be to emphasize just how hard he was working on their behalf, though Max wondered if all this bureaucratic bustle was actually on someone else's account.

Fradgley was sandwiched between Max and Ashley on the rear seat, while Appleby sat beside the driver, puffing at a pipe and cast-ing occasional glances at Max over his shoulder. *Let the silly little man talk himself dry*, his wary half-smile seemed to communicate. *Then you and I can get down to business.* All he actually said in the course of the journey, though, was a remark on the weather, after rain had begun to pelt the windscreen. 'Paris in the spring can be rather overrated, you'll find.'

L'Hôpital Militaire, Boulevard de Port-Royal, was an echoing warren of a place, the air tinged with disinfectant, the corridors peopled by sombre nurses and amputees from the war learning to

39

walk with only one leg – or none at all. The mortuary was in a distant, largely silent wing, where no nurses were to be seen, only overalled functionaries apparently immune to the prevailing chill.

Sir Henry's body was waiting for them on a trolley in a cold, windowless room. There was a taint of decay in the icy air, Max noticed. If anyone else noticed it, they did not say. But Fradgley lingered in the doorway behind them, as if reluctant to come too close.

An attendant raised the sheet covering Sir Henry's face. The right side of his head was covered by a bandage, but there was no doubt it was him, altered though he was by death: the eyes closed, the mouth unsmiling, the spirit gone.

'He suffered a severe brain injury in the fall,' said Appleby. 'Death would have been instantaneous.'

There were various cuts and scrapes around the visible part of Sir Henry's face, bruising and swelling around his eye and rucklings of the flesh at the edge of the bandage that hinted at the damage beneath.

'Were there other injuries?' Max asked.

'Most of the bones in his body were probably broken,' Appleby replied. 'It was a long drop.'

'I think we've seen enough,' said Ashley, his voice cracking as he spoke. 'It's certainly our father.'

'We should retrieve his signet ring,' said Max. 'Mother will want to have it.'

'It'll already have been removed,' said Appleby. 'Commissioner Zamaron of the Paris police has his personal effects. We're due to collect them later from the *préfecture*.'

'Could we just check, in case it's been overlooked?'

'I'm sure Appleby knows what he's talking about, James,' said Ashley.

'Even so . . .'

Appleby shrugged and said to the attendant, '*La main gauche, s'il vous plaît.*'

The sheet was folded further back to expose Sir Henry's naked torso, a patchwork of bruises, angrily dark against his chalk-white skin. Ashley started back. 'Good God,' he exclaimed. Max took

some bitter pleasure from knowing how poorly prepared his brother was for encounters with the physical consequences of violent death, whereas he had seen much worse than this all too many times.

'As you see,' said Appleby, 'the ring's gone.'

So it was. But looking down at Sir Henry's lifeless hand, Max noticed something else. The fingernails had been cut severely short and none too carefully at that. Sir Henry had always taken pains about his appearance. Such clumsy trimming was not his work. Someone else had done it. Though whether before or after his death . . .

'Have you seen enough, Mr Maxted?' Appleby asked.

Max nodded. 'Yes. Quite enough, thank you.'

Appleby signalled to the attendant, who drew the sheet back over Sir Henry's face. Max bade his father a silent farewell, then turned away.

'We can go now.'

It was only a short drive to Carrefour Vavin, where they emerged from the car into the heart of Montparnasse. But the neighbourhood's artistic reputation was belied by a scene of workaday ordinariness. The weather was dank and cold, the shoppers and passers-by had no time to pause for intellectual banter and the café terraces were empty.

Fradgley had had much less to say for himself since visiting the mortuary and glum introspection had claimed Ashley. It was left to Appleby to direct proceedings and to Max to ask the questions that needed to be asked.

Appleby led them away from the junction, where Boulevard du Montparnasse met Boulevard Raspail, along Rue du Verger, a quieter side-street, to the entrance to an apartment building, where Appleby stopped by the door. Max noticed, rather before his brother, the brownish-red stain on the pavement.

'Is this where he fell?' he asked Appleby directly. Coyness on the point was futile.

'Yes. I'm afraid it'll take some time for all the traces to disappear.'

Max looked up. He counted seven storeys, including the parapeted attic windows set in the mansard roof. A fall from such a height could only ever be fatal. Appleby gave the doorbell a hefty yank.

'The concierge doesn't speak a word of English. But she's expecting us, so . . .'

Expectant or not, she was in no hurry. There was time for Max

to light a cigarette and another for Ashley, who then paced around tensely with his for what felt like an age before the door was opened by a small, spry, elderly woman with a pronounced stoop, who eyed them as if they might be a pack of burglars.

Fradgley addressed her in fluent French and she gave ground. They were admitted to a vast and gloomy stairwell. Appleby demanded '*la clé pour le grenier*', which she surrendered with some reluctance and much rattling of a key-chain. 'Shall we take the lift, gentlemen?' Appleby asked.

No one answered, so by default they squeezed aboard and, after a struggle with the inner door, rose through a wire shaft between the flights of stairs. Nothing was said during the ascent. Max could have asked if either Appleby or Fradgley knew what had brought Sir Henry to this place. So could Ashley. Neither did. But reticence, Max felt sure, would carry them only so far. Eventually, some facts, however unpalatable, would have to be faced.

They exited at the top, on the mansard level, and headed along the landing towards the nearest door, which Appleby unlocked with the key the concierge had given him.

'The information I can supply comes from Commissioner Zamaron. You can ask him to confirm it if you want to, when we see him later. He speaks good English. This attic room is used by the tenants to store possessions they have no space for in their apartments. They all have a key. It's supposed to be kept locked, but it was found to be unlocked when the police came here following your father's fatal fall. He had no key on his person and none was discovered in the attic. So, we must assume someone had simply neglected to lock the door, allowing him to enter unimpeded.'

Appleby pushed the door open and they followed him in. Four dormer windows facing the street lit a long, dust-moted chamber crammed with old furniture, packing-boxes and trunks. Most of the articles were stacked along the inner wall, where the ceiling was highest, allowing easy access to the windows. Appleby closed the door carefully behind them and crossed to one of the windows. He opened it, startling a pigeon outside, which took off in a burst of flapping wings that caused Fradgley to jump. He for one was not at ease. That was painfully clear.

'This window corresponds to the position on the pavement where Sir Henry was found,' said Appleby. 'There's also an accumulation of sludge and mud in the gutter behind the parapet in which the police discovered a boot print matching Sir Henry's footwear. So, there's no doubt it was from here that he fell.'

'Perhaps I could take a look,' said Max, sensing that Ashley was in no hurry to. Appleby stepped aside for him. Max hooked the window open as wide as it would go and leant out. The tiled roof sloped down from the window, as Appleby had described, to a leaded gutter behind a low brick parapet. There appeared to be numerous different boot prints in the silt clogging the gutter, mostly filled with rainwater.

'I'm afraid French policemen are no lighter-footed than their British counterparts, Mr Maxted,' said Appleby. 'There's also been quite a lot of rain since Friday night. But Zamaron tells me a good plaster cast of Sir Henry's boot print was obtained. The actual print, alas, is no longer visible.'

That was either convenient or inconvenient, Max supposed, depending on your point of view. 'How does Zamaron suggest my father climbed through the window? It would have been quite a scramble.'

'There was a chair in front of the window. One of those, I believe.' Appleby pointed to a stack of plain deal chairs. 'He could simply have stepped out.'

'Then I believe I'll do the same.'

'Would you fetch him a chair, Mr Fradgley?' Appleby asked, apparently unsurprised.

Carrying furniture, for however short a distance, did not appear to agree with Fradgley. But he did as he had been asked.

'Is this really necessary?' Ashley put in. 'It seems clear enough how Pa got on to the roof, James.'

'But not why.'

Ashley's expression signalled strongly that he was not sure he wanted to know why. But his own diffidence embarrassed him. It was a legitimate question.

Apparently taking pity on him, Appleby said, 'Commissioner

Zamaron is in possession of information that may point to an explanation, Sir Ashley.'

'The information is not altogether edifying,' said Fradgley.

'I think we'd better hear it, even so,' Max responded, drawing a reluctant nod of approval from his brother.

'Very well.' Appleby smiled grimly. 'We're all men of the world, I trust. I'm obliged to speak plainly. According to the concierge, Sir Henry regularly visited a war widow, one Madame Dombreux, who occupies an apartment on the third floor. Madame Dombreux told the concierge she was giving Sir Henry French lessons.'

'French lessons?' Ashley spluttered. 'But . . .'

'How old is Madame Dombreux?' Max enquired calmly.

'Like many war widows, Mr Maxted, she is not old at all. I haven't met her myself. Zamaron described her as . . . *très jolie.*'

'Good God,' murmured Ashley.

'Also like many war widows, Madame Dombreux must support herself as best she can. She has a poorly paid job in the ticket office at Montparnasse station. It wouldn't be surprising if she sought to . . . supplement her income.'

'By giving French lessons.'

'Exactly so.'

'In the evening, no doubt.'

'No doubt.'

'This is disgusting,' Ashley grumbled.

'It may not be, Sir Ashley,' said Fradgley. 'It could all be entirely above board.'

'So it could,' Appleby agreed. 'The fact is that Sir Henry called here frequently. That much we know for certain.'

'But I don't imagine he frequently went on to the roof,' said Max. 'Does Zamaron have an explanation for that?'

Appleby sighed. 'He does.'

'Which we aren't going to find palatable either?'

'I'm afraid not. Zamaron's responsible for overseeing foreign residents in Paris. Hence his involvement in this matter. He happens to know that the attic room in the building opposite is the studio of an Italian artist named Spataro. Zamaron knows a lot of

45

artists. He seems to fancy himself as something of a connoisseur, as you'll see later. He believes Madame Dombreux sometimes models for Spataro. Make of that what you will. What he makes of it is that Sir Henry may have suspected she did rather more than pose for Spataro and that he went on to the roof on Friday night in order to spy on them, then . . . slipped.'

Ashley groaned and gave ground. 'We certainly can't relay such a story to our mother, Mr Appleby. It would be . . . impossible.'

'Then I suggest you invent a more acceptable alternative.'

'The commissioner's lurid speculations will form no part of any official conclusion on the circumstances of your father's death, Sir Ashley,' said Fradgley. 'You may rest assured of that.'

'Is Madame Dombreux likely to be at home at this hour, gentlemen?' Max enquired.

'Most likely not,' Appleby replied. 'And, frankly, I'm not sure what you'd gain by speaking to her.'

'We don't want to speak to her,' Ashley declared, apparently believing it was for him to declare their wishes in such matters.

Max had already decided he would speak to the woman with or without Appleby's assistance. He did not bother to contradict his brother, but turned back to the window.

He could see at a glance that the parapet blocked the view of the attic of the building opposite. Out on the roof it would be a different matter, of course. To that extent, Zamaron's theory was sound enough. 'I believe I'll take that look outside even so,' he announced in a deliberately nonchalant tone. 'Since we're here.'

He stepped up on to the chair and out through the open window. It was quite a stretch down to the gutter. It was not difficult to imagine his father taking a fatal misstep out there at night.

Max steadied himself against the roof and stood upright. Paris stretched grey and smoke-wreathed around him. There was the Eiffel Tower away to his right. Below, a tram was clattering round a curve in the tracks in Carrefour Vavin. And directly opposite were the windows of the attic Sir Henry had supposedly climbed out there to see into. Max could not make out much of the interior. The windows were uncurtained but dirty. Something that might have been an easel draped in a sheet stood at one end of the room.

Rectangular, stacked shapes that could have been paintings were also visible. Beyond that . . . nothing.

If Spataro fulfilled the archetype of a Montparnasse artist, he was probably asleep. At night, with lights burning within, it could have been very different. Had his father seen what he had feared he would see? Or worse than he had feared? Shock could have played its part in the disaster that overtook him. If so, it was a pitiful end.

The cooing of a pigeon close by drew Max's attention to the chimney-stack behind him. He turned and glanced up at the bird, perched by one of the pots. The stack formed part of a wall supporting it and chimneys of the next building. Max noticed there were skylights set in the roof just below the apex, serving a second attic above the one he had just emerged from.

At that moment, a pale glimmer of sunlight pierced the prevailing gloom and was reflected off the rain-slicked roof. Something sparkled in Max's field of view and he realized there were fragments of broken glass scattered across the tiles immediately below the nearest skylight. Then he saw that one of the panes in the skylight was broken. How had that come about? he wondered. How – and when?

Grasping the wooden finial above the window, he hauled himself up past the dormer roof.

'Where are you going, Mr Maxted?' Appleby called, leaning out to follow his progress.

'There's a broken window up here.'

'One of the policemen probably put his boot through it. They're a clumsy lot. Watch your step, now.'

'I will, I will.'

Max doubted if any of the police had climbed up to the skylight. It was an awkward scramble, with little available in the way of foot- or hand-holds. One wrong move and Max could conceivably go the way of his father. A glance behind him was hardly reassuring.

But flying over the battlefields of Flanders in wire-and-canvas biplanes had immunized him against vertigo. He made it to the skylight with nothing worse than a few short slips to show for it. A

hole had certainly been punched in one of the panes. A piece of wood had been nailed beneath the remnants of the pane to keep the weather out. It was obvious no policeman's boot was responsible for the damage, however. The fragments of glass on the roof proved the skylight had been broken from inside, not outside. It was puzzling – very puzzling.

He peered down through the undamaged pane into a cramped roof space. The boarded floor he could see below was thick with dust, pierced in places by assorted footprints. The footprints themselves were entirely free of dust. They had clearly been made recently – probably no longer ago than Friday.

A fatal accident in the circumstances envisaged by Commissioner Zamaron was plausible, he could not deny. But there were enough oddities and inconsistencies to suggest that something else might have happened, though what that might be he could not yet imagine. He needed to learn more. And he would, whatever Ashley said.

He slithered back down to the attic window and cast another glance towards Spataro's studio. There was still no movement there. It struck Max that if anyone had seen what happened to Sir Henry, it could only be Spataro. He would have had a perfect view – if he had been looking.

'Seen enough, Mr Maxted?' Appleby called.

'Quite enough, thank you.' Max clambered back in through the window and brushed himself down.

'Satisfied?' Ashley asked sharply, frowning at him ominously.

'I believe I am, yes.'

'Then perhaps we should be going.'

They left the attic, Appleby locking up carefully behind them, and headed for the lift. As they reached it, Ashley said suddenly, 'No sense our cramming in there again like sardines. You go ahead, gentlemen. My brother and I will walk down.'

Ashley brushed aside Fradgley's offer to give up his place in the lift. Appleby made no such offer. The expression on his face suggested he knew, as did Max, that Ashley had decided a quiet word between brothers was now in order.

*

The lift groaned and clanked arthritically down its wire shaft as Ashley and Max began a slow descent of the stairs. Max lit a cigarette and waited for Ashley to declare his position. He did not have to wait long.

'I was afraid it would be something like this, you know. Falling to his death while spying on some tart he'd become besotted with. I mean to say, it's pathetic.'

'You seem to be assuming it's true.'

'Of course it's true. How else do you explain a man of Pa's age prancing around on a roof in the middle of the night?'

'I don't. Yet. But perhaps we should speak to Madame Dombreux before we make our minds up.'

'Absolutely not. Give her the slightest encouragement and she'll be trying to blackmail us.'

'With what?'

'I don't know. *Billets doux* Pa was stupid enough to send her, perhaps.'

'But—'

'Listen to me very carefully, James. I don't want any word of this – any breath – to reach Mother.'

'Neither do I, if Zamaron's version of events is correct.'

'It's obviously correct. Fortunately, no one has any interest in bringing those events to public attention. Appleby and Fradgley are trying to avoid embarrassing our delegation here. And it sounds as if this fellow Zamaron has been told to help them do that. So, we must do everything we can to cooperate with them. Don't ask any challenging questions. And don't look down your nose in that way you have that implies you don't believe a single thing you're being told.'

'Look down my nose? I never—'

'If you want to make yourself useful, think of something we can tell Mother that will go some way towards accounting for what happened to Pa without mentioning this Dombreux woman.'

'I'll do my best.'

'You'd better. Pa's left us a truly horrible mess to clear up. It can be done. But only if we stick together. I need your support, James. Your loyalty to our family.' Ashley looked round at

49

him as he traversed the next landing. 'Can I be assured of it?'

'Of course you can.'

'Good. I'm glad to hear it.'

No doubt he was. But Max was aware that their definitions of family loyalty did not necessarily coincide. In the end, Max would abide faithfully by his definition, not Ashley's. He understood himself well enough to know that it could be no other way.

POLICE HEADQUARTERS ON THE ÎLE DE LA CITÉ WAS A MASSIVE old mansarded building facing Notre-Dame. It was so noisy and crowded that it was hard to tell who among the gabbling, form-flapping throng might be police officers, complainants or suspected criminals. Max for one was glad of a guide through the maze of narrow corridors and echoing stairways. It was clearly not Appleby's first visit to the premises. The several greetings he exchanged along the way suggested he was a regular caller.

This was confirmed when they reached the relative haven of Commissioner Zamaron's office. He was a small, wiry, moustachioed man, with a mop of suspiciously dark hair and a policemanly combination of affability and perceptiveness. Disarmingly, he and Appleby were on first-name terms – '*Bonjour, Horace*,' and 'Good morning, Léon,' no less.

Appleby had alerted them to Zamaron's supposed connoisseur-ship and it was immediately apparent. Paintings covered the walls – landscapes, still lifes and portraits in contrasting styles. Were they payments in kind for favours done? Max wondered. He could not resist whispering to Ashley, 'I expect he keeps the nudes at home.' Ashley pretended not to hear him.

There had been a telephone call for Fradgley from the Embassy, Zamaron reported in his very passable English. Fradgley took him-self off to return the call.

That left Zamaron to offer Max and Ashley coffee, condolences and his personal assurances of discretion and dutifulness. 'Horace has told you what I believe occurred, *messieurs*? *Très bien*. We do

51

not need to speak more of it. A tragic accident is a tragic accident. Everything is arranged. The, er ... *travail administratif* ... has been dealt with.'

'He means the paperwork's in place, gentlemen,' said Appleby. 'When will they be able to take Sir Henry's body back to England, Léon?'

'Whenever you wish. Tomorrow?'

'That would suit us very well,' said Ashley. 'We're very grateful for your ... expeditiousness.'

'Think nothing of it.'

'The paperwork,' Ashley pressed, 'will include a death certificate, I take it?'

'But of course. One has already been sent from the Mairie to the Embassy. No doubt Monsieur Fradgley is being told of this by his office.'

'And what does it state as the cause of death?'

'The cause of death?'

'French death certificates don't necessarily specify one, Sir Ashley,' said Appleby with a smile.

'Really?' Max put in.

Appleby's smile broadened. 'Really.'

'Sir Henry's possessions – those found on him – I have here.' Zamaron opened a drawer in his desk and took out a bulging manilla envelope. 'You will want to have them.'

'Indeed,' said Ashley gravely.

'I regret I must ask you to sign a receipt.'

Zamaron's doleful expression implied his regret was genuine. Max could not but admire the man's delicacy. It was only marginally sullied by the impression that he was enjoying himself rather a lot.

Zamaron handed the receipt to Ashley, who held it out for Max to see. It was printed in French, naturally. Their father's possessions had been listed in abominable handwriting, also in French. *Un portefeuille. Une montre. Un mouchoir. Une paire de boutons de manchette. Une épingle à cravate. Un peigne. Une chevalière. 41fr.*

'You should check it's all there, *messieurs*,' said Zamaron, when neither showed any inclination to do so.

Max sat forward and slid the contents of the envelope out on to the desk. There they were, each item instantly familiar: the leather wallet, the silver pocket-watch, the monogrammed handkerchief and cufflinks, the tie-pin, the humble comb, the signet ring. They were Sir Henry Maxted's props and accessories that he had carried around the world.

'All present and correct,' said Max quietly.

'Count the money, if you would be so good, *monsieur*.'

Max sighed and counted. Forty-one francs there were. He turned to Ashley. 'Will you sign for it or shall I?'

'I'll do it,' said Ashley. He had reddened slightly and his eyes had moistened, as if the sight of his father's effects, arranged on a police-station desk, had moved him more deeply than viewing the old man's corpse on a mortuary slab. There was something in that, Max would have agreed. He could not really have explained why.

Ashley signed on the dotted line and Max loaded the items back into the envelope. An awkward silence loomed. Zamaron looked at Appleby and Appleby looked at Max. Ashley blew his nose. Zamaron made a meal of folding the receipt. And Max decided to put a toe into some untested waters. 'You collect art, commissioner?'

'I do, Monsieur Maxted, I do.' Zamaron sounded pleased by the question and allowed himself a self-satisfied glance around his walls.

'Is there any of Spataro's work here?'

Ashley stiffened, but remained silent. Zamaron, meanwhile, appeared blithely undismayed. He was on first-name terms with his favourite artists as well, it soon transpired. 'I cannot show Raffaele's paintings here. They are too—'

'Explicit?'

'*Non, non*. They are too big. Raffaele, he . . . paints on a grand scale.'

'But he does paints nudes, doesn't he?'

'Er, sometimes. Not always. He is . . . versatile.'

'And something of a ladies' man?'

Zamaron leant back in his chair and gazed studiously at Max. 'He is Italian, Monsieur Maxted. He has a reputation, like many of

his countrymen. But it was my understanding that you and Sir Ashley did not wish to enquire deeply into—'

'We don't, commissioner,' Ashley interrupted, with a glare at Max. 'We don't require any more information than we already have. Isn't that so, James?'

Max shrugged. 'Yes. Of course. I was just—'

The door rattled open and Fradgley came in, sparing Max the need to complete his sentence. 'I'm pleased to say that all the documentation we require to facilitate the collection of Sir Henry's body from the hospital is now to hand, gentlemen,' Fradgley announced, looking every bit as pleased as he claimed to be. 'There is a reliable firm of undertakers we customarily use in such situations as this. They can arrange everything and deliver the deceased to the Gare du Nord to be carried on the train you elect to travel home on.'

'They're thinking of tomorrow, Fradgley,' said Appleby.

'That should present no difficulty. The documents are waiting at the Embassy and the undertakers will be available at your convenience.'

'Excellent,' said Ashley.

So it was, in its way, thought Max. The Paris police and the British Embassy were surpassing themselves in the cause of a speedy resolution to the awkward matter of Sir Henry Maxted's fatal fall. It was hard not to be impressed. And it was equally difficult not to ponder what chances the truth had of making itself heard amidst all this speed and efficiency.

'Is there anything else I can do for you, *messieurs*?' Zamaron enquired, in a tone that presumed the answer would be no.

'One point does occur to me,' said Max in the same instant that Ashley opened his mouth to speak.

Ashley rounded on him. 'What?'

'It's simply that there's no key among our father's possessions, commissioner.'

'No key?' Zamaron frowned in puzzlement.

'Well, I'm merely wondering how our father gained entry to the apartment building on Friday night. I assume it's locked at night.'

'For heaven's sake, James,' spluttered Ashley, 'haven't we—'

'*Non, non,*' Zamaron cut in. 'Monsieur Maxted asks a good question. The building is locked at night, *oui*. The concierge, Madame Mesnet, assures me of this. But she is forgetful. She likes to take a drink. She may have forgotten to lock the door. Or else Sir Henry had a key, given to him by Madame Dombreux, which slipped from his pocket when he fell and was . . . not noticed on the pavement.'

'Yes,' Max conceded. 'I suppose one of those explanations must be correct.'

'You're satisfied on the point, then?' Ashley asked, glaring at him.

'Yes. As far as one can be.'

'Good. Well, I'm sure Commissioner Zamaron is a busy man. I think we've taken up enough of his time, don't you?'

ASHLEY WAS CLEARLY SEETHING WITH IRRITATION AT MAX – ALL the more because he could not express it – when they left Police Headquarters and travelled to the British Embassy. There the atmosphere was calm and orderly, hushed, it struck Max, almost ecclesiastical.

Fradgley had Sir Henry's passport and his travel-hardened leather suitcase, packed with his belongings from his room at the Hotel Majestic, waiting in his office for them to collect. More crucially, he had a tranche of documents – permits of one kind or another, some in duplicate, some in triplicate, and the terse but essential death certificate. From an administrative viewpoint, nothing now stood in the way of Sir Henry's posthumous repatriation to his homeland.

Fradgley suggested they should repair promptly to the undertaker he recommended in order to arrange the next stage in the process. To this they readily agreed. Appleby explained he would not be accompanying them. 'I don't think there's anything more I can do for you, gentlemen.' They did not argue.

As he left, Appleby said, looking at Max as he spoke, 'If you do find you need me, I can be contacted via the security office at the Majestic.'

Ashley hardly seemed to be listening. But Max was.

Their business at the undertaker's was handled with sombre efficiency. Monsieur Prettre, *entrepreneur de pompes funèbres* of the fourth generation (with the daguerreotyped likeness of his

56

great-grandfather casting a faded gaze over his shoulder) assured them of his best and swiftest attention. He saw no reason why they could not take their father home on Tuesday's noon train. He suggested they telephone him later to confirm everything was in order.

Through gritted teeth (it seemed to Max) Fradgley offered them lunch 'at the Embassy's expense' after they had left the undertaker's. If this was intended as an acknowledgement of the service Sir Henry had rendered his country over the years, Max reckoned it erred on the side of paltriness.

The conversation over lunch was as dull as the food. Handshakes afterwards on the pavement outside the restaurant marked, Max assumed, the end of their dealings with Fradgley, but it transpired he was assuming too much.

'I'll be at the Gare du Nord tomorrow to see you off, gentlemen,' the wretched man announced. 'And to ensure there aren't any last-minute hitches. You can't take any chances with the French.'

Ashley interpreted this as a further indication of the lengths the Embassy was going to in order to smooth their path. If anyone's path was being smoothed, Max thought it more likely to be Fradgley's. But much of Ashley's anger at him for asking unhelpful questions at unhelpful times had dissipated, so he chose not to offer this interpretation.

A somewhat testier version of the discussion they had had on their way out of 8 Rue du Verger ensued as they walked back to the Mazarin through the dank grey afternoon. But Max was well aware it would have been testier still a few hours earlier.

'You don't seem to appreciate, James, just how helpful these people are being.'

'Oh, I do, Ashley, believe me.'

'Then why must you keep provoking them?'

'I thought they might think it odd if one of us didn't query a few things.'

'What is there to query apart from Pa's sanity? How he can have put himself in such a situation is beyond me.'

'*La femme fatale*. I believe it's an old story.'

'Well, it's not a story we can allow Mother to hear.'

'I agree.'

'Then act as if you agree. And apply your mind to the problem of what we're going to tell her.'

'I will.'

'Good. Because we don't have long to think of something.'

They assuredly did not. Max claimed, accurately enough, that a walk would help clear his mind on the subject. He left Ashley at the door of the Mazarin with a tentative agreement to dine together later. Ashley had telegrams to send, to the undertaker in Epsom their family used and to their mother, alerting her to the imminence of their return. There was plenty to keep him busy.

There was plenty to occupy Max too, though it was not exactly what he had led his brother to suppose. As soon as he was out of sight of the Mazarin, he headed for the river. He was going back to Montparnasse.

William Fradgley would not have been pleased to know this. Fortunately for his peace of mind, he believed Sir Ashley Maxted had his brother's inquisitiveness well under control. He was in the process of telling Appleby so even as Max was striding across the Pont de l'Alma.

'They'll be gone tomorrow, Appleby, and the problem of Sir Henry with them.'

'You think so?' Appleby's rumbling voice was turned into a growl by the crackly telephone line from the Majestic.

'Of course. Why not?'

'The younger brother. James. He worries me.'

'You worry too much.'

'That's my job, Fradgley. To worry. The last thing we want during the conference is a scandal.'

'It's also the last thing Sir Henry's family wants.'

'But there's more than one kind of scandal. And Sir Henry tupping a young widow is far from the worst.'

'What a coarse turn of phrase you people do have.'

'It must arise from the sort of fixes we have to get *you* people out of.'

'I don't know what—'

'Have you heard anything from *le Deuxième Bureau*?'

'No. Should I have?'

'They may have been keeping an eye on Madame Dombreux.'

'Surely whatever her husband was up to was buried with him in Russia.'

'Perhaps. Perhaps not. Certainty's hard to come by in my line of business.'

Fradgley sighed. 'I'll put the Maxted brothers on the train tomorrow, Appleby. Along with their late father. As far as I'm concerned, my involvement in this matter ends there.'

'I wish I could believe mine will too.'

'Well, I must get on.'

'Yes, yes. I'm sure there are memos you need to write. Good afternoon to you.'

Max had set himself a brisk pace and was at the Gare Montparnasse within half an hour. He had no way of knowing whether Madame Dombreux would be on duty, but was happy to take his chances. If she had already gone, he would simply have to press on to 8 Rue du Verger.

He could not see the cashiers clearly behind their grilled windows, but, after annoying several people by dodging from one queue to another, he found the one he was looking for.

The cashier was a young woman, dressed in an unflattering grey uniform. But, as Max drew closer, it became ever more obvious that she was really quite beautiful.

Her dark hair was gathered beneath her uniform cap. Her face was pale and heart-shaped and only a cast of weariness in her looks disguised her attractiveness. She kept her cool green eyes trained on the tickets and the money in front of her. Her expression was grave, her exchanges with passengers minimally polite. Max would have guessed, even without knowing, that she was someone only misfortune and adverse circumstances had reduced to issuing train tickets for a living. She had been bred for better.

*

He reached the head of the queue and drew her gaze by the simple means of saying nothing.

'*Oui, monsieur?*' she prompted, her voice soft and serious.

'Madame Dombreux?'

She frowned and looked at him more intently. Then she covered her mouth in surprise. He heard her sharp intake of breath. Somehow, she knew who he was.

'I'm James Maxted.'

'Of course. You have Henry's eyes.'

Her direct, unflinching reference to his father and the perfection of her English, in which an accent was barely detectable, took him aback. For a moment, he merely stared at her.

'I'm sorry,' she said. 'I did not mean to—'

'I need to speak to you.'

'Yes.' She nodded. 'And I to you. But we cannot speak here. Meet me in the Café du Dôme at a quarter to seven. It is on Carrefour Vavin.'

WITH TIME TO KILL, MAX WENT INTO A CAFÉ OPPOSITE THE station, where he drank two coffees and smoked several cigarettes. The light outside started to fail and the streets became slowly busier as workers began their homeward journeys. Well-filled trams rattled by at intervals. He pondered the enigma of Madame Dombreux and her relationship with his father. *You have Henry's eyes.* The phrase lingered in his thoughts, along with the manner in which she had spoken it. Whatever she had been to Sir Henry, it surely amounted to more than he had been led to believe.

It was a short walk along Boulevard du Montparnasse to Carrefour Vavin. He diverted to Rue du Verger and paused to stare up at the roof of number 8. It was growing dark now. Lamplight gleamed from some of the windows. It was easy to convince himself Madame Mesnet was peering out at him from one of them. He headed on.

There were several cafés spaced around the junction. The Café du Dôme appeared to be the busiest, with one or two hardy souls braving the terrace. Inside, most of the tables were occupied. There was laughter and shoulder-clapping banter and a miasma of cigarette smoke. Max could hear the click of billiard balls from an inner room. He found a perch on one of the banquettes close to the entrance and ordered a beer. He looked at his watch and wondered what he would say when she arrived.

A quarter of an hour slowly passed. Then a large, bulky figure entered the café, colliding with Max's table as he did so. He uttered

61

no apology, probably because he had not noticed. He was a huge man, made to look huger still by a flapping, frayed tweed suit and wild head of hair, complete with bushy beard. He headed straight for the bar, waving his hand in acknowledgement as someone shouted his name. '*Eh, Raffaele!*'

Several of those standing at the bar greeted him familiarly. And his response clinched his identity. '*Buonasera . . . mes amis.*' A brandy was downed in mid-sentence and another promptly ordered.

It was both an opportunity not to be missed and one fraught with difficulties. For all his bonhomie, Spataro looked every bit as volatile as an Italian artist might be expected to. Perhaps the shrewdest course of action would be to wait and see how he reacted to Madame Dombreux's arrival.

But shrewdness sat ill with Max's impatience to learn as much as he could before he was obliged to leave Paris. He stood up and threaded his way to the bar.

'Raffaele Spataro?' There was no response until Max had added a tap on the arm – an arm that felt like a solid mass of muscle. 'Raffaele Spataro?'

'*Si.*' Spataro swung round and looked at him. '*C'est moi.*'

'I'm James Maxted.'

'You are English.'

'Yes. Could I have a word with you?'

'Ah. Words. That is all the English have.'

'I don't think the Germans would agree with you there.'

The remark seemed to make Spataro take stock of Max for the first time. 'Do you want to buy me a drink, *mio amico*?'

'I'd be happy to.'

Spataro laughed. 'Then I leave you to pay for my brandy.' He drained his second glass and smacked it down on the bar. '*Grazie mille*. I must go.'

'Wait.' Max laid a restraining hand on Spataro's elbow. 'I'd like to ask you a few questions about the death in Rue du Verger on Friday night.'

'What is that to you?'

'The man who died was my father. Sir Henry Maxted.'

'Then I am sorry for you. But I know nothing.'

'Your studio faces the roof he supposedly fell from.'

'Supposedly? What is "supposedly"? He fell.'

'Did you see it happen?'

Spataro shook Max off and gave him a glare in which there was just a hint of fear beneath the menace. 'I saw nothing.'

'You're sure?'

'*Si.* I am sure.'

'You don't look it.'

Spataro's eyes widened. Suddenly, he grabbed Max by the tie and collar. Max felt his feet being raised from the floor. He smiled, which seemed to baffle the Italian. 'What is funny?'

'You are, Raffaele. It's a good thing you're an artist, because you'd make a rotten actor.'

Spataro's face darkened and his grip on Max tightened. Then there was a shout from behind the bar. The *patron* intervened in a reproving volley of Franco-Italian that seemed to register with Spataro as something he was bound to take note of. He scowled and ground his teeth, then released Max and held up his hands in a placatory fashion. But it was the management of a favourite watering hole he was placating, not Max. 'Leave me alone,' he growled. Then he spun on his heel and stalked out.

Max rather expected the *patron* to give him his marching orders too. But he was positively sympathetic, refusing to let Max pay for Spataro's brandies and referring to '*les artistes*' with an expressive roll of the eyes.

One of the other customers massed at the bar spoke reasonable English and claimed to know someone who knew one of those who had found Sir Henry's body. 'A terrible thing, *monsieur*. Have the police found out what happened?' Max assured him they had not. '*Naturellement*,' came the cynical response.

Max decided to finish his beer outside. It was growing cold, but that hardly mattered. He wanted to be able to suggest to Madame Dombreux that they go elsewhere for their talk. After his encounter with Spataro, he felt too conspicuous for comfort at the Dôme.

He was not kept waiting long, but her arrival surprised him nonetheless. He was expecting her to approach from the direction of the station and to be recognizable by her uniform. Instead, she appeared suddenly beside him, dressed in her own clothes: skirt, coat and cloche hat. She had evidently gone home first.

'Why are you out here?' she asked at once.

'I met your friend Spataro. He got a little . . . loud.'

'Raffaele Spataro?'

'The very same.'

'He's no friend of mine.'

'That's not what Commissioner Zamaron says.'

She frowned at him and shook her head, as if surpassingly sorry that he should believe whatever Zamaron had told him. 'Why are you here, James?' Her freedom with his first name was disarming in its effect.

'I want to know why my father died.'

'You do?'

'Yes.'

'Well, so do I.' Her eyes brimmed with tears. 'I am sorry. I loved him. His death like that . . . was so awful.' She dabbed away some of her tears with a handkerchief.

'I didn't mean to upset you, *madame*.'

'But you want the truth.'

'Yes.'

'And your brother? Madame Mesnet told me of your visit. I notice he isn't with you. Does he want the truth?'

Max shrugged. 'I can't speak for him.'

'Will you buy me a brandy, James? I feel a little . . .'

'Of course. Is there somewhere else we can go? We'll attract a lot of attention here.'

'Yes. The Parnasse. Next door. It's quieter.'

THE CAFÉ PARNASSE WAS, AS SHE HAD PROMISED, QUIETER THAN the Dôme: fewer customers, less badinage, calmer altogether. Max watched her sip her brandy and went on watching her as he flicked his lighter for her cigarette. She was older than he by a few years. And some of those years had been hard ones, costing her much of the bloom she must once have had. She was beautiful, but no longer flawless. The cuff of her blouse beneath her check jacket was ever-so-slightly frayed. There was weariness in her looks and sadness in her eyes.

'Call me Corinne,' she said softly.

'In that case, you'd better call me Max. I'm only James to my family.'

'Max it is. The name suits you. Henry said you flew in the war.'

'I did.'

'Do you miss it?'

'The war? Or the flying?'

'Both. Or either.'

'I haven't flown a plane since I was shot down in April of 'seventeen. That's nearly two years. I missed it dreadfully at first. Now . . . it's not so bad.'

'And you'll be flying again soon, won't you?'

'Ah. Pa told you about that, did he?'

She did not answer. But Sir Henry had told her everything, of course. Max felt strangely certain of that. He was damned if he would embarrass himself or Corinne Dombreux by asking her to admit she and his father – her senior by at least thirty years – had

65

been lovers. She had said she loved him and that was enough. Nor was it hard to understand what might have attracted Sir Henry to her. She had an air of mystery and a hint of fragility likely to attract many men – including Max, come to that.

'You speak very good English, Corinne. I'd hardly know you were French.'

'My mother was English. And I went to school there. Both my parents wanted me to be the perfect English lady.'

'You say that as if you disappointed them.'

'Living here, as I do, isn't what they had in mind for me. It's not what I had in mind for myself.'

'How did it come about?'

'I married the wrong man, Max. I am the widow of the infamous Pierre Dombreux.'

'I've never heard of him.'

'I wish no one had.'

'What did he do to earn his infamy?'

'He betrayed his country . . . so they say.'

'How?'

'He was a diplomat, like Henry. My parents were very pleased when I married him. So was I. I loved him. I thought he loved me. He was posted to the embassy in St Petersburg. I went with him.'

'And that's where you met my father?'

'Yes. There was nothing between us at first, except friendship, which flourished despite the difference in our ages. And a friend-ship is what it would have remained if Pierre had been faithful to me. But he was not. And he did little to hide it. Henry was a source of strength when I most needed it. He was the only friend I had in the whole of St Petersburg – Petrograd, as it was by then. When Pierre learnt of our closeness – which was entirely innocent at that point, though precious to me nonetheless – he sent me home to Paris in disgrace.

'My parents believed every lie he told them. They disowned me. This was in the autumn of 1917, just before the Bolsheviks seized power in Russia. The war was going badly. I had our apartment to live in, but no money. I found work as a seamstress. It was hard. I received a second schooling: in what the world is like for a woman

66

with no place in society. And there was worse to come. In March last year, when the Bolsheviks made peace with Germany, Pierre was accused of prompting them to do so by revealing secret plans the French government had supposedly approved for Japan to seize Vladivostok.

'The first I knew of it was when the papers named him as a traitor. He had gone missing, it was reported. A few days later, I had a telegram from the embassy in Petrograd. His body had been pulled out of the Griboedov canal. He'd been shot through the head.'

'Good God. That must have been a terrible shock for you.'

'I'm not asking for sympathy.' There was a flash of anger in her eyes. Her pride in herself had been dented by misfortune. But it had not been destroyed.

'I'll be sure not to offer any.'

Corinne frowned at him. 'You're a lot like your father, you know.'

'My mother's forever complaining of how *un*like him I am.'

'Henry always said she misunderstood him.'

'They'd grown apart, Corinne. You must know that.'

'Yes. Of course. I can only speak of the Henry I knew. We wrote to each other after I left Petrograd. And he came to see me after he left himself, early last year.' (Was that when their relationship had moved beyond the platonic? Max wondered. Or had his father waited until she was a widow?) 'When he saw how I was living, he began sending me money, which I'm ashamed to say I accepted. I was evicted from Pierre's apartment after his death. That's when I moved here. I took the job at the station to try to make myself independent. I took other jobs as well.'

'Including modelling?'

'Yes. Do you want to know how many artists I posed for in the nude, Max? Is that it?'

'The only artist I'm interested in is Raffaele Spataro.'

'He was one of them,' she acknowledged with a sigh.

'Did it stop at posing?'

'He'd have liked to take it further. I didn't let him. I know what you've been told: that Henry fell from the roof because he was

spying on Spataro to see if I was with him. It's nonsense. I wasn't there. I haven't done any modelling since Henry came to Paris. And I only modelled for Raffaele Spataro once. He's a lecher and a liar. He probably encouraged Zamaron to believe I spent the night with him to burnish his reputation as the Casanova of Montparnasse.' She shook her head. 'It would be laughable if it weren't so serious. Please don't entertain the notion that I betrayed your father. It's the last thing I'd have done.'

'Why was he there that night, Corinne?'

She took a sip of brandy and looked Max in the eye. 'He was there every night. I surely don't have to spell it out.'

'How did he get into the building?'

'He had a key.'

'None was found on him.'

'He left it in my apartment. I found it when I returned.'

'Returned from where?'

'Nantes. My sister lives there. I received a telegram at the station just as I was about to go off duty saying she was dangerously ill. I travelled to Nantes at once, but the journey took hours, of course. I knew Henry would be waiting for me, but there was nothing I could do. When I arrived, I discovered the telegram was a hoax. My sister wasn't ill at all. And she wasn't pleased to see me. I'd missed the last train back by then, so, somewhat reluctantly, she let me stay overnight. I think she suspected I was making a clumsy attempt to effect a reconciliation. Little good it would have done me. I took the first train back in the morning. And when I reached home . . .'

'You think someone lured you away?'

'It didn't occur to me at the time, but my sister had no way of knowing where I worked. Yet the telegram was sent from Nantes. Someone went to great lengths to arrange my absence that night.'

'Knowing my father would then be there alone.'

'Yes. Exactly.'

'You realize what you're suggesting?'

'He was murdered, Max. I haven't a doubt of that.'

So, she had come out and said what he had already begun to suspect himself. It was murder. And murder changed everything. If

it was true, it could not go unavenged. 'You must have told Zamaron where you were.'

'Naturally I told him, but he doesn't believe me. Spataro says I was with him. That's good enough for Commissioner Zamaron.'

'Surely your sister—'

'He assumes she's helping me out of a hole by saying I was in Nantes. Not that she *has* said that, as far as I know. I don't think he's actually asked her.'

'Why on earth not?'

'Because he doesn't need to. For his purposes, it's enough that Henry might have suspected I was with Raffaele Spataro. Zamaron isn't conducting a criminal inquiry. That's the beauty of his theory from his point of view. It means he doesn't have to amass evidence or test alibis. He doesn't have to do anything.'

'We'll see about that.'

'Don't waste your time with the police. They don't want to know. Zamaron's not his own master. The unexplained murder of a member of the British delegation to the peace conference could turn into a scandal. They're afraid the press – and others – will start suggesting it had something to do with the conference itself.'

'Could it have?'

'I don't know. Neither do they. So, it's safer to write it off as an accident.'

Max lit a cigarette and considered the point. 'How sure are you that he was murdered, Corinne?'

'You mean how sure can I make you?'

He smiled drily. 'I suppose I do.'

'Henry left the apartment in a hurry. He didn't lock the door behind him. He didn't take his overcoat. He was chasing something . . . someone.'

'An intruder?'

'Maybe.'

'When I went up on the roof, I noticed that one of the skylights was broken. From the inside.'

'I noticed that too.'

Max was not surprised to learn Corinne had been on the roof.

What else, he wondered, had she done in pursuit of her lover's murderer?

'Did they let you see Henry's body, Max?'

'Of course.'

'They wouldn't let me. There were excuses about the severity of his injuries. When I persisted, I was told I had no right to see him because I wasn't a relative. And I won't be able to go to his funeral either, will I?'

Max shook his head sorrowfully. 'No.'

'I don't expect you to approve of our relationship. But I loved him. And now I've lost him. To a murderer no one is prepared to admit even exists.'

'I'm prepared to admit it.'

She looked at him, her eyes suddenly full of hope. 'You are?'

'Someone cut Pa's fingernails, Corinne. They made a pretty poor job of it. He certainly didn't do it himself. It must have been done after his death. Probably at the mortuary. The question is: why?'

'Do you have an answer?'

'If there was a struggle on the roof, if Pa came to grips with an assailant . . .'

'There could have been blood or skin of the assailant under his fingernails?'

Max nodded. 'That's what I'm thinking.'

She sipped her brandy and thought for a moment, then said, 'We must go to my apartment.'

'Why?'

'There's something I need to show you. I wasn't sure, but now . . .' There was a decisiveness in her gaze that had not been there before. 'Now I'm sure.'

MERCIFULLY, THE CONCIERGE DID NOT STIR WHEN THEY entered 8 Rue du Verger. They took the stairs to Corinne's apartment. 'Quieter than the lift,' she explained. That was amply proven when the sound of someone entering the building reached them as they neared the third floor. It was shortly followed by the lift clanking noisily into motion. 'Monsieur Miette, second floor back,' Corinne murmured, apparently knowing all her neighbours merely by their footfalls.

Her apartment was small, though sufficient, he supposed, for a single occupier. It was neat and clean, simply but comfortably furnished, though with few personal touches. There were no photographs on display and no paintings on the walls. Corinne's domestic existence had been pared down to essentials.

One item that was clearly inessential swiftly attracted his attention, however: a box of Cuban cigars on the mantelpiece. It could only have been left there by his father.

'He would often wait for me here,' Corinne said quietly, following the direction of Max's gaze. 'He knew the times of my shifts. He'd sit there' – she pointed to a buttoned-leather armchair beneath a standard lamp – 'and smoke a cigar and read a newspaper while he waited. I could smell the cigar from the stairs. I'd know by its aroma that I'd see him smiling at me as I opened the door.'

Ashley would be scandalized by such revelations of their father's secret life, of course. Max might have been himself. Instead, he found them curiously touching. Sir Henry the old romantic was a novel but endearing figure to him.

'There was still a trace of the aroma when I returned here on Saturday,' Corinne continued in a wistful tone. 'But it's gone now.'

'What did you want to show me?' Max asked, as eager to know as he was to change the subject.

'This.' She took a piece of paper from her handbag and passed it to him.

He frowned at her. 'I thought it was something here, in the apartment.'

'I couldn't risk showing it to you in the café, in case we were being watched.'

'*Watched?*'

'The apartment was searched while I was at work yesterday. I wasn't supposed to notice. But they weren't careful enough. Fortunately, I didn't leave that piece of paper here.'

'What is it?'

'See for yourself. I found it on the table by Henry's—' She broke off. 'On the table by the armchair. You'll recognize the handwriting.'

It was his father's, unmistakably: a list of some kind. Corinne lit the lamp for Max to read it by.

It was written in pencil and seemed to represent a rough financial calculation:

Capital	4,000
Mortgage	3,000
Seals	3,000
Trust	c 5,000
Chinese box	c 5,000
Contingencies Memo	c 5,000
F.L.	c 5,000
	c 30,000

'Do you know what this is about?' Max asked, turning to Corinne.

'No. I don't think he intended me or anyone else to read it. He'd probably have destroyed it if he hadn't been interrupted.'

'By whoever killed him?'

72

'That's how I see it.'

'Thirty thousand pounds is a hell of a lot of money.'

'I know.'

'Did he say anything to you that implied he was trying to raise a sum like this?'

'No.'

Max looked at the list again. *Capital*. Sir Henry might have had savings of £4,000. It was certainly possible. *Mortgage*. He had nothing to mortgage apart from Gresscombe Place. Surely he would not have done that without telling Lady Maxted; Ashley would know if he had. *Seals*. What that might refer to Max could not guess. Likewise *Trust*, unless there was some family fund no one had ever mentioned to him, which was not inconceivable. *Chinese box* was a Chinese puzzle in its own right, as were *Contingencies Memo* and *F.L.* The first three figures were definite amounts, the next four estimates.

'Do you mind if I copy this?'

'Go ahead.'

Max fished a piece of paper from his wallet and jotted down the details. 'I'll show the list to my brother. It might mean something to him.'

'I'd rather you didn't.'

'Why not?'

'It's difficult to explain, but . . .'

'What?'

She looked down. 'Henry said Ashley wasn't to be trusted.'

'He said that? When?'

'I don't know. Some time back, I asked him about the two of you . . . and how you got on. I . . .' She shook her head. 'I'm sorry. You must think I had no business discussing you with your father. And you're right, of course.'

'What did he say, Corinne? Just tell me.'

She hesitated a moment longer, then answered him. 'I've already told you. Ashley wasn't to be trusted.'

'Is that all?'

'No. He also said he thought you were made of the right stuff.' She glanced directly at Max. 'I'm very much hoping he was right.

73

You're the only person I've shown that to. It's the only clue I have as to why Henry may have been murdered. You should weigh the risks very carefully before you share the information with anyone else. As you said, thirty thousand pounds is a lot of money.'

'What would he have wanted it for?'

'I don't know. But something happened about a month ago. It changed Henry. Not towards me, but inside himself. His thoughts were often elsewhere. As if he was turning a problem over in his mind. He said the delegation was working him hard, but that wasn't it. Something else was going on. Something else altogether. He went to London the week after your visit and—'

'He went to London?'

'Yes. He was away three nights. He said he'd been recalled to the Foreign Office for consultations.'

'That can't be right. He wouldn't have gone back to England without seeing my mother. And as I understand it most of the Foreign Office is here in Paris. He didn't need to go to London to consult his lords and masters.'

'It's what he told me, Max. And I believed him. But now . . . I'm not so sure.'

'When was this exactly?'

'He left . . . two weeks ago today.'

Max pulled out his pocket-diary. 'That would have been . . . Monday the tenth.'

'Yes.'

'I saw him here in Paris on Thursday the sixth. He said nothing about it then.'

'He can't have wanted you to know.'

'But why not?'

The only reply Corinne could manage was a shake of the head. Then she frowned and said, 'Your diary.'

'What about it?'

'Henry had a pocket-diary too. With a coat of arms on the front.'

'Official issue of some kind, I imagine.'

'It had a little pencil in the spine.'

'What of it?'

'He didn't carry any other pencil.'

'Corinne, I—'

'Did the police give you everything they found on him, Max?'

'Yes. They did.'

'Was there a pocket-diary?'

'No.'

'There should have been. He didn't leave it here. And he wouldn't have left it at the Majestic. Besides, I'm sure he used the pencil to write this list.'

Max felt sure she was right. Sir Henry's pocket-diary had been removed. But who had taken it? And why?

'The French police didn't know what they were looking for. If they had, the list would probably have gone too. It took a while for someone to arrange a thorough search of this apartment. By then it was too late.'

'Damn them all,' Max declared, his mind suddenly made up. 'I'm not going to let them get away with this.'

'But who are "they"?'

'That's what I mean to find out. Did you ever see any of the diary entries?'

'As far as I know, Henry only used it to record appointments in connection with his duties for the delegation.'

'Do you remember him mentioning any of the names of the people he met?'

'Well, there was a Brazilian delegate he saw quite a bit of called Ribeiro. They knew one another from Henry's time in Rio. And he often referred to a man called Norris whom he reported to in the British delegation. There was a Japanese delegate he was acquainted with as well, though I can't recall his name, I'm afraid.'

'What about Ireton? Did he ever talk about him? An American. Travis Ireton.'

There was a gleam of recognition in Corinne's gaze. 'Yes. Ireton. I remember. We met him at the races at St-Cloud. A strange sort of fellow, with a lopsided stance . . . and a scar on his face.'

'That's him.'

'How do you know him?'

'He was at the Ritz the evening I dined there with Pa. We had a brief word. He was in the company of some Rumanians.'

'Really? The people he was at St-Cloud with were fellow Americans, I think.'

'I asked him if he was attached to the American delegation and got a pretty evasive answer. I had the impression he was some kind of . . . fixer.'

'What does that mean?'

Max smiled. 'I'm not sure. Next time, I'll press him to be more specific about what he does.'

'I may be able to tell you how to contact him.'

Max looked at her in surprise. 'How?'

'He's a womanizer. A girl can always tell. Clumsy flirtation usually confirms it, as it did at St-Cloud. He slipped me his card. "In case you want to call round" was how he put it.'

'And you still have it?'

'I believe I do.'

Corinne crossed to the bureau in the corner of the room, delved in a flower-patterned china pot and returned, smiling triumphantly. It was the first time Max had seen her smile and a surpassingly lovely sight it was. He had a glimpse then of the pleasure his father must have taken from her company.

'Here it is.' She handed the card to him.

Travis R. Ireton
For all your needs in post-war Paris:
une cité des possibilités

Ireton Associates
33 Rue des Pyramides, Paris
Telegrams: Trireton, Paris
Telephone: Central 48-99

'"A city of possibilities",' Max mused as he slipped the card into his wallet. 'I wonder what he means by that.'

'You'll have to ask him.'

'I intend to.'

'I'd like to be there when you do.'

'It'll be better if I handle this on my own: man to man.' And

safer for Corinne, he reflected. If Sir Henry really had been murdered, seeking out the reason was likely to be dangerous.

She knew that, of course. 'Are you trying to protect me, Max?' she asked. 'I don't want you to, you know.'

'I'm sure you don't. But if I'm to pursue this, I must do it alone.'

'Are you worried I'll get in your way?'

'I'm more worried that the irregular nature of your relationship with my father could put me in a difficult position.'

She flinched. The words had hurt her, as Max had intended. If the cost of keeping her out of harm's way was to have her think him a prude, so be it.

'I'm sorry, Corinne, but I can't allow my family to think you and I have become allies.'

'No.' She composed herself. 'I suppose you can't.'

'I'm grateful for the information you've given me. I'll make the best use of it I can. And I'll let you know what I learn.'

'That would be kind of you.'

'Now I think I should be going, don't you?'

She nodded. In her expression there was realism as well as disappointment. It seemed he had succeeded in lowering her opinion of him. 'Yes. Of course.'

MAX FOUND ASHLEY CONSUMING A SOLITARY MEAL IN THE restaurant of the Mazarin and looking none too happy about it.

'Where have you been till this time?' Ashley growled. Fortunately he launched into a summary of how arrangements for the funeral stood without requiring Max to answer that question.

Max ordered fish and let Ashley talk himself out on the subjects of their father's extraordinary lack of judgement ('No fool like an old fool'), the cooperativeness of the French authorities ('Surprisingly obliging lot') and the thorny issue of what they were to tell their mother ('We have to think of something, damn it').

Then, as the meal drew towards a close, Max broached the subject that had been on his mind all along.

'I need to have a word with you in private, Ashley.'

His brother was instantly suspicious. 'What about?'

'This is no place to discuss it.'

'I don't want you creating difficulties, Max.'

'I know you don't.'

'But you're going to create some anyway. Is that it?'

'Shall we go to my room or yours?'

Ashley flung his napkin down tetchily on the table. 'Mine.'

There was a predictable explosion of fury from Ashley when he realized Max had been to see Corinne Dombreux. Eventually and reluctantly, however, he agreed to hear what Max had to say.

It seemed to Max as he spoke that the evidence of foul play was

irrefutable, or at the very least far stronger than the evidence that Sir Henry had died accidentally. The shorn fingernails; the missing diary; the broken skylight; the hoax telegram; the searching of Corinne's apartment; the mysterious list: they all told the same story.

But it was not a story Ashley had any intention of believing. His sullen silence as Max laid the facts before him suggested as much. And, when Max had finished, he wasted no time in making his position clear.

'I don't understand the way your mind works, James, I truly don't. We agreed it was in the family's best interests to ensure no scandal attached itself to Pa's death. Now here you are doing your damnedest to sabotage that effort. Perhaps the Dombreux woman has dazzled you just as she dazzled Pa. Well, I don't propose to entertain her lies for a moment. She persuaded her sister to provide her with an alibi for her liaison with this Italian painter and you swallow it hook, line and sinker. Thank the lord Zamaron isn't so credulous. You have only her word for it that her apartment's been searched, but what if it has? As the widow of a known traitor I should think she bears careful watching. A broken skylight is a broken skylight and nothing more. You don't know when it was broken or by whom. As for Pa's fingernails, I never noticed they were badly or clumsily trimmed.'

'That's because you didn't look at them,' Max cut in.

'I didn't need to. It's ridiculous to suggest the state of his finger-nails can have any bearing on this.'

'You know it isn't ridiculous. He was always fastidious about such things.'

'It's a pity he wasn't fastidious about his choice of female company.'

'What about his diary, Ashley? How do you account for it being removed?'

'It wasn't among the items the police handed over because it wasn't found on him. It is as simple as that.'

'Then where is it?'

'We don't know it ever existed. I don't recall him using one when he was at Gresscombe. The Dombreux woman may have invented

79

it, just as she's invented Pa's trip to England two weeks ago. Or . . .' A thought struck him. 'It could be in there, of course.' He pointed to Sir Henry's suitcase, standing in the corner of the room.

'Have you looked inside?'

'No.' Ashley's expression implied there had clearly been no good reason to.

'Well, perhaps we better had.'

Max opened the case and laid it on the floor. He had no expectation of finding anything of interest. Appleby had already had ample opportunity to examine the contents of Sir Henry's room at the Majestic and remove anything significant. His expectation was duly fulfilled. The case held only clothes and toiletries. He delved into every corner and into every pocket of the jackets and trousers. There was nothing else.

'No diary,' he said, closing the case.

'Then she made it up,' came Ashley's fatuous response.

'And the list? Did she make that up? The original's in Pa's hand-writing. I saw it for myself.'

'There's no mortgage on Gresscombe Place, James. And no secret family trust. It's balderdash.'

'You think Pa wrote the list for no reason?'

'I think we can't hope to know the reason. A man's bound to leave a few minor mysteries behind him when he dies as suddenly and unexpectedly as Pa did.'

'So, you refuse to accept he may have been murdered?'

'The suggestion's preposterous. Why would anyone want to murder him?'

'That's what I mean to find out.'

'Fortunately, there's no time for you to make a nuisance of your-self by trying. We leave on the noon train tomorrow.'

'That won't be possible, I'm afraid.'

'What?' Ashley stared at him incredulously, though why he should be so surprised Max did not understand. The logic of what he had said was obvious and it did not involve leaving Paris in the near future.

'I believe Pa may well have been murdered, Ashley. That doesn't appear to bother you or the police or the Foreign Office. But it does

80

bother me. And I intend to do everything in my power to establish the truth of what happened to him.'

Ashley reddened ominously. 'I had your word – your solemn word – that you'd help me protect our family's good name.'

'I am protecting it. By seeking justice for a member of it.'

'You'll be on that train tomorrow.'

'I will not.'

'Mother expects us *both* to take Pa home.'

'She'll understand why I've stayed.'

'She most certainly won't.'

'I'm not leaving, Ashley. You may as well face it.'

'I'm warning you, James.' Ashley jabbed a forefinger threateningly in Max's direction. 'Defy me in this and there'll be consequences. You need my agreement to open your damned flying school, remember.'

'I felt sure you wouldn't allow me to forget it.'

'Stay here and you *can* forget it.'

So, it had come to that, as Max had feared it would. 'I can't trust someone who's willing to let his father's probable murder be brushed under the carpet, Ashley. You scuttle back to England and spread whatever lies you like about me. I'll stay here. And do my duty.'

MAX FELT AS IF A HEAVY AND IRKSOME BURDEN HAD BEEN lifted from his shoulders following his altercation with Ashley. It was no longer necessary to pretend they were acting in concert. The use of Gresscombe land for a flying school had ceased to be a carrot dangling in front of his nose. He had always been one to chafe at limitations on his freedom. Now he need chafe no more.

He was aware that the effort of planning for the future, something he had not needed to do during the war, had oppressed him of late. It was not his forte. He was a man of action and of instinct. The RFC had found him valuable on that account, but there had seemed no call for his particular strengths in the peacetime world. His father's murder – he did not seriously doubt it *was* murder – had changed all that. He was about to revert to what he did best.

He rose early next morning and fired off a couple of telegrams. The first was to Sam. He did not want to break the bad news to him by cable, so contented himself with a holding message. *Delayed in Paris for indefinite period.* The second telegram was to his mother, worded to alert her to what he was trying to accomplish. *Will remain in Paris until possible to report true version of events.* He was confident she would see through whatever misrepresentations Ashley attempted. He was only doing what she had assured him she expected him to do. He breakfasted at a nearby café, having no wish to risk a frosty encounter with Ashley at the hotel. There he considered his position. He was tempted to proceed directly to the offices of Ireton Associates, but thinking fondly of Sam, as he had

that morning, reminded him of the value of thoroughness. It could be, he knew, the difference between life and death.

A hot afternoon in the summer of 1916, waiting to go on patrol, had exhausted even Max's capacity for dozing and lazing. Hearing that Sergeant Twentyman was still working on his plane, he had gone to find out why.

Sam was alone in the maintenance hangar, fiddling with the control wires for the elevator and rudder on Max's Sopwith Camel. 'Haven't you finished with her yet, Twentyman?' Max demanded.

'Not quite, sir,' Sam replied, without turning round.

'Why are you so much slower than the other riggers?'

'I'm not, sir. I just do more than they do.'

'More of what, damn it?'

'Checking, sir.' Sam did turn round now, his smile flashing through a face darkened by oil and sunburn. 'It's surprising what you find.'

'And what have you found?'

'Nothing you need to worry about, sir. Now I've checked, she won't let you down.'

'But if you hadn't she would have?'

'Might've, sir. Easily might've. And I'd never have forgiven myself if she had. There's not much I can do about the Hun. But at least I can check everything for you, can't I?'

Whether Max would be able to carry out the check he wanted to remained to be seen. He could only trust to luck. But it was still early enough to hope he would catch the staff of the Majestic on the hop.

The detective on the door looked promisingly bleary-eyed. Max confidently asserted that 'Mr Appleby' had approved his visit. This seemed to impress the detective, who, after scrutinizing Max's passport, took him in to the reception desk.

By chance, the clerk on duty was the same man Max had met there before. He recognized Max and offered his respectful condolences. He also confirmed that Sir Henry's room had not yet been reallocated.

'So,' said Max, 'there can be no objection to my taking a look at it.' He deliberately phrased this as a statement rather than a question.

'What are you looking *for*, sir?' the detective asked.

'I simply wish to satisfy myself that all my late father's effects have been removed. My mother would never forgive me if anything of sentimental value was left behind.'

The detective mulled this over for a moment, then gave his reluctant consent. There was a delay while a colleague of his was summoned to escort Max. 'Can't have you wandering around the hotel on your own, sir. You might get lost.' The clerk supplied the key and they set off.

The colleague was younger and friendlier and considerably tubbier. He introduced himself in the course of a lengthy tramp up two separate flights of stairs and along various winding corridors as Sergeant Benson, drafted in from the Suffolk constabulary, who was enjoying himself in Paris – 'as far as they'll let me, sir, if you catch my drift'. He was considerably out of breath by the time they reached Sir Henry's room.

It was at the back of the hotel, with a view of chimney-stacks and little else, smaller than Max had expected and poorly lit. Sir Henry's relative unimportance in the British delegation was depressingly obvious.

'Looks pretty empty . . . to me, sir,' Benson panted.

'I'll just make sure.' Max embarked on a careful inspection of the desk, wardrobe, chest of drawers and bedside cabinet. It revealed nothing. He crouched down for a view under the bed and saw only dust and what might have been mouse droppings. He did not know what he was looking for, of course, nor if there was anything to be looked for. But he knew his father to be cautious, if not secretive, by nature, despite the ample evidence of his recent recklessness. It would not have surprised Max to discover that the old man had hidden something there. It was becoming clear he had hidden a great deal about his life of late.

Max was himself no stranger to hiding things. It had been a valuable skill in the camp. Rising to his feet, he remembered the

84

role of bunk-posts in concealing material from the guards. Surreptitiously sawing off the top of the posts supporting the prisoners' bunks and hollowing out their interiors created a space in which all manner of articles could be stashed. Max recalled mentioning this when recounting some of his POW experiences to his father during their dinner at the Ritz.

The bed in Sir Henry's room had stout brass posts topped with umbrella-shaped finials. Max was standing close to one of the posts at the head of the bed. He grasped the finial and gave it a speculative twist. There was brief resistance, then it began to unscrew.

'You certainly do believe in making sure, sir,' said Benson.

'May as well, while I'm here.' Max completed the unscrewing and lifted the finial off. He peered into the hollow post and saw nothing, though it was too dark to be sure. 'You don't have a torch, do you?' he asked.

'Not on me, sir. I'd have to go back downstairs to fetch one.'

'Would it be too much trouble?'

Benson gave a put-upon sigh. 'I suppose not. You'd better come with me.'

'If you insist.'

Benson frowned. 'Oh well, perhaps it'd be all right if you just waited here. I'll be as quick as I can.'

'Thanks.'

Benson set off and Max tossed the finial down on the bed. He lit a cigarette and wondered how long the sergeant would be. He strongly suspected he had sent him on a pointless journey. There was surely nothing to be found. He sat down on the bed.

The depression of the mattress caused the finial to roll off the coverlet and fall to the floor with a clunk. Max bent forward to pick it up. Then he stopped.

Lying next to the toppled finial was a small brass key. It had been dislodged from some crevice inside the finial by the impact. Max seized it at once and glanced guiltily round at the open door-way. But there was no one watching him.

The warding on the bit of the key suggested it fitted a Yale lock or similar. It was surprisingly heavy as it rested in Max's hand. It did not rest there for long.

Benson found Max sitting on the bed, smoking a second cigarette, when he returned, his arrival announced from some way off by his heavy tread and heavier breathing. Max thanked him for putting himself out. Armed with the torch Benson had brought, he took a look inside all four bedposts. They were all empty.

Max added further thanks as they headed downstairs. He had no wish to linger now. He had got what he had come for. True, a key was of little use if you did not know where the lock was that it fitted. But Max backed himself to find that out, one way or another, sooner or later. If there was a key, there was a lock. If there was a lock, there was something worth locking away. And he was on the trail of it.

But leaving the Majestic was not to prove as straightforward as entering it. On the last half-landing before the lobby, they nearly collided with a bulky figure hurrying up the stairs. It was Appleby.

'I gather you've been taking my name in vain, Mr Maxted.' Appleby's basilisk stare revealed a colder, harder side to the man than he had chosen to display the day before. 'Did you find what you were looking for?'

'I didn't find anything.'

'That's right, sir,' said Benson.

Appleby ignored the sergeant's intervention and went on staring at Max. 'I think you and I need to have a word.'

APPLEBY HAD A SMALL OFFICE IN THE BASEMENT OF THE HOTEL, guarded by a gorgonian secretary. He appeared to have bolted a breakfast in order to intercept Max: an egg-smeared plate and a half-drunk cup of tea stood beside two telephones on his desk. A large map of Paris, sporting a patchy forest of red-headed drawing-pins, dominated one wall. Sallow light seeped in through frosted windows set near the ceiling, along with blurred impressions of the feet and legs of passing pedestrians in the street outside.

Benson had been sent on his way with a flea in his ear, leaving Max to plead his case for himself. Appleby had left him to stew while he spoke to his secretary, then he had returned, closing the door of the office firmly behind him.

'I'll ask you again, Mr Maxted,' Appleby began, slumping down in his chair. 'Did you find what you were looking for?'

'As I've already told you,' Max replied, smiling casually at Appleby across his desk, 'I didn't find anything.'

'Using my name to gain access to your father's room suggests to me you had a compelling reason for going there.'

'I wanted to establish nothing belonging to my father had been left behind.'

'Did you have any reason to think it had?'

'No.'

'Then why the subterfuge?'

'I didn't want to bother you. I felt sure you'd have agreed to my request if I'd put it to you.'

'You didn't want to bother me? How very considerate. It won't

87

do, Mr Maxted, it really won't. You tricked Sergeant Benson into leaving you alone, presumably in order to remove whatever it was you knew to be hidden in the room without being observed.'

'It was no trick. I asked him to fetch a torch so I could look inside the bedposts.'

'And he, credulous idiot that he is, trotted off in search of one. Bedposts, my aunt Fanny. It was obviously a blind.'

How ironic, Max thought, that he should be credited with such deviousness, when the bedpost was indeed where the key had been concealed. 'If you're right, Appleby, I have this . . . hidden object . . . somewhere on my person. Do you want to search me?' He felt secure in the bluff. He could reasonably claim personal ownership of the key. Appleby would know no better.

'That won't be necessary.' Appleby took out his pipe and laboriously filled it, while looking at Max with fixed studiousness. 'What's this all about, Mr Maxted?' he enquired at last.

'Are you a police officer, Appleby? Nobody ever seems to mention your rank.'

'I'm not a Scotland Yard man, if that's what you mean. I have no official rank. Why do you ask?'

'I'd just like to know who's interrogating me.'

'No one is,' Appleby sighed. 'This is a conversation. Believe me, if it were an interrogation, you'd notice the difference. Now, are you going to tell me why you came here this morning?'

'Are you going to tell me why you're making no effort to find my father's murderer?'

Max had expected the question to ruffle Appleby. But it had no discernible effect. 'What makes you think he was murdered, Mr Maxted?'

'The same things that make you think it, I should imagine. It was the blood beneath his fingernails that first caught my attention.'

'There was no blood.'

'Yes, there was. Why else would the nails be so severely cut? Then I noticed the broken skylight at eight Rue du Verger. Broken from the inside. I'm not sure what that means, but it doesn't fit Zamaron's theory and I'm not surprised. A few words with Spataro convinced me he's lying. As I'm sure you know, Madame

Dombreux was lured away the night my father died. That alone proves there was a plot of some kind.'

Appleby puffed thoughtfully at his pipe. 'I believe we only have Madame Dombreux's word for her visit to Nantes.'

'And her sister's, if you cared to ask.'

'Blood's thicker than water. You know how it is.'

'I know how you seem determined to make it appear. It won't wash. Not with me.'

'But with your brother?'

'Ashley wants no breath of scandal. To me the scandal is allowing our father's murder to be written off as an accident.'

'A laudable attitude. But consider the national interest for a moment, as I'm sure your father would have done. The peace conference is at a delicate stage. Progress towards a treaty is far too slow. And bad news keeps coming in. This revolution in Hungary, for instance. God knows what the implications are. The Prime Minister is trying to speed things along as best he can, but to do that he has to win over both the French and the Americans. No easy task. And it certainly won't be helped by publicity being given to Sir Henry's relationship with Madame Dombreux. You're aware she's viewed with suspicion by the French authorities?'

'Because of her late husband's activities in Russia? Yes. I'm aware of it.'

'Ah. You two had a regular heart-to-heart, then. There's nothing more deceptive than candour, of course. You should bear that in mind.'

'I will.'

'An attractive woman, Madame Dombreux. There's no denying it. Eyes you could drown in. I imagine a good few men have besides your father and her late husband.'

'Do you really know anything about her?'

'I know my French colleagues believe she may have been a party to Dombreux's dealings with the Bolsheviks.'

'How could she have been? She was living here in Paris at the time. They'd separated.'

'Ah, but how long had Dombreux been working for the Reds? That's the question. And might the Dombreux' marital problems

merely have been a ploy to garner the Cheka a spy in Paris to add to the one they already had in Petrograd?'

'That's absurd.'

'Maybe, maybe not. Either way, it makes Madame Dombreux a spectacularly poor choice of mistress for a British diplomat. Some might go so far as to suggest it calls his own loyalties into question.'

Before Max could fashion a retort, there was a knock at the door. Appleby barked out a 'Come in' and Max turned to see a thin, grey-suited man of apologetic demeanour enter the room. Bespectacled, with centre-parted hair and a complexion matching his suit, he was so lacking in presence as to be almost absent.

'Mr Norris,' Appleby greeted him. 'Meet Mr Maxted.'

'My condolences in respect of your father,' said Norris, offering Max a limp hand. 'I, er, had the privilege of knowing him.'

'Mr Norris oversaw Sir Henry's work for the delegation,' Appleby explained – unnecessarily, as it happened. 'I thought his contribution to our discussion might be useful.'

Ye Gods, thought Max, how could his father have tolerated answering to this wet week of a man?

'I'm not exactly sure what I can tell you,' Norris said hesitantly.

'Tell him what Sir Henry did, man,' growled Appleby.

'Of course, of course. Well, his role here was invaluable, I can assure you, although perhaps ... by some yardsticks ... peripheral. That's by no means unusual. We've assembled a wealth of knowledge and expertise here for the Prime Minister and his senior advisers to call upon. Inevitably, some of that ... knowledge and expertise ... is required only rarely ... though crucial when the need arises.'

'You're saying my father spent most of his time twiddling his thumbs?'

'No, no, not at all.' Norris appeared disconcerted by Max's directness. 'He was in regular contact with the Brazilian delegation.'

'In particular a Senhor Ribeiro?'

'Yes. Ribeiro. How did—'

'My father mentioned him. They knew each another from Rio.'

'Ah, yes. Sir Henry . . . spent some years in Brazil. Hence his selection . . . as a special adviser.'

'What's the Brazilians' biggest bone of contention, Mr Norris?' Appleby asked in a tone that suggested he knew the answer and found it paltry, but felt it needed spelling out nonetheless.

'Well, the principal difficulty in which we have an interest revolves around settling the fate of forty-three German merchant ships detained in Brazilian ports when Brazil declared war on Germany in . . . October 1917. Actually, they were detained earlier than that, but . . . the timing isn't strictly relevant.'

'Indeed not,' murmured Appleby.

'Well,' Norris bumbled on, 'the Brazilians claim ownership of the vessels, thirty of which they've since leased to France, but we feel, as do the French, that they should ultimately be allocated amongst the allies in proportion to the amount of merchant shipping each ally lost during the war, a calculation which would leave Brazil with far fewer than forty-three. A complication is that by leasing some of the vessels France could be deemed to have acknowledged that they belong to Brazil, something we obviously don't accept.'

'And what was Sir Henry doing about this?' Appleby asked wearily.

'Essentially, his task was to monitor the strength of Brazilian feeling on the issue and the success or otherwise of their efforts to win support for their cause, while seeking to persuade them to accept a compromise that would prevent the problem becoming an obstacle to the conclusion of an overall peace treaty. Seeking to formulate such a compromise involved him in discussions with the French, obviously, as well as the Americans, who see themselves to some degree as champions of their continental neighbours. They've already sided with them, for instance, over the question of the exchange rate to be applied to payments owing to various Brazilian coffee producers for consignments of coffee trapped in German-controlled ports in August 1914. The German mark has depreciated drastically since then, of course, hence—'

'Thank you, Mr Norris,' Appleby cut in. 'We'll leave the coffee question for another day. I can't stand the stuff, so I've no

91

sympathy for anyone involved in the trade. Would it be true to say, in conclusion, that Sir Henry's work for the delegation, though important in the narrow context you've described, was routine, normal and uncontroversial?'

'Why . . . yes. Of course.'

'I trust that's clear, Mr Maxted?'

Max nodded. 'Yes.' So it was. Which proved nothing as far as he was concerned.

'The Brazilian delegation is based at the Plaza Athénée in Avenue Montaigne,' said Norris. 'I'm sure Senhor Ribeiro . . . as an old friend of your father's . . . would be pleased to make your acquaintance, Mr Maxted.'

'A kind thought,' said Appleby, 'but Mr Maxted isn't staying in Paris long enough to act on it, I'm afraid.'

'That isn't necessarily true,' said Max.

'I understood you and your brother were catching the noon train to London.'

'I'm staying here. *Pro tem.*'

'You are?'

'I can't leave with so much unresolved, Appleby. Surely you can see that.'

Appleby ground the stem of his pipe between his teeth and stared hard at Max for a moment, then said, 'Thank you for your time, Mr Norris. We need detain you no longer.'

He went on staring at Max while Norris took his leave, a procedure prolonged and complicated by a collision with the hat-stand and an apologetic retrieval of Appleby's trilby from the floor. Eventually, he was gone.

'Won't you be attending your father's funeral, Mr Maxted?' Appleby asked, still chewing at his pipe.

'The funeral won't be for a couple of days at least.'

'And what can you accomplish here in a couple of days?'

'That remains to be seen.'

'You'd be better advised to leave this kind of thing to the professionals, you really would.'

'Meaning you and the local police?'

'Precisely.'

'Who propose to treat my father's murder as a bizarre and undignified accident.'

'I've explained to you why that's in everyone's best interests. You were assured Zamaron's theory about what took Sir Henry on to the roof of that building will never figure in any official verdict, an assurance with which your brother seemed, I have to say, quite content. And he is now, I need hardly point out, the head of your family.'

'He must follow the dictates of his conscience, as must I.'

'So, this is an issue of conscience for you, is it?'

'I intend to leave no stone unturned in my search for my father's murderer. You may take that as a definitive statement of my position. And now . . .'

Max started from his chair, but was halted by Appleby raising his hand and by a slight but significant change in the man's expression. He looked suddenly solicitous.

'As a pilot, you were fortunate to survive the war, Mr Maxted. I'd urge you to make the most of your good fortune. You have a life to enjoy. Don't waste it.'

'What are you trying to say, Appleby?'

'I can't guarantee your safety if you stay here.'

'I'm not asking you to.'

'Paris is full of thieves, vagrants, beggars, con men, crooks and desperadoes. Go looking for trouble and you'll be sure to find it.'

'It's the truth I'm after, not trouble.'

'They're often the same thing, in my experience. Let me give you some advice, as one who's seen more of the world than you have. Give this up. Go home, bury your father and forget whatever folly led him to his death. It's good advice, believe me.' Appleby sighed. 'But entirely futile, of course.'

'Yes.' Max smiled. 'It is.'

MAX WAS IN A HURRY NOW, EMBOLDENED BY THE RESULT OF HIS visit to the Majestic. He took the Métro – which impressed him no more favourably than the London Underground – from Etoile to the Tuileries and walked up Rue des Pyramides to number 33.

The offices of Ireton Associates were on the first floor of a handsome building near the junction with Avenue de l'Opéra. Max hardly knew what to expect. What he found was a small and apparently lethargic operation in the charge of a polite but unsmiling American secretary. She was middle-aged and school-marmish, chestnut hair helmeted to her head, eyes gleaming behind alarmingly winged horn-rimmed glasses. Her posture hinted at tight corsetry beneath the thick layers of tweed.

'Mr Ireton isn't here at present, sir,' she explained. 'And he sees no one without an appointment.'

'Perhaps I could make one.'

'May I ask what this is in connection with?'

'It concerns my late father, Sir Henry Maxted.'

'You're his son?'

'I am. James Maxted.'

'My condolences, Mr Maxted. I heard of your father's death. Such a sad thing.'

'Indeed. I—'

Max broke off and looked round. A flicker in the secretary's gaze had alerted him to a movement behind him. A large, not to say enormous, man in a dark hat and overcoat was standing in the

94

corridor that led from neighbouring rooms to the main door. He might have moved on castors, given how noiselessly he had arrived there, which was all the more surprising considering the vastness of his build. He had craggy, weather-beaten features and a sorrowful expression. His nose looked as if it had been broken, possibly more than once. Max felt eerily certain it had not been broken in a sporting endeavour.

'Is there anything you need, Mr Morahan?' the secretary asked, sounding genuinely anxious on the point.

'Nothing,' came the softly growled reply. (Morahan was clearly also American.) 'But you might like to call Travis.' A faint nod in Max's direction implied he was the reason for the suggestion.

'Just what I was thinking.'

'I'll see you later.' With that, and a touch of his hat, Morahan glided out.

'Bear with me, Mr Maxted,' the secretary said, returning her attention to Max. 'I'll see if I can reach Mr Ireton.'

She spoke to the operator in fluent French, too fluently for Max to follow. As she waited to be connected, he glanced out through the window beside her desk. He saw Morahan emerge from the building on to the pavement, towering over other pedestrians in his long black coat. He paused to light a cigarette, then strode across the road and vanished down the steps leading to the Pyramides Métro station.

The secretary began speaking, presumably to Ireton, though she did not use his name. 'I have a Mr James Maxted here . . . That's correct . . . Yes . . . Sure.' She offered Max the phone without further explanation. He took it.

'Travis Ireton?'

'The same. You're the son I met at the Ritz?'

'I am.'

'Terrible shame about your father.'

'Yes. It is.'

'You want to meet?'

'I was hoping to. I—'

'We should, I agree. But I'm spread thin today. Can you come to the office at . . . six thirty?'

'I can, yes.'

'We'll talk then. Put Malory back on, would you?'

Whether Malory was the secretary's Christian name or surname was unclear. Max handed the phone to her and she began taking notes on a pad, contributing little more than 'Yes' and 'Uh-huh' as the conversation proceeded.

It took Max a minute or so to realize that she regarded him as a matter satisfactorily dealt with. His farewell nod was barely acknowledged.

Appleby's mood had not improved following Max's departure from the Majestic. His conviction that the young man had stolen a march on him was only one reason. The other was the telegram he had received shortly afterwards. He had not anticipated a peremptory summons to the godhead in London and was annoyed with himself on that account alone. He should have foreseen such a development. The Maxted affair, he concluded over a contemplative pipe, was going to require a greater share of his attention than he had so far devoted to it.

A knock at his door heralded the arrival of Lamb, the most intelligent and reliable of his operatives. He was young and moon-faced, with the mild demeanour of a bank clerk. But a keen brain ticked away inside his head. He was perfect for this line of work, taking quiet pleasure from the invisibility of his achievements and requiring little in the way of overt praise.

'Is there a flap on, sir?' Lamb disingenuously enquired.

'I have to go to London. A flying visit, I hope. I want some surveillance put in hand in my absence. This fellow.' Appleby slid a photograph culled from RFC records across his desk. 'James Maxted. Younger son of the late Sir Henry Maxted.'

'Ah. The faller.'

'As the mighty can sometimes become. We have to pick up the pieces. Maxted's staying at the Mazarin in Rue Coligny. Tail him from there. Stick with him wherever he goes, but stay out of sight. I'll want as much detail as possible.'

'You'll have it, sir.'

'If he gets into any trouble . . .'

'Yes, sir?'

Appleby deliberated for a moment, then replied. 'Don't intervene.'

With time on his hands, Max decided to see his father off at the Gare du Nord. He did so in his own way, having no wish for a further exchange of angry words with Ashley. There was a side-entrance to the station for goods and mail. And it was there that he witnessed the arrival of a hearse bearing the name *Prettre et fils, pompes funèbres*. It was discreetly managed, with a full half hour to spare before the departure of the noon train to London. Monsieur Prettre had been as good as his word.

After seeing the coffin unloaded and wheeled into the station, suitably draped, on a trolley, Max went round to the front of the building. He had spied out a café on the other side of the street, from where he could watch taxis come and go.

He did not have to wait long for one to discharge Ashley. He was accompanied by Fradgley, who looked flustered and fretful. Max amused himself by attributing Fradgley's distracted appearance to the fact that only one of the Maxted brothers was with him. But he was aware that his amusement would rebound on him if he accomplished nothing by remaining in Paris.

He watched the station clock move slowly towards noon, calculating that Fradgley's reappearance would tell him when the train had left.

Then, to his surprise, he recognized someone else clambering out of a taxi: Appleby. And the fellow was carrying a travelling bag, as if intent on taking the train to London himself.

Max could scarcely credit that such was Appleby's intention. But noon passed and the train left. He knew that because Fradgley emerged on to the forecourt at five past the hour – alone. There was no sign of Appleby.

After Fradgley had boarded a cab and vanished, Max left the café and set off southwards on foot, turning over in his mind the mystery of Appleby's sudden departure. It was far from reassuring to know that Ashley would have Appleby's company for the next

seven hours. In his efforts to persuade Ashley that their father really had been murdered, Max had revealed more than he wanted Appleby to know. He could not rely on his brother to keep such information to himself. But there was absolutely nothing he could do about it now.

IRETON WAS WAITING FOR MAX WHEN HE ARRIVED AT 33 RUE DES Pyramides that evening – waiting, indeed, at the head of the stairs, with a glass of whisky in his hand and a broad smile on his face. He breezily conferred first-name terms on their acquaintance while ushering Max into his offices.

'Malory's a wondrous manageress of my affairs,' Ireton explained as he poured Max a Scotch and persuaded him to sample an American cigarette, 'but she can be a little stern, especially in the a.m., if you know what I mean.'

'It's good of you to see me.'

'Not at all. Your father's death was a terrible waste. I want you to know most particularly how sorry I am.'

'Thank you.'

'We could have done this at the Ritz or the Crillon.' Ireton led Max through to an inner office, where a fire was blazing. There were armchairs arranged around it. 'But I thought you'd value some privacy.'

'That was considerate of you.'

'Do the police have a theory to account for what happened?'

'Nothing I'd dignify with the word "theory".'

'That so?' They sat down and Ireton went on smiling, but was frowning slightly now as well, as if unsure quite what to make of Max. 'Well, it was a damn shame, however it came about. Do you have any ideas yourself?'

'I believe my father was murdered, Travis.'

'You do?' The frown deepened.

'Yes.'

'I see. Well, that's . . .' Then the frown lifted. He spread a hand expressively. 'That's what I surmised, Max. Henry wasn't an accident-prone man. I wouldn't have mentioned it if you were set on buying the police's cockamamie version of events, but since you're not . . .'

'You know what their version of events is?'

'I do.'

'You're well-informed, I must say.'

'I make it my business to be. Matter of fact, it *is* my business to be.'

' "All your needs in post-war Paris". It's a broad remit.'

Ireton chuckled. 'As broad as it's long. What do you need, Max?'

'Evidence of who murdered my father and why.'

'Which you think I can supply?'

'I don't know. But then I don't know what dealings you had with him.'

'No. I guess not.' Ireton took a long draw on his cigarette. 'What I do is a little hard to define. You could say I trade in the commodity that most of the delegates and journalists and speculators and hangers-on who've gathered here spend most of their time trying to lay their hands on. Information. *Timely* information. By which I mean they hear it from me before it becomes common knowledge. For that advantage they're willing to pay. That, simply put, is my business. Your prime minister took himself and his senior advisers off to Fontainebleau last weekend to thrash out a new policy on the peace treaty. A lot of people who weren't there wanted to know what they'd settled on before it was made public. They turned to me. And suffice to say they weren't disappointed.'

'How did you pull that off?'

'It's what I do, Max. It's my living. Has been for a good many years. I go wherever information is most in demand. Just now that's Paris, luckily for me.' He broke off to tong some coal on to the fire. 'Though I'd be grateful for more springlike weather. *Paris au printemps*, hey? This isn't what I had in mind, let me tell you.'

'Isn't there a shortage of coal in the city? My hotel's cold as charity.'

'Oh, yes, there's a shortage.' Ireton grinned blithely. 'But I think better when I'm warm, so scrimping's out of the question. So it should be for you. I bet you dreamt of creature comforts like a roaring fire when you were a POW. I bet you reckoned you were owed them for laying your life on the line for your country.'

Max did not deny it, though the truth was that he had volunteered less for patriotic reasons than for the chance it had given him of flying on a daily basis. He had missed that in the camp rather more keenly than a glowing hearth.

'I saw some action in Cuba in 'ninety-eight,' Ireton went on. 'I realized then that I had no gift for self-denial. My talents lie else-where.' He pitched the butt of his cigarette into the fire and lit another. 'And I believe we should all make the most of our talents.'

'About my father, Travis . . .' Max engaged Ireton eye to eye as he accepted a second cigarette. The time for sparring was over. 'What exactly were your dealings with him?'

'OK.' Ireton relaxed into his chair. 'Cards on the table. Naturally, I buy information as well as sell it. I'm a broker. People come to me because I enable them to trade anonymously. The governments or organizations they work for wouldn't necessarily approve of what they're doing. It isn't illegal, but it could be regarded as unethical, even disloyal. My discretion is one of the things I charge for. It's one the things I'm *known* for. My clients rely on it. You understand? It's not a trivial matter.'

'Was my father a client of yours?'

'He might have been.'

'As a buyer or a seller?'

'How would you feel if I said Henry was active in the infor-mation market?'

'Incredulous. He would never have betrayed his country.'

'Betrayal's a strong word. Most of the material I deal in falls well short of earth-shattering. Henry was in regular contact with the Brazilian delegation. The other South American delegations – Bolivia, Ecuador, Peru, Uruguay – would all like to know more about Brazil's negotiating tactics. And vice versa, of course. The outcome of this conference isn't going to be affected in the slightest way by trading small amounts of such information.'

'Are you saying that's what my father did?'

'Would it be so terrible if he had?'

Could it be true? Max was aware that his incredulity was founded on his knowledge of his father's character. But he could not help wondering if his knowledge amounted to anything more than a set of conventional – and quite possibly false – assumptions. 'It would be terrible if it led to his death.'

'Nothing Henry worked on was important enough to get him murdered, Max, it truly wasn't.'

'What was, then?'

'I'm not sure. But . . .'

'But what?'

Ireton fell silent for a long, thoughtful moment, then said, 'To share my suspicions with you involves letting you know more about my activities than is frankly wise, considering you and I are barely acquainted. I'd like to help you, largely because I liked and admired Henry and reckon he'd probably want me to help you. But I can't allow myself to be swayed by sentiment.'

'What *would* sway you?' There had to be something, Max reckoned. Otherwise why would Ireton have agreed to meet him in the first place?

'A demonstration of your trustworthiness, Max.' Ireton nodded for emphasis. 'That's what I need.'

'What did you have in mind?'

'A small service I'd repay with my confidence in you. I'm always happier if both sides have a bargain to honour.'

'And this service is?'

'The collection of an item from a man I'd prefer not to meet face to face. A simple matter. It shouldn't cause you any difficulty.'

Words were cheap, of course. Max was not blind to the possibility that he was being led on. Ireton might have nothing of value to disclose and see this as a way of solving a bothersome problem. 'Why not send one of your associates? Morahan, for instance.'

'Ah, yes, you met Schools earlier, didn't you? Well, I could send him, but that wouldn't tell me whether you're the sort of person I can rely on, now would it? Look at this from my point of view, Max. It's a question of establishing your *bona fides*. I have to be

sure of you. I can't proceed unless I am. You'll be taking a risk, of course. You only have my word for it that I can help you discover who may have murdered Henry. But you're not a stranger to risks and I don't believe for a moment you mean to shy away from this one. So, shall I tell you the name of the man I want you to meet and where and when I want you to meet him – or not?'

Sɪʀ Hᴇɴʀʏ Mᴀxᴛᴇᴅ ʜᴀᴅ ᴄᴏᴍᴇ ʜᴏᴍᴇ. Hᴇ ʀᴇᴘᴏꜱᴇᴅ ᴛʜᴀᴛ ɴɪɢʜᴛ in the library at Gresscombe Place. The delivery of his body in a stout oak coffin had been efficiently managed by the local undertaker. It had taken place late in the evening, at the conclusion of a lengthy journey from Paris that had left Ashley exhausted and fit only for bed.

Lydia was by contrast feeling far from sleepy. Her curiosity about her brother-in-law's reasons for remaining in Paris had thus far been held in check. Now, in the privacy of their bedroom, she proceeded to bombard her heavy-lidded husband with questions.

'Surely he understands there will be a price to pay for defying you in this manner, darling?'

'Oh, he understands. He just doesn't seem to care.'

'Doesn't he care about the good name of his own family? Or his father's reputation?'

Ashley's answering sigh converted itself into an irrepressible yawn. He had informed Lydia earlier, during a snatched quarter of an hour alone together, of the French police's theory concerning Sir Henry's death. To his mother he had offered only their official bafflement, having despaired of inventing any plausible alternative. 'James has convinced himself Pa was murdered. He says he means to bring the murderer to justice.'

'He wasn't murdered, though, was he?'

'I don't think so. But, if he was, it will have been for some scandalous reason we're all better off not knowing about. Pa made a prize fool of himself in Paris and suffered for it.'

'That doesn't mean *we* have to suffer for it as well, darling. Think of your poor mother.' Lydia was not in fact thinking of her mother-in-law at all, but even to Ashley she did not care to reveal the full extent of her callousness.

'James said he was determined to uncover the truth at all costs.'

'How typically perverse of him. As if the truth were all that mattered.'

'I felt sure my say-so regarding those fields he needs for his flying school would suffice to keep him in line.'

'You left him in no doubt that he'd forfeit the land if he went on with this?'

'I made it very clear to him. It had no effect.'

'How can he be so indifferent to his own best interests?'

'I don't know. I'd blame the war, but he's always been the same.'

'Do you think he'll come back for the funeral?'

'The day after tomorrow? I doubt it. I shall cable him with the details in the morning and leave it to him.'

'His absence will be so embarrassing, darling. How will we explain it?'

'We'll say he's ill. What other excuse can we offer? Cutting his own father's funeral is a damn poor show.'

'And raising a stink in Paris will only make matters worse. What can we do to bring him to heel?'

'Nothing. But don't worry unduly. I'm assured by those who know that his enquiries will hit a brick wall. Eventually, he'll be forced to admit defeat.'

'And then?'

'Then?' Ashley ineffectually stifled another yawn. 'He'll come home, I suppose. With his tail between his legs.'

In the few minutes between turning off the light and his descent into slumber, Ashley was visited by a frisson of doubt concerning his professed certainty that James would fail in his quest for the truth. The fellow was too stubborn and resourceful to be written off. Appleby, who had travelled with Ashley from Paris to London, had pooh-poohed the grounds for suspicion James had presented to Ashley. ('This list sounds like something and nothing to me, Sir

105

Ashley. Your brother is wasting his time.') But, upon reflection, Appleby had perhaps overdone the pooh-poohing. And the reason he had given for being on the train – a 'family emergency' – was rather too pat for comfort. Should Ashley have been more guarded in what he said? It was a worrying question, since he found it difficult now to recall just what he had said. Damn Appleby *and* James, he thought. And with that he plunged into a deep sleep.

At that moment Lady Maxted was standing beside the trestle-mounted coffin in the library, gazing down at the death-masked face of her late husband. Part of his head was concealed by a thick white veil, to spare her the sight of his fatal brain injury. What remained visible were recognizably the features of Sir Henry Maxted, but Henry the man was gone, lost to her entirely.

She had displayed as much disappointment at the news that James had remained in Paris as she had judged Ashley and Lydia would expect. And she had allowed Ashley to give an obviously inadequate account of what he had accomplished there. Altogether, she had played the part of the meek and pliant widow quite shamelessly.

From the pocket of her dress she took the telegram James had sent her that morning. She unfolded it and reread the message. *Will remain in Paris until possible to report true version of events.* Then her gaze returned to the never-again-to-open eyes of Sir Henry Maxted. 'He has pledged himself for you, Henry,' she murmured. 'He will not let you down.'

At the same moment, glumly installed with a pint of Bass in a smoky corner of the public bar of the Rose and Crown, Walthamstow, Sam Twentyman pulled from his pocket the telegram he had also received from Max earlier that day. He reread the message for the umpteenth time. *Delayed in Paris for indefinite period.* No address was supplied for a reply.

'You're trying to let me down lightly, aren't you, sir?' Sam murmured as he put the telegram away again. He sensed the flying school he had set his sights on slipping fast from his future. And without it that future looked bleak. Ill-advisedly, as he now saw, he

had paid Miller a deposit on the planes he had persuaded Max they should buy and would forfeit it if they did not conclude the purchase within ten days. It was money he could not afford to spend. But that was not the worst of it, not by a long way. If Max abandoned his plans for a flying school, Sam would be condemned to a lick-spittle role in his father's bakery business. The prospect appalled him. To avoid it he found it hard to imagine what he would not be willing to do.

And that was not his only concern. *Delayed in Paris for indefinite period* was a message that said more than it was intended to. It sounded to him as if Max was in trouble – or soon would be. He needed Sam's help whether he knew it or not. That had often been the case in the war. Apparently, it still was.

'Flying solo's no good without a mechanic you can rely on, sir,' Sam mused. 'You should know that.'

Also at the same moment, two hundred miles away, in Paris, Corinne Dombreux was walking along Rue du Verger, on her way home from an evening shift at the ticket office at the Gare Montparnasse. She was tired and in low spirits. The shock of Henry's death had faded, but the grief of losing him was an ache she could not ease. She was relying on Max to discover who had murdered his father and why, but she did not know when she would next hear from him or whether he would be able to achieve anything. It might only make her life more difficult if he did. The authorities regarded her with acute suspicion. They could move against her at any time. Nothing about her existence was secure. Pierre had bequeathed her only adversity and notoriety. And she did not know how much longer she could face both of them down.

As she approached number 8, a massive figure suddenly detached itself from the deep shadow of a doorway opposite and lurched across the street towards her. 'Corinne,' Spataro called. '*Attends un peu.*'

'I have nothing to say to you,' she responded, quickening her pace.

But he was too fast for her. To her surprise, she realized that he was, for once, stone-cold sober. He did not sway as he blocked her

107

path. There was no brandy on his breath. And he did not slur his words.

'*Ecoutes-moi, Corinne*. I beg you.'

'Why should I?'

'What I have done. It gives me . . . a bad conscience.'

'So it should.'

'I want to put it right.' He grasped her by the arm. '*Tu capisci?* I want to put it right.'

THE MEETING HAD BEEN ARRANGED AT SHORT NOTICE AND AT an hour the expressions of several people round the table suggested was unreasonably early. Appleby was not one of them. The older he grew, the less sleep he needed. He suspected the same was true of C, who surveyed the select gathering from the head of the table. He had the advantage of living on the premises, of course. Secret Service Headquarters was C's home as well as his place of work. Appleby was far from sure he envied him such an arrangement, difficult though the journey to Whitehall Court had been from his sister's home in Eltham.

The war – and the work rate it had committed him to – had taken its toll on C, who looked frailer and older than when Appleby had last seen him. Rumour had it that he had never recovered from the death of his son. It might be so, Appleby conceded. He too had lost a son in the conflict and did not delude himself that he was unmarked by the tragedy. But neither he nor C was the sort of man to dwell on such matters. Stoicism was their philosophy of choice.

'Be so good as to remind everyone of the evidence that Lemmer may be in Paris, would you, Appleby?' C prompted, fixing a beady eye on him over the rim of his teacup.

'Certainly, sir.' He risked a glance at the grim-set faces of the others: four of them, of varying degrees of seniority, representing the Military, Aviation, Naval and Political sections. None appeared either overtly hostile or supportive. But that counted for little in a service where overtness was actively discouraged. The search for

Fritz Lemmer, fugitive head of the German Secret Service's spy network, had involved them all at various stages since the end of the war. They were likely to resent the credit for tracking him down devolving upon Appleby – if indeed he had tracked him down. 'The evidence stems from material relating to the late Sir Henry Maxted. Murdered, we believe, though officially his death's to be treated as an accident.'

'The PM won't want to hear that a member of our delegation has been murdered,' remarked Political.

'Which is why he won't hear it,' Appleby continued. 'But there's no doubt in my mind Sir Henry was murdered.'

'We'll take that as read,' said C. 'Proceed with the Lemmer dimension.'

'Very good, sir. The first point to bear in mind is that Sir Henry knew Lemmer from his time in Japan. He was a second secretary in Tokyo while Lemmer was a naval attaché at the German Embassy. It's certain they'd have met at receptions and the like. Lemmer cut his teeth in Tokyo, of course, with the attempted assassination of the Tsarevich. I've been able to examine Sir Henry's pocket-diary for the period he spent in Paris. Most of the entries are routine appointments. But on the nineteenth of February there's a circled set of initials: F.L.'

'Could mean anything,' growled Naval.

'Or it could mean Fritz Lemmer.'

'Thin. Very thin.'

'Rather like the air the fellow disappeared into last November,' remarked Aviation.

'Exactly,' said Appleby. 'He has to have gone somewhere. Why not Paris?'

'Never mind why not,' said C. '*Why?*'

'In my submission, sir,' Appleby replied, 'because that's where the people he recruited are.'

'What can they do for him now?'

'Who can say? I think we'd all agree Lemmer's a master strategist.'

'Oh, yes,' groaned Military.

'But the show's over,' said Naval. 'The government he worked for has ceased to exist.'

'They lost the war, but maybe Lemmer thinks they can still win the peace.'

'What exactly do you mean?' asked C.

'I'm not sure, sir. But I am sure Sir Henry Maxted's murder is crucial. The initials F.L. also crop up on a list he made, apparently of sources of money. He valued F.L. at five thousand pounds.'

Naval scowled. 'Could Maxted have been one of Lemmer's people?'

'It's possible. But—'

'You made no mention of this list in your report,' C cut in.

'No, sir. I only learnt of it yesterday, from Sir Ashley Maxted, Sir Henry's eldest son.'

'What else was on the list?'

'The Trust.'

There was a quiver of disquiet round the table. 'The Tsarists *and* Lemmer?' Political winced. 'A toxic mixture.'

'Sir Henry's last posting was in Petrograd.'

'And you say the woman he was involved with is the widow of the French turncoat, Dombreux?' C shook his head. 'This is potentially very serious.'

'I can only agree, sir. Whether Sir Henry was receiving payments from Lemmer *and* the Trust, or hoping to profit from them in some other way, is unclear.' Even less clear to Appleby were the meaning and significance of other items on the list. He was reluctant to mention them for fear of being drawn into unwise conjecture. Fortunately, no one seemed inclined to press him on the point.

'What view is the *Deuxième Bureau* taking of Maxted's death?' enquired Military.

'A cautious one. They'd prefer to believe it wasn't murder. Even to admit the possibility would raise unwelcome questions about the security and integrity of the conference.'

'Show the Frogs a sand dune and they'll stick their heads in it,' complained Aviation.

'Aren't you confusing frogs with ostriches?' Political asked, smiling faintly.

But Aviation was not smiling. 'Shouldn't your section have

forewarned us of this? There must have been rumours about Lemmer's whereabouts.'

'None pointing to Paris.'

'Where, then?'

'Switzerland, since you ask.'

'Never mind that for now,' said C firmly. 'We will proceed on the assumption that Lemmer is in Paris. He's not a man I want on the loose any longer than I can help it. His detention is a high priority, not least because of the rotten apples he may enable us to identify. We cannot be seen to be turning Paris upside down in search of him, however. I want nothing to be done that will bring our inquiries to the attention of the French, or, worse still, the Americans. Nor do I wish to trouble the PM with this, until we know we're on firm ground. Everything we do must be discreet and deniable.'

'A tall order,' said Political.

'Indeed. But Appleby has a suggestion.'

All eyes turned on Appleby. He did not flinch. 'Sir Henry's younger son, James Maxted. Twenty-seven-year-old former pilot. Cool-headed and courageous, according to his RFC CO. Served two years on the Western Front and spent a year in a POW camp after being shot down. I've met him and I'd rate him A for nerve and pluck. He believes his father was murdered and left me in no doubt he means to bring the murderer to justice.'

Political looked askance. 'You're proposing to use an amateur?'

'*Use* is the operative word. We steer him towards Lemmer and see what he turns up. If he lands himself in trouble with the French authorities, we disown him.'

'He's more likely to end up dead in a back alley,' said Military.

'Then disowning him won't be difficult. He's going to try his damnedest to uncover the truth, regardless of the consequences. I've tried warning him off. It had no effect. I conclude our best course of action is to give him a scent to follow and see where it leads.'

'Riskier for him than for us,' said Naval.

'Keeping track of him will be the trickiest part,' observed Political.

'I will need a few extra men,' Appleby admitted. 'Purely for surveillance.'

'An important point,' said C. 'You can have your extra men, but it must be an exclusively eyes-and-ears operation – apart from yourself – unless and until we have a confirmed sighting of Lemmer.'

'Understood, sir.'

'I rather think this is the best we can do in the circumstances, gentlemen.' C glanced round the table. 'Any suggestions, reservations or objections?'

There were none. Appleby was not surprised. This was an assignment he could either make a success of, in which case it would be taken over by others, along with the credit, or a howling flop of, in which case the blame would be his to wallow in. Such were the rules he was bound to play by.

'Very well,' C declared. 'You have conditional approval, Appleby.'

'Thank you, sir.' Though whether he had anything to be grateful for, Appleby was far from sure.

OVER A SOLITARY BREAKFAST IN THE GLOOMY DINING-ROOM OF the Mazarin, Max contemplated what he had achieved so far in his search for the truth. It did not amount to much. He had a conditional promise of illuminating information from Travis Ireton, but the condition was the running of an errand that evening that might prove less straightforward than Ireton had claimed. Max had held back from contacting Sir Henry's Brazilian acquaintance, Ribeiro, in case Ireton told him something he should know before speaking to the man, but he was not prepared to let another day slip by without doing so. As for Sir Henry's Japanese acquaintance, Max had hoped Ireton would be able to identify him. Frustrating though it was, he reckoned he should wait on that possibility.

He had just lit a cigarette to accompany his coffee and begun to consider the question of how early he could reasonably present himself at the Brazilians' hotel when a waistcoated porter entered the dining-room and steered a direct course to his table.

He inclined himself by Max's elbow for a discreet word. 'Monsieur Maxted, there is a lady wishing to see you. She says the matter is urgent.'

'Her name?'

The porter's voice sank to a whisper, as if he well knew whose widow the lady was. 'Madame Dombreux.'

She was waiting for him in the lobby, anonymously dressed, eyes downcast, doing her best to attract as little attention as possible.

114

Max suggested they step outside and she agreed with no more than a nod.

The morning was cold and bright, the slanting sunlight blurred by traffic fumes. They walked slowly away from the hotel, until they had covered enough distance to speak freely.

'Have you found anything out yet, Max?'

'No. You'd have heard from me if I had.'

'What about Ireton?'

'I'm in the process of winning his confidence.' He did not think she needed to know how that was to be done.

'Perhaps you don't need to.'

'What do you mean?'

'I may have some good news.'

'Really?'

'Yes. Really.'

'Why don't we step in here?' Max indicated the café they were passing. Custom looked to be thin enough to afford them some privacy and he was feeling cold without his coat.

They went in and settled at a table near the door. 'So,' he prompted her. 'The good news is?'

'Spataro says he will recant.'

Max knew he must have looked as he felt: surprised and dubious in equal measures. 'When did he say this?'

'Last night. He stopped me on my way home and told me his conscience wouldn't allow him to continue lying about me.'

'I didn't know he had a conscience.'

'Neither did I. But apparently he does, buried under all that bombast, vanity and drunkenness. He seemed genuinely ashamed of himself.'

'This is—' Max broke off at the approach of the waiter. They ordered coffee. 'This is unexpected, to put it mildly.'

Corinne smiled and looked more relaxed than Max had so far seen her. The loveliness that had drawn his father to her blossomed before him. 'You see what this means, Max? The police will have to accept Henry didn't go on to the roof to spy on me. Which means they'll have to accept he was murdered.'

Max was not confident the police would be willing to go that far.

But without Spataro's evidence they might eventually be forced to. 'When will he tell them he's changing his story?'

'Today. He promised me he'll see Zamaron as soon as possible.'

'And how will he explain himself?'

'He was blackmailed into claiming I was with him. He wouldn't reveal what grubby secret from his past had caught up with him. I imagine there are quite a few. He wouldn't name his blackmailer either. He said it would be dangerous for me to know.'

'So it might. But we have to find out who it was, Corinne. The police will certainly press him on the point.'

'They won't welcome his change of heart, will they?'

'No. They won't.' Their coffees arrived. Max stared down at his pensively.

'I thought you'd be pleased.'

He saw in her eyes the disappointment with his reaction. She wanted him to share her optimism. And he would have liked to be able to. But he did not trust Spataro *or* the police. 'I'll be pleased when Spataro formally withdraws his statement and Zamaron admits he's dealing with a murder.'

'I honestly think we can rely on Spataro, Max. I've never known him to be as . . . well, as earnest as he was last night.'

'Maybe I should go and make sure his earnestness is still intact.'

'Don't do that.' She touched his hand. 'You'll offend him even if you don't mean to. Absurd as it might seem, he regards himself as a man of honour. I'm confident he'll do as he promised. But it must be on his own terms.'

'I suppose you're right.' On balance, he supposed she was. Let Spataro make his grand gesture of contrition. Then, when it was safely on the record, would be the time to demand more from him.

'You won't go to see him, then?'

'You have my word.' He patted her forearm. The reassurance he intended to convey was met by something profoundly disquieting: a sense also of his susceptibility. His father's ghost hovered benignly behind her. 'I'll leave well alone.'

'Good.' Corinne moved her arm away from him in order to drink her coffee. Max wondered whether that was the only reason.

She glanced up at the clock over the counter. 'I must go,' she said, draining her cup.

'Duty calls?'

'I'm afraid so.'

'How will you get to Montparnasse?'

'Métro. There's a *Ligne Cinq* station just round the corner.'

'I'll walk you there.'

They were at Boissière station within minutes, delayed only by a mendicant not-so-old soldier into whose feebly clutched biscuit-tin Corinne dropped several coins. The act reminded Max how swiftly he had come to ignore the human flotsam of the war washed up on the city's streets.

'Every time I see a man like that I realize how trifling my troubles really are,' said Corinne as they moved on. 'It must strike you too: how easily you could have been killed in the war.'

'It struck me every day I returned from a mission in one piece. One of my squadron leaders, Fred Collins, used to say to me, "You're lucky to be alive, Maxted. Make it count."'

'It's a good philosophy.'

'I try to live by it.'

'We all should. What does Mr Collins do now?'

Max remembered then, in all its clarity, the day Collins had died. But he had no wish to speak of it. 'I don't know. Something he enjoys, I hope.'

They had crossed Avenue Kléber and were standing at the head of the stairs leading down into the Métro station. Corinne turned and looked at him. 'Zamaron will be in no hurry to tell me I've been vindicated. I suspect you'll hear from him before I do.'

'I'll let you know as soon as I hear anything.'

'I'll either be at work or at home.'

'Don't worry. I'll find you.'

'I'll be waiting.'

To his surprise, she kissed him lightly on the cheek, then hurried down the stairs, glancing back at him and raising a hand as she turned a corner and vanished from sight.

A TELEGRAM FROM ASHLEY WAS WAITING FOR MAX BACK AT THE Mazarin. He read it with some dread, though it contained nothing he could not have foreseen. *Funeral fixed for noon tomorrow St Martins. Your presence hoped for.* He could reply, explaining why he would not be there. But Ashley already knew the reason and so did their mother. It would have to go unanswered.

Whatever Spataro said to Zamaron and whenever he said it, Max did not propose simply to wait on events. He went up to his room to fetch his hat and coat, intending to proceed directly to the Hotel Plaza Athénée in search of Ribeiro. But Ribeiro, it transpired, was already in search of him. A letter on Plaza Athénée notepaper had arrived for Max during his brief trip upstairs. It was handwritten, in a sprawling script.

26 March 1919

Dear Mr Maxted,
I had the honour to be a friend of your late father over many years. I was greatly saddened to learn of his death. Mr Norris has told me you are to be in Paris for a few more days at least. I should like to speak to you. I hope it is convenient for you to join me for luncheon at my hotel at one this afternoon. Please let me know if it is not. Please accept also my heartfelt condolences.
Sincerely yours,
Baltazar Ribeiro

Max sent back a note, accepting Ribeiro's invitation, then wandered out into the city, the morning empty before him. As yet, he had only a glut of questions about his father and a dearth of answers. He walked to the Eiffel Tower and took the lift to the top. From there he could see the whole city. But to see was not enough. He needed to understand. And he was as far as ever from doing so. But he had some reason to hope that might change before the day was out.

Baltazar Ribeiro was a stout, white-haired, extravagantly moustachioed man of about Sir Henry Maxted's age, impeccably dressed in a dove-grey suit with wing-collar and pearl tie-pin. He greeted Max with elaborate courtesy in grammatically perfect but heavily accented English and repeated his written condolences with every sign that they were genuine, tears brimming in his eyes as he spoke of his old friend.

'I first met your father more than twenty years ago, when he arrived at the embassy in Rio. I was new to the city myself. You could say we discovered Rio together.' Ribeiro smiled as he spoke, something the lines around his eyes and mouth suggested he did often. 'It seemed such a happy chance when I learnt that he too was in Paris for the peace conference. I am more sorry than I can say for this terrible accident. When is the funeral to be? I should like to attend if I can.'

'The funeral's tomorrow,' Max replied. 'In Surrey.'

Ribeiro was struck briefly silent. And in the panelled quietude of the Plaza Athénée's restaurant, where there were more waiters than customers, his silence was almost tangible.

'If it is tomorrow, in Surrey,' he resumed eventually, in a puzzled tone, 'why are you still in Paris?'

'I'm not going to be there.'

Ribeiro's puzzlement only deepened. 'Why not?'

'Because my father's death wasn't an accident, *senhor*. He was murdered. And it's more important that I stay here to find his murderer than I please my family by going home to see him buried.'

Ribeiro's smile had become a deep frown. 'I do not understand. Mr Norris said nothing of murder.'

'Mr Norris said what he'd been told to say. I imagine he's built his career on doing that.'

'But why should he have been told to say what is not true?'

'The unsolved murder of a member of one of the principal delegations to the peace conference would ruffle too many feathers. The authorities have agreed it should be regarded as an accident.'

'If this is so—'

'It is so, *senhor*. Would you like me to explain how I can be sure of that?'

Ribeiro nodded solemnly. 'I would.'

Max set out the evidence calmly and logically. He made no bones about his father's relationship with Corinne, though he did not name her. The revelation did not appear to surprise Ribeiro, who listened patiently, sipping his wine and picking at his food distractedly. Max said nothing of the list Sir Henry had left behind, nor of the key concealed in his room at the Majestic. The facts he could swear to would have to speak for themselves. Old friend of Sir Henry's or not, Ribeiro was still an unknown quantity.

'This is scandalous,' he said when Max had finished. 'They propose to regard Henry's death as a . . . stupid fall . . . when actually he was murdered?'

'That's the size of it.'

'I knew of Henry's . . . *caso amoroso*. He spoke of it to me a few times, though I could have guessed from how happy he was. She felt genuinely for him, you say?'

'She did.'

'Then I am very sorry for her. How is she?'

'She's coping bravely. And she's as determined as I am to establish the truth.'

'But what could that be? Why would anyone want to murder Henry? He had no enemies.'

'Are you sure?'

Ribeiro shrugged. 'If he did, he was careful to ensure I knew nothing of them. He made none in Brazil, I'm certain. He was a popular figure in the diplomatic community. I enrolled him in the Jockey Club. Everyone liked him. And everyone who knew him will be sorry to hear of his death.'

'He had more troublesome postings than Rio.'

'It is true. St Petersburg in the middle of a revolution must have been grim. And dangerous. He told me it was often unsafe to walk the streets. Ah!' A thought had struck Ribeiro. 'You know many Tsarists fled to Paris after the Bolsheviks took over?'

'Yes.'

'They live in the streets around the Orthodox Cathedral in Rue Daru. There are so many of them the area is called Little Russia. Henry told me this. I went to see for myself and it is true. Now I think about it, he said to me once that they had caused him some embarrassment.'

'How?'

'There is a bookshop run by a man called . . . I cannot remember his name. It begins with a B . . . I think. He asked Henry for help. There is an organization the bookseller is a member of, dedicated to restoring the monarchy. It is called the Trust.'

'The *what*?'

'The Trust. You have heard of it?'

Yes. Max had heard of it, though until this moment he was unaware of the fact. The Trust had been worth £5,000 to Sir Henry. But how? And why? 'I know nothing about such an organization, *senhor*,' Max said, adroitly avoiding the need to lie. 'What help did they want from my father?'

'They hoped he would speak to Lloyd George and Balfour on their behalf. This man B had known Henry slightly in St Petersburg. Henry could do nothing for him, of course, even if he had wanted to. He joked that they thought he was far more important than he actually was. But, still, perhaps they felt . . . insulted . . . by his refusal.'

'To the extent of murdering him?'

'It is unlikely, I agree.'

But it was not so unlikely if Sir Henry's dealings with the Trust had gone further than a polite refusal to lobby the Prime Minister and the Foreign Secretary for them. What exactly did £5,000 buy? 'Are you sure you can't remember the bookseller's name, *senhor*?'

'It is gone. But it does not matter. His name is over the door of the shop. In Russian, obviously.'

121

'I'll find him.'

'Be careful.'

Max smiled. 'I can't afford to be *too* careful.'

'The Russians.' Ribeiro sighed. 'We had an emperor in Brazil. We let him go into exile when the republic was created. We did not feel the need to slaughter the entire royal family. The Russians are . . . an extreme people.'

'Do you know who my father was acquainted with in the Japanese delegation, *senhor*?'

'Kuroda.' Ribeiro nodded. 'I had forgotten him. Yes. Henry knew him from his time at the embassy in Tokyo. You were born there, of course.'

'I was, yes.'

'I have not met Kuroda. I have not met any of the Japanese. They keep to themselves. And Kuroda is not a politician.'

'What, then?'

'A policeman, I think.' Ribeiro snapped his fingers. 'And there is a Russian connection.'

'There is?'

'Yes. When the Tsar the Russians killed last year was crown prince – Tsarevich – he visited Japan. There was an attempt on his life. Henry was in Tokyo at the time. He gave this policeman – Kuroda – some small assistance with the investigation of the crime.'

'What sort of assistance?'

'He did not say. And I did not ask. It seemed, as he talked of it, unimportant. It was very long ago. You will speak to Kuroda?'

'I'll speak to anyone in Paris who knew my father.'

'There will not be many who knew him well.'

'As one of those who did . . .' Max grimaced. 'I have an awkward question to ask.'

Ribeiro spread his arms wide. 'Ask it.'

'Was my father short of money?'

'Money? Your father? No. He . . . spent . . . freely when we were together.'

'He had no need to . . . raise funds?'

For the first time in their conversation, Max sensed disquiet on

122

his host's part. Ribeiro smiled, but not quite as easily or genuinely as before. Until this moment, he had been candid and open. Now there was the slightest tinge of circumspection in his eyes and his voice. 'I cannot think of any reason for Henry to raise funds, as you put it. You have some reason?'

'Nothing definite.'

'Then . . .'

'I mean to follow every clue, however faint.'

'You should.' Ribeiro sounded fatalistic, as if he knew, as perhaps he did, that it would be futile to seek to discourage Max. 'Henry was a good friend and a good man. If he was murdered . . .'

'He was murdered.'

Ribeiro's expression had become solemn and serious. 'Then, as his son, you must seek to avenge him. And as his friend . . . I shall help you if I can.'

NUMEROUS BRANDIES HAD CONCLUDED MAX'S LUNCH WITH Baltazar Ribeiro. Disappointed that he would not be able to attend his old friend's funeral, Ribeiro had insisted they toast his memory countless times as he called to mind various incidents from their friendship. Racecourse mishaps and nightclub escapades Max could hardly associate with his father had flowed from Ribeiro's alcohol-loosened tongue. 'We both left it late in life to sow our wild oats, Max.' (Max had persuaded Ribeiro to address him by his nickname, though the Brazilian's accent made it sound like Mags.) 'I lived in Manaus until I was forty, deep in Amazonia. My father made his fortune from rubber and paid for me to become a lawyer. I married another rubber baron's daughter and led a respectable, hard-working life. Then I was selected to replace one of the province's congressmen who had died and off I went to Rio, two thousand kilometres away. I had never been to the capital before. My family stayed behind in Manaus. It was a little the same for Henry. We became a pair of middle-aged playboys. We had a lot of fun, Max, more than our fair share. Oh, yes, they were great days. I miss them. And I miss my friend, your father.'

Max was aware, when he left the Plaza Athénée, that he was drunk and not necessarily the best judge of his own actions. He realized that proceeding directly to Little Russia in search of bookseller B was unwise and impetuous. But he went anyway, reckoning the walk there through the chill afternoon air would sober him up.

The chill afternoon air in fact made little impression. He reached

the neighbourhood of the multi-domed St-Alexandre-Nevsky Orthodox Cathedral under no illusion as to his condition. But he was not going to turn back now.

Many of the shops and cafés in the area sported signs in the Russian alphabet. He heard more Russian spoken by passers-by than French. In a side-street off Rue Daru, he came upon a book-seller's premises and used the Ancient Greek he remembered from his schooldays to make a rough transliteration of the proprietor's name: Bukayev. He was in the right place. But Bukayev was not. The shop was closed.

No opening hours were displayed. The interior looked dusty and barely businesslike. Bukayev probably came and went much as he pleased, Max surmised. This was confirmed by a grizzled old man in a heavy overcoat and fur hat who stopped at the sight of Max peering through the shop window. After a futile foray in Russian, he switched to French.

'*Le magasin est quelquefois ouvert, quelquefois fermé, monsieur.*'

'*Vous connaissez Bukayev, monsieur?*' Max asked.

'*Un peu.*' A little was not a lot. But it was better than nothing.

'*Où habite-t-il?*'

'*Là.*' The man gestured to the windows above the shop.

That was something. Bukayev lived on the premises. He would have to return eventually. But Max could not wait. He too would have to return.

It was probably for the best, Max concluded as he headed for the Mazarin. He needed to sleep off the brandies Ribeiro had plied him with before addressing himself to the task Ireton had set him. And he half-hoped good news might be waiting for him at the hotel in the form of a message from Zamaron. Bukayev would keep.

As James Maxted, late of the Royal Flying Corps, was striding a touch unsteadily along the eighth arrondissement streets of Paris, another youthful RFC veteran, Sam Twentyman, was walking up the drive of Gresscombe Place, in Surrey. Any unsteadiness he displayed was due to nervousness rather than alcohol. Only force of circumstance had led him to travel there from Walthamstow. He

125

knew Max would not want him to visit his family, but the telegram he had received had left him with little choice in the matter.

A maid answered the door. Sam asked if he could speak to Sir Ashley Maxted on an urgent matter concerning his brother and she admitted him to a darkened hallway. The house was quiet, oppressively so, as he waited. He knew, of course, that the family would be in mourning. He reminded himself to bear that fact in mind.

Eventually, the maid returned and reported that Sir Ashley was busy in his study, but could spare Sam a few moments of his time. She escorted him to a room towards the back of the house.

Sir Ashley was walking up and down by a window overlooking rain-prinked lawns and shrubbery. There were enough papers scattered on his desk to suggest he really was busy. His greeting was barely polite. Sam's condolences were brusquely acknowledged. A handshake was out of the question.

'You're Twentyman?'

'Yes, Sir Ashley. I was in the RFC with your—'

'Yes, yes, I know that. James has mentioned you to me. What can I do for you?'

'I wonder, has Lieutenant Maxted also mentioned our . . . business plans?'

The question raised a scowl on Sir Ashley's face. 'He may have.'

'I'm worried about how our plans . . . stand at present.'

'Are you really?'

'I understand Lieutenant Maxted—'

'You can drop the "Lieutenant",' Sir Ashley cut in testily. 'My brother's a civilian these days.'

'Yes. Of course. I, er . . .'

'What exactly do you want, Twentyman?'

'I understand . . . Mr Maxted . . . is in Paris. I had a telegram from him suggesting he . . . might be there for some time.'

Sir Ashley's face darkened ominously. The scowl rearranged itself, but remained a scowl. 'Indeed,' was all he said, though it was evident he might have liked to say more.

'Can you tell me where in Paris I could find him?'

'You're thinking of going there?'

'Yes. I am.'

'I shouldn't if I were you.'

'No?'

Sir Ashley shook his head. 'No.'

'Why not?'

'The land my brother needs for this flying school you and he had hopes of establishing . . . is unlikely to be available.'

'Oh.'

'You have a trade you can turn your hand to, Twentyman?'

'Not exactly, Sir Ashley, no.'

'Well, I should advise you to find one.'

Sam could think of nothing to say to that. He shifted awkwardly from one foot to the other. He badly wanted not to believe that his hopes for the future were to be dashed.

'If there's nothing else I can do for you . . .' Sir Ashley glanced dismissively towards the door.

Sam steeled himself. 'Mr Maxted's address . . . in Paris?'

'You still want it?'

'If . . . If you don't mind.'

'Why should I mind?' Sir Ashley stalked to his desk, ripped a sheet of paper from a pad and wrote on it, then handed it to Sam. 'There you are.'

'Thank you. I'm . . . much obliged.'

'Is that all?'

'Well, I was just wondering . . . if you could tell me . . . what's keeping Mr Maxted . . . in Paris.'

'What's keeping him there?'

'Er . . . yes.'

'If you want to find that out, Twentyman, I suggest you waste some money I suspect you don't have by going to Paris and asking him.'

'Right.' Sam swallowed a tart riposte. 'I see.'

'Do you? I doubt it. Now, you really must excuse me. I have my father's funeral to arrange.'

For a second, when the alarm clock woke him, Max thought it was early morning rather than early evening. The twilight falling greyly

through the windows of his hotel room could have denoted either. Then where and when and why took urgent hold of his mind and he leapt up from the bed. The time had come to do what he had agreed to do for Ireton. He set aside caution and apprehensiveness as he had done every day of his war service. In his experience, they only slowed a man's reactions. And speedy reactions could be the difference between life and death. Nothing as elemental as that, he felt certain, awaited him in Auteuil. In all likelihood, it would be as simple an errand as Ireton had predicted. At all events, he would soon find out.

He fastened his shoes decisively, donned his hat and coat and set out.

It was not until the train from Epsom reached Waterloo and Sam stepped out on to the platform that he decided to go through with it. Even then, absolute certainty only descended on him as he threaded his way through the surging mass of homebound commuters filling the concourse. He retrieved the bag he had deposited earlier in the day at the left-luggage office and knew beyond a shadow of a doubt that he had not packed it in vain. He would head for Westminster Bridge when he left the station and reach Victoria in time for a bite to eat before the Paris sleeper was due to depart. 'In for a penny, in for a pound, Sam,' he murmured to himself as he went on his way. 'You're better off chewing croissants than baking buns.' Already, he felt better for knowing that he was not going home.

Just as it had for the bustling commuters at Waterloo, so the working day had ended for Corinne Dombreux. She was confident Spataro had spoken to Zamaron by now, but until she had some confirmation of that she would remain anxious and fretful. Urging calm upon herself, she walked slowly home by her normal route.

The black Citroën parked by the kerb outside 8 Rue du Verger had no police markings, but was familiar to her as a model used by the higher echelons of the *préfecture*. This, it seemed to her, could only indicate that Spataro had indeed said his piece.

As she neared the car, the passenger door opened and

Commissioner Zamaron stepped out. He looked sombre and serious, as well he might, considering the coach and horses Spataro's change of heart had driven through his absurd explanation for Sir Henry's death. Corinne lengthened her stride and looked hopefully towards him.

MAX TRIED HIS LEVEL BEST NOT TO LOOK AT THE CLOCK TOO often as he waited for Monsieur Buisson in the Café Sans Souci. The establishment was only a short walk from Gare d'Auteuil. Many of its customers were on their way home from wherever they worked. There was a high degree of coming and going. By lingering as long as he already had over his coffee and hair-of-the-dog cognac, Max felt he had made himself more conspicuous than was wise. And his perusal of the copy of *Le Figaro* he had brought with him for camouflage was beginning to feel unsustainable.

Every time the door of the café opened – which was frequently – Max glanced across at the newcomer. Ireton had told him Buisson would be carrying a cardboard map-tube. He would join Max at his table long enough to down a coffee, then leave – without the tube. A few minutes later, Max would also leave – with the tube. It really was exceedingly simple. All Max had to say to Buisson was '*Monsieur Ireton vous prie d'accepter ses excuses.*' Buisson, in all likelihood, would say nothing.

But the clock told Max, when he succumbed to temptation and looked at it, that Buisson was nearly a quarter of an hour late. Much longer and the delay would assume ominous proportions. Max sighed and decided to light another cigarette.

Just as he took out his cigarette-case, the door hinge gave a now familiar squeak. He glanced across the café. And there was Buisson, a portly, middle-aged man with flushed jowls and small eyes peering anxiously from beneath the brim of his hat. He held a briefcase and furled umbrella in one hand. The map-tube was

thrust under his other arm like a swollen swagger-stick. Max rubbed his brow with his left hand, the signal Ireton had instructed him to use. Buisson nodded and moved in his direction.

He sat down with a sigh reminiscent of a slowly deflating bicycle tyre and laid the map-tube on the vacant chair between them. '*Bonsoir,*' he murmured, slipping off his hat to reveal a head of pomaded hair. Max noticed two symmetrical rivulets of sweat working their way down his temples. The sight was nether edifying nor reassuring.

'*Bonsoir,*' said Max. '*Monsieur Ireton vous prie d'accepter ses excuses.*'

'*Ses excuses,*' echoed Buisson. He took out a handkerchief and dabbed his moist upper lip. '*Bien entendu.*' He cast Max a skittering, panicky glance. Then, suddenly, without waiting to order the coffee that would have given his presence in the café a semblance of normality, he stood up, grabbed his hat, briefcase and umbrella and made for the door.

A second later, he was through it and gone. The waiter who had been bearing down on their table shrugged and retreated. Max went ahead and lit his cigarette with studied calmness. He glanced down at the map-tube. There it was, left as agreed. But Buisson's discomposure could hardly have been less in keeping with the supposed simplicity of its delivery. Something was wrong, something to which the pointer, he sensed, was Buisson's reaction to Ireton's absence: '*Bien entendu.*' He understood, apparently. But Max did not.

He finished his cigarette, inspected the bill and laid down enough coins to cover it. Then, taking the map-tube with him, he rose and walked casually across to the coat hooks at the rear of the café. He balanced the tube on one of the hooks while he put on his coat and hat, then retrieved it. He was ready to leave.

But Max had no intention of leaving by the front door. He had already reconnoitred an emergency exit and, though he could not be sure whether the emergency was real or imagined, he had decided to use it.

He slipped through the door leading to the toilets, but ignored the steps leading down to them and pressed on through another

door marked DEFENSE D'ENTRER into a decrepit storage room and out of that via a dank and dripping stairwell into a rear courtyard.

There was no lighting. He trod cautiously on the slimy cobbles and reached the corner of the building where an alley led to the street. No one was visible. A car drove slowly past as he watched, the engine labouring. He saw no cause for alarm and moved into the alley.

As he did so, a caped and uniformed policeman stepped into the mouth of the alley and looked straight at him. '*Ici*,' he shouted.

Max turned and ran. He heard the shrill blast of the policeman's whistle behind him and a percussion of footfalls. The rendezvous at the café had been a trap. He had not walked directly into it, but he was scarcely out of it either.

There was a glimmer of light ahead on the far side of the courtyard. A street lamp he could not see dimly illuminated the exposed flank of a half-demolished building. There was a scalable wall ahead of him and a void beyond it that promised escape. He ran towards it, unable to see what might be in his path, and collided blindly with a cart stowed in the corner of the yard.

Ignoring the sharp pain in his knee where he had struck the cart, he glanced back and saw several milling figures in the alley. He had only seconds to elude his pursuers. He stuffed the map-tube inside his coat, jumped up on to the cart and launched himself at the top of the wall.

It was all that remained of an originally higher wall. The surface was jagged and crumbling. Max found a clawing hand-and-foothold and virtually fell over it, descending into a rubble-strewn demolition site. His hat fell off in the process. He could not see it in the darkness and had no time to look for it. He hobbled through an invisible chaos of toppled bricks and other debris to a narrow street where there was at least some light, chanced his arm on a right turn and broke into a jog, suppressing the desire to run headlong for fear of the noise his shoes would make on the cobbles. There were shouts behind him that sounded promisingly confused, but no sound of actual pursuit. He jogged on, favouring the more shadowy side of the street.

He could see a junction with a wider street about fifty yards

further on, but fifty yards was a long way. Sure enough, the police had negotiated the wall and the demolition site before he had covered the distance. There were loud shouts behind him. Torch beams flashed. Whistles shrieked. They had spotted him.

As he reached the junction, a dark saloon car appeared, bursting out of the night from nowhere, headlamps blazing. It swerved across the road and skidded to a halt at the kerbside next to him. Through an open window, a familiar voice addressed him. 'Get in.' It was Schools Morahan.

For a second, Max hesitated, then wrenched the rear door of the car open and threw himself in.

The car started away with a squeal of tyres and a surge of acceleration, pushing Max back against the seat.

'Where . . . where did you come from?' he panted.

'The right place at the right time. There's nothing I could have done for you if you'd walked out the front door of the café. You're smarter than you look. And I see you got the package.'

The map-tube was protruding from Max's coat. He pulled it out and dropped it on to the seat beside him, then nearly fell on to it when Morahan took a sharp left, followed shortly by a right and another right along quiet, poorly lit side-streets.

'What's in the tube?' Max demanded.

'Couldn't tell you. Ask Travis.'

'Did he know he was sending me into a trap?'

'He had doubts about Buisson's reliability. Seems he was right.'

'So, to hell with me?'

'Not quite. I came to get you, didn't I?'

'They could easily have caught me.'

'But they didn't.'

Another abrupt left turn took them on to a broad road running alongside a railway viaduct. Morahan seemed to relax. The road was straight and clear ahead, but he slowed slightly and blithely lit a cigarette.

'No one's following us. The *flics* who were chasing you were on foot and they won't have been able to get a car on our tail. You can relax.'

'Thanks so much.'

'Don't mention it.'

'Are you taking me to meet Travis?'

'No. I reckon back to your hotel's best. See Travis in the morning. You won't feel so hard done by then.'

'You want to bet?'

'If you like.'

It was hard to sustain the anger Max felt for the way he had been manipulated in the face of Morahan's cool-nerved off-handedness. And, though he would not have admitted as much, he had actually rather enjoyed himself. It was good to be back in action – albeit a very different kind of action from his days in the RFC. He sighed and rubbed his throbbing knee. 'Who is Buisson?'

'Something middle-ranking at the conference printing works.'

'What does he supply – secret documents?'

'Ask Travis.'

'Maybe I'll just keep the tube and see for myself what it contains.'

'I can't let you do that.' Morahan glanced at Max over his shoulder, the shadows inside the car rendering his expression indecipherable. 'And we don't want the evening going sour on you, do we?'

MAX WAS ROUSED THE FOLLOWING MORNING NOT BY THE alarm clock but by the telephone. Looking at the clock, he saw it was only just gone seven. The merest trickle of daylight was edging round the curtains. After the evening he had had, it was an awakening he would have preferred to be postponed indefinitely. But the hope instantly seized him that the call related to Spataro, news of whose recantation was overdue. He grabbed the receiver.

'Hello?'

'Is that you, sir?'

'What?'

'It's Sam here, sir.'

Good God, it was Sam Twentyman. Max sought in vain for a plausible explanation. Surely he could not be calling from London. 'What? Where are you?'

'Downstairs.'

'You're here? In Paris?'

'Yes, sir. Arrived on the sleeper a couple of hours ago. Not too early for you, am I?'

Max stumbled down to the lobby with his thoughts whirling. He was still bemusingly exhilarated by his close shave in Auteuil, but he was well aware that the incident illustrated just how duplicitous Ireton could be. He was also troubled by the continuing silence where Spataro was concerned. Sam's sudden appearance was a complication he would have preferred to avoid. He had not expected his friend to run him to earth, though he knew why he

135

had. The sad truth was that Sam would soon discover he had had a wasted journey. Max supposed he should have spared him that.

There was a surprise in store for Max, however. He realized when he reached the lobby and caught sight of Sam, travel-weary and tousled but smiling the same old dependable Twentyman smile, that he was damnably pleased to see him. He piloted him out to the café he had taken Corinne to the previous morning and stood him a breakfast he looked in sore need of.

Max contented himself with coffee and cigarettes and listened with mounting concern to Sam's account of the difficult, not to say expensive, week he had had. In Sam's mind, the flying school was clearly still a viable proposition, notwithstanding Ashley's ominous utterances. Max had not appreciated just how heavily he was relying on it. Allowing him to continue relying on it was unconscionable.

'I'm sorry, Sam,' he said at last. 'You should understand that Surrey Wings is almost certainly a non-starter.'

'A *non-starter*?' It was obvious from his tone that Sam did not want to believe it. 'Why?'

And so Max set out the reasons. They hinged on the whole question of his father's death. Another surprising realization came to him as he explained why he was certain Sir Henry had been murdered and how he had so antagonized Ashley by maintaining as much that there was no possibility of Gresscombe land being used for their flying school. The realization was not a new one. Max had simply forgotten the bond of trust that he had established with Sam during the war. The plain fact was that Sam Twentyman had probably saved his life a dozen times in a dozen different ways by his assiduousness and ingenuity. He had never once let Max down. And there was no one else of whom that was true.

'I have to stay in Paris until I get to the bottom of this, Sam. You can see that, can't you?'

Sam nodded. 'I see it, right enough. That brother of yours, sir, if you don't mind me saying, is—'

'A first-class shit. I know. But he's cock of the walk now. And you were lucky. You didn't meet my sister-in-law. She pulls the strings. And she doesn't like me one little bit.'

'Sisters-in-law can be like that.'

'I'm afraid we're going to have to abandon our plans. I'm sorry, but there it is.'

'I was hoping you wouldn't say that, sir.'

'I know. Look, Sam, why don't you stay at the Mazarin tonight and see a bit of gay Paree before you head back? We can paint the town red tonight. I'll pay for your accommodation and you'll be home in time to reclaim the deposit on those blessed planes.'

'Ah, home.' Sam looked wistful. 'Not sure I've properly got one of those any more.'

'Maybe there's some other pilot you served with who'd be interested in starting a flying school.'

'None I'd trust further than they could fly without an engine.'

'It's a bugger, Sam, I know.' Max spread his hand sorrowfully. 'There's nothing I can do.'

'I appreciate that, sir. And I appreciate the offer of a night in Paris. It's handsome of you. I'll take you up on it.'

'Capital. Let's get you booked in, then I must run.'

'This Ireton, sir . . .'

'You're going to tell me he sounds like a wrong 'un.'

'Well, if the scrape you got into last night is anything to go by . . .'

'I'll be on my guard, don't worry. I won't let him pull a stunt like that again.'

'Seems to me you need as much looking after here as you did at the Front.'

'Possibly. But, fortunately for you, looking after me is no longer your job. Whatever trouble I may get into, I'll have to get myself out of it.'

After securing Sam a room at the Mazarin, and wishing him a pleasant day's sightseeing, Max took a cab to 33 Rue des Pyramides, where Malory, dressed this morning in a fractionally lighter shade of tweed, informed him that he was expected (as well he might be, Max thought) and should go straight into Ireton's office.

'Morning, Max.' Ireton greeted him with a broad smile and an

expansive gesture that raised loose lassos of smoke from his cigarette. 'How are you feeling?'

'I think sore would capture it in your vernacular.'

'Ah. Schools said you seemed to be limping when he left you last night. But you've bounded in here in sprightly fashion, so I guess you're nursing nothing worse than a few bruises.'

'No thanks to you.'

'That's hardly fair. I chose a meeting-place with a rear exit, didn't I?'

'But you didn't tell me I'd need to use it.'

'Call it an initiative test.'

'I call it being set up like a decoy duck.'

'You sound angrier than you look. More fun than you'd have expected, was it, Max? Maybe it stirred a few happy memories of dogfights over no man's land.'

'You lied to me, Travis.'

'Not at all. It should and could have gone as simply as I said. But obviously they rumbled Buisson and he told them everything.'

'And what's everything?'

'I've been paying him to supply me with copies of the proofs of Supreme Council minutes and consultative papers so that my clients can have advance notice of how the great and not necessarily good plan to carve up their nations. It's his word against mine as far as that goes, of course, since I didn't walk obligingly into the trap last night and the person who did got clean away. So, all's well that ends well. Or as well as it can be, considering the documents Buisson gave you are certain to be fakes and now I have to recruit someone to replace him, which won't be easy. Rumour has it they're going to limit the decision-making from here on to a new Council of Four – Clemenceau, Lloyd George, Orlando, Wilson – because there have been too many leaks.' Ireton grinned. 'You could say I'm a victim of my own success.'

'My heart bleeds for you.'

'Don't take it like that. Sit down, Max. I'm a man of my word. You deliver for me; I deliver for you.'

With a show of reluctance, Max sat down. 'Do you know who killed my father?'

'No. But I might know *why* he was killed. Ever heard of Fritz Lemmer?'

'No.'

'I'm not surprised. Lemmer would be disappointed if you had. He was the Kaiser's spymaster. Well, maybe he still is, in a sense. A former naval officer turned intelligence-gatherer. A shadowy figure, by choice and need. Thirty years in the game, apparently.'

'What game?'

'Spying. Sabotage. Assassinations. You name it, he's had a finger in it. So they say.'

'What's he to do with my father?'

'Well, the thing is this. Cigarette, by the way?' Ireton proffered his case.

'I prefer my own brand.' Max studiously took out one of his Wills and lit it. 'The thing is?' he prompted.

'Delicate, Max, delicate. Like I told you the other day, Henry's put a few pieces of information my way since this conference began. Nothing treasonable, I assure you, just . . . titbits.'

'And like *I* told *you*, I don't believe it.'

'You're going to have to if you want to find out who killed him. The fact is, Henry was eager to raise money. I don't know why. Maybe to set up Corinne Dombreux in the manner to which he thought she should become accustomed. He wasn't typical of my sources of information, far from it, and the information he supplied was minor stuff. Then, just last week, he offered me something in an altogether different league. Or, rather, he offered me some*one*. Lemmer.'

'What do you mean?'

'Lemmer vanished last November, around the time the Kaiser decamped to Holland. Since then his whereabouts have preyed on a lot of people's minds. The word is that he recruited spies for Germany in every European government. He probably didn't stop at Europe either. Nobody except Lemmer knows who they were and they're mostly still in place, presumably hoping and praying their well-paid work for the Kaiser never comes to light. The question is . . .'

'Where is Lemmer?'

'Exactly. Where is he? And what's he up to? Maybe he's still in touch with his agents, many of whom could be here in Paris, negotiating on their countries' behalf. You see how significant that could be? Whose interests are they really serving? Maybe Lemmer's trying to soften the peace terms for Germany, or sow discord among the Allies. There's no way to tell. The Americans, the British, the French and all the others would like to lay hands on Lemmer and sweat the truth out of him. But they can't find him. Which means his whereabouts constitute a very valuable commodity. Off-hand, I can't think of a more valuable one.'

'And that's what my father was offering you.'

'In a nutshell, yes.'

'But how would he know where Lemmer was?'

'It seems improbable, I grant you. But not when you think about it. Lemmer is notoriously elusive, not to mention camera-shy. There are precious few people who know what he looks like. Henry happens to have been one.'

'How?'

'Lemmer was a naval attaché at the German Embassy in Tokyo in the early nineties. He hadn't perfected his knack for invisibility then. Henry met him several times, apparently. So, when he told me he'd seen Lemmer here, in Paris, I was inclined to believe him. And happy to agree to act as his broker.'

'Pa said he knew where Lemmer was? An actual address?'

'Not quite. He said he was in a position to lure Lemmer to a meeting. That would have been enough.'

'What could he lure Lemmer with?'

'He didn't say. But he assured me it could be done. For a fee.'

'How big a fee?'

'I never got the chance to find out how high an interested party might have been prepared to go. Before I could open negotiations, Henry was killed. It would have been some auction, though. Remember, Lemmer could tell a government not only who the traitors are in their own ranks but who they are in other govern-ments' ranks. And with the right persuasion a traitor in one cause can be recruited to a different cause. Lemmer would be quite a catch.'

'Do you think he killed my father?'

'It's possible. Not personally, of course. He hires people to do that kind of thing for him. Alternatively, word of what Henry was trying to sell might have reached one of Lemmer's agents, who had good cause to fear exposure.'

'How would word have reached them?'

'I made some inquiries, as Henry asked me to.' Ireton shrugged. 'I'd be sorry to think that action on my part led to his death, but I warned him of the risks he was running and he insisted on going ahead.'

'Who did you make these inquiries with?'

'I spoke to them in strictest confidence. It wouldn't be fair to identify them.'

'Who are they?'

'Like I say, I can't—'

'Who the hell are they?' Max jumped up and leant across the desk. 'I want their names.'

Ireton did not flinch, though he frowned slightly as he looked up at Max. 'I think I've told you as much as I agreed to. More from me requires more from you. We share an interest in Fritz Lemmer, Max. I don't delude myself that you've told me everything you've found out about your father's activities. You'd have been a fool to. By the same token, I can't be expected to disclose everything I know or suspect at this stage. We have to learn to trust one another, you and I. We have to pool our resources. We have to collaborate.' The frown faded, to be replaced by the scar-distorted smile. 'Now, how does that sound to you?'

Max was under no illusions about the bargain he struck with Ireton. 'You want me to find Lemmer for you, don't you, Travis? Then you can sell his whereabouts to the highest bidder. I take all the risks. You take all the rewards.'

'Not at all.' Ireton looked shocked by the suggestion. 'I'd be happy to split the proceeds fifty-fifty. If that's what you want.'

'I'm not interested in turning a profit. I'm interested in finding my father's murderer.'

'I know. But you may as well take your share. If only to deprive me of it. I'm sure you wouldn't class me as a good cause. Now, let's get down to it, shall we? I sounded out three people about Henry's proposition. I didn't name Henry. It was all done on a hypothetical basis. But if one of them – or an associate they confided in – knew of my links with Henry and Henry's knowledge of Lemmer, they might have figured out who my source was. That seems to me the likeliest explanation for Henry's murder. But if you confront these people and start throwing accusations around they'll know I pointed you in their direction. Given what happened to Henry, that could have unhealthy consequences for me. You follow?'

'I could say I found their names along with Lemmer's on a list I came across amongst my father's possessions.'

'That's good. You appear to have a real talent for this kind of thing, Max. A list. I like that.'

'So, who were the three?'

'Not so fast. I need to be sure you don't drop me in it. I also need to know what, if anything, you learn from them about Lemmer.'

'I won't mention you. And I'll tell you whatever I find out.'

'I have your word on that?'

'Of course.'

Ireton smiled, as if genuinely amused. 'Sadly, in this serpent-pit of a world we inhabit, the word of an English gentleman is no longer sufficient to quell all doubts in such matters. Schools will go with you when you meet them. He occasionally works freelance as a bodyguard, so the arrangement shouldn't arouse any suspicion.'

'If you think that's necessary . . .'

'Oh, I do.'

Max had no choice, as Ireton must have known, but to agree. 'All right, then.'

'Fine. We have a deal.' To Max's surprise, Ireton offered him his hand. They shook. 'OK. We'll take them in the original order. Kuroda, at the Japanese delegation.'

'*Kuroda?*' Max was genuinely surprised, but also disappointed. The first name he had been given was one he already knew.

'You've heard of him?'

'Corinne told me my father knew him.'

'Did she? Well, that's interesting.'

Max had the distinct impression his acquaintance with Corinne was well known to Ireton, though for some reason he did not want to admit it. 'I guess it's no surprise. Kuroda's certainly old enough to have met Henry when he was in Japan.'

'Why did you go to him?'

'Because there's a persistent rumour Lemmer was behind a plot to assassinate the then Tsarevich when he visited Japan in 1891. His visit was supposed to smooth Russo-Jap relations, but the assassination attempt scotched that mighty effectively. A big feather in Lemmer's cap and an even bigger grudge for the Japs to bear. So, I thought they might be willing to pay over the odds for a chance to grab him.'

'And were they?'

'Hard to tell. Kuroda's the epitome of the inscrutable Oriental. But he didn't deny they'd be interested. He wasn't going to ignore the matter, that was clear. You need to establish what he did – who else he consulted, for instance. Play on your role as the loyal son

143

seeking justice for his dead father. The Japs have a soft spot for that kind of thing.'

'It's not a role,' Max snapped.

Ireton was unabashed. 'All the better, then. I suggest you and Schools call on him at the delegation's hotel this evening.'

'*This evening?* What's wrong with this morning?'

'Schools is tied up all day. I won't get a chance to brief him until later.'

'I can't wait that long.'

'Sorry, but you'll have to. That's the deal.'

'Who are the other two you sounded out?'

Ireton looked almost pained. 'Come on, Max. I wasn't born yesterday. Neither were you, though a lot closer to yesterday than I was, I grant you. If I tell you who the others are now, there's nothing to stop you approaching them on your own. No, no. We see how you get on with Kuroda. And we take it from there. One step at a time.'

Max gave brief but serious consideration to grabbing Ireton by the throat and trying to force the other names out of him. He felt certain the American was stringing him along for devious reasons of his own. But he could not afford to yield to temptation. There was too much at stake. 'Very well,' he said through gritted teeth.

'Meet Schools here at six.' Ireton beamed. 'OK?'

Max left Ireton's offices burning with impatience. His search for the truth seemed to be diverted or delayed at every turn.

His first thought was to return to the Mazarin and find out whether any message had reached him from Zamaron regarding Spataro. But a second thought saw him divert to Little Russia. Perhaps the morning would find Bukayev manning his bookshop.

The bookshop was open, but Bukayev was nowhere to be seen. The jingling of the bell as Max entered brought a sombre, heavy-featured young woman scurrying out of an office to the rear. She had raven-black hair, tied back severely, and was dressed mostly in black as well.

She addressed him in Russian, understandably enough, since the

144

books filling the ceiling-high shelves all had titles printed in the Cyrillic alphabet.

'I am looking for Mr Bukayev,' he said, slowly and distinctly.

To his relief, she switched to English in response. 'Ah. He is not here.'

'Do you know when he'll be back?'

'A few days, maybe. He is out of Paris.'

'*Damn it all to hell!*' The strength of his reaction surprised her. She took a step back. He raised a hand apologetically. 'I'm sorry. I badly wanted to talk to him.'

'What about?'

'It concerns my late father, Sir Henry Maxted.'

'You are Sir Henry Maxted's son?'

'Yes. I—'

The jingling of the doorbell and the warning look he caught in her eyes cut him off. A bulky, bull-necked man in a tightly belted raincoat and pork-pie hat entered the shop. '*Dobroe utro,*' he growled.

The young woman returned the greeting in half-hearted fashion and watched the man as he began a slow prowl of the shelves. Then she looked at Max and spoke to him quietly, to his bemusement, in French. '*Un instant, s'il vous plaît.*' Her expression and the change of language combined to urge caution on him.

She hurried into the office and returned a moment later, carrying a pencil and a notepad. She offered them to Max, her glance shifting to monitor the movements of the newcomer. '*Votre nom et votre adresse, monsieur?*' she prompted.

'*D'accord,*' he mustered, taking the pencil and pad. He wrote the information down and handed them back.

'*Merci, monsieur,*' she said, smiling briskly. And that, her smile conveyed, was all she had to say – for now.

A brisk walk took Max back to the Mazarin. The morning was wearing on and soon, he knew, the mourners would be gathering in Epsom for his father's funeral. There would be many muttered questions about his absence and no one would have an adequate answer. Many would assume the worst. He wished it could be

otherwise. But it could not. He had chosen his course. And he would steer it.

Vindication of a sort was waiting for him at the hotel. There was, at last, a message. *Please telephone Mr Appleby as soon as possible.* Max was only half surprised Appleby had been left to convey the news to him. Zamaron was probably too embarrassed, given his explanation for Sir Henry's death would now be in tatters. Max hurried up to his room and put a call through to the Majestic straight away.

The switchboard left him hanging for a moment, then he was connected. 'Mr Maxted?' came Appleby's gravelly greeting.

'Yes. It's me. I didn't know you were back in Paris.'

'Ah. I suppose your brother mentioned my trip to London. I returned on the sleeper last night.'

'And heard of an unexpected development?'

'Yes. I did. You already know?'

'I was forewarned that Spataro was going to withdraw his claim about Corinne spending the night with him.'

'Who told you that?'

'Corinne.'

'Really?' Appleby sounded genuinely puzzled.

'That is why you called me, isn't it?'

'No. No, I'm afraid it isn't. Spataro hasn't withdrawn his claim. And he isn't going to now.'

'What do you mean?'

'He's dead, Mr Maxted. Murdered, in his apartment, the night before last. His body was discovered yesterday.'

'*Murdered?*'

'Yes. And the police have arrested Madame Dombreux.'

6 'I THOUGHT YOU MIGHT LIKE TO ACCOMPANY ME WHEN I TAKE A look at the murder scene, Mr Maxted,' Appleby went on, his tone of voice sounding bizarrely normal to Max in the light of what he had just said. 'You won't get in there on your own and I know you'll have lots of questions, so do you want to come with me? It's now or never, I'm afraid. I'm operating on a tight schedule.'

'Yes,' Max murmured. 'I'll come.'

'What?'

'*I'll come with you.*'

'Good. I'll pick you up in . . . a quarter of an hour?'

'All right. A quarter of an hour.'

'See you shortly, then. Sorry, by the way, if this was a bit of a facer. I was surprised myself.'

Surprised? Yes, Max thought as he stared at the receiver before hanging up. He was that too. Surprised and shocked and horrified. Corinne had not murdered Spataro. He was surer of that than of most things. Good God, the man was already dead when she came to report his change of heart. He was already dead and she had not known it. A trap had been closing around her. And she had not known that either. But she knew it now. And so did Max.

'Are you still there, Lamb?' Appleby asked, returning his attention to the other telephone on his desk.

'Yes, sir.'

'I think I can give you a few hours off. You deserve it after the shoe leather you've expended over the last couple of days. I'm taking Maxted to Montparnasse.'

'Righto, sir.'

'Pick up his trail later at Ireton's. I think we can safely assume he'll find his way back there.'

'I should say so, sir.'

'Good work so far, Lamb. Well done.'

'Thank you, sir.'

The hearse drew away from Gresscombe Place under a pewter sky through flecks of snow blown on an icy wind. No words passed between the passengers in the limousine that followed it. The two Ladies Maxted, Winifred and Lydia, occupied the rear seat. They were veiled and enveloped in black. The middle seat, behind the driver, was shared by Sir Ashley and Winifred's brother, George, black-suited and sombre, although in George's case sombreness did not extend to sobriety. Ashley could smell the whisky on his uncle's breath quite clearly. There had evidently been more than the one stiffener he had admitted to.

Ashley, though he would never have confessed as much, would have quite liked to join George in a glass, not merely to render the funeral service and the committal of his father's body to the Surrey earth less harrowing, but also to quench some of the anxiety his earlier telephone conversation with the family's lawyer had left him with.

He should never have made the call, of course. Lydia had chivvied him into it. 'Stir the fellow up, darling, or we'll be waiting for ever to settle your father's estate.' It had been apparent from Mellish's tone that he did not consider the discussion of such issues before the funeral to be entirely seemly. 'I was going to suggest that I call at the house tomorrow morning, Sir Ashley, when I can set out the testamentary position in full.' It had hardly been possible to argue with that. But Ashley had pressed for an assurance that everything would be straightforward – and had not received one. 'I would prefer to say nothing further about the provisions of Sir Henry's will until tomorrow.'

Damn the fellow. Why did he have to be so tight-lipped? Ashley knew the terms of the will as well as he did. At least, he supposed he did. But now, watching the hearse move slowly along the drive ahead of them, he was not as certain on the point as he would have wanted to be.

Max made his view of the matter known to Appleby while they were still standing in the lobby of the Hotel Mazarin. 'I don't believe for a moment that Corinne murdered Raffaele Spataro, Appleby. The very idea is absurd.'

'Sometimes facts force us to believe what we can't imagine,' Appleby countered in his irritatingly sympathetic manner. 'That's why I suggested we go and inspect the scene of the crime for ourselves.'

'Nothing's going to change my mind.'

'Don't be too sure. We seldom know others as well as we think we do. I've often been surprised by what people are capable of *in extremis*.'

'Corinne had no reason to kill Spataro. He was about to confirm her version of events the night my father died, for God's sake.'

'We only have her word for that.'

'You think she killed the man, then calmly came here and told me he was about to retract his statement?'

'I'll tell you what I think on the way there. We're wasting time, Mr Maxted.'

They walked out to the car and started away. Appleby closed the glass screen between them and the driver and painstakingly lit his pipe while Max waited impatiently for him to explain.

'Zamaron told me of Madame Dombreux's claim that Spataro meant to change his story,' Appleby said eventually, 'though she doesn't seem to have mentioned discussing it with you, which is odd. The fact is that she has to account for being the last person seen with Spataro before he was found shot dead—'

'*Shot?*'

'Yes. With a revolver he owned. The poor sap supplied his own murder weapon.'

'You're seriously suggesting Corinne talked her way into Spataro's apartment, grabbed his gun – knowing, presumably, where he kept it and that he kept it loaded – then . . . what?'

Appleby sighed. 'I'm not suggesting anything, Mr Maxted. Do you want to hear me out?'

Max also sighed. 'Yes, yes. Go ahead.'

'Thank you. Now, this is the sequence of events as I understand them. Three passers-by who know Spataro by sight saw him entering his apartment building at seven Rue du Verger at about ten o'clock Tuesday evening. He was in the company of a woman matching Madame Dombreux's description. She doesn't deny meeting him at that time, although she says they parted in the vestibule of the building and she does deny going up to his apartment.

'Spataro was a notoriously inconsiderate neighbour. He often played loud music on his gramophone late into the night. Jazz, usually. Zamaron's theory is that the fatal shots were fired while the gramophone was operating and hence not heard, although they may have been heard and . . . simply ignored. Bumps and thumps on the ceiling went with living below him, apparently. Everyone knew about the gun, by the way. There were complaints about him taking pot-shots at pigeons from his window. Zamaron gave him a ticking-off, but allowed him a good deal of artistic licence.

'Noise was one thing, but the tenant of the apartment below Spataro's wasn't prepared to overlook a brownish-red stain that appeared on his ceiling overnight. He thought it looked like blood and he was right. He got no answer when he knocked on Spataro's door. He went off to work, asking the concierge to investigate in his absence. After several failed efforts to raise Spataro, she used her pass key to enter the apartment. She found him lying dead on the floor. He'd been shot three times in the chest and stomach, causing extensive bleeding, and once in the head. Not a pretty sight, I imagine.

'The gun was lying by his right hand and first thoughts were that he'd killed himself. But it was soon realized the shots had been fired from a distance of several feet at least. It was clearly murder, unconvincingly disguised as suicide. The murderer had

worn gloves, in order to avoid leaving fingerprints on the gun.'

'How can the police know that?' Max cut in.

'Because the murderer threw the gloves on the fire before leaving the apartment. Gunpowder residue could have been detected on them if they hadn't been burnt. As it happens, the fire died too quickly to destroy them completely. They're a pair of fine-leather ladies' gloves, in Madame Dombreux's size.'

'Is that the only evidence they have against her?'

'She was seen going into the building with Spataro shortly before the murder was committed. She was known to be angry with him for telling the police they were lovers. By claiming he meant to withdraw that statement, she might have hoped to persuade us that someone else killed him in order to prevent him doing so.'

'And mightn't they have done?'

'The someone in question being another woman, presumably, with the same glove size as Madame Dombreux?'

'The police can't know the gloves were actually worn by the murderer, Appleby. They may have been left there to incriminate Corinne.'

'They may have, it's true, but only as part of an elaborate conspiracy for the existence of which there's not a scrap of evidence. The police aren't looking for any other suspects. As far as they're concerned, they've caught Spataro's killer.'

'They're wrong.'

'See if you're as sure about that after we've taken a look at the apartment. From what Zamaron tells me, you may not be.'

Number 7 Rue du Verger was in many respects a mirror image of 8 Rue du Verger, though somewhat smarter in its common parts, gleaming brass and glowing marble attesting to more assiduous housekeeping. The concierge was younger and friendlier, though understandably downcast. '*C'était épouvantable à voir, messieurs*,' she averred as she escorted them to the lift. A terrible thing to see? Max felt sure it had been.

The entrance to Spataro's apartment was on the sixth floor. A notice from the *préfecture* had been pinned to the door, forbidding entry. But Appleby had the key and official permission. They went straight in.

What they entered was the world of Raffaele Spataro. Bright colours were everywhere, in rugs and upholstery and tapestries, not to mention the numerous huge and gaudy paintings. Leopard- and tiger-skins had been draped and strewn around as well. The man had lived in a jungle of strident shapes and tones. The paintings were a mixture of still lifes and nudes, the fruits ripe, the men muscular, the women broad-hipped and big-breasted.

'I think we can safely say Spataro wasn't keen on self-restraint,' Appleby remarked. He stopped at the foot of a staircase that led up to a large hatch in the ceiling. 'This communicates with his studio on the floor above. We'll take a look up there later.'

Appleby led the way into the drawing-room. There was no relief from the kaleidoscopic excess of Spataro's taste in furnishings and decoration. Tableloads of liquor and disorderly piles of news-papers and magazines compounded the chaos. What were surely

several years' worth of party invitations filled the mantelpiece, with the overflow tucked into the frame of the gigantic mirror above it.

In the centre of the room a clearance had been made, exposing floorboards darkly stained with blood. The extent of the stain took Max aback. It was at least six feet across. 'He was a big fellow,' said Appleby. 'A lot of blood will have come out of him.'

'So I see.'

'I gather there was a rug it soaked through that they took away for evidence. Oh, and there's the famous gramophone.'

The machine stood on a sideboard, flanked by a stack of records. There was one already on the turntable. Appleby lifted it off and peered at the label.

'Proof the Devil doesn't always have the best tunes,' he said, dropping it back into place.

'Where do the police think he was shot from?' Max asked.

'From just about where you are now.'

Max looked down at his feet, though what he expected to see he could not have said. Corinne had not killed Spataro, but someone had. Someone had stood where Max was standing and gunned Spataro down in cold blood. And then the hot blood had flowed.

'I imagine she stepped closer after he'd fallen and finished him off with the shot to the head. While this' – Appleby nodded back to the gramophone – 'was caterwauling away.'

'Corinne didn't do it, Appleby.'

'So you keep saying. The police say otherwise.'

'Does she have a lawyer to defend her?'

'Not yet, as far as I know. Under wartime regulations, I believe they can hold her without charge, let alone legal representation, for as long as they like.'

'But the war's over.'

'Not legally. Until there's a treaty, we're all still theoretically at war.'

'Can I see her?'

'That would be up to Zamaron. And what good would it do? She'll protest her innocence. And you'll believe her.'

'I already believe her. First my father, now Spataro. It's the work of the same man. Surely that's obvious.'

'Let's go upstairs. I'm told it's well worth a look.'

They went back out into the hall. The hatch leading to the studio was operated by a pulley fitted to the wall at the foot of the stairs. Appleby wound the handle and the hatch slowly rose until it engaged with a hook vertically above them. Then he gestured for Max to go on up.

The studio was lower-ceilinged than the apartment owing to the angle of the mansard roof, and the windows were smaller, but it seemed larger and airier on account of its bareness. The walls were white and furnishings were few. Spataro's paintings, on the other hand, were many.

They were propped and stacked around the studio, the route between them leading in a series of diagonals to a far corner lit by windows from both sides of the building, where an easel was set up on a dais, next to a chair and a low table supporting a spinney of paintbrushes sprouting from old jam jars.

'Looks like he painted many more than he sold,' Appleby remarked as he followed Max in the direction of the easel. There was a clunk as his foot struck an empty wine bottle, one of many dotted around the room.

Max stepped up on to the dais and looked through the street-facing window. There, on the other side of Rue du Verger, was the mansarded top floor of number 8, from which Sir Henry had fallen to his death. Spataro would have had a clear view of the event, if he had happened to be looking.

'Zamaron advised me to pay particular attention to the paintings behind the easel,' said Appleby. 'The stack there.'

There were a dozen or so leaning against the wall, covered in a paint-spattered sheet. Max moved across to them and tugged the sheet away.

And there was Corinne. Max recognized her at once, despite the distortions and exaggerations of Spataro's technique. She was depicted sitting on a chair, a coat draped loosely around her shoulders. She was otherwise naked, apart from a pair of shoes.

Her legs were crossed to preserve a hint of modesty, but her breasts were fully exposed.

She had not denied modelling for Spataro, but confronting the proof of it was still a shock for Max. He told himself to accept what he saw as an artwork and nothing more. But acceptance did not obligingly follow.

'She's all woman, isn't she?' murmured Appleby.

'Why don't you—' Whirling round to be met by Appleby's confoundedly bland gaze, Max fell suddenly silent. Losing his temper now would help no one, Corinne least of all.

'Shall we take a look at the others, Mr Maxted?'

Max moved the first picture aside, bracing himself for more of the same. But on the second canvas there was only a faint pencil sketch of a woman who might have become a likeness of Corinne in a finished painting but was now only a series of suggestive lines: a nude, naturally, reclining on a couch.

The third canvas was another sketch of another nude, crouching on all fours on the low table. And the remaining canvases were blank.

'Work in progress, you think?' Appleby asked.

'She only modelled for him once,' Max said stubbornly, leaning the canvases back against the wall and replacing the sheet.

'Once, twice or umpteen times, it's proof she knew Spataro . . . how shall we put it? . . . on terms a man who loved her might resent.'

'There are lots of artists in Montparnasse, Appleby, and lots of artists' models.'

'I wouldn't like it. And I bet Sir Henry didn't like it either.'

'There was nothing between Corinne and Spataro.'

'That's the problem, isn't it?' Appleby pointed with the stem of his pipe at the shrouded paintings. 'There may have been *literally* nothing between them.'

Max broke away and stared disconsolately through the window. Less than a week ago, on the rooftop opposite, the drama that had led him to this place had been set in motion. He had resolved to avenge his father's murder, but all that had happened so far was a second murder – and a second injustice. He wanted an enemy he

could engage with, a target to fix in his sights before he pressed his triggers. But the sky was empty. There was no foe to be seen.

'Penny for them,' said Appleby, standing so close behind him that his pipe smoke drifted over Max's shoulder.

'I miss knowing who I'm supposed to be fighting.'

'You seldom see more than the shadow of your opponent in my game, Mr Maxted.'

'And what is your game, Appleby?'

'I'm here to protect the British delegation to the peace conference from any threat that may present itself.'

'What are you – Secret Service?'

'If I were, I wouldn't admit it.'

'And you're not admitting it, I notice.'

'It'll be the guillotine for Madame Dombreux if she's convicted of murdering Spataro.'

'She's innocent. You know that, don't you?'

'I know my first duty is to our delegation. And for that reason – not because I find it hard to believe a beautiful young woman is capable of murder – I have to consider the possibility . . . that you're right.'

Max turned and stated at Appleby in amazement. 'What?'

Appleby allowed himself a tentative smile. 'There are suspicious aspects to Sir Henry's death, as you pointed out. And this business with the gloves does have a contrived look about it. Also . . .' He frowned. 'I had an interesting chat with your brother on the train on Tuesday. It must have occurred to you that Sir Ashley would mention the list you found. I can't help noticing you haven't mentioned it to me.'

'All right. So you know about the list.'

'In Sir Henry's handwriting?'

'Yes.'

'Mind if I see it?'

'What makes you think I carry it around with me?'

'I doubt you'd leave it in your hotel room. I doubt you'd leave it anywhere.' Appleby held out his hand. 'I'd be very grateful if you showed it to me, Mr Maxted.'

Max hesitated, then reached into his pocket. He took out the list

and passed it to Appleby. 'It's only a copy. Corinne has the original.'

'*Had*, you mean. The police have probably got it now. Unless they've sent it on to *le Deuxième Bureau*.'

'Who?'

'The French Secret Service.' Appleby ran his eye down the list. 'It's a worrying possibility, since this is considerably more enlightening than the entries in Sir Henry's diary.'

For all that the admission was casually made, Max did not doubt it was carefully calculated. 'So, you admit you removed the diary from his personal effects before they were delivered to us?'

'It was a potential source of vital information. It was always my intention to return it once I'd had an opportunity to evaluate the entries.' Appleby delved inside his coat and pulled out the diary: pocket-sized, bound in blue leather, with a lion-and-unicorn crest on the front and a small pencil in the spine. 'Routine appointments only, I'm afraid. Nothing significant.' He passed it to Max as he spoke. But he held on to the list. 'This, on the other hand, could be very significant.'

'Did you tell my brother that?'

'Certainly not. It would only have confused him. And I assume you don't really want him interfering.' Appleby returned the list. 'Made any progress interpreting those items?'

'Some.'

'Really?'

'Enough to know you must understand at least a couple of them yourself.'

'Must I?'

'The Trust, for example.'

Appleby nodded. 'A Russian monarchist organization based here in Paris.'

'And F.L.?'

'They're the initials of the man who ran the Kaiser's spy network.'

'Fritz Lemmer.'

'The very same. Not a commonly known name, of course. How did you come by it?'

157

'I asked around.'

'Around thirty-three Rue des Pyramides, perhaps?'

Max held a poker face. 'Why there?'

'Because your father recorded a few appointments at that address, with one Travis Ireton, proprietor of Ireton Associates, known to us as a broker of illicitly obtained information. According to your brother, you met Ireton when you visited your father earlier this month.' (Max silently and expressionlessly cursed Ashley's inability to keep his mouth shut.) 'I assume you've been to see him since. He'd know who Lemmer is. I should warn you that Ireton's the sort who likes other people to do his dirty work. I suppose that's why the French authorities have failed so far to pin anything on him. Zamaron told me they had particularly high hopes of catching him last night in the act of taking delivery of proofs smuggled out of the conference printing works down in Auteuil. But he sent someone in his place and, as it happens, that someone managed to give the police the slip. They think he was an Englishman.'

'Really?'

'Yes. He lost his hat climbing over a wall. There was a London hatter's label inside the crown.' (How fortunate it was, Max reflected, that he had not bought the hat in Epsom.) Appleby shuddered theatrically. 'Cold today, isn't it?'

'I hadn't noticed.'

'That'll be why you came out without your hat, I suppose.'

'Do you know what the Contingencies Memo is?' Max asked, eager to revert to the subject of the list.

'No.'

'Or the Chinese box?'

'Not for certain. But if I had to hazard a guess . . .'

'Why don't you?'

Appleby smiled faintly. 'All right. The head of the Chinese delegation, Lou Tseng-Tsiang, visited Tokyo on his way here for talks with the Japanese government. While he was in Tokyo, a box of secret documents he was carrying went missing. Stolen by the Japanese, presumably. But who knows? There are so many thieves in this world. And so many secret documents. Your father served a

couple of years at the embassy in Tokyo, of course. He'd have known how things work there.'

'What exactly are you suggesting?'

'Nothing. It's all too vague to base a suggestion on. But Sir Henry was swimming in uncharted waters. That much is clear, I think. And any involvement with Fritz Lemmer would have been highly dangerous.'

'I might have to involve myself with him if I'm to get to the bottom of this.'

'Which I advised you against attempting to do. I suppose Madame Dombreux's arrest makes it certain you'll go on with it, though.'

'It was already certain. It's just more urgent now.'

'There are a lot of people looking for Lemmer, Mr Maxted, and a lot of people who don't want him found.'

'Which camp are you in?'

'The former, of course.'

'Then help me track him down.'

'Most of the people looking for Lemmer are better qualified for the task than you are, so I'd say your chances of success are negligible. Besides, there's not much I can do in the way of help. I've received no firm indication that Lemmer's in Paris, though that's only to be expected where such a slippery fellow's concerned. A firm indication of his whereabouts would probably be a false trail. He was in Tokyo at the same time as Sir Henry, as I expect you're aware. Their acquaintance may have given Sir Henry an advantage of some kind, but as to what kind . . . I don't know.'

'Who might know?'

'If I were you, I'd start with Masataka Kuroda at the Japanese delegation.'

Of course. Kuroda. All roads seemed to lead to him. 'I already know about Kuroda, Appleby. He knew my father. And he blames Lemmer for an assassination attempt against the late Tsar when he visited Japan in 1891.'

'Good. No need for me to fill you in, then.'

'If you think he's such a promising source . . .'

'Why haven't I sounded him out about Lemmer myself? It's a

fair question. The truth is there are limits to what I can do here in Paris. The French are a touchy lot and Downing Street doesn't want anything done that might put their backs up. Openly mounting inquiries about Lemmer would soon have me treading on *le Deuxième Bureau*'s toes, I'm afraid.'

So, that was it. First Ireton. Now Appleby. They both wanted Lemmer. And they both wanted Max to do the finding.

'There's another issue,' Appleby went on. 'Kuroda plays his cards close to his chest. He'd tell me nothing, however nicely I asked. But you're the son of Sir Henry Maxted, a man he admired and respected. As a matter of honour, he might be more forthcoming with you. If he proves to be, I could give you my expert advice on how to use any information you glean.'

'You seem to be doing what you accused Ireton of, Appleby: arranging for someone else to do your dirty work.'

'Ah, but, unlike Ireton, it's because circumstances oblige me to.'

'All right. I'll see Kuroda. And I'll report back to you. But I also want to see Corinne. Think you can arrange that for me?'

Appleby took a reflective puff on his pipe, then said, 'I think I probably can, yes.' His gaze drifted round the studio before returning to Max. 'One thing.'

'What?'

'Go carefully, won't you? I don't want to have to escort Sir Ashley round the scene of your murder.'

'No need to worry on that score. Ashley will think it's suicide.'

TO ANY NEUTRAL OBSERVER, ALONG WITH ALMOST ALL OF THE mourners, the funeral of Sir Henry Maxted would have appeared to pass as a textbook example of such ceremonies: dignified, orderly and respectful. The hymns and readings were well-chosen, the graveside observances well-handled. The old diplomat was seen off as diplomatically as he might have wished, with no mention of the circumstances of his death beyond their sudden and tragic nature.

Appearances, however, as so often, were deceptive. The presence of one of those attending gave George Clissold, as soon as he saw him, a sobering jolt. He communicated the news to his sister as they followed Sir Henry's coffin out of the church at the end of the service.

'Brigham's here, Win,' he whispered.

'What?'

'Brigham. He's among the mourners.' George did not warn her against looking around to confirm the point. He knew she would never betray herself in such a way.

A nod of acknowledgement and a frown of puzzlement were the only visible reactions Lady Maxted allowed herself. But George was aware that she would be displeased, if not alarmed, by the turn of events. And already she would be considering how to deal with it.

Lionel Brigham remained, in his sixtieth year, a handsome figure of a man, perhaps, in fact, more handsome than he had ever been.

Greying hair and heavier smile lines suited his rugged features. He had not run to fat in middle age, thanks to indulging in a range of energetic pursuits when not pacing the corridors of power in Whitehall. Fencing, swimming and real tennis were three of those. Rumour would have added womanizing as a fourth. He had never married nor seemed inclined to. He was not the marrying kind.

He was acquainted with many of those attending the funeral, drawn as they mostly were from the retired ranks of the diplomatic service. He told them he had been sent from Paris to represent the F.O. and would be hurrying back to attend to his duties at the peace conference. He was a busy and important man. No one could have doubted that. He was not the retiring kind.

He had been four years ahead of George at Eton and George marvelled that what the fellow had been then he essentially still was: arrogant and easy to admire. George would ordinarily have enjoyed the company of such a man. But he was a protective brother for all his other faults. He did not intend to allow Brigham to upset Winifred any more than she was bound to be upset on such a day. He found a moment as the mourners moved away from the graveside after the committal to have a quick and quiet word with him.

'Surprised to see you here, Brigham.'

'Sorry I didn't cable. Rather a last-minute decision as to who would come over.'

'Odd you should be chosen, though.'

'We go where we're sent in the service, George. We're not our own master.'

'Strange. That's exactly what I thought you were: your own master.'

'How's Winifred bearing up?'

'As you'd expect.'

'I'd like to speak to her before I return to Paris.'

'You'll see her at the house.'

'I meant alone.'

'That won't—'

'Tell her, George, there's a good fellow.' Brigham eyed him from close range. 'And tell her it's important.'

Max sat in a café in the Rue de Rivoli, his newly purchased fedora hanging with his coat on the nearby hat-stand, the knowledge heavy in his heart that at that very moment his father's funeral was drawing to its sombre close in Surrey.

He sipped his coffee and drew on his cigarette as he worked his way carefully through the pages of his father's diary. Appleby was right, damn him. It was merely a record of appointments which on their own revealed little. Corinne's name appeared nowhere. The commonest entries related to meetings with either Ribeiro or Norris. Sir Henry had apparently met Ireton just twice. He had recorded and circled the tantalizing initials F.L. on Wednesday, 19th February, but nothing else that day to explain why. There might have been other meetings, of course – and with other people – he had not recorded. Many days were blank, especially in recent weeks. There was no clue as to what he had done in London earlier in the month, nor even confirmation that it was London he had gone to. With an irritated sigh, Max closed the diary and thrust it into his pocket. No wonder Appleby had been willing to return it.

He drained his coffee, stubbed out his cigarette, flung down some coins and went to fetch his coat and his brand-new hat. There was nothing he could do before the evening, when he and Morahan were due to pay an unannounced call on Kuroda, so hurrying was pointless. But he hurried nonetheless. Walking was better than sitting and thinking to no effect.

When he reached Place de la Concorde, he paused, waiting for a gap in the traffic before he crossed to the island in the middle of the square where the Egyptian obelisk stood. He became suddenly aware of a twitching at his sleeve and turned to find a young dark-skinned man dressed in various unmatching items of military uniform smiling at him and holding out his hand importunately.

Max guessed the man – hardly more than a boy, really, to judge by his build and complexion – was an Arab of some kind, most likely Algerian. He had seen more than a few like him begging on the streets, the residue of France's colonial army. This one was

163

different, though: less downcast, less beaten. His smile was not so much ingratiating as interrogative.

It was cold and Max had no wish to linger. He doled out a few coins and moved on, receiving no thanks beyond a faint and somehow condescending inclination of the young man's head.

Had he looked back, which he did not, he would have seen that the young man continued to watch him as he made his way to the far side of the square. And the ingratiating smile faded slowly from his face as he did so.

Halfway along the Champs-Elysées towards the Rond Point, Max tugged down the brim of his hat and turned up the collar of his coat to ward off the chill wind. As he thrust his hands into his pockets, he felt an unfamiliar object in one of them. He stopped, took off his glove and fished it out. It was a piece of paper wrapped around a small pebble. He had no knowledge of how it had got there, but immediately suspected the young Arab. He moved to the side of the pavement and carefully flattened it out.

When it lay open in his palm, he saw the message that someone had written on it in pencilled capitals: LEAVE PARIS OR DIE.

Max raced back to the Place de la Concorde, but the young Arab was nowhere to be seen. He scoured the square and the terrace of the Jardin des Tuileries in vain. The messenger had gone. But his message remained.

WINIFRED, LADY MAXTED, SELDOM HAD OCCASION TO VISIT the billiard-room at Gresscombe Place. It was reserved for gentlemen's after-dinner entertainment, of which there had been little since before the war. Lionel Brigham had contested a few frames there in the days when he had been a frequent visitor to the house and perhaps it was for old times' sake that he had suggested it as a rendezvous.

Most of the mourners still sipping sherry and swapping memories of Sir Henry Maxted in the drawing-room charitably assumed Lady Maxted had slipped away in order to compose herself after the stress and strain of the funeral. This was certainly what George led Ashley and Lydia to believe. 'Give her ten minutes and she'll be right as rain,' he assured them, before heading off in search of some whisky. And he fervently hoped it would be so.

But George, of course, had no idea what Brigham wanted to discuss with Winifred in private. Neither did Winifred, though various disturbing possibilities did occur to her as she made her way along the corridor that led to the billiard-room. She regarded his presence at the funeral as both suspicious and insensitive, which sadly did not conflict with what she knew of his character.

He was leaning over the table with his long, supple fingers steadying the cue for some ambitious snooker shot when she entered the room. As he pulled away and stood upright to greet her, she was reminded of all the reasons she had been drawn to him in the first place. He was a handsome devil and was well aware of it.

165

He was the kind of man women were attracted to, in part because they knew they could not trust him.

'Winifred,' he said, bestowing upon her his rakish smile. 'It's good of you to spare me a little of your time.'

'Why are you here, Lionel?'

'To tender the Foreign Secretary's official condolences on the passing of a distinguished diplomat. Along with my personal condolences, of course. Henry's death must have been a shock for you.'

'A letter would have sufficed.'

'That would have seemed cold and unfeeling in view of our . . .' his eyes twinkled beneath his bushy eyebrows as he selected a suitable phrase '. . . old association.'

'It would have seemed appropriate to me.'

'Then I'm sorry to have disappointed you.'

'Really? I find it hard to believe you've ever been truly sorry for anything.'

'A word of advice, Winifred, now you've embarked on widowhood. Don't burden yourself with regrets.'

He laid the cue on the table and took a few steps towards her. She stiffened, though she did not retreat. She could recall only too well the thrill of his touch – the electric tremor that had coursed through her body when he had folded her in his arms. But there were other sensations to recall as well. And ultimately they were stronger.

'Do you remember that day—'

'I remember every day,' she cut in. 'From the beginning to the end.'

'Ah, but perhaps we haven't yet reached the end.'

'What do you want, Lionel?'

'A word . . . about James.'

'He couldn't be with us today.'

'For his father's funeral? That's shabby by any standards. Someone said he was ill. I didn't disabuse them of the notion, which I thought was good of me. Considering I know he's in Paris, digging into the circumstances of Henry's death.'

'If you know where he is, why did you ask?'

'I didn't.' Brigham treated her to a superior smile. 'What I said was that I wanted to talk to you about him.'

Winifred gave him a look that spoke of her impatience and her distaste in equal measure. 'Please come to the point, Lionel. I must rejoin the mourning party soon or it will look odd.'

'And we can't have that, can we? Very well. I'm concerned James may blunder into danger while he goes looking for a murderer who doesn't exist. Word has it Henry kept sinister company in Paris. The sort of people who don't take kindly to being cross-questioned.'

'What do you want me to do?'

'Call him off. In his own best interests.'

'You surely don't think he'd come home at my bidding? He risked his life every day in the Royal Flying Corps. I honestly believe he enjoyed it. The more perilous a situation is, the more he seems to relish it.'

'James isn't up against the likes of the Red Baron in Paris, Winifred. These people don't play by gentlemanly rules of combat.'

'You speak as if you're personally acquainted with them.'

'I keep my ear to the ground. It's what I'm paid to do.'

'You're not paid to be concerned for James's welfare, though. So, why are you?'

'You know why.'

The old scandalous whisperings were almost audible in Winifred's ears. Brigham had always seemed indifferent as to whether they were accurate. He had left it late – far too late, she was tempted to say – to confront the issue. 'You are not James's father, Lionel.'

'Is that so? My arithmetic must be defective, then. But I don't think it is. I took the trouble to check his date of birth in RFC records, you see. The fifth of May, 1891. He must have been conceived in late July or early August, 1890. Henry was in Tokyo all summer. But you—'

'I know where I was.'

'Yes. And I know where I was too.'

'You're not his father.'

'There was no one else, Winifred. You didn't have the spirit for that kind of game.'

'You make that sound like an insult.'

'The only insult here is to my intelligence. I'd hoped for better from you than a blank and illogical denial, I must admit.'

'Why would it matter to you even if it were true? I doubt you've ever faced a responsibility in your life unless you were forced to. Certainly not a paternal one.'

He took another step closer. She did not drop her gaze. 'You don't think very highly of me, do you?'

'Why would I? I assume you don't think very highly of yourself.'

'If you're expecting me to apologize for—'

'I assure you I'm not expecting that. Merely a better explanation than you've so far given of why you're here.'

'Isn't it obvious?'

'Not to me.'

'As a man grows older, he's bound to take stock of his life and to wonder what he has to show for the years he's spent on this Earth. To know I have a son—'

'You don't have one by me.'

'It's a miracle he came through the war in one piece. Don't let him throw his life away trying to avenge a murder that never happened.'

'How can you be sure it never happened?'

Brigham lowered his voice. 'The truth is known, Winifred. And a damned discreditable truth it is too. Ashley's in possession of the facts. Squeeze them out of him, if you must. But tell James to leave Paris. Now.'

'You don't seem to understand, Lionel. He won't take any notice of me.'

'But you're not even going to try, are you?'

'No. I'm not.'

'If you won't, perhaps I'll have to.'

'How do you propose to influence him?'

'By pointing out that Henry wasn't his natural father.'

'And that you are?'

'You leave me no choice in the matter.'

'Oh dear.' Winifred sighed, more, it seemed, in disappointment than sorrow. 'Need I remind you that we weren't always as discreet

as we should have been? James was a perceptive boy. I'm fairly certain he drew his own conclusion long ago – the same entirely false conclusion you've drawn. But evidently he still regards Henry as his father in every important sense. He'll probably laugh in your face. I'd do the same myself if I were less governed by my upbringing.'

'My God.' Brigham stared at her as if glimpsing her true character for the first time. 'You're a hard woman.'

'If I am, who made me so?'

'Whoever his father may have been, you're his mother. Don't you care what happens to him?'

'Of course I do. But he'll do as he sees fit. He always has and he always will. I'm proud of him for that. He has my full confidence. In everything he does.' She looked Brigham in the eye. 'Is that plain enough for you?'

Sᴀᴍ ʜᴀᴅ ɴᴏᴛ ʀᴇᴛᴜʀɴᴇᴅ ꜰʀᴏᴍ ʜɪꜱ ꜱɪɢʜᴛꜱᴇᴇɪɴɢ ᴡʜᴇɴ Mᴀx ꜱᴇᴛ off to meet Morahan. Max slipped a note under his door explaining that the night on the town he had suggested might not be possible after all. Sam would understand. He was an understanding fellow.

The evening was colder than the day. There were flecks of snow in the flurries of rain that fell from the moonless sky. Max set a stiff pace to Rue des Pyramides to warm himself, trying not to wonder what it was like to face a second night in a police cell with no certain way of knowing that anyone in the outside world knew of your plight. Such was Corinne's dire situation. He had her to seek justice for now, as well as his father.

Morahan was waiting for him at Ireton's offices, as agreed, but Ireton himself was nowhere to be seen. Malory was on station, however. She and Morahan were drinking cocoa in an atmosphere bordering, somewhat bewilderingly, on the cosily convivial.

Malory's secretarial role extended, it soon became apparent, to a keen appreciation of all the business of Ireton Associates. The smile with which she accompanied her favourable comment on Max's new hat was unmistakably mischievous. 'It makes you look like a real *gentilhomme*, Mr Maxted,' she said.

'We weren't the only ones expecting to see you,' Morahan observed, with a glance through the window.

'What do you mean?'

'You have a friend. He's in a doorway on the other side of the street.'

'What?' Max moved towards the window to see for himself, but Morahan signalled for him to stay where he was.

'No sense in letting him see you're on to him. He's probably been with you for a couple of days.'

'That's ridiculous. I—'

'What's ridiculous is how easy I expect you've made it for him. The question is: what do we do about it? He looks English to me.'

'How can you possibly tell that?'

'The shoes. And the way he stands. Leaning without slouching. One of Appleby's men, I'd guess. I assumed we'd walk to the Bristol. It's in the Place Vendôme. But I can fetch the car and take a detour if you think we need to lose him.'

Max sighed. 'There's no point. Appleby knows I'm going to see Kuroda. He actually advised me to.'

'Ah. Take the shadow along, then.'

'Yes. I suppose so.'

'You know what they say, Mr Maxted,' trilled Malory. 'You can be sure you're going in the right direction when people follow you.'

It was easier for Max to obey Morahan's instruction not to look behind him for a glimpse of Appleby's man thanks to the pace he had to walk at in order to keep up with the giant American's loping stride. Morahan was a reassuring presence, with his vast build, his air of confidence and a voice that rumbled within him like a ship's engine. Max had taken him for an underling of Ireton's, but now, as they talked, he was not so sure. Perhaps theirs was more in the way of a partnership.

'Has Travis explained Kuroda's background to you, Schools?'

'I wouldn't work with Travis if he didn't tell me what I needed to know.'

'And how long have you worked with him?'

'Long enough.'

'Where did your paths first cross – Cuba?'

'Good guess.'

'You know him well, then?'

'Better than most.'

'Can I trust him?'

Morahan chuckled. 'I trust him.'

'That's not quite what I asked.'

'It's the best I can do.'

'Tell me, did you ever meet my father?'

'Yuh, I met him.'

'What did you think of him?'

'I thought he had the look.'

'The look?'

'A lot of guys his age fold their hand and leave the table. Quit while they're ahead, is how they'd put it. Something dies in them then. A light goes out. You can see it gone from their eyes. It never comes back. But Henry still had it. He hadn't left the table. He was still in the game.'

'That's good, is it?'

'It's the only way to be.'

The hushed and somnolent atmosphere of the Hotel Bristol hardly suggested it was serving as the headquarters of one of the peace conference's most important delegations. According to the newspapers Max had forced himself to read, Japan had been eased to the sidelines by the recent establishment of the Council of Four. It no longer had any say in the really important decisions, which were taken by Wilson, Clemenceau, Lloyd George and Orlando behind closed doors. The reaction to this of the leader of the Japanese delegation, Marquis Saionji, was unknown. He eschewed all public utterances.

If Masataka Kuroda proved equally tight-lipped, Max and Morahan were likely to have had a wasted journey. But unannounced or not, they were courteously received by a tiny hand-wringing functionary. He explained that Commissioner Kuroda (the title suggested he was indeed a police officer) was 'elsewhere'. Mention of Sir Henry's name and Max's relationship to him prompted a telephone call to the elsewhere in question. The functionary reported that Kuroda could not leave where he was – but they were welcome to join him there.

It was a large neo-classical house near Parc Monceau. The hefty bodyguards on the door suggested to Max that this was where

Marquis Saionji was resting his venerable bones while in Paris, although no one said as much and they were not encouraged to ask.

Kuroda received them in the library, surrounded by shelf-loads of leather-bound tomes lit by one oil lamp and the flickering glow of a well-banked fire. He was unusually tall for his race, thin to the point of emaciation and impeccably dressed, more like a courtier than a policeman. He could have been any age between fifty-five and seventy with his narrow face, solemn eyes, close-cropped grey hair and incipient stoop. He was standing when they entered and made no move to sit down. Nor did he invite them to do so. Max had the impression the library was not his customary domain in the house. Perhaps he was not expected to receive visitors there at all.

He offered Max his condolences in a stiff and formal fashion, without any hint that he knew Sir Henry personally. He and Morahan had clearly met before, something the American had omitted to mention, although Max suspected he would have justified that on the simple grounds that he had not been asked. Kuroda enquired after Ireton – his pronunciation rendering Morahan as Mohan and Ireton as Iton – as well as a Miss Hollander, whom Max belatedly identified as Malory. Kuroda was particularly insistent that his good wishes should be passed on to her. Morahan explained that Ireton had recommended him to Max as a bodyguard, though whether Kuroda was entirely convinced by the explanation was unclear.

'You are Sir Henry's younger son, Mr Maxted?' he asked, the effect of his attention being suddenly turned on Max rather like that of a torch being shone in his eyes. 'You were a pilot in the war?'

'Yes. I was.'

'To soar above the ground of the enemy. This must be a wonderful thing.'

'It would be more wonderful if the enemy weren't also soaring.'

To Max's surprise, Kuroda laughed. 'Ah. Good. Yes. You are right. And you are here to discuss . . . a soaring enemy?'

'In a sense. I found your name on a list in my father's handwriting. I wondered if he'd discussed anything important with you.'

Kuroda frowned. 'Not directly. But a certain matter was broached through an intermediary.'

'Can you tell me who that intermediary was?'

Kuroda glanced at Morahan, who gave a nod of consent. 'It was Mr Ireton. Though he did not say he was speaking to me on Sir Henry's behalf. I deduced it from the subject Mr Ireton raised with me and from the fact that I heard no more from him about it following Sir Henry's death.'

'Was the subject . . . Fritz Lemmer?'

'Ah.' Kuroda sounded rather more surprised than he looked. 'You know about Lemmer.' (He was Lemma to him, of course.)

'I do.'

Kuroda nodded. 'He was the subject, yes.' Another glance at Morahan seemed to draw a favourable response. 'Mr Ireton said he represented someone willing to sell information that would enable the buyer to locate Lemmer. Sir Henry, I concluded, was the seller.'

'I believe he may have been murdered to silence him about Lemmer, Mr Kuroda.'

'This is as I surmised. You blame Lemmer himself?'

'Maybe.'

Kuroda nodded thoughtfully. 'An invisible opponent is the hardest to judge. Is he cleverer than we think or not as clever as we fear? It has taken me nearly thirty years to measure the cleverness of Fritz Lemmer.'

'And how do you rate him?'

'Dangerous, Mr Maxted. Very dangerous. He lays traps for the unwary. Those who pursue him become his prisoners.'

'Was my father his prisoner?'

'I do not think so.'

'Could he have been responsible for my father's murder?'

'Of course. But in general he kills no one unless their death serves a purpose. And I see no purpose in Sir Henry's death.'

'If he knew Lemmer's whereabouts . . .'

'Then it would be simpler for Lemmer to alter his location. And I have reached the conclusion that the secret of his success is not the complexity we see . . . but the simplicity he sees.'

'You were presumably keen to acquire the information Travis offered you.'

'Oh, yes. I assured him I would outbid all other interested parties.'

'You blame Lemmer for an assassination attempt against the Tsarevich in Tokyo in 1891?'

'It was not in Tokyo, Mr Maxted. The Tsarevich was in Kyoto at the time. He was due in Tokyo the following day. But he never visited the capital. After the attack, which he was lucky to survive, he returned directly to Russia. The visit was a chance for Japan and Russia to settle their differences. Instead, it only deepened them. Without that attempt on his life, there might have been no war between Japan and Russia in 1904. Then no humiliating defeat for Russia, no revolution simmering in her cities, no Bolshevik takeover, no massacre of the Tsar and his family. Lemmer rears consequences as others rear canaries. He enjoys their plumage. Yes, I blame him for that. For all of that. Others think I am mistaken. They believe the assassination attempt was organized by Japanese reactionaries. And it was. But Lemmer was behind it. One of those reactionaries worked for him. I know which one, though I cannot prove it. I hope to, one day. But I have been hoping for a long time.'

'And Lemmer's been a thorn in your side ever since then?'

'He has been a thorn in the side of many.'

'Have you ever met him?'

'No. He left Tokyo before I obtained any evidence to suggest he had organized the assassination attempt. Sir Henry knew him, of course. They were fellow diplomats. He told me what he could about him. But it was not much. Lemmer is a highly secretive man.'

'Did you see anything of my father while you were both here in Paris?'

'I met him once only. I wish now I had seen more of him. But my duties for the delegation are quite demanding.' Kuroda smiled thinly. 'You would be surprised at the trouble young men of high rank can get themselves into when sent abroad to represent their nation.'

'Then there's the added burden of a seventy-year-old head of delegation who brings his twenty-year-old mistress with him,' Morahan remarked.

Kuroda's smile grew thinner still. 'You are misinformed, Mr Morahan. My lord Saionji does not celebrate his seventieth birthday until later this year.'

'When you met my father,' Max pressed on, 'did he mention Lemmer?'

'No. If he had . . . I would have advised him to be very careful.'

'And did you discuss Travis Ireton's offer of information with anyone?' This was the crux of the issue. And Max did not doubt Kuroda would know it was.

'I have no way of knowing how many spies Lemmer has who still work for him, Mr Maxted. I cannot be certain who may be such a spy or who may not. The Emperor has sent more than fifty people here to negotiate for him. If you ask me is a spy of Lemmer among them, I answer yes. If you ask me how many there may be, I say I do not know. A man who reveals a secret to someone he cannot trust is a fool. I am responsible for the security of the Emperor's delegation. I cannot afford to trust anyone.'

'That sounds like a no,' said Morahan.

Kuroda nodded. 'It was intended to.' He looked at Max. 'You suspect someone heard of Mr Ireton's offer of information, calculated that Sir Henry was the source and determined to silence him?'

'Yes.'

Another nod. 'I agree. You should suspect anyone Mr Ireton discussed the matter with. Including me. Unless, of course, you trust me. Then and then only can you believe me.' He smiled. 'Have you any more questions, Mr Maxted?'

'Just one. When you met my father, did he mention the box of secret documents stolen from the head of the Chinese delegation while he was in Tokyo?'

A slight narrowing of his gaze was the only hint of surprise on Kuroda's part. And it might not have been surprise at all. 'No. He did not.'

'Between ourselves, Masataka,' said Morahan, 'did your people steal that box?'

'If we had, we would not admit it. If we had not, we would know that our denial would not be believed.'

'That sounds like a yes-no-maybe.'

Kuroda nodded. 'It was intended to.'

IT WOULD HAVE BEEN EASY FOR MAX TO DISMISS THE MEETING with Kuroda as pointless. Certainly, he had learnt little he did not already know. But the strangest thing had nonetheless happened. He found he believed every word Kuroda had said. No responsibility for Sir Henry's death could be laid at his door.

Morahan seemed to feel the same. 'For a man who speaks mostly in riddles, he makes himself remarkably plain.'

'He told no one. I'm sure of it.'

'Me too.'

'Who's next?'

'Ask Travis. I'm to report to him tomorrow morning at nine. You should join us.'

'But you know already, don't you?'

'It's Travis's show. You'll have to let him run it. Your shadow's still with us, by the way.' They were walking south-west along Rue de Monceau. The night was cold and quiet. The wind had dropped. There were few other pedestrians. Glancing back, Max saw only splashes of lamplight and dark shapes between. 'If you want something done about him, let me know.'

'What sort of something?'

'Nothing fatal.'

'Glad to hear it. I'll bear your offer in mind.'

'You do that.'

Morahan took to the Métro at Alma station, leaving Max – and his shadow – to carry on to the Mazarin without him. Irritated by the

assumption Appleby and Morahan seemed to share that he was ill-equipped to deal with such surveillance, Max headed along Rue de Bassano, turned left at the first opportunity and covered thirty yards or so, then spun on his heel and marched smartly back. There was a man, damn it, moving towards him, who adroitly crossed the street and melted into the darkness as Max approached.

'Going my way?' Max called after him. 'Maybe we can walk together.'

There was no response. And there was nothing to see. Max went after him, but all the doorways he checked were empty. The fellow was smart, no question.

Max made his way back to the corner of Rue de Bassano, where he stopped, lit a cigarette and waited for him to reappear. He did not. There was a sound far off that could have been a footfall, then another, resembling a stumble of some kind. Even shadows evidently had to watch their step in the dark. But he did not show himself.

'Hello?' Max called, walking slowly towards the sound.

Again, there was no response. Nothing stirred. There were no more footfalls.

Then a door opened a short distance ahead of Max. In a brief spill of light, a portly, heavily clad man emerged, trailing a tiny dog on a lead. The door closed behind them and they pottered off in the direction the sounds had come from.

As Max watched, they proceeded along the street, the man emitting occasional squeaks that were presumably comprehensible to the dog, the dog snuffling occasionally in response. They paused at a lamp-post for the dog to urinate, then moved on. If they passed anyone lurking in a doorway, they did not appear to notice.

'To hell with this,' Max muttered, throwing down his cigarette. He headed back once again to Rue de Bassano. And he did not look over his shoulder.

There were two messages waiting for Max at the Mazarin, which was two more than he was expecting. Both surprised him in their different ways. The first he opened was addressed to him in handwriting he recognized as Sam's.

178

Sir,
I'm going with someone who's anxious to meet you to a
nightclub called Le Sagittaire. We'll wait for you there. The
hotel can direct you.
Sam

According to the reception clerk, Sam had left about an hour
before, accompanied by a woman he described under questioning
as 'Slavic'. It had to be the young woman from Bukayev's bookshop. There were simply no other candidates, though how Sam had
fallen in with her he could not imagine.

The second message had been telephoned in. It was from
Kuroda. The time recorded on it by the clerk suggested he had
made the call very shortly after they had parted.

M. Kuroda asks you to meet him in Parc Monceau – near
the west entrance – at 11.15 tomorrow morning.

Max put to the back of his mind the mystery of why Kuroda
wanted to meet him again and headed straight out, armed with
directions from the clerk, who permitted himself a meaningful twitch
of one eyebrow when he described Le Sagittaire as *très animé*.

It was a basement establishment close to the Champs-Elysées, full
of noise, smoke and couples of varying ages and races. A band was
playing music Appleby would definitely not have approved of,
though those dancing to it definitely did. Sagittarius himself was
depicted in a vast mural, reflected in an equally vast mirror on the
wall facing it. There was a palpable air of permissiveness about
the place. Black men were wrapped around white women, white
men around black women. Some of the men were old enough to be
their partners' grandfathers. And some of the women, it struck
Max, were probably not women at all. Ashley, he felt sure, would
have been appalled.

On the far side of the dance floor from the jazz band was a bar
and a gathering of tables. Sam waved to Max as he approached.
Sam was red-faced and grinning and clearly far from sober. His

companion was, as Max had surmised, the young woman from the bookshop, looking much more glamorous and indeed much more Russian with her black hair flowing over her shoulders. Her skin was even paler than Max remembered, almost white in the lamplight, so much so that the red bow on her black dress looked like a splash of blood.

'Ah, there you are, sir,' Sam slurred. 'Just in time. I'm running out of stories to entertain Nadia with.'

'Nadia Bukayeva,' the young woman said, extending a hand she appeared to expect Max to kiss. He was happy to oblige. 'I could not tell you earlier. Igor Bukayev is my uncle.'

'Delighted to make your acquaintance.' Max sat down, lit a cigarette and engaged Sam in interrogative eye contact.

'Drop of wine, sir? There's plenty.'

'You've certainly had plenty, by the look of you.'

'He is not your batman now, Max,' said Nadia, reprovingly but genially.

'He never was, actually.'

'He says you were a very daring pilot.'

'Poppycock. I was as cautious as they come. I wouldn't still be alive otherwise.'

'That is English modesty, yes?'

'That's what it is, right enough,' said Sam.

A waiter hove to and Max ordered a whisky. 'Are you a regular here, *mademoiselle*?' he asked Nadia.

'Nadia, please. We have become very informal, Sam and I.' She squeezed Sam's knee, inducing a blush that was visible even through the flush of wine.

'Nadia was asking after you when I got back to the hotel, sir. I didn't think you'd want me to let her just wander off.'

'So we came here to wait for you,' said Nadia. 'And, no, I am not a regular. More . . . an occasional.'

'Is it always like this?'

'Usually livelier.'

'Really?' Max glanced around. 'Livelier than this, eh?'

'They know how to have fun, don't they, sir?' said Sam. 'There are some sights here I never thought to see.'

180

'And in some cases you're not exactly sure what it is you're seeing.'

'Exactly, sir.'

The whisky arrived. 'Cheers.'

'Cheers.' Sam gulped down a mouthful of wine. 'It's been quite a day.'

'I bet it has.'

''Scuse me, sir – Nadia.' Sam rose unsteadily to his feet and stifled a belch. 'I've got to point Willy at the wall.' He stumbled off.

'Who is Willy?' asked Nadia.

'No one you know,' Max murmured, watching Sam navigate his meandering way towards a door beyond the bar.

'We need to talk, Max.' Nadia's voice was suddenly so close to Max's ear that he jumped in surprise.

He turned to find her staring at him intently. She was more serious now – more like the earnest bookshop assistant he had met earlier. 'This is hardly the place for a quiet chat, Nadia,' he pointed out.

'Can you hear what I'm saying?' Her lips were nearly touching his ear lobe. She was speaking at normal volume, but the noise around them reduced her words to a whisper that was nonetheless clearly audible.

He nodded. 'Of course I can hear you.'

'Then this is the place. No one else will hear. And anyone who sees us will think I am trying to talk you into bed.'

'But you're not, are you?'

'Do you want me to?'

Max smiled, unable to decide whether she was flirting with him or rebuking him. Maybe Sam had had the same problem. 'I want you to tell me why you came to the hotel to see me.'

'Because my uncle disappeared last Saturday, Max. Just a few hours after he heard your father was dead. I do not know where he is. I am very worried about him.'

'You've no idea where he might be?'

'No. I do not even know if he is still alive. But when the news came to him of Sir Henry's death, he was full of fear. I know that much.'

181

'What did he have to be frightened of?'

'My uncle is a leading member of a secret organization dedicated to the overthrow of the Bolsheviks and the restoration of royalty in Russia.'

'The Trust.'

'You have heard of it?'

'It doesn't seem to be that big a secret.'

'No. Probably it is not. Russians talk. It is one of our vices. Sir Henry had information about the Trust that he offered to sell to my uncle. Did you know this?'

Max still found it hard to believe his father had been engaged in such activities, but it seemed he was going to have to accustom himself to the idea. 'What sort of information?'

'There is a traitor inside the Trust. The Cheka know our plans before we know them ourselves. We are being destroyed from within. Sir Henry told my uncle he knew who the traitor was. He was given the name by Pierre Dombreux.'

'But Dombreux was working for the Bolsheviks.'

'Maybe he was. Maybe he wasn't. Maybe he was playing a double game. It is a dangerous thing to do.'

'So it seems.'

'We must know who the traitor is, Max. Did Sir Henry leave any sort of . . . record?'

'Nothing that will help you.'

'But will you help us, Max? If you discover the name . . .'

'I'll tell you. And you won't have to pay me for it.'

'Thank you.' She bowed her head and rested it on his shoulder. She murmured something into the muffling cloth of his jacket. For a moment, he thought she was crying.

'Don't upset yourself.' He raised her chin gently.

She looked at him with her large, dark soulful eyes. 'I am afraid, Max. And you also should be afraid.'

Max thought of the note the young Arab had secreted in his pocket and smiled. 'You're probably right. But I seem to have lost the knack.'

WHEN HE BELATEDLY REJOINED THEM, SAM MADE NO EFFORT to deny that he felt dead on his feet. 'It's been a long day and no mistake.'

Max insisted on settling the bill and they promptly took their leave of Le Sagittaire.

'You head back to the Mazarin, Sam,' Max said once they were outside. 'I'll escort Nadia home.'

Ordinarily, Sam would have managed some kind of knowing wink at that. But he really was exhausted. Max suspected much of what he had eaten and drunk in the course of the evening had recently left him by the emergency exit. 'Righto, sir.' With that he staggered off.

It was not far to Bukayev's bookshop. The streets were generally quiet. Snow was gently falling. In Little Russia, it was quieter still and the snow heavier.

'It is a little like St Petersburg here tonight,' said Nadia as they approached the shop.

'You grew up in St Petersburg?'

'Yes. And I miss it every day.'

'Do you have any family apart from your uncle?'

'No. My father and my two brothers were killed in the war. My mother died of a broken heart. Uncle Igor is all I have left.'

'I hope you'll hear from him soon.'

'I hope also. I do not enjoy being alone.'

They stopped at the door of the shop. There was an appeal – an

invitation – in Nadia's gaze Max could have chosen to pretend he had not noticed. But the warmth and softness of her body were easy to imagine. And he wanted in that instant to do more than imagine them.

'Will you come in?'

He hesitated, then nodded. And she turned and unlocked the door.

Max was aware that the man Appleby had instructed to tail him had almost certainly followed him from the Mazarin to Le Sagittaire and on to the bookshop. Staying with Nadia was in part an act of defiance: a statement that he did not care what they knew or thought they knew about him. The rest was a simple surrender to the sensuality of the moment. Nadia needed him and he needed her. And the need was urgent.

He left as dawn was breaking. Nadia lay in bed, watching him dress. Neither spoke. Words, after their urgent couplings, seemed wholly redundant. He did not even kiss her goodbye. But in the looks that passed between them they exchanged a fitting farewell.

The snow had stopped overnight and most of it had dissolved into slush. The streets were deserted and Max wondered if his shadow was still with him. He would have had a bone-chilling vigil outside the bookshop if he was. There was no sign of him that Max could detect. But that, he well knew, was hardly decisive.

Back at the Mazarin, Max took a bath and was still towelling himself down when there was a knock at the door. He opened it to find Sam outside in charge of a breakfast trolley.

'I ordered enough for both of us, sir,' he said, sounding unwontedly chirpy. 'There's nothing like bacon and eggs after a night on the tiles.'

'It's you who overdid it, Sam, not me.'

'If you say so, sir.'

'But I am confoundedly hungry. And that bacon smells good. Wheel it in.'

Sam obliged. Max flung on his dressing-gown and they set to.

'I've something to tell you, sir,' Sam swiftly announced, munching on a sausage. 'I'd have told you last night, but I wasn't firing on all cylinders.'

'So I noticed.'

'Fact is, I may have found myself a job.'

'You mean here – in Paris?'

'Yeah.'

'But how? What sort of job?'

'Well, I thought rather than go gawping at the sights yesterday I'd do something a bit more . . . constructive.'

'Which was?'

'Like you'll know, I'm sure, a lot of the meetings to do with the peace conference are held at the French Foreign Office on the Key Dorsey. I went down there and had a chat with some of the chauffeurs. They hang around most of the day, apparently. Got myself into a card game with the British drivers and helped one of them out with a distributor problem he was having. Turns out the chief mechanic they brought over from London's gone and died of the Spanish flu and they're desperate to find someone to replace him.'

'So you volunteered?'

'I'm to meet the bloke who hires and fires this morning. The pay's not bad and room and board at the Majestic's thrown in.' Sam grinned. 'Seems like you might be stuck with me, sir.'

'What about the deposit on those planes?'

'I'll cable Miller cancelling the order. I reckon I can trust him to pay me back when I get home.'

'You've got it all worked out, I see.'

'Cars are child's play compared with planes, sir. It'll be money for old rope. I should be able to spare some time to help you out. If you need me to.'

'It's a kind offer, Sam.' It had struck Max, in fact, that having a trusted ally lodging at the British delegation hotel might prove invaluable. 'But everything's much more complicated than it was this time yesterday.'

Max told Sam then about Spataro's murder and Corinne's arrest. Sam was clearly shocked by the developments. It hardly

required a genius to deduce that investigating Sir Henry's death was a riskier enterprise than Max had originally supposed. And that was before the death threat delivered to him by the young Arab was taken into consideration. He showed Sam the note.

'It gets straight to the point, doesn't it?'

'But I notice you're still here, sir.'

'I've never been one to walk away from a scrap.'

'Or fly away, as I recall.'

'I don't really want to drag you into this, Sam.'

'But you reckon Kaiser Bill's spymaster is behind it all, don't you, sir?'

'Well, I—'

'Which makes it my patriotic duty to lend a hand. If I can. And I haven't given up on the flying school yet. You'll be no use to me dead.'

'Nor much alive, I suspect.'

Sam frowned. 'You reckon the boy who slipped you the note was an Arab?'

'Yes. What of it?'

'It's funny, that's all. The drivers were talking about a spate of burglaries at the delegation hotels. Petty stuff, apparently. But not so petty if you're the victim, I suppose. Anyhow, the papers have given the burglar a name: the Singe.'

'The what?'

'Singe.'

'Do you mean *le Singe* – the Monkey?'

'Ah. That'll be it. He gets in through windows so high up no one thinks they need to be closed.'

'Does he now?' Max remembered standing on the roof of 8 Rue du Verger trying to understand what had led Sir Henry to his death. 'I wonder how he gets to those windows.'

'Over the roof, maybe.'

'My thoughts exactly. But where are the Arab connections?'

'A few people have caught a glimpse of the burglar – well, someone they think must be the burglar. They say he's small and dark-skinned – Arab-looking.'

'Is that so?'

'So, d'you want me to ask a few more questions about the Monkey – after I've got my feet under the table at the Majestic?'

Max smiled. 'It seems to me I'm powerless to prevent you.'

Sam nodded. 'That you are, sir. But I thought it only polite to ask.'

IRETON SEEMED MONUMENTALLY UNSURPRISED BY HOW LITTLE Max had learnt from Kuroda. It seemed to Max, indeed, that it was just as he had expected, perhaps even as he had hoped. If stringing Max along to no purpose was Ireton's objective, it had been well served. If not, it was hard to understand why the American should look so pleased with himself.

Morahan had the decency to appear at least mildly disappointed as he confirmed Max's account of their evening's work. Malory served coffee and smiled appreciatively when Max passed on Kuroda's good wishes. 'He really is a charming gentleman,' she declared, ignoring Ireton's sarcastic scowl.

What Max did not pass on, of course, was news of Kuroda's later contact with him. He reckoned it was only fair to play Ireton at his own game. For the same reason he made no mention of Spataro's murder and Corinne's arrest. He did not seriously doubt that Ireton knew of these events. But he was damned if he would give him the satisfaction of being the first to refer to them.

'Are you going to tell me the next person you approached after Kuroda?' Max asked bluntly as soon as Malory had left them to it.

'I agree Kuroda was never likely to have breathed a word to any-one,' said Ireton, answering an entirely different question. 'But we had to rule him out. You can see that, can't you, Max?'

'I can see it was convenient for you to use me to rule him out for you. Who did you approach next?'

'Like Kuroda told you, he said he'd outbid anyone else who was interested. I took him at his word. But I needed other bidders, of course, to drive up the price he'd be willing to pay.'

'*Who?*'

'Where's the money in this world, Max, since most European countries have bankrupted themselves waging the war to end war? In my homeland, of course. The good old US of A. The American delegation was the obvious place to turn in search of a big fat bid. So, that's what I did.'

Max sighed. 'You may as well give me his name.'

'No need. I've arranged to have lunch with him at the Crillon. I've told him there's someone I want him to meet. You. But he doesn't know who you are and it wouldn't be fair to put you one up on him. Be at the Crillon at one o'clock and I'll introduce you to each other. Then we'll see what you can get out of him. He's less tight-lipped and a whole lot less cautious than Kuroda.' Ireton treated Max to one of his misshapen grins. 'He could be our man. So don't be late.'

Ireton soon excused himself on the grounds of a pressing engagement elsewhere, leaving Max to finish the coffee-pot with Morahan, who seemed in no hurry to be on his way. Max was emboldened to ask him a favour.

'About my shadow, Schools?'

'You want to lose him?'

'I want to be able to lose him when I choose to.'

'There are a few simple methods. You're on foot. So is he. That makes any form of transport your friend. Hire a taxi when there are no others about. Hop on a tram just as it's leaving. Likewise the Métro. There's a good chance you can give him the slip, at least temporarily. He can pick you up again at your hotel, of course. So, what you really need to do is to put a face to him. The Métro's probably best for that. Board a train, then jump off just as the doors are closing. Either he shows himself by jumping off as well or he stays on and loses you. I shouldn't bother trying that this morning, though.'

'Why not?'

'I watched you come in. You're not being tailed today, Max. Maybe Appleby's decided it's not worth the bother.'

'You're sure?'

Morahan shrugged. 'It's possible he's put a smarter operator on your case, I suppose. Maybe more than one man, but that's a heavy investment. I can't see Appleby running to it.'

'Why would he call it off?'

'I can't say. Maybe you should ask him.'

Morahan walked Max out. Max paused on his way at the door of Malory's office to wish her a good morning.

'Are you likely to see Mr Kuroda again?' she asked.

'She has a soft spot for our Japanese friend,' said Morahan, coming unintentionally to Max's rescue.

Malory blushed slightly and pursed her lips in irritation, though whether with herself or Morahan was unclear. 'I've enjoyed talking to him about his country, that's all. It brings back some happy memories.'

'You've been to Japan?' Max asked, surprised by the possibility.

Malory sighed, more sorrowfully than nostalgically. 'I may as well tell you, if only to deny Schools the pleasure of relating it.'

'I never speak about you to anyone without your permission, Malory,' said Morahan, sounding offended by the suggestion.

'No? Well, that may be so,' conceded Malory. 'In which case I apologize.'

'Apology accepted. I'll be seeing you, Max.' With that Morahan retreated in the direction of his own office.

'Oh lord,' said Malory. 'I believe I've hurt his feelings.'

'I believe you may have.'

Malory looked at Max then with a frown of concentration, as if properly assessing him for the first time. 'Travis said you were born in Tokyo.'

'He's disturbingly well-informed.'

'But it's true?'

'Yes. I have no memories of the city, though. We left when I was only a few months old. It could as easily have been Timbuktu. You've been there?'

'Tokyo? Yes. Timbuktu? No.'

They both laughed. Some of Malory Hollander's artfully concealed vivacity broke briefly from cover.

'What took you to Japan, Malory?'

'I was a Lutheran missionary. Very young and very naive. I believed it was my duty to spread the word of God. And I set about my duty with the kind of energy only the very young and very naive possess. I'm pained to recall how insensitive I was, forcing pamphlets and prayer-meetings on all those polite, restrained and contented Shintoists and Buddhists. I'm lucky no one tossed a rock at my head. I wouldn't blame them now if they had.'

'How long did you last?'

'Three years. Three wasted years. Except that I learnt how beautiful the country is and how remarkable its people are. I gained much more from the experience than they did.'

'Does that mean you know how Kuroda's mind works?'

'Goodness, no. But it does mean I know better than to try to understand how it works. The greatest honour the Japanese do us is to refrain from telling us how stupid they think we are. I told Travis that once.'

'How did he take it?'

'He said he likes it when someone thinks he's stupid. It makes it easier to outwit them.'

'I doubt he'd find it easy to outwit Kuroda.'

'I doubt that too.'

'Do you ever think of going back to Japan?'

'I will, one day.' Malory smiled brightly at him, then added, bafflingly, 'Something tells me you will too.'

Max found it hard to believe he really was no longer under surveillance, despite Morahan's confidence on the point. He went down into Pyramides Métro station, bought a ticket to Gare de l'Est and waited on the platform with a smattering of other passengers, none of whom seemed to pay him the slightest attention. He gave them a lot of his, and elicited nothing in the way of a suspicious reaction. Then the train rolled in and everyone climbed aboard.

Max stood inside the doors for a few moments, then stepped back out. There was time for anyone following him to do the same, but no one moved. The doors closed. The train rolled out. And Max was alone on the platform.

GILBERT MELLISH, SURREY SOLICITOR, POSSESSOR OF A FINELY honed professional manner, a balding dome of a head, an aldermanly paunch and an expression of practised neutrality, settled himself in the armchair to which he had been directed and pulled a bulging file from his briefcase. He gazed at his audience through thick-lensed glasses that magnified his eyes disquietingly, and cleared his throat.

The widow, brother-in-law, eldest son and daughter-in-law of his late lamented client, Sir Henry Maxted, were gathered in a semicircle around him. Of Sir Henry's younger son there was no sign and Mellish had as yet sought no clarification of Sir Ashley's statement that 'My brother can't be with us.'

Winifred, the Dowager Lady Maxted, appeared calm and composed. Her brother, George Clissold, sat beside her, regarding Mellish through heavy lids. Sir Ashley was altogether more alert, sitting upright in his chair and fiddling with his tie. He had made no reference to the somewhat testy telephone conversation he had had with Mellish two days previously, though the frown on the face of Lydia, the junior Lady Maxted, suggested she for one was well aware of it. Mellish's correctitude had evidently failed to meet with her approval.

'It's my understanding that you're all familiar with Sir Henry's wishes for the disposition of his estate,' Mellish said by way of preamble.

'Yes,' said Ashley. 'We are.'

'Gresscombe Place and the entailed farmland is yours, Sir

Ashley, along with five sixths of the income it generates, one sixth being reserved for your mother.'

'Henry laid these matters before us some years ago, Mr Mellish,' said Winifred. 'There is no confusion on anyone's part.'

'Indeed not.'

'There are no other beneficiaries, then,' said Lydia.

Mellish wondered if she was thinking of herself, but was inclined to suspect she was more concerned about her absent brother-in-law. He nodded. 'There are not.'

'I have the death certificate issued by the French authorities, Mellish,' said Ashley. 'Armed with that, I assume you can set about applying for probate.'

'Ah, there a small complication arises, I'm afraid.'

Ashley frowned. 'Why?'

'My firm has not been appointed as an executor of the will.'

'A mere detail. As executor, I will—'

'Neither have you, Sir Ashley.'

There was a brief, shocked silence. Winifred stiffened. George opened his eyes. Lydia stared. And Ashley glowered. 'What the devil are you talking about?'

'You are not an executor, Sir Ashley. Only an executor can apply for probate and in due course implement the provisions of the will. I'm sorry, but there it is.'

'A moment ago you said you understood we were fully aware of Sir Henry's wishes,' said Lydia.

'For the disposition of his estate, yes. Nothing has been changed there. Only in the matter of the executorship did Sir Henry make an alteration.'

'When did he do this, Mr Mellish?' asked Winifred.

'The revised will is dated . . .' Mellish broke off to consult the document. 'The twelfth of March.'

'March this year?' Ashley snapped.

'Er, yes.'

'But that's only . . . a few weeks ago.'

'Indeed.'

'How is this possible? He'd been in Paris since early January.'

'Not all the time, self-evidently. He telephoned me from his

London club on, let me see . . .' There was a rustling of papers. 'Yes. On Tuesday the eleventh. He said he wanted urgently to make an amendment to his will and would call on me the following day to do so.'

'He came to Epsom?'

'Yes.'

'But—'

'You must be mistaken,' Lydia cut in. 'He wouldn't have come to Epsom without contacting us.'

'He came, Lady Maxted, I assure you. Having the revised will typed there and then so that it could be signed and witnessed the same day placed something of a strain on my secretarial resources. I well recall the occasion.'

'Henry was in the country,' said George. 'I saw him myself.'

Ashley turned on him. '*What?*'

'In London. The eleventh, you say, Mellish?' George nodded. 'Yes, that sounds about right.'

'You *saw* him?'

'I did. At some distance. In Lombard Street. I thought I must be mistaken, but clearly I wasn't.'

'Did you know about this, Mother?'

'Yes, my dear. George told me.'

'Well, you might have told me.'

'I didn't consider it important.'

'*Not important?*'

'Who is the executor, Mellish?' George asked, ignoring Ashley. 'You may as well put us out of our misery.'

'It's James,' said Winifred quietly.

'James?' Ashley's tone had now acquired a timbre of horror.

'You are correct, Lady Maxted,' said Mellish. 'Mr James Maxted is the sole executor of Sir Henry's will.'

'Good God,' Ashley exclaimed, 'this . . . this is . . .'

'Intolerable,' said Lydia. 'That is what it is.'

'Sometimes the intolerable must be tolerated,' said Winifred.

Ashley glared at her. 'How can you take this so calmly?'

'I imagine the appointment is legally unchallengeable,' Winifred replied.

'Indeed so,' said Mellish.

'Then to take it other than calmly would be futile.'

But calmness clearly did not commend itself to Ashley, who squirmed and grimaced helplessly. 'I assume James could renounce the executorship if he wished,' said Lydia tightly.

'He could,' Mellish responded. 'Do you know of some reason why he might wish to?'

'Well, he's currently abroad and didn't return even for his father's funeral. That hardly suggests he's a natural choice for the role.'

'Be that as it may, Lady Maxted, Sir Henry's wishes were very clear on the point. If you can furnish me with an address for your brother, Sir Ashley, I'll—'

'Much good that'll do you.'

'But you can tell me where he is?'

'Yes, yes, damn it. Hotel Mazarin, Rue Coligny, Paris. Unless he's moved on to God knows where.'

'We have no reason to doubt his presence there, Mr Mellish,' said Winifred with some emphasis.

'Then I shall communicate with him as soon as possible,' said Mellish. 'As regards his suitability or inclination, I'll certainly offer my firm's services for the settlement of the estate.'

'He'll probably plump for that,' said George. 'He won't want to bog himself down in paperwork.'

'Let's hope not,' said Ashley, stroking his forehead gloomily.

'I'll need the death certificate you mentioned, Sir Ashley,' said Mellish, smiling uneasily.

'Yes, yes, very well.' Ashley hauled himself to his feet and headed for the door.

'Tell me, Mr Mellish,' said Lydia as soon as her husband had left the room, 'if, purely for the sake of argument, James *did* renounce the executorship, who would replace him?'

'The courts would appoint an administrator, Lady Maxted.'

'And who would that be?'

'Normally, the residuary legatee. In this case, Sir Ashley.'

'And in that event, we would be much where we were, in testamentary terms, before Sir Henry made the recent alteration to his will?'

'We would be *exactly* where we were.'

'I see.' Lydia nodded thoughtfully. 'Excuse me for a moment, would you all?' With that, she rose and bustled from the room.

Winifred watched her depart, then turned back to Mellish with a smile. 'We should have offered you tea, Mr Mellish. Would you care for a cup?'

'Or a glass of something stronger?' George suggested.

Lydia caught up with Ashley in his study. He already had the death certificate in his hand and was about to leave. She closed the door behind her, clasped his arm and fixed him with a purposeful stare.

'As executor, James is likely to prove an appalling nuisance,' she said. 'It's simply not to be borne.'

'I know,' Ashley groaned. 'But what's to be done?'

'If he renounced the executorship, you'd take over, according to Mellish.'

'Why would he renounce it?'

'To secure the land he needs for his wretched flying school.'

'I've already told him that's out of the question.'

'You're going to have to change your mind, darling.' Her grip on his arm tightened. 'Or at least pretend to.'

THE PARC MONCEAU LOOKED BOTH SPRINGLIKE AND WINTRY IN pallid sunshine. The snow lay in half-thawed patches between colourfully blossomed beds of flowers. The keen wind did not encourage the pram-pushing nannies to loiter and the benches flanking the path Max followed into the park were empty.

He had taken care to arrive exactly on time, suspecting Kuroda would be punctual, and was soon rewarded by the sight of the Japanese detective walking towards him. He was wearing a Homburg, gloves, scarf and heavy overcoat and was carrying an umbrella, though no rain was threatening.

'Good morning, Mr Maxted,' Kuroda said as they met.

'Good morning, Mr Kuroda. Why don't you call me Max? Everyone does.'

'Your father did not.'

'Everyone except my family.'

'Aha. Very well. Come then, Max. I had thought we would sit and talk, but we must walk if my teeth are not to chatter.'

They headed at a brisk pace towards the gate Max had entered by. 'And what should I call you? Mr Kuroda? Commissioner? Masataka?'

'I had the honour to know your father as Henry and to be known by him as Masataka. You are the son of my friend. Therefore . . .'

'Masataka it is.'

Kuroda gave a formal little nod of approval.

'I was surprised to get your message last night, Masataka.'

'Why? You must have calculated that I could not speak without constraint in the presence of Mr Morahan.'

'I wasn't sure you wanted to speak without constraint.'

'Henry would wish me to advise you candidly, Max. I do not walk with you here this morning as a loyal servant of the Emperor. I walk with you here this morning to give you my counsel.'

'I'll take it, gratefully.'

'Then first we must acknowledge the facts. Neither you nor Mr Morahan referred to the murder of Raffaele Spataro and the arrest of Corinne Dombreux. Yet those events flow from the same source as the murder of your father. You agree?'

'Yes.'

'I believe you are in considerable danger. Have you received any threats to your life?'

Max sighed. 'Yes.'

'Which you have disregarded?'

'I'm staying in Paris until I learn the truth.'

'Your resolve is commendable. It may also be fatal. But why do you suppose the threat to your life has not yet been acted upon?'

'They think I can be frightened off.'

'They hope you can. Their difficulty is that your murder would make it hard for the police to continue to pretend that Henry's death was accidental or that Madame Dombreux murdered Spataro. That is why they stay their hand – for the moment.'

'Do you know who they are?'

'You are caught in a web. And Lemmer is the spider at its centre. That is all I can be sure of.'

They reached the gate. Max paused to light a cigarette. Kuroda declined his offer of one. They turned and began to retrace their steps.

'Henry sought in his last weeks to sell valuable pieces of information he possessed to various people. The whereabouts of Fritz Lemmer was only one such piece of information. You are aware of this, I think.'

'I am. I didn't know you were.'

'My duties require me to be aware of many things. Henry's behaviour suggested desperation to me. He was a professional

199

diplomat. This auction of secrets was a contradiction of all he stood for. Have you discovered what drove him to it?'

'No.'

'Well, perhaps it is not your most pressing problem. Do you know what else besides his knowledge of Lemmer he hoped to profit from?'

'I have a few . . . indications.'

'Do any of those indications point to a matter that might involve my delegation?'

Max nodded. 'Yes.'

'And that matter was?'

'Something he referred to as the Chinese box. Meaning, I assume, the boxload of secret documents stolen from the head of the Chinese delegation when he stopped off in Tokyo on his way here.'

'I assume that also.'

'Stolen by your lot, according to Appleby.'

'My lot?' Kuroda chuckled drily. 'There he is mistaken.'

'Who, then?'

'I greatly fear the thief, whether or not he was Japanese, acted on instructions from Lemmer.'

'Why would Lemmer want the documents?'

'To answer that question I must entrust you with a state secret, Max. I should not, of course. It is most unwise, most . . . irresponsible. But if I don't, I estimate your chances of leaving Paris alive will be close to zero.'

'It can't be that bad.'

Kuroda cast him a sidelong glance that might have been one of pity. 'I have serious doubts about the wisdom of discussing this matter with you. You could ease those doubts by assuring me that you will disclose what I am about to tell you to no one else . . . unless to do so becomes the difference between life and death.'

'You have my word.'

'Thank you. I will hold you to it. Now, the Chinese box. There is a game played in China in which a series of wooden boxes must be fitted inside each other. It can only be done in one specific sequence. The difficulty arises from the minute differences in the

200

size and shape of each box. This is what we are doing, Max: puzzling over sizes and shapes. There is only one solution to the puzzle. And this, I believe, is that solution.

'Lemmer's calculation from the start of the war was that the only hope Germany had of winning was to outflank its enemies. He planned to do this by neutralizing some of them and turning others into allies. So, he gave the Bolsheviks secret support to bring down the Tsar and plunge Russia into chaos. And he sought to persuade Japan to change sides. Japan's entry into the war had been a strategic disaster for Germany. They lost their Pacific naval base at Tsingtao and the island colonies it protected. Lemmer understood that if and when the United States joined in, Germany was doomed, unless Japan by then was an ally. Japan could distract the Americans, by threatening Hawaii and the Philippines. So, through agents in China, which was still neutral then, he offered the Japanese government a deal: as much territory as they wanted in eastern Russia and the Pacific, including Australia and New Zealand, in return for an alliance with Germany. From some viewpoints, it was an attractive offer. And I must tell you it was seriously considered.'

'How seriously?'

'I believe the stolen box contained a copy of a letter sent by Prime Minister Juichi to the German Foreign Minister, Zimmermann, accepting the offer. If the evidence of this letter was made public, it would have a catastrophic effect on Japan's relations with the United States and Great Britain. It might even lead to Japan's expulsion from the peace conference. The consequences of that are hard to judge. But they would be extremely grave.'

'How would such a letter have ended up in the hands of the Chinese?'

'Remember that since the Last Emperor abdicated, there have been two governments in China, struggling for mastery. I believe the letter was part of the bargain struck between the Peking government and Sun Yat-sen's rival administration in Canton when they formed a joint delegation to the peace conference. Canton was the route chosen by Lemmer for secret communication with Japan because Sun was financially dependent on Germany. The letter

201

never reached Zimmermann, in fact, because the German high command chose to launch unrestricted submarine warfare in an attempt to crush Britain. This and a clumsy attempt to draw Mexico into the conflict led inevitably to a declaration of war by the United States. I imagine Lemmer was horrified by the stupidity of the Kaiser's senior advisers. Count Juichi was also horrified. He withdrew his agreement and tried to retrieve the letter. Sun said it had been destroyed, but no one in Tokyo believed him. We are sure he used it to buy representation here. It would have won China many concessions from Japan if it had not been stolen. Sun would have gained credit for those concessions. Now he probably curses the foolishness of Lou Tseng-Tsiang for letting the Japanese rob him. And we Japanese must let Lou – and Sun – believe he was robbed by us. We are thought to be more cunning and devious than we truly are. Misfortune is a cruel flatterer.'

They had reached a crossroads in the centre of the park and now turned right, towards the distant southern exit. 'There is something I don't understand,' said Max after they had covered ten yards or so in silence. 'How could my father know about any of this?'

'Lemmer threads his agents together as if they are pearls on a string. In a time of war, communications are vital, but also fragile. I believe Lemmer's principal agent in Russia was a conduit for the overtures he made to Japan. And I believe Pierre Dombreux was that agent.'

'Dombreux?'

'There is no better camouflage than to be thought to have betrayed your country to another when in truth you have betrayed them both to a third.'

If Kuroda was right, Max realized at once, Dombreux might have known about the Trust as well as the stolen Chinese documents. 'You're suggesting Dombreux confided in my father?'

'Yes, I am. A triangle has three sides. It is a rule of geometry. Dombreux and his wife. Madame Dombreux and Henry. Henry and Dombreux. We must ask ourselves what passed between them in the months after the Bolsheviks seized power in Russia. Lemmer's Japanese plan had misfired. Maybe he blamed Dombreux. And maybe Dombreux knew the Bolsheviks doubted

202

his loyalty. The wolves were prowling at the edge of the wood. Soon they would close in on the dwindling camp fire. He was a frightened man with much to fear. I am not sure which of his masters, if any, he was truly loyal to: Lemmer, the Bolsheviks or *la belle France*. And I am not sure if he was as heartless a husband as he appears to have been. Perhaps he sensed his doom approaching and gave Henry some of his secrets in the hope that they would enable him to protect Madame Dombreux.'

'If so, it didn't work, did it?'

'No. Henry was outmatched. As you are. There is something else I must tell you, Max. It is a hard thing to say. This matter of Count Juichi's letter and Lemmer's probable responsibility for its theft is a very serious threat to the Japanese government. An order has been given. A man has been engaged. An assassin. He is a master of his craft.'

'What has he been engaged to do?'

'Find Lemmer. Kill him. Retrieve the letter. And kill anyone else who knows what it contains.'

'I see.'

'That is why you must speak of it to no one. For there is no one you can trust absolutely. You are a blind man who has crossed the path of a tiger. And a hunting tiger makes no sound. His name is Tarn. I know nothing else about him except his reputation.'

'Which is?'

'Formidable.'

'You think he killed my father?'

'It is possible. Yet, strictly speaking, it would have been illogical, unless Henry had first told him where Lemmer was hiding. And Tarn has not found Lemmer yet. That much is certain.'

'Does he work alone?'

Kuroda glanced round at Max in surprise. 'What makes you ask?'

'That death threat I ignored was delivered to me by an Arab boy.'

'A boy? Or simply a slightly built young man?'

'Hard to say.'

'There is a rumour that Tarn employs an assistant who could be the person you describe.'

'Le Singe.'

'You have been reading the newspapers. Yes. Le Singe. It could be him. Or someone like him.'

'What would Tarn use him for?'

'Reconnaissance. Surveillance. Gaining entry to buildings.'

'But according to the papers he's an opportunist burglar.'

'Maybe he is. When Tarn does not need him.'

'Is Tarn a Frenchman?'

'I do not know.'

'Would Ireton know?'

'It is possible. He knows many things. That is why I have dealt with him from time to time. But I doubt he would be willing to help you. He would consider it dangerous to attract Tarn's attention. And he would be right.'

They were nearing the southern gate. Kuroda stopped and Max pulled up beside him. They turned and looked at each other. Max lit another cigarette. 'As my self-appointed counsellor, Masataka, what do you suggest I do?'

'Leave Paris.'

'And if I don't?'

'Confront your enemy. He has given you some time – probably not much – to acknowledge his superiority and retreat. If you do not intend to do so, then you must attack him.'

'But first I must find him.'

Kuroda nodded. 'So you must.'

'What chance do you give me?'

'A slim one. Though no slimmer than the chance that we should ever have met. We can never see the ends of the roads our choices lead us down until we reach them. I chose long ago, as a young Tokyo police officer, to volunteer for special attachment to a foreign police force. I was sent to London and spent a year at Scotland Yard. That is how I came to learn English and to love the writings of Scott and Dickens and Hardy. It is why, after I returned to Japan, I was assigned to investigate the activities of foreign residents in our country. And it is why I find myself in Paris today, standing with you here, in the cold spring sunshine. The future is not written, Max. It is a blank parchment. What I will eventually

read of you on it, or you of me, cannot be known. Until the time comes.'

'And meanwhile?'

'Tread softly. But tread swiftly.' Kuroda laid a hand on Max's shoulder. 'That is your self-appointed counsellor's considered advice.'

MAX SURVEYED THE THINLY PEOPLED BREADTH OF THE PLACE de la Concorde, wondering if he would see the young Arab again. But he was nowhere in sight. Outside the entrance to the pillared and porticoed Hôtel de Crillon, however, Travis Ireton was very much in evidence, smoking a cigarette and gazing about him as he prowled up and down.

'You made it, then,' he said, smiling crookedly as Max approached.

'There was no danger I wouldn't.'

'I guess not, though danger's often where you don't expect to find it.'

'Shall we go in?'

'Sure. But before we do . . .'

'Yes?'

'Back me up in everything I say, won't you, Max? It's important we stick to the script.'

'And what is the script?'

'You're a smart fellow. You'll soon catch on.'

As at the Majestic, there were guards on the door of the Crillon. These were big, burly American guards. Ireton was obviously well-known to them, however. He and Max were admitted without difficulty.

The marbled splendour of the lobby was only outdone by the mirrored and frescoed ornateness of the restaurant, but the Americans had contrived to lay a heavy transatlantic hand on

the hotel's Parisian elegance. The food being consumed and the largeness and loudness of those consuming it clashed rudely with the surroundings. The very smell of the place was wrong.

Walter Ennis, their host, was a tall, good-looking, middle-aged man who would have looked better still for the loss of several stones of fat which even an expertly cut suit could not disguise. He was flushed and uneasy in his manner, though superficially jovial. His shirt collar strained round a roll of pink flesh where his neck should have been and there was a disagreeable sweatiness to his handshake. Max had the impression the Martini he was drinking was not his first of the day.

They joined him in his choice of aperitif and Ireton managed some deft introductions. He and Ennis, it transpired, had been schoolfriends in Baltimore, but Ireton had not, he shamelessly lamented, followed Ennis's path to Yale and government service. Ennis himself proffered neatly phrased condolences when he realized whose son Max was.

'I met your father a couple of times at meetings of our Latin American committee. A real gentleman. I was awful sorry to hear about his death, I truly was.'

Max thanked him and kept a studiously straight face as Ireton explained that it was Max who had proposed the three of them meet. 'He was insistent, actually, Walter. But evasive about the reason, aside from the fact that it concerns his father.'

It was clear to Max that Ennis did not like the sound of that. But he smiled gamely as they ordered their meals and moved on to a second Martini (or third or fourth, in his case). Ireton piled on the agony by asking Ennis how he thought President Wilson would respond to continued French claims for the Saar coalfields. Ennis's reaction suggested he felt this was an improper question in such company. Exasperation with his old schoolfriend, fuelled by alcohol on an empty stomach, began to exhibit itself. And Max soon became an additional target.

'What *exactly* can I do for you, Max? I reckon it's time you said your piece.'

'You're right, Walter. If I've delayed explaining myself it's because the situation's a little . . . foggy.'

'Nothing like sunlight to clear fog,' said Ireton. 'We need a few shafts of it, don't we, Walter?'

'That we do,' said Ennis.

'Then let me supply them,' said Max, keeping his tone relaxed and unassertive. 'Firstly, you should know my father's death wasn't an accident, as reported in the press. He was murdered.'

'You don't mean it.'

'He does,' said Ireton. 'This part I know.'

'I'm determined to find his murderer and see him answer for his crime.'

Ennis eyed Max queasily. 'Well, I guess you would be.'

Their lunches arrived at that moment. Ennis had ordered a steak, but his expression implied regret that he had not asked for it to be well done. Blood was evidently not what he wanted to confront on his plate.

'I found a list of names in my father's handwriting,' Max went on. 'You're both on it. I thought I'd start by asking why you thought that might be.'

'Depends what kind of list we're talking about, I imagine,' said Ireton.

'It's hard to tell. But it's one of the few clues I have to follow. There are figures on it as well. It almost looks as if you . . . owed him money.'

Ireton's eyes widened at this piece of improvisation. Ennis's complexion darkened a shade. It was closer to red now than pink. 'I didn't owe Henry any money,' he said emphatically.

'Nor me,' said Ireton.

'Maybe we could see this list.'

'I'm afraid I don't have it with me.'

'Well, that's a shame. You're not giving us a lot to go on, are you?'

'Would some of the other names he listed help?'

'They might.'

'Lemmer.'

Ennis frowned unconvincingly. 'Lemmer? I don't think . . .'

'You know who he is, Walter. You both do.'

'No sense denying it, I guess,' said Ireton, drawing a glare from Ennis.

'I wondered if you two were in some kind of negotiation with my father . . . for information about Lemmer.'

'What makes you think that?' Ennis asked levelly.

'Well, I assume the whereabouts of the Kaiser's spymaster would be of interest to a senior member of the US delegation such as yourself, Walter.'

'You do, do you?'

'My father knew Lemmer from the time when they were both in Japan in the early nineties. He was one of very few people familiar with his appearance. That may be what got him murdered.'

'That's quite a leap you're taking, Max.'

'Were you in discussion with him about Lemmer?'

Ennis glanced at Ireton, who shrugged unhelpfully. He sighed. 'Travis here suggested Henry might know where Lemmer was and asked if I'd be interested, on behalf of the State department, in buying the information.'

'Henry asked me to put out some feelers,' said Ireton. 'So I did.'

'Did you express any interest, Walter?' Max pressed.

'Of course.'

'And did you consult anyone else about it?'

'Why do you ask?'

'I'm wondering if someone tipped Lemmer off, you see.'

Ennis's eyes narrowed. 'Are you making some kind of accusation?'

'Not yet.'

'I'm not sure I like the direction this conversation is taking.'

'Sorry about that. But murder's a disagreeable business. So's spying, of course. I gather there were people at all levels of every government in Lemmer's pay.' Max could have stopped there. But he was conscious of Kuroda's warning that he did not have un-limited time to play with. 'Let me throw another name on the list at you. Tarn.'

'Tarn?' Ireton looked at him in frank surprise.

'I don't know who you're referring to,' Ennis declared.

'No?'

'No.' Ennis flung down his fork with a clatter, tossed his napkin on to the table and stood up. 'You're going to have to excuse me for a few minutes, gentlemen. Eat on without me. I'll be back directly.'

As he headed out of the restaurant, Ireton took a sip of wine and frowned at Max. 'You seem to have got under his skin.'

'I wonder why.'

'Maybe because he doesn't like being accused of treason.'

'Is that how it sounded?'

'Wasn't it meant to? And what was that about Tarn? Where'd you—'

'Excuse me, Travis.' Max rose from his chair. Speed was of the essence. It had suddenly occurred to him that he might profit from speaking to Ennis alone. 'There's something I have to attend to.'

Max guessed Ennis had gone to the toilets and emerged into the reception area wondering where they might be. But, no, Ennis was standing at the desk directly ahead of him. Max saw the clerk take a key from the pigeon-holes behind him and hand it to Ennis, who turned and hastened towards the lifts.

Max took a slow waltz round a pillar to avoid the American's eye-line. The lifts were definitely his destination. He must be going up to his room. But why?

As soon as Ennis was out of sight, Max marched confidently across to the desk. Descrying objects at a distance was a vital skill for a pilot in wartime and he was blessed with twenty-twenty vision. He knew which pigeon-hole had contained Ennis's key and noted the number on the fobs of keys dangling in the holes either side of it as he approached. A swift calculation revealed that Ennis was going up to room 221. Max pulled up as if he had just remembered something, turned and headed for the stairs.

During the early, trivial stages of their conversation, Ennis had bemoaned 'the slow as a snail elevators' in the hotel, so Max was not surprised, on reaching the second floor and following the signs, to see the American opening the door of his room and going in. He was clearly in a hurry and Max could hear his heavy, wheezy breathing.

In fact, he was in so much of a hurry that he did not check the

door was closed behind him, merely pushed it to as he entered. The latch did not engage. Max lengthened his stride.

He reached the door, pushed it carefully open and stepped inside. The room was vast, white-panelled and high-ceilinged, with tall windows looking out on to the Place de la Concorde. For a second, Max could not see where Ennis was. He actually heard his voice, barking into the telephone, before he spotted him, stooping over the desk next to one of the windows.

'Yes, it's me . . . Sir Henry's boy is the problem. He's downstairs. He's been making a nuisance of himself . . . Easy for you to say. It's me who has to carry it off . . . You'd better remember my problems are your problems . . . He mentioned Tarn, damn it . . . All right . . . God damn it, I said *all right* . . . Yes, yes . . . Yes. I'll be there.'

Ennis crashed the receiver down so heavily the telephone toppled off the desk. With a curse, he bent down and hoisted it back into place. Then he turned and saw Max.

'What the—'

'Who was that you were speaking to, Walter?'

'None of your damn business.'

'I must beg to differ, since it's me you were discussing.'

'Get out of here.'

'Not until you've told me who you were speaking to.'

Ennis grabbed the telephone and rattled the switch-hook. 'Ennis, room two twenty-one,' he announced to whoever had responded. 'I need a couple of guards up here to deal with an intru—'

He was cut off by Max wrenching the phone out of his hand, so violently the wire was pulled out of the wall behind the desk. Max tossed the instrument aside and stared into Ennis's eyes. The man was frightened, probably not just of Max. His face was lightly sheened with sweat and he was struggling for breath.

'Get out . . . while you still can, Maxted,' he panted. 'You're in . . . way over your head.'

'No. You're describing yourself, Walter. I know exactly what I'm doing.'

'If you did . . . you'd quit now.'

'Who were you speaking to when I came in?'

'Go to hell.'

211

Ennis was obviously not going to answer any questions voluntarily. Max decided to see whether a little discomfort would loosen his tongue. He punched him hard in his bulging stomach. Ennis went over like a sack of flour, sagging on to his knees with a spluttering groan.

'Who was it, Walter?' Max demanded, kneeling beside him. 'I need the name.'

Ennis's head fell forward. His face was a purplish red. He was choking and coughing. Max thought he might be about to vomit, but now was not the moment to show him any mercy.

'*Who was it?*'

'You don't . . . understand,' Ennis gasped. 'You . . . haven't got . . . a chance in hell.'

'We'll see—'

There was suddenly a noise behind him of running, booted feet. Shadows fell across them. In the next instant something blunt and heavy struck the back of Max's head with stunning force. And he went down with it, into a pool of darkness.

TRY AS HE MIGHT TO DISGUISE IT, THERE WAS NO QUESTION THAT Shuttleworth, i/c support services for the British delegation to the peace conference, regarded Sam as the answer to his prayers. He needed someone with the technical expertise to keep the delegation's fleet of cars on the road who was also capable of controlling a squad of junior mechanics. A former RFC NCO engineer with impeccable credentials fitted the bill perfectly. And, as Sam pointed out, he could start straight away.

'Tomorrow morning?' Shuttleworth asked.

'Yes,' Sam replied.

'The job's yours.'

'You did say there'd be accommodation, didn't you, sir?'

'Certainly. Bed *and* board.' Shuttleworth consulted a chart hanging on the wall behind his desk. 'Your predecessor shared a room with Jenkins, who's down with the flu himself, so I can't put you in there. Let's see . . .' He sucked his pen for a moment or two, then made a telephone call. 'McLeod? Shuttleworth here. I need accommodation for a new chief mechanic. Is two eight five still empty? . . . Good . . . Yes . . . Twentyman, S . . . Got that? . . . Good . . . You'll see to it, then? . . . Thank you.' He put the telephone down and smiled at Sam. 'Another dead man's making way for you, Twentyman. But don't worry. He didn't actually croak in the room. And you'll have it to yourself, which is a bonus.'

Sam's gaze strayed to the wall chart. On it were several grids of numbered boxes, with names written in them, some crossed out and substituted with others. The name in box 285 had been crossed out,

213

but no new name had yet been entered. And the old one was still legible. *Maxted, Sir H*.

'I'm sure the room will be fine, sir,' Sam said quietly.

Sam paid a visit to the garage before he left the Majestic. The junior mechanics seemed a decent bunch. He had encountered less promising material in the RFC on numerous occasions. It wouldn't take long to knock them into shape.

He walked back to the Mazarin to collect his belongings and leave a note for Max suggesting they meet that evening. Whether they would, he had no way of knowing. It depended on what Max discovered in the course of the day – and, he supposed, on just how alluring Max found Nadia Bukaycva. Sam regretted having been too drunk to offer any kind of competition for her favours, although he did not delude himself that the result would have been different, however sober he had been. A Russian monarchist like Nadia was bound to be a snob at heart. She would always prefer an officer.

Several large men in overcoats and hats were gathered at the reception desk when Sam entered the Mazarin. The discussion they were having with the clerk was not exactly heated, but it was certainly warm. One of them, who was older than his companions and seemed to be in charge, was speaking slowly and very firmly. He sounded as if he was keeping his temper with some difficulty.

'A man's been killed, *monsieur*, and I'd ask you to bear that in mind. You say you've no idea where Mr Maxted is or when he's likely to be back?'

Mention of the name Maxted stopped Sam in his tracks. The clerk knew he was acquainted with Max and Sam was not at all sure he wanted to be drawn into the exchanges. He turned towards the door. But it was too late.

'There is Mr Maxted's friend, Mr Twentyman,' the clerk wailed. 'Perhaps he can help you.'

One of the large men cut off Sam's retreat. He turned back to be

met by the stern gaze of the clerk's interrogator-in-chief. 'Mr Twentyman?'

'Er, yes. That's me.'

'I'm looking for James Maxted. It's a matter of considerable urgency.'

'Sorry. I don't know where he is.'

'But you are a friend of his?'

'Well, yes. We . . . were in the war together.'

'Were you indeed? Mr Maxted's kept very quiet about you, I must say. My name's Appleby. Perhaps you've heard of me.'

Sam had heard of him. Appleby. Secret Service bigwig. Not to be trifled with, especially not by the likes of Sam. 'Lieutenant Maxted doesn't—'

'Lieutenant, is it? I see. The bonds of war are close, aren't they? If Maxted chose to confide in anyone, I suspect it would be you.'

'If he did, sir, I'd respect his confidence.'

Appleby gave him a narrow-eyed stare. 'So you would, I'm sure.'

Sam heard the telephone behind the desk ring. The clerk answered it. 'If you don't mind me asking, sir,' Sam ventured, 'who's been killed?'

'A young fellow I had high hopes of. Found dead this morning, not far from here. Throat cut from ear to ear. Your Mr Maxted could have been the last person to see him alive.'

'Wouldn't his murderer have been the last person to see him alive, sir?'

'You're a sharp one, aren't you, Twentyman? You're quite right, of course. But maybe Mr Maxted and the murderer are one and the same. Now, where is he?'

'I already—'

'*Mr Appleby!*' the clerk shouted. Appleby whirled round and looked at him. 'This call is for you. From the Majestic.'

Appleby leant across the counter and took the telephone. As he did so, the illogical fear formed in Sam's mind that Shuttleworth was on the other end of the line. Sam might be about to lose his job before he had even started it. But the caller was not Shuttleworth.

'Appleby here . . . Yes, Jones, what is it? . . . What? . . . At the Crillon? . . . He did what? . . . What was he thinking of? . . . No, no.

215

I realize you don't know. . . . I'll go straight there . . . Yes. Thank you.'

Appleby thrust the phone back at the clerk and rounded on Sam. 'Your Mr Maxted's been a busy boy, Twentyman. Caught roughing up a member of the American delegation. What have you got to say to that?'

'I expect he deserved it, sir.'

'You do, do you? Well, let's go and find out. You're coming with me.'

THE CLAUSTROPHOBIC ATMOSPHERE IN ONE OF THE BASEMENT rooms of the Hôtel de Crillon was largely due to the number of occupants. In a space appropriate to a large store cupboard, four men were seated around a shabby desk, while two more men, dressed in US military police uniforms and built like the foothills of the Rockies, were stationed outside in the corridor, either side of the doorway itself.

Max was the one holding a bag of ice against a tender spot behind his left ear. Despite this encumbrance, he was smoking a cigarette and looking strangely at ease. The same could not be said of Sam, who was also smoking, but with transparent nervousness. The haze of their smoke had been turned to a deep fug by the effluvium of Appleby's pipe. He was on the other side of the desk from them, seated next to an intimidating slab of a man with short-cropped blond hair and piercing blue eyes. He was Frank Carver, Appleby's opposite number at the American delegation. And he alone was not smoking. Instead his prognathous jaws were champing rhythmically on a stick of gum.

'You're in a tight spot, Mr Maxted,' Carver said, with no apparent irony. 'I advise full cooperation. Unless you want us to hand you over to the French police.'

'If you decide to do that,' said Max, 'I want you to remember Sam here knew nothing about my visit to Walter Ennis. He has no share in the responsibility for what happened.'

'We'll be the judge of that,' said Appleby. 'He's your alibi for when Lamb was murdered and therefore inherently suspect.'

217

'I'm sorry about your man, Appleby,' said Max. 'I had no idea you were having me tailed.' That was not actually true, of course, but he and Sam had had to do some judicious editing of the facts on a nod-and-a-wink basis. 'It's not just Sam's word, though, is it? If the poor fellow had his throat cut, his murderer would have been covered in blood. I'm sure the clerk at the Mazarin would have noticed that when I called there.'

'With Lamb dead, I have no independent verification of your movements since yesterday afternoon.'

'That's hardly my fault.'

'They say Paris is a hotbed of crime with this conference going on,' Sam contributed. 'Maybe Mr Lamb just happened to be in the wrong place at the wrong time.'

'No. That's you, Mr Twentyman,' said Carver. 'Keep it in mind, won't you?'

'Are you sure you chose the right man for the job, Appleby?' Max asked provocatively. 'It seems clear Lamb was out of his depth.'

Appleby's teeth ground into the stem of his pipe as he stared at Max. 'Leave me to dwell on that question when I write to his parents.'

'I am sorry. We both are, aren't we, Sam?'

'Yes, sir.'

'The war's inured us to sudden death, I'm afraid.'

'This might go easier if you explained to Mr Maxted why you were having him tailed, Horace,' said Carver.

Max smiled faintly at Appleby. They were on treacherous ground. Carver wanted to know all that lay behind Max's fight with Ennis. But Max felt sure Appleby did not want to tell him.

'I was concerned for your safety, Mr Maxted, in view of the unexplained circumstances of your father's death and that of Raffaele Spataro,' said Appleby.

'The police have Corinne Dombreux in custody for that, don't they?' queried Carver.

'I'm not convinced by the case against her.'

Carver absorbed Appleby's reply with a twitch of one eyebrow, then looked across at Max. 'Why did you come to see Ennis, Mr Maxted?'

'I found his name on a list written by my father. I wanted to know how they were acquainted.'

'Was Travis Ireton's name also on the list?'

'Yes. It was. I asked him to arrange the meeting.'

'Good of him to oblige. I'll be seeing Mr Ireton, you can be sure of that. It's unfortunate he'd already left the hotel when we went looking for him.' Unfortunate, perhaps, Max reckoned, but entirely characteristic. 'Why did you go up to Ennis's room?'

'It was clear to me from his reaction to my questions that he was hiding something. I followed him out of the restaurant to see what he might be willing to say without Ireton sitting next to him. I saw him taking the lift up to his room and I decided to catch up with him there.'

'Where there wouldn't be any witnesses.'

'I wanted to talk to him alone. I don't deny that. I caught him making a phone call. He was demanding that whoever he was speaking to get me off his back.'

'So you say.'

'Doesn't your switchboard operator have any idea who he was calling?'

'There are calls being made and received here all the time, Mr Maxted. We installed a lot of extra lines to cope with the traffic when we moved in. No one knows who Ennis called, if he called anyone, apart from the guardroom when you started threatening him, that is.'

'Have you asked him?'

'I haven't had the chance. He slipped out after you'd been taken away. When he comes back, I'll ask him for a full account of what took place.'

'Are you sure he's coming back?'

'Why wouldn't he be?'

'Because he's running scared. I might have been able to find out *who* he's scared of if I'd had longer with him.'

'One of the other people named on your father's list, maybe.' Carver stared at Max challengingly. 'Who are they, Mr Maxted?'

'Kuroda. Ribeiro. Norris. I've spoken to them. None of them reacted the way Ennis did.'

'So, what it comes down to is that you reckon Ennis was mixed up in your father's murder.'

'Maybe.'

'Have you given me the name of everyone on that list?'

'Yes.'

'Could I see it?'

'I destroyed it.'

'Why in hell would you do that?'

'I thought it might be something it was dangerous to be found in possession of.'

'Well, that's a reasonable assumption, considering danger seems to hover round you like flies round horse shit – which I'm thinking is what you're serving up here today.'

'You don't believe me?'

'I don't believe you're telling me the whole story, Mr Maxted. Not anything close to the whole story.' Carver looked round at Appleby. 'Maybe we should have a word in private, Horace.'

'Certainly.' Appleby nodded and cast Max a fleeting glance of highly provisional approbation. There was an unspoken agreement between them to keep Lemmer's name out of this for as long as they could. Max did not seriously believe Appleby suspected him of Lamb's murder. Their alliance, such as it was, remained in place.

Carver and Appleby left the room. Silence settled in the smoke-laden air. The guards swapped places either side of the door. Max and Sam had much to discuss, but were in no position to discuss it. Max sighed and discarded the ice-bag. Water oozed out on to the desk.

'You should keep that on, sir,' said Sam. 'There's nothing like ice for a bruise.'

'Thank you, matron.'

'You know I'm right, sir.'

'God damn it.' Max snatched up the ice-bag and reapplied it to his head. 'Happy?'

'Not exactly.'

'How did the job interview go?'

'I start tomorrow. Assuming I ever get out of here.'

'You will, Sam, don't worry. Leave it to Appleby.'

Rather to Sam's surprise, Max's words proved prophetic. When Appleby and Carver returned about ten minutes later, Carver announced the questioning was at an end.

'In Ennis's absence, I propose to regard your . . . scuffle . . . as a private altercation. I'll pursue the matter with him when he returns to the hotel and I'll check your account with Ireton, so don't think you've heard the last of this, Mr Maxted. Or you, Mr Twentyman.'

'I don't see where—' Sam began. But he was cut off by Appleby.

'I'll walk the two of you out. Shall we go?'

No further word was spoken until Max, Sam and Appleby were standing out on the Place de la Concorde, some distance from the entrance to the Crillon. The men who had accompanied Appleby earlier were waiting in a car at the corner of Rue Royale. Appleby made a meal of relighting his pipe and gazed pensively in the direction of the National Assembly, on the far side of the Seine.

'I really am sorry about Lamb, Appleby,' said Max. 'Believe it or not.'

'You should be. It was your fault as much as mine.'

'I don't see how I'm to blame.'

'They killed him to demonstrate their reach and capability. And to send a message. This was left in his pocket.' Appleby pulled a piece of paper from inside his coat and handed it to Max. It was folded in half, with JAMES MAXTED written in pencilled capitals on one flap. Max unfolded it to read the message inside. LEAVE PARIS OR DIE – FINAL WARNING. 'I take it from the wording that this isn't the first such threat you've received.'

'You take it correctly.'

'Blimey,' said Sam, peering at the note over Max's shoulder.

Max passed it back to Appleby. 'Did you tell Carver about this?'

'I told Carver as little as possible. But the same doesn't apply to you and Twentyman, does it?'

'You can trust Sam.'

'You mean I have to because you do.'

'We're playing for the same team, Mr Appleby,' said Sam. He sensed it would be better to enlighten Appleby about his new job before anyone else did, so on he went. 'I work for the British delegation, just like you do. Meet your new chief mechanic.'

'You?'

'They don't come better qualified.'

Appleby frowned sceptically at Sam, then turned to Max. 'Listen to me very carefully. I may not know what you've been doing since Lamb was killed, but those who killed him probably do. And this threat' – he flapped the note in Max's face – 'isn't an idle one.'

'I'm aware of that.'

'I don't want the Americans pursuing Lemmer in their size-twelve boots. I don't want the French on his trail either. I want *you* to find him. But you don't have long to pull it off.'

'I know. That's why I tried to force the pace with Ennis.'

'You think he's one of Lemmer's spies?'

'It would explain why he cut and run.'

'If you're right, I can't keep Carver in the dark indefinitely.' Appleby forced a smile. 'It wouldn't be good for Anglo-American relations.'

'How did you persuade him to let us go?'

'I said we were more likely to get to the bottom of this with you on the loose. Which is true, of course.'

'Don't put anyone else on my tail, Appleby. It's too dangerous.'

'In the circumstances, I'm forced to agree with you.'

'I'll keep you fully informed of what I learn.'

'I doubt that. But remember, you won't be able to tackle Lemmer without help from me. It would be a fatal mistake to think you can. Do you actually have any more leads to follow?'

'A few.'

'Courtesy of Ireton?'

'He's useful.'

'He probably thinks the same of you.'

'What about Corinne? Can I visit her?'

Appleby sighed heavily. 'Yes. It wasn't easy to arrange, let me tell you. But I managed to fix it with Zamaron.'

'Thank you. When?'

Appleby consulted his watch. 'There's no time like the present.'

'Fine.' Max gave a grim little smile. 'As things stand, it's probably the only time I've got.'

LEAVING SAM TO GET ON WITH HIS MOVE FROM THE MAZARIN TO the Majestic, Max set off for Police Headquarters with Appleby. Sam's parting shot was a pained comment on the rattly note of their car engine. 'I'll have 'em all running sweeter than that by next week, I guarantee it.'

'He will too,' said Max, glancing back at Sam's receding figure on the edge of the broad pavement as they accelerated away across the Place de la Concorde.

Appleby groaned. 'If I had any sense, I'd veto his appointment. Allowing you to have an informant on the delegation's payroll is plain reckless.'

'This whole thing's reckless, Appleby. And as far as I know I'm working for you *gratis*, so it seems only fair for Sam to draw a wage.'

'Well, Twentyman's employment isn't high on my agenda, Mr Maxted, so—'

'Why don't you call me Max, like everyone else?'

'All right. Max. Did Ennis give you anything to go on?'

'Not really. But I've been thinking about the circumstances of my father's fatal fall. I mean the *exact* circumstances.'

'And?'

'Could le Singe be involved?'

'Ah. You've heard about him, have you?'

'A burglar who comes and goes by rooftops and high windows. He fits the bill, doesn't he?'

'A burglar isn't generally a murderer. They're very different lines of work.'

'Are you sure?'

'Well, if you want to learn more about le Singe . . . Max . . . ask your friend Ireton. I have reason to believe he may have used le Singe to procure secret documents for him on several occasions.'

'Really? Well, I'll certainly do that.'

Max considered what he knew of Travis Ireton as the car sped east along the Quai des Tuileries. He had supposed Ireton was on no one's side but his own. Could he have misread the man, though? Ireton had certainly contrived to obstruct Max's enquiries while claiming to want to help him. Was he covering someone's tracks – perhaps his own? Max was going to have to find out. Soon.

Zamaron was not available at Police HQ, but he had left word that Max was to be allowed to visit Corinne Dombreux. His permission came with a condition attached, though – one Appleby had chosen not to mention until now.

'You can't see her on your own, Max. I have to be there as well. Apparently, Léon doesn't trust you not to engage in some form of criminal conspiracy with Madame Dombreux.'

'Are you sure this isn't your condition, Appleby? It gives you a chance to question her.'

'That's true. But, no, it was Léon's idea.'

'Or so you let him think.'

'You're getting very suspicious, aren't you?'

'I need to be suspicious.'

'Well, I won't disagree with you there.'

The room they were taken to was a small, bare chamber buried in the dank basement of the building. Chairs were arranged either side of a table nearly as wide as the room: two on one side, one on the other, closer to the door. They took the two and waited.

A few minutes slowly elapsed, then Corinne arrived, escorted by a grim-faced policewoman. Corinne was wearing a shapeless grey dress. She looked pale and anxious. The smile she gave Max was a fragile shaft of hope. He rose to greet her and the policewoman barked out, '*Ne pas toucher*'. Meekly, he sat down again.

'I'm so sorry about all of this, Corinne,' he said, looking directly at her.

'Commissioner Zamaron insisted I be here, *madame*,' said Appleby.

Corinne glanced at Appleby, then sat down in the chair facing them. She gazed soulfully at Max across the table. 'I'm glad you came, Max,' she said softly. 'But you should forget me and leave Paris. I'm beyond your help.'

'I don't accept that. And I'm going nowhere until you're free.'

'Have you been mistreated, *madame*?' Appleby asked.

She shook her head. 'Not in the sense you mean.'

'I'm getting closer to the truth all the time, Corinne,' said Max. 'If I'm successful, they'll have to release you.'

'Have charges been mentioned to you?' asked Appleby.

'No.'

'Have you seen a lawyer?'

'No.'

'Have you asked to see one?'

Corinne looked at him witheringly. 'It's been made very clear to me that under wartime regulations I have no rights, Mr Appleby. I assume *le Deuxième Bureau* are pulling the strings.'

'I think that's a sound assumption, *madame*. Your marriage to a known traitor—'

'Was he a traitor, Corinne?' Max cut in. 'Do you really believe Pierre betrayed his country?'

'It's what they told me. I'm not sure what to believe about where Pierre's loyalties truly lay.'

'For what it's worth, *madame*,' said Appleby, 'I don't think you killed Raffaele Spataro.'

'But your influence on *le Deuxième Bureau* or the Ministry of Justice is . . . what?'

'Negligible, I'm afraid.'

'Then I will remain here until they decide to charge and try me. And then . . .'

'It won't come to that,' said Max. 'I won't let it.'

'If you cause them enough trouble, Max, they'll deal with you much as they've dealt with me.'

'Commissioner Zamaron is a conscientious police officer,' said Appleby. 'He won't ignore hard evidence that serves to exonerate you.'

'But there isn't any, is there?' Strangely, Corinne seemed harder-headed than her visitors. 'Motive, means and opportunity. I believe they're what the police look for in these matters. And I appear to have had all three.' She looked at Max. 'You've been to the apartment?'

'Yes.'

'You saw his paintings?'

'I did.'

'Of course you did.' She looked away then. 'I'm sorry I posed for him. If I'd known . . .'

'You have nothing to apologize for.'

'Henry really would be proud of you, you know.' Tears glistened in her eyes. She wiped them away with the sleeve of her dress.

Max longed to reach out and comfort her. A guilty memory came into his mind then of his night with Nadia Bukayeva. The guilt was multi-layered, for there had been a moment when he had begun to call Nadia Corinne. He had stifled the word and Nadia had been too absorbed in her own pleasure to notice. But he knew. He knew and he could not forget.

'Don't take any risks on my account, Max. Please. I'm not worth it.'

'Did Pierre – or my father – ever mention a man called Fritz Lemmer?'

'No. Who is he?'

'F.L., Corinne. The initials on the list.'

'I know about the list, *madame*,' said Appleby.

Corinne registered mild surprise at that, but did not dwell on it. 'I've never heard the name before,' she declared. 'Is he . . . responsible for Henry's death?'

'He may be. But—'

'*Fini*,' the policewoman interrupted, gesturing at a watch she had pulled out of her tunic.

'No one told me there was a time limit,' Max protested. 'Appleby?'

227

Appleby shrugged. 'Rules and regulations. There's nothing I can do.'

'He's right, Max,' said Corinne. 'There's nothing you can do either. Please—'

'*Le temps est épuisé*,' the policewoman announced, advancing to Corinne's shoulder.

Corinne stood up, holding Max's gaze. 'The only thing that could make this worse is if I hear you've come to harm, Max. If you won't agree to leave Paris—'

'*Allons-y*,' snapped the policewoman, leading her away by the arm.

She did not resist.

'I'll be careful,' Max called after her. But he did not intend to be careful. He never had been. And he knew he could not help Corinne by changing now.

Max could find nothing to say to Appleby after Corinne had gone. And Appleby had the decency to let him stay silent as they made their way upstairs and out into the courtyard where the car was waiting.

'I'll walk from here,' Max announced.

Appleby looked unsurprised. 'Apart from giving Madame Dombreux something to worry about – your safety – what do you reckon that visit accomplished, Max?'

'I don't judge everything I do by what it accomplishes, Appleby. Sometimes I just . . . do.'

'And what are you going to *do* next?'

'Keep pushing. Until I can see who's pushing back.'

MAX PURGED SOME OF HIS ANGER AND FRUSTRATION BY walking so fast other pedestrians on the darkening streets made way for him with alarmed looks on their faces. He suspected his expression told its own story. The time had come to demand of Travis Ireton some direct answers to some direct questions.

But at 33 Rue des Pyramides Malory Hollander had bad news for him. 'Travis said you might call by, Max,' she said, treating him to her knowing smile. 'I'm afraid he's had to leave town.'

'*What?*'

'An influential personage is arriving from New York to join the American delegation. Travis is anxious to meet him when his ship docks at Brest tomorrow morning. His train should have left' – she adjusted her glasses to study the clock – 'about forty minutes ago.'

Max shook his head morosely. 'Damn the fellow.'

'I'm sorry. It was a last-minute decision.'

'Oh, I'm sure it was.'

'Settle for a word with me, Max?' came Morahan's voice, floating into the room from the open doorway. 'We can help ourselves to some of Travis's Scotch and stoke up his fire, provided Malory swears not to split on us.'

'And I do so swear,' said Malory. 'Provided I get a nip of the Scotch too.'

Morahan delivered a small glass of the strong stuff to Malory, then ushered Max into Ireton's office, where he closed the door and poured distinctly larger measures for the two of them. Then he

tonged a few knobs of coal on to the fire and pokered it back into life.

'Travis told me what happened at the Crillon,' he said, leaning back in Ireton's chair with his long legs stretched out before him. 'I guess it looks to you like he's made himself scarce to dodge having to answer any of your questions.'

'Well, hasn't he?'

'It's not just you. Carver's been here as well. You met him, right?'

'Oh, yes.'

'Travis reckons Ennis is your man, based on his behaviour when you challenged him – and his subsequent bolt. But the scene you made risks Travis's contacts with all levels of the American delegation getting more attention than he'd welcome right now. So, he thought it best to take himself out of the picture for a while.'

'Has he really gone to Brest?'

'I doubt it, since that's where he has Malory telling everyone he's gone. Deauville, maybe? Or Monte Carlo? He likes to keep his hand in at the baccarat table.'

'I need to find out as much about Walter Ennis as I can as quickly as possible, Schools. Whether he's one of Lemmer's spies or not, he's certainly up to no good.'

'I don't doubt you're right about that.'

'And Travis knows him well, doesn't he?'

Morahan nodded. 'Better than most. They go back a long way.'

'And now they've both gone to ground. What do you make of that?'

'Not what I get the feeling *you* make of it. Travis isn't in cahoots with Walter Ennis, Max. He just doesn't want Carver prying into his business and reckons being unavailable for a grilling is the best way to prevent that. He calculates Carver will lose interest in him as soon as he tracks Ennis down.'

'Maybe so. But that doesn't help me.'

'No. And I'm sorry for that. But if Ennis was responsible for your father's murder, Carver will be better placed than you to extract a confession from him.'

'So, you suggest I just sit back and wait for Ennis to be apprehended and Travis to return to Paris?'

'It might be the safest thing to do.'

'But you're assuming he will be apprehended and that he really was responsible for my father's murder. I can't afford to assume anything, Schools. That's the other thing I want to discuss with Travis, you see: who the third person was he spoke to on my father's behalf.'

Morahan drained his glass and lit a cigarette, frowning thoughtfully as he did so. 'Travis said I was to tell you he's convinced, based on what happened at the Crillon, that Ennis is the man you're looking for. That being so, he sees no merit in naming the third person he approached.'

Max sprang to his feet to expend some of his irritation. He leant on the mantelpiece, swore heartily and took a kick at the fender, dislodging a coal into the grate, where it blazed and sputtered.

Morahan rose slowly from his chair, grasped the tongs and returned the coal to the fire. He stood where he was then, one foot on the edge of the grate, and aimed his level gaze at Max. 'What do you want to know, Max?' he asked quietly.

'The name of the third person Travis spoke to.'

'I can't give you that.'

'More than your job's worth, is it?'

'Travis doesn't employ me, Max. I work *with* him, not *for* him. I think I explained that to you before.'

'With or for, it still means you keep his secrets.'

'If I promise to stay silent about something, I stay silent. As it happens, I genuinely don't have the name to give you. You have my word on that, which I hope you'll accept.'

Morahan's earnestness brooked no challenge. Max was forced to acknowledge as much. He took a deep breath. 'All right, Schools. I believe you.'

'Good.'

'Do you have any idea who he might be?'

'No. But I can tell you this. Travis said he thought Carver would be able to identify him eventually if he sought help from Appleby.'

'Appleby?'

'The implication's clear, isn't it? The man you're looking for must be a member of the British delegation.'

FATIGUE AND FURY MADE FOR STRANGE COMPANIONS. MAX left 33 Rue des Pyramides as wearied by the events of the day as he was enraged by them. At every turn he was blocked, delayed or deflected. He trusted what Kuroda and Morahan had told him. For the rest there was only a torrent of doubt. Ennis's escape and Ireton's departure stood as rebukes to his foresight. And then there were the messages from whoever had commissioned his father's murder. *Leave Paris. Final warning.* He would not allow himself to be intimidated. He would not flee the city. But, if he stayed, what could he actually accomplish?

Max's intention was to speak to Appleby as soon as possible. The phone call Ennis had made from his room at the Crillon proved he was part of a conspiracy of some kind. The member of the British delegation Ireton had contacted might also be part of it. In Ennis's absence, his was the more promising trail to follow. And Appleby was the man to guide Max along it, preferably before he did the same for Carver.

But Max was flying on little more than fumes. He needed a hot bath and a good meal. The water at the Mazarin was seldom more than lukewarm and the food indifferent, but they would have to suffice. He found a taxi in the Place Vendôme and asked to be taken straight there.

'There's a gentleman waiting for you in the writing-room, *monsieur*,' the clerk announced as he handed Max his key.

'Who is he?'

'I regret, *monsieur*, he did not give his name. He is English and known to you, he said. That is all I can tell you.'

Max was in no mood to be trifled with. He strode into the writing-room with no clear expectations of who might be waiting for him. But at the sight of his visitor he pulled up sharp.

Lionel Brigham. Of all the people Max would have preferred not to meet again, this handsome, cocksure, smooth-mannered roué was surely the one he wanted most of all to avoid. An irksomely frequent guest at Gresscombe Place during Max's youth, Brigham had been too close to Lady Maxted for too long to ignore. There was no doubt in Max's mind that they had been lovers. And he believed there was cause to suspect Brigham might actually be his father. It was a possibility he had spoken of to no one. It was a possibility, indeed, that he had done his level best to put out of his mind, though it was undeniable that it had tainted his relationship with his mother. Unvoiced resentments were ultimately, he had discovered, the most poisonous kind.

'James,' said Brigham, rising a touch stiffly to his feet and extending a hand. 'It's good to see you.'

'Brigham.' Max accepted the handshake coolly. 'What brings you here?'

'To Paris, you mean? Or to your hotel? As to the former, I'm here with the delegation.'

God rot the man, thought Max, cursing himself for his failure to anticipate that Brigham might be in Paris. He could always be relied upon to insinuate himself into a gathering of the great and the good, even though he was neither. 'I suppose I thought you'd retired,' Max said, with a hint of disparagement.

'No such luck.'

'And what are you doing for the delegation?'

'Oh, nothing very interesting.'

'To what do I owe this visit, then?'

'I wanted to offer you my condolences on Henry's death. Such a terrible thing.'

'Indeed.'

'I was surprised not to see you at the funeral.'

God rot the man twice over, thought Max. Why could he not just leave the Maxted family alone? 'I was detained here.'

'So I gather.'

'And I'm really rather busy, so—'

'We need to talk, James, you and I.'

There was a faintly menacing twinkle in Brigham's blue-grey eyes. Max ignored it as best he could. 'We do?'

'A confidential talk. I drove myself here. Would it be asking too much for you to step out to my car? I won't keep you long.'

The car was a sleek black Daimler, parked just round the corner from the Mazarin. Brigham proposed they drive down to the Seine. 'It'll be quiet by the river,' he said.

He filled the brief journey with an account of the funeral he had attended but Max had not. Irony, and something more sinister, clung to his words.

Max remembered a day he had tried hard to forget, when he had returned home from Eton one hot Saturday afternoon in the summer of 1907. The house had been filled with silence, the staff nowhere to be found. He had called a general hello in the hall. There had been no immediate response. Then Brigham had appeared at the head of the stairs, looking less well-groomed than usual, and had come down to greet him. 'Your mother's resting,' he had said. And that was all he had said. She had joined them on the terrace a short time later, her normal imperturbability mysteriously mislaid. 'You should have told us when you'd be arriving, James.' Yes. He should have. He really should. And he only wished he had.

A later remark of his father's had alerted Max to the most disturbing of all possibilities. Sir Henry had been reminiscing about life in Japan. 'Your mother found her first Japanese summer a great trial,' he had said. 'I took pity and sent her to spend the second with friends in Kashmir.' The remark had ticked away in Max's mind like a time-bomb. It only required simple arithmetic to calculate that a child born in the spring of 1891, as he was, must have been conceived in the summer of 1890 – the summer of his mother's sojourn in Kashmir.

*

Brigham drove to the river bank beyond the Palais du Trocadéro and stopped near the Pont d'Iéna. The Eiffel Tower stretched up into the night sky on the opposite bank. He snapped open a cigarette-case and offered Max a smoke. Max pointedly expressed a preference for his own brand. Brigham declined the chance to take offence and they both lit up.

'Damnably cold for the time of year,' said Brigham, coughing over his first draw.

'Perhaps you're going down with flu,' said Max. 'There's a lot of it about.'

'Yes. It carried off poor old Sykes. But I don't think it'll get me. You needn't worry.'

'I shan't.'

'It's actually yourself you should worry about. I've heard what you've been up to, James. You're playing with fire.'

'Where have you heard what I've been . . . "up to"?'

'There's more gossip circulating in this city than French francs. I asked around. And learnt you too are asking around. You should let Henry rest in peace. That's the sincere advice of someone who wishes you to come to no harm.'

'Meaning you?'

'Your mother would never forgive me if I let you stray into trouble for lack of a word to the wise.'

'Did she ask you to deliver this word?'

'No, no. Though only because, I sensed when I met her, that she feared you'd ignore any pleas emanating from her.'

'And you think I'm likelier to heed a warning from you?'

'I'm concerned for your welfare, James. I always have been. You're out of your depth here. I very strongly urge you to—'

'Give it up?'

'Yes. Exactly. Give it up.'

'At whose hands do you think I might come to harm, Brigham?'

'Oh, I couldn't say. Specifically. It's just that I know you're mixed up with Appleby. And he's Secret Service. That's dirty and dangerous work. I expect he has you running all manner of risks on his account. If you got yourself killed, he could disown you just like that. As he undoubtedly would.'

Max paused long enough to encourage Brigham to believe he might be about to give ground, then said, 'Pardon me for asking, but why should that matter to you?'

'As I told you, I—'

'We're nothing to each other as far as I'm aware. You're a some-time friend of my mother's, that's all. I neither need nor desire you to be concerned about me.'

'But I am. And there it is.' Brigham looked round at Max. 'I think you know why.'

'I'd be interested in knowing why you're so anxious for me to leave Paris.'

'Because it's a hazardous place to be asking the kind of questions you're asking. Henry should never have allowed himself to become involved with Corinne Dombreux. He was courting disaster and he duly met with it. I don't want to see you make the same mistake.'

'You don't think his death was an accident, then?'

'I think it's best to say it was. For everyone's sake. Especially yours.'

'When did you last meet my father, Brigham?'

'Some weeks ago. I bumped into him at the Quai d'Orsay. I'd prob-ably have seen him more often if I'd been staying at the Majestic, but the place is such a madhouse I've found an apartment to rent near by. We were both on our way to meetings. There was no time for more than the briefest of words. I regret that now, of course.'

'Of course.'

'I gather there was an . . . incident . . . at the Crillon earlier today. Walter Ennis has gone missing.'

'Are you acquainted with him?'

'Slightly, yes. Just as I'm acquainted with scores of members of other delegations. I'm on more committees than I can count.'

'What about Travis Ireton? Are you acquainted with him?'

'Ireton?' Brigham made a show of deliberating on the point. 'No, I don't think so. I've heard the name, but . . . I can't say we've ever met.'

'He didn't approach you a couple of weeks ago asking if you'd be interested in buying some information from him?'

'Information about what?'

'If he approached you, you'd know.'

'Quite. But he didn't.'

'Ennis is a friend of his.'

'Really?'

'Perhaps Ennis approached you. On the same subject.'

'No. He didn't.'

'If that's so . . .'

'It is, I assure you.'

'Then I'm curious. You seem to have some insight into what led to my father's murder. How did you gain that, if not from him or Ennis or Ireton? Did someone else put you in the picture?'

Brigham meticulously stubbed out his cigarette and lit another. He peered through the windscreen at the caped figures of two policemen on bicycles who rode slowly round the car and turned on to the bridge. Max found himself watching them as well. One of the policemen glanced back at the car as they took the turn. 'Since that mad anarchist took a pot-shot at Clemenceau, the French have been nervous as kittens that there'll be some fearful outrage to sully their management of the conference. They're suspicious of everything. I shouldn't really be here, talking to you. It could be hard to explain, if I was called upon to do so.'

'It was your idea.'

'So it was.'

'What's the answer to my question?'

'No one put me in the picture, James. I merely made judicious enquiries. Good God, I've been in this game for nearly forty years. I know how to find things out. It requires tact, caution and connections developed and nurtured over decades. You're clearly deficient in every one of those departments. That's why you're in such danger. You're brave and determined, which is admirable. But it's not enough. In your situation, it may even be a disadvantage. Do you sail?'

'What?'

'I have a share in a villa near Cannes. I keep a boat down there, scandalously underused. A local man looks after it for me. You could go and stay in the villa, if you like. Take the boat out. Enjoy

a Provençal spring. Relax. Pamper yourself. My friends would be delighted to meet you. I might even join you there, if this conference ever ends.'

Max hardly knew what to say. The man's nerve was quite something. 'I'm not going to Cannes, Brigham. Or anywhere else. I'm staying here until I find my father's killer.'

'Or until he finds you?'

'The cards must fall where they will.'

'What a fatalistic young man you are.'

'It's what I'm resolved to do.'

'As an act of filial piety?'

'If you like.'

'The statement does you credit. But it's misplaced piety, as I think you're aware. It would seem perverse in the extreme to lose your life seeking to avenge a father who isn't actually—'

'*Don't say another word.*' The force of Max's interjection succeeded in silencing Brigham. Max turned to face him, though he could see little of his expression in the dim light that reached them from the nearest street lamp. 'I promise you this, Brigham: if I learn you were responsible in any way for my father's murder, however indirectly—'

'That's preposterous. I had nothing to with Henry's death.'

'*If* I learn that, I'll kill you. Do you understand?'

'What? You can't—'

'Be serious? Oh, but I'm being deadly serious. I want you to know that. It's not an idle threat. I can't be bought off or adopted as some kind of pet. I mean to finish what I've started. I mean to punish those who brought my father down. If you're one of them, I advise you now: do your worst before I do mine.'

'James, you've completely—'

'I'll bid you goodnight, Brigham. I'll walk back to the hotel, thanks. I need some fresh air.'

With that, Max yanked the door open and hopped out of the car. He slammed the door violently behind him and strode away across the street without a backward glance. If Brigham was his enemy, he was glad of it. Proof, one way or the other, was all he needed. Proof. And then he would act.

MAX DID NOT WALK BACK TO HIS HOTEL, AS HE HAD TOLD Brigham he would. He headed for Little Russia. The explanation he advanced to himself was that he needed to confirm Nadia was safe and well. She might have news of her uncle, or of something else that would aid his search for the truth. But he would not spend the night with her. His encounter with Brigham had left him emotionally ragged. That the fellow might be his father was a sickening possibility he had long done his level best to disregard. He wanted nothing of Brigham's. He could not, would not, acknowledge any tie, least of all of blood.

The bookshop was in darkness, but a light was burning in the room above. Max rang the bell and stepped back to let Nadia see him from the window. A lace curtain twitched, though she did not show herself. But, a few moments later, he heard a movement in the shop. And then the door opened.

She looked pale and anxious. 'Max,' she said, smiling as if it was an effort to do so.

'May I come in?'

'Ah, no.' She lowered her voice. 'A friend of my uncle and his wife are here. It is . . .'

'Awkward?'

'They will ask you many questions, Max. And they are not . . . discreet people. It is better, I think, if you do not come in.'

'I understand. Is all well?'

'Nothing has changed. I wait to hear. But I hear nothing.'

'I'm sorry. If there's anything I can do . . .'

Her voice dropped to a whisper. 'Come again soon. Last night . . .' She looked deep into his eyes. 'I need you.'

'You know where to find me. I'll say goodnight.'

'*Spokoynoy nochi*, Max.' She blew him a kiss and slowly closed the door.

Max took a long detour on his way back to the Mazarin, walking himself into a state of exhaustion on the cold and empty streets of the night-time city. It was the only way he could be sure of sleeping, with so many doubts and questions swirling in his mind.

In Sir Henry Maxted's old room at the Majestic, Sam was already sound asleep. Insomnia had always been a mystery to him, a good night's rest no more complicated than a bed to climb into. It did not even have to be a particularly comfortable bed, though this one was certainly that.

He had not been surprised to hear nothing from Max that evening, concerned though he was about him. No news was in a sense good news. He did not doubt Max would be in touch when he could. The war had only served to reinforce Sam's innate pragmatism. What would be would be.

By the same token, he did not dream much, generally waking with no memory of how his sleeping mind had occupied itself. But that was not to be the case when he came to himself on Saturday morning, with a shaft of grey morning light falling across the coverlet.

He had dreamt of le Singe, or his subconscious version of le Singe: a small, spry, dark-skinned boy dressed in ragged army fatigues, standing before him, on tiptoe it seemed, ready to dodge or spring, and pointing at him with one steady forefinger, smiling as he did so, his teeth a yellow crescent across the umber of his round, simian face. There was something white in his other hand: a stick of chalk, perhaps. The sight fleetingly transformed him into one of the teachers at Sam's old school in Walthamstow. Then there was a

blur of motion. Le Singe was a crouching figure in a window. And then he was gone.

Sam sat up and rubbed his face. The dream stayed with him, refusing to leave his mind. He looked at his alarm clock. There was still half an hour to go before the time he had set the alarm for and he wondered what had roused him. The chill air, perhaps. It was desperately cold in the room.

He glanced across at the window and saw that it was open. The stay was hanging free, though he felt sure he had secured it the night before. It had not fitted properly, though. It might have worked itself loose. He lumbered over and closed it, shivering in the chill. As he did so, he noticed a mark on the sill outside: a white cross. Had it been there before? He could not say for sure. He reopened the window and rubbed the cross with his finger. He was left with a smear of chalk on his skin.

Then he turned and started with astonishment. On the wall above the bed, while he had lain asleep, someone had chalked a message.

At the Mazarin, Max was woken by a telephone call from the lobby. Sam was downstairs, sounding breathless and perturbed. Could he come up? Max, his thoughts still fuddled by sleep, slurred out his consent and struggled into his dressing-gown.

He had hardly done so when Sam was knocking at the door. 'What the devil's the matter?' Max demanded as he let him in. 'And what time is it?'

'Bacon-and-egg time, sir, but there's something I have to tell you before you tuck into breakfast. Take a look at this. I copied it down off the wall of my room at the Majestic. Your father's old room, as it happens.'

'My father's room? What are you—' He broke off as Sam handed him a piece of paper and read the message written on it.

TELL HIS SON I NOT KNOW WE KILL HIM
AND GIVE HIM THIS – HX 4344

241

Max reread the message when Sam had finished recounting the events of the night. It seemed clear le Singe had paid him a visit. It was no dream. The chalked words on the wall and the open window proved that.

'He must be double- or triple-jointed, sir. You'd need to be able to swing from pipes and railings like a monkey from creepers in the jungle to get to the window of that room. And I reckon he's been before. That cross on the sill is his mark. It was the first night since Sir Henry's death that there was a light in the room. His first chance, as he saw it, to send you this message.'

'He seems to want to tell me he didn't know murder was part of the deal. Fine. It's his boss I'm after, anyway. But if le Singe has a conscience, it could mean he'll give us some more help. If we can only make contact with him.'

'That's what I was thinking.'

'What did you do with the writing on the wall?'

'I rubbed it out sharpish, sir. We don't want anyone else to get the benefit of it, do we?'

'No, we don't. Good work, Sam. Now, these letters and numbers. What are they supposed to mean?'

'Looks like a car registration number to me, sir. HX is the code for central London.'

'It is?'

'I thought everyone knew that.'

''Fraid not, Sam. It's an inexplicable gap in my education.'

'I checked the cars in the garage before I left. They were all brought over from London and most have HX in front of the number. But 4344 ain't among 'em.'

'And what would it mean if it were, eh?'

'I was hoping you might have some idea, sir.'

'Maybe I do.' Max tapped his front teeth thoughtfully. 'Brigham's rented an apartment, so he's not staying at the Majestic. His car wouldn't be in the hotel garage.'

'Who's Brigham, sir?'

'A senior member of the British delegation. And a nasty piece of work to boot. Our man, quite possibly. He took me for a drive last night and advised me to leave Paris in the interests of my health.'

'What was he driving, sir?'

'A Daimler. His own, I suspect.'

'Get the registration number, did you?'

Max gave Sam a pained smile. 'Incredibly, it never occurred to me.'

'Sorry, sir.'

'But it doesn't matter. Appleby can tell me where Brigham's staying. It shouldn't be difficult to find out if he's driving HX 4344. I'll go and see Appleby straight after breakfast. Do you want to join me for a bite here?'

'Kind of you, sir, but I'd better hotfoot it back to the Majestic. I have to put the mechanics through their paces this morning.'

'All right. You go. Thanks for bringing this to me so promptly, Sam.'

'Don't mention it, sir. About le Singe . . .'

'Yes?'

'He's a weird one and no mistake. I really thought I was dreaming when I saw him. And it was like he knew I'd think that. He wasn't worried a bit. He seemed . . . calm. Calm as a pail o' milk.'

'Would you know him again?'

'Oh, yes. He's a breed all to himself.'

'Maybe he'll call again.'

'If he does, I'll be ready for him.'

'Take care.'

'I will. You too, sir.'

Max grinned. 'Don't I always?'

After Sam had gone, Max bathed and shaved hurriedly, then went down to breakfast. He was halfway through a bowl of porridge and a silent rehearsal of what he was going to tell Appleby – he had already half-convinced himself Brigham's Daimler would turn out to be HX 4344 – when a clerk materialized at his elbow.

'Telephone call for you, Monsieur Maxted. A Senhor Ribeiro. Will you speak to him? He says the matter is urgent.'

Max swallowed his spoonful of porridge and stood up. 'Take me to the phone.'

*

243

'Baltazar?'

'Yes, Max. It is I. Baltazar Ribeiro. I am sorry to be calling you so early.'

'Never mind. I'm an early riser.'

'I rise early also. I sleep badly, probably because I do not take enough exercise.'

'I'm sorry to hear that. But—'

'I generally take a little walk as soon as it is light. To give me an appetite for breakfast.'

Max's lunch with Ribeiro had not left him with the impression that the Brazilian's appetite was ever likely to be deficient, but he did not dwell on the point. 'Really? Well, I—'

'As soon as I left the hotel he appeared in front of me. He must have been waiting for me. Perhaps I mentioned to him my habit of an early walk.'

'Who was waiting for you?'

'Walter Ennis. Of the American delegation.'

'*Ennis?*'

'Yes. It was him. We know each other from the confiscated-shipping committee. But that is of no importance. You know him also, I think.'

'Yes. We met yesterday.'

'He would not say what happened between you. But something bad, I assume. He looked worried and . . . not himself. He had not shaved. His clothes were creased.'

'What did he want?'

'Someone he could trust – and you could trust also – to pass a message to you from him.'

'What was the message, Baltazar?'

'He wants to meet you. This morning. He said he wants to tell you the truth. Before it is too late. His words, Max. *Before it is too late.*'

'I'll meet him. Where and when?'

'Notre-Dame, ten o'clock. Sit in the nave and wait. Go alone. If you are not alone, he will not show himself.'

'He doesn't need to worry about that. I'll be alone.'

'Max, I—'

'It's all right, Baltazar. There's nothing for you to be concerned

about. There's no danger, I assure you. We'll just talk. That's all.'

'But—'

'Thanks so much for letting me know. Goodbye.' Max put the telephone down and glanced at the clock on the wall behind the reception desk, then strode towards the stairs.

APPLEBY WAS OUT OF THE OFFICE WHEN MAX CALLED IN AT the Majestic. Cursing his luck and unable to spare the time to wait, Max headed for Etoile Métro station and his appointment at Notre-Dame.

When he crossed the bridge to the Ile de la Cité that cold, grey, sleety morning, he looked ahead at the white-flecked flank of the Préfecture de Police and wondered what sort of night Corinne had passed in her cell. He feared she did not believe he could accomplish anything on her behalf. But he was going to. One chink in his enemy's armour was all he needed. And Walter Ennis might be it.

Indigent ex-servicemen and assorted beggars were thick on the ground outside Notre-Dame, hoping for a coin or two from worshippers going in or out. Max ignored them, knowing that if he gave to one he would be expected to give to all. They looked at him with their gaunt, weary faces and he felt sorry for them. But he could not take their woes on to his shoulders. He hardened his heart and pressed on.

The interior of the cathedral was bone-numbingly chill. Max's breath frosted in the still air. The light was thin and sallow, the windows all plain glass, the stained glass having been removed for safe-keeping during the war. A few people were lighting candles, a few others praying quietly. The vast nave was filled with echoes of shuffling feet and whispering voices.

Max settled in a pew about halfway along the nave and waited. He glanced up at the high, vaulted ceiling and ahead towards the distant altar. It was possible to believe, in such a setting, that all human concerns were petty and insignificant. But Max instinctively rejected the notion. The war had not led him to reject God. But nor had God come to his aid, as far as he was aware. Flying a fragile plane into combat above the battlefields of Flanders had made him trust his own judgement and no one else's, not even the Almighty's.

Minutes ticked slowly by. Max looked at his watch. Ennis was late, assuming, of course, he had any intention of showing up at all. A cigarette would have been a welcome distraction, but he could hardly smoke in a cathedral. Max picked up the prayer-book from the shelf in front of him, then put it down again.

'You came, then.' Ennis's voice was suddenly close to Max's ear. Half-turning, he saw the American's bulky figure in the pew behind him. '*Don't look round.*' Ennis leant forward, as if to pray, resting his elbows on the back of Max's pew. 'Do you think we're safe here, Max?' he whispered. 'Do you think the people we're dealing with recognize the concept of sanctuary?'

'You tell me, Walter,' Max whispered back. 'You know them better than I do.'

'I wish to God I didn't.'

'You could have refused to take Lemmer's money, I imagine.'

'If only it had been so simple. Lemmer doesn't generally resort to anything as crude as bribery.'

'Call it what you like. You've betrayed your country.'

Ennis sighed heavily. 'That I have.'

'And you betrayed my father as well.'

'No. I swear to God I didn't. I suspected Henry was Travis's client, true enough, but I didn't tell Lemmer that.'

'What did you tell him?'

'As little as I needed to. I warned him Travis was trying to sell information concerning his whereabouts. I had to. If he'd learnt I knew that and *not* warned him . . .'

'Your neck would be on the line? Well, it's there now anyway,

247

isn't it? You're a wanted man, Walter. That's where your treachery's got you.'

'You think I don't know that? You think I don't regret every single damn thing I've ever done for Fritz Lemmer?'

'I don't know. Maybe you do. Maybe you don't. But you did those things. And as far as I can see no one forced you to.'

'You've no idea what you're talking about. Once Lemmer has you, he has you for keeps. You can't refuse to do what he tells you to do. That's suicide.'

'You won't tell me where he's hiding, then?'

'I don't *know* where he's hiding. He wouldn't trust me anywhere near as far as that. I don't think you understand what it's like to be one of his creatures. I've only met him once, in Berlin, before the war. He operates through intermediaries. I don't even know how many intermediaries there are between him and me.'

'We can start with the one you were speaking to on the telephone from your room at the Crillon.'

'We'll *start* with what I want you to do for me. I'm risking my life just by being here.'

'Why should I do anything for you, Walter?'

'Because you want to nail the people who killed your father and I can help you do that. But I need guarantees of my safety. It's a question of trust, Max. Or the lack of it. I've no way of knowing who's one of Lemmer's men and who isn't.'

'*I'm* not one of his men.'

'Exactly. What about Appleby?'

'Nor is he.'

'Are you sure?'

'Of course I'm sure. The idea's absurd.'

'It's not so absurd. But I think you're right. Appleby's on the level. He's one of very few I feel sure about. So, let's talk to him. I'll give you the names of the people who may have killed Henry, in return for safe passage out of Europe and a new identity to go with it. Think you can arrange that?'

If feather-bedding Ennis was what it took to find Lemmer, Max was confident Appleby would agree to it. 'Yes, I think I can.'

'Nothing less will do.'

'Then nothing less will be supplied.'

'It needs to happen soon. Every day I stay in Paris is one too many.'

'Come with me now. Why delay? You don't have to tell Appleby anything if he rejects your terms.'

'You obviously have no idea how his outfit operates. You get his agreement and meet me back here in four hours. That should give you enough time. Then I'll tell you how we're going to manage things. OK?'

'OK.'

'I'm leaving now. Stay here for five minutes before you leave yourself. Understood?'

'Understood.'

'I'll see you later.'

Max nodded a final acknowledgement. The pew-back sprang slightly as Ennis pushed himself upright. Then he was gone in a tattoo of heavy, hurrying footsteps.

Max had no intention of staying where he was for the five minutes Ennis had stipulated. He risked a backward glance after less than one and saw Ennis hurrying out through the door Max had entered by. It was his cue to stand up and go after him.

He was most of the way to the door when it was opened by someone else who was leaving. At that moment, there was a sharp crack of noise from outside, a burst of flapping wings as disturbed pigeons took flight, then a cry of alarm. Max knew at once the noise had been a rifle report. He started running.

The old man who had opened the door was frozen to the spot, staring straight ahead. Max brushed past him and rushed out into the daylight.

The beggars and passers-by had scattered. A figure lay motion-less about twenty yards ahead of him on the flagstoned square in front of the cathedral. It was Ennis. He was sprawled on his back and a pool of blood was spreading beneath his head. As Max ran forward, he saw that one side of his skull had been completely blasted away. He was dead. But where was his killer?

Max reached the body and stopped. He looked down at the gaping wound. It was a livid hole gouged in Ennis's brain: an

instantaneously fatal, expertly aimed shot. Where had it been fired from? From beyond the square, certainly, but where was the vantage point? The only elevated position in that direction was the Préfecture de Police. Max glanced towards it.

The multi-windowed frontage of the building met his gaze. He ran his eye up and across it. Then a movement up on the roof seized his attention. A figure was lying half in and half out of an open dormer window on the mansard level, with his rifle supported by a stand on the narrow parapet in front of him.

It was only in that instant that Max realized the peril he was in. He lunged to his left even as he heard the crack and whine of the second shot. The bullet struck the flagstone where he had just been standing. But now he was running, hard and fast, towards the trees bordering the Seine.

He felt the shot hit him before he heard it, a jolting impact in his left side. There was no immediate pain and the certainty that another shot would follow carried him in a burst of energy to the shelter of the plinth supporting Charlemagne's statue, halfway to the riverside wall.

The shot came, as he had anticipated, ripping through the air beyond the statue. He was safe where he was, but for how long? If the gunman came after him, or had an accomplice, he was finished. And he did not know how serious his wound was. There was a sensation of heat now where the bullet had hit him. He could feel blood seeping out beneath his shirt.

Then he saw the barge chugging upriver and knew it was his only chance to escape the gunman's arc of fire. He broke cover and ran towards the bridge connecting the island with the Left Bank.

The barge was passing slowly beneath the bridge as he reached the railings, its cargo covered with a tarpaulin. A bullet pinged off the railings as he clambered over them, then he was plunging towards the barge, wondering, almost neutrally, if he would make it to the vessel or fall wide and find himself in the river.

He supposed, as far as he was able, that it did not really matter much.

MAX WAS NOT DESTINED TO ESCAPE THE ILE DE LA CITÉ AFTER all. When he next became aware of his surroundings, it was early evening and he was in bed in a river-facing room of the Hôtel Dieu, the hospital that flanked the very square where Ennis had been murdered and he had narrowly avoided the same fate.

A nurse fetched a doctor, who, in stuttering English, informed him that he had knocked himself out jumping on to the barge, but the bullet that had struck him earlier had considerably steered clear of any vital organs in its passage through his body. 'You are young and 'ealthy, *monsieur*. If there is infection, you should be able to fight it. The bullet went close to, ah, your spleen, which concerns me. But . . . we will see . . . *non*?'

Max felt too weak to seek clarification. There was a policeman guarding the door to his room, but the fact that he had been shot at from the *préfecture* hardly made this reassuring. Soon enough, though, he had more visitors: Appleby, in the company of Commissioner Zamaron and a junior officer delegated to take notes.

Zamaron expressed incredulity when Max gave his account of what had happened. Max said nothing about Lemmer, suspecting Appleby would prefer him to keep silent on the real reason for his meeting with Ennis. He said Ennis had admitted to involvement in Sir Henry's murder and agreed to volunteer the details to Appleby in return for safe passage out of Paris. It was the truth, but not the whole truth.

A rifleman operating from the roof of the *préfecture* was too

much for Zamaron to swallow, however. '*Impossible*,' he said several times. But Max knew there were dozens of witnesses to the direction of the shots. The impossible was something Zamaron was going to have to accustom himself to. He was non-committal when Max suggested the incident proved Corinne innocent of Spataro's murder. 'I will consider the evidence carefully,' was all he would say. 'It is for the magistrate to decide.'

Eventually, Zamaron and his junior left, but Appleby remained. He drew up a chair beside the bed and plonked himself down in it. 'You didn't take long to get yourself shot, I must say,' he remarked. 'There are those who are going to remind me they predicted employing an amateur would end like this.'

'Nothing's ended,' Max objected. 'I'll soon be on my feet again.'

'And back in the cross-hairs of whoever killed Ennis. I'm not sure you're safe on the streets, Max.'

'Ennis was offering us Lemmer in exchange for the safe conduct I told Zamaron about. I reckoned bringing him in was worth a few risks.'

Appleby sighed. 'The likelihood is Ennis thought he was setting you up to be killed, little realizing he was a target as well. As for firing at you from the *préfecture*, I imagine the choice of location was designed to warn Zamaron he'd be wise not to ask too many questions. The place is more like a railway station than a police station, anyway. There are always too many people milling about for anyone to keep track of. *Impossible* it certainly wasn't.'

'I'm not going to give up. In fact, I reckon this shows I'm making progress.'

'Towards an early grave, certainly. It's an unwelcome development, Max, and not just because it nearly cost you your life. Ennis was a senior member of the American delegation. He was very publicly murdered. The press will want to know what's going on. I'm going to try to keep your name out of it, but it won't be easy. It may not even be possible, though, as you see, I had Zamaron fix you up with your own room to give you as much privacy as possible. I can't afford to have my department's involvement widely known. There are the Americans themselves to be considered as

252

well. Carver will certainly want to question you. I'll hold him off as long as I can. He mustn't discover we're after Lemmer. You understand?'

'Don't worry. I can handle Carver. I'll give him the same story I gave Zamaron. Meanwhile, there's a member of the *British* delegation I need you to check up on.'

'Brigham?'

'Yes. How did you know?'

'Twentyman told me. He's waiting outside, anxious to reassure himself you're not going to die. I'll send him in when I leave. I'll find out the registration number of Brigham's car, but even if it is HX 4344 that won't give me any justification to do more than ask him a few gentle questions.'

'For God's sake, Appleby, it's obviously *significant*. Brigham's up to something. He tried to talk me into leaving Paris.'

'Perhaps he was concerned for your welfare. With good reason, as it turns out. I'll look into it, all right? But Brigham's well-connected. He's said to have the ear of the Foreign Secretary. I have to tread carefully.'

'Well, I don't have to.'

'No. And I'm sure you won't, once you're up and about. You can try and persuade me to give you his address then. Meanwhile, you need to rest. I'm putting one of my men on your door. Just to make sure the police do their job. Incidentally, Carver tells me Ireton's done a disappearing act.'

'Apparently so.'

'He obviously doesn't think Paris is a healthy place to be these days. And by the look of you he's right.'

'I intend to make it unhealthy for Lemmer.' Max paused, then asked, 'Can you get me a gun, Appleby?'

Appleby's eyebrows twitched in surprise. 'It's not what most people in hospital ask for.'

'I want it for when I leave. Which will be sooner than the doctor recommends, if I have my way.'

'As you no doubt will.'

'The gun?'

Appleby chewed his unlit pipe and contemplated the request for

a moment. Then he said, 'It could only be for self-defence. But then . . . I suppose you may have need of quite a bit of that.'

'It seems so.'

Appleby nodded. 'I'll see what I can do.'

Sam had brought food and a few toiletries, for which Max was grateful, though whatever the doctor had prescribed to dull the pain of his wound had dulled his appetite as well. He was almost as pleased to see Sam as Sam was to see him, though he hid it rather better.

'Mr Appleby said you got off lightly in the circumstances, sir.'

'He must have a curious definition of "getting off lightly".'

'I told him about Mr Brigham.'

'I know. He mentioned it.'

'Thing is, sir, I didn't get the feeling he was going to do much about it.'

'Neither did I. Brigham has friends in high places, Sam. Appleby can't afford to tread on their toes.'

'Luckily for you you've got a friend in a low place, then. I'll scout round the streets tonight. Mr Brigham's apartment can't be far from the Majestic and it's not likely a garage goes with it. So, I may be able to find his car. If it's HX 4344 . . .'

'Yes? What then?'

Sam tapped the side of his nose. 'I've had an idea.'

Max groaned. 'Lord save us.'

'You know what they say. If Mahomet won't come to the mountain . . .'

'What's that supposed to mean?'

'Don't worry, sir. Just leave it to me.'

MAX FELL ASLEEP THAT NIGHT WATCHING SNOW FALLING OVER the Seine. Access to his room was guarded by a French policeman and a British Secret Service representative built in keeping with his name, Burley. Max felt as weak as a baby, but was confident a night's rest would revive him. The attempt to kill him he took as a back-handed compliment. They were frightened of him. And he was determined to give them good cause to be. First, though, he had to sleep.

The snow that grew heavier as the night deepened did not deter Sam, but it did complicate his tasks. There were quite a few cars parked on the streets of the eighth arrondissement, but the accumulation of snow meant their registration numbers were mostly illegible. Sam began his circuit from the Majestic diligently brushing the snow off every number, but his gloves were soon sodden and his fingers numb, so he abandoned that in favour of looking for Daimlers in particular and English makes in general. His ability to distinguish them at a glance from French cars was far from infallible, however. His clothes were not warm enough and he cursed the Parisian spring weather with many muttered profanities as he trudged along. Despite reviving halts for coffee and brandy at various bars, HX 4344 remained frustratingly elusive.

While clasping his coffee-cup between his frozen hands in one such bar, puffing suspiciously on a French cigarette, Sam acknowledged to himself that he had bitten off more than he could chew. Many of the apartment buildings he had passed had inner

courtyards, where a car could be stowed out of sight. There were stables as well, and a few garages, to be considered. Not to mention the possibility that HX 4344 was simply elsewhere that evening. It seemed likelier that he would catch pneumonia than a sight of the damned thing.

If it even existed, of course. Perhaps it was not a registration number at all. Perhaps le Singe had played a trick on him. *Cheeky monkey*, Sam thought, smiling grimly at his own play on words.

Eventually, Sam took pity on himself and suspended the search. It was as he approached the Arc de Triomphe for the third or fourth time that he decided he should quit while he was behind. But returning to the solitude of his room at the Majestic with his tail between his legs did not appeal to him. Little Russia was a shortish walk away along Avenue Hoche. He did not know precisely how matters stood between Max and Nadia Bukayeva, but he felt sure she would want to be told what had happened, although naturally Sam would claim ignorance of the events that had led to the shooting. It was not yet midnight and he did not suppose Nadia was one to be wrapped up in bed with cocoa at ten. She was a creature of the night if he had ever met one. And she might even be pleased to see him.

It was as he turned into Rue Daru and saw the domes of the Orthodox Cathedral ahead of him through the flurrying snow that Sam heard the throaty note of a car engine behind him and was shortly afterwards splattered about the ankles with slush from the gutter as a sleek black Daimler purred past.

Sam broke into a squelching trot to keep the car in sight. The registration number was displayed on a curved plate fixed to the spare tyre on the boot, but was obscured by snow. The car slowed ahead of him and turned left into the next side-street, the very side-street, in fact, where Sam knew Bukayev's bookshop was located. He put a spurt on.

He heard a car door slam as he neared the corner and, rounding it, saw a hatted, trench-coated figure hurrying away from the Daimler, now standing at the kerbside, its engine ticking.

The bookshop was halfway along the street on the opposite side and the man steered a straight course towards it. Sam stopped running and moved into the deep shadow of an unlit doorway. The car was only a few feet from him, but still he could not make out the number. Whatever the number, though, there was something about this he did not like. And he felt sure Max would like it even less.

There were lights burning in the rooms above the shop. The man reached the door and rang the bell. A curtain twitched above. Sam thought he glimpsed Nadia's face, though he could not have sworn to it. A few moments later, the door opened. There was a murmured exchange of words. Then the man stepped inside and the door closed behind him.

'You naughty girl,' Sam said under his breath. 'Not playing fair with us, are you?' He walked hastily to the rear of the Daimler and brushed the snow off the numberplate. It was HX 4344.

Sam returned to the shelter of the doorway and stood there for several minutes, considering what he should do next. His original plan had been designed to prove Brigham drove HX 4344, but he reckoned that was now clear. The question was what he should do about it. On balance, there was still a lot to be said for obliging Brigham to bring the Daimler to the Majestic for repair. It would establish his ownership as an unchallengeable fact, though quite what it would establish beyond that Sam did not know.

He looked up at the illuminated windows of the rooms above the bookshop. He had misread Nadia Bukayeva. So had Max. It would be preferable to believe she was merely indiscriminate with her favours than what Sam actually suspected: that some greater treachery altogether was afoot.

He could delay no longer. Either he went through with it or not. 'Get on with it, lad,' he told himself, with sudden decisiveness. He left the doorway and advanced to the front of the Daimler. He looked both ways along the street and was reassured. The coast was clear. He rested his hand gently on the warm bonnet of the car. For what he had in mind, it would be easier to open her up. That risked drawing the attention of anyone passing by. And if Brigham happened to glance out of the window . . . No. It was going to be

a cold and wet scramble beneath the engine, but there was nothing else for it. After another glance in both directions, he crouched down on the snowy pavement and crawled gingerly into the space between the kerb and the chassis of the car.

Max woke, at what stage of the night he could not have said, aware that something had changed – for the worse. He was bathed in sweat, his heart was fluttering, his head pounding, every part of his body pulsing with heat. He was in the grip of a fever the like of which he had never known. Moving a single muscle demanded more concentration and effort than he felt capable of exerting. There was a small bell on the bedside table for him to summon help if he needed it and there was no question that he did need help. He managed to bend his neck so that he could see the bell. The next challenge was to reach out and grasp it. He stared long and hard at it, pulling together the small amount of strength he had. Then he forced himself up on one elbow and stretched out his hand. He noticed that his fingers were trembling like leaves in a breeze. They touched the bell, but he could not seem to control them enough to take hold of it. It toppled over, rolled to the edge of the table and dropped to the floor. And Max fell back against the pillow. He could do no more.

WHEN SAM WENT TO VISIT MAX THE FOLLOWING MORNING, HE was horrified to learn of the deterioration in his condition. The doctor on duty was too busy to speak to him and none of the nurses spoke English. '*Une fièvre*' was mentioned, which Sam assumed meant a fever, since Max was clearly in the grip of one and too far gone to communicate. Burley, the Secret Service man Appleby had put on the door to Max's room, told Sam the doctor had said earlier that the bullet wound had led to blood poisoning and that 'the next twenty-four hours will be critical'.

Sam was still gloomily mulling this over when Carver and a couple of men built like wardrobes arrived in the hope of questioning Max. Their frustration that this would not be possible was more in evidence than any concern about the patient's prospects. Carver turned to Sam as a substitute, but was to be disappointed.

'I wasn't there, sir. I don't know what Mr Ennis may have said before he was shot. I didn't even know Mr Maxted was planning to meet him.'

'I thought you lived in the guy's hip pocket.'

'He's never told me everything that's in his mind. He probably reckons it's safer for me to be kept in the dark.'

'But what if I don't believe you *are* in the dark?'

'Then I suppose you won't believe anything I say.'

'A US diplomat has been gunned down in broad daylight, Twentyman. I need to find out why. If turning you upside down and shaking you to see what falls out is what it takes, I'll do it.'

'I'm sure you will, sir. But nothing will fall out.'

Carver closed in and prodded Sam so hard in the shoulder that he was propelled back a step. 'The dumb act's fine, Twentyman, so long as you really are dumb. If not, you're storing up a whole lot of trouble for yourself. You can trust me on that. Because I'm one of the places the trouble will be coming from.'

'I'm sure Mr Maxted can explain everything when he's well enough.'

'You are, are you? Well, for your sake I hope he's well enough pretty damn soon.'

'I hope that too, sir.'

Carver held Sam with a glare for several seconds, then broke away and led his far from merry men off down the echoing stairs from the landing where he and Sam had exchanged words.

Sam leant on the banister-rail and watched them descend in a surge of coat-tails and jutting fedoras. They reached the ground floor and vanished from sight.

He did not move away, however. He stayed where he was, gazing into the vortex of the stairwell, wondering what to do for the best.

Then, to his astonishment, Nadia Bukayeva moved into view on the next landing down. She had clearly been waiting for Carver and his crew to leave. She looked up at him and frowned, then headed up the stairs.

'Why did you not tell me what happened to Max?' she asked as she reached him. 'I went to the Mazarin to see him this morning. They gave me the news there.'

'I'm sorry,' said Sam, flustered and well aware that he probably looked it. 'I would have . . . got in touch with you today . . .'

'How is he?' she cut in, clasping his arm. She looked genuinely worried. Sam had to force himself to remember what he had seen the night before.

'The wound isn't serious. Or it wasn't. They think he's contracted blood poisoning. He has a bad fever.'

'Can I see him?'

'Well, I . . .'

'I must.'

Sam decided to let the nurses decide the issue. Nadia talked her way past them in fluent French, charming Burley along the way. Max was sleeping when they entered his room, though hardly peacefully. Nadia stroked his hand and murmured what sounded to Sam like a prayer. She left with tears in her eyes. He would not have doubted her for a moment but for knowing more of her than she had cause to suppose. She was a consummate actress. He could not deny that.

'Can we go outside and talk, Sam?' she asked, drying her eyes. 'Please tell me as much as you can about what happened. And then . . . there is something I want to tell you. It is why I went to see Max this morning. I need help.' She looked at him with an expression of utter sincerity. 'Will you help me, Sam? There is no one else I can turn to.'

'Try Brigham,' he was tempted to say. But he said no such thing.

They went out into the inner courtyard of the hospital. The sky above them was pure blue, but the air was cold and snow lay in thick carpets on the lawns. In milder weather, recovering patients might have been taking tentative strolls there with friends or relatives. As it was, they were alone.

Sam offered Nadia a cigarette, which she gladly accepted. He held the match for her, noticing how her hand trembled as she clasped the cigarette. She pulled the fur collar of her coat up around her soft, pale cheeks and looked, gazing at him through a drift of smoke, quite breathtakingly lovely.

He told her then the little he felt he should about the circumstances of the shooting, proclaiming as much ignorance to her as he had to Carver. 'He'd have explained it all to me afterwards,' he said, referring to Max's rendezvous with Ennis. 'But he hasn't been well enough to.'

'Will he live, Sam?'

'I'll back him to. He's a tough nut.'

'I will pray for him. You should pray for him also.'

'He wouldn't want me to.'

'Do it, Sam. You do not need to tell him.' She smiled encouragingly.

261

'All right, then. I will.' And he would – in his own way. 'This help you need, Nadia . . .'

'It is about my uncle. He has been missing for more than a week.'

'Have you had some news of him?'

'News? Maybe. I do not know what to call it. A man called Brigham—'

'Brigham?'

'Yes. Lionel Brigham. He is a member of the British delegation. You have met him?'

'No. But I've heard of him.'

'He has visited my uncle a few times. And they have met a few more times in other places. I do not know what business my uncle has with him. He has never said. But last night Brigham came to see me.'

'He did?' Sam commenced a rapid reassessment of events. Perhaps Nadia's allegiances were not to be doubted after all.

'Why are you frowning?'

'Am I? Sorry.' He made an effort to relax his features. 'Go on.'

'I do not like Brigham. There is something in his eyes. Something . . . I cannot say what it is.'

'But you don't like it.'

'Are you laughing at me, Sam?'

'No. Of course I'm not.'

'First you frown. Then you smile.'

'Sorry. Just . . . tell me what Brigham said.'

'He said he is in contact with people who know where my uncle is. He said they had asked him to give me a message. If I want to see my uncle again, I should go to the railway bridge over the Canal de l'Ourcq at Quai de la Sambre.'

'Where's that?'

'Out in the nineteenth arrondissement, near the city walls. I do not know exactly. But I must go there.'

'Of course. You want me to come with you?'

'That is the strange thing. Brigham advised me to take a friend. "You may need help," he said.'

'What did he mean by that?'

'He would not explain. He would not explain anything. "Go soon, my dear," he said. "You should not delay."'

'Then we shouldn't.'

'But what will we find?'

'Wondering won't help you, Nadia. Let's go.'

Nadia seemed grateful for Sam's decisiveness. As they hurried out of the hospital, they passed the main enquiries office, where misanthropic functionaries dispensed grudging directions to visitors through a small window. One such visitor was turning away from the window with a disappointed scowl when he heard Sam speaking English and scurried over to buttonhole him.

'Sounds like you and me are from the same neck of the woods, squire,' he said in a cockney accent, laying a detaining hand on Sam's elbow as he did so.

The man was small and scrawny, with skittering, inquisitive eyes. Sam did not like the look of him. 'Small world,' he mumbled, endeavouring to disengage himself.

'Been visiting someone?'

'Why else would we be here?' Nadia asked icily.

'That's what I was thinking. Expect you've heard about yesterday's shooting. Just along from here, in front of the cathedral. Like the Wild West, they say.'

'Do they?'

'Point is, rumour has it the so-called innocent bystander they brought in here with a bullet wound is English. Thought you might be friends of his.'

'Can't help you,' said Sam.

'Sure about that, squire? Caution understandable, o' course, but there could be money in it for you. I'm with the *Daily Mail*. Phelps is the name.' Sam found Phelps' card had suddenly and magically materialized in his palm. 'We're doing a Paris edition during the conference. You've probably seen it. Always on the lookout for material. Lord Northcliffe's given us a generous budget. You could be in for a slice of it if—'

'We're not interested.' Sam thrust the card back into Phelps' hand and pressed on towards the door.

'Didn't catch your name, squire,' Phelps called after them. But Sam did not respond.

'Are you really not interested, Sam?' Nadia asked once they were outside. 'He probably would pay you well.'

'Not well enough.'

'How can you be sure?'

'Because you can't put a price on self-respect.'

'Ah, no.' She looked at him with what appeared to be genuine admiration. 'You cannot, of course.'

Sam grinned. 'Specially when you haven't got too much of it to start with.'

THEY TOOK THE MÉTRO TO GARE DE L'EST, THEN ON TO THE END of *Ligne* 7 at Porte de la Villette. From there they headed along the boulevard that followed the line of the city wall south, with the railway line to their right. The sky was blue and the lying snow a dazzling white, but the east wind cut like a knife. Beyond the railway line was the city's main abattoir, inactive on a Sunday, but emanating nonetheless a sharp, fetid tang that soured the air.

They reached the Canal de l'Ourcq where it ran in from the east and turned on to Quai de la Sambre. The railway was directly ahead of them. Beyond lay the rear of the abattoir and more bridges linking it with the meat market on the other side of the canal. Several barges were moored along the bank, but the towpath was empty. It was no place for strolling and certainly not for taking the air.

'Why have we been brought here?' murmured Nadia as they approached the railway bridge.

'There's got to be a reason,' said Sam. 'Didn't Brigham even hint at what it could be?'

' "If you want to see your uncle again, go there," ' Nadia replied. 'That is all he said.'

'And here we are.'

They reached the bridge and moved into the shadow of the arch. Out of the sun, it was colder by several degrees. Water was dripping from the ironwork above them on to the path and into the canal, where a thin skin of ice had formed along the bank.

Nadia shuddered. 'There is nothing here,' she said, her breath clouding before her.

'There must be.' Sam looked ahead, then back the way they had come. There was not a soul in sight and not a vessel moving on the canal. It had all the elements of a fool's errand. But Brigham had surely been in earnest. This was where he had said they should go and this was where they were: the very spot.

'I thought someone would be waiting for us,' said Nadia. 'I even hoped Uncle Igor would be here. But there is no one.'

'They couldn't predict when we'd arrive,' Sam reasoned. 'Perhaps they've watched us approach and will show themselves now we're here.'

Nadia walked out into the sunlight on the other side of the bridge and gazed around. 'Where could they be watching from?'

Sam joined her. 'I don't know,' he admitted, surveying the desolate scene. 'We just have to wait.'

'For how long?'

'I don't know that either.' A fear he suspected might be far from irrational suddenly gripped Sam. They had been lured to this place for some reason, even if it was not the reason Brigham had given. Someone could be watching them from any number of vantage points. And that someone could be the man who had killed Ennis and wounded Max. 'Let's wait under the bridge.'

'Why? It's warmer here.'

'But it's also more exposed.' He grasped Nadia by the arm and led her back into the shadow of the arch.

'You think this is a trap?' she whispered, her voice quavering with alarm.

'I'm probably wrong. It's just—'

Sam broke off. His eye had been caught by a movement at the water's edge on the other side of the canal. A bubble, lit by a shaft of sunlight, had come to the surface and burst. As he watched, there came another. These bubbles were rising in a patch of ice-free water around a rope tied to a mooring-ring on the towpath. And the rope was taut. There was clearly something heavy on the end of it, beneath the water.

'What is it?' asked Nadia. 'What are you looking at?'

'I'm not sure. Wait here.'

Sam took off at a sprint. He wanted to reach the other side of

the canal before Nadia jumped to the same conclusion he had. If it was the right conclusion, she should be spared it if at all possible.

He ran to the footbridge by the city wall, crossed it and raced back to the bridge. It took him only a few minutes to cover the distance. When he arrived, Nadia stared across at him with an anxious frown.

'What is it, Sam?' she called.

'Probably nothing,' he called back, bending by the mooring-ring and tugging at the rope. But it was not nothing. A shape stirred in the murky depths of the water. Peering down, Sam made out what looked like a large, bell-shaped sack. He could not simply pull it to the surface. It was too heavy. He heaved at it unavailingly for several seconds, then gave up.

'I am coming over,' Nadia called.

'No. Stay there.'

'I am coming over.' And, so saying, she set off.

'I hope this isn't what I think it is,' Sam muttered to himself. Looking along the towpath, he saw an iron ladder fixed to the bank just beyond the bridge. If he could drag the sack as far as that, he would be able to come to grips with it.

He untied the knot round the mooring-ring, took the weight of the sack and looped the rope around his waist so as not to lose his grip, then started walking backwards along the path.

It was slow progress and Nadia had overtaken him by the time he had reached it. She said nothing to him, her face gripped by a dawning realization she clearly could not bring herself to express. Instead, she grasped the rope and pulled along with him.

She lost her footing at one point and fell against him, but assured him through gritted teeth that she was all right. They set to again and eventually reached the ladder, where Sam tied the rope to the top of the stile.

There was nothing to be gained by delay, reluctant as he was to take the next step. It either was what he feared or it was not. Bracing himself against the chill of the water, he climbed down the ladder.

He winced as the freezing water seeped inside his boots and trousers. It was above his knees by the time he was able to reach the

267

sack. He took out his penknife, opened it and stabbed a hole in the material, then sawed upwards to create a slit.

A large bubble of air emerged. As it reached the surface, Sam was enveloped in a foul stench. He coughed and spluttered and, glancing up, saw Nadia cover her mouth and nose. Then he looked down at the sack again and saw something white and swollen flop out through the slit.

It was the head of a man.

'I'M VERY SORRY FOR YOUR LOSS, MISS BUKAYEVA,' APPLEBY said, in a gentler tone than Sam was used to from him.

'*Moi aussi, mademoiselle,*' said Commissioner Zamaron.

They were in Zamaron's office at the Préfecture de Police, surrounded by his art collection and enveloped in an atmosphere of sombre diligence. Several hours had passed since the discovery of Igor Bukayev's body in a sack weighed down with rocks, suspended in the Canal de l'Ourcq. The deceased had been taken to a mortuary, where a pathologist was attempting to determine the cause of death.

Nadia had maintained rigid control of her emotions since her initial horror at what she and Sam had found. She spoke quietly and formally and generally avoided eye contact. The only signs of her inner turmoil were the constant clasping and unclasping of her hands.

She and Sam had explained what had led them to the canal without any need of misrepresentation, although Sam had naturally omitted to mention meddling with Brigham's car. The facts appeared to speak for themselves. Lionel Brigham of the British delegation to the peace conference was implicated in the murder of Igor Bukayev and quite possibly in the murders of Sir Henry Maxted, Raffaele Spataro and Walter Ennis.

The enormity of the allegations against Brigham was clearly a factor in the solicitous but non-committal attitudes of Appleby and Zamaron. Officially, the Paris police still regarded Sir Henry's death as an accident and Corinne Dombreux was being held by them as a suspect in the murder of Spataro. As for Ennis, they were looking for a killer who had had the audacity to strike from their

269

own headquarters. All in all, Sam reckoned Zamaron was a man with several headaches and no aspirins.

Zamaron had an additional difficulty where Brigham was concerned, as he was at pains to explain to Nadia. 'All the officials the British have brought here have diplomatic immunity, *mademoiselle*. I could not even question Monsieur Brigham without the agreement of . . .' He turned to Appleby for clarification.

'The Permanent Under-Secretary,' Appleby dolefully specified. 'He'd need a lot of persuading.'

'And forgive me, *mademoiselle*, but it would be . . . *comment dirait-on ça?* . . . it would be your account against his for what he said when he visited you last night.'

'Assuming he admits visiting you at all,' said Appleby.

Sam said nothing. He had not told Nadia – and he did not want to – that he had been in Little Russia the night before. He would have to tell Appleby, though – as soon as possible.

'He knows the people who murdered my uncle,' said Nadia with quiet gravity. 'You must make him tell you who they are.'

'We'll try, miss,' said Appleby.

'Can *you* question him?'

'I certainly intend to. But I can't force him to answer my questions.'

'Unless the Permanent Whatsit says he must?' suggested Sam. 'Is that the size of it, Mr A?'

Appleby glowered at him. 'How succinctly you put it, Twentyman.'

'This must be dealt with at the political level, *mademoiselle*,' said Zamaron. 'I will refer the problem to my superiors, who will refer it to their superiors at the Ministère de Justice. There are the Americans to be also considered in the matter of Monsieur Ennis.'

'Any progress there, Léon?' Appleby asked in a tone that suggested he assumed there had not been.

'*Non.* How the man who shot Ennis entered and left this building is still . . . without explanation.'

'You seem to be telling me, gentlemen,' said Nadia, 'that there is nothing you can do.'

'*Non, non.* We will investigate all the circumstances of your

270

uncle's death, *mademoiselle*. We will seek witnesses. We will search for clues. And we will provide you with protection.'

'I'll get as much as I can out of Brigham, miss,' said Appleby. 'You have my word on that.'

'If you had seen what Mr Twentyman and I saw . . . you would not tread so softly.'

'Unfortunately, we're obliged to.'

'And I will be obliged to tell my uncle's friends that his murderers may be able to hide behind . . . diplomatic immunity.'

'Not if I can help it.'

'But can you help it, Mr Appleby? That is the question.' With that, Nadia rose to her feet. 'I must go home now. There is much to be arranged.'

'I have a car waiting for you, *mademoiselle*,' said Zamaron, rising hurriedly himself.

'*Merci, monsieur.*' She turned to Sam. 'You will tell Max what has happened . . . when he is better?'

'Of course.'

'For all you did, Sam . . . I am grateful.'

'Don't mention it.'

'This way, *mademoiselle*,' said Zamaron, ushering her out.

For a moment, Sam found himself alone with Appleby. 'Brigham definitely visited Nadia last night, Mr A,' he said. 'I saw him park the Daimler and go in.'

'HX 4344?'

'The very same.'

'I've confirmed it's his car. Nadia doesn't know you were spying on her, I assume?'

'I wasn't exactly spying.'

'But she doesn't know?'

'No.'

'You mightn't remain the knight in shining armour in her eyes if she found out.'

'You have to squeeze the truth out of Brigham, sir. He's in this up to his neck.'

'And four people are dead.'

'That's right. There's Madame Dombreux as well. She obviously

271

didn't kill Spataro. You should twist the commissioner's arm to get her released.'

'How kind of you to tell me my job, Twentyman.'

'I didn't mean to do that.'

'No? Well, I—'

Appleby broke off as Zamaron rejoined them, wearily rubbing his forehead. '*Mon Dieu*,' he moaned, 'what a day!'

Appleby caught his eye. 'What a *week*!'

'You will interrogate Brigham, Horace?'

'It won't amount to an interrogation, I'm afraid.'

'But . . .'

'I'll do my best.'

'You will need to. The politicians will not want to connect these killings.'

'I know.'

'Why not?' asked Sam.

'Leave Léon alone, Twentyman. He has enough problems on his plate without being cross-questioned by the likes of you. I'll tell you as much as you need to know – outside.'

They went down into the courtyard, where Appleby's car was waiting. He told the driver to take a stroll, while they sat in the back. He obviously wanted no witnesses to what he had to say, which did not strike Sam as promising.

'Murder's not uncommon in this city, Twentyman,' Appleby began, chewing on his unlit pipe. 'The French are a passionate lot. And the war's left a good many guns in the wrong hands. Sir Henry's death really could have been an accident. Madame Dombreux really could have killed Spataro. And the Russians are notorious for score-settling, so Bukayev could be a victim of something in that line. As for Ennis, well, his murder's hard to explain, I grant you, without imagining a conspiracy to be at work. But Carver will find a way round that, if he's told to.'

'And will he be told to?'

'In all likelihood, yes. To acknowledge the existence of some kind of conspiracy stemming from the presence of past or present German spies within the delegations would be to acknowledge a

threat to the validity of the peace conference. It could even lead to its suspension.'

'Crikey.'

'Exactly.'

'I expect our leaders would move heaven and earth to avoid that.'

'They would. And they will.'

'What are you going to do, then?'

'Question Brigham before he has a chance to hide behind the skirts of the Permanent Under-Secretary. If I can persuade him to give himself away . . .'

'Max seems to think he's a wily operator.'

'No doubt he is. But I have a few wiles of my own.'

'I'm sure you do, sir.'

Appleby glanced sharply at Sam. 'Do you mean to be sarcastic, Twentyman, or is it just your natural tone?'

'You'd have to ask my old mum for a ruling on that, sir.'

'Since Max trusts you, I have little choice but to do the same, at least while he's *hors de combat*. Don't think that trust is any more than highly provisional, though.'

'Oh, I wouldn't dream of it, sir.'

'If Max doesn't pull through—'

'Don't say that, sir.'

Appleby paused in deference to the sincerity of Sam's interruption. He sucked on his pipe for a thoughtful moment, then said, 'I was using Max to do things I'm not free to do for fear of sparking a diplomatic incident. You understand that, don't you, Twentyman?'

'I do, sir, yes.'

'So . . .'

'Is there something you want *me* to do for you?'

Appleby sighed. 'Much against my better judgement . . . yes.'

Sam had readily agreed to Appleby's request, but was not entirely confident of his ability to talk his way into an audience with Baltazar Ribeiro of the Brazilian delegation. He did not lack for nerve, but his appearance and accent often encouraged his social superiors to treat him disdainfully. He would have to tread both boldly and carefully: a tricky combination, to put it mildly.

As it turned out, however, an audience was delivered to him on a plate. When he repaired to the Hôtel Dieu to see whether there had been any improvement in Max's condition, Burley surprised him with the announcement that Max had a visitor. 'Brazilian gent by the name of Ribeiro: senior member of their delegation. Not the sort of bloke you turn away.'

Sam went into the room and found a large, smartly dressed man sitting in a bedside chair that was obviously too small for him, gazing anxiously at Max, who was drifting feverishly in and out of sleep and probably unaware that there was anyone with him at all.

Ribeiro's tanned skin and thick white hair gave him a vigorous appearance, but he was breathing heavily, perhaps because he was upset by the state he had found his old friend's son in – or perhaps because he felt responsible for it. He was clad in a voluminous green overcoat and was turning a string of rosary beads fretfully in his fingers.

'Senhor Ribeiro?' Sam asked.

'*Sim.*' Ribeiro turned a pair of rheumy eyes in Sam's direction. '*O que?*'

'My name's Twentyman. I'm a friend of Max's.'

274

'You are?'

'I served under him in the war.'

'Ah. I understand.' Ribeiro rose and clasped Sam's hand in both of his, grinding a rosary bead into Sam's thumb in the process. 'This is very bad. I am saddened to see him so ill.'

'How did you hear about it?'

'Ah . . .' Ribeiro hesitated.

'Max told me everything, *senhor*. I know you passed him the message from Ennis.'

'Poor Ennis. To die like that, here, in the centre of Paris. You served under Max in the war, you say?'

'Yes. Perhaps . . . we could go somewhere for a quiet word, sir.'

Sam piloted Ribeiro to a cheerless and sparsely populated canteen in the bowels of the building. Ribeiro revealed en route that he had heard of Ennis's demise on the conference grapevine. The murder of a delegate had a lot of people worried. 'And they will remain worried, until the authorities can assure them the crime had nothing to do with the business of the conference.'

Naturally, Ribeiro had been rather more than worried, since he it was who had told Max that Ennis would be waiting for him at Notre-Dame. Learning a so-called bystander had been wounded, he had feared the worst. And he had been right to.

'I blame myself for passing the message,' he said glumly as they reached the canteen. 'I should have refused.'

'Max was glad to get the chance to meet Ennis, *senhor*,' Sam consoled him. 'It wasn't your fault.'

Ribeiro appeared unconvinced and the coffee the canteen supplied seemed to do nothing to lift his spirits.

'I wanted to ask you exactly what Ennis said when he called round at your hotel yesterday morning, *senhor*,' Sam ventured.

'It was as I told Max. It was not a long conversation. Ennis was frightened, though he would not say what he was frightened of. He only wanted to be sure I would contact Max and—'

'You asked him what he was frightened of?'

'Yes. He only shook his head.'

'Nothing else?'

275

Ribeiro raised his coffee-cup, but put it down again without drinking. He frowned thoughtfully. '"What is wrong, Walter?" I asked. Yes. That is what I said. "What is wrong?" And he shook his head. And I asked again. And he gave me such a tired look. He was weary to his core. "Contingencies, Baltazar," he said. "It's the ones you can't foresee that get you in the end."'

'Contingencies?'

'Yes. Contingencies.'

'But what did he mean?'

'I do not know. He would say no more than that. I asked if I could help him. He shook his head again and walked away.'

Contingencies. There had been something about them on Sir Henry's list. Sam could not exactly remember what. But the word had been there all right.

'Does it mean anything to you, Mr Twentyman?'

'No, *senhor*. But it might mean something to Max.'

'Will he recover? I spoke to a doctor who came in while I was there. He shrugged his shoulders a great deal. It is a habit of the French I do not like. He gave Max *une chance sur deux*. Fifty-fifty, you would call it. Not good.'

'Not so bad either. He faced worse odds than that every day he flew in the war.'

Ribeiro raised a smile at that. 'You hearten me, Mr Twentyman. You are better for me than the doctor is for Max, I think. This coffee, incidentally, is undrinkable. Do they sell brandy here?'

'I'll ask.'

Sam went up to the counter and enquired pessimistically after cognac. To his surprise, it was forthcoming. The phrase *Contingencies Memo* sprang suddenly into his mind as he watched the serving woman dispense the liquor. Yes. That was the item on Sir Henry's list. Valuable, like every other item on it.

When Sam returned to the table with the brandy, he found Ribeiro fiddling with his rosary beads again. He looked as if the cares of the whole city were resting on his shoulders. 'Thank you,' he said, raising the glass and taking a sip. He set it down again with a heavy sigh. 'My father, God rest his soul, once told me a happy man is a man without friends. What do you think, Mr Twentyman?'

'Did your father have many friends?'

'Oh, yes. And some of them caused him great problems. He had a generous nature. When the rubber boom ended, many of his friends asked him for help. He lent them money, which some of them never repaid. But what do you do when a friend asks you for help? Turn him away? No. Of course not.'

Sam had the distinct impression Ribeiro was really talking about himself rather than his father. Who was the friend he had not turned away? And what had he asked for? 'You and Sir Henry went back a long way, isn't that right, *senhor*?'

'Yes.' Ribeiro took another sip of brandy. 'It is.'

'You tell me if I've got the wrong end of the stick, but was there something Sir Henry asked you to do that you regret doing now?'

Ribeiro stared at him in silence for a moment. He went on staring at him as he smoothed down his moustache. Then he said, 'What did you do in the RFC, Mr Twentyman?'

'I kept the planes running.'

'How did you do that?'

'I know engines, *senhor*. I could tell from the sound of them if there was something wrong before it actually went wrong. It's a knack. You've either got it or you haven't.'

'And you have it?'

'Yes.'

'I must be careful what I say to you. You have good ears. There is a difference between listening and hearing and it seems you know the difference. I cannot speak to you of what passed between me and Henry. It would not be right. But I will speak to Max. After what has happened to him, I must, as soon as he is well enough, which I pray to God will be soon.'

'Can I tell him what you'll be speaking to him about?'

Ribeiro nodded solemnly. 'You can. Tell him I know why Henry was trying to raise so much money. Tell him I know what he was planning to spend it on.'

LIONEL BRIGHAM ENTERED FRADGLEY'S OFFICE AT THE BRITISH Embassy that evening with the air of one unconvinced that anything Fradgley wanted to discuss could be urgent enough to justify an interruption of his normal Sunday routine. His expression suggested he would swiftly be demanding an explanation from Fradgley for this summons 'on a matter of the utmost importance' with a distinct presumption that it was unlikely, in his judgement, to be important enough.

The few members of staff on duty at the Embassy had been unable to enlighten Brigham in the slightest degree, other than to confirm that Fradgley was on the premises. Strangely, however, upon knocking at the door and going on in without waiting for a response, Brigham was dismayed to discover that the room was empty, the chair behind the broad desk untenanted, no one's eyes but those of the King in a framed photograph on the wall trained upon him.

'Damn it all,' Brigham remarked in his bafflement. 'What the devil's the fellow playing at?'

'Ah, there you are.' Through a doorway in the far corner of the room, leading Brigham knew not where, a figure suddenly advanced, beaming in welcome. It was Horace Appleby of the Secret Service, a man Brigham had done his best to steer well clear of. He regarded the Secret Service as an unwise and unwarranted innovation – a johnny-come-lately to the business of government which he would have preferred not to have come at all.

'There's clearly been some mistake,' said Brigham, with as

much nonchalance as he could muster. 'I'm here to see Fradgley.'

'Presently indisposed,' said Appleby, clamping an unlit pipe between his teeth. 'But even if he had been here, it's you and I who'd have done most of the talking. Shall we sit down?'

'No need. I won't be staying.'

'Please, Mr Brigham. Take a seat.' Appleby subsided into the chair behind the desk and gestured towards the chair facing him.

'There's really nothing we need to discuss, Appleby. I think I'll be going.'

'As you wish. I can't force you to stay. But there are some questions you're going to have to answer sooner or later. Very serious questions. It'd be in your own interests to hear what they are.'

Appleby was still gesturing towards the vacant chair. Brigham hesitated a little longer, then shrugged and sat down. He took out a cigarette and lit it. 'I'll give you until I finish this.'

Appleby smiled, but said nothing. His only response was to fill his pipe and light it, in a leisurely routine that declared he would not allow Brigham to set the terms of their exchanges. Then he smiled again.

'Perhaps I could ask you a question, Appleby,' said Brigham. 'Your outfit's been going, what, ten years? Can you point to one single achievement of lasting value that you've chalked up in that time? We managed to rule an empire for two centuries without . . . whatever it is you people do. Extraordinary, isn't it?'

'How would you describe your dealings with Igor Bukayev, Mr Brigham?'

'What?'

'Igor Bukayev,' Appleby repeated. 'How would—'

'I heard what you said.'

'Then perhaps you'd oblige me with an answer.'

'I don't have dealings with him,' Brigham said, slowly and carefully.

'But you do know him?'

'He's a politically active member of the Russian exile community. It would be surprising if I hadn't come across him.'

'When did you last come across him?'

'I don't know. Some reception or other.'

'A long way from the Canal de l'Ourcq, I assume.'

'The Canal de l'Ourcq?'

'Yes. Out in the nineteenth arrondissement.'

'You've lost me, Appleby. You probably know more about canals than I do. Father a bargee, was he?'

Appleby sent up a plume of smoke and studied Brigham intently through the haze of it. 'Bukayev's body was found earlier today in a sack suspended in the Canal de l'Ourcq, Mr Brigham. Do you want to make a joke out of that?'

'Good God.' Brigham's expression switched to one of horror. 'Bukayev's dead?'

'Yes. Just like Walter Ennis.'

'I heard about Ennis. Shocking business. But ... did he have something to do with Bukayev?'

'You tell me.'

Brigham frowned heavily. 'What are you driving at, Appleby? I'd be grateful if you simply came out and said it.'

'You've admitted an acquaintance with Igor Bukayev. What about his niece, Nadia Bukayeva?'

Brigham's expression darkened. 'His niece?'

'Do you know her, Mr Brigham? Yes or no?

'I may have met her a few times. In the company of her uncle.'

'Ever been alone with her?'

'What are you implying?'

'Have you or haven't you?'

Brigham weighed the question for a moment, then said, 'Not that I recall.'

'Really? I wouldn't have put you down as a man of fallible recollection, I must say. And last night isn't long ago, now is it?'

'Last night?'

'You were seen.'

Brigham flinched. 'You have her under surveillance?'

'What we have is independent verification of her claim that you visited her last night.'

'She told you?'

'She did. She also told us you passed on a message to her, a

280

message that led her to the Canal de l'Ourcq this morning – and a terrible discovery.'

'*I* passed on a message?'

'Do you deny it?'

'Certainly I deny it.' The colour in Brigham's face and the tone of his voice suggested denial was very much what he was about. 'This is preposterous. I visited her, yes. I considered it ungentlemanly to volunteer the fact to you, but in the light of her outrageous allegation I no longer feel obliged to protect her reputation. I went to see her, at her prior invitation, for reasons the tenor of that invitation made clear enough. I spent an hour or so with her. She mentioned her uncle had left Paris for a few days. She said nothing else about him. And I said nothing about him at all.'

'Let me get this straight.' Appleby removed his pipe from his mouth and pointed the stem at Brigham. 'The purpose of your visit was . . . sexual?'

'If you insist on being specific about such matters, yes.'

'You're old enough to be her father.'

'I don't believe I have to defend myself in this regard, Appleby. I'm a bachelor. I enjoy the company of women. And Nadia Bukayeva enjoyed *my* company. There's nothing else to be said.'

'Except that she tells a very different story. And someone must have passed the message about Bukayev to her. Otherwise she wouldn't have known where to go.'

'Whoever it was, it wasn't me.'

'You contend she's lying?'

'I don't contend. She simply is.'

'Why would she do that?'

'To avoid naming the person who really passed the message, presumably.'

Appleby replaced the pipe in his mouth and relit it. 'Your work for the delegation has touched on our policy towards the Bolshevik regime, I believe. A committee you sit on formulated advice to the Prime Minister concerning the strategy to be adopted by our negotiators if the proposed meeting with Russian representatives at Prinkipo had gone ahead.'

281

'What of it?'

'Involving yourself with the niece of a well-known Tsarist could be seen in the circumstances as compromising. Highly compromising, I'd say.'

'You can probably cause me some embarrassment, Appleby. But nothing worse. I think you'll find I have more friends than you do.'

'More highly placed friends, you mean?'

'They tell me you were a policeman before you joined the Secret Service. I can believe it. There's definitely something plodding about you. The uniform must have suited you.'

'They tell *me* you took some leave last week in order to attend Sir Henry Maxted's funeral. Is that correct?'

'It is.'

'So, you won't deny being acquainted with him?'

'Certainly not.'

'Or Walter Ennis?'

'I met the fellow at various meetings.'

'Your acquaintances are an unlucky lot, aren't they?'

'What do you mean?'

'Well, so many of them come to a sticky end.'

Brigham lit another cigarette and gave Appleby a long, contemptuous look. 'And so many more of them don't.'

'Do you know Sir Henry's son, James Maxted?'

'Of course. I'm a friend of the family.'

'Are you indeed? Then you'll have been sorry to hear of his condition.'

'His . . . condition?'

'I assume you're aware he was injured during the Ennis shooting.'

'No.' Brigham's face drained of colour. He appeared genuinely shocked. 'I was not aware of it.'

'He's in the Hôtel Dieu, fighting for his life.'

'Good God. Are you saying . . . he may not survive?'

'It was a relatively minor wound. But septicaemia's the problem now. I wouldn't like to say what his chances are.'

'Does his mother know about this?'

'He said he preferred not to worry her.'

'But . . .'

'You look upset, Mr Brigham.'

'I am upset, God damn it.' Brigham jumped up from his chair. 'I'd better go and see how he is for myself.'

'I'm afraid I can't allow that.'

'What?' Brigham glared at Appleby. 'What the devil do you mean?'

'There's good reason to suppose the man who killed Ennis hoped to kill young Maxted as well. I've placed a guard on his room at the hospital. In view of the suspicious nature of your involvement in this matter, I can't authorize you to visit him.'

'You think I might try to kill him?'

'Your loyalties are unclear, Mr Brigham. Therefore your actions are unpredictable.'

'My God, you have a nerve.' Brigham brought his fist down on the blotter in front of Appleby, setting the lids of the bottles rattling in Fradgley's inkstand but making no discernible impact on Appleby's composure. 'I shall be lodging a formal complaint about your conduct – and your damned insinuations.'

'Please do. I've already notified the Permanent Under-Secretary of my concerns about you. I await his response.'

'His response will be to tell Cumming to bring you to heel.'

Appleby puffed at his pipe and smiled up at Brigham. It was unusual to hear C referred to by his actual surname. It could be regarded as calculatedly disrespectful, as Appleby suspected it was intended to be. But he did not rise to the bait. 'As to that,' he said in an amicable tone, 'we shall see, shan't we?'

THE BREAKING OF MAX'S FEVER WAS LIKE THE PASSING OF A
storm. All, in an instant, was clear and calm. He lay in his bed
at the Hôtel Dieu, conscious of himself for the first time in some
indeterminate period. It was dark beyond the window of his
room, but which night it was he had no way of judging. He felt
cool and serene, though so weak he could barely raise his
hand to his brow. The sleep he fell into then was a soft, healing
slumber.

He was aware of a nurse hovering over him at some point, checking his temperature and the dressing on his wound and murmuring
'*Très bien*'. He opened his eyes and tried to speak to her. She smiled
at him and patted his hand. '*Dormez tranquille, monsieur.*'

Max vaguely supposed a doctor would come to see him in the
morning. But it was still dark outside when gentle pressure on his
shoulder woke him and he became aware of a white-coated
presence beside the bed.

Max did not recognize the doctor, though it was hard to make
out his features, silhouetted as he was against the dim light from the
doorway. There was no other light. Someone had turned off
the bedside lamp. He could just discern a suit and bow-tie
beneath the white coat. The man was grey-haired and bearded and
wearing some distinctive, apple-scented cologne. His face was
entirely in shadow.

'Doctor?' Max murmured.

'I am a doctor, yes.' The voice was low and silky, but the accent

284

was not French. It was altogether more middle European. 'Though not of medicine.'

'I'm . . . sorry?'

'Don't apologize, Max. You've not been well, though now, I'm glad to say, you appear to be recovering. It is actually for me to apologize to you. I was not responsible for Saturday's . . . *coup de main* . . . but those who were are to some degree under my control. I regret that it occurred. There was a certain amount of panic when it was realized Ennis might tell all. He had made himself a threat to the safety of several people. Their reaction was understandable but excessive. We cannot have assassinations on the streets of Paris. It is altogether too conspicuous.'

'Who are you?'

'I think you know who I am. I was acquainted with your father. We met in Tokyo . . . thirty years ago.'

Max was seized by the conviction that the man sitting at his bedside was none other than Fritz Lemmer. He tried to push himself upright, but did not have the strength. He opened his mouth to cry out, but a hand was clamped over it.

'They would not believe you, Max. They would think you were still delirious. I am Doctor Wahlen from Strasbourg, helping out here at the request of the Director. Nod your head if you are willing to continue our conversation without raising the alarm. It would be to your advantage to do so, I assure you.'

Max nodded and the hand was removed. He lay where he was, his chest heaving from the effort he had made to rise. He was by no means certain that he could shout for help even if he wanted to.

'I am sorry for your father's death, Max. I rather admired Henry. He was incorruptible but surprisingly imaginative. Encountering him here in Paris was the sheerest misfortune. He had no business catching a tram so early in the morning. It was simply bad luck. Even so, I would not have expected him to recognize me. I tried to ignore him, to pretend I did not know him. I sensed the attempt was in vain, but I hoped he would realize that to move against me would be extremely risky. And why should he take such a risk, after all? Patriotism surely has its limits. I stood there, in the crowded tram, ignoring his stare, refusing to engage with him eye to eye. We

285

did not speak. There was no acknowledgement. I thought of the last time we had met. A reception at the Russian Embassy in Tokyo, shortly before the Tsarevich's visit, in the spring of 1891. I wonder if he thought of it also. I will confess to you that I would have liked to talk to him about those days. I cannot tell you how earnestly I hoped he would not pursue me. For his sake as well as mine.'

'You expect me . . . to believe that?'

'It is the truth. Of course, I did not know then that he was involved with Madame Dombreux, although naturally I was aware he had been acquainted with her late husband. Pierre Dombreux is something of a puzzle, to me as he is to others. I thought I had him in the palm of my hand. But no. It seems he served several masters, none of them loyally. If he trusted anyone, it was Henry. That was my difficulty when I encountered Henry. How much of what Dombreux knew did he know? It was the lure he planned to use to trap me. I cannot complain. The hunter must always expect to be hunted. There is no divine law that dictates the prey may not turn upon the predator. Still, it is a dangerous game, as Henry discovered, though I suspect that came as no surprise to him. Patriotism was not his motivation. Hence my miscalculation. He wanted to profit from what he knew about me. Do you know why he needed so much money? I confess I do not. He was not a mercenary man. There must have been a compelling reason. Strictly speaking, it is irrelevant, at least to me. But it would be interesting to know.'

'You . . . murdered . . . him.' Max had to force the words out.

'Agents of mine neutralized the threat he represented. They acted with my approval, at least initially. Henry's fatal accident and Spataro's death, apparently at the hands of Madame Dombreux, constituted a coherent, not to say elegant, solution to several related problems. You could say they were actions forced upon us. The attack on you and Ennis was clumsy by comparison. I did not sanction it. There will be repercussions, you may be assured, for those who instigated it. But there it is. I still have power. My resources, however, are undeniably diminished. I am the functioning arm of an empire that no longer exists. The Kaiser's realm has shrunk to a castle in the Netherlands. So, what end do I

serve now? It is an important question, as much for you as for me.'

'Why should I . . . give a damn?'

'Because you impress me, Max. You are single-minded, courageous and resourceful. We would work well together. Many of my people think you are as big a threat to their survival as your father was. They will not allow such a threat to hang above them. But if you come over to us, the threat is dissolved. You enjoy my protection. You join my secret army. You become one of my lieutenants.'

'Not . . . in a million years.'

'Do not decide so hastily. Rest here and recover. And while you do so, reflect. You can trust no one except me. I speak the truth. Everyone else dissembles, one way or the other. Oh, there is your tame mechanic, of course, Twentyman. He is loyal to you, I admit. That makes him vulnerable. What would you be willing to do to guarantee his continued well-being? Think about that also. A man of principle is always compromised by his friendships. For myself, I have no friends, no lovers, no confidants. I learnt the hard way that I could afford no such entanglements.'

Max stared hard at where he judged Lemmer's eyes to be. 'Go to hell.'

'If there is one, I undoubtedly will. But there is much to be done before I confront the hereafter. To business. Your clothes are in that wardrobe over there.' Lemmer pointed his finger against the light. 'I have examined the contents of your pockets. The list is interesting, is it not? Henry was certainly budgeting for an expensive, not to say extravagant, purchase. Whatever can it have been? The Trust and the Chinese box were to be expected. But I was surprised he had knowledge of the Contingencies Memorandum. He really was prepared to burn his boats, wasn't he? And then there is the key.'

Max groaned. There, before him, held in Lemmer's fingers, was the key Max had found in the bedpost in his father's room at the Majestic.

'Still looking for the lock it fits, are you, Max? I'll make you an offer. Find it before I do and you can have the key back. Provided I have first sight of whatever Henry locked away. Work with me. Not for, but with. You'll enjoy it, I promise, just as you enjoyed the

war. I know, I know. It should have been terrible, and so it was. But still it raised you up, didn't it? It should have destroyed you. But you were forged by the fire, not consumed. I see that in you as clear as noon. It is a great asset. Don't waste it. Learn to use it. Let me teach you how to use it. I am sorry Henry had to die. I can help you make more of his death than anything simple revenge can bring you.'

'When I'm strong enough . . .'

'Yes?'

'I'll find you . . . and kill you.'

'Bravo.' Lemmer patted Max on the shoulder. 'You prove my point for me, Max. Don't worry. You'll come to see the sense of my argument, I'm sure of it. Go back to sleep. But remember what I've said. I must go now. Doctor Wahlen has other calls to make. I hope we will see each other again. The means of communicating with me will be made known to you in due course. I will kill you if you force me to. But I will not betray you. That is my pledge.'

As Lemmer stood up, Max made a feeble grab for the hand in which he held the key. But he was far too slow. He grasped only thin air and felt himself falling from the bed.

Lemmer caught him and heaved him back, panting, against the pillows. 'Rest, Max. Rest and reflect. Then you will understand. Then you will know I'm right. *Gute Nacht.*'

Sᴀᴍ's ꜰɪʀsᴛ ꜰᴜʟʟʏ ꜰᴜɴᴄᴛɪᴏɴɪɴɢ ᴅᴀʏ ɪɴ ᴄʜᴀʀɢᴇ ᴏꜰ ᴛʜᴇ delegation garage, which occupied converted stables at the rear of the Majestic, was bound to be a busy and demanding one. There was no prospect of being able to visit Max until the evening. An early telephone call to the Hôtel Dieu had set Sam's mind at rest, however. Max's fever had broken. He was much improved. He was, Sam gathered, out of the woods.

Appleby had received similar tidings and had decided, in a moment of soft-heartedness, to deliver them to Sam in person. But, when he found the delegation's new chief mechanic whistling while he worked, he guessed those tidings had already reached him.

'I'll call in on him later today, Twentyman. Any message?'

'Let those nurses tend him like a babe, Mr A. That'd be my advice. I'll see him as soon as I've finished here, which won't be till late, judging by the way your drivers hammer these engines.'

'They're not *my* drivers.'

'Aren't you part of the establishment, then, sir?'

'A moot point, Twentyman. Decidedly moot.'

'What about Brigham?' Sam asked, lowering his voice, though he hardly needed to in the general hubbub of the maintenance bay.

'The matter's being dealt with, as I'll be sure to tell Max. I'll also tell him about Bukayev. Suffocated before he was dumped in the canal, according to the pathologist.'

'Does Miss Bukayeva know?'

'Zamaron will inform her.'

'The poor chick. Will Zamaron let Madame Dombreux go now?'

'Things don't happen that quickly, Twentyman. You'll have to be patient. And so will Max.'

Some things did happen quickly, however, as Appleby discovered when he returned to his office. A summons had arrived in his absence. The Permanent Under-Secretary wanted to see him. 'Without delay, sir,' Appleby's secretary informed him with some emphasis.

Lord Hardinge of Penshurst, His Majesty's Permanent Under-Secretary of State for Foreign Affairs, received Appleby in his first-floor office at the nearby Hôtel Astoria, where he enjoyed some respite from the toing and froing of the Majestic. He was a tall, lean, quietly spoken man of austere bearing, who wore authority like a favourite coat. He clearly regarded Appleby as a form of life he should not properly be required to engage with. But he was too polite to say so.

Appleby was aware that Hardinge had overseen the creation of the Secret Service back in 1909. C was therefore beholden to him and he was obviously not a man to be trifled with. Whether he regretted allowing the establishment of an autonomous intelligence-gathering organization under the aegis of the Foreign Office was bemusingly unclear.

'Do you know why I agreed to C's proposal that you be sent here, Appleby?' Hardinge opened.

'My understanding was that you were anxious to avoid secret information finding its way to other delegations and interested parties, my lord.'

'Indeed. For what would such leaking of information constitute?'

'It would undermine confidence in the delegation's decision-making procedures.'

'And if it became publicly known?'

'There would be a scandal.'

'Precisely, Appleby. A scandal. The avoidance of such is, so far as I am concerned, the principal purpose your posting here was intended to serve.'

'As to—'

'I can hardly imagine a greater scandal than the implication of a senior civil servant in a multiple murder inquiry, can you?'

Appleby offered a pained grimace by way of reply.

'Well, can you?'

'No, my lord.'

'I read your memorandum concerning Brigham and the allegations of Miss Bukayeva with considerable perturbation. I intended to discuss the matter with you today. It did not occur to me that you would seek to question Brigham directly before we had had that discussion.'

Appleby shifted uneasily in his chair. He would have liked to light his pipe, if only to serve as a distraction. But he hardly felt he could in Hardinge's headmasterly presence.

'Brigham came to see me last night, after your meeting with him at the Embassy. He felt you had exceeded your authority by interrogating him and I'm bound to say I agree with him, as I shall make clear to C in due course. Would you care to defend yourself against the charge?'

Appleby cleared his throat. 'It's sometimes important to question a suspect before he has a chance to prepare himself.'

'A suspect in what?'

'I've yet to establish the full extent of Brigham's involvement in the recent spate of violent deaths, but I'm certain he is involved.'

'Sir Henry Maxted, Raffaele Spataro, Walter Ennis and Igor Bukayev. They are the spate you refer to?'

'Yes. Along with my late assistant, Thomas Lamb.'

'In your memorandum, you mentioned a man called Fritz Lemmer, whom you described, somewhat melodramatically, as "the Kaiser's spymaster".'

'It's hardly melodramatic, my lord, merely accurate.'

'In essence, you believe Brigham to be one of Lemmer's spies?'

'I regard it as highly probable.'

'How would you wish to proceed?'

'I'd like him placed in some form of detention, my lord, so I can question him at length and in detail.'

'But who is to detain him, here in Paris?'

'If you withdrew his immunity, the French police could—'

'Absolutely not. The precedent such a move would set is un-conscionable. There will be no detention, Appleby. The evidence you have amassed against Brigham is insufficient to justify any-thing of the kind. His liaison with Miss Bukayeva certainly demonstrates poor judgement on his part, but there is no reason – no reason whatever – to believe her version of events over his.'

'I can't agree, my lord. The circumstances of the discovery of Bukayev's body clearly suggest Brigham acted at the very least as a messenger for whoever murdered him.'

'And that would be Lemmer, or those acting on Lemmer's behalf?'

'Yes.'

Hardinge sighed. 'If I allowed the French to take Brigham into custody, I'd be reading a *Figaro* editorial alleging our delegation was a nest of spies before the week was out. And by next week the work of the delegation would have disintegrated in the face of a *Daily Mail*-orchestrated witch-hunt. You seem to have no conception of how serious the ramifications of this matter could be.'

'I certainly don't think Brigham was Lemmer's only recruit in Whitehall, my lord.'

'No. I'm sure you don't.'

'The ramifications *are* serious.'

'They would be, if I gave you your head.'

'With respect, my lord, I—'

'Don't tell me you take your orders from C, Appleby. I'm well aware of that. I'm also well aware of the source of C's funding, for the simple reason that I control it. Brigham is an incorrigible philanderer. He has behaved very foolishly, but not, I judge, traitorously, far less treasonably. I have sent him back to London to cool his heels.'

'You've sent him to London?'

'I have. He can do no harm there, even supposing he has a mind to. I cannot say he was any happier to go than you appear to be to hear of his going. But I'm satisfied it was for the best.'

'Well, my lord, I—'

'Have grave reservations. Yes, no doubt you do. But I am bound to take a circumspect view. The Germany Brigham may or may not have spied for no longer exists. I think even you will agree Lemmer is not acting on behalf of the present government in Berlin. I am therefore satisfied that the integrity of the conference is not threatened by the tragic consequences of whatever manner of falling-out there may have been among his former acolytes.'

Appleby summoned a deep breath, and with it his courage, then said, 'I believe you ignore this matter at your peril, my lord.'

'I am not ignoring it, Appleby. I am setting it to one side. If C decides to have Brigham questioned in London, I will not stand in his way. But here I must have quietude. The business of the conference demands it. Is that clear?'

Appleby frowned heavily. 'It is, my lord.'

'Assess the situation for C's benefit as you see fit. But I want no further harassment of senior civil servants, or minor ones, come to that, without my explicit prior approval, which you can assume will not be forthcoming. Is that also clear?'

Appleby nodded grimly. 'Yes, my lord.'

'Excellent.' Hardinge permitted himself a thin smile. 'Then I'll bid you good morning.'

THE DOCTOR WHO CAME ON DUTY ON MONDAY MORNING
expressed his pleasure and satisfaction at Max's emergence from
his fever. 'You have strength, *monsieur*. It is not so common since the
war. You will be leaving us on two feet, I think. *Très bien, très bien.*'

Max made no reference to his nocturnal visit from Dr Wahlen.
He knew Lemmer was right. No one would credit such a story.
Telling it might only delay Max's discharge from the hospital. And
he wanted to be out of there as soon as possible.

A tentative foray as far as the door of his room proved he would
not be striding out just yet, however. The nurse who helped him
back into bed recommended *bouillon de boeuf* for breakfast and a
lot more rest. It was not what Max wanted to hear. But he was in
no position to contest the logic of it.

Burley assured Max that Appleby would be along to see him later.
But his first visitor of the day turned out to be Schools Morahan.
Even sitting down, he seemed to tower over the bed. Max was
pleased to see him, though. And Morahan was evidently pleased to
see him as well.

'I was more or less convinced you'd get yourself killed, Max. I'm
glad you didn't quite pull it off. Malory sends her love.'

'What about Ireton?'

'We've had a cable. He's staying away in light of what happened
to you and Ennis. Especially Ennis. *Deem it wise to lie low until all
blows over.*' Morahan smiled mirthlessly. 'Travis never was at his
best under fire.'

'Where did he cable from?'

'Nowhere you'll want to follow him to. If Carver quizzes you, as I'm sure he will, refer him to me. I guess you don't need to know who in the British delegation Travis spoke to now, though, anyhow. It was Ennis who blabbed, right?'

'Wrong, actually. I—'

Max broke off as one of the more senior nurses entered in full sail. 'Your ... *notaire* ... is here, Monsieur Maxted. *Une affaire urgente*. You want to see him?'

'Found yourself a lawyer, Max?' Morahan asked.

'Apparently. Yes. Please show him in. Whoever he is.'

The nurse frowned and went to fetch him. 'I'll leave you to it,' said Morahan. 'If there's anything I can do for you when you get out of here, you be sure to let me know.'

Morahan's helpfulness continued to puzzle Max, but he had no time to consider it further. The lawyer who bustled in as Morahan left was, to his surprise, none other than the Maxteds' family solicitor, Gilbert Mellish, a long way from his normal Surrey stamping ground.

'Mr Mellish! What are you doing here?'

'They told me at the Mazarin you were in hospital following a shooting, Mr Maxted. I'm relieved to find you looking so well.'

'I was lucky. But what I meant was: what are you doing in Paris?'

Mellish, considerably breathless from rushing around the city and climbing the stairs of the Hôtel Dieu, subsided into the bed-side chair, cradling a bulging briefcase on his lap. 'Does your mother know of your injury, Mr Maxted?'

'No. And I'd like to keep it that way.'

Mellish squirmed uneasily, but did not dispute the matter. 'As you please.'

'You still haven't told me why you're here.'

'Your father appointed you executor of his will, Mr Maxted. I assumed you'd attend his funeral and I planned to inform you afterwards, though obviously not quite this—'

'He appointed me executor?' Max was as astonished as he supposed he must look.

'Indeed.'

'Not Ashley?'

'No. Though that reminds me . . .' Mellish fished a letter out of his briefcase. 'Sir Ashley asked me to deliver this to you.'

Max took the letter and thumbed it open. It was in Ashley's handwriting on Gresscombe Place headed paper, dated 28th March – the day after their father's funeral and presumably the day Ashley had made the unwelcome discovery that Max, not he, was executor of Sir Henry's estate.

Dear James,

I am sorry that we parted in Paris on somewhat acrimonious terms. I have subsequently regretted implying that I would not allow you to use any Gresscombe land for your proposed flying school. I would certainly not wish to stand in your way where that is concerned. Lydia and I both—

Max cast the letter aside, unfinished. 'How did Ashley take the news, Mr Mellish?'

'He was . . . surprised.'

'And my sister-in-law?'

'I believe she expressed some doubt about whether you would want to accept the appointment.'

'I have a choice?'

'You do.' Mellish leant forward. 'I should perhaps explain that beyond the executorship you are not mentioned in Sir Henry's will. There is no bequest to you.'

'Everything goes to Ashley?'

'Bar an allowance to your mother, yes. I have a copy for your perusal.' Mellish flourished the document. 'Shall I?' He made to place it on the bedside cabinet. Max nodded his assent. 'You can, er, study it at your leisure.'

'I expected no inheritance, Mr Mellish. My father was a firm believer in the principle of primogeniture.'

'Can I take it you'll act as executor?'

'I'm a poor choice. As I'm sure my brother and sister-in-law have already told you. Frankly, it's a baffling decision on Pa's part. He gave me no inkling of it.'

'Nor me, Mr Maxted. He revised his will to accommodate your appointment as recently as the twelfth of this month.'

'So that's why he went back to England at such short notice.'

'Ah. You knew of the visit?'

'Only that it occurred. Not the reason. Until now.'

'There may have been several reasons. I've had a letter from the curator of the county museum.' Mellish made another extraction from his briefcase. 'It appears that after visiting my office on the twelfth Sir Henry proceeded to Guildford, where he reclaimed some ancient artefacts loaned to the museum by his father. The curator wants to know if they're likely to be returned to their keeping following Sir Henry's death. That would be a matter for, er, his executor, of course.'

'Ancient artefacts, you say?'

'Sumerian cylinder-seals, to be precise.'

'Seals?'

'Yes. You've seen them?'

'No.' Max sighed. 'And I doubt the curator will again.'

'Oh?'

'I think Pa probably sold them.'

'Really?' Mellish looked pained as well as puzzled. 'Well, you may wish to tell the curator that.'

'I can't act as executor, Mr Mellish. I don't have the time. Judging by his letter, Ashley's anxious to persuade me to renounce the role, so I may as well oblige him.' A few short weeks ago, Max would have fought tooth and nail for his and Sam's flying school. Now it hardly seemed to matter. It belonged to a different world – a different life. 'Where do I sign?'

Mellish adjusted his glasses and peered at Max. 'Sign what, Mr Maxted?'

'Whatever I have to sign to give up the executorship.'

'Well, I . . .'

'You said I had a choice.'

'Indeed. I can certainly prepare a letter of renunciation. You'd need to sign it in my presence, or more appropriately in the presence of some other notary public, so that it can be formally lodged with the probate registry. But that may not be necessary. I

can handle all administrative matters pertaining to the settlement of Sir Henry's estate if you instruct me to do so. The demands on your time and attention would be minimal.'

'Even minimal's probably more than I can manage.'

'But there is something else you have to consider, Mr Maxted. In many respects, it's why I've travelled to Paris. This.' Yet another document emerged from the briefcase, clutched in Mellish's sausage-fingered hand. 'Sir Henry did more than revise his will when he came to see me on the twelfth. He dictated and signed quite specific instructions relating to an item of his property not mentioned in the will. Mentioned or not, of course, it still forms part of Sir Ashley's inheritance, but, as executor, it falls to you to take the steps required to classify it as an asset of the deceased.'

Max grimaced. 'What?'

'Sir Henry lodged the item – or items – in a safe-deposit box at a bank here in Paris. But he did so under an assumed name, hence the procedural difficulty. The letter he left with me overcomes that difficulty, however. It supplies the name and address of the bank, the number of the safe-deposit box and his pseudonym: Farngold. That should be sufficient to gain you access. There will have been a key also. Did you come across one amongst his possessions that might fit such a box?'

Max's heart sank. Oh, yes, he had come across the key. Hidden, discovered . . . and lost. 'I don't have it,' he said levelly.

'No matter. The will identifies you as his executor and the letter authorizes you to take charge of the contents of the box. As soon as you're fit enough to leave the hospital, I would recommend you contact' – Mellish consulted the letter – 'la Banque Ornal and claim the property, whatever it might be.'

'Pa gave no clue?'

'None. But he left me in little doubt that it was very important to him. And possibly . . .'

'Yes?'

'To you as well, Mr Maxted, if I'm to be frank.'

'He said that?'

'No. It was an impression I had. But a forceful impression, certainly. The use of a pseudonym is also indicative of . . .' Mellish

cleared his throat and fell silent, unable, it seemed, to frame his idea of what such a precaution might point to.

'Where is la Banque Ornal, Mr Mellish?'

Mellish glanced at the letter. 'Rue Vivienne, second arrondissement.'

'Not far.'

'No? Well, once you've recovered sufficiently, I suggest—'

'Hang that, Mr Mellish.' Max pushed himself up, threw back the blankets and swung his feet to the floor. 'I'm going now. There's no time to be lost.'

TIME TO BE LOST OR NOT, MAX DID NOT ACHIEVE AN instantaneous departure from the Hôtel Dieu. The doctor who had congratulated him on riding out his fever was fetched to caution him against leaving. 'You need to rest, *monsieur*. *Se reposer.*' It did not help Max's cause that Mellish urged the same. 'Leave it until tomorrow at least, Mr Maxted. I can wait.'

But Max could not wait. And Mellish admitted that nothing short of a personal visit to the bank would suffice. Eventually, a compromise was agreed. Max would not actually discharge himself, merely travel to the bank with Mellish, then return to the hospital.

As it turned out, Burley went with them. Having failed to contact Appleby by telephone, he decided it made no sense to guard a room whose occupant had left it. Max suffered the indignity of being conveyed in a wheelchair down in the lift to the ground floor, then along the corridors to the main entrance, where a taxi was waiting.

Quitting the chair as he exited into the open air, he was relieved to discover that he could walk short distances without difficulty, despite shortness of breath and a disquieting rubberiness in his legs. He felt better just for being out of hospital, though the coldness of the weather came as a shock. They squeezed into the taxi and set off.

Burley did not accompany them into the bank, whose ornate frontage seemed to persuade him that Max would be safe enough

300

inside. The premises were certainly imposing, with high ceilings, classical frescos, *grand siècle* furnishings and lavishly marbled acreages of space.

They were received courteously, but the response to their request, once it had been understood, was far from speedy. They were kept waiting for close to half an hour before being ushered into the office of *le directeur*. Mellish chose to interpret the delay as no more than typical French dilatoriness, but Max had begun to fear a more sinister explanation. The involvement of the bank's senior officer did nothing to reassure him.

There were elaborate introductions. The director's surname was Charretier-Ornal. He was evidently some semi-detached member of the founding family. He did not look like a man who had worked his way up through the business counting francs and cashing cheques. There was nothing remotely clerical about him. His manner was smooth and confident, with the barest undertow of discomposure.

He read English as well as he spoke it and swiftly perused the various documents Mellish presented: the will, the death certificate, the letter of authorization. He tut-tutted as if he had detected a discrepancy before returning them, prompting Mellish to ask if something was wrong.

'The documents indicate that the Monsieur Farngold who rented box number 2576 was actually Sir Henry Maxted, who died on the twenty-first of this month,' said Charretier-Ornal, speaking slowly and carefully. 'That is your contention, *messieurs*?'

'It's not a contention,' said Max. 'It's a fact.'

'*Oui*. A fact. As you say, Monsieur Maxted. My condolences to you. I read of Sir Henry's death in the newspaper. A great tragedy.'

'You realized he was the man known to your bank as Farngold?'

'*Non, non. Pas du tout*. Monsieur Farngold was a customer like any other. We did not know it was . . . *un pseudonyme*. I never met him. The transaction was . . . routine. There was no reason for us to question his identity.'

'Well,' said Mellish, 'I trust you accept that, as Sir Henry's executor, Mr Maxted is entitled to access to box 2576.'

'*Bien sûr*. I accept it. But you must understand, *messieurs*, that

the conditions we agreed with Monsieur Farngold – Sir Henry – were simple as regards to access. They were our standard conditions. He would unlock the box in private using the key supplied to him when he first rented it.'

'We don't have the key,' said Max.

'But you can open the box,' said Mellish. 'There must be provision for that to be done if the key is lost.'

'*Mais oui*. There is provision. But that is not the problem.'

'What *is* the problem?' Max pressed.

Charretier-Ornal pursed his lips and frowned. A moment passed. Then he said, 'There was access to the box earlier this morning.'

'What?'

'A man claiming to be Monsieur Farngold came here at' – he consulted a note – 'ten thirty. He gave my staff no reason to doubt he was who he said he was. His signature matched the specimen. He had the key to the box. He was given access to it. He left at' – another consultation – 'ten fifty.'

It was as Max had feared. Lemmer had got there before them. He sank his face in his hand. 'Oh God,' he murmured.

'I must emphasize that we proceeded strictly according to the conditions of use. There was no ... *déviation. Voyez vous-même.*'

Charretier-Ornal thrust under Max's nose a form bearing a signature in the name of H. Farngold that undeniably reminded Max of his father's handwriting. Another form swiftly followed: the specimen. They were a close match. Not exact – for how could they be? – but close enough to satisfy a credulous bank clerk on a humdrum Monday morning. Max almost felt sorry for the blustering director. They had all been outclassed.

'If the man was an impostor—'

'He was either that or a ghost, *monsieur*.' Max smiled grimly at Charretier-Ornal. 'Take your pick.'

'A friend of your father, perhaps, obeying some ... dying wish.'

'My father died in a fall from a roof, *monsieur*. He had no time for dying wishes.'

'This is all highly unsatisfactory,' said Mellish. 'You appear to

have allowed an unknown third party access to Sir Henry's property.'

Charretier-Ornal scowled at the implication of incompetence. 'Sir Henry must have given the third party, as you call him, the key – *et le pseudonyme*. We cannot be responsible.'

'As to that, it'll be for—'

'Never mind who's responsible,' Max cut in. 'Did the man claiming to be Farngold empty the box?'

Charretier-Ornal shrugged. 'I cannot say. The boxes are opened in private, as I explained to you. We do not know what they contain.'

'Can we see what this one contains now?'

Silence briefly intervened. Charretier-Ornal looked momentarily indecisive. Then he said, '*Oui*. Let us all go and see.'

Charretier-Ornal spoke to someone on his telephone – too quickly for Max to follow what was said – then they descended to the bank's vault. A clerk who had been hovering outside the director's office fell in with them to unlock various doors along the way. A second man, less smartly dressed and introduced by Charretier-Ornal as '*notre serrurier* – our locksmith' joined them en route. Charretier-Ornal set a brisk, impatient pace, before realizing that the corpulent Mellish and the ailing Max could not keep up with him.

'You do not look well, Monsieur Maxted,' he remarked.

'I feel better than I look.'

'That is good. May I repeat my condolences on your loss.'

'You can repeat them, by all means. But they won't help.'

They reached the room housing the safe-deposit boxes. Three walls were lined with numbered, lockable steel hatches of varying sizes. The clerk had a key for the hatch numbered 2576 and removed the box that was inside.

The box, also of steel, was about three feet deep, a foot wide and a foot high. The clerk laid it on the table in the centre of the room. He said something to Charretier-Ornal in French as he did so.

'What was that?' Max queried.

Charretier-Ornal grimaced. 'He said it feels light.'

'Is he the one who brought the man claiming to be Farngold down here earlier?'

'He is.'

'Can he describe him?'

There was an exchange in French. Charretier-Ornal's glum expression remained glum throughout. Then: 'A man of sixty years or about, he thinks. English, he also thinks. Not fat. Not thin. Not tall. Not short. There was nothing to remember about him. Grey hair. Beard. He spoke quietly.' The director shrugged. '*C'est tout.*'

'Do you know who he is, Mr Maxted?' Mellish asked.

Max nodded. 'I believe I do.' He looked at the locksmith. '*Ouvrez la boîte, s'il vous plaît.*'

It required a wave of the hand from Charretier-Ornal before the locksmith swung into action. Within a few minutes, he had removed the lock. The clerk prepared to raise the lid. And they all stepped forward to see what might be inside.

It was as Max had known it would be.

ACCORDING TO SAM, WHO HAD SEEN A LOT OF PILOTS COME and, sadly, go, one of Max's most valuable assets was his optimism. 'It might sound stupid to you, sir,' he had once said under a cerulean sky into which Max was about to take off, 'but I reckon those who expect to survive usually do.'

Well, Max had survived the war, true to Sam's prediction, albeit half of it in a POW camp. And he was by nature an optimist, sometimes to his own surprise. Sitting in the vault of la Banque Ornal that morning, staring at the empty safe-deposit box on the table in front of him, he wondered how long it would be before he finally abandoned the notion of bringing his father's murderers to justice. He should perhaps have despaired there and then.

He did not contribute to the increasingly tetchy discussion between Mellish and Charretier-Ornal about responsibility for allowing an impostor access to the safe-deposit box. It was a redundant debate. The fox had had his run of the hen-coop. And he had not even left a few feathers behind him.

How had Lemmer discovered the pseudonym Sir Henry had used? How had he been able to forge his signature so convincingly? How, come to that, had he known which bank Sir Henry had used? The questions only illustrated the scope of Lemmer's power. He was always at least one step ahead of his pursuers. Several steps, in this case.

'I'm not going back to the hospital,' Max announced as he and Mellish, the latter still grumbling pointlessly about the bank's

305

ineptitude, walked out to rejoin Burley. 'The doctor said all I need is rest. I can get that at the Mazarin.'

'What?' Mellish gaped at him.

'I'm not going back to the hospital.'

'That's surely unwise,' said Mellish.

'*Definitely* unwise,' Burley contributed.

'You're right, of course.' Max drew in a lungful of Parisian air and knew that, however short of his best he currently was, retreating to a bed at the Hôtel Dieu was not to be countenanced. 'But then unwise is what I mean to be.'

Burley had not been idle during Max and Mellish's sojourn at the bank. He had telephoned Appleby again and this time got through to him. He made another call when they reached the Mazarin. Appleby, he reported, had a lot to discuss with Max, wherever he chose to rest, and would be with him within the hour.

The hour passed swiftly, as Max took a gingerly bath, applied a fresh bandage to his wound, and recovered as best he could from the disproportionate effort involved. He would have told any other man behaving as he was that he was being a damn fool. But he could not help that. He was not going to give in, even to his own frailty.

It was hard to tell whether Appleby's downcast expression when he arrived was due to Max's appearance or the tidings he had brought. 'Do you want to know how you look?' he asked as he slumped down in the only armchair in the room and watched Max lower himself on to the edge of the bed.

Max came to rest with a wince. 'No.'

'Good. Because I've quite enough bad news to deliver as it is.'

'You'd better get on with it, then.'

So Appleby did, relating the discovery of Igor Bukayev's body in the Canal de l'Ourcq, Nadia Bukayeva's allegations against Brigham and Brigham's subsequent departure for London. 'I've been officially warned off, Max. Brigham's boss outranks my boss. My hands are tied.'

'It sounds like Sam's been busy on my behalf while I've been laid

up. I must thank him. And I must proffer my condolences to Nadia as well.'

'Well, perhaps you can console each other for your misfortunes. Although I wouldn't try anything too energetic in your present condition. Burley tells me you think it was Lemmer who emptied Sir Henry's safe-deposit box. In person, would that be?'

'Maybe. I'm not sure.' Max was not ready to tell anyone, even Appleby, about his encounter with Lemmer. He was not sure Appleby would believe him. He had difficulty believing it himself. 'Without whatever the box contained, though, and with Ennis dead, Brigham's the only possible source of information about Lemmer's network. If you can't squeeze anything out of him, I'll have to.'

'How?'

'I think I can find a way under his defences.' Brigham's weakness was his belief that he was Max's father. That was what Max would play on, reluctant as he was to do so. 'Leave it to me. I'll follow him to London and give it my best shot.'

'How soon will you be fit enough to travel?'

'I'll go on tonight's sleeper.'

'Being shaken around on that won't do you much good. And then there's the Channel crossing.'

'Is there a storm forecast?'

'Not that I know of.'

'Then don't worry about me. I only need you to do a couple of things for me.'

'What?'

'Get me the gun you promised before I leave.'

'I didn't promise anything.'

Max gave Appleby a straight look. 'Just get it, OK?'

Appleby sighed. 'Very well.'

'And can you organize the ticket?'

'All right. But you'll be on your own, you know. In every sense of the word.'

'Oh, I know. But that doesn't matter. Actually, it's how I prefer it.'

*

307

Max had a meal sent up to him and planned to take a nap afterwards, before going to the Majestic to speak to Sam. In the event, he plunged into a deep sleep and was woken by Sam coming to see him at the end of his working day. It was already early evening. Anxious as he was to set off, time was slipping through his fingers like sand.

'You should still be in the hospital, sir,' Sam said, frowning at Max with obvious concern. 'Mr Appleby said you were off to London tonight. You never are, are you?'

'Needs must, Sam.'

'You're going after Brigham?'

'Someone has to.'

'But you're not well enough. It's plain to see.'

Max strode less than fluidly across to the dressing-table and peered at himself in the mirror. 'A little pale, I grant you. A steak supper will see me right. Care to join me?'

'More than happy to, sir. But there's something I have to tell you first.'

'Appleby filled me in on everything, Sam. You did well and I'm very grateful. Finding Bukayev as you did can't have been pleasant. You can tell me all about it over a stiff drink.'

'This is something Mr Appleby doesn't know about, sir.'

'It is?'

'And in the circumstances . . . I don't think it'll wait.'

As they left the Mazarin, the reception clerk presented Max with a letter that had been handed in for him. The envelope contained his ticket for the sleeper to London and a note from Appleby. *I will meet you with the other at the station tonight.*

'What's the "other", sir?' Sam asked, craning over his shoulder as they exited on to the street.

'A bath-chair, I expect. Everyone's convinced I'm an invalid.' Max suspected Sam would worry about him all the more if he knew he was going to be carrying a gun.

'But you *are* an invalid, sir, that's the trouble. Maybe I ought to go with you.'

'And walk out on your new job? I wouldn't hear of it. I'll see my doctor when I get to London. He can do any patching-up that's needed.'

'You'll have a relapse if you overdo it.'

'I'm not letting Brigham off the hook, Sam. You may as well accept it. Now, find us a cab, there's a good fellow. Ordinarily, I'd walk to the Plaza Athénée, but as it is . . .'

'I'll find one, sir. You just stay there.'

Baltazar Ribeiro was dressing for dinner when they were admitted to his suite at the Plaza Athénée. His delight at seeing Max up and about was considerable, although it was swiftly followed by concern. 'Sit, sit,' he said, ushering Max to a couch.

'Before he falls down, eh, *senhor*?' said Sam. 'I have tried to tell him.'

'And as I've already told Sam, I can't afford to rest. I've lost enough time lying in that hospital already.'

'Drink a little brandy,' said Ribeiro, fumbling with a bottle and some glasses. 'It gives strength when you need it.'

Max did not argue and accepted a tot. 'I expect you can guess why we're here, Baltazar,' he said, swallowing some down.

'Of course. I meant what I said to Mr Twentyman yesterday. It is time to share the secret with you, Max, and I am glad to have the chance – glad because you are well enough to be told.' Ribeiro drew up a couple of armchairs, one for himself, one for Sam, and sat down. He drank some of his brandy and gazed earnestly at Max. 'Henry was my friend. I did not feel I could tell you this when we first met because he had trusted me to tell no one. But so much has happened since then that I think now you should know. Still, it is not easy. I feel I am . . . betraying him.'

'I understand,' said Max. 'But if this information helps me bring his murderers to justice . . .'

'I do not see how it can do that. But at least you will know what was in his mind. In truth, it is a simple story. *O amor*. Love. He was planning a future for himself and Corinne Dombreux. He was not a rich man. His wealth was in the estate in England. He needed money of his own to give them a comfortable life somewhere. And I . . . suggested a way to get it.' Ribeiro frowned at his own folly – or that of Sir Henry. 'I inherited land in Amazonas from my elder brother, Francisco, land that had once made our family rich from the rubber it produced. But the business went into decline around the turn of the century because of competition from Asian plantations. Now the land is nothing except jungle. An Englishman is to blame for this, I must tell you. A man called Wickham smuggled thousands of rubber seeds out of Brazil that were used to start growing the crop in Malaya. Our monopoly was broken. Our rubber trees grow wild, you must understand. We did not plant them. We could not compete with the close-grown Asian plantations. The riches . . . evaporated.'

'Baltazar, I don't quite—'

'Wait, wait. I will explain. Francisco had a plan. He believed plantation rubber could be successfully grown in Brazil. It only

310

required labour to clear the land and expert knowledge of how to cultivate the crop. He bought options on several neighbouring estates and sent a trusted man to Malaya to study how it was done. Then he died. And the war came. But the options stand. I inherited them from him. I have had discussions with representatives of two large American corporations who are interested in investing in Francisco's scheme. Motor cars are the transport of the future, Max. One day everyone will want to own one. And every car has four tyres made of rubber. This could make me rich again many times over. It could have made Henry rich too. If he had lived.'

'You persuaded him to put some money into this venture?'

'I offered him the opportunity, as a friend. Firestone and Ford – there now, I have told you who the American corporations are – do not want the price of rubber to be set by Britain, France and the Netherlands, the imperial powers who control the rubber-growing areas of south-east Asia. They fear a cartel, with the price going up and up. A separate source of rubber, in Brazil, controlled by them, appeals to them greatly. They will pay handsomely to secure it. But I must take up the options if I am to be the one they pay. And for that I need liquid cash. I have some, of course. But not enough. I asked Henry if he would like to be my partner. He said yes. And he said he thought he could raise the rest of the cash we would need. I did not ask how. But I swear to you I did not think he meant to risk his life to do it.'

Max contemplated the irony of his father's fate. His relationship with Corinne was a late-life chance of happiness. Naturally, he wanted to give her all the luxuries she had been denied in recent times. Then Ribeiro came to him with a proposition that must have seemed heaven-sent. All he needed was his share of the investment. And so he turned his mind to such assets as he could trade in. It was a short list – and, as it turned out, a dangerous one. 'Where did he plan to take Corinne, Baltazar?'

'He did not say. Rio, maybe. He loved the city and would have enjoyed introducing her to it. With his share of the profit, he could have bought a grand mansion in Botafogo and a villa in Petrópolis to retreat to in the summer and a private art collection and a

racehorse and more fine clothes and jewellery than Madame Dombreux could ever have worn.'

'Is this really rubber you're talking about – or gold?'

'Rubber *is* gold to Henry Ford and Harvey Firestone, Max. They will pay whatever I ask.'

'Will you still go through with it?'

'If I can raise the money to buy the options, yes, I suppose I will. But I must be honest with you. There is profit and there is joy. They are not the same. Money is paper and the possessions you buy with it. Joy is in the spirit. And there is no joy for me in this now Henry is dead. Especially if I believe, as it seems I must, that he died because of my accursed scheme to make us both rich.'

'You shouldn't blame yourself. I'm sure my father wouldn't want you to.'

'No. He would not. He was a good man.'

'About Ennis, Baltazar . . .'

'*Sim?*'

'Sam tells me Ennis mentioned "contingencies".'

'Ah yes. He did. I do not know what he meant.'

'Does the phrase "Contingencies Memorandum" mean anything to you?'

Ribeiro shook his head. 'No. A document maybe. Something to do with the conference.'

'Something my father saw as a source of money, actually. But what exactly it was . . . or is . . .'

'I did not know he carried so many secrets. They did not weigh him down. I will say that. The last time I saw him, his heart was light.'

'Did he ever mention a man called Fritz Lemmer to you?'

'Lemmer?' Ribeiro frowned. 'Yes. I think he did. Not recently, though. Years ago, when we first knew each other, in Rio.'

'What did he say?'

'*Meu Deus!* It is so long ago. But I do remember the name. Yes, Lemmer. What was it? What was it Henry used to say?' Ribeiro stroked his moustache as he cast his mind back. 'Somehow, I think, he was involved with an assassination attempt against the Tsarevich

312

in Japan. Yes. Japan. That is where Henry knew Lemmer. You know him also?'

'I'm beginning to. He's a dangerous man. As Pa discovered.'

'I am sorry I did not tell you the whole truth when you first came to see me.'

'It wouldn't have made any difference, Baltazar. It wasn't your rubber venture that got my father killed. It's what he did to fund it.'

'Rio has the most beautiful racecourse in the world, you know, with the mountains and the bay and the clear, clear light.' Ribeiro shook his head in mourning for times past. 'Such days we had there, Henry and I.' He sighed. 'He always liked long odds. It was a weakness of his. I believe you may have inherited it.'

'You could be right.' Max rose slowly to his feet, gratified by the lack of pain in his side. 'I certainly wouldn't suggest you back me to win.'

'But you will run the course, even so?'

Max nodded. 'Oh yes. To the end.'

IN THE END, MAX HAD HIS STEAK AT THE GARE DU NORD. HE WAS tired, but oddly exhilarated. Lemmer had got the better of him so far, it was true, but Brigham was vulnerable for reasons Lemmer was almost certainly unaware of and Max was confident he could exploit the fact.

He asked Sam to tell Nadia where he was going and why. He had hoped to see her that evening, but the visit to Ribeiro had eaten into his reserves of time and energy. He also asked Sam to apologize to Mellish on his behalf for giving him no warning of his departure. Sam reiterated his opinion that a man in Max's condition should be going nowhere except the nearest hospital. But he knew Max was not going to change his mind. 'You are a stubborn so-and-so, sir, you truly are.'

Appleby arrived to see Max off with barely ten minutes to spare before the train left. Max had begun to suspect he was not going to be supplied with the promised gun, but Appleby had actually been delayed by a wrangle with Carver. 'It may be just as well you left the Hôtel Dieu when you did. He was hoping to interrogate you. Naturally, I claimed ignorance of where you'd gone.'

The revolver came with a box of ammunition. 'As far as anyone's to know,' Appleby emphasized, 'you bought this from an ex-serviceman in a bar.'

'I'll remember that.'

'What kind of marksman are you?'

'I wasn't bad with a machine-gun mounted on a Sopwith Camel.'

'Have you ever fired a revolver?'

'No. But don't worry. The other chap won't know that.'

He boarded the train with Sam, who stowed his bag in the first-class sleeping compartment Appleby had generously paid for. They shook hands before Sam got off. No words were spoken. They had said all that needed to be said. Max lit a cigarette, his first since the shooting, and waved from the window as jauntily as he could manage when the train drew out. Appleby had already left. Only Sam remained to wave back.

Max surprised himself by sleeping well as the train wound north through the night. A pink-streaked dawn was breaking as the ferry left Calais. His Channel crossing with Ashley seemed an age ago, though in fact only a week had passed since then. Time, as he knew from the contrast between active service and confinement as a POW, was a deceptively elastic commodity.

It was mid-morning when the train reached Victoria. Max felt sore and weary, despite all the sleep he had had. He made straight for the flat. Tuesday was not one of Mrs Harrison's cleaning days, so he was safe from mothering by her. A shivering fit on the ferry had subsided as rapidly as it had come and his wound seemed to be healing well. He was still several paces slower, in thought and movement, than he was used to being. He was not quite as firmly fixed in the world as he knew he should be. It was as if he was slightly drunk when in reality he was stone-cold sober – and deadly serious.

After a soothing bath and a closer shave than he could have managed on the train, he telephoned the Foreign Office. He was put through to Brigham's secretary. She was all plummy-toned unhelpfulness at first, but, after consulting Brigham at Max's insistence, she changed her tune. 'I'll put you through, Mr Maxted.'

'James?' Brigham sounded suspicious, as well he might, but also strangely solicitous. 'I'm glad to hear from you. How are you? I've been worried about you.'

'You know about the shooting?'

'Yes. I'd have come to see you if I hadn't been, well, banished in

315

effect, as a result of an absurd misunderstanding. Are you phoning from the hospital? It's an unusually good line.'

'No. I'm in London.'

'What? How's that?'

'I discharged myself. It wasn't a serious wound. I feel fine.'

'Really?'

'Really.'

'But what brings you to London?'

'You do, Brigham. I've been thinking about what you said when we met in Paris. I shouldn't have flown off the handle as I did.'

'Well, it's understandable that—'

'The fact is, I think I may have misjudged you.'

'You do?'

'It's an awkward situation. I'm sure you appreciate that.'

'Of course.'

'I wonder if we could meet and talk things through a little more calmly.'

'I'd be delighted to, my boy. When can you manage? How about lunch at my club? My unexpected return to London means I have an empty diary.'

'Lunch at your club would suit me very well.'

'Then I'll see you at the Athenaeum at one.'

Max donned an artificial persona as well as one of his better suits for lunch with Brigham. He would be reasonable, open-minded and receptive. He would imply that his brush with death had made him appreciate how justified – and genuine – Brigham's concern for his welfare was. As to their possible blood relationship, he would suggest it was a question they could never hope to answer conclusively; it might best be left open. They were men of the world. Not all marriages were happy. Not all adulteries were contemptible. Oh, yes, Max intended to be everything he needed to be to set Brigham at ease.

The ploy was remarkably successful. Brigham greeted him in the entrance hall of the Athenaeum warmly, if nervously. 'We got off

on the wrong foot last time, James. I can't tell you how pleased I am to have this chance of setting matters right.'

They went into the dining-room and sat at a window table. Brigham was well-known to the staff and other members. He was in his element, which was exactly where Max wanted him. Max ventured an apology for his behaviour when they had last met. Brigham assured him it was unnecessary. They relaxed over aperitifs. Brigham referred again to the 'misunderstanding' that had led to his departure from Paris. Max did not oblige him to elaborate.

Wine began to flow, though Max made sure more of it flowed down Brigham's throat than his. He recounted his war experiences. Brigham described the life of a diplomat. They both expended a deal of delicacy in discussing Brigham's friendship with Max's mother, while refraining from specifying what it might mean they were to each other. Neither of them mentioned Walter Ennis or Igor Bukayev. Neither spoke directly of the circumstances of Sir Henry's death.

Late in the meal, Max shifted the ground of their conversation, as he had always intended to. 'I think I may have threatened to kill you when we spoke that night in Paris, Brigham.'

'I trust you're not planning to now.' Brigham's voice was slightly slurred, his face flushed, but not with anger. He was, in fact, smiling broadly.

'No. My narrow escape at Notre-Dame has made me realize how foolishly I was behaving then.'

'I did warn you.'

'Indeed you did. I should have listened.'

'Paris may not look like a snake-pit, but that's what it is while this damned conference brings half the world's rogues to its boulevards. You were lucky not to be killed.'

'I know. Blundering around the city accusing every third person I met of involvement in Pa's murder wasn't the wisest way to proceed.'

'Probably not.'

'I've made myself a few enemies in the process.'

'Just as well you've left Paris, then.'

317

'Yes. But some of them have a long reach, I fear. One in particular.' Max lowered his voice and leant across the table. 'Fritz Lemmer.'

'Lemmer?' Brigham's eyes widened in an impressive show of surprise. 'You surely haven't crossed his path.'

'You know who he is?'

'The Secret Service do brief us from time to time, albeit reluctantly. Yes, I know who Lemmer is – and what he used to be – though I've always suspected his importance was overestimated.'

'Pa posed a threat to Lemmer. I believe that's why he was killed. And I believe it's why my life is in danger.'

'You think it is? I assumed you were just . . . in the firing line . . . when Ennis was shot.'

'I need help, Brigham. *Your* help.'

'Well, if there's anything I can do . . .'

'How do I get Lemmer off my back?'

'Perhaps, if you leave him alone, he'll leave you alone.'

'I'm afraid I may have got too close to him already for him to take that line. I think I have to send him some kind of message if I'm to persuade him to call off the dogs.'

'How do you propose to do that?'

'You know a lot of people, Brigham. I remember you told me I lacked connections. And you were right. But you have connections, don't you, built up over the years?'

'A good many, yes.'

'So, could you use them to communicate with Lemmer on my behalf?'

'With *Lemmer*?'

'Yes.'

Brigham sat back in his chair and frowned. 'You know what they say he did for the Kaiser. You know how he's supposed to operate. And now, as I understand it, he's on the run. You can't seriously suppose I have any way of approaching him.'

'Not even if my life depends on it?'

The frown deepened. 'I'd have to find someone who was – or knows someone who was – one of Lemmer's spies.'

'Or still is.'

'Exactly. Which is something no one in their right mind would admit, or even encourage another to infer. Good God, it's what Appleby more or less accused me of being on the basis of that Russian girl's crazy allegations.'

'I wouldn't ask how you managed it, Brigham. I'd simply be grateful. I just want Lemmer to understand I'm not a threat to him, as I'd be prepared to demonstrate in any way he asked.'

Brigham cocked his head in a show of perplexity. 'What do you mean by that, my boy?'

'I'm not sure. You probably know how these things work better than I do. It's just that I've begun to see the wisdom of the old saying: if you can't beat 'em, join 'em.'

'You surely wouldn't want to *join* Lemmer's operation.'

'Not as such, no. But it's effectively defunct, isn't it, with the Kaiser in exile? Lemmer's in no position to damage British interests, so doing him some small service would harm no one. You catch my drift?'

'I couldn't possibly advise you to strike terms with a man like Lemmer, James. The war may be over, but he's still an enemy of this country.'

'Friends and enemies can be a little hard to tell apart in the situation I find myself in.'

'I appreciate that, but—'

'Is there really nothing you can do for me? I don't know where else to turn.'

Surely Brigham would give ground now. Surely he could not ignore such an appeal. Max gazed pleadingly into the eyes of the man who so badly wanted to believe he was his father. And something shifted in Brigham's gaze. 'I suppose there are . . . avenues I could explore.'

'You'd be willing to do that for me?'

'Yes. But this is a delicate business.' Brigham craned forward and dropped his voice to a whisper. 'If we're to discuss it further, I'd prefer we did so in a more private setting.'

There was no one within earshot. Most of the other tables had emptied long since. But Max was not about to challenge Brigham's

logic. A more private setting would suit him very well. 'We could go to my place in town. It's in Mount Street.'

'I believe I may have been there.'

When and why Brigham had been there he was unlikely to say and Max had no wish to ask. The flat had originally been bought by Sir Henry as a pied-à-terre within easy reach of the Foreign Office. During his many long absences abroad, Lady Maxted had used it for visits to London to shop or see a play or . . . otherwise amuse herself. Max could have guessed that Brigham would have found his way there at some point, but he could not afford to indulge the distaste he felt at the thought.

'Listen, James, I ought to put in an appearance at the office this afternoon.' Brigham glanced at his watch. 'What's left of the afternoon, anyway. I'll call on you at the flat at, say, six o'clock. By then I'll have been able to give some thought to your problem. I want to help you, I really do. And I will if I possibly can.'

'I can't tell you what a relief it is to hear you say that.' What a consummate liar Max was becoming. He quite appalled himself.

'Don't worry, my boy. There's a way out of everything if you look hard enough.'

'I hope you're right.' And so another lie tripped from Max's lips. For there would be no way out of the trap he was setting for Brigham. He would see to that.

A SURPRISE AWAITED SAM IN THE REPAIR BAY OF THE garage at the Majestic that morning: a black Daimler, registration number HX 4344, with Hegg, one of the keener if not necessarily most proficient mechanics, at work on its clutch. Since, as far as Sam knew, Brigham had left Paris twenty-four hours earlier, the car's arrival was a puzzle he immediately set about solving.

'When did this come in, Billy?' he asked, joining Hegg by the open bonnet.

'Last night, just after you'd gone, Mr Twentyman. The gears are slippin' somethin' awful. But I'll fix that.'

'It's not one of our fleet cars.'

'No. The owner must've brought it with him from London. Decent bloke. None of that shoutin' and stampin' you get from some of—'

'You met him?'

'Yeah. Last night, like I say.'

'You *met* the owner? Here? Last night?'

Hegg scratched his bristly head. 'Yeah. Mr Norris. What's the problem?'

Sam had never heard of Norris. He spent several minutes in the relative privacy of his cubby-hole of an office trying to decide what to make of the development. Norris, he concluded, was probably a friend Brigham had asked to take the car in for repair in his absence. He would naturally have given Hegg the impression he was

321

the owner, probably without even meaning to. Yes. That was it. That was the only logical explanation.

After satisfying himself that there were no urgent matters requiring his attention in the garage – and with the minor mystery of Norris's stewardship of Brigham's Daimler pushed to the back of his mind – Sam slipped out to pay a call on Max's solicitor at his hotel, a short step away on the other side of the Champs-Elysées.

He found Mellish consuming breakfast in a gloomy corner of the hotel's dining-room, introduced himself and reported Max's sudden departure. 'He asked me to say how sorry he was he couldn't let you know, sir.'

'Is he really well enough to travel, Mr Twentyman?'

'He thinks he is.'

'And is he coming back here? Or should I follow him? I need to take his instructions regarding his father's estate.'

'Oh, he'll be back.'

'When?'

'Ah well, that's the question.' Sam shrugged.

And Mellish sighed. 'I see.'

Sam was tempted to press on to Little Russia and pay a call on Nadia, but he did not like to be away from his post for long. He had only just started the job, after all, and could not afford to have his reliability called into question.

As chief mechanic, however, he was blessed with a telephone. It was not difficult to find a slack moment during the morning to call Nadia at the bookshop. But there was no answer. It occurred to him then that she had probably closed the shop for a period of mourning. He would have to contact her later.

Within half an hour or so, however, he was summoned from the inspection-pit to take 'an urgent call'. Nadia was on the line.

'Max has left the Hôtel Dieu, Sam. They do not know where he is. What is happening?'

'He felt well enough to leave, so he did. He's had to go to London.'

'London? Why?'

'Could we meet later? I could explain then.'

'Yes. That would be good. You are busy until when?'

'Six o'clock or so.'

'Come to the shop then.'

'All right, I'll be there. How are you . . . bearing up?'

'It is not easy, Sam. But I must not keep you from your work. *Da*—'

'Before you go . . .' Sam cut in.

'Yes?'

'Have you heard of a man called Norris?'

'*Norrees?*'

'Yes. A member of the British delegation. A friend of Brigham's. Norris.'

'I . . . do not think so.'

'Well, never mind. It was—'

'Why are you asking?'

'It's probably nothing.'

'But possibly something?'

'Exactly. Don't worry. I'll sort it out.'

The comings and goings of members of the British and Dominions delegations were, as Shuttleworth had warned Sam when appointing him, usually but not always predictable. Monday had gone smoothly and calmly, as had half of Tuesday. From noon onwards, however, there was a sudden surge of demand for cars to shuttle important (and some not so important) personages between the Majestic, the Quai d'Orsay, the Crillon, the Edward VII (head-quarters of the Italians) and the Place des États-Unis (home from home of President Wilson). The Council of Four, reliable rumour had it, had resolved to despatch a peace mission to Budapest in an attempt to bring the new Bolshevik government in Hungary to heel. The emissaries were to leave that evening, so a procession of cars to the Gare de l'Est was bound to follow. Ensuring enough roadworthy vehicles would be available became Sam's sole pre-occupation for the next few hours and drove apparent trivialities such as Norris's claim to Brigham's Daimler far from his thoughts.

*

In London, Max had to rest on a bench in St James's Square, and another in Berkeley Square, on his way back to the flat. Lunch with Brigham, and the mental manoeuvrings his plan had committed him to, had drained his limited resources. He reckoned it was just as well he had several hours in which to prepare himself for the second round. His wound was not paining him, but he remained well below par, with all manner of disquieting symptoms to remind him of the fact. Bizarrely, he seemed to have lost his taste for tobacco, as several unsatisfactory attempts at smoking had demonstrated. But he felt certain persistence would cure that.

Entering the flat, Max was momentarily convinced someone had been there in his absence. The memory of le Singe's singular talents for covert entry prompted him to check every window. There was nothing amiss, far less ajar, yet certainty that all was well eluded him. He could not convince himself one way or the other that the doors of the various rooms were or were not as he had left them. He went down to the porter and questioned him, accomplishing nothing but to leave the poor man worried about Max's state of mind. He returned to the flat and checked the exit from the kitchen on to the service stairs. Nothing seemed wrong. Yet nothing seemed quite right either. After starting at his own reflection, glimpsed in the bathroom mirror as he walked past the open doorway of the room, he forcefully told himself enough was enough. He lay down on his bed and tried to sleep, convinced he would not be able to. But he was wrong. Sleep came soon enough, pouncing as if from nowhere.

Sam had reconciled himself to being late for his visit to Nadia. It was well past six o'clock when he finally left the garage, with most of the cars back and no problems reported. He had squeezed in a wash and brush-up earlier, so there was nothing to detain him. It was only as he was on his way out that he remembered the Norris puzzle, which he had intended to mention to Appleby. He diverted to Appleby's office in order to do so, but found it empty. He scrawled a note and propped it against the ashtray on the desk:

Mr A: I meant to tell you HX 4344 is in the garage. It was brought in last night by Mr Norris. Not important, I suppose?

Twentyman

It was a cold evening. But the thought of seeing Nadia again warmed Sam as he hurried round Place de l'Etoile and turned up Avenue Hoche. He was not worried. He did not think Mr Norris, whoever he might be, was important in any way at all.

MAX WAS WOKEN BY THE RINGING OF THE DOORBELL. HIS first reaction was surprise that he had slept so long. Squinting at the bedside clock, he saw that it was a few minutes past six. Obviously Brigham had arrived and been sent up to the flat by the porter. The doorbell rang a second time.

It was as Max pushed himself up that he realized something was wrong. A weight dragged on his right wrist. He could not at first believe what he saw when he looked towards it. He was handcuffed to the bedpost. He stared at the short stretch of chain between the cuffs in sheer astonishment. Was he dreaming? He tugged at the chain. No. He was not.

'James?' Brigham's voice carried from the hall. He was inside the flat. But how? 'James? Where are you?'

'*Brigham*,' Max shouted. 'How did you get in?'

'The door was ajar. When you didn't answer the bell . . . Where are you?'

'In the bedroom.'

'Are you unwell?' Max heard Brigham's footfalls in the passage as he hurried towards him.

'Be careful. There may be someone else here.'

'Someone else? Who?'

'I don't know. But—'

Brigham reached the open door of the bedroom and stared in, amazed. 'What the devil's going on?'

'I'm not sure.' Max rubbed his forehead with his free hand. It

326

was true. He was not sure of anything. 'I woke . . . to find myself like this.'

Brigham entered the room and moved to the bedpost. 'I don't understand,' he said. 'What do you mean? How could this have happened?'

Max had no answer to give. But one came, nonetheless, delivered in a low, husky voice. 'I did it.'

Max looked up. Brigham turned round. A man was standing in the doorway: short, thin and dressed in the trousers and waist-coat of a black suit, with a dark shirt and a black bow-tie. He was narrow-faced and virtually chinless, with a beaked nose and a prominent brow that cast his eyes in shadow. His dark, receding hair was short and lacquered. Altogether, he should have looked unimposingly bank-clerkish, but the way he held himself and the arrogance of his stare would have created a far from unimposing impression, even without the gun he was holding.

'What the devil . . .?' Brigham began, taking half a step forward.

'Stop,' said the newcomer, raising the gun slightly and pointing it at Brigham. Brigham stopped. 'Move when I tell you only. Or I will shoot you.' He sounded deadly serious. His accent and syntax were not English, though what his nationality was Max could not have said with any certainty. The gun looked strangely familiar, though. It was either the same model as the revolver Appleby had supplied – or the very same revolver.

'What do you want?' Brigham demanded.

'Information.'

'We'll, er, help you if we can.' Brigham glanced back at Max and winked, hoping, it seemed, to reassure him that they could talk their way out of this. 'Won't we?'

Max rose to his feet, sliding the handcuff up the bedpost until it was stopped by the cross-rail at the top. He looked straight at the man with the gun, determined to give him no ground. 'You're Tarn, aren't you?'

The man's reaction – or lack of it – confirmed Max was right. This was Tarn, the hired assassin, Kuroda's 'hunting tiger'. 'Sit down, Mr Maxted. Please. Or I shoot Mr Brigham. With your

gun.' He was wearing fine back leather gloves, Max noticed. He would leave no fingerprints.

'The noise of a gunshot will carry though the building,' Max countered. 'The police will be called.'

'Too late for Mr Brigham. And for you.' Tarn pointed the gun at Brigham's head. 'Please. Sit down.'

'Do as he asks, Max,' said Brigham. 'For God's sake.'

'All right.' Max sat down.

'What do you want to know?' Brigham asked, his voice cracking with anxiety.

'Where is Lemmer?' Tarn asked calmly.

'Who?'

'Lemmer. Please. You work for him, Mr Brigham. You know where he is. Have you told Mr Maxted?'

'No. That is, I don't work for anyone called Lemmer. I've no idea what you're talking about.'

'What will I do to make you tell me, Mr Brigham? You have an idea of that, maybe?'

'I don't work for Lemmer. I'm a British diplomat, for heaven's sake. You have no right to threaten us like this.' Brigham looked round at Max. 'You know this man, Max?'

'He's the assassin, Brigham. Do I really need to tell you? He killed my father. And Raffaele Spataro. Walter Ennis, too.'

Tarn spat dismissively. 'Ennis was not me.'

'But the others?'

'Mr Brigham knows about the others. He hired me.'

'I did no such thing,' Brigham blustered. 'This is outrageous. I've never met you before in my life.'

'You sent your man to me. You paid the fee.'

'What "man"?'

'Where is Lemmer? You will tell me, please. The *Japonais* pay bigger than you. For them I end Lemmer. Where is he?'

'I don't work for Lemmer. I don't know where he is.'

'Tell him, Brigham,' said Max. 'He'll kill you if you don't.'

'I can't tell him what I don't know.' Brigham stared imploringly at Max. 'You surely don't believe I hired this, this . . . creature . . . to kill Henry?'

Brigham was angry as well as frightened. And somewhere beneath both of those emotions, written starkly on his face, Max glimpsed a truth he would never otherwise have credited. Brigham did not work for Lemmer. He had not hired Tarn.

'Enough,' Tarn cut in. 'You will tell me where Lemmer is, Mr Brigham. You will tell me everything. I will make you tell me. Come this way.' He stepped back and signalled with the gun for Brigham to leave the room.

'Where are you taking me?'

'Walk in front of me, please. Now.'

'He can't help you, Tarn,' said Max. 'Don't you see? He truly doesn't know.'

'He knows. And soon I will know.'

'Who approached you? Who said he was Brigham's man?'

'If you shout for help, Mr Maxted, I will kill Mr Brigham, then you. And no one probably will hear your shouts. But they will find your bodies later. Your gun, remember. Murder and suicide. That is how the police will think it was.'

'And if I stay silent?'

'I will let you live, maybe.'

'Do as he says, Max,' said Brigham, looking back at him from the passage. 'It's our only hope. If I can convince him I'm telling the truth . . .'

'Enough,' said Tarn. 'Move, Mr Brigham. Or I shoot you here.'

Brigham shook his head despairingly and started walking. Tarn followed. They could have covered only a few yards, though that was enough to take them out of Max's sight, before Tarn spoke again.

'Go into the *salle de bain*.'

They entered the bathroom. Max heard their footsteps echo against the marbled floor.

'Put this on your left wrist, Mr Brigham.' Max heard something click – another pair of handcuffs, he surmised. 'Get in.'

'In the bath?'

'Now.' There was a pause, during which, Max imagined, Brigham did as he had been told. Then: 'Put it round the pipe and

329

fix it to your right wrist.' There was another click and a rattle of metal against metal. 'Kneel down, Mr Brigham.'

'What for?'

'Kneel down. Please.'

A moment passed. Then there was a thump and a cry of pain.

'Are you all right, Brigham?' Max called.

'Tell him, Mr Brigham,' said Tarn.

'I . . . I'm all right.'

'Now tell *me*. Where is Lemmer?'

'I don't know.'

'You know.'

'As God's my witness, I don't.'

'You will tell me.'

'I can't. *I don't know*.'

There was a sudden, indecipherable sound. Then Max heard a gurgling, scrabbling noise. And Tarn's voice: '*Tell me*.'

'Leave him alone, Tarn,' Max shouted. 'He doesn't work for Lemmer.'

'Do you work for Lemmer, Mr Maxted?' Tarn responded, raising his voice above Brigham's spluttering and choking.

'What are you doing to him?' Max wrenched at the handcuffs. But they were firmly fixed. He could not move so much as a pace from the bed.

'*Do you work for Lemmer?*'

'No. Of course I don't. Neither does Brigham.'

'I think he does. Well, Mr Brigham?'

The choking ceased and gave way to coughing. Tarn had given Brigham a moment to recover – and to confess. But it was only a moment.

'Well?'

'I don't . . . know where Lemmer is. You must . . .'

'*You must believe me*,' Max imagined Brigham had been about to say. The irony was that now, too late to help either of them, Max did believe him. Somehow, he had got the wrong man. So had Tarn. But Tarn did not know that yet. And Max suspected it would take Brigham's death – and his too – to make him understand.

'*Where is Lemmer?*'

THERE WERE NO CUSTOMERS IN THE SHOP WHEN SAM ENTERED. Nadia emerged from the rear office to greet him. She was dressed in black, as usual, but this was the sombre, unrelieved black of mourning, and she was paler than he recalled. The smile that might once have warmed her expression was missing. There was something tremulous about her – fear, he suspected, fused with grief.

'I am glad to see you, Sam,' she said, kissing him lightly on the cheek.

'Are you alone here, Nadia?'

'Yes.' She looked puzzled. 'Of course.'

'Didn't Zamaron say he was going to give you protection? I expected to see a bobby outside.'

'Bobby?'

'Policeman.'

'Ah. Yes. There were two. I sent them away.'

'Why?'

'My uncle's friends are nervous people, Sam. They do not like the police. They would doubt my loyalty if they saw I was being guarded by the French authorities.'

'They would?'

'Doubt and exile march together. Now, come upstairs. I will close the shop.'

Sam had not been in Nadia's flat before. It appeared to contain almost as many books as the shop, along with a lumber-room's

331

worth of china, paintings and extravagantly framed mirrors.

'My uncle brought from Russia only the things he said he could not live without,' Nadia explained, following Sam's gaze. 'Now they will live without him.'

'Will you stay here, running the shop?'

'I am not sure. Tell me about Max, please. I need to understand what is happening.'

It did not take Sam long to explain that Max had gone to London in pursuit of Brigham. Nadia expressed concerns he could only echo about how fit Max was to undertake such a journey.

'I am worried for him,' she said.

'You and me both,' Sam admitted.

'Whenever I close my eyes, I see my uncle in that sack in the canal,' she said, shaking her head sadly.

'It was a horrible thing. You shouldn't have had to see it.'

'But I did.' She stroked her neck reflectively. 'Do you have a cigarette, Sam?'

He pulled out a pack and offered her one with an apologetic grimace. 'They're French. I ran out of Woodbines.'

'Woodbines?'

'Proper British fags.'

'Ah. I see. These are fine. Thank you.'

He lit the cigarette for her and one for himself.

'What did you mean about the other man – Norrees?'

'Norris. A friend of Brigham's, as far as I can tell. He brought the car in yesterday for repair.'

'What car?'

'Brigham's Daimler.' Sam remembered then that he had not told Nadia about his encounter with le Singe. Evidently, neither had Max. And something he could not quite have defined deterred him from doing so now. 'It was the registration number of the car that first put Max on to him,' he continued inaccurately.

'Why is the number important?'

'I'm . . . not sure.' Sam was floundering. 'Max didn't say.'

'Does he think this . . . Norris . . . is an accomplice of Brigham's?'

'He's got no reason to.'

'If they are friends . . .'

332

'Max doesn't know that yet.'

'Ah. I see. But you must tell him, of course. It may be important.'

'Oh, I will. As soon as he gets back.'

'We should take a drink for his safe return. Will you have a glass of wine with me, Sam?'

'I'd be happy to.'

'Sit down. I will bring the wine. Make yourself comfortable.'

She went into the kitchen at the rear of the flat, leaving Sam to choose a fireside armchair. He finished his cigarette and lit another, gazing up at a murky oil painting above the mantelpiece of a stern, hawk-nosed figure in the naval uniform of a bygone era.

'Relative of yours?' he asked, when Nadia returned with the wine.

'Yes. The most famous of them all. Admiral Viktor Vitalevich Bukayev. A lover of Catherine the Great, if you believe the stories that are told.'

'And do you believe them?'

'When I want to.' She handed him his glass and raised hers. 'For Max's safe return.'

They drank the toast. The wine was strong and peppery and hit some kind of spot, though Sam would very much have preferred a pint of Bass. Nadia sat down opposite him.

'Max told you about the Trust, Sam, yes?'

'Your organization? Yes, he did.'

'Not mine. My uncle's. There is a traitor in it who must be found.'

'Do you reckon your uncle rumbled who the traitor was?'

'Rumbled?'

'Worked out. Found out.'

'Ah. Yes. I think so. I think that is why he was killed.'

'Maybe Max can get the name out of Brigham.'

'Maybe. Yes. Or out of Norris.'

'Well, it's possible, I sh . . . sh . . .' Sam rubbed his eyes. 'Sorry. It's been a busy day. It must've taken more out of me than I thought. Thish wine's gone shtraight to my . . . head. I . . .'

'You look tired, Sam. Maybe you are hungry also. I can give you something to eat, if you want.'

'No, that'sh . . . that'sh . . .' Sam made to set his glass down in the grate, but tipped it over in the process. He heard it smash on the tiles, but the sound seemed to come from some more distant place. He felt queasy and woozy all at once. 'Shorree,' he managed to say in a slow, slurred voice that he did not recognize as his own. He tried to push himself up from the chair. But his legs gave way beneath him.

He half-fell, half-rolled, to the floor, where he was aware of little beyond the musty smell of the rug he found himself lying on. He looked up, but could focus on nothing. The room was a blur. Nadia was nowhere to be seen.

Then he heard her speak. But she was not speaking to him. 'You can come in now. He is—'

But he heard no more.

'He is helpless,' said Nadia, turning to look towards the kitchen.

A thin, grey-suited man walked into the room. His face was pinched and narrow, his mouth pursed, his eye piscinely moist behind the lenses of his round-framed glassed. 'So I see,' he said quietly.

'What will you do with him?'

Herbert Norris stood for a moment, gazing down at Sam, who was sprawled unconscious on the floor. He tapped his lips thoughtfully and frowned.

'You should not have taken the car to the hotel garage,' said Nadia, with an edge of reproof in her tone.

Norris looked mildly at her. 'You should have told me he worked there, my dear.'

'I did not think it was important.'

'Ah, well, the things we think unimportant are often the things that catch us out, don't you find? To be honest, I had no idea they were interested in the car at all. I can't quite understand why they were. But never mind. Once Tarn has dealt with young Maxted – and we've disposed of Twentyman here – Appleby will have no reason to suspect me.'

'What about *me*?'

'You have nothing to worry about. Your performance as the

grieving niece is entirely convincing. The Trust will be more of a problem for you than Appleby. I shall recommend you be allowed to leave Paris. I'm sure we can recruit another informant among your fellow exiles. They generally spend so much and earn so little that corrupting them is child's play.'

'You do not respect my people, do you?'

'I respect professionalism, my dear, wherever I find it.'

'Is that why you use Tarn?'

'I certainly wish others would take note of how thorough the man is. He'd never be associated with anything as crass as the Ennis shooting.'

'But he is outside the organization. He is not bound to us.'

'He does what we pay him to do. And he does it well. Killing Appleby's man was unnecessary, perhaps, but I can forgive him the odd surrender to vanity.'

'What if he discovers you have misled him?'

'Why should he care? His fee's generous enough to console him for any minor misrepresentation. He's altogether ideal for our purposes.' Norris sighed. 'But even Tarn can't be in two places at once. Twentyman falls to us.'

'What are you going to do with him?'

'Dobson will arrive here shortly with a large packing case. We'll stow Twentyman in it and remove him. You needn't concern yourself with what happens to him after that.'

'I would like to know.'

'Why?'

Nadia looked down at Sam. 'He is not a bad man. I do not want him to suffer.'

'If only bad men suffered in this business, my dear, it would be easier on all our consciences. But that's not how it is. As it happens, he'll have drowned long before the effect of the drug wears off, so his will be a painless quietus. He's as good as dead already.'

EXACTLY TWO MONTHS EARLIER, ALMOST TO THE HOUR, SAM WAS struggling with a recalcitrant carburettor on one of Twentyman & Son's bread vans in the yard behind their bakery in Walthamstow. Darkness had long since fallen. He was working with the aid of a lamp on a trailing wire suspended from an adjacent post. It was cold and damp and everyone else had gone. By rights, he should have gone himself. But Sam was in no hurry to return to the family home, where his welcome back from the war had failed to match the touching vision of loved ones' reunions relayed in the newspapers. His brother viewed him as a cuckoo in the nest, while his sister regarded him as a rival for a position in the business she had earmarked for her fiancé, a man who had braved shot and shell in the trenches while Sam, as she saw it, had lazed around airy hangars in the French countryside polishing propellers.

The truth was that Sam would have been delighted to grant his siblings' generally unspoken (but occasionally muttered) wishes and take himself off to a different job and a home of his own. But he was constrained by penury and the harsh fact that an expertise in the workings of aero-engines was a qualification for nothing bar unemployment in the brave new post-war world. The Royal Air Force (as the RFC had become in the last months of his service) had jettisoned him – and many others like him – with perfunctory thanks and little ceremony. He was on his own now. His father would say otherwise, so too his brother, but that was how it seemed to him. The loaves might rise in the bakery. But he would not.

336

'Buggeration,' he swore, as he gave his already bruised thumb another knock with the spanner. He sucked the joint to ease the pain and wondered if he should abandon the task. Some deliveries tomorrow would just have to be late. That was all there was to it, apart, of course, from the apportionment of blame. That would be his to bear, without question.

'Sam?'

It was a voice Sam did not immediately recognize, calling from the open wicket door in the gate that led to the street. He moved clear of the van and peered towards it. 'Who's there?'

'It's me, Sam.' A figure in a hat and overcoat stepped through the door and walked towards him. 'Max.'

'Who?'

'James Maxted, Sam.' The newcomer reached the pool of light cast by the lamp, whipped off his hat and smiled – a familiar, self-mocking, defiant smile. 'Don't you remember me?'

'Bloody hell, sir, it's you.' Sam grinned inanely. 'You're a sight for sore eyes and no mistake. I never expected to see you again.'

'I've been in a POW camp. You didn't think I was dead, did you?'

'No. We got the word you were all right. I just . . . didn't reckon our paths would ever cross again.'

'Well, here I am.'

'How'd you find me?'

'You told me often enough your family ran a bakery in Walthamstow. It wasn't difficult.'

'I'm surprised you made the effort.'

'Now I have, how about a drink to celebrate surviving the war?'

Sam's grin broadened still further. 'That sounds just the ticket, sir.'

They adjourned to the Rose and Crown, where Sam had eked out several mournful pints since his homecoming. But Max was paying and eking was not what either of them had in mind.

The first pint vanished while they did little more than laugh and joke and savour the sweetness of the moment. Comparing notes on Max's experiences as a POW and the remainder of the aerial war as seen from Sam's fly-on-the-ground point of view occupied them

for most of the second. Then Max surprised Sam by reminding him of a conversation they had had a few weeks before he was shot down.

'We talked about what we might do after the war, if you recall.'

'We did that, sir, yes.' Sam had not forgotten. The miserable couple of months he had spent at the bakery had ensured he had been in no danger of doing that. 'We settled on a flying school, didn't we?'

'Yes. An attractive idea at the time. Flying without being shot at. And being paid by others to show them how to do it.'

'I bet a good few of our old comrades had the same idea.'

'No doubt. But what have they done about it?'

'Sweet FA, I should think, sir.'

'Exactly. And why do you suppose that might be?'

'Oh, the usual reasons. No money. No land. No balls.'

'You'd need a natural flyer who's also a good communicator, backed up by a smart mechanic, a nice flat piece of land within easy reach of London and enough capital to set the operation up and see it through some lean times.'

'You've got it about right there, sir.'

'So, you'd better stop calling me "sir" and switch to "Max".'

'Why's that, then?'

'Because we're not in the RFC any more, or whatever they call it now.'

'RAF, sir.'

'"Max".'

Sam grimaced. 'I'll never get the hang of that, sir.'

'Well, try, for God's sake. We're going to be partners.'

'We are?'

'Unless you tell me your heart's in the bakery business.'

'No, sir. Too much of the wrong kind of dough.'

'I virtually was an instructor for a lot of the younger pilots.'

'You were, sir. And a damn good one.'

'You're the best mechanic the squadron ever had.'

'Well . . .

'Spare me the false modesty. I think I'll be able to twist my old dad's arm into leasing us some land near Epsom.'

'Sounds perfect.'

'And I have a little money put by.'

Sam took a deep swallow of beer and looked Max in the eye. 'I'd work my socks off, sir.'

'I know you would, Sam. I know you *will*.'

'They're practically giving planes away out at Hendon. Engines and parts too. The lot.'

'What do you say, then?'

'You really mean it?'

'Of course. You don't think I came all the way out here just for the pleasure of your company, do you? We could make a go of this, Sam. I know it. Are you game?'

'You bet I am.'

'You won't regret it.'

'Neither will you, sir.'

'I think this calls for a toast.' Max ordered Scotch for them both. They clinked glasses. 'To the future.'

'To the future,' Sam echoed.

They downed the drinks in one and smiled at each other. In that moment of blind optimism, the future they had drunk to looked long, bright and inviting.

But it was not to be.

THE WORLD TURNS ON A SIXPENCE. NOTHING CAN BE FORETOLD. Certainty lies only in the actual.

A figure drifted gently into Max's field of vision while his attention was fixed on what was happening in the bathroom. It was only a sudden draught from the window that made him look round. Then he started in surprise.

It was le Singe: a small, agile, dark-skinned boy, wearing bits and pieces of army uniform and a cautious smile. He raised a hand and pressed his forefinger against his lips. His eyes were wide, his gaze eloquent: '*Do not speak; do not move.*' Max stared at him and frowned a question: '*What then?*'

The boy stepped past him so nimbly it was as if his feet were not touching the floor. He lowered his finger from his mouth and opened his hand. A small key was lodged in his palm. He smiled more broadly still and nodded in confirmation of Max's guess.

'Where is Lemmer?' Tarn's voice carried from the bathroom.

'I . . . don't . . . know,' came Brigham's answer in a series of strangulated gasps.

'You will tell me.'

The choking began again. Max looked at le Singe. The boy grasped the handcuff attached to Max's wrist, slid the key into the lock and released it, then lifted it away carefully so that it did not rattle against the post. He gave a final nod. '*I have done what I can for you,*' it seemed to declare.

Max returned the nod, then moved. There was no time to reflect

340

or consider. He had the advantage now. And he meant to take it.

Brigham was kneeling in the bath, his arms stretched ahead of him, his wrists handcuffed to the pipe supporting the taps. Tarn was crouched over him, tightening a narrow strap round his throat. The sound coming from Brigham was a spluttering, sputtering struggle for breath, for life itself. Tarn might give him another chance to speak. But it would make no difference even if he did. Brigham could not tell him what he wanted to know.

The gun would make a difference, though. Tarn had left it on the laundry basket next to the washhand-basin. He could easily reach back and grab it if he decided to finish Brigham with a bullet. But it was not in his hand at that moment.

Max had not survived as a fighter pilot by hesitating in a crisis. He strode forward and seized the gun.

Tarn sensed some movement behind him. He swung round, flinching in alarm and amazement as he registered Max's presence in the room.

Max raised the gun as Tarn lunged at him. The barrel was pointing straight at Tarn's forehead as he pulled the trigger. He could not miss.

And he did not.

Dobson's muscularity had been as useful to Norris in the recent past as his taciturnity. He arrived as promptly as Norris had assured Nadia he would, unloaded a large, empty packing case from the back of his van and carried it into the shop and up to the flat. He said nothing, grunting some kind of greeting to Nadia and various acknowledgements of orders from Norris. They bundled the inert and unconscious Sam into the crate, nailed it shut and, with Dobson doing the lion's share of the humping and heaving, carried it back down to the van.

Norris told him to wait while he returned to the flat for a parting word with Nadia. With his cargo safely stowed, Dobson stood behind the van, lit a cigarette and, smoking it, wondered idly what the exact nature of Norris's relationship with Nadia might be and whether there would be time for a second cigarette.

His wonderings were rudely interrupted by a sharp blow with a cosh to the back of his neck, eliciting one of his limited range of grunts. He went down like a sack of coke from a coal-lorry.

Norris was in the midst of urging Nadia to remain calm in the days ahead, and patient with regard to his efforts to arrange her departure from Paris, when he heard the engine of the van cough into life. He rushed to the window, just in time to see it pull away, leaving a sprawled figure in the street behind it.

Schools Morahan was attuned to the need to act decisively when circumstances required it. He had not anticipated such circumstances would arise that evening, but he was not unduly surprised. Life, in his experience, was generally predictable – until it ceased to be. Malory had given him the name of the member of the British delegation Ireton had approached on Sir Henry's behalf because she, like Morahan, was worried about what would happen to Max when he left hospital. She had overheard a telephone conversation between Ireton and Herbert Norris that left no room for doubt in the matter. She was also acquainted with a secretary at the British delegation who had access to the addresses of delegation members not lodging at the Majestic or neighbouring hotels. This was only what Morahan would have expected. Malory Hollander was a woman of greater resourcefulness than Ireton seemed to appreciate. The fact that Norris was sharing a flat in the 16th arrondissement with Lionel Brigham had struck Morahan as nothing less than sinister in light of Brigham's banishment from Paris.

He went to the Hôtel Dieu to warn Max of Norris's possible role in events, only to be told Max had already left, as he had the Mazarin by the time Morahan reached it. Morahan proceeded to Norris's address in the 16th with no great hopes of accomplishing anything, but arrived just as Norris was leaving and followed him to Little Russia. He knew Nadia Bukayeva slightly because of her late uncle's dealings with Ireton and had never trusted her. Her associations with Norris only confirmed his doubts about her. He saw Sam Twentyman go into the shop and not come out. A little later, a man drove up in a van and carried a large packing case up to Nadia's flat. Then he returned, with Norris helping him to carry

the case, now clearly much heavier. What was inside? Morahan reckoned he could guess. And he always backed his own guesses.

Morahan drove fast to the Avenue Hoche and pulled in under a street lamp. He climbed out, hurried round to the back of the van, yanked the doors open and clambered in beside the packing case. There was a tool-box inside the van as well. He grabbed a jemmy and levered the lid off the crate, the nails tearing loose as he let his strength tell. Tossing the lid aside, he shone a torch in on Sam and checked he was still breathing. He was, though deeply unconscious. Several slaps to his cheeks brought no response. Drugged, Morahan concluded. He would need medical attention. There was nothing for it but to drive him to the Hôtel Dieu. It was frustrating not to be able to settle matters with Norris and the treacherous Nadia, but Morahan was well aware that he could not afford to declare his loyalties too openly. There were sleeping dogs that must be left to lie, while there were others, awake and barking, that must be brought to heel. He clambered back out of the van, returned to the cab and drove away.

Weakness began to overtake Max as he coped with the aftermath of Tarn's death. He had been carried to this point on a surge of adrenalin. Now his limbs felt rubbery and his wound twinged at every move. He found the key to the other pair of handcuffs in Tarn's pocket and released Brigham, reduced by his ordeal to a stumbling, mumbling old man. Nothing coherent was said by either of them as Max helped him out of the bath and led him slowly to the bedroom, where he laid him on the bed. Le Singe was gone, as Max had known he would be. Had he stayed long enough to witness the death of his master? Max would have needed to understand the working of the boy's mind better than he did to answer that question.

There was a lot of Tarn's blood on Brigham and spatters of it on Max too. Tarn himself, his head split by the bullet Max had fired at point-blank range, was a dark, bleeding, spreadeagled form in the bathroom. Max leant against the door-jamb and gazed in at the body as he recovered his breath from the effort of moving Brigham.

343

He felt no satisfaction at having slain his father's murderer. He had wanted to learn the full truth of the night Sir Henry had died and feared now he never would. Tarn had snatched the chance away by forcing Max to kill him and the identity of those who had hired Tarn was more elusive than ever, now Brigham's innocence had been so starkly demonstrated. Sir Henry's assassin had covered his tracks by dying in them.

Max stumbled on along the passage to the drawing-room, where he telephoned for an ambulance – Brigham would certainly need one even if shock was the worst of what he was suffering from – and then called the police. He had shot a man dead. There would be many questions asked of him. He might even be arrested, though he felt sure he would be vindicated by what Brigham had to say, as soon as he was capable of saying it. He could not quite grasp in his mind all the ramifications of what had happened. He would simply have to await them.

He poured himself a Scotch and one for Brigham as well, which he watered, then set off back to the bedroom with the glasses, taking a couple of gulps from his as he went.

Brigham moaned some kind of recognition as Max entered the room and set the glasses down on the beside table. 'There's an ambulance on the way,' Max said, surprised by his own hoarseness. 'They won't be long. Do you want a little whisky?'

But Brigham seemed not to have heard. He frowned and feebly raised his hand, as if trying to point.

Max turned and looked at the wall facing the bed. And there, in chalked letters, he saw le Singe's parting message.

MAX MIGHT EASILY HAVE BEEN ARRESTED, BUT HE LOOKED little better than Brigham when the police arrived. In the event, they were both packed off to St Thomas' Hospital, with constables in tow.

After a doctor had satisfied himself that Max was no worse than badly shaken, though certainly in need of bed-rest in view of his wound and recent fever, a fox-faced Scotland Yard inspector by the name of Denslow invited him to explain what had happened. Max adhered as closely as possible to the truth. Tarn was a hired assassin who would have killed them both if they had not killed him first. He made no mention of le Singe, having no wish to set the police on his saviour's trail and secure in the knowledge that Brigham had not seen the boy. He claimed Tarn had foolishly left the key to the handcuffs within reach. As for any message Brigham might later say he had seen written on the bedroom wall, Max planned to suggest, if he needed to, that it was a hallucination. He had already ensured it was no longer visible.

Max referred Denslow to Appleby for confirmation that he had been trying to track down his father's murderer in Paris and had followed Brigham to London under the misapprehension that Brigham was party to the murder. Appleby's Secret Service credentials had a satisfyingly intimidating effect on the inspector, who undertook to contact him as soon as possible.

Soon translated into an hour, which was as long as it took Denslow to return with the news that Appleby had vouched for Max and would be on his way to London to do so in person as

345

soon as he had dealt with 'a related incident' in Paris. As to the nature of that incident, Denslow was in the dark. He clearly had no desire to become embroiled in Secret Service business and began treating Max with exaggerated respect. 'We'll just wait until you feel well enough to make a formal statement, Mr Maxted.'

A terrible conclusion formed in Max's mind as he drifted in and out of sleep that night. Brigham's innocence, amply demonstrated by his ordeal at Tarn's hands, pointed to Nadia's guilt. Brigham had told her nothing about her uncle. Nor had anyone else. She had not needed to be told. She had consented to Igor Bukayev's murder. She might even have engineered it. And she had probably implicated Brigham at the behest of whoever in the British delegation Ireton had sounded out on Sir Henry's behalf. But why in that case had le Singe given them the registration number of Brigham's car? Unless . . .

Max was feeling quite well enough the following morning to undertake a short walk along the corridor to Brigham's room. He found Brigham bruised and weary, but eager to express his gratitude.

'You saved my life, James,' he said, his voice reduced to a hoarse whisper by the damage Tarn had inflicted on him. 'I can't thank you enough.'

'I saved my own too. It was self-preservation, really.'

'That fellow . . . Tarn . . . killed Henry?'

'I believe so. He was paid to do it by those who feared they might be exposed as spies working for Fritz Lemmer.'

'But . . . Tarn was looking for Lemmer.'

'The Japanese paid better. He said so himself.'

'And you . . . thought I was one of . . . Lemmer's people?'

'Yes. I was trying to give you enough rope to hang yourself.'

'I may be many things, James, but I'm not a traitor. The idea's absurd.'

'It didn't seem so absurd at the time. Especially not when Nadia Bukayeva said her piece.'

'So, I have my . . . liking for the ladies . . . to blame for this, do I?'

'Someone in the British delegation was pulling Nadia's strings, I'm sure of it. Tell me, does anyone else drive your car?'

'My car?'

'The Daimler. HX 4344.'

'You know . . . the registration number?'

'Does anyone else drive it?'

'Well, since you ask . . .'

'Yes?'

'The chap I share the apartment with in Paris. I let him use it . . . from time to time.'

'Who is he?'

'Herbie Norris.'

'*Norris?*'

'Yes. You know him?'

Norris. So, that was it. The meek maundering Mr Norris was not at all what he had chosen to appear. 'I know him,' Max said dolefully. Though all that flowed from such knowledge was far from clear to him. Had le Singe set out to mislead them, acting on Norris's orders? Or had he been misled himself?

'Are you saying . . . Herbie Norris works for Lemmer?'

'It looks like it.'

'Good God.'

'I'll alert Appleby as soon as I can.'

Brigham shook his head in disbelief, wincing at the effect on his throat and coughing so badly Max had to fetch him a glass of water. 'Thanks . . . my boy,' he gasped, after talking a few soothing sips. 'Norris is simply the last man I'd have thought capable of . . . spying. He seemed . . . straight as a die and . . .' He smiled weakly. 'And dull as dishwater.'

'It probably suited him to have you think that.'

'Of course. And it's . . . surprisingly easy . . . to misread people, isn't it, James?' Brigham looked Max in the eye and held his smile.

'Yes.' Max nodded – a small enough gesture, but full of meaning, a meaning neither of them could mistake. 'It is.'

'I'll make the police understand . . . you had no choice but to shoot Tarn. It was . . . him or us.'

'That it was.'

'What about the writing . . . on the wall? Will you tell them about that?'

'I'd rather not.'

'It was . . . intended for you, wasn't it?'

'I think it was, yes.'

'Would you prefer me . . . not to mention it?'

'Very much.'

'I won't, then.'

'Thank you.' Max nodded his appreciation, which was more genuine than he could ever have imagined it would be of any act of Brigham's.

'You're not going to tell me what it said, are you?'

'I don't know what it said. I don't even know what language it was written in.'

'Japanese.'

'Really?'

'I think so. I can't read Japanese script, of course, but . . . I recognized it. And Tarn . . . was working for the Japanese, wasn't he?'

'So he said.'

'Now Tarn's dead, will you . . . drop this?'

'Maybe.'

'Or maybe not.' Brigham looked at Max knowingly.

'I should leave you to rest.'

Max stood up, relieved Brigham had said nothing, even indirectly, about the possibility that they were father and son. He no longer suspected Brigham of any responsibility for Sir Henry's murder. But that did not mean he was no longer suspicious of him in other ways. His view of the man had become disconcertingly complicated since their life-and-death struggle with Tarn.

'I'm glad—' Max began. Then words deserted him.

'When I'm back on my feet,' said Brigham, 'I'll probably . . . go down to Cannes . . . for a while. They can cope in Paris without me.'

'I'm sure they can.'

'I don't suppose . . .' Brigham gazed up at Max and found the answer in his face. 'No. Of course not.'

Max returned to his room and went to the cabinet where his clothes were hung. From his jacket pocket he took the piece of wallpaper he had unceremoniously torn from the bedroom wall at the flat and looked again at what had been written on it.

ファーンゴールト

Was it really Japanese, he wondered. Brigham had seemed in little doubt. But le Singe was more likely to be fluent in Arabic than Japanese. How could he have written it? And what did it mean?

As to that, Max knew who would be able to tell him. And he would ask him, just as soon as he could.

MAX CHARMED A NURSE INTO HELPING HIM SEND A TELEGRAM to Appleby, warning him Norris was the rotten apple in the barrel. When Appleby arrived at the hospital that evening, however, Max realized he must have left Paris before the telegram had reached him. But, strangely, he already knew about Norris.

'You don't need to worry about him, Max. He no longer poses any kind of threat. I'll explain why when you've told me what happened here. Inspector Denslow seems . . . confused.'

Max did his best on that front, admitting for Appleby's benefit the role le Singe had played in events, but instinctively avoiding any mention of the message on the wall. He wanted to know what the message said before he told anyone about it.

'I'll call in at Scotland Yard tomorrow and have a word with Denslow's boss,' said Appleby when Max had finished. 'I've already spoken to him on the blower and I'm confident there'll be no charges brought against you. Killing Tarn could be regarded as a public service. You'll have to appear at the inquest, of course, along with Brigham. But that'll be a formality.'

'I want to get back to Paris as soon as possible.'

'I'm sure you do. And you'll want to hear my news, as well.'

'Is it good news?'

'Some of it is, yes. Which is probably as much as we can ever hope for in this life.'

Appleby's account began with Sam's impulsive decision – inspired, as it turned out – to sabotage Brigham's Daimler. The car's

subsequent delivery to the Majestic garage for repairs, not by Brigham but by Norris, initiated a chain of events that led to Sam walking into a trap in Nadia Bukayeva's flat.

'Norris must have decided to eliminate Twentyman for fear his plan to cast suspicion on Brigham would fall apart once we discovered he had the use of the Daimler. I think le Singe was trying to tell you the driver of that car was your enemy, you see. What he didn't know was that there were two drivers. And what Norris didn't know was that Morahan had followed him to Little Russia, so was able to intervene before they could dump Twentyman in the Seine.'

'How's Sam now?'

'Recuperating at the Hôtel Dieu. The drug they used left him pretty groggy, but he'll soon be up and about. He asked me to say hello.'

'Good old Sam.'

'And good old Morahan. Why he should have bothered to involve himself I don't really understand, but I'm glad he did. Twentyman had left me a note about Norris's use of the car, but it would have been far too late for him by the time I read it. As it was, Morahan telephoned me from the hospital and put me in the picture.'

'Have you got Norris in custody? Is that what you meant about him no longer posing a threat?'

'I couldn't have taken him into custody even if I'd had the chance, Max. Nor could the French police. I'd been warned off by the Permanent Under-Secretary and Foreign Office staff enjoy diplomatic immunity, remember.'

'Nadia Bukayeva doesn't, though.'

'Good point. And one not lost on me. I hoiked Zamaron out of bed and persuaded him he should arrest her for conspiracy to murder Twentyman and probable complicity in her uncle's murder as well. Time was of the essence, of course. I was afraid she'd already have done a bunk.'

'And had she?'

'Oh, yes. It looked like she'd packed some clothes before leaving. I think we can assume she's not planning to return to Paris in the near future.'

'She must have been the traitor in the Trust Pa was offering to identify.'

'That's how I read it. But working for Lemmer rather than the Cheka. Or maybe for Lemmer as well as the Cheka.'

'Had Norris gone too?'

'Not exactly. Though gone he certainly had in one sense.'

'What do you mean?'

'We found him in Nadia's flat, Max. Him and his assistant, Dobson. Both shot dead.'

'Nadia killed them?'

'Who else? She must have ice in her veins. I imagine she opted for a scorched-earth policy once she realized Norris's plans were miscarrying. Perhaps she calculated he'd decide to kill her rather than risk her confessing all under interrogation, improbable though it seems to me that any interrogator could get more out of her than she was willing to give. Whatever her reasons, though, she carried it off efficiently. Two clean head shots. Bang bang, they're dead.'

'And she got away?'

'Clean away, I regret to say.'

Appleby sighed and thrust his pipe, with which he had been fiddling, back into his pocket, apparently concluding that lighting it in a hospital was out of the question. But he burrowed in his bag and pulled out a bottle of whisky with a satisfied smirk that suggested he regarded it as a more than adequate substitute. A grubby tumbler also emerged, inscribed SE & CR, evidently purloined from the train. He poured himself a generous measure and sloshed some into Max's water glass.

'Your health, Max.'

'Well, despite the setting, I don't feel too bad. And being the subject of a police inquiry does get you a private room here, so I'm not complaining.' Max raised his glass and took a sip. 'Even so, I'd have discharged myself by now if I had a home to go to. Denslow put the flat out of bounds.'

'He tells me he's finished with the flat now. And you could always visit your family, of course.'

'Not a good idea. As soon as the police are off my back, I'll head

for Paris. Tomorrow, I hope, if you can do your stuff at Scotland Yard.'

'You don't really need to go back to Paris, Max. You've killed the man who killed your father. The man who hired the killer is also dead. And Zamaron's confident the magistrate will approve Madame Dombreux's release now it's obvious Spataro was one of Tarn's victims. You've done all that could have been expected of you – more, frankly, than I thought you were capable of.'

'But Norris was only one of many spies in Lemmer's network. And your condition for helping me, as I recall, was that I track down Lemmer for you.'

'With Norris dead and Miss Bukayeva gone with the wind, I'd put your chances of doing that at close to zero. I could and maybe I should encourage you to persist. It's what my boss would expect me to do. You might turn up some other spies and they might take us closer to Lemmer. But you've had several narrow escapes already.' Appleby paused and looked at Max thoughtfully, then went on. 'My son would be the same age as you, if he hadn't been killed at Loos, you know. He was a volunteer too.'

'You've never mentioned him before.'

'No occasion to. I shouldn't drink Scotch, really. It makes me sentimental. Oh, before I forget, you might like to know what I've found out about the Contingencies Memorandum. It's keeping Carver and a few others in the American delegation awake at night. No one will give me chapter and verse, but I gather it's a document in which President Wilson sets out variations to be made to his supposedly inviolable Fourteen Points – his much-vaunted programme for world peace – if certain contingencies arise during the peace conference. Some of those variations wouldn't paint him in an honourable light. If it reached the press, there'd be hell to pay. So, if your father got hold of an authentic copy . . .'

'It would have fetched a high price at auction, so to speak.'

'It would. And if it was in that safe-deposit box of his . . .'

'It might already be in Lemmer's possession.'

'Indeed it might.'

'Doesn't that possibility worry you?'

'Personally, no. Why should I care if he throws a spanner in the

conference works? Departmentally, I should probably hope he does. American embarrassment equals British advantage.' Appleby shrugged and topped up his glass. 'Peace is almost as dirty a business as war.'

'You should drink Scotch more often, Appleby. It mellows you.'

Appleby grunted, apparently considering mellowness an accusation bordering on the insulting. 'Have you found out what your father was raising money *for* yet?'

'Corinne Dombreux and a comfortable life with her, probably in Brazil. He planned to invest the money in a business venture of Ribeiro's.'

'Ah.' Appleby looked almost disappointed. 'So that was all it was.'

Or was it? After Appleby had gone, Max turned out the light and lay watching raindrops forming at intervals on the uncurtained window of his room. The sky beyond the window was black, the rain falling from clouds he could not see. The truth, it struck him, was like that, revealing itself, if at all, only by its effect on something else. He had the sense that there was a greater, darker truth beyond all that he had so far learnt. Why had his father appointed him his executor if not to discover what that was? Had the safe-deposit box hidden the secret? Or was it hidden somewhere else, still waiting to be found? If Max gave up now, he would never know for certain, never quite be able to dismiss from his mind the fear that he had turned his back on what his father had died for. And that, he knew, he could not bear.

MAX HAD PERSUADED APPLEBY IT WOULD BE BEST IF THEY went to Scotland Yard together the following morning. The doctor who had treated him on his admission raised no more than a token objection to discharging him and conjectured that Brigham would be fit enough to leave within a few days as well. 'You should go gently, though, Mr Maxted. You have youth on your side, of course, but the body takes its own sweet time to recover from the sort of thing you've put it through lately, young or not.'

Max assured the doctor he would lead a quiet life for the next few weeks, which he had no intention of doing. He headed for the flat first, for a change of clothes, where he was intercepted by the head porter, anxious for a word about the events of the night before last. Max brushed the poor fellow off with an assurance that there would be no further visits from the police, then hurried on to Scotland Yard.

Appleby was waiting for him at the bottom of Whitehall, puffing contentedly at his pipe. He led Max into Metropolitan Police headquarters with the air of a man returning to his natural domain. Several people they passed greeted him cheerfully. Their destination was the office of Chief Superintendent Mappin, a genial fellow with a booming voice who also seemed pleased to see Appleby – and Max, to judge by his warm handshake and prompt assurance that his force were not about to cause problems for a young gentleman who had saved the life of a senior civil servant and despatched a foreign assassin into the bargain. 'Tarn, you think his name was? Well, we'll ask our French colleagues if they

know him. Then the Belgians, if they don't. Then . . . Well, maybe someone will claim him, maybe they won't. I take it we can agree, Horace, that we're all better off without him?'

'Very much so, Bill. We think he was responsible for several murders in Paris. A nasty piece of work in every way.'

'And the fewer of those we have on the streets of London, the happier I am. The coroner will have the final say, of course, Mr Maxted, but we'll tell him we're satisfied you killed Tarn in self-defence. We'll need a signed statement from you before you leave and you'll be required to give evidence at the inquest in due course. Oh, and we'll have to hang on to the gun until then. Strictly speaking, you don't have a licence for it, but we'll overlook that, shall we? Forgot to hand it in when you were demobbed, I dare say, like a lot of you chaps.'

'I was certainly glad of it on Tuesday night, Chief Superintendent,' said Max.

'I'm sure you were, Mr Maxted. Glad and no mistake.'

Accommodating as Mappin was, Max was not able to leave Scotland Yard before the morning had stretched into the afternoon. The dictating, typing and signing of a statement absorbed a laborious couple of hours and he was also fingerprinted – 'for the purposes of elimination', according to Denslow.

Appleby left while Max was waiting for his statement to be typed. They exchanged parting words in a corridor.

'If you decide not to go back to Paris, Max, I'll understand.' It was as close as Appleby seemed able to come to repeating his advice of the night before.

'I'll be on tonight's sleeper,' said Max. He wanted no misunderstanding on the point.

'Then you'll be ahead of me by twenty-fours hours. As a personal favour, try not to get into any more trouble before I catch up with you.'

Max smiled. 'I will try.'

He returned to Mount Street to pack his bag, only to encounter the head porter again. Mrs Harrison had been and gone, considerably

put out by the state she had found the flat in and alarmed in particular by the bloodstains in the bathroom.

But Mrs Harrison had not been the only caller. A *Daily Mail* reporter had been there, asking questions. 'We had a lot of trouble getting rid of him, Mr Maxted, I don't mind telling you. I shouldn't be surprised if he came back.' Max proffered an apology and decided to spend most of his time elsewhere before boarding the sleeper.

The reporter was not the end of it, however. 'Your solicitor's been looking for you as well.' Of course. Mellish was still expecting to be given some kind of instructions about the estate. It was predictable – though Max had failed to predict it – that he would come to London. Unfortunately, as the head porter revealed, Mellish had met Mrs Harrison. He therefore knew everything that had happened. He might easily take it into his head to inform Ashley, a complication Max could do without.

He hastened up to the flat and telephoned the solicitor's office in Epsom, hoping Mellish had returned there by now. But he had not. Max left a message, asking him to take no action until they had spoken. He could only hope that would cover it.

He went to Victoria station and bought a ticket for the eight o'clock sleeper, then took himself off to the Tate Gallery, where he spent more time in the tea-room than he did admiring the art, a commodity for which he had never had much use. Rain forced him on to a bus for the return journey to Victoria. The Londoners he was jammed in with grumbled about the weather and the coal shortage and the incompetence of the government – concerns that seemed a million miles away to Max.

The concourse at Victoria was bustling with commuters and luggage-laden Continental travellers. Max bought some cigarettes for the journey – though, oddly, he had still not quite recovered his taste for them – and headed for the departures board.

'James!'

He recognized George Clissold's voice with some surprise and turned to see his uncle approaching through the crowd. 'Uncle George? What are you doing here?'

'Looking for you, my lad, at your mother's bidding. She wants to speak to you.'

'But—'

'She's waiting for us in the station hotel. And she's already waited long enough to test her temper.'

'I have a train to catch.'

'I know. But it doesn't leave for half an hour yet. Shall we?'

Max had no choice but to walk with George in the direction of the hotel entrance. He was not ready to face his mother, but it seemed he was going to have to.

'How did you find me?' he asked as they steered as straight a course as they could contrive through the streams of arriving and departing passengers.

'Mellish alerted your mother to your latest brush with death.' *Damn the fellow*, thought Max. Why had he had to go and do that? 'He mentioned you got yourself shot in Paris as well. Win's a phlegmatic character, but it's fair to say she's worried about you. You should have kept her informed, James, you really should.'

'I was trying *not* to worry her.'

'Well, you failed, I'm afraid. She's been to Mount Street and extracted all the details from the porters. She's also visited Brigham.'

'She has?'

'Let's not pretend we don't both know about Win and that blighter. I can only hope she doesn't start seeing him again now he's done something vaguely heroic. You were the one who saved the day, though, weren't you?'

'Well, I—'

'Yet here you are, scuttling off back to Paris without a by-your-leave. Win guessed that's what you'd do. It was her idea to come here. You're a far bigger mystery to me than you are to her. Have you found out what got Henry killed?'

'Yes. And Mother won't enjoy hearing about it. I suppose I . . .'

'Wanted to spare her the truth?'

'As long as I could, yes.'

'Well, my lad, the time's come. You're just going to have to spit it out.'

Lady Maxted was waiting, with tea set before her, in a quiet, palm-dotted lounge of the hotel. She greeted Max with a frown that blended pride at his derring-do with bafflement at his eagerness to slip back to France without telling her what he had learnt. But there was something else in her gaze as well: relief.

'You look better than I'd feared, James. Mr Mellish said you'd been *shot*.'

'That makes it sound worse than it was. I'm fine.'

'And this appalling attack you and Mr Brigham were so lucky to survive?'

'We were lucky, yes. But survive we did, with nothing worse than a few bruises to show for it.'

'You've uncovered the truth about Henry's death, haven't you?'

Denial was pointless. 'Yes, Mother, I have.'

'When you left Gresscombe Place last month, you promised to tell me what you learnt before you told anyone else.'

'I still don't know everything. I didn't want to . . .'

'Shock me?'

Max forced himself to look her in the eye. 'It's not an altogether pretty story.'

'I never thought it would be.'

'Even so . . .'

'I think I'd better hear it, James. Ashley doesn't know I'm here, by the way. I didn't alert him to Mr Mellish's call. So, I'll be free to decide whether to disclose any information you give me to him and Lydia – or not. Don't imagine I'm unappreciative of the efforts you've made and the risks you've taken. But I'm entitled, as your mother, as your father's widow, to be told what led Henry to his death. And don't worry about missing your train either. George and I will be travelling with you to Dover. That should give us all the time we need.'

PROMISING THE WHOLE TRUTH WAS EASIER THAN DELIVERING IT. Even as Max recounted to his mother what he had discovered in Paris, he was aware of omitting almost as much as he revealed. Lady Maxted seemed to be aware of this as well. She did not press for information about the woman Sir Henry had planned to spend his retirement with. Nor did she ask for details of his scheme to raise money to fund their life together. It was enough, apparently, for her to know why he had been murdered and by whom – that his murderer was dead and that the man who had commissioned his murder was also dead. Justice, after a fashion, had been served. And of that she was glad in her own sombre, reflective way.

It was not as simple as that, of course. Norris was not the only agent of Lemmer's to whom Sir Henry had posed a threat. The decision to set Tarn on him must have been a collective one. There were guilty men – and women, in the case of Nadia Bukayeva – who had escaped punishment and would probably continue to do so. Lady Maxted understood that and urged her son to accept it, as she was willing to.

'These other people may still see you as a threat, James, may they not?'

'They may.'

'Then why return to Paris? Staying away would draw a line under the affair. And if what you say – and what I infer – about the sort of people they are is correct, a line must be drawn somewhere. You cannot pursue them all.'

'There are some loose ends I have to tie up.'

'So, you will come home soon?'

'I'm not sure how long it will take.'

'I can persuade Ashley to allocate the land you need for your flying school, you know. Lydia doesn't call every tune. And the executorship gives you something to bargain with, as perhaps your father foresaw.'

'I can't think about any of that now, Mother. I can't predict what I may yet learn – and where learning it may lead me.'

'At what point does bravery become foolishness, James?'

'When you overstep a mark you can't see until you've over-stepped it.'

'Is that thought meant to comfort me?'

'I won't lie to you, Mother. That's probably the only comfort I can offer.'

They parted in wind and rain on the platform at Dover Marine station. George had gone to secure a taxi to take him and Lady Maxted to the Lord Warden Hotel, where they planned to stay overnight before returning to London. Max would soon have to board the steamer for Boulogne. He thought everything had been said that needed to be said. But his mother, though she trusted her brother in all matters, had one last thing she wished to say to her son – and to her son alone.

'I am aware what Lionel believes he is to you, James, and my conversation with him yesterday left me in little doubt that you are aware of it too.'

'There's no call to speak of it, Mother.'

'You thought him a traitor.'

'And he's not a traitor. I was ready to believe the worst of him. I was wrong. I admit it.'

'I am not concerned with that. A man who behaves as he does must expect to be misjudged. What concerns me is the possibility that you will credit his claim of . . . a blood relationship . . . because you now know he is not quite as bad as you thought him.'

'I really don't—'

'There is something I must tell you, James.'

Max looked at his mother, her expression veiled by the shadow

361

of her hat and the rain-blurred glare of the station lamps. 'Are you sure?' he asked levelly.

'Absolutely. Lionel Brigham is not your father. Believe me in this if in nothing else. If I had a Bible with me, I would be willing to swear upon it. You are Henry's son. There is no margin for doubt or uncertainty. You are his son and no other man's.'

No margin for doubt or uncertainty? How could that be? Sir Henry had unwittingly revealed to Max where his mother had spent the summer of his conception. Either she was lying to him now, which he could hardly believe, or there was something he was not being told. And this possibility was only strengthened by what she said next.

'Honesty is always partial, James. No two people can or should reveal everything of themselves to each other. I will not be interrogated about this. Nor will I interrogate you about those many things you have chosen, wisely or not, to keep from me. But you are Henry's son. That is the truth. Carry it with you – along with your mother's love – in whatever trials still await you.'

It was a rough crossing and a largely sleepless journey followed from Boulogne to Paris, as Max analysed his mother's words in search of what he took to be their hidden meaning. It still eluded him. And sleep came, perversely, just as the train was entering the Gare du Nord.

He was not required to vacate his cabin for another hour, which he dozed through, before breakfasting in the station café. He bought a copy of the Paris edition of the *Daily Mail* and forced himself to read it. There was nothing yet about Tarn, which came as a relief. The editorial was a dire warning against leniency towards Germany. Max could not help wondering if Lemmer planned to use any of the material he had removed from the safe-deposit box to win some concessions for his country. It was a worrying thought. But there was nothing he could do about it. Whatever advantage access to the box had handed to Lemmer was his to exploit.

Max went straight to the Mazarin from the station and dropped off his bag, then headed for the Majestic. He found Sam just where he

had expected to find him, supervising work in the hotel's garage.

'They winkled you out of the hospital, then,' said Max, soft-footing his way to Sam through the clamour of tuning engines and then surprising him.

'It's you, sir,' Sam responded, whirling round to greet him with a broad smile. 'Alive and well, I'm relieved to see.'

'The feeling's mutual, Sam.' They shook hands warmly. 'I gather we've both been in the wars.'

'You can say that again.'

'Can you spare me a few minutes?'

''Course I can. I'll make us some tea. Come into my parlour.'

Sam fired off some parting instructions to the mechanic he had been talking to, then led the way to his tiny office, where he had rigged up a Primus stove.

'I've managed to get hold of some English tea,' he proudly announced, setting the kettle to boil and lighting a cigarette. 'Smoke, sir?'

'No, thanks. But tea will slip down a treat.'

They sat down, Max in the only chair, Sam on an upturned box, and regarded each other with smiling bemusement. 'Mr Appleby told me you'd gone and killed Tarn, sir. But not how you'd managed it.'

'I had help, Sam. From le Singe. Without it I wouldn't have survived.'

'What's his game, sir?'

'I don't know. But I'm glad he's playing it. I owe him my life. I gather you owe Morahan yours.'

'That's right, sir. We're a lucky couple of beggars.'

'I'm afraid I read Brigham wrong.'

'And we both read Nadia wrong.'

'So, we're gullible as well as lucky.'

'That's about the size of it. But better gullible than unlucky, don't you reckon?'

Max nodded. 'I do.'

They swapped stories of their narrow escapes as they drank tea from enamel mugs. From Sam, Max did not withhold le Singe's

message. He showed him the scrap of wallpaper with the Japanese characters written on it.

'Does that really mean something, sir?' Sam asked.

'Yes. And I intend to find out what.'

'You're not dropping it, then, with Tarn and that turncoat Norris both dead?'

'Did you think I would?'

'Not really, sir. I never expect you to take the easy course.'

'I'm sorry you had such a rough time of it in my absence, Sam. If I'd been here—'

'It mightn't have turned out as well as it did. And it wasn't that rough. I never knew my life was in danger until after it stopped being. I came to in the hospital to find my forehead being stroked by a nurse with the face of an angel, telling me I'd nearly suffocated and should take it easy. It wasn't difficult to do as she said. The worst was learning Nadia was a snake in the grass.'

'There's treachery everywhere you look, I'm afraid.'

'And salvation in strange places. I still don't understand why Mr Morahan stepped in. I'm just thankful he did.'

'I plan to ask him. But I don't expect to learn much. He keeps his own counsel.'

'That he does, sir. But I'd be happy to hear what he tells you – even if it doesn't amount to anything – over a glass or three this evening.'

'Good idea. We've both earnt a night on the spree.'

'See your family while you were in Blighty, did you, sir?'

'I met my mother.'

'I don't suppose the subject of those fields your dad earmarked for you cropped up, did it?'

Max offered no immediate answer. He drained his mug and set it down by the kettle, then gazed out through the glass-panelled door into the maintenance bay. 'I couldn't drag you away from all this, Sam,' he said at last. 'You're doing your country such sterling service.'

'You mean you *won't* drag me away.'

'I mean I don't know what the future holds.' Max turned to Sam

and grinned. 'Apart from standing you more drinks than will be good for you this evening.'

MAX ENTERED THE OUTER OFFICE OF IRETON ASSOCIATES AT 33 Rue des Pyramides, to find Schools Morahan and Malory Hollander discussing horse-racing form, with laughter bubbling in their voices. Max had a fleeting impression, not for the first time, that they shared some secret purpose over and above their work for Travis Ireton, that they were partners in an enterprise whose significance eclipsed their everyday concerns – and of which they would never speak.

The impression was all the more fleeting because of the pleasure they took at his arrival. Malory kissed him and Morahan pumped his hand.

'I knew Tarn by reputation, Max,' said Morahan. 'I'd never have expected you to be able to outwit him.'

'I was lucky. And so was Sam.'

'He was. Sometimes, though not often enough, fortune smiles on the righteous.'

'I want to thank you for what you did.'

'I just happened to be in the right place at the right time.'

'It didn't just happen, though, did it? I gather you both decided I needed looking after and Sam was the beneficiary.'

'We were glad to be of service.'

'Would Travis have approved?'

'We didn't ask him,' said Malory. 'That's what happens when you make yourself elusive.'

'He's still lying low?'

'He is,' said Morahan. 'But he's back in Paris. Business would

366

suffer if he stayed away any longer. You won't be seeing him here for a while, though. Carver mistakenly thinks Travis knew about Ennis's dealing with Lemmer and wants to sweat the details out of him. So Travis is keeping out of his way. I'm meeting him this afternoon at Enghien racetrack. He feels safe in a crowd. Malory's just been picking me a winner from the paper.'

'Héliad in the four o'clock,' said Malory. 'The track will suit him.'

'We'll see about that. Any message for Travis, Max?'

'None you'd care to pass on.'

Morahan smiled. 'Understood.'

'Grand as it is to see you, Max,' said Malory, 'you really shouldn't stay.'

'She's right,' Morahan sighed. 'Carver's stationed a guy in the café across the street to monitor comings and goings here. He'll report your arrival and I'd guess Carver would take a long talk with you as second best to one with Travis.'

Max had no wish to encounter Carver. At the very least the man would waste a lot of Max's time. 'I'd better make myself scarce, then.'

'Have you heard about Corinne Dombreux?'

'What?'

'Commissioner Zamaron regards me as his new-found *meilleur ami* since I helped him wrap up those several murder cases that have been cluttering his desk. Best of all from his point of view, and thanks to you as well as Nadia Bukayeva, the principal suspects are all dead. Never mind that Norris probably didn't hire Tarn on his own initiative—'

'Or that Tarn didn't shoot Ennis.'

Morahan looked surprised and curious. 'He didn't?'

Max shook his head. 'No. But what about Corinne?'

'Oh, I pointed out to my buddy Léon that she's obviously innocent and that by arranging her early release he could avoid being obliged to look for the police officers who might have dosed up the evidence against her. This very morning he telephoned me to report that the magistrate's set her free.' Morahan glanced up at the clock. 'She's probably on her way home already.'

'*Ligne Trois* from Concorde to Notre-Dame-des-Champs would be your quickest route,' said Malory.

'Give her my regards when you see her,' Morahan continued.

'You've met Corinne, Schools?' Max asked.

'Once, yes.'

'How did that come about?'

'She called by here one day hoping to see Travis. He was out. She got me instead.'

'What did she want with Travis?'

'She never actually said. I advised her to make an appointment. It was only later that I discovered she knew Henry. So, if I was guessing, I'd say she was anxious about his dealings with Travis and planned to charm Travis into telling her what those dealings were.'

'And did she make an appointment?'

'Yes,' said Malory. 'Travis told me to invite her to have lunch with him if she called again, as she duly did.' She flicked open the desk diary in front of her. 'Wednesday, March twelfth. Café Voltaire, Place de l'Odéon.'

'The twelfth?' Sir Henry had been in England that day, changing his will and reclaiming his father's Sumerian antiquities. Corinne had never mentioned lunch with Ireton. She had never mentioned meeting him after their encounter at St-Cloud. 'Did Travis say what happened?'

'Not that I recall. But then I doubt I asked.'

'Schools?'

'Nope.'

'If you want to dodge Carver, Max,' Malory said softly, 'you really should go.'

'Yes. Of course. One other thing, though. Do you speak Japanese, Malory?'

'I picked up a few of the basics.'

'What about reading it?'

'Are you kidding? Have you seen what Japanese looks like?'

Impulsively, Max took the scrap of wallpaper out of his pocket and showed her le Singe's message. 'Like this?'

Malory squinted at the markings, then nodded. 'Yes. Just like that.'

'Any idea what it means?'

'No. Except . . .'

'What?'

'Well, there are no *kanji* in it. It's mostly *katakana*, I think, so that suggests it's a foreign word translated into Japanese.'

'Really?'

'Probably.'

'Kuroda could tell you what it says,' suggested Morahan.

'Just what I was thinking. Where would I be likeliest to find him, d'you think?'

'Now?'

'Or later.'

'There's a Council of Five meeting today. It's a sop to Japan for being excluded from the Council of Four. Their delegates will be out in force. So, he'll probably be with them at the Quai d'Orsay until . . .'

'Some time after Héliad romps home in the four o'clock at Enghien,' said Malory with a superior smirk. 'Is that writing on a fragment of wallpaper, Max?'

'Yes, it is.'

'Where's the wall it came off?' asked Morahan.

Max did not answer. All he said as he strode towards the door was, 'I must go.'

'Then go well,' Morahan called after him.

'Amen to that,' murmured Malory.

As Max hurried away from 33 Rue des Pyramides in Paris, heading, as Malory had recommended, for Concorde Métro station, Appleby advanced slowly into C's office at British Secret Service Headquarters in London.

Nine days had passed since C had approved his proposal to use Max as a means of tracking down Lemmer. The plan had so far failed to achieve its desired result. It had produced other effects, however, not all of them to C's liking, as his forbidding expression and the absence of any other member of staff served to confirm. What he had to say – and what Appleby might say in response – he evidently did not judge suitable for committee consumption.

369

'Sit down, Appleby, sit down,' C began in a tone he may have intended to be neutral, but which somehow carried gruffness at its edges. He closed a file he had been studying. 'I've just taken a look at the minutes of last week's meeting to remind myself of the conditions upon which I approved your operation.'

'Oh, yes, sir?'

'The justification you advanced for using James Maxted as a proxy in the search for Lemmer was that we could disown him if we needed to.'

'Indeed, sir and—'

'I specifically told you to avoid drawing our inquiries to the attention of the French authorities and *at all costs* to keep the Americans out of it.'

'Yes, sir,' said Appleby glumly. The course of their discussion was set and it was not set fair.

'I must congratulate you. I cannot recall in the admittedly short history of this department an operation that has miscarried so comprehensively and so quickly. I have had Lord Hardinge bending my ear about your harassment of senior civil servants and reminding me that my budget for this year is still only provisional. I have had the commissioner of the Metropolitan Police reporting that you conferred departmental privilege on Maxted in respect of their investigation of a homicide at an address in Mayfair earlier this week. The US Department of State has been in touch with the Foreign Office seeking information they believe we may possess about Lemmer's whereabouts following the assassination of a member of the American delegation in Paris last Saturday. The *Deuxième Bureau* wants to know what we have to say about the murders of two members of *our* delegation last Tuesday. One of our own men, a promising young agent whose father I know personally, is also dead. Meanwhile, extreme measures are having to be taken to hold the press at bay. And Lemmer, I feel sure you will confirm, is as elusive now as he was when you last sat in this room.'

Silence settled over them, moderated by C's stertorous breathing. He appeared to be waiting for Appleby to mount a defence, with little expectation that it would be adequate.

'Well, sir—'

'Yes?'

'Things obviously haven't gone as I'd hoped.'

'I should perhaps add understatement to the list of your talents when I next review your personal file,' said C unsmilingly.

'There have been some valuable outcomes.'

'Pray apprise me of them.'

'We've exposed one of Lemmer's agents in our delegation.'

'But sadly he's not available for interrogation.'

'No, sir. Nor is Lemmer's agent in the American delegation. But the damage the Americans have suffered is greater than any done to us. I believe Lemmer now has information likely to prove very embarrassing to them.'

'The Contingencies Memorandum?'

'Yes. The Japanese may also be in difficulties.'

'Because of these Chinese documents you think he's procured?'

'Yes. I suggest the French can be fended off by demanding an explanation from them for the bungling at best, the sabotage at worst, of inquiries into the death of Maxted's father.'

'Sir Henry. The lovesick old fool – if I read your report correctly – who set this disastrous sequence of events in motion.'

'It may be he was that, sir. Or it may be he wanted to be thought that.'

'What are you implying?'

'I believe there's more to be discovered yet about Sir Henry and his dealings with Pierre Dombreux.'

'Who we assume was another of Lemmer's spies?'

'Yes, sir. But it is only an assumption.'

'As is your claim that Lemmer had penetrated all the leading delegations in Paris.'

'We know about Norris and Ennis, sir. There are bound to be others. If we can take one of them alive, we may find a trail that leads to Lemmer.'

'A faint hope, Appleby, considering that I imagine you'd start looking for these "others" by investigating Norris's known friends and associates. Lord Hardinge wouldn't allow that, I'm afraid. It would be more than my job's worth, never mind yours.'

371

'It's the obvious way to proceed, sir.'

'Then you'll have to find an *un*obvious way. Before you try, speculate for my benefit about Lemmer's motives. His network, however extensive, no longer serves any purpose. The Berlin government has no use for him, even supposing he has any use for them. And our fly on the wall at the Kaiser's court-in-exile assures us they have no contact with him at all. So, what is he trying to achieve – and for whom?'

'I don't know, sir. Frankly, that's what we should probably be most worried about. Lemmer has a plan. It's in his nature. He's plotting to some end. But what that end might be . . .'

'Why did you disobey my orders where young Maxted was concerned, Appleby?' A frown like a brewing storm had taken over C's never entirely benign features. 'You were supposed to disown him if anything went wrong, as I think we can agree it did.'

'He risked his life for us, sir, and nearly lost it – twice.'

'That's your explanation?'

'Yes, sir.' Appleby braced himself. 'It is.'

'Mmm.' The frown lightened – marginally but significantly. 'The gesture does you credit, Appleby, even if nothing else does in this sorry affair. We cannot simply wash our hands of those who help us for noble reasons, however advantageous it might be to do so. Can Maxted be of further use to us?'

'It's hard to see how, sir.'

'Yet he worsted Tarn, a seasoned killer.'

'He did, sir, though not without assistance.'

'From le Singe?'

'So he said, sir.'

'And whose side is le Singe on?'

'Difficult to judge, sir. We know almost nothing about him. He's . . . a rumour made flesh.'

'More flesh and less rumour is what we need all round, Appleby.'

'What do you want me to do, sir?'

'Return to Paris, for the time being. The situation in the Council of Four is tense, as I'm sure you're aware. It's perhaps fortunate for us that the PM's too busy wrangling with Clemenceau over the Rhineland to give any attention to our problem with Lemmer.

We'll keep our heads down for a while and review the situation in a month or so. But talking of heads, I'll be candid. Yours may well have to roll.'

Appleby was unsurprised. He had taken too many chances. He had offended too many powerful people. 'I stand by my report, sir.'

'Good. Backing down won't help you. I'm not sure what would, short of a breakthrough on the Lemmer front. Think you can pull one off?'

'With my hands tied as they are, sir? No. But . . .'

'Never say die, eh?' C's gaze narrowed to a squint. 'At your age, you could opt to retire now the war's over. But I dare say you haven't a great deal to retire *to.*'

'I'd prefer to stay on, sir.'

'Yes. Of course you would. Well, we'll see.' C sighed heavily. 'That'll be all for now, Appleby. You can go.'

'Thank you, sir.'

As Appleby rose to leave, C cast him a strange, almost pitying look. He seemed about to add something, then changed his mind and flapped a dismissive hand towards the door, through which, a moment later, Appleby retreated.

It WAS NOT CLEAR TO MAX WHETHER MADAME MESNET recognized him or not. But she admitted him to 8 Rue du Verger readily enough and confirmed, somewhat grudgingly, that Corinne was in. '*Madame Dombreux? Oui, monsieur. Elle est à la maison. Au troisième étage.*'

He climbed the stairs to her door, accompanied, it seemed to him, by his father's ghost. It was easy to imagine Sir Henry walking up with him, breathing heavily, rocking slightly in that arthritic way he had, humming to himself some old music-hall tune as they went. For an instant, Max was convinced he smelt the old man's cigar smoke drifting past him.

They reached the door. And Max was alone. He knocked.

There was no response, though he was certain he had heard a movement inside the apartment. He knocked again and called her name. 'Corinne? It's Max.'

There was an interval of silence. Then the door opened and she looked out at him. She was pale and hollow-eyed. But to see her in her own clothes rather than the grey smock she had worn while in custody was a relief. There was disbelief in her gaze and more vulnerability than there had been before. Confinement had left its mark. She had not known, of course, how long she would be held. She had not known Max would be as good as his word and win her liberation.

'Can I come in?' he asked lamely.

'Of course.' Tears sprang suddenly into her eyes. 'I'm sorry. Please.' She stepped back, dabbing away the tears with a handkerchief.

374

He entered and closed the door. 'How are you?' he asked, horrified by his own banality.

'Oh, Max.' She hugged him then, clinging tightly to him. 'I never thought this day would come.'

'I told you it would.'

'I didn't dare believe you.' She broke away, but held him by the hands as she looked at him. 'Is it all true? The man who killed Henry is dead and the man who paid him to kill Henry is also dead?'

'Yes. It's true.'

'And you are well and safe?'

'As you see.'

'You look thinner, Max. And your colour is not so good. They tell me you were shot.'

'A flesh wound. I'm fine.' He smiled. 'Though tender when hugged.'

'I'm sorry. I didn't—'

'No, no. It's all right. You're not quite your old self yet either, Corinne. We've both been through the wringer, haven't we?'

'They said you were in London. When did you get back?'

'This morning. I came here as soon as I heard you'd been freed.' He glanced past her, his attention taken by something he could see through the open door of the bedroom at the end of the passage. A suitcase was open on the bed, with clothes and other articles piled in and around it. He frowned in puzzlement. 'Are you . . . going away?'

Corinne let go of him and nodded solemnly. 'I have to. It's a condition of my release. I must leave Paris immediately and stay away for the duration of the peace conference. It was made very clear to me that if I refused they would continue to hold me.'

'But on what charge? I thought the police had admitted you were innocent.'

'Of poor Raffaele's murder, yes. But I can be accused of complicity in Pierre's alleged treason at any time they wish and detained indefinitely under emergency wartime regulations. And the war cannot officially end while the conference continues.'

'Where will you go?'

'Nantes, to begin with. My sister has agreed to take me in, probably against her better judgement. I won't stay with her for long. Though where I'll go from there . . .' She shook her head. 'I simply don't know.'

'But you'll write and tell me when you're settled?'

'If you want me to.'

'Of course I want you to.' Max wondered if, like him, Corinne had imagined a possible future in which they were not so far apart. Irony was knotted around them. But for his father, they would never have met. And but for his father, he might have spoken some of the words that had formed in his mind.

'Then I'll write. But to what address?'

'I'm not sure. My solicitor will know where to find me. Write to him.' He took Mellish's card from his wallet and handed it to her. 'You will, won't you?'

'Yes.' She smiled. 'I promise.'

'When will you set off?'

'This afternoon.'

'So soon?'

'I was advised to leave without delay. I have no choice but to comply.'

'Do you have time for lunch with me before you go?'

'Oh, Max, there's such a lot I have to sort out. Lunch would be lovely, but . . .'

'Say you'll come.' He smiled defiantly at her. 'There's so much I have to tell you.'

'Tell me now.'

'Only if you agree to lunch.'

She gave in and smiled back at him. 'All right.'

She had made coffee and there was more than enough for two. They sat drinking it by the window of the sitting-room. The window was half-open and the sounds of the city – clopping hoofs, rumbling carts, rattling trams, barking dogs, raised human voices – filtered in around them. As Max recounted his experiences of the previous ten days, he made excuses to himself for resorting to minor misrepresentations in order to avoid mentioning certain

376

things – such as his night with Nadia Bukayeva and his wish to believe the worst of Brigham because he might be his son – on the grounds that they changed nothing materially. The truth of why Sir Henry had been killed and by whom and at whose instigation was established now, doubtful though it was that it would ever be formally acknowledged.

'Tarn wasn't simply an assassin,' Max explained. 'He specialized in disguising his murders as accidents – or as the acts of others. I suppose Norris and his accomplices feared Pa might have confided in you, so Tarn planned to silence you as well, by having you take the blame for Spataro's murder, which also conveniently disposed of a false witness against you before he could change his story.'

'And Henry took all the risks he did so that he and I could live in luxury?'

'Apparently so. His money was tied up in the estate in Surrey and I suppose he didn't think it would be fair to the family to try to take any out. Ribeiro's scheme promised an independent source of wealth.'

'But I would have gone anywhere with him, even if he'd been penniless. He must have known that.'

'He probably did, Corinne. But he wanted you to enjoy the finer things in life after being denied them for so long.'

'Instead of which, Henry is dead and I am homeless and jobless.' She looked away, out through the window.

Max saw her chin trembling from the effort it took her not to cry. He stretched forward and took her hand. 'I'm sorry.'

She squeezed his in return, then let go. 'I had plenty of time to think while I was in custody,' she said, her voice thick with emotion. 'I suppose I always knew Henry carried secrets with him of which he would never speak. And I suppose I knew those secrets were dangerous. When he went to London, I didn't really believe he'd been recalled to the Foreign Office. I never told you before – I didn't want you to doubt my loyalty to him – but while he was away—'

'You went to see Ireton.'

'You *know*?'

'Morahan told me. Just this morning.'

'Ah, Mr Morahan.'

'He sends his regards. He said you wanted to know what dealings Pa had with Ireton.'

'Yes. I met Ireton for lunch in the hope of finding out. It was a waste of time. Mine *and* his. It soon became clear we had different expectations of each other. He said a lot. But he told me nothing. Except, of course, what I already knew: that he would steal me from Henry if he could, or even share me with him.' She shuddered. 'He is not an honourable man.'

'As his behaviour since has confirmed.'

'Henry should have known better than to do business with him.'

'There's no one else in that particular business.'

'No. I suppose there isn't. I wonder, though, if there wasn't something else Henry was trying to arrange through someone other than Ireton.'

'What makes you think so?'

'The Arab boy who saved your life. Le Singe. You said he can travel across roofs, up and down sheer walls and in and out of high windows.'

'Better than any gymnast.'

'Then it must have been le Singe Henry was chasing when he went up on to the roof. No one else could have got in here so easily. Tarn used the boy to lure Henry on to the roof and then . . .'

'Pushed him off.'

'Yes.' She shook her head, surprised by her own reactions, it seemed. 'I'm glad you killed Tarn, Max, however useful he might have been alive. I'm glad he had a split second in which to understand that he was going to pay for what he'd done.'

'I don't think le Singe realized what was going to happen. He's been trying to make amends for it ever since.'

'But why did Henry go after him, Max? That's what I can't stop asking myself. *Why?*'

'I don't know.'

Max had told only Sam about the message on the wall in London. He had kept it from Corinne so far, assuring himself that he should find out what the message meant before disclosing it to her. That was not the only reason for his reticence, though. Corinne

was surely right. There was a secret within the other secrets Sir Henry had borne. Max could sense it. He could almost smell it, as distinctly as the cigar smoke he had imagined on the stairs. But he could not see it. He could not touch it.

'Do you think you will ever know?' Corinne asked.

'I think I will, yes. One day.'

Before leaving, Max borrowed the key to the attic and retraced the steps his father had taken on the last night of his life, reasoning out the sequence of events as he went. The pursuit: le Singe swift and agile, Sir Henry slow and lumbering. Le Singe would have had to hold himself back, so that Sir Henry could not fail to know where he had gone. Then, as Sir Henry entered the attic, le Singe broke the skylight in the loft space above and scrambled out on to the roof. Sir Henry followed, through the window ahead of him, emerging in the gulley behind the parapet and turning to—

Tarn struck. Not cleanly, though. There was a struggle. But the younger, stronger man prevailed. Sir Henry was pushed back over the parapet. He lost his footing. He fell.

Max stood where he had stood once before on the roof, the city spread around him like an arena. He stared out and down into the air his father had fallen though.

There was nothing to see. He looked up, towards the apex of the roof, where le Singe could have crouched and watched as the deed played itself out. There was nothing to see there either. Except the blank sky. Against which the mind could paint any picture it cared to – until the true one was known.

THE COUNCIL OF FIVE MEETING HAD BROUGHT A HORDE OF functionaries to the French Foreign Ministry on the Quai d'Orsay. Max had to join a lengthy queue for a word with the *portier* who controlled access to the building beyond the entrance hall. Military police were guarding the stairs and corridors. No one was going any further without a good reason.

Just as Max was wondering whether he would be able to persuade the *portier* to send a message to Kuroda, he saw the representative of the Japanese delegation he and Morahan had spoken to at the Hotel Bristol descending the main staircase, wringing his hands as ever. He appeared to be on his way out of the building.

Max intercepted him as he headed across the hall. 'Excuse me. You may not remember me. We met last week, at the Bristol. I was—'

'Ah yes.' The man nodded in recognition and gazed at Max through circular steel-framed glasses. 'You were looking for Commissioner Kuroda.'

'That's right. I—'

'Your name is Maxted. You were with Mr Morahan.'

'You have a good memory.'

'It is part of my job, Mr Maxted. To remember things.'

'I'm looking for Commissioner Kuroda again. Is he here?'

'Ah, no. I am sorry. He is not here. I do not know where he is. I will see him later, though. If you want me to give him a message . . .'

'How much later is that likely to be?'

'I cannot say. He is busy with many things.'

'It's rather an urgent matter.'

'Can I help?'

Max hesitated. He contemplated having to wait another day for an answer to the question that had been burning inside him for far too long already. He could not do it. It was a simple matter of translation. It was not really important who did the translating. 'That's kind of you, Mr . . .'

'Yamanaka.' The name came with a courtly bow.

'Well, Mr Yamanaka, the thing is this.' Max took out the scrap of wallpaper and showed him the message. 'Can you tell me what this says?'

Yamanaka peered at it. 'Of course. It is written in Japanese. You cannot read it?'

'No.'

'It is a Japanese translation of an English word. An English surname, I think.'

'Really?'

'I think so, yes.'

'What is the surname?'

'Farngold.'

Max wandered out into the open expanse of the Esplanade des Invalides, thoughts whirling in his head. *Farngold.* Suddenly, the name had meaning – significance. It was not – it had never been – merely the pseudonym Sir Henry had used for renting a safe-deposit box at the Banque Ornal. It was a door, opening on to a hidden world. Like a row of dominoes, the consequences of the discovery toppled in Max's mind. Sir Henry had appointed him as his executor not only because of what the box contained, but because of the name it was held under. Lemmer had guessed he would use the name because they shared the knowledge of its importance. *Farngold.* Written by le Singe in Japanese, a language he surely neither spoke nor wrote. But Japan was where Sir Henry and Lemmer had first met. And that was where the secret must have been spawned, nearly thirty years in the past. *Farngold.* It was the answer, if only he knew the question.

Max was not optimistic that Corinne would ever have heard Sir Henry mention the name Farngold, but he certainly intended to find out. They had arranged to meet for an early lunch at La Closerie des Lilas in Boulevard du Montparnasse. Max arrived shortly before 12.30 and bagged a prime table.

As he waited for Corinne, he leafed through the café's copy of *Le Figaro*. His eye was taken by an article on an inner page under the headline *Le Marquis Saionji et la maîtresse indiscrète*. As far as he could glean, Ohana, the '*très jeune*' mistress of the '*vénérable*' head of the Japanese delegation to the peace conference, was embarrassing her '*vieux protecteur*' with her lack of reticence and might be to blame for Japan's exclusion from the new all-powerful Council of Four. Max wondered if this explained Kuroda's absence from the Quai d'Orsay. If so, he was not to be envied. Silencing a loose-tongued geisha did not sound like an easy task.

Absorbed in the effort of translating the article, Max was surprised by the sudden appearance at his table of a meek, tubby, balding, placid-featured man in a tight-fitting suit that looked to have seen better days. 'Monsieur Maxted?'

'Yes.'

'My name is Miette. I am a neighbour of Madame Dombreux. I work near by.'

'You do?'

'Madame Dombreux asked me to give you this.' He handed Max a letter. 'Please excuse me.'

With that Miette was gone, leaving Max to open the envelope bearing his name and to read the letter it contained.

My dear Max,

I have set off early for Nantes. By the time Monsieur Miette delivers this to you, my train will have left. I am so sorry to disappoint you. I could not bear to exchange farewells with you. I feel it is better to go now, before the little courage I have deserts me. You should stop looking for answers. There must always be some that elude one in this life. Go home. You have avenged Henry. That is enough. Leave the past

behind. Make a future for yourself, as I will try to do for myself.

Corinne

Glancing down, Max noticed that there was something else in the envelope. He slid it out on to the table.

Mellish's card. Corinne wanted him to understand clearly that he would not hear from her again. She had made her decision and was going to live by it.

Despite what Corinne had said in the letter, Max hurried from the café to the Gare Montparnasse. He scoured the concourse and the waiting-room. There was no sign of her. And a clerk confirmed a train for Nantes had left half an hour previously. She was gone.

It took a visit to 8 Rue du Verger to convince himself of the fact, though. '*Partie, monsieur*,' Madame Mesnet insisted. '*Partie sans espoir de retour*.' She had gone. And she was not coming back.

MAX HEADED NORTH, BACK TOWARDS THE QUAI D'ORSAY. HE had no particular destination in mind. What he should do next he could not decide. He forced himself to address the question: was Corinne right to draw a line under what had happened and seek a new start in life elsewhere? Quite possibly, he could not deny. The clue he was following now was faint and perhaps illusory. Farngold might be just a pseudonym after all.

But he did not believe that. And it was not in his nature to let such uncertainty rest. He might be forced to eventually. Until he was, though . . .

He crossed the river at the Pont de la Concorde, then struck west to the Plaza Athénée, reasoning that Sir Henry might have talked about Farngold to his old friend and confidant, Baltazar Ribeiro.

They informed him at the desk that Ribeiro was in the hotel, but busily engaged with a working lunch in a private room. Max prevailed upon them to send a message in, requesting a few minutes of Ribeiro's time. He said he would wait outside.

'Max!'

Ribeiro emerged at a half-charge into the frail spring sunshine on the Avenue Montaigne and beamed at Max as if seeing him was the best thing that had happened to him all day, as perhaps it was.

'I have been worried about you,' Ribeiro declared, breathing heavily. 'It is a relief to see you looking so well.'

'I'm sorry to call you out of a meeting, Baltazar. If the matter had been less urgent . . .'

'Does this concern Herbert Norris?'

'You've heard about him?'

'Of course. I knew him. He was the British delegation's representative on the shipping committee. It is rumoured that he was implicated in Henry's murder. Is it true?'

'I'm afraid so, yes.' Max was aware he owed Ribeiro a fuller explanation of events than he currently had the energy or inclination to supply. 'I'd like to be able to tell you everything I've learnt, Baltazar, and I will, but I simply don't have the time at present. What I wanted to ask you now was whether my father ever mentioned to you someone called Farngold.'

'Farngold?'

'F-A-R-N-G-O-L-D.'

Ribeiro frowned, then shook his head. 'No. I do not think so. It is not a name I remember.'

'You remembered Lemmer.'

'Yes, I did. But not this name. It is important, yes?'

'Very.'

'So, it has not ended with Norris?'

Max shook his head. 'No. It hasn't.'

Max headed for the Mazarin because, for the moment at least, he could think of nowhere else to go.

He was barely aware of his surroundings as he approached the hotel and as a result nearly walked into the car door that opened across his path when he was only a few yards from the entrance.

Frank Carver glared out at him from the rear seat of the vehicle. 'I'd like a word with you, Mr Maxted,' he said grimly.

Max sighed. He felt tired and dispirited and in no mood to fend off questions from Carver. But it seemed he had no choice in the matter. 'I can't help you,' he said simply.

'Let me be the judge of that. Get in and we can talk while Joe drives us around town.'

'Must I?'

'I can't force you to. But I'll keep after you if you don't, getting

grouchier all the time. So, why not do us both a favour and climb aboard?'

The drive was a circular tour of the 8th arrondissement. Their discussion had its circularities too. Carver was convinced Max knew more than he was willing to admit about Sir Henry's involvement with Lemmer's network of spies. He also blamed Max for Lemmer's possible acquisition of a document – the Contingencies Memorandum, obviously, though he never referred to it as such. And he suspected Max of working for or with Ireton in some unspecified capacity. Max made it as clear as he could that he had only ever acted in pursuit of the truth about his father's death. He was not responsible for all that had flowed from that.

'It's over, Carver. Tarn's dead. So's Norris. I've done as much as I can for my father. And there's nothing I can do for you.'

'Why'd you come back to Paris, then? Why are you still in contact with Ireton?'

'I'm not. I went to his office this morning to thank Morahan for saving the life of my friend, Sam Twentyman. And I came back to Paris to see Sam.'

'Bull. You're up to something. The French may have decided to close the book on this, but I can't afford to. There are too many unanswered questions.'

'I agree. But I don't have any of the answers to give you.'

'Why do I find that so hard to believe?'

'I don't know. Maybe you're too cynical for your own good.'

'If I learn you're holding out on me . . .'

'You won't, because I'm not.'

'No? Well, for as long as you stay in Paris, I'll assume you are. So don't think you've seen the last of me. I'll be watching you. Waiting for that false move I bet you'll make in the end.'

Silence fell between them. The car drove on slowly along the Champs-Elysées, approaching the Rond-Point for the second time. A few moments passed. Then Max said, 'Can I get out now?'

MAX SET OFF SOUTH ALONG AVENUE D'ANTIN. HE HAD ONLY covered twenty yards or so when a car pulled in beside him. Fearing Carver had changed his mind and wanted to ask him some more questions, he put his head down and kept on walking.

'Max!'

It was not Carver's voice and not his aggressive tone either. Max turned round to find himself looking at the overcoated and smiling figure of Masataka Kuroda, standing by the stationary vehicle.

'Can I walk with you, Max? I was waiting for you at your hotel. We have been following you.' He nodded to the car. 'Did you enjoy your tour with Mr Carver?'

'Hardly.' Max returned Kuroda's smile and shook his hand. 'It's good to see you, Masataka.'

'You also, Max. Shall we walk?'

'Yes. Let's.'

Kuroda said something to his driver in Japanese and the car started away. He and Max fell in together and carried on along the avenue.

'I assume Yamanaka told you I was looking for you earlier.'

'He did. And that you had something you wanted to be translated.'

'He did the honours.'

'Farngold.'

'That's right. Does the name mean anything to you?'

'I cannot say it does. May I see . . . the piece of paper?'

'Certainly.' Max took the scrap of wallpaper from his pocket and unfolded it for Kuroda to look at.

Kuroda squinted at the writing for a few seconds. 'Strange,' he said. 'Very strange. May I ask where it came from?'

'My flat in London.'

'Ah. Where you killed Tarn?'

'You know about that?'

'Of course. His death is a blow to those in my government who hoped he would eliminate Lemmer. It has caused consternation. They hired the finest archer, only for an arrow to sprout from his chest.'

'I was lucky, Masataka, that's all.'

'All? You should not speak so lightly of luck, Max. I am more glad than I can say that you survived. I expected to hear of *your* death, not Tarn's. Luck is a gift from the gods. You should be grateful for it.'

'I am, believe me.'

'It gives you a chance to extricate yourself from the intrigues surrounding Lemmer. Those who authorized the hiring of Tarn are shamed by his failure. Those opposed to such extreme action are therefore in the ascendant. While they remain so, you would do well to leave the fray.'

'But what if there's more to be discovered?'

'About Farngold, for instance?'

'Exactly.'

'Who wrote the name?'

'I didn't see it done.'

'Was it le Singe?'

'It seems unlikely he'd know how to write anything in Japanese.'

'Unlikely, but not impossible. There is a rumour that he has been employed to enter hotels and offices used by various delegations in order to examine documents and memorize their contents. It seems he may have what is called a photographic memory. It is even possible that the burglaries he is supposed to have committed were intended to distract attention from the real purpose of his activities. If this is true, he may be capable of reproducing a word he had seen written in Japanese without understanding what it means.'

388

'Who's rumoured to be his employer, Masataka?'

'No one knows. But you and I could hazard a guess.'

'Lemmer.'

'It may be so. Ultimately, that is. Presumably, Lemmer would have engaged his services through intermediaries. Tarn must have known what le Singe was doing, remember, but it did not help him find Lemmer. One may see the strings on the puppet, while the hand pulling the strings remains invisible.'

'Still, it's surely no coincidence that the word was written in the language of the country where Lemmer and my father first met.'

'You think Farngold – whoever or whatever it is – connects Henry with Lemmer?'

'I think it may.'

'And how will you find out if it does or not?'

'I don't know yet.'

'Maybe you will never know.'

'Maybe I won't.'

'Then consider well the wisdom of abandoning your search. You are young. Life lies before you, with all its pleasures and fulfilments. You deserve to enjoy it. Why not allow yourself to do so?'

'Because I don't like giving up before I have to.'

'No.' Kuroda patted Max on the arm, almost paternally, as if imparting some resigned reflection on Sir Henry's behalf. 'And you will not give up, of course.'

They parted at the Pont des Invalides, where Kuroda crossed the river, heading for the Quai d'Orsay. Max watched him go, a tall, thin, courtly figure, moving at his own pace though the Parisian afternoon. His advice was sound. Max had accomplished more than could reasonably have been expected of him. He had defied the odds. He had won.

But he had no sense of victory. Nadia had escaped. Lemmer was unscathed. And le Singe's message still pointed to an untold truth. He could not simply walk away.

No one was lying in wait at the Mazarin this time. But still the reception clerk had a surprise for him. 'There is a parcel for

389

you, Monsieur Maxted.' He lifted it out from beneath the desk.

It was about the size of a shoe box, wrapped in brown paper and fastened with string. Max's name was written on it in large capitals. There was no address. It had not come through the post.

'When was this delivered?'

'A couple of hours ago, *monsieur*.'

'Who by?'

'He did not give his name. He said you would be expecting it.'

'"Expecting it". He said that?'

'*Oui, monsieur*.'

'What did he look like?'

'Er ... *quelconque*; ordinary. He was ... well-dressed. Not young. Grey-haired, with a beard. And glasses. He spoke quietly. You know him?'

THE PARCEL HELD MONEY: LOTS OF IT. THE BUNDLES OF banknotes spilt out on to the bed in Max's room at the Mazarin and he gazed at the heap in astonishment. It amounted to thousands of pounds, as far as he could tell, though there were more US dollars and French francs than sterling. Lemmer had told the reception clerk Max would be expecting to receive it. But he had not been, of course. He had not foreseen this, not remotely.

His first thought was that it was a crude bribe. Then it came to him. It belonged to his father. It was Sir Henry's stockpile of money from the safe-deposit box at the Banque Ornal – and now, with bizarre appropriateness, delivered to his executor. The gesture was pure Lemmer. He had not wanted the money. He had wanted the documents the box held. Now he had them, Max was welcome to the cash.

There was no explanatory note. Max sifted through the bundles in search of one, though he felt sure he would search in vain. Lemmer trusted him to understand the message. The money had been wrapped in a sheet of newspaper: Max pulled it free from beneath the bundles and cast it aside.

As he did so, he noticed that someone had ringed in bright-red ink an advertisement on what was the back page of the previous Sunday's edition of *Le Petit Journal*.

MALADIES INTIMES. Guérison rapide peu coûteuse.
Consultations gratuites par docteurs-spécialistes.
Discrétion absolue. Pharmacie Claverie, 24 Boulevard de
Sébastopol, Paris.

391

The phrase *Discrétion absolue* had been underlined in red as well. It might mean nothing. A sheet of newspaper was a sheet of newspaper, a marked advertisement nothing out of the ordinary. But did anything really mean nothing in the world of Fritz Lemmer? Max doubted it. He doubted it very much.

He locked the money in his suitcase and headed out.

There was no queue at the counter of the Pharmacie Claverie. A mild-mannered man in a white coat faced Max across it with a smile that contrived to be both welcoming and discreet. *'Bonjour, monsieur. Vous desirez?'*

'Bonjour. I, er . . . *Je m'appelle Maxted.* James Maxted.'

'Ah, Monsieur Maxted.' The pharmacist seemed to know the name. *'Attendez un moment.'* He bustled off into a room behind him, reappearing a few seconds later with a small dark-brown bottle in his hand. *'Votre ordonnance.'* He passed it to Max with a broadening of his smile.

'C'est . . . pour moi?'

'Oui, monsieur.'

'Mais . . .'

'C'est tout, monsieur.' The pharmacist nodded emphatically, not to say dismissively. *'Merci beaucoup.'*

Max did not examine the bottle until he was outside, though it felt suspiciously light. Sure enough, there were no pills inside, just a plug of cotton wool and, beneath it, a tightly folded piece of paper.

It was a page torn from a railway timetable, showing services from Paris to Melun, a place he had never heard of, via numerous other places he had never heard of. The column listing the timings for one of the services – the 11.35 departure from the Gare de Lyon – had been outlined in red.

As Max set off back along the quai towards his hotel in Paris, pondering how to respond to what he did not doubt was an invitation from Lemmer, a very different kind of invitation was being considered by his mother in the drawing-room at Gresscombe Place in Surrey.

'Would you care to explain why you told us nothing about this, Mother?' Ashley asked snappishly.

'Ashley is head of the family now,' put in Lydia, quite unnecessarily, since Lady Maxted was well aware of his status.

'I'm bound to ask *when* you intended to inform us,' Ashley continued. 'But for the letter I had from Fradgley telling me the French police had changed their minds about how Pa met his death and my subsequent telephone conversation with Mellish, we might still be in ignorance of these appalling events. We were horrified to learn that James had actually killed a man – in the London flat, of all places. Such shocks aren't good for Lydia in her present condition.'

'Have you been to the flat?' asked Lydia. 'What state is it in?'

'Is it your unborn child you're concerned about?' Lady Maxted responded. 'Or the redecoration bill?'

'What we're concerned about, Mother,' said Ashley, with heavy deliberation, 'is limiting the damage to our family's reputation that James may have caused by involving himself in such . . . mayhem.'

'He killed an intruder in self-defence. And the French police are evidently satisfied, based on what Mr Fradgley has written to you, that the intruder in question murdered Henry. I'm bound to say that we should all be grateful to James for what he has achieved. Don't forget he also saved Mr Brigham's life.'

'But to shoot a man through the head,' gasped Lydia. 'It's . . . too awful for words.'

'Then spare yourself the distress of finding any words, my dear. Many men shot other men through the head in the war. We regard them as heroes and rightly so. James has done what he swore to do. I for one am proud of him.'

'I still don't understand why you didn't tell me what had happened as soon as you heard of it from Mellish,' Ashley complained.

'I knew how you would react. It was an emergency. I needed a calm atmosphere in which to address the matter.'

'Calm atmosphere? What the—'

'And I had George to advise me.'

'This isn't good enough, Mother,' Ashley declared, in something

393

close to a shout, adding a slap of his hand on the arm of his chair for emphasis. 'It really isn't.'

'Where is James now?' Lydia demanded.

'He's gone back to Paris.'

'Why?'

'He said there were some loose ends he wanted to tie up.'

'Loose ends?' spluttered Ashley. 'Hasn't he caused enough trouble?'

'He seems to think not.'

'Good God Almighty. He's insufferable, completely insufferable.'

'Did he say anything about the executorship before he left?' asked Lydia.

'The executorship?' Lady Maxted affected a vagueness of tone calculated to rile her daughter-in-law.

'Yes. The executorship.'

Lady Maxted paused theatrically, then said, 'As a matter of fact . . . I don't believe we spoke of it.'

'More money than either of us has ever seen before,' said Max a few hours later, opening the suitcase in his room at the Mazarin to show Sam Sir Henry's hoard of cash.

Sam whistled in disbelief. 'And more than I'll ever see again. That's for sure.'

'Lemmer certainly has his own way of doing things.'

'I'm sorry to hear that, sir.'

'Why?'

'It means you'll go after him. Just like you always went after the Boche pilots who had the biggest reputations. It's in your blood.'

'If I go after him, it'll be to learn the truth – the whole truth – about my father.'

'Understood, sir. Still, it's a pity.'

'What is?'

'The flying school. I'm sure we could have made a success of it.'

Max smiled. 'We still can. You're wrong about never seeing this much money again, Sam. Legally, it belongs to my brother, but he can go hang. I intend to salt it away so that you and I can start that

flying school eventually. Ashley's never going to give us those fields at Gresscombe, so we'll need to buy land as well as planes when the time comes.'

'Are you sure that's a good idea, sir? I mean—'

'As I recall, we were both sure it was a good idea when we talked it over at the Rose and Crown. You haven't changed your mind, have you?'

Sam looked aghast. 'Changed my mind? 'Course not. But . . . all this money. I, er . . .'

'Let me worry about the money.' Max clapped Sam on the shoulder. 'I can't predict how long it's going to take me to do what I have to do, Sam. The question is: are you willing to wait? You could always look for another partner.'

'You're joking, aren't you, sir?' Sam grinned. 'I'll never find anyone else I'd want to go into business with who'd actually be willing to go into business with me.'

'Rubbish.'

'It's the truth, sir. So, like my girl said to me before I went off to war: "I'll wait for you." But unlike her, I mean it. Anyway, I've got a job until this conference ends, haven't I? The way they're going, I reckon they could still be here come Christmas. And Paris is definitely one up on Walthamstow. The way I see it, I'm sitting pretty.'

'Good man.' Spontaneously they shook hands, confirming the renewal of their bargain. 'I doubt you'll see much of me for quite a while after tonight, Sam. You appreciate that, don't you?'

'I do, sir.' Sam knew better than to ask any questions about Max's pursuit of Lemmer. And Max liked him all the more because of it. 'You'll take care, won't you?'

'Of course. When did I ever not?'

'You don't want me to answer that, do you, sir?'

'Absolutely not. Now, to more serious matters.' Max pulled several notes out of a bundle of French francs and slipped them into his pocket, then closed the suitcase and locked it. 'It's time to go and get roaring drunk, I think, don't you?'

APPLEBY WAS SLEEPILY AWARE OF HIS TRAIN'S ARRIVAL AT THE Gare du Nord early the following morning, but he intended to doze on for an hour or so before emerging into the Parisian dawn. He distinctly recalled telling the steward so and was therefore none too pleased to be roused by a persistent knocking at the door of his cabin. 'Go away,' he bellowed. '*Va-t'en!*' But it did no good. Eventually, he hauled himself out of his bunk and opened the door.

'Good morning, Appleby,' said Max, beaming in at him. His voice may have been gravelly, but his chin had the smoothness of one who had already bathed and shaved. 'Can I buy you breakfast?'

They adjourned to the station café. Neither, it transpired, had much of an appetite. Coffee and his pipe satisfied Appleby's needs. It was coffee for Max too, supplemented by brandy. 'Hair of the dog,' he explained, without elaboration.

'Are you leaving Paris already?' Appleby asked, nodding to the suitcase Max was carrying with him.

'Maybe. I don't actually know.'

'It's too early for riddles.'

'I'll keep it plain and simple, then. How did your meeting at HQ go?'

'Not well, thanks to your exploits. My ears are still ringing from the reprimand.'

'Sorry about that.'

Appleby grunted. 'It can't be helped.'

'Ah, but perhaps it can. I have a proposition for you.'

Appleby's gaze narrowed. 'Go on.'

'Lemmer wants me to work for him.'

'*What?*'

'He came to see me while I was laid up at the Hôtel Dieu. Turned up at my bedside in the middle of the night, masquerading as a doctor.'

'Are you joking, Max?'

'No. I didn't tell anyone about it at the time because I didn't think they'd believe me. But it was him. Softly spoken, mild-mannered man. Beard and glasses. Professorial air.'

Appleby nodded slowly in amazement. 'So they say.'

'He offered me exciting and lucrative employment.'

'As a spy?'

'Something in that line. He said I'd enjoy the work.'

'And what did you say?'

'I told him to go to hell.'

'So I should hope.'

'But now . . .'

'Yes?'

'He's contacted me again since I came back to Paris. Indirectly. The offer's still open. You could even say he's made payment in advance. The suitcase contains the money he found in my father's safe-deposit box. Lemmer wanted the documents that were in it, of course, not the money. He's returned it to me as a gesture of good will. I was hoping you'd agree to bank it for me. In an account where it can be held for the duration.'

'The duration?' Appleby sat back in his chair and looked thoughtfully at Max. 'What have you got in mind?'

'There's something I haven't come to grips with yet that connects Lemmer with my father – some secret they shared, dating back to their days in Japan, I suspect. I mean to find out what it is. And I'm not going to stop until I do. Which is why I've decided to accept Lemmer's offer.'

'*Accept* his offer?'

'It's the only way I can get close enough to him to get to the heart of the mystery and maybe live to tell the tale. Don't you see,

Appleby? Working for Lemmer gives me the protection I need. It gives me a chance. I have to take it.'

'All I can see is that Lemmer's an enemy of our country. And anyone who works for him is guilty of treason. Do you really want to tell me that's what you propose to engage in?'

'Of course not.' Max leant across the table and fixed Appleby with his gaze. It was vital there be no misunderstanding between them. 'I'm telling you because I can accomplish something else beyond teasing out the truth about my father. I can learn what Lemmer intends to do with his spy network now the war's over – what plans he has, what plots he's hatching. And I can learn who's in his network. This is your chance as well as mine, Appleby. I can be your man on the inside. I can bring him down for you.'

Appleby looked at Max fondly, almost sorrowfully. 'Have you any conception of how dangerous what you're suggesting would be? Lemmer's bound to be doubtful of your loyalty. He's going to require ample proof of it. And any evidence to the contrary – the faintest suggestion that you're feeding information to me – will be fatal for you. Literally fatal.'

'I'll have to tread carefully, then. And trust you to do the same.'

'You've obviously already made your mind up.'

'It's a unique opportunity, Appleby. You're not going to refuse to help me, are you?'

Appleby took a fretful chew on his pipe, then said, 'No. Of course I'm not. As a representative of the Secret Service, I should do everything in my power to encourage you. And, if it comes to it, I will. But as you and I sit here this morning, Max, I say this to you. Don't do it. One way or the other, it'll destroy you. Let your father's secrets rest with him. Walk away. While you still can.'

Max smiled softly and shook his head. 'But I can't, you see. That's the point. I *can't* walk away.'

Appleby sighed. 'Then be it on your own head.'

'So, you *will* help me?'

Another sigh. 'Yes. But what we're discussing is no job for an amateur. And that's what you are.'

'Teach me a few of your professional tricks, then.'

'I'd have to get approval from the top for an operation like this,

Max. I couldn't discuss covert communication methods with you without authorization. And without some mastery of those methods you'd be sunk.'

'What are you talking about? Codes? Invisible ink?'

'That sort of thing, yes.'

'We used lemon juice at school.'

'It's no laughing matter.'

'I'm not laughing.' Max looked at his watch. 'You've got about five hours to turn me into a spy.'

'*Five hours?*'

'It's all I have, I'm afraid. Delaying my response would make Lemmer suspicious before I even started.'

'I couldn't get authorization in that time, let alone train you to any level of competence.'

'I'm a quick learner. And this is an emergency.'

'For God's sake, I've already had my knuckles rapped for letting you wreak havoc. Do you seriously expect me to go out on a limb for you again?'

'Lemmer's the target, Appleby. I'm just the arrow. How badly do you want him? How badly do your bosses want him? Playing it by the book won't work. This is our chance. Our only chance. Now. Today. What's it to be? Yes or no?'

A lengthy silence followed as they pondered each other's seriousness of purpose. Then Appleby groaned. 'Five hours, you say?'

'Yes.'

'Well, we'd better look lively, then, hadn't we?'

MAX STEPPED DOWN FROM THE TRAM IN FRONT OF THE GARE de Lyon, travelling bag in hand. He checked his watch by the station clock. It was twenty past eleven and he was neither early nor late. Warm spring sunshine fell hearteningly on his face as he walked unhurriedly towards the station entrance.

He paused in his progress by a post-box, where he took a letter out of his pocket and glanced at the name and address he had written on the envelope – *G. A. Mellish, Esq, Mellish & Co., 119a High Street, Epsom, Surrey, Angleterre* – before dropping it into the slot.

Max entered the station, made his way to the ticket office and bought a first-class single to Melun, then consulted the departures board to learn which platform his train was leaving from. Next he wandered across to a news-stand and bought a copy of *Le Figaro*. The Paris editions of several British and American newspapers were also available, but he had no wish to advertise his foreignness.

He strolled, with every appearance of casualness, to the platform where the train was waiting. It was not a popular service. There were few other passengers. He climbed aboard, glancing at his watch as he did so. In no more than a few minutes, the train would leave. He could disembark before then and walk back out of the station into the safe and secure normality of one version of the rest of his life. But he was not going to. His course was set.

He sat down. He had the compartment to himself, though, strangely, he felt as if he was being watched. He opened the

400

newspaper, but crooked his wrist so that he could follow the ticking down of the minutes to 11.35.

11.35 came. And 11.35 went. So did 11.36. At 11.37, there was a shrill blast on a whistle and a general slamming of doors. Then, at the last moment, the door of his compartment was yanked open and a man jumped in, slamming it shut behind him. The train was already moving. Max was no longer alone.

The man was of about Max's age, lean, sallow-skinned and narrow-shouldered. He was wearing a raincoat, despite the mildness of the day, which he did not take off. He removed only his hat as he sat down, diagonally opposite Max. He had thinning, sandy-coloured hair and a pinched, raw-boned face. He was breathing heavily, presumably because he had had to run for the train, and the cigarette he immediately lit activated a phlegmy cough. He unfolded a newspaper and began reading it.

The train lumbered out of the station, past goods sidings and warehouses. Max settled back in his seat. All he could do now was wait upon events. Lemmer would show his hand when he wanted to and not before.

Perhaps he already had, in the form of Max's tardy fellow passenger. Perhaps not. Time would tell.

The train stopped at every station as it slowly lurched and wheezed its way out of the city and south through a succession of villages separated by flat, open countryside.

With the other occupant of the compartment buried in his paper, Max began to assume nothing would happen until he reached Melun. He relaxed and closed his eyes, wondering if he would be able to catch up on any of the sleep he had missed the night before. He had always been a ready catnapper.

'*Excusez-moi, monsieur!*'

How long Max had dozed – whether he had dozed at all, indeed – was unclear to him. His fellow passenger had tapped him on the knee with his newspaper and now, blinking across at him, Max saw that he had an unlit cigarette in his mouth and was waggling a matchbox to demonstrate that it was empty.

'*Pouvez-vous me donner du feu?*'

Max delved in his jacket, produced a box of his own and obliged the fellow with a light.

'*Merci, monsieur.*' The man took a draw on the cigarette, coughed, then said, 'Next stop, Max.'

'What?'

'Next stop.'

The train was slowing, though only green fields were visible through the window. The man turned his newspaper in his hand so that Max could see the back page. He had seen it before. It was the previous Sunday's edition of *Le Petit Journal.*

'*Discrétion absolue,*' the man murmured.

The train slowed still further, the roof of a small station coming into view as it juddered to a halt. Max stood up, pulled his bag down from the luggage-rack and moved towards the door, only to discover that his companion had already opened it for him.

He stepped out on to the platform and looked back, thinking there might be some last signal or direction. But the man did not so much as glance at him as he slammed the door.

Max saw only one other passenger disembark – a middle-aged man wearing a tweed suit. The guard blew his whistle and the train cranked back into motion.

There were a couple of cottages next to the station. Otherwise it was surrounded by fields, though the roofs of the village it evidently served were visible in the distance. A lane marked by a line of poplars led away from the station towards them.

The noise of the train faded as Max followed the tweed-suited man along the platform to the ticket office. The man turned through a narrow gateway next to it into a small courtyard at the front of the station, lifted a bicycle out from behind a bush, attached clips to his trousers and climbed on to the machine, then pedalled slowly away along the lane, glancing back at Max as he went.

Max watched him go. Rural quietude descended. Only birdsong reached him on the gentle breeze. He lit a cigarette and smoked it through as he paced up and down, wondering if somehow this had all been a wild-goose chase.

Then he heard the thrumbling note of a car engine approaching along the lane from the direction of the village. He strode forward for a view of the vehicle.

It was a small Peugeot two-seater. And he recognized the driver.

The car pulled in beside him and stopped. 'Hello, Max,' said Nadia Bukayeva, gazing at him from beneath the brim of her fur-fringed hat. 'You are surprised to see me, yes?'

'Why are you here?'

'He sent me to collect you.'

It was futile to pretend he did not know who had sent her. But there was something he genuinely did not know. 'Why you?'

'To test you, I think. Maybe to test me also. I was shocked when he told me. Why are you coming over to us?'

Max had expected to be asked the question sooner or later. But he had not expected Nadia Bukayeva to be the one who asked it. He steeled himself. 'The offer was too good to refuse.'

'Of course. It always is. But remember: no one will trust you until you prove you can be trusted. That is how it is for all of us.'

'Did Norris trust you?'

'I did what I had to do. That is how it is also. But I am glad Sam did not die.'

Max looked her in the eye. 'You should be.'

'Because otherwise you would kill me, yes?'

Max did not reply, but went on looking at her. She did not flinch. And neither did he.

'Will you come with me now?'

'Where are we going?'

'To meet him. He is not far. He is waiting for you.'

'Very well.' Max tossed his bag into the dicky seat and climbed in beside her. 'Let's go.'

Nadia nodded, put the car into gear and started away.

As the car crossed the bridge over the railway line, a shadow detached itself from the larger shadow of the station canopy: a slightly built, dark-skinned young man, dressed in weather-stained army clothes. He briefly shaded his eyes to check the progress of

the car, then he turned and moved swiftly along the platform towards the gate into the courtyard.

TO BE CONTINUED

AUTHOR'S NOTE

None of the recorded history of the Paris Peace Conference of 1919 has been altered in this novel. Real people, places and events have been depicted as accurately as possible. I am indebted to the authors of numerous books on the subject for the insights they gave me, most notably Margaret Macmillan (*Paris 1919*) and the late Harold Nicolson (*Peacemaking, 1919*). In truth, the conjuring up of the past, whether for fictional or non-fictional purposes, can never be precise. But I am grateful to the staff of the Bibliothèque Historique de la Ville de Paris for helping me make it as precise as it could be in this case. I am also grateful to my good friend Toru Sasaki for providing the Japanese translation of the surname Farngold.

ABOUT THE AUTHOR

Robert Goddard was born in Hampshire and read History at Cambridge. His first novel, *Past Caring*, was an instant bestseller. Since then his books have captivated readers worldwide with their edge-of-the-seat pace and their labyrinthine plotting. The first Harry Barnett novel, *Into the Blue*, was winner of the first WHSmith Thumping Good Read Award and was dramatized for TV, starring John Thaw. His thriller *Long Time Coming* won an Edgar in the Mystery Writers of America awards.